To Move A Nation

TO MOVE A NATION

The Politics of Foreign Policy in the Administration of John F. Kennedy

by

ROGER HILSMAN

"I believe in an America that is on the march—an America respected by all nations, friends and foes alike—an America that is moving, choosing, doing, dreaming. . . ."

—JOHN F. KENNEDY

Garden City, New York

DOUBLEDAY & COMPANY, INC.

1967

Library of Congress Catalog Card Number 67–10407
Copyright © 1964, 1967 by Roger Hilsman
All Rights Reserved
Printed in the United States of America
First Edition

To Eleanor, especially, but also to
Hoyt, Amy, Ashby, and even Sarah—
none of whom ever had a chance to ask
what they could do for their country,
but were very quickly told.

CONTENTS

Part V
THE CUBAN MISSILE CRISIS

Part VI
THE CONGO CRISIS

Part VII
THE UNITED STATES AND COMMUNIST CHINA

Part VIII
INDONESIA, MALAYSIA, AND CONFRONTATION

Part IX
VIETNAM

Part X
THE MAKING AND MANAGING OF FOREIGN POLICY

List of Maps

List of Maps

THE WASHINGTON CENTER OF FOREIGN POLICY RESEARCH
School of Advanced International Studies
The Johns Hopkins University

THE INSTITUTE OF WAR AND PEACE STUDIES
School of International Affairs
Columbia University

This book was jointly sponsored by the Washington Center of Foreign Policy Research, of the Johns Hopkins School of Advanced International Studies, under whose auspices it was begun, and the Institute of War and Peace Studies, of the Columbia University School of International Affairs, under whose auspices it was completed.

The Washington Center conducts studies in the theory and practice of international relations and on problems of American foreign policy. It provides a setting where practitioners and theoreticians in foreign affairs can meet to their mutual advantage. Other books of the Washington Center are: Arnold Wolfers, ed., *Alliance Policy in the Cold War* (1959); Lawrence W. Martin, ed., *Neutralism and Non-Alignment* (1962); George Liska, *Nations in Alliance* (1962); Arnold Wolfers, *Discord and Collaboration* (1962); David Wainhouse, *Remnants of Empire* (1964); George Liska, *Europe Ascendant* (1964); Arnold Wolfers, ed., *Changing East-West Relations and the Unity of the West* (1964); Charles Burton Marshall, *The Exercise of Sovereignty* (1965), and *The Cold War* (1965); David Wainhouse, *International Peace Observation* (1966); Arnold Wolfers, Robert Osgood, *et al, The United States in a Disarmed World* (1966).

The Institute of War and Peace Studies has concentrated its research primarily on national security policy, on the contributions of the various social sciences to the understanding of international relations, and on theories of international relations. Other books from the institute are: Alfred Vagts, *Defense and Diplomacy* (1956); Seymour Melman, ed., *Inspection for Disarmament* (1958); William T. R. Fox, ed., *Theoretical Aspects of International Relations* (1959); Kenneth N. Waltz, *Man, the State, and War* (1959); Samuel P. Huntington, *The Common Defense: Strategic Programs in National Politics* (1961); Samuel P. Huntington, ed., *Changing Patterns of Military Politics* (1962); Warner R. Schilling, Paul Y. Hammond, and Glenn H. Snyder, *Strategy, Politics, and Defense Budgets* (1962); Amitai Etzioni, *Political Unification* (1965); Annette B. Fox and William T. R. Fox, *NATO and the Range of American Choice* (1966); Demetrios Caraley, *The Politics of Military Unification* (1966); Glenn H. Snyder, *Stockpiling Strategic Materials; Politics and National Defense* (1966). The Institute of War and Peace Studies and the Russian Institute jointly sponsored the publication of *Political Power USA/USSR* (1964) by Zbigniew Brzezinski and Samuel P. Huntington.

Prefatory Note

THIS BOOK had its origins in a Rockefeller Foundation grant given to me in 1958 to study the politics of policy-making in foreign affairs. The research was based on case study material of foreign policy decisions in the Truman and Eisenhower administrations, including interviews with various officials in both administrations. The hope was for some theoretical insights into the nature of the policy-making process.

Before the study was completed, however, John F. Kennedy was elected President, and I joined his administration, first serving as Director of the Bureau of Intelligence and Research in the State Department, and later as Assistant Secretary of State for Far Eastern Affairs. As a result, I had the opportunity to become a participant, instead of simply an outside observer, in a number of foreign policy decisions.

These experiences were invaluable background for the essentially theoretical, political science study I had begun, and I had hopes of returning to it some day. Had the Kennedy administration ended in a normal way, I would probably have done so, leaving any book that I might write about the Kennedy administration itself to the far future. For the President would have written his own book if he had lived, and any contribution those who served him could make would have followed his book and merely supplemented it. Now, however, there is an obligation on those who know different segments of the story to see that their knowledge is not lost. In the circumstances, it seemed desirable that my book should serve not only its original theoretical purpose but also this additional purpose of relating the history of those foreign policy decisions of the Kennedy administration of which I had some personal knowledge. The book, in consequence, changed from a theoretical study based on case study materials to one in which the case studies themselves are prominent.

Because of my own participation in these decisions, this book is also somewhat of a personal memoir. As it turns out, this is not without utility. For one thing, it helps to make the decisions of government real and understandable. But there are more important utilities. Foreign policy is made by human beings, with human hopes and fears, human greatness and human failings. The interaction of personality is often the

decisive factor in shaping decisions, and the anecdotes of personal
memoirs are sometimes the only source of information about incidents
that may have changed the history of a decision. Finally, as so many
scholars turned participant have learned to their sorrow, historical documents have sometimes crippling limitations, and for some materials
personal memories are the only source. Many documents, for example,
are attempts at accommodation rather than a true reflection of a position
—like pedestrians crossing a street, they make allowances for the
direction and momentum of the oncoming stream of other pedestrians
and alter their own course to accommodate. There is also much that is
left out of documents, especially in a telephonic age. And, finally, statesmen today are so terribly conscious that historians will soon be along to
pore over their documents and judge their actions that they are tempted
to write the documents with this fact in mind.

In attempting to serve all these several purposes one runs the danger
of fully satisfying none. But the advantages of a multiple approach seem
worth the risk, and this book in consequence attempts to combine all
three. In part, it is a theoretical study in political science; in part, it is
history; and in part, it is a memoir.

There was a temptation to broaden the book to include the whole of
foreign policy in Kennedy's administration. But if the particular case
studies, such as those on Laos, Cuba, Vietnam, are to have full utility
for students of the policy-making process and if they are to have the
authority and richness that will make them instructive about how and
why these decisions were made the way they were, then it seemed
important that I stick to those subjects of which I had substantial
personal knowledge. As a consequence, the book makes no attempt to
deal with a number of large and very important problems of foreign
policy during Kennedy's administration—Berlin, for example, or arms
control or the Alliance for Progress.

Even in the problems that are covered, my personal knowledge was
inevitably incomplete. No single person, not even the President himself,
can personally be acquainted with every facet of a large and complicated issue of foreign policy. He cannot, for example, be in Saigon
and Washington simultaneously. Most foreign policy problems, furthermore, are continuing. The Congo crisis began in the Eisenhower administration, reached a climax in the Kennedy administration, and before it
finally died out had extended into the Johnson administration. No single
high official in the United States was continuously involved. The individual official came into responsibility, struggled with the problem for a
time, and then responsibility passed to someone else. I was not involved in the decisions of the Eisenhower administration about the
Congo, and I was only lightly involved in the earlier decisions of the
Kennedy administration. Consequently, I have had to deal with these

parts of the Congo story and the parts of the other cases in which I was less deeply involved through the ordinary methods of historical research and analysis.

In some of the case studies I have gone into the historical background more deeply than in others. In some of the cases, too, I have dealt with periods in which I was deeply involved in greater detail than in others. In both instances, this was a result of a judgment about the importance of the subject. Vietnam policy and China policy, for example, have been treated at greater length than any of the others.

In the first chapter of the book, I try to set the scene in a theoretical sense. Historical writing of any kind is inevitably a process of selecting some material and passing over other material. The reader is entitled to know the basis of selection, and this chapter attempts to outline the theory of the politics of policy-making that underpins the case study chapters on Laos, Cuba, Vietnam, and so on.

Except for this inevitable process of selection, however, I have tried to write the case study chapters "straight" and "flat"—with as little speculation on theoretical implications as possible. Other scholars who are interested in the politics of policy-making may draw different theoretical conclusions from these cases, and even though the process of selection itself, as I said, is mainly determined by the theoretical approach used, it seemed better to separate my own formal attempt at theorizing from the case study chapters and put it at the end of the book, in chapters 35 and 36.

The professional political scientist might find it interesting that the analytical model of the policy-making process offered here does not differ radically from that outlined in some of my earlier articles on the subject.* One might have hoped for some entirely new and fundamentally different theoretical schema to come out of such experiences. But in one sense the less dramatic result is comforting—the outside observer can apparently reach as valid conclusions as the inside participant. However, I do hope that I have been able to make some useful refinements to the model offered and perhaps to have added some secondary theoretical hypotheses that are new and worthwhile.

Another cost of trying to do several things at once and especially of the decision to put my own more formal theorizing at the end is that continuity and the provision of transitions from one set of case study chapters to another are bigger problems than they might have been. The different issues of foreign policy related in this book frequently over-

* "Congressional-Executive Relations and the Foreign Policy Consensus," in the *American Political Science Review*, September 1958, and "The Foreign Policy Consensus: An Interim Research Report," in the *Journal of Conflict Resolution*, December 1959.

lapped in time, and a straight chronological approach has not been possible. For this reason it would have been useful to have the additional unifying theme of a theoretical treatment scattered though each of the case study chapters.

But the problems of foreign policy also overlap in the real world. Some problems present themselves in great detail, others in sketchy outline. Some problems come to the decision-maker in a logical order, in others he learns of the important aspects after action has been taken based on the unimportant. If this book is sometimes a little disjointed in its presentation because of the approach chosen—the decision to attempt a multiple approach as well as the decision to put the theorizing at the end—then I can only console myself that it is more like the real world than it otherwise would have been.

The events described in this book are recent enough to cause me to have had the entire manuscript gone over by qualified specialists to ensure that it contained no information impinging on national security. Within the limits of national security and of protecting individuals, however, I have tried to give a full account.

Although documents cannot be trusted to give the whole story, as I say, they do have their utilities. Accordingly, I have also made provisions to answer any questions that future scholars may have about sources of various quotations and statements which have been omitted for reasons either of security or of protecting individuals by seeing to it that copies of all documents, memoranda for the record, notes of meetings, telephone conversations, and so on that were used in the preparation of this book were included in my personal papers, which have been deposited in the Kennedy Library. To the best of my knowledge and belief, there is no significant statement in the book that does not have some grounding in a contemporary document, although the document in some instances might be notes or a memorandum for the record rather than a more formal piece of paper.

One final word. This is a story of battles, battles over national policy. The policy issues were excruciatingly important, at least once concerning matters that could conceivably have resulted in the "incineration of the northern hemisphere." Given the difficulty of the problems, it was inevitable and even desirable that the participants in these battles disagreed in their judgments. Given the importance of the stakes involved, it was entirely appropriate that they fought hard and passionately—indeed, it would be cause for dismay if it were otherwise. But anyone who has been involved in such battles knows that these matters are never black and white, that there are persuasive arguments on both sides, and that the final judgments are always close. But no matter how hard a man who has been a participant may try to be fair, he cannot help but present the case for his own side more fully and vigorously than he does the case for his opponents. Along with the accounts of other participants in historical events who have written of their experiences, my account here also has this failing. But let me be clear on one point—and very specific, too. I was on the winning side in some of the policy debates described in this book and on the losing side in others, including one, lost after President Kennedy's death, that turned out to be among the most important of all— Vietnam. I still believe the side that ultimately lost the battle on Vietnam was right, and I would argue that subsequent events lend support to their case. But there was a good and reasonable argument on the other side, even though I did not agree with it then and still do not. Given the stake and involvement that many now have in the escalation of the struggle in Vietnam there may be some temptation to interpret the analysis advanced in this book as raising a question about the motives of the people involved. Such an interpretation would be wrong. In the Vietnam case, as in the others, the people on both sides of the argument were honest, intelligent, reasonable, and patriotic men struggling manfully with mean and intricate problems of the highest importance. In short, although there is at least one hero in this story, there are no villains at all.

ROGER HILSMAN

Hamburg Cove, Lyme, Connecticut
Morningside Heights, New York City, New York

Acknowledgments

THIS BOOK would not have been written without the encouragement, understanding, and academic entrepreneurship of Arnold Wolfers, then Director of the Washington Center of Foreign Policy Research, of the Johns Hopkins School of Advanced International Studies, and of William T. R. Fox, Director of the Institute of War and Peace Studies, of the Columbia University School of International Affairs. I am more grateful to them both than I can express.

Warner R. Schilling, Bernard C. Cohen, Henry F. Graff, and Michael V. Forrestal went over the entire manuscript, and I owe each of them the deepest thanks for their highly professional advice and criticism.

Others who read portions of the manuscript on which they had special knowledge and expertise were Andrew W. Cordier, Howard P. Jones, Wayne A. Wilcox, Donald S. Zagoria, Thomas A. Cassilly, Edmund A. Gullion, James C. Thomson, Jr., and Arnold Wolfers.

Various officials who are still in government also read chapters dealing with matters on which they are expert or in which they participated. Even though I cannot thank them publicly, I am most deeply grateful for their help and advice.

Others who read the entire manuscript or substantial portions of it from a more general point of view are Eleanor H. Hilsman, David Webster, Robert M. Sussler, Phoebe and Douglas J. Bennet, Alba Della Fazia, and Deirdre Henderson. I am grateful for their advice and suggestions.

My gratitude also goes to the Rockefeller Foundation for a grant in 1958 that permitted my initial study of the politics of policy-making.

During that initial period of research, I received encouragement and help of various kinds from L. Quincy Mumford, Ernest S. Griffith, Hugh L. Elsbree, Burnis Walker, Merlin H. Nipe, and Valarie Griffith—all of the Library of Congress.

Also during that initial period, three graduate students in a special seminar at the School of Advanced International Studies did valuable case study work—Howard Bliss, Stevan S. Conner, and Nicholas Platt. Emmy Clubb helped enormously as research assistant. Mary Lampson, Elaine Clark, and Robert Anderson contributed with secretarial and other work.

For the past two years, Patsy Spykman Winer served as research assistant, and I am most grateful for her patient and imaginative efforts.

Also during the past two years, secretarial help of many kinds was required, for which I am grateful to Dorothy Herbert especially and to Suzanne Abromson Joiner and Dorothy Psomiades. Both Karen Rich and Carol Tyler also helped in the earlier stages.

A special kind of thanks goes to Harriet F. Pilpel for her legal and other advice, both of which were always good.

My thanks also go to Kenneth McCormick and Lawrence Freundlich of Doubleday, who not only served as editors but gave muchly appreciated encouragement.

Finally, I am grateful to the men and women of the Bureau of Intelligence and Research, in the State Department, and the Bureau of Far Eastern Affairs, who shared in these events and to whom I owe much.

I

THE POLITICS OF
POLICY-MAKING

"The members of the Cabinet are a President's natural enemies."
—CHARLES G. DAWES, *Vice-President of the United States*

CHAPTER 1

Policy-Making Is Politics

IN THE YEARS following World War II, Princeton University established what was probably the most unlikely university post in the Western world—a professorship combining sculpture and boxing. The job was set up for a man named Joseph Brown, who was equally competent in both fields and who was drawn to things that called for both talents. As a boxer, he was interested in strong bodies, and as a sculptor he was interested in strong lines. Designing playground equipment combined the two nicely, and Professor Brown conceived and built some unusual pieces in free-form concrete. But his greatest achievement came when he discovered nylon rope woven around a core of steel wire. He built a spider web of this special rope in the shape of a pyramid, and then tightened the strands until each was in vibrating tension with every other. The results were dramatic: if an impish child in a crowd of climbers plucked a strand on one side of the pyramid, some startled innocent on the other would find himself flung violently in several directions at once. The taut nylon web was so intricately interwoven that there was no sure way of telling who had been the original culprit, so the game of retaliation and counterretaliation usually led to what can be described as complex pandemonium. But since most of the children succeeded in hanging on and the one or two who didn't were never more than shaken up, the apparatus was a huge success.

But Professor Brown's greatest pride was neither in the fun nor the body-building, but in what he liked to call the educational contribution. "The children," he said, "learn two profound truths about life. The first is that there are so-and-so's in the world. The second, and more important, is that it's not easy to be sure just who they are."

In these two respects, if in no other, Washington resembles life. Anyone who has lived and worked there knows beyond doubt that the town is full of so-and-so's. But it would be impossible to get agreement on a definitive list.

"Washington," I remember Secretary of State Dean Rusk saying when one of our colleagues was cruelly and unfairly attacked in the press, "is an *evil* town." It is, but not because the people who inhabit it are evil by nature, but because of the struggle that is inherent in the fact that the capital of a nation is the nerve center of the nation's power. Where power is, there also are conflict and turmoil. Thus the reasons that Washington is the way it is lie deep in the heart of both the nature of the business of Washington and of the political and governmental process by which that business is carried out.

DECISIONS

The business of Washington is making decisions that move a nation, decisions about the direction American society should go and decisions about how and where and for what purposes the awesome power— economic, political, and military—of this, the world's most powerful nation, shall be used. The decisions are about social security and medicare and labor laws and the rules for conducting business and manufacture. Or they are about moving a nation toward war or peace—a test ban treaty, intervening in Vietnam, the UN in the Congo, or Soviet nuclear missiles in Cuba. Where the power to move a nation is, there also are the great decisions.

What is decided is policy. It is policy about problems and issues that may make or break powerful interests in our society—organized labor or the medical profession or the massive interests represented by the "military-industrial complex" that President Eisenhower warned about in his farewell address. Or it is policy that will cost American lives in some foreign jungle and result either in our continued survival and success as a nation or, conceivably, in our downfall in a nuclear holocaust that takes much of the rest of the world with us. In the business of Washington, the stakes are high.

THE PROCESS OF POLICY-MAKING

The nature and importance of the business done in Washington are obvious. The process by which that business is done and the nation is moved is more obscure.

As Americans, with our flair for the mechanical and love of efficiency combined with a moralistic Puritan heritage, we would like to think not only that policy-making is a conscious and deliberate act, one of analyzing problems and systematically examining grand alternatives in all their implications, but also that the alternative chosen is aimed at achieving overarching ends that serve a high moral purpose. Evidence that there is confusion about goals or evidence that the goals themselves may be competing or mutually incompatible is disquieting, and we hear repeated calls for a renewed national purpose, for a unifying ideology with an appeal abroad that will rival Communism, or for a national strategy that will fill both functions and set the guidelines for all of policy. As Americans, we think it only reasonable that the procedures for making national decisions should be orderly, with clear lines of responsibility and authority. We assume that what we call the "decisions" of government are in fact decisions—discrete acts, with recognizable beginnings and sharp, decisive endings. We like to think of policy as rationalized, in the economist's sense of the word, with each step leading logically and economically to the next. We want to be able to find out who makes decisions, to feel that they are the proper, official, and authorized persons, and to know that the really big decisions will be made at the top, by the President and his principal advisers in the formal assemblage of the Cabinet or the National Security Council and with the Congress exercising its full and formal powers. And we feel that the entire decision-making process ought to be a dignified, even majestic progression, with each of the participants having roles and powers so well and precisely defined that they can be held accountable for their actions by their superiors and eventually by the electorate.

The reality, of course, is quite different. Put dramatically, it could be argued that few, if any, of the decisions of government are either decisive or final. Very often policy is the sum of a congeries of separate or only vaguely related actions. On other occasions, it is an uneasy, even internally inconsistent compromise among competing goals or an incompatible mixture of alternative means for achieving a single goal. There is no systematic and comprehensive study of all the implications of the grand alternatives—nor can there be. A government does not decide to inaugurate the nuclear age, but only to try to build an atomic bomb before its enemy does. It does not make a formal decision to become a welfare state, but only to take each of a series of steps—to experiment with an income tax at some safely innocuous level like 3 per cent, to alleviate the hardship of men who have lost their jobs in a depression with a few weeks of unemployment compensation, or to lighten the old age of industrial workers with a tentative program of social security benefits. Rather than through grand decisions on grand alternatives, policy changes seem to come through a series of slight modifications of existing policy, with the new policy emerging slowly and haltingly by small and usually tentative steps, a process of trial and error in which policy zigs and zags, reverses itself, and then moves forward in a series of incremental steps.[1] Sometimes policies are formulated and duly ratified only to be skewed to an entirely different direction and purpose by those carrying them out—or they are never carried out at all. And sometimes issues are endlessly debated with nothing at all being resolved until both the problem and the debaters disappear under the relentless pyramiding of events.

THE POWER OF THE PRESIDENT

One result of all this is that in spite of the great power they wield, presidents can very rarely command, even within what is supposedly their most nearly absolute domain, the Executive Branch itself. President Truman, as he contemplated turning the presidency over to Eisenhower, used to say, "He'll sit here and he'll say, 'Do this! Do that!' And nothing will happen. Poor Ike—it won't be a bit like the Army."[2]

Presidents, being human, sometimes find the system frustrating. Once at a press conference, President Kennedy surprised us all by answering a question about allied trade with Cuba with a promise to take certain measures that were still under discussion. "Well!" he said afterward with some exasperation. "Today I actually made a little policy." But mainly, presidents maneuver, persuade, and pressure—using all the levers, powers, and influences they can muster. And most presidents recognize that this is what they must do. On another occasion, for example, midway in the Vietnam crisis, there had been a morning meeting of the National Security Council in the Cabinet room of the White House at which several decisions that seemed to mark a watershed had finally been taken. After the meeting, Secretary of Defense Robert S. McNamara, the Chairman of the Joint Chiefs of Staff, Maxwell D. Taylor, Presidential Assistants McGeorge Bundy and Michael V. Forrestal and I repaired to the Situation Room just off Bundy's office in the basement of the White House to draft a cable reflecting the decisions. We were finished by early afternoon, but by that time the President was involved with thirty or forty congressmen in a bill-signing ceremony and a pile of other work he had to move, and only Bundy, Forrestal, and I waited until he was free to get his final okay. The three of us trooped into his oval office through the curved side door from the room his private secretary, Mrs. Lincoln, occupied and found the President rocking away in his chair before the fireplace, reading and signing the last of a pile of letters. He looked up and grinned. "And now," he said, "we have the 'inner club.' "

After he had cleared the cable and the three of us were walking down the hall, I asked Bundy if what the President had meant was that we now had in one room the people who were *really* familiar with the problem. "Yes," said Bundy, "but also something more. It's a private joke of his: he meant that, but also that now we had together the people who had known all along what we would do about the problem, and who had been pulling and hauling, debating and discussing for no other purpose than to keep the government together, to get all the others to come around."

On some occasions presidents do not succeed in getting the others to come around, and they must then either pay the political costs of public disunity or make some concession to achieve the unity of compromise. In the Kennedy administration, for example, the State Department was convinced that high-level visits to Vietnam were politically bad. They felt, in particular, that visits by so high-ranking an official as Secretary of Defense McNamara would get United States prestige hooked too tightly to the roller coaster of events in Vietnam in spite of the fact that we had only limited influence on those events. Visits by so high-ranking an official would also tend to make a bad situation look even worse by showing our concern too openly. And, finally, such visits would tend to make a Vietnamese struggle conducted with only our aid and advice look in the world's eyes like a purely American war.

The President was only too well aware of these probable consequences, but in the circumstances, he indicated that he was prepared to pay the price. For the only way of keeping the higher-ranking military officers in the Pentagon from an increasingly public display of discontent with the President's decision not to enlarge the war was to keep the Secretary of Defense fully content with the policy. And the only way to do that, apparently, was to let him see for himself.

On some occasions, the President clearly makes the decision, even if he cannot make it exactly as he might wish. On other occasions, the decision is just as clearly made by Congress. But in action after action, responsibility for decision is as fluid and restless as quicksilver, and there seems to be neither a person nor an organization on whom it can be fixed. At times the point of decision seems to have escaped into the labyrinth of governmental machinery, beyond layers and layers of bureaucracy. Other times it seems never to have reached the government, but remained in either the wider domain of a public opinion created by the press or in the narrower domain dominated by the maneuverings of special interests.

TURMOIL

Just as our desire to know who makes a decision is frustrated, so is our hope that the process of policy-making will be dignified. A decision, in fact, may be little more than a signal that starts a public brawl by people who want to reverse it. President Eisenhower's "New Look" decision to concentrate on air power at the expense of ground forces, for example, had no visible result for the first year except semipublic fights with the Joint Chiefs of Staff, an eruption of the so-called "Colonels' revolt," and frequent leaks of top secret information. The whole strategy was completely reversed when the Kennedy administration came into responsibility in 1961, and the reversal was fought by the same technique of leaks, but this time it was Air Force rather than Army partisans doing the leaking. At the very beginning of the Kennedy administration, for example, Rusk wrote McNamara a memorandum seeking an interdepartmental discussion of the basic problem, and a distorted version of the memo was promptly given to Air Force sympathizers in the press in an obvious attempt at sabotage.

Leaks, of course, are the first and most blatant signs of battle, and they are endemic in the policy process. When it became clear, for example, that the report of the Gaither Committee, set up by Eisenhower in 1957 to study civil defense in terms of the whole of nuclear strategy, would be critical of the "New Look" and the entire Eisenhower defense policy, the crucial battle between the different factions within the administration took place, not on the substance of the report, but on the issue of whether there would be two hundred top secret copies of the report or only two. For everyone knew without saying so that if the President did not accept the Gaither Committee's recommendations, it might be possible to keep the report from leaking to the press if there were only two copies, but never if there were two hundred. The committee won the battle, and two hundred top secret copies were distributed within the Executive Branch. The President did not accept the recommendations; and, sure enough, within a few days Chalmers Roberts of the Washington *Post* was able to write a story, covering almost two newspaper pages, that contained an accurate and comprehensive version of both the top secret report and its recommendations.

Not surprisingly, it was these continual leaks that especially puzzled and angered Eisenhower. In 1955, he said, "For some two years and three months I have been plagued by inexplicable undiscovered leaks in this Government." But so are all presidents, before and after Eisenhower. Not only are there leaks of secret information, but leaks that distort secret information so as to present a special view that is often totally false. There flows out of Washington a continuous stream of rumor, tales of bickering, speculation, stories of selfish interest, charges and countercharges. Abusive rivalries arise between the government agencies engaged in making policy, and even within a single agency different factions battle, each seeking allies in other agencies, among the members of Congress, from interest associations, and among the press. Officialdom, whether civil or military, is hardly neutral. It speaks, and inevitably it speaks as an advocate. The Army battles for ground forces, the Air Force for bombers; the "Europe faction" in the State Department for policy benefiting NATO, and the "Africa faction" for anticolonialist policies unsettling to our relations with Europe. All of these many interests, organizations, and institutions—inside and outside the government—are joined in a struggle over the goals of governmental policy and over the means by which these goals shall be achieved. Instead of unity, there is conflict. Instead of a majestic progression, there are erratic zigs and zags. Instead of clarity and decisiveness, there are tangle and turmoil, instead of order, confusion.

SOURCES OF THE TURMOIL

But even though we deplore the disorder and confusion, the seeming disloyalty of leaks, the noise and untidiness, and all the rest, it would be well to look more deeply into the nature of the process before condemning it.

Partly, of course, the turbulence derives from the nature of our constitution itself. As Richard E. Neustadt has pointed out, the constitutional convention of 1787 did not really create a government of "separated powers" as we have been taught, but a government of separated institutions sharing powers.[3] The Executive, for example, is clearly part of the legislative process—almost all major bills today are drafted and put forward by the Executive department concerned, and the President still has the veto. The courts, too, legislate—much to the annoyance of many congressmen, especially die-hard segregationists. And the Congress is equally involved in administration, in both its investigative function and its appropriation of money and oversight of spending. To the head of a department or agency, the Congress, with its power to reward and punish, is as much his boss as is the President. And some agency heads can build enough power on the Hill to put themselves beyond the reach of a President even to fire them—as J. Edgar Hoover succeeded in doing with his job as director of the FBI. Different institutions sharing powers, getting involved in each others' business, provide the checks and balances sought by the founding fathers and many other benefits besides. But they also contribute to the phenomenon of turbulence.

THE MULTIPLICITY OF ACTORS

Still another dimension is the now familiar fact that many more people are involved in the process of government than merely those who hold the duly constituted official positions. It is no accident that the press, for example, is so often called the "fourth branch of government." The press plays a role in the process of governance. It performs functions which are a necessary part of the process and which it sometimes performs well and sometimes badly.

There are also lobbies, the spokesmen of special interests of every kind and description from oil producers and farmers to the Navy League and Women Strike for Peace. Their efforts on Capitol Hill are more familiar, but the lobbies work just as hard to influence the Executive, although in different ways. In any case, they play a role in the process of governance and perform necessary functions, often for good but sometimes for evil.

And there are others who play a role. The academic world, the world of research in the universities, has an influence and participates in the process, both formally and informally. In the presidential campaigns of

1960 and 1964, for example, no candidate could be without his own
team of university advisers—Kennedy and Nixon each had such a team,
and so did both Johnson and Goldwater. Most of the more effective senators on Capitol Hill have academic friends, experts in the universities,
whom they regularly consult. And there is a whole new set of institutions
doing research of all kinds on contract with the government, organizations
staffed with people who have governmental clearances for secret work but
who are neither in the armed services nor the civil service—quasi-governmental organizations such as the RAND Corporation, in Santa Monica,
California, the Institute of Defense Analyses, in Washington, and the
Hudson Institute, just outside New York. All of these people and organizations influence policy. Although not accountable to the electorate, they
have power and they are as much a part of the governmental process as
the traditional legislative, judicial, and executive branches of government. There are many more people involved in making policy than those
who hold official positions, in sum, and they have more subtle ways for
shaping policy.

POLICY CONVICTIONS

But all this is only the beginning. Among the principal findings of a
British government committee appointed to study the powers of ministers
was that most men find it easier to go against their own pecuniary interests than they do to go against a deep conviction on policy. As we have
said, in the business of Washington, the stakes are high and the issues
fundamental, both to our society and to the question of war and peace
for the entire world. In such circumstances it is not surprising that passions run strong and full. It is not even surprising that men occasionally
feel so deeply that they take matters into their own hands, leaking secret
materials to the Congress or the press in an attempt to force the President
to adopt what they are convinced is the only right path, the salvation of
the nation. When in the late 1950s, for example, intelligence officials
leaked secret information foreshadowing an upcoming "missile gap" to
Democratic senators and sympathetic members of the press, it was not
because they were disloyal, but because they were deeply convinced that
the nation was in peril. They had tried and failed to convince the top
levels of the Eisenhower administration of the validity of their projections,
and they felt completely justified in taking matters into their own hands
by going over the President's head to Congress, the press, and the public. Colonel Billy Mitchell was doing the same in the 1920s when he
provoked a court-martial so he could present the case for air power to
the nation at large. But none of this is new. Throughout history, the motive for such deeds—for mankind's greatest achievements, but also, unhappily, for mankind's greatest crimes—has rarely been to benefit the

individual, but for the glory of something the individual thinks of as bigger than himself, for his God, his nation, or his ideology.

There is nothing in this to nullify the point that selfish interests are also involved in these decisions, and that the decisions affect such powerful interests as labor, the farmers, the medical profession, and the "military-industrial complex." But society is made up of its different parts, and it is not merely a rationalization when farmers, for example, argue that a healthy nation depends on a healthy agriculture. There is nothing wrong in the people of a democracy expressing their interests, their values, hopes, and fears through "interest" organizations. How else, save through some such hierarchy of representative organizations, can the needs and desires of so many millions of people be aggregated?

Nor is there anything wrong in the fact that the bureaucracy itself is divided, that it represents special interests, and that its parts speak as advocates, fighting hard for their constituencies. The Department of Labor is inevitably and rightly more oriented toward workingmen than management; the Bureau of Mines more toward extractive industry than the industrial users of minerals; the Children's Bureau more toward restrictions on employers than permissiveness. Indeed some segments of society that are poorly organized for exercising leverage on either public opinion or the Congress would have a much smaller voice if the bureaucracy of the federal government did not represent their interests, and many of the long-range, more general interests of society as a whole have no other spokesman at all. But all this also contributes to the turbulence of the Washington scene.

INADEQUACY OF KNOWLEDGE

Still another dimension of the confusion and turbulence of the policy-making process is the complexity of the problems and the inadequacy of our knowledge of how and why things work in the social affairs of men, our limited capacity to foresee developments that bring problems or to predict the consequences of whatever action we do take. Partly this is because in the field of foreign affairs, especially, there are so many other people and nations involved, friends and enemies, with goals of their own and tactics of their own. But it is more than this. More and better understanding will not always or necessarily lead to sure solutions to knotty problems, but it sometimes does. If our understanding of the workings of a modern industrial economy had been better in the 1920s, the Great Depression could very probably have been avoided; and if our knowledge had been only slightly greater in the 1930s than it was, the measures to meet the Depression would probably have been more effective and quicker-acting. Winston Churchill called World War II the "unnecessary war," by which he meant that if we had better understood what Hitler

and Nazism were really about and particularly their compelling dynamism leading toward war, it would have been politically possible to take
the necessary preventive measures—which however hard and costly,
would have been better than the horror of what actually occurred.

When knowledge is inadequate, when problems are complex, and especially when they are also new—presenting a challenge with which there
has been no experience—there is in such circumstances room to spare
for disagreement, conflict, and turmoil. It is not the only cause of disagreement, much less the central cause, but it is one of them. McGeorge
Bundy once said that policy in Vietnam was "the most divisive issue in
the Kennedy administration." He meant *inside* the administration, and he
was right. And the cause of the dissension was precisely inadequate understanding and a failure of analysis. Modern guerrilla warfare, as the
Communists practice it, is *internal* war, an ambiguous aggression that
avoids direct and open attack violating international frontiers but combines terror, subversion, and political action with hit-and-run guerrilla
raids and ambush. It is new to the Western world, and not yet fully
understood. In the Kennedy administration there were those who saw it
as a modified form of traditional war, but war nevertheless to be fought
primarily with traditional military measures. Others saw guerrilla warfare as essentially political in nature, aimed at winning the people while
terrorizing the government, and they believed that in fighting against a
guerrilla insurgency military measures should be subordinated to political action. But there was simply not enough knowledge and experience
with such matters to prove who was right, and the struggle within the
administration became increasingly bitter.

POLICY-MAKING IS POLITICS

These are some of the facets of policy-making and the decisions that
move nations—separate institutions sharing powers, the press, experts,
and others who influence policy without holding formal power, selfish and
unselfish interest groups that exert a different kind of power, the difficulties and complexities of analysis, prediction, and judgment. These many
facets help to explain the turmoil, and they flag a warning to those who
would be cynical about Washington and the hurly-burly that is disquieting
or even repugnant to so many. But they do not completely explain even
the surface phenomena of Washington, nor is what explanation they do
give completely satisfying. As Americans, we aspire to a rationalized system of government and policy-making. This implies that a nation can
pursue a single set of clearly perceived and generally agreed-to goals, as
a business organization is supposed to pursue profits. Yet is this realistic?
Is the problem of making policy in a highly diversified mass society
really one of relating the different steps in making a decision to a single

set of goals or is it precisely one of choosing goals—of choosing goals not in the abstract but in the convoluted context of ongoing events, with inadequate information, incomplete knowledge and understanding, and insufficient power—and doing so, in all probability, while we are pitted against opposition both at home and abroad? If so, the making of national decisions is not a problem for the efficiency expert, or of assembling different pieces of policy logically as if the product were an automobile. Policy faces inward as much as outward, seeking to reconcile conflicting goals, to adjust aspirations to available means, and to accommodate the different advocates of these competing goals and aspirations to one another. It is here that the essence of policy-making seems to lie, in a process that is in its deepest sense political.

Recognizing the political nature of policy-making might help us to a better understanding of the diversity and seeming inconsistency of the goals that national policy must serve. It might also help us to understand the powerful but sometimes hidden forces through which these competing goals are reconciled, why the pushes and pulls of these crosscurrents are sometimes dampened or obscured, and why they are sometimes so fiercely public. Even the roles of such "unrational" procedures as bargaining and power might also become more clear.

President Kennedy once said, "There will always be the dark and tangled stretches in the decision-making process—mysterious even to those who may be most intimately involved . . ."[4] Yet it is equally true that we can understand better than we now do how a nation is moved and that better understanding can lead to more effective policy and perhaps even to improvements in the policy-making process itself. Understanding comes in looking at the vital stuff of events themselves, in the interaction of the President, the Congress, the press, and special interests and in the rivalries of the great Executive departments, State, Defense, and the Central Intelligence Agency, as they clash in the actual making of policy, in the crucible of events—in the struggle over organizational mandates, in the crisis of Soviet nuclear missiles in Cuba, of the Congo, Laos, and the guerrilla struggle in Vietnam.

NOTES

[1] See Charles E. Lindblom, "The Science of 'Muddling Through,'" *Public Administration Review*, XIX, 1959, and his book *The Intelligence of Democracy*, 1965.
[2] Richard E. Neustadt, *Presidential Power*, 1960, p. 9.
[3] Richard E. Neustadt, *op. cit.*, p. 33.
[4] In his foreword to Theodore C. Sorensen's *Decision-Making in the White House*, Columbia University Press, 1963.

II

THE ORGANIZATIONAL STRUGGLE

"The processes of government have sometimes been described as a struggle for power among those holding public office. I am convinced that this is true only in a certain formal and bureaucratic sense, having to do with appropriations, job descriptions, trappings of prestige, water bottles and things of that sort. There is another struggle of far more consequence, the effort to diffuse or avoid responsibility. Power gravitates to those who are willing to make decisions and live with the results, simply because there are so many who readily yield to the intrepid few who take their duties seriously.

"On this particular point the Department of State is entering, I think, something of a new phase in its existence. We are expected to take charge."

—DEAN RUSK *to the policy-making officers of the Department of State, February 20, 1961*

"President Kennedy's favorite quotation from Dante was that the hottest corner of hell was reserved for those who preserved their neutrality in times of moral crisis."

—ROBERT F. KENNEDY *to the students of Columbia University, October 5, 1964*

CHAPTER 2

Theory: Power to the State Department

DEAN ACHESON used to tell a story about Chief Justice Taft relating a conversation he had just had with an eminent man about the "machinery" of government. "And you know," Taft said with wonder in his voice, "he really does believe it *is* machinery."

Of one thing we can be sure: it isn't machinery. There was a day when political scientists spent a great deal of their time on organization charts, moving boxes here and there in accordance with principles based on a distinction between "administration" and "management," on the one hand, and "policy" and "politics," on the other. They do no longer.

Arguments about organization can arouse high passion. Partly this is because organizational struggles are struggles for personal power and position. The outcome of the battle can be a more or less formal confirmation of who ended up with power over what kind of policy. Not everyone, however, strives for power. As Secretary Rusk suggested in the words quoted at the beginning of this section there are many men who are more concerned with the trappings and titles of power than with the substance, and there is also an effort to diffuse and evade responsibility. Part of the organizational shuffling in Washington, in other words, is a scramble to get off target zero.

But the struggle over organization in Washington is also considerably more than an attempt either to acquire personal power or to evade it. Apart from very obvious efficiencies or inefficiencies, in so complicated a business as the making of national policy there is probably no good or bad organization except in terms of what one regards as good or bad policy.[1] By making it easier for some people to have access than others, by providing for the accumulation of one kind of information and not another, or by following procedures that let some problems rise to the top of the government's agenda before others—in all these ways some organizational arrangements facilitate certain kinds of policy and other organizational arrangements facilitate other kinds of policy. One example was when Theodore Roosevelt tried to establish conservation of natural resources as national policy in place of the older, "homesteading" policy of creating incentives for clearing the forests and peopling the land. The old organizational arrangements provided easy channels for lumbering and other exploitative interests to express their preferences and almost none for "conservationist" interests to express theirs. There were almost no mechanisms for gathering the kind of information that would permit governmental decisions to conserve rather than exploit. The result was that President Roosevelt could not really change from a policy of encouraging "homesteading" to a policy of encouraging "conservation" until he changed the organization dealing with the problem.

So whether one thinks a certain organizational arrangement is "good" or "bad" depends on what one thinks of the kind of policy it facilitates. And this, too, has its repercussions. We have said that policy-making is essentially a political process, by which the multiplicity of goals and values in a free and diverse society are reconciled and the debate over means and ends is distilled into a politically viable consensus on a workable policy. But if some organizational arrangements facilitate certain kinds of policy and other arrangements facilitate other kinds, then organization is also politics in still another guise—which accounts for the passion that men so often bring to procedural and organizational matters.

The struggle within the Kennedy administration over the overorganization of national security affairs went on for almost a full year after President Kennedy took office, and it had all the passion one would expect before things settled down to a more or less stable balance. But the struggle had begun long before, in the form of debates on Capitol Hill and elsewhere about the organizational arrangements Eisenhower had made in his administration and about suggestions for still more changes that would require legislation.

THE EISENHOWER ADMINISTRATION

President Eisenhower, of course, had grown up with military administrative procedures, and although he had had extensive experience with high policy, it was not of a kind to make him doubt the soundness of military procedures. His experience with high policy had been in wartime. There is no doubt that he had his share of international political problems, beginning with Admiral Darlan in North Africa. But in time of war the over-all goal of winning a victory mutes the raw politics of reconciling a multiplicity of competing goals and hostile interests that is the stuff of day-by-day affairs. President Eisenhower, accordingly, took the set of institutions he had inherited and made them into something very similar to the formalized, hierarchical military procedures with which he was so familiar.

And what he had inherited—the basic National Security Council structure set up by the act of 1947—had also had military roots. Franklin D. Roosevelt had had a free and easy style that plucked advice and information from every conceivable and even casual source, and he had also built competition into the relationship between departments, cabinet ministers, and his personal staff. Out of the competition and glorious disorder he could develop policy alternatives, test them on a wide variety of people, and ensure that it was he who made the choices at his timing and not someone else. But such a style often left one or another department, agency, or high official out of what he felt he should legitimately be in. The NSC setup came out of studies in the Pentagon, sponsored mainly by James V. Forrestal, Secretary of the Navy and later the first Secretary of Defense, and it was designed to make sure that all the major departments, and especially the Department of Defense, had a regular voice. It tried to pin down future presidents in a way that Roosevelt would never permit himself to be pinned down, and the NSC was as much a reaction to Roosevelt, the man, and his way of operating as the amendment limiting presidents to two terms. The NSC, in fact, has been called "Forrestal's Revenge" in what is only half a jest.[2] For Forrestal was trying to ensure a Defense Department voice in foreign policy to make sure that our strength was consistent with our commitments.

To the basic NSC structure, Eisenhower added a Planning Board and an Operations Coordinating Board. Thus policy in the Eisenhower administration was made by a hierarchy of interdepartmental committees, proceeding step by step up the ladder until it arrived at the NSC itself, which met weekly with the President as chairman. Then, after a formal decision, the Operations Coordinating Board took over with monthly, quarterly, and annual reviews, including mountains of follow-up memoranda, to ensure that each department and agency carried out the approved policy.[3]

There were indications that President Eisenhower and other top members of his administration were considering going even further along these lines—for proposals kept circulating in Washington for creating a second vice-president, to be in charge of foreign affairs, for strengthening the NSC, or for increasing the power of the Special Assistant to the President for National Security Affairs (a post held in the Eisenhower administration by Robert Cutler and Gordon Grey and in the Kennedy administration by McGeorge Bundy).

The idea behind the Eisenhower way of organizing the government was that the top men should save their strength and wisdom for what the officials lower down were unable to decide, and the pressure was toward reconciling differences at as low a level in the hierarchy as possible so as to give the top leadership an agreed "best" solution. The assumption behind this notion was that an administration is a "team"—one of President Eisenhower's favorite words—rather like an idealized British cabinet that had common interests and ideology.

In a sense, the assumption was correct, for such an organizational arrangement did tend to produce the kind of basically conservative policies that the dominant elements of the Eisenhower administration desired. It naturally discouraged new and innovating policies by its pressure for agreement on a "best" solution—which usually resulted in agreement on the lowest common denominator of competing departmental interests and concerns. In foreign policy, particularly, its effect was to emphasize policies supporting the *status quo,* with a high value on "stability."

THE DEMOCRATS ATTACK

Long before the end of the Eisenhower administration, the Democrats began to attack the Republicans' organizational ideas and to develop some of their own. Dean Acheson, as the last Democratic Secretary of State, summed up their views in an article entitled "Thoughts about Thought in High Places."[4] When Dulles had taken over as Secretary, Acheson recalled, he had said that he intended to organize the Department of State so that he would have time to think. Ridiculing the idea that in policy-making thought could be so divorced from action, Acheson predicted that the result would always be as it had been with the Eisenhower NSC structure—to cut the chief off from his principal officers and interpose a "coordinating staff" between them and the chief. "The result," Acheson wrote, "will be that he will have to see just as many people, but they will be the wrong people."

As for the idea that the purpose of good organization is to see that as many problems as possible are decided as low in the hierarchy as possible—in the form of "agreed" papers—Acheson argued the exact opposite. The true purpose of good organization, he maintained, was to furnish, where there was any doubt at all about the wise course, not agreed papers, but "disagreed" papers. The need, Acheson felt, was for papers in which the issues are laid out and the alternatives argued as fully and persuasively as the different advocates knew how. The Democrats' position, in sum, was that trying to make a decision-making body out of the NSC had been a failure. For there are differing interests in the different departments, and it is the true job of these departments to defend these interests as best they can. To ask these same people to decide on the "best" solution is to ask them to find the lowest common denominator, to invite them to reconcile differences by papering them over with a policy so general as neither to serve nor damage the interests of the competing participants.

THE ACADEMIC COMMUNITY

The academic community also weighed in against the Eisenhower administration's reliance on the NSC structure, and ridiculed the suggestions for strengthening it further and for creating "czars" such as a vice-president for foreign affairs.[5] An example was an article summarizing discussions a group of us held at the time—a group including Herman Kahn, then of Princeton; James E. King, Jr., of Johns Hopkins; H. Field Haviland and Charles A. H. Thomson, of Brookings; Evron Kirkpatrick, of the American Political Science Association; Jeffrey Kitchen and George Tanham, of the RAND Corporation; Joseph E. Slater, of the Ford Foundation; Ernest W. Lefever, and others.[6] Our conclusion was that any attempt to "strengthen" the NSC would tend to erect more obstacles than it would remove. Measures like creating a vice-president for foreign affairs, we felt, would put still another layer between the President and the problems which only he could decide, and add still more to the pressures for agreed positions at the cost of clarity and concreteness. No good, we were convinced, could come of creating a rival for the Secretary of State in the area of his own responsibility, for policy-making is not the kind of work that is necessarily facilitated by a czar. The expediter with extraordinary powers may often be the answer to a production problem or to getting a crash program on the road. But producing policy is different from producing hardware and does not yield to the same expedients. The NSC is a device by which the different departments concerned with national security can meet, discuss their problems and differences, reconcile unimportant disagreements, and when it comes to major disagreements at least poke holes in each others' arguments—all in the presence and for the benefit of the President. Its function, we argued, is that of a forum for debate and through debate that of a channel for information. But nothing more.

Our conclusion was that any attempt to make the NSC into something more than this—into a true decision-making body similar, for example, to the cabinet in the British parliamentary system—would probably be frustrated. In the first place, the President, unlike the British Prime Minister, does not need the direct support of his cabinet secretaries and fellow party members in the legislature to continue in office, and cabinet secretaries in the United States do not represent segments of political power in quite the same way as ministers do in Britain. In the second place, the argument continued, for many policies a wider consent seems to be needed than can be represented in a body like the NSC, and such a body is hardly suitable for making the bilateral arrangements that may be necessary in developing that wider consent, for bargaining, or for the weighing and balancing of power that a political process entails. The question, we concluded, was not so much one of organization, but of policy and purpose—the existing arrangements could be made to produce "good" policy or "bad" policy, depending on who used them, for what purpose, and how.

CONGRESS AND THE JACKSON SUBCOMMITTEE

Perhaps the most important work of all that contributed to the thinking of the Kennedy administration on organizational problems, however, was done in Congress, by the Jackson Subcommittee. It was an outstanding example of a creative, responsible, and constructive use of the congressional power to investigate, conduct studies, and explore.

Senator Henry M. Jackson's Subcommittee on National Policy Machinery of the Committee on Government Operations, to give its official title, began work in July 1959, with a staff that included J. Kenneth Mansfield, a Yale-trained political scientist who had worked for several years on the staff of the Joint Committee on Atomic Energy; Dorothy Fosdick, a former professor at Smith and former member of the State Department's Policy Planning Staff; and Robert W. Tufts, a professor at Oberlin and also a former member of the Policy Planning Staff. Hearings were conducted with men like Robert A. Lovett, Nelson Rockefeller, Admiral Arthur W. Radford, General Maxwell D. Taylor, and the then Secretaries of State, Defense, and Treasury. The results were a series of reports that began to come out in the fall of 1960 and early spring of 1961—perfectly timed to influence the organizational struggles of the new administration.

The subcommittee's conclusions were blunt and to the point. Any idea of radical additions to the existing policy machinery or of "super-cabinet officers and super-staffs" was rejected. "Our best hope," the final report read, "lies in making our traditional policy machinery work better—not in trading it in for some new model." The subcommittee harshly criticized the heavy undergrowth of interdepartmental committees clustered around the NSC and particularly the cumbersome Operations Coordinating Board. "The case for abolishing the OCB," said the subcommittee's report on NSC structure, "is strong." But the major theme was that no task was more urgent than improving the effectiveness of the Department of State. The subcommittee pushed hard for better people down the line, for "take charge" men, particularly at the Assistant Secretary level, but it pushed even harder for the idea that the State Department should *lead*. "In our system," the final report read, "there can be no satisfactory substitute for a Secretary of State willing and able to exercise his leadership across the full range of national security matters . . ."

THE KENNEDY ADMINISTRATION

If the organizational arrangements of the Eisenhower administration produced *status quo* policies and discouraged innovation, the Kennedy administration wanted something different. The Kennedy administration was activist in foreign policy, oriented to the emerging peoples and the new nationalisms, and determined to attempt to shape events. If the object was to produce policies for these purposes, it seemed to make sense to put power in the hands of those whose responsibilities would make them politically oriented and concerned with the whole of foreign problems—the Department of State.

In any case, President Kennedy seemed to agree with this general approach, and he moved rapidly to clear the organizational decks. Within a month of taking office, he abolished the Operations Coordinating Board and relegated the Planning Board to what became a luncheon discussion group. In his statement announcing the action, the President said that his administration planned to do the board's work in other ways. "First," he said, "we will center responsibility for much of the Board's work in the Secretary of State. He expects to rely particularly on the Assistant Secretaries in charge of regional bureaus, and they in turn will consult closely with other departments and agencies. This will be our ordinary rule for continuing coordination of our work in relation to a country or area." Something over forty-five interdepartmental committees died with the OCB, and the White House killed another thirty or forty in the next few weeks. Instead of regular weekly meetings, the NSC met only for special problems; and there were only sixteen such occasions in the first six months. Thus the general thrust was to give responsibility for leadership to the Department of State.

In a letter to Senator Jackson, whose subcommittee was following up its earlier work, McGeorge Bundy summed up the changes the new administration had made in the NSC structure, and, again, the theme was that responsibility was being given to the Department of State. Recalling that Robert Cutler, the principal Eisenhower aide in the NSC, had praised the flexibility of the NSC structure, and had stressed that "each President may use the Council as he finds most suitable at a given time," Bundy said that three specific changes had occurred in the Kennedy administration. The first was that the NSC met less often than in the Eisenhower administration—only sixteen times in the first six months, as mentioned above. Bundy went on to describe smaller, less formal meetings in which many of the same people were present—which in fact eventually developed into what was called the "Executive Committee" at the time of the Cuban missile crisis a year later.

Bundy regarded the abolition of the Operations Coordinating Board as the second major development. Arguing that this was not in any sense a downgrading of the tasks of co-ordination and follow-up, but a move to eliminate an instrument that did not match the style of the new administration, Bundy went on to say that the OCB was a committee in which no member had authority over any other, and that its work could be better done in other ways. "The most important of these other ways,"

Bundy wrote, "is an increased reliance on the leadership of the Department of State."

The third change Bundy described was the new administration's action to rub out the distinction between planning and operations in the work of the White House staff. Under Kennedy this staff was smaller than it was under the previous administration and, according to Bundy, more closely knit. "Their job," he wrote, "is to help the President, not to supersede or supplement any of the high officials who hold the line responsibilities in the executive departments and agencies. . . . Heavy responsibilities for operation, for coordination, and for diplomatic relations can be and are delegated to the Department of State. Full use of all the powers of leadership can be and is expected in other departments and agencies. There remains a crushing burden of responsibility, and of sheer work, on the President himself; there remains also the steady flow of questions, of ideas, of executive energy which a strong President will give off like sparks. If his Cabinet officers are to be free to do their own work, the President's work must be done—to the extent that he cannot do it himself—by staff officers under his direct oversight."

RUSK'S SPEECH TO THE POLICY-MAKING OFFICERS

At President Kennedy's instigation, Secretary of State Dean Rusk made a speech to the policy-making officers of the State Department summing up the new administration's expectations and stressing above all that the State Department was expected to lead, to "take charge." Describing a world of change, the Secretary called upon the officers of the Department to assume the "leadership of change," to reduce the "infant mortality rate of ideas," to assume responsibility not only for the formulation but the active co-ordination of policy. "We have a President," he said, "with great interest in foreign affairs. We have a President who will rely heavily upon the Department of State for the conduct of our foreign relations. This will not be a passive reliance but an active expectation on his part that this Department will in fact take charge of foreign policy." The recent executive order which abolished the Operations Coordinating Board, he went on to say, bore witness to the fact that the Department of State was expected to assume leadership of foreign policy. In consequence, an enormous responsibility fell upon the State Department, not only in developing policies but in seeing that they were carried out.

The climax of the speech came in the paragraph quoted at the beginning of this section—the ringing words in which the Secretary declared that power gravitates to those who are willing to make decisions and called upon the Department of State to be among those "intrepid few."

It was exactly to encourage new ideas and a "take charge" approach that we understood our task to be in the Bureau of Intelligence and Research, and I had my secretary type out the Secretary's words on a card, which I kept on the corner of my desk. A good friend, Richard E. Neustadt, an authority on the presidency whose book had impressed President Kennedy and who was serving as a consultant in the organizing phase of the new administration, was in my office a few days later. Suddenly, during our talk, he noticed the card and especially the phrase that the Department of State was "expected to take charge."

"My God, I hope it does," Neustadt said with an intensity of feeling that startled me. "If the Secretary and the Department don't catch and run with this ball, we will all be paying for the failure."

Both the Bay of Pigs and Vietnam came to be haunting symbols of what we had to pay for the failure, but that was later. For several weeks I kept the card on my desk. But gradually it became a painful reminder of what Neustadt had said rather than an inspiration. For it was increasingly clear that the State Department and the Secretary did not have a very firm grip on the ball, nor were they going to run with it.

NOTES

[1] On this point see Warner R. Schilling, "The Politics of National Defense: Fiscal 1950," in Warner R. Schilling, Paul Hammond, and Glenn Snyder, *Strategy, Politics, and Defense Budgets*, 1962, pp. 16–17.

[2] Richard E. Neustadt, "Approaches to Staffing the Presidency: Notes on FDR and JFK," *American Political Science Review*, December 1963.

[3] For a description of the workings of the NSC structure during the Eisenhower administration, see Robert Cutler, "The Development of the National Security Council," *Foreign Affairs*, April 1956.

[4] Dean Acheson, "Thoughts about Thought in High Places," New York *Times Magazine*, October 11, 1959.

[5] A representative sample would include the following: Hans Morganthau, "Can We Entrust Defense to a Committee?," New York *Times Magazine*, June 7, 1959; Don K. Price, edited, for the American Assembly, *The Secretary of State*, 1960; George F. Kennan, "America's Administrative Response to Its World Problems," *Daedalus*, vol. 87, No. 2, Spring 1958; Henry A. Kissinger, "The Policy-maker and the Intellectual," *Reporter*, March 5, 1959; W. W. Rostow, "The Fallacy of the Fertile Gondolas," *Harvard Alumni Bulletin*, May 25, 1957; Paul H. Nitze, "Organization for National Policy Planning in the United States," a paper presented to the American Political Science Association, September 1959.

[6] Roger Hilsman, "Planning for National Security: A Proposal," *Bulletin of the Atomic Scientists*, March 1960.

CHAPTER 3

Practice: Failure and the Bay of Pigs

THE FIRST opportunity for decisive action came in the matter of appointments. But in the State Department, unlike the rest of the New Frontier, even the process of filling the vacancies with new presidential appointees seemed to belie the calls for action. President Kennedy had set up "Operation Talent Hunt" under his brother-in-law, Sargent Shriver, with instructions to turn up people with ability without regard to party or how they voted in the election. The idea worked, too, producing the names of men like Robert S. McNamara, whom no one had ever thought of for governmental office, and a number of brilliant younger men like Nicholas J. Katzenbach, who went into the Department of Justice, and Alain Enthoven and Charles Hitch, both of the RAND Corporation, who went into the Defense Department. Working with Chester Bowles, who had Shriver's same bold approach, the "Talent Hunt" group turned up equally good suggestions for the State Department—from down the line in the foreign service as well as from the outside. The names included men like Edwin O. Reischauer, Ambassador to Japan; Teodoro Moscoso, Ambassador to Venezuela first and then Director of the Alliance for Progress; Abram Chayes, Legal Adviser; Lincoln Gordon, Ambassador to Brazil; Ben S. Stephansky, up from the Foreign Service to be Ambassador to Bolivia; Edmund A. Gullion, also from the Foreign Service to be Ambassador to the Congo; J. Kenneth Galbraith, Ambassador to India; William Attwood, Ambassador to Guinea; Edwin M. Martin, also a career officer, who eventually became Assistant Secretary for Latin American Affairs; and so on.

But in the case of the State Department, there were unaccountable delays after Bowles and the "Talent Hunt" people had made their recommendations to the Secretary of State. Very few of the recommendations were vetoed in the end, the one conspicuous case being Walt W. Rostow, whose appointment as head of the Policy Planning Staff Rusk finally did not accept. But the long, agonizing delays caused pain to the prospective appointees and wonder in the ranks of the career people. Both Abram Chayes, who became Legal Adviser, and J. Kenneth Galbraith, who became Ambassador to India, for example, had been very close to President Kennedy before and during the campaign. Yet their appointments were delayed so long that press leaks began to cause speculation that they were for some reason being sabotaged. In one case, this was exactly what happened. Douglass Cater had been proposed as Assistant Secretary for Public Affairs in the State Department. But his appointment was stalled, there were leaks to the press, and the outside opposition to his appointment had plenty of time to muster enough pressure to kill it.

Much the same thing happened in policy matters. Crises arose, but rather than the State Department "taking charge," it seemed ill-prepared and occasionally befuddled. The Secretary himself seemed to want to hold back, and everyone else began to hold back too. To force action, the President began to appoint interdepartmental "task forces." One of the first of these was on Latin American matters, and the President chose Adolf Berle, the old New Dealer, as chairman, giving him at the same time a position as a special White House aide. When the State Department's response to the growing crisis in Berlin remained halting and timid, the President not only decided on another task force, but in choosing a chairman reached past the State Department to Paul Nitze, then Assistant Secretary of Defense for International Security Affairs. At the urgings of the Secretary of Defense, Robert S. McNamara, a Vietnam task force was also set up—under the chairmanship of Roswell Gilpatric, the Deputy Secretary of Defense. Power was not going to the State Department, but away from it.

The career people down the line in the State Department watched all this with wonder. The President was making phone calls to desk men, the White House staff was calling for new ideas, and there was throughout the rest of Washington a surge of excitement and stirrings of movement. There were plenty of able career people with ideas, but they hesitated longer than people in the other agencies about putting them forward. As they watched the actions taken those first few weeks, they were not at all sure just how much the Secretary of State meant of what he had said about the State Department "taking charge."

THE OPERATIONS CENTER

One effort the State Department did make and the Secretary supported was the new Operations Center. The Defense Department had its War Room, which served as a central nerve center, fully manned, and equipped with twenty-four-hour-a-day communications to United States military installations all over the world. Even the CIA had modern communications and coding equipment. But the State Department was hopelessly behind. Its cryptographic equipment was obsolescent, which slowed communications, and it had no central situation room at all. If a crisis arose in the middle of the night, a communications clerk would telephone a duty officer at his home, who would dress, drive to the Department, read the cable, and then decide whether to wake up someone higher on the ladder with the authority to act. By the time the process was completed, so much time had passed that the officer who could take action was usually at work anyway. Secretary Rusk directed that the Department should set up a room with communications tickers hooked to the military networks, scrambler phones, and so on, and man it with middle-grade foreign service officers who could at least make judgments about urgency in the middle of the night.

Hope began to grow that the "Op Center," as it came to be called, would be the answer to the State Department's problems. The Secretary appointed a very senior career foreign service officer and former ambassador, Theodore C. Achilles, to head the center, and issued instructions that the task forces were to be "housed" there. Achilles, who had been about to retire, looked very much like the popular stereotype of the old-time foreign service officer. Never without a pipe, he spoke slowly and judiciously between puffs, and had a general air of tweediness. In an effort to give the center a boost and at least some of the youth and vigor of the New Frontier, Stephen Smith, the President's thirty-two-year-old brother-in-law was persuaded to join the center as Achilles' deputy, although unforeseen personal circumstances prevented him from remaining in the position for more than a short time.

The improved communications and a place from which crises could be managed at night or on weekends were a great help. But the Op Center was really just a gimmick, and hardly a substitute for the active, driving leadership that was needed if the State Department was to meet its new responsibilities successfully. What made matters worse was that Achilles assumed that the center would take on regular substantive responsibilities as well as being a service center for others. And this caused trouble for the men who would mean the difference in making foreign policy effective—the regional Assistant Secretaries of State.

ROLE OF THE ASSISTANT SECRETARIES

There are five regional Assistant Secretaries of State—African Affairs, European Affairs, Latin American Affairs, Far Eastern Affairs, and Near Eastern and South Asian Affairs. Rusk himself on several occasions before and after he became Secretary stressed that the job of Assistant Secretary was "the crucial post in terms of the art of management of policy in our relations with the rest of the world."[1] To anyone who knows the State Department's work, the point is obviously sound. The Secretary of State can give very broad guidance, as well as leadership. He can manage a particular crisis, if he has the specialized knowledge and the desire to do it, as Secretary Dulles managed the Quemoy-Matsu crisis of

1958. As a practical matter, Secretaries of State have also taken over the day-by-day management of two or three of the most important continuing problems. In the post-World War II world, for example, most Secretaries of State have for obvious reasons made relations with the Soviet Union their principal concern, as well as the concomitant liaison with the United Kingdom, France, and Germany. But the foreign affairs of a great power are too extensive for one man to manage them all.

On the other hand, significant items of foreign policy cannot be managed at a level lower than a member of an administration, a man who is appointed by the President and who is therefore in a position at least to begin to inject into policy the broad political considerations which must peculiarly concern the President. What I mean is such considerations as the effect on different segments of the American society and the special interest groups that are involved, what the Congress, the press, and the mass of the people will accept, and how much effort will have to be made to develop the kind of consensus and public support that will be needed. Only the President can apply this kind of broad political judgment to policy in any final sense. But each of the five regional Assistant Secretaries is important precisely because he is the President's appointee, and as such he is the junction at which all strands of policy—political, military, economic, and diplomatic—first come together. His is the *first* level in government that can begin to apply these broad political considerations to policy and the management of foreign affairs. Paul H. Nitze, former head of the Policy Planning Staff, meant the same thing when he once said to me long before the Kennedy administration came to responsibility, "Never underestimate the importance of the regional Assistant Secretary. He's the first person on the ladder who can *commit* the United States of America."

What the Op Center's move into substantive matters did was to dilute the authority of the regional Assistant Secretaries without in any way lessening their responsibility. The Assistant Secretaries still had to take the rap, but the Op Center was one more office with a policy position that had to be considered, one more office that had to be "co-ordinated," one more representative to be invited to departmental meetings that were already overcrowded with representatives from the Policy Planning Council, Public Affairs, Intelligence, Congressional Relations, Politico-Military Affairs, and so on. And it compounded the problem of *inter*-departmental meetings, where the Assistant Secretary frequently had to try to continue to be the focal point in competition with high-ranking generals or civilian Secretaries or Assistant Secretaries from the Department of Defense and equally powerful and ambitious representatives from Treasury, the Agency for International Development, or the Central Intelligence Agency. What the State Department needed was vigorous and aggressive—even belligerent—support for the Assistant Secretary in asserting the Department's primacy in both the formulation and execution of policy, as the President desired, not a further dilution of his authority within the department itself.

Then, in the midst of all the organizational maneuvering came the Bay of Pigs debacle in the last part of April 1961. If some extra-galactic observer with a wisdom and insight undreamed of on earth were asked to comment on the Bay of Pigs affair, he might well say that it was through this comparatively small disaster, though disaster it clearly was, that President Kennedy learned the lessons that enabled him to avoid a much greater, nuclear disaster a year and a half later by managing the Cuban missile crisis with such a sure and steady hand. If so, the price may have been cheap. But the Bay of Pigs was a failure on Kennedy's part, nevertheless, and he learned that no President may ever completely trust the experts—whether military experts at the Pentagon or intelligence experts in the CIA. And the Bay of Pigs also revealed to the President just how far the State Department had fallen short of taking up the role of leadership he had assigned to it.

In retrospect it seems clear that three separate factors contributed to the Bay of Pigs decision. There was, first of all, a new administration presented with an extraordinarily chancy scheme at the very outset of its term of office, before the new men had had any time to get shaken down and accustomed to working together.

The second factor requires some background. The plans with which the new administration was confronted—to use a Cuban refugee force that the preceding administration had armed and trained—were put forward by three holdovers from that preceding administration. One was Allen Dulles, the Director of the CIA; the second was Richard M. Bissell, Jr., a deputy director of CIA, and the third was General Lyman L. Lemnitzer, Chairman of the Joint Chiefs of Staff. Allen Dulles had been an important official in the United States Government off and on since the twenties, and he was probably the most experienced intelligence officer the United States had ever had. Bissell was a brilliant economist and government executive whom President Kennedy had known for several years and so admired and respected that he would very probably have made him Director of the CIA when Dulles eventually retired. Lemnitzer was the senior general on active duty with the Army; he had had forty years' service and at the time of the Bay of Pigs he occupied the highest post that a military man might reach in time of peace, the chairmanship of the Joint Chiefs of Staff. It was my good fortune to know and work with all three of these outstanding men, and particularly Allen Dulles, for whom I developed an affection as well as admiration. Yet all three are human, and while their abilities were obvious to the new administration, what was not so obvious was that all three, and especially Dulles and Bissell, had become emotionally involved. All three may have felt some guilt for the original loss of Cuba to Castro's Communism, but in any case they were so deeply involved in the development of the Cuban invasion plans that they were no longer able to see clearly or to judge soundly. There was so deep a commitment, indeed, that there was an unconscious effort to confine consideration of the proposed operation to as small a number of people as possible, so as to avoid too harsh or thorough a scrutiny of the plans.

A single anecdote will illustrate the point. As Director of Intelligence and Research of the Department of State at the time, I held a position whose incumbent, obviously, would normally be involved in the consideration of such matters. Yet although I had known of the existence of the Cuban refugee force—mainly from articles in the press—I knew nothing of the plans to use the force until one day in a meeting Allen Dulles let drop a remark that made me realize something was up. I went straight to the Secretary of State and told him what I had learned. I reminded him what he already knew from his own military experience, that an invasion on a hostile shore was probably the most difficult of all military operations, and that if the CIA expected the brigade of a thousand Cuban refugees to win against Castro's two-hundred-thousand-man militia, the assumption must be that the Cuban people would rise. I was no expert on Cuba, but there were plenty of people in the Bureau of Intelligence and Research who were, and I asked the Secretary for permission to put them to work on the question. "I'm sorry," he replied, "but I can't let you. This is being too tightly held."

My personal lesson from the Bay of Pigs is that in such circumstances an official should not ask to be permitted to do a study, but should simply go ahead with whatever study seems necessary on his own authority. The specialists in the Intelligence Bureau were all cleared for top secret, and there was no risk from them of a break in security. But the point of the incident is that the Secretary of State was forced by what seems to me to have been CIA's excessive security restrictions to make a judgment without the benefit of advice from his own intelligence staff. And I suspect the same held true for the others who were asked for their approval. Robert Amory, Jr., the Deputy Director of CIA for Intelligence, for example, who was in charge of intelligence research and estimates, was also kept in the dark. This meant that the President was denied the judgment of CIA's own estimators on the research side of the organization. And I would not be surprised to learn that the Joint Chiefs of Staff were also required to give a judgment without benefit of the advice of experts on their own staffs.

The third factor in the Bay of Pigs decision was the failure of the State Department to play its role in forcing full weight to be given to political considerations.

The proposal to use the Cuban refugee forces posed a peculiarly delicate political problem for President Kennedy. He had specifically and repeatedly ruled out the use of American forces in overthrowing Castro during the hard-fought presidential campaign. Yet when he came into office he found well-advanced plans to use the Cuban refugee force in a landing at Trinidad, a harbor on the southern coast, almost three hundred miles from Havana. This plan would require some U.S. participation—although supposedly so little that if the operation were successful, the American role could plausibly be denied. President Kennedy nevertheless decided to stand on his campaign statements that there would be no U.S. troops involved. Dulles and Bissell then developed a new set of plans at a different landing place, the Bay of Pigs, and they assured the President that the operation would be successful without any U.S. involvement at all.

The decisive question was whether the operation would really be successful. The President might have great doubts himself, but if he said "No" to an operation to get rid of Communist Castro that had been prepared by the previous administration, and that was fully supported by the career military and intelligence experts, the fact of his saying, "No" would promptly leak to the Republicans—and his administration, plastered with a label of "weakness," would never get off the ground in the great enterprises he had set for it. If the State Department and the Secretary stood up strong and clear against the plan, then he, the President, would have a choice. But whatever opposition that did come from the Secretary of State and his department was neither strong nor clear. The only course for a President in such circumstances is to delay, not to say, "No," but to say, "Maybe," or "We'll see"—laying down whatever conditions he feels necessary, such as the assurances about the use of American troops, until he is as certain as a man can be that the outcome will be successful or until the proposal dies without his ever having had to say, "No."

But presidents have used delaying tactics before, and there are counter-tactics. The pressures and the sense of urgency began to mount. There were reports that Cubans were being trained behind the Iron Curtain to fly Soviet MIG fighter planes and that MIGs were on their way to Cuba, and Dulles and Bissell interpreted these reports to mean that if an invasion were to succeed, it must be mounted soon. Another argument was that the Cuban refugee forces were at their peak of morale and training and would begin to go downhill fast if they were not soon used. It was mentioned that the weather could be expected to turn less favorable to the operation shortly—and so on.

The Secretary of State had to be away for a few days late in March, and Chester Bowles, as Acting Secretary, learned of the plans. He was horrified, and on March 31 he wrote a long memorandum to Rusk urging that the State Department take a strong stand against the whole idea. Although Rusk was apparently reluctant to start out as Secretary of State with a head-on clash with the CIA and the military, he seems to have made some sort of attempt to get the operation played down, so that it would look less like an invasion and more like just another infiltration of reinforcements to the tiny anti-Castro guerrilla force in the hills. Or so Bowles understood.

THE "SECOND STRIKE"

After it was all over the people down the line in CIA tried to excuse the failure of the operation in both official briefings and in unofficial leaks to the press on the grounds that everything would have been all right if the second bombing strike had not been canceled. After a while all this effort to put the blame for failure on the cancellation of the second strike began to remind me of a supply sergeant I knew in World War II. Whenever a C-47 from his squadron went down, he would list all the lost, strayed, or stolen items still on his books as part of the cargo —until he overdid it once and someone added up the weights and discovered that a C-47 so heavily loaded couldn't have gotten off the ground. The "second strike" of the Bay of Pigs was very much like that C-47: in hindsight, at least, it was expected to carry quite a load. The argument was that it was Castro's air attacks that defeated the landing force, that the first strike got half of Castro's planes, and that a second strike would have gotten the rest.[2] A first strike may achieve surprise and succeed in knocking out 50 per cent of a number of planes parked in the open at a single airport when no war was on and no attack was expected. But a second strike, twenty-four hours later, when the planes have been dispersed, hidden, and protected, has no hope at all of achieving such total surprise. And the overwhelming point is that if Castro's air attacks on the beachhead had not crushed the one-thousand-man landing force, the two-hundred-thousand-man army of militiamen that followed would certainly have done so.

The cancellation of the "second strike" did not doom the Bay of Pigs operation. It was doomed from the beginning, and the true failure was in not seeing this when the decision was made. President Kennedy failed in trusting too much the judgment of experts whose expertise was inevitably parochial. He failed in not realizing the emotional commitment of Dulles and Bissell and, in not realizing the dangers in the very newness of the new administration. Dulles and Bissell failed in letting themselves become emotionally involved. The Joint Chiefs failed in not insisting on a more thorough military study and in not pointing out the military risks. And the Secretary of State failed in refusing to take a strong stand and in not insisting that experts who had a contribution to make should be allowed to make it. Above all, both the Secretary and the department failed to make the case for political considerations that should have been made. They failed to take up the role of leadership that the President had expected of them.

THE ATTACK ON THE STATE DEPARTMENT

Certainly one of the conclusions that President Kennedy himself drew from his reflection on the Bay of Pigs in the weeks that followed was that something had to be done about the State Department. What could he do if the State Department continued to fail to rise to the challenge, or, alternatively, how could he force them to rise to it?

The air in Washington soon got tangy with the smell of impending bloodshed, and the press began to nose out bits and pieces of information on the nature of the President's dissatisfaction, to try to interpret what was in his mind, and to try to influence any action he might take. The town buzzed with rumors and the press reported most of them. The first target was the more or less anonymous "State Department." The President referred to the department privately as a "bowl of jelly" and the word got around. The press reported that the Latin American bureau was full of "confusion and lack of direction."[3] They said that the Far Eastern bureau was "wishy-washy" and little more than a lackey of Chiang Kai-shek and the Nationalist Chinese.[4] And there were specifics. The story went the rounds that Ambassador Galbraith asked for instructions from the department on a question to be raised with Nehru and got such a collection of clichés that he made a point of showing it to the President—who threw it all in the wastebasket. In a press conference on July 19 the President publicly expressed concern at the weeks it had taken to reply to the note Khrushchev had handed him at Vienna on June 4—a total of forty-three days. He put it off mainly on the problems of having to consult with the other members of NATO—jesting that Napoleon had once said that he won his victories because his enemies were a group of allies —but there was enough of a hint of dissatisfaction with the State Department to set the press off to find the full story. It was simple enough. As one newsman reported it, the Soviet note said nothing new, so the reply could be nothing but a standard assertion of United States claims, and all that could be demanded was "speed, clarity, briskness, and possibly eloquence." When the department's reply was finally ready, it had not one of the possible virtues, and although it had indeed been necessary to consult with some of our allies, these took "nowhere near as long as the consultations between one State Department desk and another."[5]

Actually, what had added insult to injury was that some language that Kennedy himself had suggested for the note was ignored, and the President was forced to use it only as a covering statement when the note was issued to the press.

The only part of the department that came in for any praise in the period from the Bay of Pigs to Thanksgiving, 1961, was the Bureau of African Affairs and G. Mennen Williams, the former Governor of Michigan who had been named Assistant Secretary before any other State Department appointment had been made, including that of Secretary Rusk. It was reported that Williams had indeed taken charge, and that he had inspired a once demoralized staff. "American policy on the Congo," one member of the Bureau of African Affairs is reported to have said, "used to be run by the Pentagon, the CIA, the European desks, everyone but us; but now we're running it."[6]

ON THE SECRETARY

The second target was the Secretary of State himself. The Washington *Post* reported that inside the department, on Capitol Hill, and in the White House itself Rusk was credited with every quality for the secretaryship with the exception of "vigorous leadership and assertiveness."[7] Rusk was described as being "unassertive and conventional" in one article which went on to say that although he had built a reputation for "careful competence" the President's confidence in him had been shaken by his reluctance to take a strong position on Cuba.[8] Another reporter, summing up press accounts, said that Rusk's "cautious, undramatic" approach did not endear him to the press, who used words like "loner" and "compulsive insider" to describe him and who accused him of failing to take decisive stands on anything—Cuba, Laos, Berlin, or even to defend his colleagues and subordinates when they were attacked.[9] Even James Reston and the normally staid New York *Times* joined in. When Chester Bowles came under fire, Reston suggested that Bowles was being made the fall guy for Rusk's failures. "Rusk himself said in March that the President expected the Department to take charge of foreign policy," Reston wrote, "and if it hasn't done so, then it is not the responsibility of Bowles."[10]

The rumor mill added its contribution in the form of a raft of vicious and malicious political jokes, usually not very funny but always cruel. One story going the rounds at the time, for example, had a White House aide asking what the Secretary of State thought about a high policy matter, and the other inquiring whether anyone had ever discovered what the Secretary thought about anything. And there were many others.

One story, however, was repeated so persistently that it was more carefully noted by the old Washington hands than any of the others. "How do you fire a Secretary of State," the President was supposed to have been overheard asking, "who never does anything, good or bad?"

AND ON CHESTER BOWLES

The third target, of course, was Chester Bowles, the Under Secretary of State. Bowles had done good work for the President during the campaign, advising him on foreign policy matters. Since taking over as Under Secretary he had taken on the job of rejuvenating not only the department but the missions overseas, and he had brought a creative imagination and a wide acquaintanceship in the field of foreign affairs to the task of bringing in new people. A whole new slate of remarkably able, young, and vigorous ambassadors and departmental officers, from both within the foreign service and from the outside, had been appointed by the New Frontier and much of the credit for this belonged to Bowles. He had gone out to the posts and missions to explain the new policies and to give the men in the field some sense of the movement the new administration was giving to United States foreign policy and of his own excitement at the prospects ahead. He had in those few months done more than any other man in the administration to correct the imbalance that had existed in the previous administration between the State Department and the Central Intelligence Agency. And it was he more than anyone else who brought into the day-by-day workings of the State Department the concern of the New Frontier with the importance of the emerging nations of Africa, Asia, the Middle East, and Latin America. Yet Bowles was a natural target for some of the more conservative members of Congress and the press. Even though he had been quiet and in the background as Under Secretary, his past advocacy of foreign aid, of the importance of the emerging peoples during and after his ambassadorship to India, and so on labeled him a "militant liberal" in conservative eyes. His work as Chairman of the Democratic Platform Committee in a year that gave prominence to both foreign policy and civil rights further alienated the conservatives, especially the Southerners. And the very effectiveness of his work to give the State Department and the foreign service a new vigor came to hurt him. For those attacking Bowles were further inspired by old-guard foreign service officers being eased into a retirement that they blamed on Bowles and his emphasis on new and younger blood. The attackers even made sly use of the fact that Bowles had been right on the biggest foreign policy crisis so far, the Bay of Pigs. For they suggested that it was Bowles himself who had leaked to the press the fact that he had opposed the operation.

Not surprisingly, the attack on Bowles quickly got enmeshed with organizational matters, concentrating on the known fact that the President was dissatisfied with the State Department and arguing that the cause of the trouble was that the department was not being well administered. The anti-Bowles argument was that a "strong managerial hand at the top level" was lacking but that Rusk couldn't be blamed because the Secretary had to concentrate on "policy" while the Under Secretary concentrated on "administration." In actual fact, Bowles had done more to give direction to the rambling State Department bureaucracy than anyone else, more to streamline it, and more to make its procedures efficient. And he also had had more executive experience than anyone else in the department. He had made a great deal of money in private business, meeting many "payrolls" in the process; he had headed OPA during World War II; he had been Governor of Connecticut—jobs that were challenges precisely of skill in administration, and he had met them with great success. It was the patent unfairness of an attack on Bowles's capacity and performance as an administrator that had prompted Reston and the New York *Times* to come to his defense.

But it was also true that Bowles was somewhat out of tune with the New Frontier. The men in the administration of Kennedy's age and intellectual bent thought of themselves as liberals, but as hardheaded and pragmatic liberals. Even though Bowles's ideas and policies were virtually identical to their own, his expression of them was too high-flown, too idealistically stated. In actuality, President Kennedy agreed with Bowles on many issues—even on some of the more controversial ones. But Kennedy was looking for economy, crispness, and precision in words and rapidity and decisiveness in action—and Bowles tended to overgeneralization in words and to be less interested in action than in articulating grand policy. Finally, even though Bowles did not leak to the press the fact that he had opposed the Bay of Pigs operation, he had said as much to friends—which others felt was not appropriate at a time when the new administration was in its first major trouble.

Even those who counted themselves as Bowles's particular friends began to feel that he had probably been miscast as Under Secretary. They had felt before that a deputy's job did not give Bowles the scope and authority to exercise his talents, and they now began to feel that a man of his stature and vision would have a difficult time bringing himself down to the backstairs maneuvering, manipulating, and bureaucratic in-fighting that was going to have to be done by the Under Secretary if the department was to hold its own against the Pentagon and the CIA when the Secretary of State himself was a man whose personal style was to remain aloof.

In any case, the rumors turned out to be very near the mark. As Arthur M. Schlesinger, Jr., later reported, the President decided that shifting the Secretary of State would "constitute too severe a comment on his original judgment."[11] The President decided to shift Bowles instead.

But when the decision began to leak, the conservatives, within and outside the administration, who opposed Bowles for his policy views, made too much of the fact that he was being replaced. The liberals in the press and on Capitol Hill counterattacked with outrage and the headlines grew even bigger. If Bowles were shifted under this kind of publicity barrage, it would be politically embarrassing. The Republicans and conservative Democrats would regard his ouster as their first scalp, and the administration would appear either to be giving way to petty resentment over Bowles' having been right about the Bay of Pigs and letting it be known, or of caving in to right-wing pressures. At his news conference on July 19, 1961, the President, in response to a question, praised Bowles and his contribution, and went on to say, "My judgment is now that he should stay as Under Secretary of State, and if there's going to be any change, I'll make it very clear at the time." The significance of the word "now" was not missed.

Over the next four months, there was renewed pressure from the White House for the State Department to be faster and more responsive and pressure from within the State Department itself to reassert the department's primacy of interest in the task forces, such as the ones on Berlin and Vietnam. Paul Nitze had handled the Berlin task force with tact— holding the meetings, for example, in the State Department, even though he was an Assistant Secretary of Defense—and this made the readjustment easier than it might have been. But the matter still required some maneuvering. As an interim measure, Foy D. Kohler, who was Assistant Secretary of State for European Affairs, was appointed full-time chairman of the task force in place of Nitze, and the rest of his responsibilities were turned over to his deputy, William R. Tyler. The final solution had to wait until Kohler became ambassador to Moscow in July of 1962. Tyler then became Assistant Secretary and Martin Hillenbrand, one of Tyler's deputies, quietly took over the chairmanship of the task force while remaining under the jurisdiction of the Assistant Secretary—the normal situation. The Vietnam task force underwent a similar transformation.

But these moves did no more than restore the flow of day-by-day work to regular channels and eliminate the confusion caused by the original disruption. Something more fundamental would be needed to revitalize the State Department, to make it more responsive to the President's needs, and to ensure that it would be able to provide the central leadership and co-ordination that had been intended to be the State Department's responsibility. In the interregnum, the President considered a variety of alternatives. One possibility was to remove the entire top command at State and start over. Another was to give up the idea of making the State Department *primus inter pares* and center the function of leadership and co-ordination in the White House. But whichever alternative the President finally chose, it had to take into account the personalities involved—Dean Rusk, Robert S. McNamara, McGeorge Bundy, John A. McCone, the man chosen to replace Allen Dulles as Director of CIA, and, finally, the President himself.

NOTES

[1] This particular quote is from his testimony before the Jackson Subcommittee on December 11, 1963.

[2] For example, see Charles J. V. Murphy, "Cuba, the Record Set Straight," *Fortune*, September 1961, which bears the earmarks of a story inspired by deliberate—and somewhat distorted—leaks from CIA. There also was a suggestion that the planes of the "second strike" could also have knocked out the causeways over which Castro brought his tanks to the battle—as they flew home from knocking out the air force!

[3] The Washington *Post*, June 7, 1961.

[4] Washington *Star*, in an article summing up earlier events, November 27, 1961.

[5] Richard Rovere, "Letter From Washington," *The New Yorker*, December 9, 1961.

[6] Joseph Kraft, "Come-back of the State Department," *Harper's* magazine, November 1961.

[7] Washington *Post*, July 15, 1961.

[8] *New Republic*, "Disarray at State," July 24, 1961.

[9] Kraft, *op. cit.*

[10] New York *Times*, July 19, 1961.

[11] Arthur M. Schlesinger, Jr., *A Thousand Days*, p. 436.

CHAPTER 4

Personalities: Cunning Men or Wise?

"A SINGLE MAN," President Kennedy used to say, "can make a difference." There are more choices at more crossroads in the course of events than students of the broad sweep of history might realize. The choices are rarely presented as grand alternatives, but show themselves as a series of incremental shifts and for this very reason, the instinctive, gut reaction—the individual personality—has particular scope. "Nothing doth more harm in a state," Francis Bacon said, "than that cunning men pass for wise." If President Kennedy was going to move the nation and so the world, as he was dedicated to doing, he had either to gather around himself a group of men whose instinctive, "personality" reaction in tight spots would be in the same direction as his own or he had to find a way of relating the existing personalities to each other in such a way as to accomplish that purpose. He had to relate the different personalities to each other in a way that would permit him to make the necessary adjustments and compensations, to push this man, restrain that, to substitute this strength for that weakness.

The personality equation with which President Kennedy had to deal at this time had five main variables, as mentioned above, Dean Rusk, Robert S. McNamara, McGeorge Bundy, John A. McCone, and the President himself.

DEAN RUSK

Dean Rusk was born and raised in Cherokee County, one of the poorest and most backward in all Georgia, the son of a Presbyterian minister who had been forced to turn from the ministry to farming because of a throat ailment. Winning a Rhodes scholarship to Oxford, Rusk worked his way up. He taught for six years at Mills College in California, rising to be dean of the faculty. Ordered to active duty as a reserve officer in World War II, he reached the rank of colonel. After the war, he served as a civilian aide in both the Pentagon and the State Department. Later, as Secretary of State, he was fond of saying that he had served as much of his working life in the Pentagon as anywhere else in the government. In 1947, he settled down at the State Department and rose steadily until by the end of the Truman administration, he was serving as Assistant

Secretary of State for Far Eastern Affairs. He was then offered and accepted the post of President of the Rockefeller Foundation, which he held from 1952 until 1960.

Rusk brought to the secretaryship an extraordinary intelligence, which was displayed not in flashing brilliance, but in judiciousness and especially in a capacity to keep simultaneously in mind all the many facets of the inherently multifaceted problems with which the State Department deals. It could be argued, in fact, that his reputation for extreme cautiousness was really his capacity to see so many sides of a question at the same time and hence his unwillingness to reduce it to the kind of simplified fundamentals that are conducive to decisive action. A man of great physical stamina, Rusk worked longer hours, more days a week than any other Secretary in history. He is supposed to have taken only four days off in four years.

Rusk also brought to the job a sweet and gentle wit, and he would laugh with crinkled eyes, chuckling in a suppressed bubbling as if he were trying to hold the lid on a whole pot of laughter. I remember once a very serious-minded young man asked Rusk if it were true that it was his ambition to go down in history as the Secretary of State who solved the Berlin crisis. "No," said Rusk, crinkling, "I'm not quite that vain. But I do want to go down in history as one of those Secretaries of State who succeeded in passing the Berlin crisis on to his successor!"

Rusk gave the secretaryship more of a sense of dignity and protocol than it had had since the days of Cordell Hull, and also great tact. And his wit helped here, too. When he finally decided to try to get the Vietnamese task force back under the State Department wing, he was able to turn the trick with a phrase. "If you want Vietnam," he said to McNamara, "give me the marines."

Rusk was also reserved and acutely shy. So many of his new colleagues had so much trouble feeling that they had any personal relationship with him that it came to be a constant subject of conversation. Finally, people in the State Department began to understand that he was neither incompatible nor cold, but that he was in some way afraid of being involved with people. For he was stiffest and most uncomfortable when he felt most drawn to another person or grateful to him. Rusk was often accused in the press of being "a man who likes to veil his thoughts and reserve his judgment until the last moment," which some critics felt prevented him from exercising leadership in the State Department.[1] But even though Rusk did, indeed, tend to veil his thoughts, he did so because of his difficulty in reaching out to other people, his concern to keep his defenses intact, and his discomfort in the presence of candor and openness.

This apparent coldness and the tendency to hold back his own views made some of Rusk's colleagues wonder what would happen when the

going got rough, as it was bound to get, and just how far he would go to
support them. When Bowles was under fire, Rusk stayed on the periphery,
and within the Department there was inevitably talk about loyalty being
a two-way street—"Loyalty is hilly, and it has to go down if it is going
to go up." But here again those who worked close to Rusk began to
realize that the trouble was not disloyalty to those under him, but the fear
of involvement with people combined with an intelligence that highlighted
complexities rather than ordering them. Increasingly, the people in the
State Department began to realize what the columnist Joseph Kraft later
put into words. Writing after Kennedy's death, Kraft noted that Rusk had
been criticized for turning on a number of State Department men who
had been prominent in pushing foreign policy initiatives during the Kennedy administration, but that the criticism was an exaggeration. "It was
certainly not a case of ditching subordinates who once had his support,"
Kraft wrote. "He had never really supported them in the first place."[2]
Rusk had not been opposed to the foreign policy initiatives taken in the
Kennedy administration. But neither had he pushed them. In personality,
in intelligence, and in philosophy, Rusk was a superb counselor, but he
could not bring himself to be an advocate.

Rusk's relations with the press were always correct, but they were
never good. Newsmen need sharp, clear-cut statements of administration
thinking and policy, highlighting change in particular, and Rusk's instinct
was the exact opposite. His natural tendency was to mask his thinking
and to smooth over change particularly, and he had a great skill with the
diplomatist's technique of using words that obscure rather than reveal.
To the press, both his obfuscation and his quietness were maddening. It
was often observed that Rusk's most-used expression was "low-key."
There were bets at high odds that sooner or later he would direct that
something should be played "high-key." But he never did.

On one occasion a member of the John Birch society called Rusk a
"Red" along with practically everyone else in public life, including Dwight
D. Eisenhower, and the next morning Rusk gave a cheery, "Good morning, comrades," to his colleagues at the staff meeting. An aide later related the incident to a columnist who was doing a sympathetic story,
thinking it was an endearing example of Rusk's wit. And so it was. But
Rusk himself was upset and especially troubled that one of his personal
aides would relate anything he had said at the staff meeting to the press.

On another occasion, one of his senior public relations advisers gave
some of the press a briefing on a cable to the Soviets that showed Rusk
at his toughest, precisely to counter a raft of stories that the Secretary
was "soft" or "indecisive." Since the Soviets were putting out to the press
what their own position had been, it seemed a logical countermove; but
Rusk regarded the briefing as a disastrous "leak."

The press respected Rusk for his judiciousness, his experience, and his steadiness. But they often got very angry about his attitude toward them and their function, and this frequently resulted in bitter comments. Some of these went beyond criticizing his being too "low-key" or "faceless" for a public figure. "There are two facts about Dean Rusk that are revealing," said one particularly critical newsman. "The first is that he was Assistant Secretary of State for Far Eastern Affairs during the Korean War. The second is that no one even remembers it."

ROBERT S. MCNAMARA

If the main lineaments of Rusk's personality were judiciousness, reserve, caution, and an intelligence that was sensitive to all sides of multifaceted problems in almost paralyzing detail, Robert S. McNamara was opposite in a number of fundamental ways. Born and brought up in California, McNamara went to the University of California at Berkeley, where he won a Phi Beta Kappa, and then on to the Harvard Business School. He did so well at Harvard that he moved straight from being a student to a post on the faculty. During the war, he rose to the rank of lieutenant colonel in the Air Force. He worked with the new management technique, "statistical control," and after the war was one of a group of the so-called "whiz kids" who sold themselves as a package, with the Ford Motor Company being the highest bidder. At Ford he rose steadily, until by 1960, when President Kennedy picked him for Secretary of Defense, he had been made Ford's president.

The one thing Rusk and McNamara had in common when they came to Washington in 1960 was an exceptionally high degree of intelligence. But where Rusk's intelligence focused on the subtle and the complex, McNamara's catalogued and simplified, working best with numbers and statistics. He tended to brush away broad political and strategic arguments, and to concentrate on what could be quantified—money, men, guns, and ammunition. "Management is accounting," a somewhat curmudgeony older New Frontiersman said in despair, "and McNamara is the best accountant I've ever seen. He may turn out to be the best Secretary of Defense, too, but when it comes to international politics statistics are not enough."

McNamara was an extraordinarily able man, a brilliantly efficient man. But he was not a wise man. "The issue about the Secretary of Defense," James Reston wrote much later, "is not over his inefficiency, but his decisive efficiency in putting over dubious policies. . . . He is tidy, he is confident, and he has the sincerity of an Old Testament prophet, but something is missing: some element of personal doubt, some respect for human weakness, some knowledge of history."

But even though the State Department might despair at McNamara's interventions into international politics, his creative leadership at the Defense Department was magnificent. He rebuilt the whole armed services, for the first time in its modern history giving the military establishment a coherent, flexible strategy, a rational weapons policy, and an effective co-operation among the services. He vastly increased the effectiveness of the military establishment, and while this is a different kind of achievement from that of Forrestal and Elihu Root, who brought the defense establishment into tune with political needs, it may well rank as high.

The press frequently accused McNamara of being "cold," "power-hungry," and "domineering." As Secretary of Defense, he was on occasion all of these things, but he was bold in his conceptions, and vigorous in their execution. Where Rusk was hesitant and tentative, McNamara was crisp, decisive, and almost totally lacking in self-doubt. In his field, he was superb; the risk was when he roamed beyond his field, and the concern of a President was to exercise care that his neighbors' fields did not develop vacuums into which McNamara's energy and self-confidence would thrust.

MCGEORGE BUNDY

Where Rusk and McNamara came from essentially humble backgrounds, McGeorge Bundy was as close to being an aristocrat as America can produce. He was born of a Boston family of inherited means, and his mother was related to the Lowells. His father, Harvey Bundy, was for seven years an assistant to Henry L. Stimson, who served both as Secretary of State and Secretary of War. The younger Bundy later acted as co-author with Stimson in helping him write his memoirs, and he came to regard Stimson as a sort of super-father on whom he modeled himself as much as on his own father. Thus the young Bundy grew up in an atmosphere of power, of affairs of state, and while still a child came to know the men and women who acted in national events. It is not surprising that he measured himself against those he watched, and developed ambitions to take a place for himself at high councils.

In World War II, Bundy saw it all again from a different angle as aide-de-camp to Admiral Alan G. Kirk in London and at the Normandy landings. He had graduated from Yale with high marks—both going to Yale and getting high marks were family traditions—and after the war he began to teach at Harvard. In only four years, at the exceptionally young age of thirty-four, he was made dean of the faculty. Bundy, too, came to Washington with an extraordinary intelligence—more brilliant, in fact, than either McNamara or Rusk. He was, perhaps, as able a man as any in Washington at the time.

Given his family connections and high native ability, it was only natural that Bundy would be accused of arrogance. One press account, for example called him "self-confident to the point of arrogance, intelligent to the point of intimidation."[3]

And he also had an air of impatience, a brusque, no-nonsense manner and a way of speaking shortly and sharply, even sarcastically, when he was in a hurry or merely tense, that gave the charge credibility and made him seem to ride roughshod over anyone who wasn't quite so quick as he. Yet Bundy probably had more thoughtfulness, more warmth reaching out toward other people than either Rusk or McNamara. I remember one incident that illustrated the point in particular. During the Cuban missile crisis, Thomas L. Hughes, who was Deputy Director of Intelligence and Research, was sent to New York to brief over three hundred congressmen, senators, and governors from all over the eastern seaboard. But when Hughes arrived, the *Times* already had everything that was in his briefing, including the pictures of Soviet missiles, which had been released the night before. Disturbed, Hughes phoned me to point out that it would do the administration no good if all these key congressmen felt they had come such distances for nothing.

The President's plan called for stopping a Soviet oil tanker, which would obviously have no arms, as the first test of the blockade, and then letting it proceed. This had just been done, at 8:00 A.M. that morning, when the Soviet tanker *Bucharest* had been stopped, and although there were some tricky aspects to announcing the fact, I understood the information would be released within an hour, probably even before the briefing was over. There was some risk that a congressman would spill it to the press prematurely, but the briefing, after all, was classified, and there were big "Secret" signs all over the hall. On my own authority, I told Hughes to go ahead. Not long afterward, Representative James E. Van Zandt, of Pennsylvania, who was running for the Senate and who was eager for publicity, rushed out of the secret briefing and made a statement to the press about the Soviet ship being stopped.[4] As it happened, the President had not yet released the information but had called a special meeting to consider the very question of how to handle the release. The tickers of Mr. Van Zandt's statement arrived in the middle of the meeting, and the President was furious. He began trying to reach Hughes, who by this time was at La Guardia and who found himself somewhat discomfited at being paged for a call from the President of the United States. Learning of all this, I quickly called the President myself to tell him that the responsibility for the error was mine, not Hughes's. The President, taut and concerned, gave me a tongue-lashing that made the wires sizzle, and my morale, when I was finally permitted to hang up, was very low. But within fifteen minutes, McGeorge Bundy called. "I was in the room when the President was . . . er, talking to you," he said, "and I just wanted to say that it has happened to all of us. This little hot spot will quickly cool, and you should realize that the President would not have permitted himself that kind of blow-off if you were not one of these he regards highly and fully trusts." My gratitude for Bundy's call was complete, and so is my conviction that Bundy is a man of warmth and thoughtfulness.

JOHN A. MCCONE

John A. McCone was chosen to replace Allen Dulles in October of 1961. I had not known him before and read the press accounts of the considerable opposition to his appointment with increasing uneasiness. McCone was an Irish Catholic Republican, a very rich shipbuilder from California, and many of us were afraid the administration was buying trouble.

Kennedy himself had long ago found out that rich Catholics tended to support his conservative Protestant opponents rather than accept even his pragmatic liberalism. After a testimonial dinner to the memory of Al Smith given by Cardinal Spellman, for example, where the audience had been pro-Nixon, Kennedy had remarked with ironic amusement that "when the chips are down, money counts more than religion."[5] Kennedy was committed to correcting the imbalance between the ground and air forces created by the concept of "massive retaliation," yet McCone in an interview only two years earlier had recalled that he had believed in the concept of "massive retaliation" when he had been Under Secretary of the Air Force in the Truman administration and that he still did. In addition, McCone was reputed to be so militantly anti-Communist that some of his opponents were convinced that his intelligence reporting to the President would be colored. There were people on Capitol Hill who felt that when McCone had been Chairman of the Atomic Energy Commission, during the Eisenhower administration, he not only had worked busily against Eisenhower's and Dulles' attempts to get an atomic test ban treaty, but that he had at times gone beyond the limits of what they considered loyal opposition.

Just at this time, a famous columnist asked me to lunch—and I discovered that his purpose was to repeat all that I had read and, in addition, to tell me that to McCone power was everything. "McCone," the columnist concluded, "is an 'alley fighter' who will stop at nothing."

This columnist was a serious man whom I admired, and I decided to phone Senator Henry M. Jackson, who had spent long years on the Joint Committee for Atomic Energy as a member of both the House and the Senate, and whose judgment I greatly respected. The Senator, I learned, heartily approved of the appointment. He felt that McCone was a slugger and although he could indeed be an alley fighter if he needed to, the people on the Joint Committee had found him fair and the most co-operative Chairman of the AEC they had ever had. Although not as urbane and sophisticated as Allen Dulles, McCone, in the Senator's judgment, was

sensible and open-minded. And both the Senator and his staff felt that I
would like McCone as a man.

Over the next two months, as we worked together on the United States
Intelligence Board and in co-ordinating matters between the State Department and the CIA, I got to know McCone fairly well, and I did indeed
come to like him as a man. He was very ambitious, but disarmingly
candid about it. Very soon after he arrived, to give an example, I was
offered a professorship in international politics at a large university that
was the kind of post I had always regarded as ideal, and after much
soul-searching I decided to accept. Both McCone's ambition and his
candor are illustrated in the argument he used to try to dissuade me. "I intend to be a power in this administration and to give the whole intelligence
community a bigger voice. Having a fellow like you at State would be a
big help, and if you stay you'll have a bigger voice, too." Laughing, I
told McCone that it was probably a good thing I was going, because my
own view was that, although intelligence should have an important voice,
in my judgment it was already big enough and that it was the State Department whose voice had to be enlarged. But it was typical of McCone
that he welcomed the notion of some resistance at the State Department,
too.

McCone was tough and a hard-liner, as people said, but it was a sensible
and reasonable toughness by and large, and his intelligence judgments
and policy predilections were toward a selective, discriminating application of toughness, tailored to the particular situation. When we differed in
our judgments, as we did on occasion, I also found him candid and fair-
minded. I'm sure there was a streak of the alley fighter in McCone, but
there was also a rough and ready sense of decency.

JOHN F. KENNEDY

But the President himself was undoubtedly the most extraordinary personality of them all. Quick in mind and sophisticated, Kennedy was a man
who was vastly charming, but who also had a sprightly, earthy, even
impish Irish wit. And when he was angry he could command profanities
just as effectively as that old soldier Eisenhower. Roosevelt's biographer,
Robert Sherwood, in commenting on the motives behind a decision about
which Roosevelt had left neither written nor spoken record, said that he,
Sherwood, could not begin to speculate about what went on in that "heavily
forested interior." Certainly, Kennedy's was equally profuse. He was interested in ideas and theories, but not for their own sake. His interest was
aroused only when the ideas had some practical consequence, only if they
could make it possible to shape the world, to accomplish something. He
was energetic and full of life, yet he was often in physical agony. I remember once slipping into his office to brief him before an important

foreign visitor arrived. His little son, John, not quite three, had been rollicking in his office with pillows from the couches and had left one on the floor. As I talked, the President stooped to pick it up, but had to catch himself against the desk in pain. Yet a minute later he was forceful and vigorous.

His joy in his children was obvious, and so were his love and tenderness for his wife. Not long before the President's death, I had occasion to take a foreign visitor to see him. It was one of Washington's golden autumn days, the French doors leading from the oval office to the garden were open, and as he rocked the President's gaze was drawn again and again to the lovely garden and sunlight. Suddenly, Jackie appeared in the distance, in a skirt and sweater and loafers, with the two dogs galloping off and back. The President, with pride and tenderness in his eyes, jumped up and called her over to be introduced, loafers and all.

Courage and excellence he admired especially—even in opponents. I remember shortly after the Cuban missile crisis, he agreed to tape a long TV interview with Sander Vanocur on Sunday evening, December 17, and he asked me to come chat with him that morning about the Soviet mood, bringing along one of the bureau's Soviet specialists. I took Joseph Neubert, a career foreign service officer who had done a brilliant job of analysis during the crisis, and when we arrived the President was seated in the alcove at the end of the Indian room with the morning light pouring in through the glass and the Sunday papers scattered all around him, reading Khrushchev's long speech defending his decision to withdraw the missiles. As we came in, the President looked up. "Listen to this," he said, and he read us examples of the images Khrushchev had used in his speech—that there was during the crisis "a smell of burning" in the air and that the West might be a "paper tiger," but it had nuclear teeth. "Now those," he said, "are first-rate," and he proceeded to telephone Arthur Schlesinger to twit him about how good his rival speech writers in the Kremlin were.

He had the capacity to see the complications in a world whose inconsistencies surpassed comprehension yet he had strong convictions on where we ought to be trying to move it all. He had patience and a pragmatic willingness to settle for the possible, to see the other side of questions and to provide opponents a way out. Yet he wanted to change the world and was eager to get on with the change. Much has been written about John F. Kennedy as a man, as a friend, a statesman—and much will yet be. Still, I think his greatest, almost magical quality was the ability to inspire men to help in bringing about this change, to "get America moving again"—the capacity to expose where we had fallen short as a nation and to excite the best that was in us to achieve the best of what we are still capable of . . . And yet somehow, Kennedy was able to do all this without sentimentality, to do it with both style and taste, and without

letting either the excitement or the idealism cloy. Often there was wit—
as when he wrote a balloon-pricking parody of his own inaugural address—and always there was a skeptical questioning and a cool, unruf-
fled pragmatism that included not only patience but a willingness to compromise, to make a world of diversity with room for all.

The question was how the President was going to be able to relate all
these personalities to each other and to himself in a way that would maximize strengths and compensate for weaknesses, in a positive way that
would further what he wanted his administration to accomplish. He had
to make use of McNamara's aggressive energy, yet somehow keep him
out of matters in which he had neither knowledge nor talent. He had to
draw on Rusk's judiciousness, but find some other device to energize the
Department of State. McCone's qualities as a fighter would make him
invaluable in keeping the intelligence community in line, but the President
had also to be sure that McCone did not stray beyond those responsibilities,
as well as to find means to ensure that intelligence estimates and reports
continued to be balanced and objective if there was indeed the risk some
people feared in McCone's militant anti-Communism. And he had to use
the outstanding ability and intelligence that Bundy offered without letting
the White House staff take over the responsibilities of everyone else.

NOTES

1 Joseph Alsop, "The Decision-Making Process," The New York *Herald Tribune,*
July 14, 1961.

2 Joseph Kraft, "The Enigma of Dean Rusk," *Harper's* magazine, July 1965.

3 *Time,* June 25, 1965.

4 The fact that Van Zandt had violated security may have had nothing to do with
his defeat, but it was mentioned in the elections.

5 Arthur M. Schlesinger, Jr., *op. cit.,* p. 72.

CHAPTER 5

Solution: The "Thanksgiving Day Massacre"

As WASHINGTON speculated as to how President Kennedy would mesh all these disparate personalities together, deal with the disarray at the State Department, and put some order into the still-floundering top command of his administration, the President continued to keep his own counsel.

Then, in late November 1961, with apparent suddenness, he acted. The town of Washington and the press, caught by surprise, called it the "Thanksgiving Day Massacre" at the State Department. Chester Bowles was removed from the job of Under Secretary and given a meaningless title as the President's Special Representative and Adviser on African, Asian, and Latin American Affairs to make room for George W. Ball, former Under Secretary of State for Economic Affairs, to become Rusk's deputy as the principal Under Secretary. George C. McGhee moved to Ball's position and Walt W. Rostow came over from the White House to be Assistant Secretary for Policy Planning (with Rusk reversing his earlier action of killing this same appointment when it had first been proposed at the beginning of the Kennedy administration). W. Averell Harriman took over the post of Assistant Secretary for Far Eastern Affairs, and two others also came over from the White House—Frederick G. Dutton, to be Assistant Secretary for Congressional Relations, and in the post of Deputy Assistant Secretary for Latin American Affairs, Richard N. Goodwin—the bright, no-nonsense, twenty-eight-year-old Harvard Law School graduate who had made it his business to needle the State Department into getting the Alliance for Progress going and who had become a controversial figure in the process.

Neither the town of Washington nor the press quite knew what to make of it all. The first reaction was the inevitable political joke. There were no policy or power implications at all, the gag went. It was just that Rusk was so quiet the President had to send all those people over from the White House so he would have *somebody* at the State Department to talk to. But political jokes aside, there were varying interpretations. One of the Washington papers described the moves as the "formal culmination of several months effort to revitalize the Department without at the same time causing a blow-up inside the Democratic party," since Bowles was so heavily identified with the Democratic liberal wing.[1] James Reston and the New York *Times* saw it as basically just a readjustment of personalities to correct the hurried political appointments made at the beginning of the administration. The President, Reston surmised, had apparently reached the conclusion that the way to make foreign policy effective was to take those on his White House staff on whom he had been relying so heavily and put them in the State Department.[2] Walter Lippmann, on the other hand, saw it as a fundamental change, centering power finally in the State Department. "As I read the terms of the reorganization," he wrote, "they mean that the State Department has grown so much stronger than the original arrangement, when so much power was centered in the White House staff, that this [original] arrangement may come to be thought of in the future as a stopgap arrangement to compensate for the initial weakness of the State Department."[3]

From my own position as Director of Intelligence and Research of the Department of State, the meaning was not at all clear. Responding to the call from the President and the Secretary for the Department of State to take the leadership of foreign policy, we had reorganized and reoriented the Bureau of Intelligence and Research to do its part—reducing and streamlining the bureau from over 700 people to less than 350, and at the same time developing a philosophy of policy-oriented research and intelligence papers that were brief and pointed to replace the lengthy and somewhat plodding tomes that had been the rule. And we were also struggling to try to put the department into a position where its voice carried proper weight in the decisions of the intelligence community and the CIA—in decisions about operations, like the Bay of Pigs, and about research and estimating, such as the National Intelligence Estimates. The men and women in the bureau had been magnificent—they had responded with an excitement and enthusiasm that had them working long hours and producing exactly the right kind of crisp, taut, to-the-point analyses that were needed. Bundy reported that the President liked the result, that he read our papers and used them. But "hard-hitting," and "policy-oriented" papers were bound to trample on some toes. A paper about policy toward Japan, for example, would not be realistic if it did not raise questions about the somewhat dictatorial way we were administering Okinawa and our military bases there; and a paper on the Congo to be worth anything would have to come to grips with the question of Portugal and the importance to NATO of our bases in the Azores. And all of this would inevitably raise hackles in the Pentagon, in segments of the CIA, and in one or another bureau of the State Department itself. What worried us was that although we knew this was what the President wanted, he was not close enough to the daily battles to help when the crunches came, and we were not at all sure that the support would be forthcoming from within the State Department itself. We had a big stake in knowing just what was foreshadowed by the shuffle of personalities in the State Department and how the President intended to operate in the future.

THE PRESIDENT EXPLAINS

As it happened, I ended up hearing the explanation from the President himself in an episode sparked by my decision to accept the university position mentioned earlier. When the President heard that I had decided to leave, he asked to see me, setting the date for January 10.

Although I had met the President once or twice when he was still Senator from Massachusetts and had seen him occasionally since, my relationship with him had been indirect and professional rather than direct and personal. But it was still going to be awkward. As Chief of the Foreign Affairs Division of the Library of Congress's Legislative Reference Service, I had written a number of memoranda on defense and foreign policy for him during the campaign and had helped as a consultant to his staff and to the group of his academic advisers in Cambridge. The President had remembered my work for him and when his staff and the people in the "talent hunt" operation had put up my name for the post of Director of Intelligence and Research at the State Department, it was the President who had recommended my appointment to Rusk.[4] In the circumstances, it was not going to be easy—as Thomas L. Hughes, the Deputy Director of the Intelligence Bureau and an old friend, said, "John F. Kennedy will simply not understand why anyone would want to leave the action and power of Washington for the reflective life in a university."

It was the day before the President had to deliver the annual State of the Union message, a time of frantic busyness, and the hustle and bustle outside the President's office contrasted sharply with his own relaxed air. "Tell me about this university job," he said, "and why you want to resign." I gave him the details, pointing out that a professorship had long been what I had been headed for, that a top post in international politics in a major university did not open up very often, and that, once filled, it would probably not become vacant again for a decade. I then went on to tell him of the reorganization of the Bureau of Intelligence and Research, of my pride in the work the bureau had been doing, and, in what was probably too obvious an attempt to influence the choice of a successor, of my confidence that Hughes could carry on the work as well as I. "It will be no surprise to you, sir," I said finally, "that getting things done in the State Department has its frustrations and in my judgment this job of revamping the Bureau of Intelligence and Research has been carried about as far as it probably can. So I would like to get back to my basic career."

To my surprise, the President merely nodded and proceeded to tell me that he had just been reading the latest issue of the *Marine Corps Gazette,* which was devoted entirely to guerrilla warfare and which included a speech of mine called "Internal War: The New Communist Tactic."[5] I had led an OSS guerrilla group behind the enemy lines in Burma in World War II and had thought a good deal about both the political and military aspects of guerrilla warfare. For almost forty-five minutes, we had a spirited conversation—the President firing questions about my wartime experiences, exchanging arguments with me on the theory of fighting and meeting guerrilla wars, and repeating his own conviction that the most likely and immediate threat from the Communists was neither nuclear war nor large-scale conventional wars, as in Korea, but the more subtle, ambiguous threat of the guerrilla. To meet this threat, new military tactics had to be developed, which he hoped the Special Forces would do. But new political tactics also had to be devised, and, most importantly, the two —the military and the political—had to be meshed together and blended.

The subject of guerrillas exhausted, the President abruptly turned to what he had called me to see him about, and, as part of the counter-argument, he proceeded to give an explanation of the "Thanksgiving Day Massacre" and how he intended to work in the future. It was done succinctly and somewhat elliptically, which was understandable in the circumstances, but the meaning was clear. He had had his troubles with the State Department, and the Secretary was certainly "no Dean Acheson." Everyone had his own style and people above as well as below always had to do some adapting. He had found that he was going to have to work with people at the action level in the State Department, and there were now a number of people at that level with whom he would be working closely. Hopefully, in this way we could get on with the job.

What the President suggested was that he was moving toward a more direct and personal supervision of foreign affairs. Certainly, he thought foreign affairs were central to his concern. He used to say that a domestic failure could hurt the country, but a failure in foreign affairs could kill it. And he was also fascinated with the subject, concerned even in the management of details. Later, when I was Assistant Secretary for Far Eastern Affairs, for example, he phoned so frequently about one or another development he had read about in the morning paper that I was forced to rise earlier in the morning so I could get to the newspapers before he got to me. And he had convictions about where the world ought to be headed and a determination to try to move it in that direction.

But I doubt very much that President Kennedy set out to be his own Secretary of State, as has sometimes been alleged, or that he had conducted his search for a man with this in mind. I believe he was looking for the most experienced and able man he could find—without, of course, taking on someone with serious political liabilities—and that on balance Dean Rusk most closely filled the bill of any of the men available.

It is, perhaps, one of the drawbacks of our system of government that so few men can acquire the combination of experience in both foreign affairs and domestic politics needed by a Secretary of State and that, consequently, a President has so few choices. President Kennedy needed a man, first of all, who had competency and stature in the field of foreign affairs. If that man also had political experience and was himself a public figure who could bring public support without political liability, so much the better. Lincoln found such a man in Seward—once Seward stopped thinking that it was he who really should have been in the White House, and began to be the President's man. President Harrison tried with James G. Blaine, the Mr. Republican of his day—but Blaine never really stepped down to be the President's man. Truman tried and failed for the same reason with James F. Byrnes, who always felt that Truman had gotten the Vice-Presidential nomination that he Byrnes, had really deserved. Truman finally found Dean Acheson, who had some public stature and was well known at least to the makers of public opinion, the press, and the Congress, if not to the public at large. And Acheson had also had very considerable experience in foreign affairs. Eisenhower had found almost exactly the same combination in John Foster Dulles, although he was perhaps even better known to the public, since there had been much speculation four years earlier that he would be Dewey's choice for Secretary if Dewey were elected in 1948. But each of these Presidents as a practical political matter never had more than a half a dozen men to choose from.

The names mentioned for Secretary of State at the time President Kennedy was choosing his cabinet were Adlai Stevenson, the Democratic candidate for President in 1952 and 1956; J. William Fulbright, Senator from Arkansas and Chairman of the Senate Foreign Relations Committee; Chester Bowles, former Governor of Connecticut, Ambassador to India, and head of OPA; W. Averell Harriman, former Governor of New York, Ambassador to Moscow and London, and head of the Marshall Plan; and Robert A. Lovett, who had served both as Under Secretary of State and as Secretary of Defense in former administrations. All these men brought public stature as well as competency and experience in foreign affairs. But all were disqualified for one reason or another. Stevenson might be just as hard to handle as Blaine or Byrnes, and the opposition in Congress to his liberal views and the reputation he had acquired for indecisiveness might balance off the considerable public support he brought to the job. Harriman was felt to be too old; Bowles was judged too liberal to get along well with Congress; and the fact that Fulbright was a Southerner would make it difficult for him to carry out United States foreign policy in Asia and Africa. President Kennedy offered Lovett the job, but his health was such that he could not accept. Thus in the end the President chose Dean Rusk—who had been Assistant Secretary of State for Far Eastern Affairs in the Truman administration and Assistant Secretary for International Organization Affairs, as well as President of the Rockefeller Foundation in the meantime—as the most experienced and highly recommended man among a second group of those who had neither the stature nor were so well known as the front runners.

Robert S. McNamara came to the job of Secretary of Defense in much the same way, and neither had been known to the President beforehand. Thus the President, as he suggested, was confronted with a set of personalities to which he had to adjust, just as they had to adjust to him.

THE WHITE HOUSE AND THE DEFENSE DEPARTMENT

The adjustment to the Defense Department was rather straightforward. President Kennedy had very well developed ideas about strategic matters, fully formed in the great national debate on "massive retaliation," the "missile gap," and so on that took place over the six years from 1954 to 1960. He believed in balanced forces, and the capacity for "flexible response." In McNamara, he found a Secretary of Defense who shared his views, who had the imagination to push those views even further down the line of their logical development, and who had the will for strong leadership. "I see my position here as being that of a leader, not a judge," McNamara once said. "I'm here to originate and stimulate new ideas and programs, not just to referee arguments and harmonize interests. Using deliberate analysis to force alternative programs to the surface, and then making explicit choices among them is fundamental."[6]

Kennedy could comfortably let McNamara be "Secretary of Defense" while he remained as "President"—giving broad policy direction, taking care through a variety of means, including an active White House staff, that he was made aware of the policy issues and alternatives down the line in the Defense Department in time for him to intervene effectively when and if he chose. The only problem which required exceptional care was that McNamara's boundless energy and formidable ability, as mentioned above, sometimes tempted him to use whatever military component there was in a political problem as a beachhead. Occasionally he extended the beachhead until he came very near to dominating the whole affair— as, for example, relations with Europe at the time of the Berlin crisis, the political situation in Saigon on a later day, or relations with India following the Chinese attack. Such vigorous excursions by those charged with military responsibilities into foreign political affairs is not necessarily bad—just as equally vigorous excursions by the State Department into military and strategic matters might at times be good—so long as there are strong and knowledgeable men in the one department defending political considerations and equally strong and knowledgeable men defending military considerations in the other. But it does require an alert President in constant supervision.

It was Bundy's job to police this area where political and military considerations overlap and to keep the administration together. In the Kennedy administration, Bundy avoided being an advocate of policy, although he frequently acted as judge, as on occasion did everyone who attended meetings at the White House. His role in the period leading up to a decision was to be the midwife of policy, to anticipate problems coming up, to see that the staff work was fully done, that all departments, agencies, and segments of the administration that had a legitimate concern had a full opportunity to present their views, and that no aspect of the problem itself was neglected. Then, after the decision, his responsibility was to follow through, to see that each department did its part in implementing the policy, but especially to see that the *President's* interests were protected.

Thus to some extent, it was Bundy and the White House staff who performed the function of ensuring that issues were exposed, that policy alternatives were developed and not masked over, and that the President had the opportunity to make choices and at his timing. But, like Roosevelt, Kennedy made sure to build a certain amount of competition into the relationships between departments. Again, an anecdote will illustrate. In the early spring of 1963, President Kennedy made George C. McGhee Ambassador to Germany, promoting Averell Harriman to the post vacated by McGhee of Under Secretary for Political Affairs and me to the post of Assistant Secretary for Far Eastern Affairs, vacated by Harriman. When Rusk called to tell me of the switch, he said that the "policy-oriented" papers for which I had been responsible as Director of Intelligence had, as we had anticipated, trampled on some toes, especially in the Defense Department. Rusk then went on to say that he had assured the Pentagon that I would refrain from intruding into military and strategic matters in my new post as Assistant Secretary for Far Eastern Affairs.

Pausing, Rusk then said, softly, "Assistant Secretary for Far Eastern Affairs . . . it's a tough job." I knew how very true that was, and I was so bemused at the enormity of the responsibilities of the job that I neglected to question how it could be done without becoming involved in strategic matters—which were so tightly interwoven with the diplomatic and political, especially in Southeast Asia. But the minute I got back to my desk, the phone rang from the White House. "By now," said a voice, "you will have been told that you are to be the new Assistant Secretary for Far Eastern Affairs." I said that I had. "You will also have been told to refrain from intruding into military and strategic matters." I admitted this, too. "Well," said the voice, "the President wants you to understand that it was precisely because you have stood up to the Defense Department that you were chosen, and that he expects you to continue."

ADJUSTING TO THE STATE DEPARTMENT

President Kennedy's adjustment to the State Department was more complicated. And this was partly because Rusk's conception of his job was more complicated than McNamara's.

Rusk's conception of the job was also less easy to identify. His method of operation was puzzling. Instructions, for example, might come to me as Assistant Secretary from the White House to prepare for a National Security Council meeting with the President later that week, say, on a matter dealing with Korea. From previous work with the President I might have some idea of the direction of his thinking. Often, he might have telephoned me himself. In the usual case, however, I would get a sense of the President's general views from Michael V. Forrestal, who was working directly with the President and McGeorge Bundy as White House aide on Far Eastern matters. As a rule, Forrestal saw the President almost every day and Bundy and me often several times a day.

Averell Harriman had continuing responsibility for Far Eastern matters among the Under Secretaries, and I would either call or meet with Harriman as soon as possible. Harriman would cogitate out loud, debate vigorously with anyone present, and sometimes seem to stick stubbornly to a wrongheaded position. Then, he might suddenly switch, for Harriman had an unusual objectivity and generosity toward others and their views— he was a man who could and frequently did change his mind under the weight of argument. I remember thinking in those days that Harriman had a true sense of history. There are, I suppose, those who feel that a nation as large and powerful as the United States can simply dictate the course of history and force events to its will, although I doubt if anyone who has held some measure of responsibility for directing American foreign policy can believe it. There are clearly others, and some of these may well hold high office, who sense history as massive, inevitable, and irresistible—like the slow but overwhelming push of a gigantic glacier— and that the task of statesmen is to adapt the policies of their country to that inexorable flow of events. But a true sense of history, it seems to me, and greatness in a statesman, is the capacity to discriminate, to know when one can manage history and when one must adapt to it. Harriman always asked two questions: first, "What course do we want events to take?" and then, "Do we have the power to bring it about?"

I would always try to provide the Secretary of State an opportunity to have a preliminary meeting with Harriman and me—and sometimes one of the two other Under Secretaries, George Ball or U. Alexis Johnson, if the subject matter cut into areas for which they were responsible or if Ball were Acting Secretary in Rusk's absence. In these preliminary meetings Rusk asked penetrating questions that frequently caused us to re-examine our position, but what puzzled me was how rarely he expressed his own conclusions on policy, much less issue directives.

Between the preliminary meeting with Rusk and the day of the meeting with the President—which might have been only twenty-four hours later and was sometimes less—I worked with the office directors and desk officers in the Far East Bureau, checking with Harriman and Forrestal, and developing a policy to be recommended to the President. The usual practice in the department was to meet with the Secretary an hour before the White House meeting to go over our position, and we would frequently ride over together in the Secretary's car, continuing our conversation. But even at this meeting, just before seeing the President, the Secretary's position did not always become clear. Although there were, again, penetrating questions, I frequently left for the White House not knowing whether the Secretary really approved of what was being recommended or disapproved.

Other Assistant Secretaries apparently had similar experiences, and at times it went the same when we arrived at the meeting in the White House. Not infrequently, the Secretary would present an introductory analysis of the problem and then turn the floor over to the Assistant Secretary to present the "State Department's position"—which seemed to imply that there might also be a "Secretary of State's position" that was different from the "State Department's position." More often than not, the Assistant Secretary would find himself in a somewhat unequal contest—ranged against not only the Secretary of Defense and the Director of the Central Intelligence Agency, for example, but a bevy of four-star generals. For although the generals might look choleric, there was only one position from the Pentagon.

I found the first such experience unsettling. But shortly thereafter, I had occasion to go to the Secretary to warn him of a serious problem that had arisen over which he would obviously want to exercise general supervision from the outset. "No," he said, "I'm going to stick to being Secretary of State." It was only when I had thoroughly pondered this remark that I began to understand Rusk's conception of the role of the secretaryship, to realize that his conception was logical and internally consistent; and to recognize that, like all other organizational notions, it had advantages as well as disadvantages.

Dean Acheson, clearly, would have agreed with the idea developed by the incoming administration that the Secretary of State should be leader and advocate of policy, which would require him to manage the State Department itself, and that at the same time its Secretary should be the chief co-ordinator of those policies that cut across several departments in the area of foreign affairs, because of the pre-eminence of political considerations over the economic or military. It was probably because Acheson saw it this way that his name had come to Kennedy's mind in our conversation. Acheson also understood the implications of this view in terms of how exposed a Secretary who tries to be advocate and leader can be to public and congressional attack. He once wrote that in Washington the President and the Secretary of State were "working in an environment where some of the methods would have aroused the envy of the Borgias."[7] He also understood the other set of implications, what such a role requires *from* the Secretary of State if he is to be the co-ordinator of policy and maintain the pre-eminence of the political over the economic and the military. When a foreign colleague once asked him to name the quality most required in an American Secretary of State, he replied, "The killer instinct." When Acheson was faced with a very ambitious Secretary of Defense who reached aggressively beyond the Pentagon for dominance over the whole spectrum of policy, he forced a showdown and before it was over, true to his "killer instinct," his opponent, Louis Johnson, had been fired.

Rusk, on the other hand, seemed to feel that it was inappropriate for the Secretary of State to do battle in the name of the Department, even for the important cause of maintaining the pre-eminence of political considerations. He was proud of having a "partnership" with the Defense Department, which itself became the subject of barbed comment that went the rounds in Washington—as a quote from a White House aide: "He and McNamara are partners all right—only he's the junior partner."

But, like all these political jokes that so persistently followed Rusk, this was most unfair. McNamara quite obviously respected Rusk's judgment and knowledge, and no matter how peremptory his attitude or how "here-are-the-facts" dogmatic, McNamara always stopped to listen when Rusk spoke.

Rather than doing battle in the name of the State Department, or even representing it, Rusk seemed to see himself as standing somewhat apart, more as a personal adviser to the President than as representing any particular point of view, even the political. He seemed to view the Secretary not as the maker and advocate of policy, but, at the President's side, as a judge. Thus the President, in Rusk's view, should give leadership in terms of over-all goals and objectives, in terms of grand policy. The Assistant Secretaries, concentrating on particular regions, should be the formulators and advocates of specific policies and the managers of the State Department. But the position of Secretary of State he seemed to see as being above all this and apart from it, permitting the incumbent to sit alongside the President in judgment precisely because he was free of the restraints and commitments of representing a department.

Not many people would share Rusk's view of the secretaryship, but it seems to me to be a perfectly logical and reasonable view, providing a meaningful and useful role around which a President can build an effective organizational arrangement. Rusk has been much criticized. For my part, however, although I was occasionally discomfited by the mode of operation to which his critics objected, I believe that, consistent with his own conception of the role of the Secretary of State, Rusk served John F. Kennedy well. He represented a point of view, corresponding closely with responsible conservative opinion among congressmen, that it was essential for Kennedy to consider. Patiently and with calm dignity, he explained the complexities of the world and our policies to the men on Capitol Hill, and earned their respect for himself and, by and large, their co-operation for the Kennedy administration. And by his modesty and restraint he made easier the President's task of keeping the great departments and their sometimes imperious leaders working together toward a common goal.

And so it settled down to what seemed to be a stable arrangement and set of personalities. In defense matters, the President worked mainly with McNamara, relying on McNamara himself and on Bundy and the White House staff to keep open his own options for choice. In the State Department, he made full use of Rusk's talents as a judge, as adviser, as representative on Capitol Hill, and, I am convinced, respected his judgment. But it was the President himself who was, in McNamara's phrase, the "leader, not the judge" at the State Department, who was there "to originate and stimulate new ideas and programs, not just to referee arguments and harmonize interests." This task, as well as the task of co-ordinating and managing the whole range of security policy that he had intended to assign to the State Department, he assumed himself. For although he had not sought to be his own Secretary of State, in the end he had no other choice.

NOTES

[1] Washington *Evening Star*, November 27, 1961.

[2] James Reston, the New York *Times*, November 27, 1961.

[3] Walter Lippmann, the Washington *Post*, November 28, 1961.

[4] Rusk, whose diplomatic sense rarely failed him, made one of his few slips on this occasion. Although Rusk was only forty when Truman had made him Assistant Secretary for International Organization Affairs, he was uneasy about the youthfulness of Kennedy's appointees, and when my name came up in a telephone conversation between Rusk in Washington and Kennedy in Palm Beach, someone who was present later told me, Rusk apparently said that there was one disadvantage—youth. "How old is he?" the President asked. "Only forty-one," Rusk replied. There was a pause, and the President said, "Well, I'm forty-three, and I'm President. . . ."

[5] The President's enthusiasm, in fact, encouraged the *Gazette* to expand the issue and publish it as a book, with Kennedy's letter to the editor as the preface. See *The Guerrilla—And How to Fight Him*, edited by Lieutenant Colonel T. N. Greene, 1962.

[6] W. W. Kaufmann, *The McNamara Strategy*, 1964, p. 171.

[7] Dean Acheson, "The President and the Secretary of State," in the American Assembly's *The Secretary of State*, 1960.

III

PRESIDENT KENNEDY
AND THE CIA

"We have grown up as a nation respected for our free institutions and for our ability to maintain a free and open society. There is something about the way the CIA has been functioning that is casting a shadow over our historic position . . ."
—PRESIDENT HARRY S TRUMAN,
December 22, 1963

"The euphoria of secrecy goes to the head . . . I have known men, prudent in other respects, who became drunk with it. It induces an unbalancing sense of power. It is not of consequence whether one is hugging to oneself a secret about one's own side or about the other. It is not uncommon to run across men, superficially commonplace and unextravagant, who are letting their judgment run wild because they are hoarding a secret about the other side— quite forgetting that someone on the other side, almost indistinguishable from themselves, is hoarding a precisely similar secret about them. It takes a very strong head to keep secrets for years, and not go slightly mad. It isn't wise to be advised by anyone slightly mad."

—C. P. SNOW, *Science and Government, 1961*

CHAPTER 6

The Problem of CIA

"It's a hell of a way to learn things," President Kennedy said immediately after the Bay of Pigs, "but I have learned one thing from this business—that is, that we will have to deal with the CIA."

That something was wrong about the CIA had become increasingly clear for several years. When President Kennedy was still a senator, he and everyone else on Capitol Hill, where it was all common gossip, had known the general outlines of a number of fiascoes—aid to the 1958 rebellion in Indonesia, where an American pilot, Allen L. Pope, was still held prisoner; the allegation that CIA was deeply involved in maintaining Chinese Nationalist, Kuomintang troops on the territory of Burma; and a variety of situations, such as Laos, where the CIA was reported to be pursuing policies undercutting the ambassador.

Kennedy had also been aware that the trouble was more fundamental than particular mistakes. President Truman, who had been responsible for setting up the CIA some years later expressed the nature of this concern in a public statement. "For some time I have been disturbed," he wrote, "by the way CIA has been diverted from its original assignment. It has become an operational and at times a policy-making arm of the government." Truman went on to say that he never had any thought when he set up the CIA that it would be injected into peacetime cloak-and-dagger operations, but that he intended for it to be confined to intelligence work. "Some of the complications and embarrassment that I think we have experienced are in part attributable to the fact that this quiet intelligence arm of the President has been so removed from its intended role that it is being interpreted as a symbol of sinister and mysterious foreign intrigue—and a subject for Cold War enemy propaganda." President Truman's conclusion was that he would like to see the CIA restored to its original assignment as the intelligence arm of the President. "We have grown up as a nation," he wrote, "respected for our free institutions and for our ability to maintain a free and open society. There is something about the way the CIA has been functioning that is casting a shadow over our historic position and I feel that we need to correct it."[1]

President Truman's role in creating the CIA makes his criticism all the more sobering. But, stiff though his criticism was, others were even harsher. Article after article in magazines and newspapers catalogued a long list of charges: that the CIA was a mass of bumbling inefficiency; that it was a citadel of extreme conservatism; that it had vast sums of money at its disposal for which it made no accounting; that it had such an extensive empire and so many employees that in some of our embassies overseas the CIA agents outnumbered regular foreign service officers; that the pervasive secrecy of intelligence activities permitted CIA to pursue its own policies without regard for the rest of the government; that when an intelligence agency combined policy and operations with intelligence-gathering, as the CIA did, there was an inevitable tendency to warp the intelligence it gathered to suit its particular policies; and that the atmosphere of plot and intrigue inevitably spilled over into the domestic arena, threatening the very system the intelligence agency was supposed to protect. Some of these charges were undoubtedly motivated by nothing more than sensationalism. But some of the concern was very real. Two responsible journalists, one the head of the *Herald Tribune*'s Washington bureau, later went so far as to write a book which charged that there were "two governments in the United States today," one visible and the other invisible. They were convinced that "the Invisible Government has achieved a quasi-independent status and a power of its own," with the result that one cannot help suspecting "that the foreign policy of the United States often works publicly in one direction and secretly through the Invisible Government in just the opposite direction"—sometimes, they seem to suggest, against the wishes of the President himself.[2]

The root fear was that the CIA represented a *Staat-im-Staat,* a state within a state, and certainly the basis for fear was there. In its network of agents overseas, the CIA had the means for gathering the necessary information on which policy must be based. In its staff of researchers and in the Board of National Estimates in Washington, which are all under the Deputy Director for Intelligence, it had a "little State Department" of people qualified to analyze that information and reach policy conclusions. Because of its method of operating out of embassies— which all intelligence services do, incidentally—it had representation abroad and contact with high officials of foreign governments through which policy could be implemented. Indeed, because the CIA could keep its men in a particular country longer than most ambassadors stay, CIA station chiefs frequently had been able to make closer friendships with prime ministers and kings and presidents than ambassadors did, and thus to be more influential. In many countries, especially the more backward countries on the firing line of Communist expansionism, where money is used freely in ways that the State Department budget does not provide for and where intrigue is a way of life, most nationals of the country sincerely believed that it was the CIA station chief who really represented the United States. The CIA also had all the facilities of an information and propaganda agency—including powerful radio transmitters. It also had independent communications facilities, as mentioned earlier, by which either information or instructions could be sent without any other part of the American government being aware of it. For the implementation of policy, indeed, the CIA had military training centers that had frequently been used to train guerrillas and on at least one occasion—for the Bay of Pigs operation—a brigade of regular troops equipped with artillery. It had airplanes and the pilots to fly them. It had naval vessels and the crews to man them. With all of this, it is not surprising that there should be fear that the CIA might develop into a state within a state.

From my own personal experience, I know that it had not and that most of the more extreme charges about CIA were not valid. Although the people in CIA, in common with all other human beings, have made mistakes, the organization possesses a more able staff than most. Far from being a haven of extreme conservatism, the CIA during the Eisenhower administration was the one place that Senator McCarthy was unable to touch in his witch hunt and was in fact the only place in the Eisenhower administration that had room for the young activists who wanted to work with youth and labor movements abroad. Through its intelligence-gathering effort, which has relied on scholarly research as much as on cloak-and-dagger operations, the CIA has played a large part, though not the only part, in making the United States Government the best informed in the world. In a patient though sometimes painful educational campaign waged through the tedious procedures by which National Intelligence Estimates are developed, it has succeeded in bringing an objectivity—and an over-all point of view rising above the parochial interests of the individual military services—that was previously unknown in the American government's analyses of events abroad. The United States, in fact, owes the men and women of the CIA an extraordinary debt.

But the CIA still represented a most serious problem, as President Truman said. And the problem was one of power.

"The National Security Act of 1947 . . . has given Intelligence," Allen Dulles once said, "a more influential position in our government than Intelligence enjoys in any other government of the world."[3] By the time the Kennedy administration came into office, Allen Dulles had been Director of the CIA for almost eight years, and the CIA's power was at an all-time high.

The CIA, first of all, had people. Where the State Department, for example, at one time had three people on its Laos desk, the CIA had six. This meant that the CIA could always afford to be represented at an interdepartmental meeting, that it could spare the manpower to prepare the papers that would dominate the meeting, and that it could explore the byways and muster the information and arguments that gave its men authority at those meetings.

What is more, the people in CIA were outstandingly able, which was itself a source of power. As mentioned above, the agency had stoutly protected its people from McCarthy and was one of the few parts of government in the Eisenhower era where new ideas were encouraged and activists permitted to do things, and these facts also helped in attracting still more active and able people. Promotion was fast.

CIA also had money. The exact amount of its budget is still secret. But various newsmen have estimated the total for all United States intelligence activities at about two billion dollars per year, and it is obvious that CIA's share of the total would be large, certainly amounting to more than the State Department had to spend per year. CIA's freedom from normal accounting and auditing procedures gave it a flexibility in the use of its money that also gave it power. Paradoxically, CIA became involved in many activities that its critics considered to be outside its legitimate purview at the urging of other agencies, such as the State Department, who would normally be responsible for the activity but whose budget did not provide for it. Buying books abroad was one example and helping the impoverished leader of a government-in-exile come to New York to present his case to the UN General Assembly was another. Unhappily, however, where both activities would be accepted as a matter of course if the State Department money had been available, they became sinister when CIA money was used.

CIA's command of information was also a source of power. Quite apart from the issue of whether or not information is bent to support a particular point of view, in Washington the first to have a tidbit of information is the first to interpret its significance, and is the first to be on the scene when discussion starts on what the policy implications of the information might be. Where information is an asset, command over information is the power to grant or withhold that asset—to a congressman or the press, for example.

Even the need for secrecy can be power. Quite apart from the phenomenon mentioned earlier that in countries where intrigue is a way of life the mere fact of being the secret intelligence service gives prestige that translates into power, the need to keep certain operations or sources of information secret gives those who "need to know" a further dimension for making judgments or understanding the why of what is happening. Those who knew of the peripheral reconnaissance flights that probed Soviet air defenses during the Eisenhower administration and the U-2 flights over the Soviet Union itself, for example, were better able to understand some of the things the Soviets were saying and doing than people who did not know of these activities.

The CIA also derived power from the fact that the function they performed, like that of the FBI, is by its nature politically appealing. The CIA was in the forefront of the Cold War. Its job was to smite our enemies, not to negotiate with them, or compromise with them, or make agreements with them. It had the appeal of patriotism. In Congress, the CIA's natural allies were also the "inner club," the power center of Congress—the men at the heart of the long-standing coalition of Southern Democrats and right-wing Republicans, the men of long tenure and conservative outlook. A natural alliance with the congressional power center, a mandate so broad that it is called upon to testify as often before the Committees on Armed Services and Science and Technology as before the Committee on Foreign Relations, and a command of secret information that can itself enhance the position of the members of the congressional committee that receives it—all of these are levers which a politically astute Director of the CIA can use to great effect on Capitol Hill. And most have done so. It is no accident that the two men John F. Kennedy immediately named as carry-overs into his new administration were J. Edgar Hoover and Allen W. Dulles.

Political leverage is power. Information is power. Secrecy is power. Speed in communications is power. Ability is power. And the sheer number of people is power. CIA had all these, and during the years of the Eisenhower administration it had still another source of power—the fact that the Secretary of State, John Foster Dulles, and the Director of the CIA, Allen W. Dulles, were brothers. Allen Dulles probably never presumed on this relationship, but it inevitably had its effects, if only because people believed it did, and behaved accordingly. When the Kennedy administration took office, resentment of the CIA in the Foreign Service and the State Department was high. They resented what they thought was high living abroad, the better communication, the more ample travel funds, and the encroachment on what was regarded as traditional State Department functions. But it was the relationship of the two brothers that had become the focus of the resentment. John Foster Dulles said that he carried the State Department in his hat, by which he meant that he did not rely very heavily on the department and its bureaucracy. Allen Dulles, on the other hand, did rely heavily on his bureaucracy. He liked to have his own man in every capital of the world, if possible, and in allied and friendly capitals, he liked to have his man on close personal terms with the chief of state, who was also in some cases under some obligation to the CIA of one form or another. As mentioned above, in many cases the CIA's station chief had been in the country much longer than the ambassador, knew more of the nationals more intimately, knew conditions in the country better, had more money to spend, more favors to do, and may well have been a more able person than the ambassador. In differences of judgment, in other words, it might well have been that the CIA man was more often right. But quite apart from the facts of the matter, many people in the department and the foreign service were convinced that CIA would win disputes no matter what the merits were, and there were persistent rumors that this or that ambassador had been relieved not for the reasons given but because he had taken issue with the judgment of the CIA station chief in his country.

What people in the State Department did not so often realize was that there was a basis for resentment in the CIA as well. CIA, as we have said, had a large number of exceptionally able people. It was undoubtedly frustrating to some of these men to have to take a back seat to some less able foreign service officer who occupied the front position solely because he was the State Department representative. The State Department was jealous of its policy-making role, and instead of leading in foreign policy it sometimes merely excluded others from participating. And as the CIA people got older, they saw a ceiling on their own advancement. Unlike a foreign service officer, a CIA career man could have little hope of ever becoming an ambassador—his long service in intelligence alone precluded it.

All these questions of morale were a matter of concern to the Kennedy administration when it came into office, but it was the greater issue of the power of CIA and its role—the problem that Truman later described —that was paramount. It was not until after the Bay of Pigs that President Kennedy felt the urgency of "dealing with the CIA," but the preliminary steps had been taken some months earlier, at the very beginning of the Kennedy administration.

NOTES

[1] Harry S Truman in an article syndicated by the North American Newspaper Alliance, as it appears in the Washington *Post*, December 22, 1963.
[2] David Wise and Thomas B. Ross, *The Invisible Government*, 1964.
[3] In a speech at Yale University, February 3, 1958.

CHAPTER 7

The Kennedy Compromise

I TOOK over my duties as the Director of the Bureau of Intelligence and Research at the State Department on February 5, 1961. A few days later, Secretary Rusk called me and David Bell, then Director of the Bureau of the Budget, to talk about the problems of the intelligence community—apparently at the instigation of the White House. Rusk began by saying that when he had worked for Secretary of War Robert P. Patterson in the period immediately following the war, they had fought hard for the idea of a centralized intelligence arrangement and had helped in setting up the CIA. On the whole, he thought the centralized intelligence setup had been more of a plus than a minus. But the White House and he both felt that it would be wise to take a close look at the interdepartmental machinery for handling CIA-State business and for seeing that foreign policy and intelligence activities were in step with each other. There were, the Secretary felt, two tasks involved. The first was for me to take a good hard look at my bureau and get it in shape to do both the job of providing the department with research and intelligence studies that were pertinent to policy and the job of representing the department effectively in the intelligence community. The second, which both the Bureau of the Budget and I should undertake, was to look at the role of the intelligence abroad and at the interdepartmental procedures for co-ordinating foreign policy and intelligence activities, to see if they were sound and how they could be improved. Although guarded and vague as these instructions were, I took them to be an assignment to look at the role of CIA and the relations between CIA and the Department of State in line with President Kennedy's call for the State Department to lead.

Taking up the task of reshaping the Bureau of Intelligence and Research, I found that the bureau had almost seven hundred people on its rolls and a budget of $5.8 million. The bureau was not an intelligence organization in the sense that it gathered information, for its entire staff was in Washington. It was responsible, first, for distributing within the State Department intelligence received from CIA or the military services —or information received from whatever source, whether an ambassador or an AP news ticker. Its second responsibility was for making political, economic, or sociological studies of conditions abroad ranging from the organization of the Communist movement in Latin America to the relative power of the different factions vying for control in Saigon. Its third responsibility was for co-ordinating State-CIA business, which sometimes involved delicate questions of intelligence operations or activities that might have perilous political repercussions. These matters are generally secret, but one example now in the public domain is the use of the U-2 reconnaissance plane for flights over the Soviet Union during the Eisenhower administration. Since the planes were based in Turkey, it is obvious that at some stage negotiations had to be conducted with the Turkish Government for landing rights for the U-2, and it was in such matters that the Bureau of Intelligence and Research had a co-ordinating role to perform between the intelligence community, on the one hand, and the regional policy bureaus in the State Department on the other. It acted as an advocate to the regional bureaus for the interests of the intelligence community and as an advocate to the intelligence community for the political interests with which the regional bureaus were concerned.

The Intelligence Bureau also represented the State Department on the United States Intelligence Board. This was an interagency committee, chaired by the Director of CIA, whose members were the Directors of Intelligence from the State Department, Defense, Army, Navy, Air, the Intelligence Staff of the Joint Chiefs of Staff, and representatives from the FBI, the Atomic Energy Commission, and the National Security Agency. It was the Intelligence Board that gave final approval to the National Intelligence Estimates after they had been developed in subordinate interagency committees. It was also the Intelligence Board that made decisions concerning intelligence priorities, the allocation of resources, and the division of labor between the different intelligence agencies.

I also discovered that the Bureau of Intelligence and Research was responsible for the political and economic sections of a series of encyclopedic reference works, called the National Intelligence Surveys, that endeavored to give the basic facts about the government, politics, transportation system, and so on of every country in the world. This project was begun in the late 1940s to avoid the trouble experienced in acquiring such basic information as the type of sand on the beaches of Iwo Jima or the height of railroad tunnels in North Africa during the planning for the invasions of World War II. A complicating factor was that this project and a similar one on biographic information were financed by a yearly transfer of funds from CIA, which meant that the bureau was dependent on CIA for about 40 per cent of its budget. It was another example of the flexibility of CIA's funds—the State Department did not have the money, but the CIA did.

The goal was to streamline the bureau and to reshape it to produce studies that contributed directly to the making of foreign policy—"policy-oriented research," as we came to call it. And it seemed obvious that the National Intelligence Survey and the reference work to develop biographic information, although useful to the government, did not contribute directly to the making of foreign policy. Both functions could also be performed more economically and efficiently if they were done centrally, by the CIA. What was more, getting rid of these functions would also end the bureau's anomalous position of being dependent on the CIA for such a substantial proportion of its budget. I decided to go ahead.

But I had not reckoned on Congress. I had Rusk's approval, but before the decision was final I had to touch base with the Bureau of the Budget, the CIA, and others. Before I could complete the rounds, there was—inevitably—a leak, and a leak designed to block the move. A national news magazine reported that I was about to sell half the personnel of the bureau "up the river"—literally up the Potomac River to the CIA headquarters at Langley, Virginia. Wayne Hayes, Chairman of the Sub-committee on State Department Organization, and the entire membership of the House Foreign Affairs Committee were furious at what they thought was a further enhancement of the power of CIA. For the Foreign Affairs Committee shared many of the State Department's resentments of the CIA, and for many of the same reasons. Knowledgeable and sensitive to the political considerations in our dealings abroad because of their work on the committee, the members decried the growth of the CIA, its ubiquitousness, and the political handicaps which the United States' seemingly excessive reliance on secret agents and cloak-and-dagger techniques brought in their wake. They also resented the fact that the CIA had a special relationship with a secret subcommittee consisting of members from the Appropriations Committee and the Armed Services Committee—by-passing the Foreign Affairs Committee on a number of matters they considered their proper responsibility. I was ordered to appear before the subcommittee the next day.

I arrived at the committee room early and sat in the place reserved for the witness at the oval table on the right of the chairman's seat in the small and crowded Foreign Affairs Committee room in the main building of the Capitol. Hayes arrived first—scowling red. When the other members arrived, I gave them a full and frank explanation, in spite of the sensitivity that interdepartmental problems always present, spelling out exactly what it was that we intended to do and why we intended to do it. The purpose, I pointed out, was to rid ourselves of pedestrian functions precisely so that we could give more foreign policy guidance to the intelligence community and do our part in the job of co-ordinating the activities of the intelligence community with foreign policy. Once this was understood the members of the committee were generous in their support, with Wayne Hayes in the forefront.

By midsummer of 1961, we had reduced the bureau by half, to fewer than 350 people, and concentrated its research functions down to three. The first was the traditional intelligence estimating, including State Department participation in the National Intelligence Estimates. The second was evaluating current developments—producing fast, informed interpretations by the best people we could find of current developments as they happened. The third function was "policy-oriented research." The purpose here was to analyze situations with foreign policy implications, keeping those policy implications precisely in the forefront. An example we used at the time, to illustrate what we meant by "policy-oriented research," was taken from the period immediately after Mossadegh, the Premier of Iran, nationalized the oil industry in 1951. An analyst in the Bureau of Intelligence and Research studying United States actions and Iranian counteractions suddenly realized that, although no one in the United States Government had specifically said so, the various American policy decisions seemed to be based on the implied assumption that if the United States succeeded in cutting down on the foreign exchange available to Mossadegh he would go broke and be forced to come to terms. When the analyst totaled up the foreign exchange that Mossadegh had at his disposal and that the United States could not affect, and added it to the economies that would naturally occur to Mossadegh, the policy implications were devastatingly obvious. It was this kind of critical, searching analysis that we were trying to encourage.

In addition to these functions of intelligence estimating, evaluating current developments, and policy-oriented research, we were also able to persuade Congress to appropriate money to begin a program for the first time in the history of the State Department for contracting studies to the universities and independent research organizations. The amount remained at less than one hundred thousand dollars—which was less than the military services spent on foreign policy studies and only a fraction of what they spent on weapons research. But it was a beginning.

Reducing the bureau by half enabled us to pick and choose the people best suited to the tasks that lay ahead. It freed us from the anomalous position of having almost half our budget supplied from CIA funds. It permitted us to rid ourselves of the more pedestrian functions and to concentrate our energies on the strategic points—the research and intelligence work that bore directly and immediately on foreign policy. In terms of the papers and research studies, the results were visible almost overnight— we began to get, as I said, just the right kind of crisp, taut, to-the-point analyses that were needed.

But the going was much rougher in the second task that Rusk had outlined in his conversation with David Bell and me, the problem of CIA's role and improving the interdepartmental machinery for co-ordinating intelligence activities and foreign policy.

For one thing, we found ourselves almost immediately preoccupied with a series of crises resulting from past failures to co-ordinate intelligence activities and foreign policy. The Bay of Pigs was one example, but there were several others. Most of these are still confidential, but one was made public in 1965 by Lee Kuan Yew, Prime Minister of Singapore, and officially admitted by the State Department, and this incident will serve to illustrate.[1] What Prime Minister Lee revealed was that late in 1960, just at the very end of the Eisenhower administration, CIA agents attempted to bribe an officer in Singapore's own intelligence unit, the Special Branch, to pass over information to them illegally. The officer informed his superiors, who instructed him to lead the CIA men on. He did lead them on, and after sufficient evidence, including tape recordings, had been piled up, the Singapore government moved in for an arrest. They caught the CIA official red-handed. There were several tense weeks, and many cables back and forth that cost a lot of late hours. The only light touch in the whole business was supplied by Carl Rowan, who had come from the newspaper world to join the new administration as Deputy Assistant Secretary for Public Affairs. One night, after we had finished a cable on press guidance in case the whole thing became public, Carl sighed heavily. "Well," he said, shaking his head, "I guess all this beats writing 'obits'—but just barely."

Prime Minister Lee was finally persuaded in the interests of the free world to release the American official being held in jail and to keep the matter quiet. But the incident irritated President Kennedy and the members of the new administration. Intelligence activities were clearly necessary. Sending a U-2 over the Soviet Union in 1960, for example, might well have been a matter of national survival. In addition to their iron curtain of almost paranoiac secrecy, which has always been in itself ominous, the Soviet Union was at that time pursuing a warlike policy threatening Berlin and all of Western Europe. There was also evidence that the Soviet Union might be drawing ahead in missiles, which would give them a fatal advantage. But in the Singapore incident, the Special Branch, which was officered in part by British officials on loan from the United Kingdom, was in constant liaison with United States intelligence officials, and there was no question that they would pass over any information affecting American security. Thus the only possible gain from this attempt to subvert a Special Branch official would be to check on how much of the more routine, less important information was ordinarily being exchanged—which hardly seemed important enough to justify the political costs if the attempt were exposed.

One such incident, taken by itself, seems unimportant and might be shrugged aside. But a hundred incidents, taken together, could be disastrous. The steady repetition left the impression that subversion and cloak-and-dagger techniques were the principal instrument of United States policy; that the United States was contemptuous of the ideals of non-intervention, constitutionality, and integrity that it professes; that the United States was willing to corrupt the countries it said it wanted to help —the impression was left, in a word, that the CIA was the real voice and power of United States foreign policy and that the narrow Cold War aims of intelligence were the principal aims of the United States itself.

The political damage is illustrated by the fact that four and a half years later, when the Singapore government, following its expulsion from Malaysia, had need to ingratiate itself with other Asian nations, the easiest way to do so was to announce the injuries it had suffered at the hands of the CIA, the "bad" side of the United States. For this was an appeal to the anti-American, anti-"imperialist" sentiment created not only by Communist propaganda but by such ill-conceived, essentially irresponsible intelligence activities typified by the Singapore incident.

All this made President Kennedy and the members of the New Frontier begin to wonder whether some people in the agency had become so enamored of the cloak-and-dagger game that they were beginning to play it for its own sake and had lost their capacity to keep intelligence activities in perspective with the rest of American values. And the fact that the CIA had not bothered to consult in advance either the State Department in Washington or the consul general and ambassador in the field rubbed salt in the wound, for it seemed to indicate that at least some people in the agency thought themselves above political control. In the White House and among some of the presidential appointees in the State Department, the incentive for trying to improve the procedures for co-ordinating intelligence activities and foreign policy increased sharply.

There were two aspects to the problem—how the State Department organized itself to handle these matters, first, and, second, the role of the CIA in the over-all context of United States foreign policy. In the intelligence business, as Allen Dulles describes in his book, a distinction is made between espionage activities and "activities belonging in the category of political or psychological warfare."[2] Sometimes called "covert political action" or simply "covert action," these latter activities can be almost anything from giving the non-Communist faction in a foreign labor union money to help them fight a Communist faction financed from Moscow or Peking to a *coup d'état* or a major rebellion, such as Dulles describes in Guatemala, which overturned the pro-Communist Arbenz regime. Each of these two types of activity, espionage and "covert action," presents a different problem of "co-ordination," according to the political consequences if something goes wrong. Certain espionage activities, of which the U-2 affair in 1960 is a conspicuous example, can have very widespread political consequences if they are discovered. Flying an airplane over another country's territory is a violation of international law. It is a flagrant and provable violation if the airplane is shot down. It is insulting to the nation and its prestige in that flying over its territory implies both actual technological superiority—impunity from being shot down—and contempt for the other nation's defenses. And flying a reconnaissance airplane over another country's territory also runs a risk of looking a little too belligerent, as if the preliminary steps are being taken for war.

Some other kinds of espionage activity, on the other hand, are regarded as part of the game, and shrugged off with a "boys-will-be-boys" attitude. Where shooting down the U-2 caused a political storm that wrecked a summit conference, the political repercussions of a Western intelligence service getting caught trying to recruit a Soviet citizen as a secret agent would hardly cause a ripple. On the other hand, if a Western intelligence service got caught trying to recruit an official of a friendly country as a secret agent, the political repercussions might be very serious.

The problem of "co-ordinating" intelligence activities with foreign policy is a problem of finding ways for the people responsible for foreign policy— in the White House and the Defense Department as well as in the State Department—to consider proposals for operations that might have serious political consequences and to weigh out the relative gains as against the probable costs. Generally speaking, the "political warfare," or "covert political action," type of activity Dulles describes has such a high potential for political disaster that every single program, no matter how innocuous it seems, is the subject of "co-ordination." As Dulles wrote in response to criticisms that CIA had gone off on its own, "The facts are that the CIA has never carried out any action of a political nature, given any support of any nature to any persons, potentates or movements, political or otherwise, without appropriate approval at a high political level in our government *outside the CIA*.[3] This is true, but it still leaves room for lots of difficulty—and part of the difficulty was the way the State Department was organized to participate in this process of granting interdepartmental approval at "a high political level."

What the Kennedy administration discovered was that the State Department was fragmented, on the grounds of secrecy, so that people approving a particular proposal did not always know of other activities that had a bearing on the possible repercussions. Traditionally, it was the Under Secretary who sat on any interdepartmental committees that met to consider such matters, and there was a small, independent group of officers who did the necessary staff work, checking out various aspects of a problem with the regional Assistant Secretary or other officer whose responsibilities would be affected. But for "intelligence" operations, the channels were quite different—going through the Director of the Bureau of Intelligence and Research in his capacity as a member of the United States Intelligence Board.

One result of this fragmentation of the State Department was that occasionally the CIA intelligence officer sponsoring a particular proposal gave way to the human temptation, when confronted with alternative channels for obtaining approval, of choosing the channel through which approval was most likely to be forthcoming, either the Under Secretary or the Intelligence Bureau. And all too frequently, the channel that was most likely to approve was the channel that was least informed about that particular problem. But the most serious consequence was that the right hand of the State Department did not always know what the left had approved, and neither in consequence had the knowledge to judge proposals fully and soundly.

Our recommendation was that all "co-ordination" staffs and procedures —both for intelligence and political action proposals—should be consolidated in the Intelligence Bureau. This meant there would be only one channel in the State Department—the Director of Intelligence and Research, who would then report to the Under Secretary and the Secretary. But the idea was immediately blocked—by Allen Dulles himself. Courtesy demanded that Dulles be consulted about the proposed change, and so did prudence. Although the way the State Department chose to organize itself would normally be the State Department's business, in this particular case Dulles might successfully exercise a veto. The National Security Act of 1947 gave the Director of CIA responsibility for protecting "intelligence sources and methods from unauthorized disclosure" and if he did not approve of these changes and anything ever went wrong, he could certainly make the State Department's position acutely uncomfortable in a practical political sense. Chester Bowles, as Under Secretary, urged that the issue be pushed to the White House if necessary, but Rusk was reluctant. And so the matter stood.

On the second aspect of the question, the role of CIA in the conduct of American foreign policy, there was, quite obviously, no easy solution. The United States was faced with hostile Communist nations that were determined, in Khrushchev's words, to "bury" us, and knowing what those hostile nations were up to was vital to the survival of the United States. The Communists were also attempting to subvert weaker, developing countries all over the world with a lavish outlay of money, goods, and people, and there were occasions when a little counteraction in the field of covert political activity might make the difference between losing a country to Communist subversion or maintaining its independence. We had to have a CIA, and this particular one, in fact, had had great successes.

Partly the trouble was the very ability of the CIA and the people in it. When ability, secrecy, and money were combined with very narrow responsibilities, the narrow responsibilities—in this case both covert political activities and secret intelligence activities—were pursued with a vigor and emphasis that was sometimes out of proportion and that made the United States appear to rely as heavily on subversion and secret service techniques as the Communists. There were too many CIA people abroad, in a word, doing too much and doing it too successfully. It is no secret that when President Kennedy took office CIA had almost as many officers abroad engaged in intelligence activities as the State Department had for the whole range of its activities. Because the CIA had people and money, they kept busy thinking up new things to do to spend the money and keep the people occupied—and all in the narrow field of secret service activities. Because they had people and money, as mentioned before, other agencies kept pushing them into activities that were peripheral to true secret service work, and those activities, too, became tainted with the aura of "intelligence" and contributed to the impression of an omnipresent, pervasive CIA—ubiquitous, active, powerful, a finger in every pie. Even their successes backfired. By 1961 so many of their feats were known that in many countries CIA was given the credit for almost everything that happened in them—good or bad.

Thus the basic trouble was that the agency was simply too powerful for the narrow function for which it was responsible. It combined in one organization just too many of the resources and instruments of foreign policy—the means to gather information in its agents abroad; the means to analyze information and develop policies and proposals in its research and analysis sections in Washington, and the means to implement policy with a whole range of instrumentalities, including CIA station chiefs with their capacity for high-level representation. Ideally, the best solution was probably along the lines the British had followed—which kept the research and analysis functions in an organization separate from the secret intelligence-gathering functions and subordinated the latter very sharply to the Foreign Office. But such a drastic move would require legislation —and that would clearly be impossible in the face of CIA's natural strength with the coalition of Southern Democrats and conservative Republicans that dominated Congress. The only thing to do was to try to bring about some reduction in the numbers of CIA people abroad and their prominence and to fight new proposals that were unrealistic or excessively risky. But this effort, too, quickly met a stone wall.

In the meantime, Bowles had run into the problem of CIA-State Department relations in his efforts to strengthen the hand of the ambassador in our posts overseas, even though this was a matter in which the President was personally interested as part of his concept of relying on the State Department for leadership. The issue revolved around a proposed letter of instructions from the President to each ambassador. The proposed instructions read, bluntly, "You are in charge of the entire United States Diplomatic Mission, and I shall expect you to supervise all of its operations. The Mission includes not only the personnel of the Department of State and the Foreign Service, but also the representatives of all other United States agencies which have programs or activities in [your country]." Although President Eisenhower, too, had sent a letter to his ambassadors at the beginning of his administration, there were significant differences of tone. But the real trouble was that in the Eisenhower administration a second letter had followed the first specifically exempting the Central Intelligence Agency from the ambassador's authority, and Bowles was refusing to agree to such a letter this time.[4]

The issue was not whether the CIA had the right to pursue their own, independent policies or to "freewheel" abroad, as so often alleged in the press. No one in CIA would ever have contended that they did. The issue was whether intelligence should have special status and the presumptive privilege of excluding ambassadors whom they considered were not fully to be trusted with the supersecrets of intelligence. Bowles maintained that any ambassador who could not be trusted should not be an ambassador, but all concerned knew that the real issue was authority, whether the ambassador should be the unquestioned, single boss or whether his power and authority should be shared.

And it was here—at stalemate—that matters stood in April of 1961, when the Bay of Pigs fiasco intervened.

Two days after the failure of the Bay of Pigs operation, President Kennedy called General Maxwell D. Taylor back from retirement to head an investigation of what had gone wrong. Also on the investigating committee were Allen Dulles, Admiral Arleigh Burke, and the President's brother, Robert F. Kennedy. Taylor had retired from his post as Chief of Staff of the Army in the Eisenhower administration in protest at the "massive retaliation" strategy and the emphasis on air forces at the expense of ground forces, and he combined military stature with considerable political acumen.

At the same time, the President re-established the President's Board of Consultants on Foreign Intelligence Activities under a new name, the President's Foreign Intelligence Advisory Board. Kennedy reappointed the same chairman that the board had had under Eisenhower, James R. Killian, and gave him an even broader mandate—to re-examine the whole range of activities in the entire intelligence community.

The Taylor Committee considered that its mandate was to look only at the Bay of Pigs operation, determine what went wrong, and make recommendations as to the future division of labor in such matters between CIA and the Defense Department. Their analysis showed that from a military point of view everything about the operation was inadequate—the number of men, their equipment, the air support, the ammunition—and the Taylor Committee concluded that an agency like the CIA was poorly suited for carrying out operations on that scale. In the future, CIA would continue to have responsibility for the kind of "covert political action" that would, for example, head off a Communist attempt to gain control of a foreign labor union. But responsibility for paramilitary operations would be assigned to a Special Warfare section of the Pentagon.

It was in the Killian Committee and the White House that discussion centered on the larger question of CIA's role in the making of policy and the conduct of foreign affairs. Within the White House staff, Arthur M. Schlesinger, Jr., spent more time on the problem than anyone else, and it was he who developed a full and reasoned set of proposals. His basic thesis was that secret activities are permissible so long as they do not affect the principles and practices of our society, and that they cease to be permissible when their effect is to corrupt these principles and practices. The original idea of CIA had been to conceal the cloak-and-dagger activities behind the much larger mass of "overt" intelligence work—research and estimating, monitoring foreign propaganda broadcasts, and so on. But what had happened was the opposite, the "covert" activities had tainted all the rest, making even the most innocent of legitimate research seem sinister. Noting this, and cataloguing the list of other excesses—too many people overseas, too much influence with too many chiefs of state abroad, sometimes in pursuit of policies different from those of the ambassador—Schlesinger argued for a drastic overhaul of the intelligence setup. What he proposed was (1) taking the research and estimating function and all other overt activities out of CIA and also taking the Bureau of Intelligence and Research out of the State Department and combining the two into a new, independent agency; and, (2) leaving CIA with its covert functions, but renaming it to escape the tarnished image and putting the new agency directly under the State Department for "policy guidance."

In the State Department, the studies that Rusk had commissioned in his conversation with David Bell and me in February pointed in the same general direction—creating a new agency that would encompass all the *overt* activities of research and estimating and leave the remainder to a renamed and truly secret intelligence service. But Rusk felt there was not time enough to conduct the interdepartmental discussions that he wanted, and he instructed me merely to make the studies available to those interested as working papers on which he had not yet had time to form a view.

In Congress and among the liberal press, there was some effort to drum up support for a fundamental reorganization of the intelligence community. The *New Republic,* for example, wanted to break up the CIA. "The fact that what amounted to policy-making responsibility on Cuba had been allowed to the CIA by President Eisenhower," the editors wrote, "was the natural end-result of a broad usurpation of power which took place, almost unnoticed, during those anomalous years when one Dulles ran the Department and the other the Agency . . . Cuba turned a searing spotlight on the phenomena of a government which has come to have in effect two State Departments."[5] And a few congressmen—notably Emilio Daddario of Connecticut—called for a "Watchdog Committee" of the Congress to oversee all intelligence activities.

At one stage, someone on the President's staff attempted to test the public view by leaking the various proposals described above to the press—a raft of stories describing especially the Schlesinger proposals appeared with a Hyannis Port dateline, where the President and his staff were spending the Fourth of July weekend. But by and large the public and congressional demand for drastic measures did not extend beyond a segment decidedly on the left of the political spectrum.

The lack of public and congressional support for far-reaching changes in the role and function of CIA meant that nothing could be done that would require legislation. In the wake of the Bay of Pigs, emotions were just too highly charged, and an attempt to get legislation would end up in a bitter fight between defenders and opponents of CIA that would hurt more than it would help. Any adjustments in the role and power of CIA would have to be made within the Executive Branch itself—and they would have to be quiet changes even then.

It was, of course, perfectly obvious to everyone that both Allen Dulles and Richard Bissell would have to leave as soon as the storm died down a bit. David Bell suggested that the President could make use of this opportunity to bring about at least a change of emphasis. What Bell had in mind was to appoint the new Director on the understanding that he would not act as operating head of the CIA but, working out of the White House, as the co-ordinator of the entire intelligence community. Then, the new Deputy Director could act as the operating head of the CIA. In this way, Bell hoped, the two hats which Allen Dulles had worn, and which had given him so much power, would be separated in practice.

When John A. McCone took over as Director of Central Intelligence, the President did tell him to keep the two hats clearly in mind and to make as much distinction as he could. But nothing really came of it.

The President also ordered a "drastic and urgent" reduction in the number of CIA men overseas in the most visible of the "official cover" positions, the term for intelligence men occupying a position in an embassy abroad ostensibly as an official of the State Department or some other government agency. A painful review was conducted and some reductions were made over the next year, but they were more than offset by increases in other places.

But there were some subtle changes that eased the problem temporarily—for the Kennedy administration at least. For what no one in Washington had failed to notice was that the Bay of Pigs debacle, the public display of the CIA's feet of clay, and, within the administration, the President's obvious disenchantment were all having an effect. On May 15, 1961, Allen Dulles called me to say that although he still had a few qualms, he was withdrawing his objections to the State Department's plan to consolidate its staffs and procedures for "co-ordinating" intelligence and political action proposals. More importantly, the letter to the ambassadors from the President giving them clear authority over all United States agencies abroad was cleared and shortly thereafter, on May 29, 1961, dispatched. Over the next few weeks, the ambassadors at all our missions overseas received briefings on the operations of all the agencies represented at their posts. Another, more subtle change also became apparent—everyone had been burned so badly by the Bay of Pigs that fewer of the "political action" kind of operation were now being proposed for interdepartmental approval and fewer still were approved. Not all of this became known immediately, but it was not long before even those of our allies who were most dependent on CIA saw the way the Washington wind was blowing. Finally, our ambassadors in those countries began to feel the change reflected in the officials with whom they dealt. When notables from these countries visited Washington, for example, they paid far fewer calls on the Director of Central Intelligence than had once been customary. CIA's power had been at least slightly reduced, in other words, even though no formal organizational changes had actually been made.

This uneasy balance was temporary at best, and it was not certain how long it would last. One threat was John McCone himself. He had said that he intended to become a "power in this administration" and the question was whether he meant in the old Allen Dulles sense in which CIA loomed large in every aspect of the conduct of foreign affairs or whether he meant to be a power in the sense of developing the agency's potential as a professional intelligence service only. The second threat was the newly established Defense Intelligence Agency, which had taken over and consolidated most of the functions of the Army's G-2, the Air Force's A-2, and the Navy's Office of Naval Intelligence. McNamara had set up the DIA as part of his attempts to unify the military services and reduce duplication between them. But the DIA grew so large so quickly, building up staffs of analysts in political and economic intelligence as well as purely military, that Washington was inevitably filled with talk of an impending struggle between the DIA and McNamara, on the one hand, and the CIA and McCone, on the other. And thus from the viewpoint of the State Department, at least, the two threats were related so as to pose a dilemma. The State Department did not want the Director of CIA to be so strong as to dominate foreign policy, but it certainly wanted him to be strong enough to prevent the Defense Intelligence Agency from dominating foreign policy.

The first test of the new balance, which came between McCone and the State Department, was ominous. Shortly after McCone arrived, he drafted a letter of instructions from the President to himself that was a very, very broad grant of authority. Alarmed at this, the new Under Secretary, George Ball, and I finally persuaded Secretary Rusk to sign a letter that, while accepting the draft as it was proposed, went on to lay down a number of qualifications. The letter made McCone mad as a hornet; he demanded that it be withdrawn—and the Secretary complied.

As it turned out, however, McCone was restrained in his use of the power of CIA. Like his predecessor, he had a voice in the policy discussions of the National Security Council, which he exercised. But he was content at that, and made no special effort to use the power of CIA to try to dominate the whole range of foreign policy. And McCone was equally restrained in exercising his power within the intelligence community. Although he argued vigorously for his own special point of view at the weekly meetings of the Intelligence Board when it considered National Intelligence Estimates, for example, he did not use the power of his office to impose his own view on the estimate.

Uneasy though it was, the balance continued to hold. For the time being, the President had at least contained the problem of CIA by the two devices of taking advantage of the atmosphere created by the Bay of Pigs debacle and by getting the right man to do the job the way he wanted it to be done. But the long-run problem of the CIA remained.

NOTES

[1] See the New York *Times,* September 2–4, 1965, and editorial September 3, 1965.
[2] Allen W. Dulles, *The Craft of Intelligence,* 1963, p. 46.
[3] Allen W. Dulles, *op. cit.,* p. 189. The emphasis is Mr. Dulles'.
[4] The existence of the second letter was revealed in the *Department of State Newsletter,* December 1961. See *"INR Report: Bureau Undergoes Changes in Thinking and Planning,"* of that issue. The initials INR stand for Bureau of Intelligence and Research.
[5] "Leashing Up the CIA," The *New Republic,* May 8, 1961.

CHAPTER 8

Secret Intelligence in a Free Society

THE CIA is not a threat to our liberties and never has been. It is composed of dedicated officers of extremely high standards of integrity and patriotism. Should anyone attempt to subvert the agency to purposes that would threaten our society, it would be members of CIA who would be the first to sound the alarm. But the real problem of CIA, the inherent tension in conducting secret intelligence in a free society, remains.

Secrecy and deception will always create problems in a free society. The Bay of Pigs, as we have seen, illustrates one aspect of this. Because of secrecy, men who had knowledge that could have contributed to the making of sounder judgments were excluded from making that contribution. Another, more subtle aspect of secrecy is the way it tends to corrode confidence among different officials and between the government and the public and the press. Adlai Stevenson at the UN was ignorant of the planned invasion of Cuba and read into the UN record a statement that the planes that had bombed Havana's airfield were "defectors" from the Cuban air forces—not knowing that he was repeating the CIA "cover" story. At the time that the U-2 was shot down in 1960, Lincoln White, the official State Department spokesman, in all innocence flatly and indignantly denied that the United States had flown a spy plane over the Soviet Union. "There was absolutely no—N-O—no deliberate attempt to violate Soviet airspace," White said. "There never has been." And he repeated the CIA "cover" story that what had been shot down was a "weather" plane that had strayed. Again, when Singapore's Prime Minister, Lee, made his charges public in 1965, the State Department spokesman denied everything—until Lee produced a letter of apology from Secretary Rusk dated 1961 and threatened to make available to the press the tape recordings the Singapore government had made when it eavesdropped on the CIA's attempted subversion. After such experiences, officials inevitably began to wonder what else they do not know and sometimes to distrust the instructions they have been given. An American ambassador to Burma during the Eisenhower administration, for example, began to feel that he was not being told the truth about CIA involvement with the Chinese Nationalist troops in northern Burma and eventually to wonder whether his official denials to the Burmese Government might be proven lies. The point is not that there was any foundation to the ambassador's suspicion but that suspicion and distrust begin to spread throughout the government and to the Congress. When I appeared before the Senate Foreign Relations Committee prior to being confirmed as Assistant Secretary for Far Eastern Affairs, for example, the question asked most persistently was, "How can we be sure that you can keep the CIA in line in the Far East—or even know what they are doing?"

And secrecy and deception sow the same mistrust and cynicism in the press. When the Indonesian Government charged during the 1958 rebellion that the rebels had received aid from the United States, the New York *Times* published a long and indignant editorial denouncing the Indonesian Government for circulating a "false report" that the United States had sanctioned aid to the rebels. "The position of the United States government," said the editorial, "has been made plain, again and again. Our Secretary of State was emphatic in his declaration that this country would not deviate from a correct neutrality. The President himself, in a news conference, reiterated this position . . . [Jakarta's] cause is not promoted by charges that are manifestly false."[1] The editorial concluded that, although most Americans did not approve of President Sukarno's "guided democracy" and his "enthusiasm to have Communist participation in his government," the United States was not ready to help "overthrow a constituted government." As more and more of the full story began to come out, the embarrassment in the *Times* editorial board was undoubtedly acute, but the real damage was a growing cynicism in the press and their doubt about the truthfulness of the official statements of their own government.

Another problem that existed in the past and will undoubtedly continue in the future is the tension between the need to engage in clandestine activities and our national reputation. A reputation for openness, respect for others, and idealism is one of our greatest political assets. But openness, respect for others, and idealism are inconsistent with the deviousness and intrigue of secret service techniques.

Allen Dulles justifies secret intelligence gathering activities—espionage and the use of devices such as the U-2—on the grounds of national survival. The Communists are avowedly out to "bury" us, and they make extensive military preparations in the utmost of secrecy. These facts alone, Dulles argues, justify our taking the measures necessary to uncover those preparations.[2] Dulles justifies our covert political activities on similar grounds. As long as the Communist countries continue to use subversive means to bring down non-Communist regimes, those who oppose the Communists must be prepared to meet the threat. But meeting it successfully, Dulles argues, means that our intelligence services must play their role early in the struggle, while the subversion is still in the plotting and organizational stage. "To act," Dulles writes, "one must have the intelligence about the plot and the plotters and have ready the technical means, overt and covert, to meet it."³ Citing the Truman and Eisenhower doctrines, which laid down policies that the United States would come to the aid of countries threatened by Communism *whose governments requested help,* Dulles goes on to enunciate a doctrine of his own. He argues that covert political action should be used to foil Communist attempts to take over a country with or without a request for help. "In Iran a Mossadegh and in Guatemala an Arbenz came to power through the usual processes of government," he writes, "and not by any Communist coup as in Czechoslovakia. Neither man at the time disclosed the intention of creating a Communist state. When this purpose became clear, support from outside was given to loyal anti-Communist elements in the respective countries . . . In each case the danger was successfully met. There again no invitation was extended by the *government* in power for outside help."⁴

In both these arguments, it seems to me, Dulles is fundamentally right. So long as the Communists themselves are openly antagonistic to the rest of the world, as they openly and avowedly are, and so long as they use the techniques of subversion to bring down governments, which they do and which they openly and avowedly advocate doing, then the countries to which they are so hostile have both a right and a duty to use the methods of secret intelligence to protect and defend themselves—where those methods are effective and appropriate and for which there is no effective and appropriate alternative.

The trouble has been, of course, that these qualifications have not always been observed. In the past we have too often used secret intelligence methods when they were *not* effective and appropriate or when there *were* effective and appropriate alternatives. "Covert political action" in particular became a fad, the answer to every kind of problem, and American agents became as ubiquitously busy as the Communists.

In the years following the establishment of CIA and especially after General Walter Bedell Smith made it an effective organization in 1950–51, the United States was first coming up against some of the perplexities of the postwar world and the Communist threat. We met the direct Communist challenge by building up our military strength and by alliances. But again and again we came up against problems that did not yield to power alone—ineffectual governments, graft, politically apathetic populations, indifferent leaders, Communist subversion, terrorism, and guerrilla warfare—or problems in which it would have been politically disastrous for a great nation to use its massive power in ways that the world would regard as petty bullying, if the giant United States, for example, directly attacked tiny Cuba. To many of the policy-makers who faced these dilemmas of foreign policy, covert action seemed a way out. We would fight Communist fire with fire. Since the action was "covert" it promised to get around the obstacles, the moral problem of "intervention," the political problem of appearing to be a bully. Covert action also had an aura of omnipotence, like James Bond, the fictional Agent 007, as if it could accomplish miracles.

But covert action was really nothing more than a gimmick. In very special circumstances, it was a useful supplement, but nothing more. It is one thing, for example, to help the Shah's supporters in Iran in their struggle against Mossadegh and his Communist allies, but it is something else again to sponsor a thousand-man invasion against Castro's Cuba, where there was no effective internal opposition. It is one thing, again, to give a covert boost to, say, the Philippines' Magsaysay, a natural leader with wide popular support, in a bid for power in the midst of national crisis created by the guerrilla terrorism of the Communist Hukbalahaps, and it is something quite different to try to create a Magsaysay by covert efforts, as we did in the 1950s with General Phoumi Nosavan in Laos.

But it was some time before these distinctions became clear. Covert action was overused as an instrument of foreign policy, and the reputation of the United States suffered more and more. "Covert" is usually defined not as completely secret, but as "plausibly deniable." But while one action might be "plausibly deniable," several hundred are not. And where one action, considered in isolation, might seem worth the cost of slightly tarnishing our image abroad, the cumulative effect of several hundred blots was to blacken it entirely. By the end of the Eisenhower administration our reputation was such that we got credit for almost everything unpleasant that happened in many countries, whether or not we were actually responsible. In Southeast Asia, for example, there was hardly a single country in which it was not widely believed that CIA had been behind some major event. The Burmese had no doubt that CIA had supported the Nationalist Chinese troops operating on their soil. The Lao believed that the CIA had created and brought down several successive governments. Sihanouk in Cambodia was convinced that the CIA had financed the effort of the so-called "Free Khmer" movement that had attempted to overthrow him. Sukarno in Indonesia had absolute proof of CIA's complicity in the 1958 rebellion. Even in France, our oldest ally and friend since it helped us in the Revolutionary War, newspapers published the charge that CIA supported the OAS generals in their attempted coup in 1961 against President de Gaulle—and Frenchmen believed it. And again in 1965, when the French Government protested that an American photo-reconnaissance plane had flown over French atomic energy installations, French newspapers charged that it had been sent there deliberately on an intelligence mission, just as the U-2 had been sent over the Soviet Union—and Frenchmen believed it. Too heavy reliance on the techniques of secret intelligence, in sum, so corroded one of our major political assets, the belief in American intentions and integrity, as to nullify much of the gain.

But if it is granted that the United States has both a right and a duty to use the methods of secret intelligence to defend itself against an avowedly hostile Communist power, there are some advantages to having the kind of centralized intelligence setup which CIA represents. Without this centralization, for example, there would be continuous disasters in the field of clandestine collection activities. Competing intelligence services would inevitably stumble over each other with ridiculous and dangerous consequences. Without this centralization, intelligence priorities would be developed by each individual service and department, instead of by the whole of the United States Government, which permits a rational measuring of cost as against gain not only in monetary but also in political terms. Finally, without this centralization CIA would not have been able to bring about the truly *national* intelligence estimates that it has, especially on the big questions of Soviet missile and nuclear strength, the Sino-Soviet dispute, and Communist intentions and probable reactions, in which all the different services and departments have educated each other. And the alternative would have been competing estimates that would have torn policy asunder.

For all these reasons, it seems best that changes in the role, functions, and powers of CIA be made slowly and deliberately. A beginning can be made, for example, by a series of not very drastic steps: (1) continue the reduction that was begun in the Kennedy administration in the number of covert action operations, reducing them down to those few that are truly "effective and appropriate and for which there is no effective and appropriate alternative"; (2) concentrate clandestine intelligence collection operations on matters of true threat to the nation and put the savings into improving the quality; (3) in step with the foregoing, reduce the numbers and visibility of CIA agents abroad and permit a freer transfer of able CIA people into the foreign service sooner; and (4) encourage the State Department both in Washington and abroad to assert its policy control and guidance more vigorously.

After these modest steps have been carried out, it will be time enough to consider more drastic measures—such as the proposal to carry through a reorganization along the lines of the British example of putting research and estimating functions in an independent agency and having a smaller, truly secret intelligence service reporting for policy guidance to the Secretary of State.

The need for the United States to engage in clandestine activities will continue and so will the tension between this need and the need to preserve the asset of belief in our intentions and integrity. Similarly, the problem of secrecy and deception in a free society will continue. But it seems to me that all these problems are more the responsibility of the policy-makers than of CIA and its particular mandate and powers. It was the policy-makers who were fundamentally responsible for making covert action a fad, and it is the policy-makers who can at least prevent secrecy and deception from coming to defeat policy. For it is on the policy-makers —the President, the Secretaries of State and Defense, the Under Secretaries, and the Assistant Secretaries—on whom responsibility ultimately rests.

NOTES

[1] The New York *Times,* May 9, 1958.
[2] Allen Dulles, *The Craft of Intelligence,* pp. 48–51.
[3] Allen Dulles, *op. cit.,* p. 234.
[4] Allen Dulles, *op. cit.,* p. 224.

IV

LAOS

"You have a row of dominoes set up, you knock over the first one, and what will happen to the last one is that it will go over very quickly. So you have a beginning of a disintegration that would have the most profound influences."

—Dwight D. Eisenhower,
News conference, April 7, 1954

"Where nature makes natural allies of all, we can demonstrate that beneficial relations are possible even with those with whom we most deeply disagree—and this must someday be the basis of world peace and world law."

—John F. Kennedy, *State of the Union Message, January 30, 1961*

CHAPTER 9

The Dominoes of Southeast Asia

ON MARCH 23, 1961, just two months after taking office, President Kennedy found himself facing the television cameras at a news conference to warn of the imminent possibility of war.

Behind the President on easels stood three maps of Laos. The first showed the area of Laos controlled by the Communists as of August 1960—essentially the two extreme northeastern provinces of Phong Saly and Sam Neua, which bordered on Communist China and North Vietnam. The second map showed the results of Communist expansion up to December 1960, which by then covered the central portion of Laos and the Plain of Jars. And the third showed the situation at the time the President was speaking, after the Communists had moved southward into the panhandle of Laos so that they controlled the whole eastern half of the country along a line that roughly marked the edge of the hills and mountains.

The President reminded his audience that the Geneva agreements of 1954 had created Laos as one of the successor states of French Indochina and had provided for its neutrality and freedom from external domination. He charged that in the military advances illustrated by the three maps, the Communist Pathet Lao had had "increasing support and direction from outside," including a large-scale airlift, mounted by the Soviet Union, and heavy weapons and combat specialists from Communist North Vietnam. "It is this new dimension of externally supported warfare," the President said, "that creates the present grave problem."

"I want to make it clear to the American people and to all of the world," the President went on, "that all we want in Laos is peace, not war; a truly neutral government, not a cold war pawn; a settlement concluded at the conference table and not on the battlefield." But if there was to be a peaceful solution, he said, the "armed attacks by externally supported Communists" had to stop. "If these attacks do not stop," he concluded in warning, "those who support a truly neutral Laos will have to consider their response. The shape of this necessary response will, of course, be carefully considered, not only here in Washington, but in the SEATO Conference with our allies . . ." The implication was war.

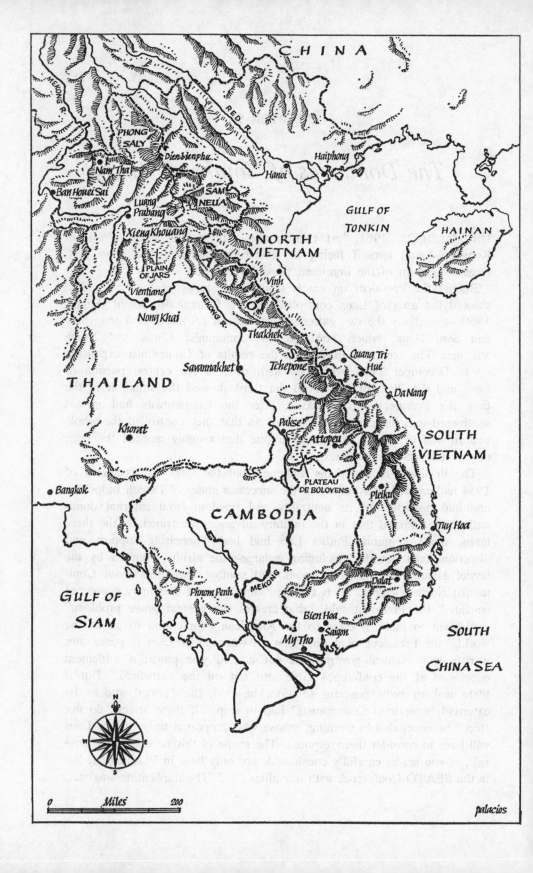

CHINA

MEKONG R.

RED R.

PHONG
SALY

Dienbienphu

Nam Tha

Ban Houei Sai

Luang
Prabang

SAM
NEUA

Xieng Khouang

PLAIN
OF JARS

Vientiane

Nong Khai

THAILAND

Khorat

Bangkok

GULF OF
SIAM

Phnom Penh

My Tho

Hanoi

Haiphong

GULF OF
TONKIN

HAINAN

NORTH
VIETNAM

Vinh

MEKONG R.

Thakhek

Savannakhet

Tchepone

Quang Tri
Hué

Da Nang

Pakse

Attopeu

SOUTH
VIETNAM

PLATEAU
DE BOLOVENS

Pleiku

CAMBODIA

Tuy Hoa

MEKONG R.

Dalat

Bien Hoa
Saigon

SOUTH
CHINA SEA

0   Miles   200

palacios

THE STRATEGIC SIGNIFICANCE OF SOUTHEAST ASIA

In the nineteenth century, the Southeast Asian peninsula—comprising Burma, Thailand, Malaya, and French Indochina—came to be the Asian arena of confrontation between the British and the French. British power extended into Burma and Malaya from India and French power embraced the several ancient kingdoms of Indochina. Thailand was in the middle, maintaining an uneasy independence as a buffer state between them. In the latter half of the twentieth century, the Southeast Asian peninsula has become the arena of confrontation between the Communist world, and particularly Communist China, on the one hand; and the West on the other, especially the United States. And in this instance, it is India that is in the political if not the geographic middle— still unclear about its role, but looming in the background.

This peninsula of mainland Southeast Asia is a salient thrusting down through the great arc of Asia, dividing Japan, Korea, the Philippines, and the basin of the China Sea from the countries of South Asia bordering on the Indian Ocean—India, Ceylon, and Pakistan.* And it pinches the sea lanes from north to south against the islands of Indonesia at the Strait of Malacca.

The peninsula itself is made up of a series of parallel north-south ridges, mammoth spurs of the Himalayan massif—the Naga Hills-Arakan chain between Burma and India, the jumbled Shan hills and mountains of Burma and Thailand, and the great Annamite chain of Indochina. Between the long mountain ridges great rivers flow southward from the Tibetan-Chinese plateau: the Mekong, the Salween, and the Irrawaddy.

Throughout this whole peninsula there are only four north-south roads —or more correctly, only four routes capable of being developed into roads. Two of the four run through Burma, down the western side of the peninsula. The first is the Ledo Road, cutting over from the Brahmaputra valley of Assam in India across the top of Burma to Kunming in China—first developed, ironically, by the Americans in World War II as a means of supplying China. The second is the old Burma Road, leading from Rangoon up past the ancient jade and ruby mines of Mogok and thence on to China. Marco Polo traveled this way on his return journey from Cathay when the route was already very, very old—for jade traveled over it in prehistoric times, just as amber traveled a similar route from the beaches of the Baltic Sea down through the Alps to the Mediterranean. A third route runs down the other side of the Southeast Asian peninsula from China to Hanoi, in North Vietnam, and thence right beside the sea on the coast of Vietnam to the very tip of Cochin

* See map pp. 276–77.

China. The fourth and final route goes down the middle of the Southeast Asian peninsula on the other side of the Annamite chain from the sea, traversing the mountains of Laos. But it is more of a potential route than an actual one. North of Luang Prabang, there are several possibilities where mountain trails could be developed into actual highways, with the most likely being the roads built by the Chinese as part of their program of aid to Laos. South of Luang Prabang, it is the existing route to Vientiane, the administrative capital of Laos, and thence southward either along the Mekong to Cambodia, South Vietnam, and the China Sea or bearing westward from Vientiane into Thailand via Khorat to Bangkok and the Gulf of Siam.

It could be argued that the strategic significance of Laos lies in the fact that it is situated astride this land-locked fourth route and that the United States interest in all four routes was not in controlling them for itself but in denying them to Communist China. In a technical, logistic sense, it is true that it was over one of these four routes that Chinese power could be most easily projected southward to dominate Southeast Asia. And circumstances focused attention on Laos. Burmese neutrality, so long as it was effective and honored, denied the Chinese the first two routes. The division of Vietnam at the seventeenth parallel denied them the third—at least for as long as South Vietnam maintained its independence, and perhaps even longer, considering the vulnerability of the coastal road to American sea power. But the potential route through Laos was highly vulnerable.

But determination and effort can create routes of communication where none exist naturally: Hannibal went through the Alps, and the Chinese attack on India in 1962 was through the Himalayas. The Chinese could come through Thailand if they wanted to make the effort, and the reason Laos was under pressure was not only because it was situated astride a possible route of communication southward but because it offered political opportunities. Like South Vietnam, Laos presented the Communists an "ex-colonial" issue that had never existed in Thailand and had died out in Burma.

THE TERRAIN

And the problem for the United States was compounded by the terrain of Laos, by the primitive state of its economy, and by its people and their politics. Laos is shaped like a caveman's club, with a knobby head in the north, and a handle extending southward. The very butt of the handle is the border with Cambodia. In the east, the border is the crest of the Annamite chain, shared for only the bottom half of the handle of the club with South Vietnam and for all the rest of both handle and head with the Communist north. On the west, the border is the Mekong

River, shared for most of the whole length of Laos with Thailand, the only exceptions being the provinces of Bassac in the south and Sayaboury in the north. One nob at the very top of the head marks a part of the border shared with Burma, and the next nob over to the east, still at the very top, is the border shared with Communist China.

The royal capital of Laos is at Luang Prabang in the north, where the valley is narrow as the Mekong makes its way through the mountains. But most of the Lao people live on the lowlands of the river farther south. One concentration is in the terrain compartment at Vientiane, located about midway between the point where the river makes a great bend to flow east for 150 miles and a second bend where it turns south again. Most of the rest of the people of Lao descent live in these southern lowlands—in villages grouped around the old market towns of Pak Sane, Thakhek, Savannakhet, and Pakse. There are also in the mountains a few scattered valleys and plateaus—of which the largest and richest is the Plain of Jars, with its market town of Xieng Khouang, not far from the center of the head of the club.* But except for these, Laos is a jumble of hills and mountains.

The lower valleys are blanketed by tropical rain forest. Tall trees standing shoulder to shoulder make such a dense canopy that the floor of the forest is in perpetual shade. Higher up the slopes of the hills, the forest is mixed with groves of softwoods and thick underbrush—grass, rhododendron, bamboo, and palms. And still higher there are pines and semitropical undergrowth reminiscent of the hill country of the American southland. Through all the forests and mountains of Laos roam wild elephant, tiger, deer, and the wild buffalo called gaur. What is probably the greatest natural game preserve left in the world, for example, is the circular Plateau de Bolovens, fifty miles in diameter and rising four thousand feet out of the Mekong lowlands in southern Laos.

The climate of Laos is dominated by the monsoon. In November, December, and January the weather is delightful, with cool, clear nights and bright, comfortable, sunny days. Then, slowly, day by day the weather gets hotter and hotter until the mighty Mekong is a trickle wending its way through cracked mud. Then suddenly in May or June the rains come. And when the rains do come, they come in torrents, coursing down the steep-sided mountains in raging floods, turning the dirt roads and trails into quagmires and washing out bridges, culverts, and fills—gullying even the very best of modern roads, which, no matter

* The jars on the Plain of Jars are, literally, jars. Two sites on the plain are littered with several hundred each. The jars themselves stand about four feet tall and are carved from solid rock, many with well-fitted lids. Their origin is a prehistoric mystery, but the most likely explanation is that they were the burial urns of some ancient people. Souphanouvong, the Communist leader, told me that Lao legend relates that the jars were already there when the Lao people first arrived.

how well engineered, require constant upkeep. A measure of the rains is what happens to the Mekong. For six months of the year it is fordable at many points in its long journey through Laos. But when the monsoon comes it begins to swell, until in September it is 30 to 40 feet deep and frequently over a mile wide.

THE PEOPLE

The people of Laos number only two million, although in area the country is almost twice the size of New York State. And of these two million, less than half are Lao. Living almost entirely in the Mekong lowlands, as we have said, the Lao, like the Thai, to whom they are closely related in language and blood, are Theravada Buddhists, and they are among the most gentle, peace-loving, and serene people in the world. Large families are the rule, and even among the French-educated elite, themselves so often sophisticates of Paris, families of ten, twelve, or fifteen children are not unusual. The rest of the population of Laos are mountain tribesmen, animist in religion, whose origin and tribe can frequently be deduced from the altitude of their villages. In the north, the mountain peoples are recent immigrants of Chinese-Mongolian background. The Yao, who live in the lower hills, came first, and then the Meo, who never live below four thousand feet, drifted down to Laos largely in the middle years of the nineteenth century. Of all the peoples inhabiting Laos, the most natural fighters are the Meo, a tough, stocky Mongolian people who have fought stubbornly to defend their villages against all comers. In the southern mountains, the tribesmen are mainly one or another branch of the darker-skinned Kha peoples, who stem from an aboriginal Indonesian stock.

The economy of Laos is simple. In the Mekong lowlands, the people live mainly in a wet-rice culture. The mountain peoples, however, follow the traditional Southeast Asian slash-and-burn technique for growing upland rice. The trees of a mountain slope are ringed and killed, and then burned off in the hot, dry season—in spite of the sparse population, in fact, the haze from this slash-and-burn technique can be so heavy over the mountains of Southeast Asia in March and April as to be a hazard to air travel. Mountain rice is then grown on the slopes so cleared and fertilized for a few years until the land wears out—and then the whole village picks up and moves on to another site, where the process is repeated.

The only other major crop in addition to rice, and undoubtedly the greatest earner of foreign exchange today, as in the time of the French, is opium. The waving fields of poppies are grown largely by the Meo, who collect the sap in gummy balls and trade the crude opium to Lao,

Chinese, Thai, or Vietnamese merchants, through whom it eventually finds its way to the world's markets, legal and illegal.

This, then, is Laos. Mountains and jungles so lightly populated that one may walk for days and see only one tiny Meo village, a cluster of bamboo huts clinging to the side of a mountain next to a steep field of upland rice. Narrow lowlands along the Mekong with green or yellow paddy fields and villages of bamboo, the mountains hung with mist in the distance. And little towns with dusty streets—Vientiane, for example, got its *second* traffic light in 1963—bamboo huts with tin roofs, a scattering of more substantial houses of "Farang" architecture, a modified French provincial style adapted to the tropics, a single movie house with a garish poster, these are towns not unlike their hot and dusty counterparts in the Southwestern United States, except for the domed Buddhist *wats,* the yellow-robed *bonzes* with shaved heads and begging bowls, and the pungent Asian smell of spice and incense.

THE POLITICS

The politics of Laos has been as varied as its terrain and people. In the nineteenth century, what is now Laos consisted of a collection of tiny principalities—the Kingdoms of Luang Prabang and Xieng Khouang, in the north, the Kingdom of Vientiane, along the middle Mekong between the two great bends, and the Kingdom of Champassak, in the south—all of which had a history of vassalage to either the Vietnamese emperor at Hué or to the king of the Thai at Bangkok.

In 1887, Auguste Pavie, an energetic and imaginative French official who became consul general at Luang Prabang, persuaded the king to abandon the Thai overlordship and become a French protectorate. From this beginning, French control was gradually extended over the whole of present-day Laos.

But everything was changed by World War II and the turmoil that followed it. For Laos, the immediate postwar history is peculiarly the history of three remarkable brothers of an ancient family, a cadet branch of the royal house of Luang Prabang—Phetsarath, Souvanna Phouma, and their half-brother, Souphanouvong. As was customary for princes of the royal blood, all three had been educated at French schools in Hanoi or Saigon and then at the University in Paris, the younger two being trained as engineers. When the Japanese broke their agreement with Vichy in March of 1945 and threw the French officials of Indochina into jail, Prince Phetsarath was Prime Minister. Immediately, he began to lay the groundwork for postwar independence, proclaiming the union of Champassak and the Kingdom of Luang Prabang as the independent Kingdom of Laos.

Phetsarath created a political party, the Lao Issara, and also formed a government—with Souvanna Phouma as Minister of Public Works. Souphanouvong, who had been in central Vietnam when the war ended, had independently taken up the task of making contact with Ho Chi Minh and the Viet Minh and getting their support. Successful in this, he set out on foot for Laos, and when he arrived in Vientiane in November, he was appointed Minister of National Defense and Commander in Chief of the Armed Services.

Over the next few months, the French forces fought their way back into Laos, and by April 1946 they had occupied all the major towns. The Lao Issara government fled to Bangkok, and from their exile they tried to keep alive a guerrilla harassment of the French occupation forces. As time wore on, the aging Phetsarath became less active, and the two other brothers diverged in their policies and allegiances. Souphanouvong, in his capacity as Commander in Chief, was not only in and out of Laos on covert trips but frequently extended his secret travels to Vietnam to maintain contact with the Viet Minh, and he became more and more closely identified with the Communists in the process. Souvanna Phouma, on the other hand, was hopeful of obtaining independence for Laos by peaceful means, and when the French granted Laos an additional measure of freedom in 1949, he joined the King for the negotiations in Paris. Souphanouvong, however, refused to go. The Lao Issara party was thereafter dissolved. The moderates returned to Laos with Souvanna, and the extremists remained in exile with Souphanouvong, who formed what became the Communist-dominated Pathet Lao and its front party, the Neo Lao Hak Xat (NLHX).

Both the Pathet Lao and the NLHX were built around Vietnamese cadres, and there is evidence that the Communist leaders of Vietnam intended from the beginning to try to maintain some sort of control over the Lao party apparatus even after it succeeded in taking over the country.[1] As time went on, it became increasingly difficult for outside observers to be sure just how much power Souphanouvong retained within the Pathet Lao and how much he had lost to men like Kaysone Phomvihan, a shadowy figure, half Lao and half Vietnamese, who seemed to represent the "Vietnamese faction" within the Communist apparatus of Laos.

In November 1951, Souvanna Phouma became Premier of the government in Laos. He vainly hoped to bring Souphanouvong into a government of national union, which he felt would be more effective in pushing the French into granting genuine independence, but he did use the pressure of the Viet Minh as an effective argument in persuading the French to grant a few additional concessions. But by this time, the fate of Laos was thoroughly intertwined with the Vietnamese war against the French.

THE BREAKUP OF INDOCHINA

When President Eisenhower turned his office over to John F. Kennedy, he said that the hardest problem he was leaving the new President was Laos. But the problem of Laos had been several years in the making, and it was part and parcel of the larger problem presented by the breakup of the French colonial empire in Indochina. In the wake of World War II, Ho Chi Minh succeeded in making himself and his Communist faction dominant in the basically nationalist and anticolonialist movement struggling against the French for Vietnamese independence. The French, blind to the tide of history, were stubbornly determined to maintain their colonial domination of Indochina, and for the first few years the Vietnamese revolutionaries made little headway. Then, in 1949, when the Chinese Communists ousted Chiang Kai-shek and took over the mainland, the situation changed. The Chinese Communists recognized Ho Chi Minh's government, and the Soviets quickly followed suit. Soon thereafter the Viet Minh—as the national independence movement was called—began to receive arms and ammunition from China, accompanied by Chinese military advisers.

For the United States, the French war in Indochina posed a dilemma. In one sense it was part of the over-all effort to contain Communism, and therefore deserving of support. But the French refusal to recognize the facts of Asian nationalism also made their effort in Indochina a senseless and hopeless struggle to maintain an outmoded colonial empire. The most that the French would do was to provide a mere façade of self-government—setting up "within the French Union" the three "Associated States" of Laos, Cambodia, and Vietnam. The American mission in Saigon was split on what they thought U.S. policy should be. Edmund A. Gullion was political counselor and he and a number of people in the aid program and the CIA were convinced that the only possible way the French could organize a successful resistance to Communist expansion was to grant Vietnam full and immediate independence. Many in Washington shared this view, and so did the young congressman John F. Kennedy. He visited the area in 1951 and spoke against the policy on his return. "In Indochina," he said, "we have allied ourselves to the desperate effort of a French regime to hang on to the remnants of empire." But what came out of the debate was a compromise that was in many ways the worst of both worlds. The United States did not intervene directly, but supported the French by using its power and political energies to deter the Chinese and other members of the Communist world from participating more directly, and by aid, both economic and military. On February 7, 1950, following Chinese and Soviet recognition of the Ho Chi Minh government, the United States under President

Truman recognized the three "Associated States" and immediately after the attack on Korea in June 1950 began a program of military assistance to them and to France. The flow of military aid soon reached massive proportions, totaling over two billion dollars by 1954. It is estimated that the United States financed 40 per cent of the total cost of France's Indochina war between 1951 and 1954, and by mid-1954 was paying for more than 75 per cent of it.

In July of 1953, General Navarre, the French commanding officer in Indochina, launched a large-scale buildup of forces which was to be followed by a dramatic offensive trumpeted to win the war in 1954–55.

DIENBIENPHU

But Navarre, like the other French generals before him, persisted in fighting the guerrilla war with large-scale conventional tactics—which permitted General Giap, the Viet Minh supreme commander, to choose just when and where he would accept the challenge to fight a conventional battle. The keystone of Navarre's strategy was an isolated village in a dish-shaped valley deep in the mountains of North Vietnam at the junction of roads from China and Laos—Dienbienphu. Still misreading the nature of guerrilla warfare, he turned Dienbienphu into a fortress—although it could be safely supplied only by air—which he liked to think of as the "cork in the bottle" that would stop the flow of supplies from China into Vietnam. Navarre put twelve thousand of the best French troops in the world into Dienbienphu, the elite parachutists, and made it a standing dare to the Viet Minh.

On January 30, 1954, Giap took up the challenge. He concentrated the bulk of his forces in the hills around Dienbienphu while other troops and thousands of peasant sympathizers began the "impossible" task of hauling artillery up over the mountainous trails by hand.

In the meantime, the French public had grown more and more weary of the war—which cost France 85,000 dead and wounded—and French politicians were forced to seek an accommodation. At a conference on Germany in Berlin, the Soviets proposed that France meet with Communist China, the United States, Great Britain, and the Soviet Union at Geneva. Secretary Dulles objected, convinced as he was that negotiating with the Chinese would be too close to recognition, but the French argued that they could not promise very much toward the defense of Europe if they failed to pursue any reasonable chance of ending the drain of the Indochina war. In the end, the five powers all agreed to meet at Geneva on April 26 to discuss both Indochina and Korea—and, to strengthen the Communist hand at the negotiations, General Giap redoubled his efforts to win a victory at Dienbienphu.

By mid-March, the French defenders at Dienbienphu were in trouble, and Washington was worried. Admiral Radford, Chairman of the American Joint Chiefs of Staff, proposed to the French high command that sixty American bombers from Clark Field in the Philippines escorted by 150 Navy fighters from the Seventh Fleet should conduct a raid on the forces ringing Dienbienphu in an attempt to "eliminate" Viet Minh artillery installations and communications—"Operation Vulture" it was named.

Vulture was another in what has become a long history of attempts to use air power, not as a supplement for ground power in Asia, but as a substitute for it—attempts to make war "immaculate," to move it up above the jungle muck and blood of ground combat to the clean blue skies. General Navarre was full of hope, and he convinced himself that a massive air strike might indeed destroy the Viet Minh artillery and that the war could still be contained. He also convinced himself that the Chinese would regard the strike as a limited American retaliation for the Chinese having helped the Viet Minh and so refrain from intervening as they had done in Korea.

In the United States, the American congressional leaders were briefed by Radford and Dulles, and they were much less hopeful. Radford maintained that one strike would do the job—but that if not, surely a second would. The congressmen were skeptical. They wanted to know whether American ground forces would have to be sent in if air strikes failed to "destroy" the enemy, as they had failed to destroy the supply lines in Korea. They wanted to know why Radford and Dulles were so sure that the Chinese Communists would not intervene. And they wanted to know whether or not our allies would stand with us in the enterprise.

In the end, the congressional leaders laid down three conditions that seemed to them essential: (1) that support to the French be multilateral; (2) that the French should speed up the process of granting Indochina its independence; and (3) that the French should agree not to withdraw their military forces from Indochina.

The Eisenhower administration was convinced that Indochina was a strategic key—it was on April 7 that President Eisenhower first spoke of the "falling domino" theory, arguing that if Indochina fell to the Communists, the other states of Southeast Asia would, in an inevitable dynamism, also fall. But the President nevertheless decided that the conditions laid down by the congressional leadership would have to be met.

The British were the linchpin of allied co-operation, and the British were completely skeptical. They did not believe that an air strike would eliminate the artillery at Dienbienphu unless atomic bombs were used—and atomic bombs would eliminate the defenders as well. The use of air power, the British were convinced, would not settle the matter but only involve American prestige and make the use of ground forces inevitable.

And neither ground forces nor air forces would get at the sources of Viet Minh strength, for the source of Viet Minh strength was popular support for independence and an end to French colonialism. What an American intervention would do, the British felt, was to repeat the whole costly business of the Korean War—including the introduction of Chinese Peoples Army Volunteers—but, unlike Korea, without the support of either the UN or the people of the country.

In Washington, the British argument gained powerful support from General Matthew Ridgway, Chief of Staff of the Army. He had sent a team of engineers, signal and communications specialists, and combat officers to Vietnam to investigate his own position that air power would not be decisive and that American ground forces on a large scale would be required, and their report persuasively marshaled the case—that the United States intervention would not be successful without ground forces fighting a sustained war similar to the fighting in the Pacific theater during World War II. It also contended that at least five divisions would be needed at the outset, rising to ten or more as the fighting progressed. It was Ridgway's contention that the United States not only deeply wished to avoid fighting a large-scale war in Asia, but that the ground forces necessary for such a war simply did not exist, due to the Eisenhower administration's "New Look" policy of replacing ground divisions with air power and substituting the strategy of "massive retaliation" for the strategy of "containment." The "New Look" policy, the Ridgway report pointed out, had reduced the Army until there were only six divisions available for intervening in Indochina, and these were under strength and incompletely equipped. It would take six to eight months to make them combat ready, and this meant they could not be deployed to Indochina until December 1954 or January 1955. There is no doubt, as Ridgway himself said, that the report "played a considerable, perhaps a decisive, part in persuading our Government not to embark on that tragic adventure."[2]

Even so, on April 23, Dulles told Anthony Eden, then British Foreign Secretary, that intelligence estimated that Dienbienphu would fall within seventy-two hours unless there was an American air strike. Dulles said that he was ready, if he had British agreement, "to recommend the President ask for 'war powers.'" But Eden would *not* agree. He later wrote in his memoirs that he "went to bed that night a troubled man," although he had been hardened to crises. "I did not believe that anything less than intervention on a Korean scale, if that, would have any effect in Indochina."

On May 7, 1954, the French forces at Dienbienphu surrendered, and on May 8, the discussions at Geneva turned to the question of Indochina. Viet Minh troops continued to push south, but both Moscow and Peking seemed to be convinced that a further military effort might provoke

American intervention after all. At the same time, they also seemed to feel that the kind of settlement that could be extracted from the Geneva negotiations would give them half of Vietnam for sure and an excellent opportunity to win the other half through political subversion. In consequence, Moscow and Peking put increasing pressure on Ho Chi Minh and the Hanoi regime—who resented the pressure so hotly as to make their resentment obvious even in the West.

In the meantime, the French Government had fallen, and Pierre Mendès-France, trying to form a new one, had asked the National Assembly to give him until July 20 to reach an agreement at Geneva. Under this deadline, the pressure on Ho Chi Minh and the Viet Minh became overwhelming, and they finally acquiesced.

The last holdout was Cambodia. Prince Sihanouk was the Cambodian chief of state and on his courageous instructions, Nong Kimny, the Cambodian representative at Geneva, resisted pressure from all the great powers, eastern and western. Throughout the night of July 20, he stuck to the position that Cambodia alone of the successor states to Indochina had no Communist Party and hence could make no agreement to recognize the Party's existence and provide for its activities. At dawn on July 21, Hanoi was eventually brought to make this final concession, too, and seventy-five days after the conference had begun, the agreements were finally signed.

THE GENEVA AGREEMENTS OF 1954

The Geneva accords consisted, first, of a joint declaration to which all the participating powers were party except South Vietnam and the United States—each of which, however, declared its intention to abide by the accords. In addition, there were a number of separate agreements signed by the various contending parties and various declarations by individual states. What this collection of agreements provided for was an end to hostilities; the independence and neutrality of Laos and Cambodia; and the setting up of international machinery to supervise the implementation of the agreements—an International Control Commission (ICC) of India, Poland, and Canada reporting to the two co-chairmen, Great Britain and the Soviet Union. Vietnam was divided at the seventeenth parallel into two "zones," neither of which should be "utilized for the resumption of hostilities." Provisions were included permitting "everyone in Vietnam to decide freely in which zone he wishes to live," but at the same time the declaration specifically stated that the demarcation line "should not in any way be interpreted as constituting a political or territorial boundary." Also, provision was made for general elections to be held under international supervision two years later, in July of 1956.

Concerning Laos, the agreements provided for the withdrawal of Viet Minh forces and the regrouping of the Communist Pathet Lao forces in the two northeastern provinces of Phong Saly and Sam Neua and their eventual reintegration into the Royal Lao Army. The Lao Government also declared its intention to "integrate all citizens, without discrimination, into the national community" and renounced military alliances and any military aid or foreign military instructors "except for the purpose of its effective territorial defense and to the extent defined by the agreement on the cessation of hostilities." France was permitted to retain two military bases in Laos, with no more than 3500 troops. Responsibility for training the Lao Army was also assigned to France, which was allowed an additional 1500 officers and men as instructors.

The Geneva agreements of 1954 did not affect the earlier agreement made between the United States and Laos as an "Associated State" and so permitted the United States to continue both economic and military aid to the Lao Government. Neither did the Geneva agreements alter the Treaty of Amity and Association, between Laos and France, which made France responsible for defending Laos against foreign aggression. But on balance the loopholes which riddled the Geneva agreements favored the Communists. The lack of rules for the ICC created endless opportunities for the Communist member, Poland, to obstruct and confuse its activities, and the requirement that all ICC decisions had to be unanimous made it possible to paralyze them. There were no provisions for creating the necessary conditions for free and fair elections in Vietnam; no procedures for integrating the dissident Pathet Lao into the Lao "national community"; no way to determine whether or not the Viet Minh forces would continue to respect the Lao national boundaries; and so on and on. A decade after these events a man who had been a member of the British delegation at Geneva remarked in wonder, "Why, you know, there wasn't anyone around that table who would have bet a farthing that any of those countries could have stayed out of the Communist bloc for even three years, much less ten."

NOTES

[1] For a public account of these matters, see Arthur J. Dommen, *Conflict in Laos,* 1964.

[2] Matthew Ridgway, *Soldier,* p. 277.

CHAPTER 10

Laos and the United States

FROM THE TIME of its birth in the Geneva agreements of 1954, Laos presented the United States with a problem of foreign policy out of all proportion to the intrinsic importance of a country so poor, so remote, and so lightly populated. But its geographic location had given Laos strategic significance and the twists and turns of history had given it political significance. The United States had to deal with Laos whether it liked the prospect or not.

THE ALTERNATIVES FOR UNITED STATES POLICY

Broadly speaking, there were three basic policy alternatives for the United States in Laos, each of which came to be associated with the name of a Lao leader. One broad alternative was the policy advocated by Prince Souvanna Phouma—a policy that looked to a genuine reconciliation of all the different factions within Laos and a true neutrality in the relations of Laos with both the Communist and Western worlds. Souvanna Phouma wanted to absorb the Pathet Lao into the Royal Lao Army and bring the Communist leaders into a Government of National Union. Diplomatic relations would be established with all nations, including members of the Communist world, and the role of the United States would be minimal, as would that of the Soviet Union. Foreign aid from both sides would be necessarily small; nation-building and modernization would go on, but slowly.

A second alternative was described as a modified form of neutrality—neutrality with an anti-Communist and pro-Western orientation. This policy came to be associated with Phoui Sananikone, head of a family just as ancient and powerful as that of Souvanna Phouma. It would permit the continued existence of the Communist party, the NLHX, but would severely restrict its activities and exclude its leaders from any participation in the government. The United States presence would be prominent; aid from the United States would continue at a high rate; and the effort to build internal strength and unity and to modernize would proceed at a fast pace.

The third alternative was the policy symbolized by Phoumi Nosavan, a general who, according to common gossip throughout Laos, had risen to power through the support of the American CIA. His was the policy of militant anti-Communism, of making Laos into an American ally in everything but name. The Pathet Lao were to be militarily defeated and the NLHX destroyed. No Communist nations would be permitted diplomatic representation. As the ally of Laos in all but name, the United States would have a large presence, and it would be required to supply substantial military backing as well as economic aid.

From the vantage point of the United States, these were the three alternatives that presented themselves and the Lao leaders that went with them. In fact, however, it was more complicated than this. From the standpoint of Lao politics, the Sananikones were conservative and anti-Communist, and probably more doctrinaire and unbending in their conservatism and anti-Communism than Phoumi ever was. Phoumi, in fact, was probably just a bit more opportunistic. The more significant differences between these two factions were rooted in Lao regionalism—Vientiane versus Savannakhet. But the different groups stepped into different policy stances as a means of attracting American support, and it was in terms of these three alternatives and personalities that the problem posed itself to the United States: Souvanna, neutrality and Communist participation in the government; Phoui, pro-Western neutrality and no participation by the Communists; or Phoumi, alliance with the United States in fact if not by treaty, and the elimination of the Communists entirely.

At one time or another in the years after 1954, the United States followed each of these three policies and on other occasions vigorously opposed each of them. Some Western newsmen confronted with the twists and turns of policy pursued both by the United States and by Laos, the long names so difficult for a Western tongue, the exotic culture, and the complexity of Lao politics termed the whole postwar history of the country a comic opera. But it also had some of the elements of a Greek tragedy, with themes and actors containing within themselves the seeds of mutual destruction.

One theme was weakness, dissension, and irresponsibility among the tiny, interrelated Lao elite.

Another theme was the timidity and helplessness of the International Control Commission (ICC) in the face of Communist intransigence and duplicity, and the failure of the idea that international organization might play a significant role in keeping the peace on the remote front lines of the Cold War.

Still another theme was the disagreement, pettiness, tension, and cross-purposes among the Western allies.

And a final theme, unfortunately, was disagreement and cross-purposes within the United States Government—among the departments and agencies in Washington and among their representatives in the American mission at Vientiane.

And on the other side of this mushy political milieu were the Communists. They, too, occasionally seemed at cross-purposes with each other, and they certainly made errors that were both serious and stupid. But in general they presented a clearer and stronger countertheme. Their forces appeared more tightly disciplined and their propaganda and diplomatic moves more skillful—but here again it was all clearly controlled and orchestrated by the tougher, more determined North Vietnamese.

THE LAO LEADERS

And the personalities were as constant as the themes. Plump, pipe-smoking, a lover of French culture, and a fiend at bridge, Souvanna Phouma was obviously a complex personality. But it seemed to me, when I met him, that here was undoubtedly a great patriot, with a deep understanding of the yearnings of his own people. Souvanna claimed to have wide popular support among his fellow Lao, especially among the peasants, but most American officials doubted his claim. There was, in fact, considerable disagreement among American officials as to just how much popular support Souvanna did actually command. Certainly he had some. No Lao leader commanded very great popular support, and perhaps the best that can be said is that Souvanna probably commanded as much as any. On the other hand, he was decidedly not popular among his fellow members of the elite, but he was respected by them, particularly for his stubborn courage. The differing opinions among the elite about Souvanna the man, in fact, often seemed to be really differing opinions about his policy. What some Lao considered wisdom in sensing the desire for unity among all Lao, including the Communists, others insisted was merely susceptibility to the influence of stronger personalities —his French-Lao wife or his Communist half-brother, Souphanouvong. What some Lao considered openness, generosity, and willingness to accommodate in the interests of national unity others considered irresponsibility if not deviousness. The United States Government, in its strong anti-Communist mood during the Eisenhower administration under Secretary Dulles, frequently thought Souvanna was untrustworthy and his policies self-deluding. Later, however, many in the United States Government came to realize that there was much truth in what Souvanna had to say about Laos and about the desire of the Lao peoples for peace and neutrality.

Souvanna's half-brother, Souphanouvong, the Communist leader, was square, stocky, energetic, and virile in appearance, and he was certainly one of the most able of the Lao leaders. I met him in January 1963, and found him an impressive figure, forceful and forthright at least in conversation. In our conversation, for example, he described in some detail the pioneering work he had done on the so-called Ho Chi Minh trails for the Vietnamese. Souphanouvong's original motives in the political course he had chosen were apparently rooted not so much in ideology as in a peculiarly virulent hatred of the French and their particular brand of colonialism, an inability to get along with the members of his own family, and a vaunting ambition. His increased associations with the Viet Minh had by 1954 probably led him to become a convinced Communist —although he continued to want to be addressed as "Your Highness" in deference to his princely title. But I came away from our meeting wondering how events might have differed if French attitudes had been more flexible in those early years.

By 1960, however, Souphanouvong's position within the Lao Communist Party was already unclear, and power was shared by others less worldly than Souphanouvong if they had not actually taken over completely. In any case, Souphanouvong continued to be important if only as a front man. He enjoyed widespread respect and even affection in the back country, which he knew so well as a result of his work with the Viet Minh and the early struggle in Laos itself, and he was probably the only Lao leader in history who had walked the length and breadth of the land, who knew the back trails and villages, and who had shared with the villagers their life of hardship.

Phoui Sananikone was an intelligent, realistic, and resourceful politician, head of an ancient and powerful family. Although opportunistic when in opposition, he acted responsibly when in power. Consistent with his policy of "pro-Western" neutrality, he adopted strong measures to combat the Communist threat inside Laos and collaborated closely with the West while maintaining at least the letter of neutrality in the Cold War. When in office as Prime Minister, Phoui was not above using his power to favor commercial enterprises in which he had an interest, and he placed representatives of his family in as many army and government positions as possible. He was frequently involved in the intrigues of Lao politics—as for example when he allied himself early in 1956 with pro-Communist factions. At the same time, he vehemently opposed the policies advocated by Souvanna as being too weak. But he was equally vigorous in opposing Phoumi Nosavan's policy of forcefully repressing the Pathet Lao and the NLHX. As head of the Sananikone clan, which was probably the wealthiest and most powerful in Laos, Phoui retained considerable political influence even when he was out of office.

Phoumi Nosavan was the only one of the major leaders of Laos who did not come from one of the old aristocratic families. He had powerful support in the Savannakhet area and he was cousin to Marshal Sarit Thanarat, benevolent dictator of Thailand until his death in 1963. But within Laos Phoumi did not have the prestige of those of princely blood. When I first met him, Phoumi appeared mild-mannered, easygoing, and unpretentious. But he was tough and stubborn in actuality and one of the most able men on the Laos scene. Strongly anti-Communist, Phoumi frequently equated opposition to his personal policies with sympathy toward Communism, and he had a propensity for high-flown, somewhat pretentious schemes. Many Lao and Americans felt he was stubborn and devious, especially in resisting advice. And he had a habit of acting without consulting his allies despite promises to do so, which made him particularly difficult for United States officials to work with. Phoumi tended to run a one-man show, and he was unwilling to delegate authority to subordinates. He was an expert at intrigue and was particularly active in the factionalism that plagued the Lao armed services. Despite reports that he diverted some Lao Government and U.S. aid funds and other charges, most observers agreed that Phoumi was honest by local standards. His basic approach to his country's problems was authoritarian, and he consistently sought to ally Laos with the West. But some Americans became increasingly convinced that he was less interested in defeating Communism than in assuring the victory of his own faction, that he was so unscrupulous and opportunistic that he came to forget the interests of his country in blindly pursuing ends and ambitions that were purely personal.

One more personality must be mentioned—King Savang Vatthana, who ascended the throne on his father's death in 1959. The King lived in the royal capital at Luang Prabang, preoccupied with the elaborate ceremonial responsibilities of a Buddhist monarch, which were relieved only occasionally by those of a constitutional monarch—opening the National Assembly or conducting the investiture of a cabinet minister. The King was often charged with indecision and described as a hand wringer. On more than one occasion, for example, he wept as he talked to visitors, bemoaning what he saw as an inevitable "demise of an ancient kingdom" caught helplessly in the grip of world forces beyond its power to affect. But over time, the King grew in both stature and statesmanship. In general, the King favored Phoumi over the other Lao leaders and Phoumi was loyal in return—despite an occasional outburst when the King's indecisiveness undercut Phoumi himself.

All these different personalities and themes, the physical handicaps, the jumbled terrain, the country's exposed position, the cross-purposes and weakness of the leadership, the inherent instabilities in an emerging nation that was not yet a true nation, the continuing threat and pressure from the Communists within Laos and from North Vietnam and China, the sometimes counterproductive effect of American aid, not to mention its frequently bad management, the pettiness and cross-purposes among the Western allies, and the equally petty cross-purposes and differences within the United States Government in Washington and in the field at critical periods—all have been part of the story of Laos.

SOUVANNA AND THE POLICY OF NEUTRALITY: 1954

The Geneva agreements were signed on July 21, 1954, and Souvanna Phouma, as Prime Minister, flew immediately to the Plain of Jars to re-establish contact with his half-brother, Souphanouvong, in pursuit of his policy of forming a government of national union and neutrality. He was confident that if the Vietnamese Communists were indeed sincere about letting Laos go its own way, then the Lao Communists could be brought back into the "national community" and nationwide elections could be held in 1955 in accordance with the declaration made at Geneva. But he made little headway for the moment. The Vietnamese cadres remained, and the Pathet Lao demanded changes in the electoral laws and other concessions in what appeared to be a search for an excuse to boycott the elections if they really were held.

What the Pathet Lao did pay serious attention to was consolidating their hold on the provinces of Phong Saly and Sam Neua, bordering North Vietnam and China, where the Geneva accords had specified that the Communists were to "regroup." The ICC was subject to Communist obstruction through the Polish member, but even so it confirmed that the Geneva accords recognized the "sovereign right of the Royal Government to establish its administration in the two northern provinces and this right is undisputed." But the Pathet Lao under North Vietnamese prodding were apparently not yet willing to give up the notion of gaining control of Laos through force, and, to maintain this option, they needed a base. They proceeded to consolidate their hold on the two provinces with ruthless dispatch, attacking and capturing two government posts, for example, when negotiations with the government about their status were still going on. Souvanna resigned as Prime Minister, and although his successor attempted to continue his policies there was no progress whatsoever.

But with the Bandung Conference of 1955, the Communist world, and especially the Chinese, began experimenting with a new, more flexible line of policy. In accordance with this new line, the North Vietnamese met separately during the conference with the Lao delegation and signed an agreement with them stating that the terms of a settlement between the Lao Government and the Pathet Lao were a question of "internal order" and that the two governments of Laos and North Vietnam intended to maintain friendly relations in accordance with the *"panch shila,"* the so-called "five principles." In this more favorable atmosphere, Souvanna again became Prime Minister in early 1956 and began again the work of trying to bring the Pathet Lao into the national community and to build a government of national union.

His negotiations with the Pathet Lao began in August of 1956 and continued for over a year. The agreement, signed in November of 1957, brought two of the Communist leaders, Souphanouvong and Phoumi Vongvichit, into the government—the first as Minister of Plans, Reconstruction, and Urbanism, and the second as Minister of Cults. The agreement recognized the NLHX as a legitimate political party, and provided for special elections to be held four months after the agreements were signed. Phong Saly and Sam Neua were turned over to the authority of the King, with elaborate arrangements for sharing provincial posts— such as, for example, providing for a Pathet Lao governor and a Vientiane deputy governor. On the military side, fifteen hundred of the Pathet Lao troops were to be integrated into the Royal Lao Army and the others were to be demobilized.

Souvanna also pursued his policy of neutrality in the larger world. He visited both Peking and Moscow in August of 1956, and won Mao Tsetung's approval of his policy of establishing diplomatic relations with neither Peking nor Taipei. He visited both Hanoi *and* Saigon. And yet he did not hide his fear of the Communist threat to his neutralist policies. "In the political field," he said in a statement in June of 1958, "the new government will strive to consolidate its prestige and maintain the Lao tradition to safeguard freedom and the complete independence of Laos. It will do all it can to check the Communists' sabotaging activities and the spread of Communist thoughts and ideas. Our neutral policy applies only to the military field. Politically speaking, we still adopt a system of constitutional monarchy and practice democracy."

From 1954, the Americans had opposed Souvanna in his attempt to form a government of national union—sometimes vehemently and harshly —and urged him instead to follow the Phoui Sananikone policy of "pro-Western" neutrality. "I struggled," the American Ambassador J. Graham Parsons later testified before a congressional committee, "for sixteen months to prevent a coalition."

THE UNITED STATES AND THE ROYAL LAO ARMY

Quite apart from the relative wisdom of Souvanna's "true" neutrality as opposed to the "pro-Western" or "anti-Communist" neutrality that the United States was urging, the American record in Laos up to that point was not good. Take, for example, the creation of the Royal Lao Army. The pressure to build this force came mainly from the United States, especially the State Department, and the United States offered both to equip the Lao Army and to finance it, paying the salaries of all its officers and men.

Many of the Lao leaders themselves were reluctant—and they might have been even more reluctant if they had fully realized how much power the United States would acquire in internal Lao affairs through financing the army. For by merely withholding the monthly payment to the troops, the United States could create the conditions for toppling any Lao Government whose policies it opposed. As it turned out, in fact, the United States used this weapon twice—to bring down the government of one Lao leader and to break the will of another.

The Pentagon also opposed creating a Lao Army. In the first place, they would not agree to any military aid program that did not provide for American military trainers and advisers as a matter of principle. But the Geneva accords on Laos, unlike those on South Vietnam, gave the French sole responsibility for giving the Lao military training to the exclusion of all other nations. Even though American military aid could legally be sent to Laos, sending American military advisers would be a violation of the Geneva agreements. In the second place, it seemed absurd to think that a tiny force of 25,000 men would have any utility against outside aggression. The only possible aggressors would be either North Vietnam, which had an army of 250,000 to 300,000, or Communist China, which had an army of several million. The Pentagon view was that the Lao should confine themselves to building the forces necessary for internal policing.

But the State Department and Secretary Dulles insisted. They did not, of course, expect the Lao to defeat an attack from either North Vietnam or China. But the Communist Pathet Lao were busy drumming up popular support in the two northern provinces, and there were some fears that they would launch a military offensive—although in retrospect the threat seems more likely to have been an expansion of political control based on winning peasant support in the villages. Then, too, an army could serve as a unifying symbol, a rallying point for patriotism, and an institution around which the forces of nationalism could coalesce. But the most important factor in the State Department's reasoning was probably the Cold War atmosphere of the time and Dulles's policy of creating military alliances around the perimeter of the Communist world. Pro-Western, anti-Communist neutrality might be the most that could be expected from a country like Laos, but it was consistent with Dulles's way of thinking that Laos should also have a military "trip wire" that could offer enough resistance to Communist aggression to dramatize it and permit outside intervention. And for these purposes, a 25,000 man army would be enough.

To accommodate to the Pentagon's insistence on having a Military Assistance Advisory Group (MAAG) in spite of the provisions of the Geneva agreements, the State Department agreed to let one be set up in disguise. The PEO, for Programs Evaluation Office, was set up as part of the economic aid mission, and the military officers wore civilian clothes—to no avail, since the deception eventually became known and hit the newspapers. But although this was politically bad, what was worse was the kind of army that was created. It seems obvious that if a small Lao

Army was to have any real utility it would be against guerrilla warfare rather than against an open, conventional attack by China or North Vietnam. But what the United States trained and equipped in Laos, as in South Vietnam, was not a counterguerrilla force, but a conventional army—twelve regular infantry battalions, twelve volunteer infantry battalions, an artillery battalion, an armored reconnaissance battalion, two parachutist battalions, a Transportation Corps, a Quartermaster Corps, and an Air Force of C-47 transport planes to which AT-6 trainers equipped as fighter-bombers were later added. It was a conventional military force, lighter than the forces typical of the traditional warfare of Western Europe, but very reminiscent of those forces. It was completely equipped with jeeps and trucks, for example, in a country that had few roads, most of which were impassable, even to a jeep, during the six months of the rainy season. It was a road-bound force facing a guerrilla enemy who stayed beyond the roads, in the mountains and jungles, traveling by trails used only by tigers, elephants, opium smugglers, and isolated tribesmen.

Inevitably, such an army became more political than anything else— a focal point for graft, the principal lever for ambitious men plotting coups, and a symbol of governmental repression in those villages to which it did, intermittently, penetrate. And such an army was probably self-defeating in its larger purpose. Giving the Lao a military weapon to meet what was at bottom a political threat probably created an issue of "American imperialism" that made the military threat more tempting.[1]

AMERICAN AID

The problem of financing this army, in a country whose economy was at a subsistence level and whose commerce was largely carried out through barter, also came to dominate the American aid program. Kip, the Lao currency, were needed to pay the soldiers. To prevent this monthly injection of currency from causing a runaway inflation, some way had to be found to bring the amount of currency in circulation into a balanced relationship with the amount of goods and services available. Taxes at the needed rate were too slippery to administer in such an underdeveloped country and would have been cruel in any case. For the effect would have been not only to take 25,000 men out of the work of producing rice and other goods and services and put them into the unproductive task of soldiering but also to make the remaining manpower take up the additional work and pay the 25,000 out of their own extra sweat, if they really could. The solution was for the United States to send commodities—rice, consumers goods, and so on—to Laos as part of the American aid program. The Lao Government would then sell the goods to merchants for kip which could be used to pay the army. The goods made available in this way would match the money supply, and inflation would be avoided. The soldiers, through U.S. financing, in effect earned foreign exchange to pay for imports of goods and food that would sop up the excess currency their own pay generated.

But the notion had other consequences. For years the commodity import program was inadequately supervised and controlled; it provided endless opportunities for graft; and it came to corrupt not only some of the individual Lao and Americans associated with it, but Lao society as a whole. The Chinese merchants were happy to make an additional payment above the price of the goods to a Lao official who would grant them a purchase license, for the difference in price of kip in Laos and in places like Hong Kong and Bangkok meant that the merchant could re-export the goods purchased and sell them abroad at a fantastic profit. In fact, the transactions eventually became so blatant that, rather than shipping the goods to Laos and then reshipping them out again, the merchants merely arranged for a customs official in Laos to issue a receipt for the goods, which really never left Bangkok. Not only did all this lead to cynicism and loss of faith in the government, but since so many of the goods never reached Laos, the program also failed in its purpose of stopping inflation. Rice, for example, doubled in price in the two years from 1955 to 1957.

And the goods that did get to Laos, combined with the graft, huge profits, and inflation had one other bad effect that had not been anticipated—that of making the gap between the towns and the villages even greater than it was before. Thus the army came to be a symbol of repression in the villages, rather than a symbol of protection; and the American aid program, dominated as it was by the need to finance the army, came to make the towns richer and the villages poorer. Yet it was in the villages that the real battle was taking place, the political battle for the allegiance of the people.

THE CIA

One other set of American activities must also be mentioned—those of the CIA, which have long since become the subject of public discussion in the Lao and American press. CIA officials were appalled by the apathy, dissension, and lack of organization among the non-Communist Lao, especially as contrasted with the tight discipline and purpose imposed on the Pathet Lao by the Vietnamese Communist cadres. To meet this threat, the CIA apparently proposed helping the Lao organize not so much a political party as a patriotic organization that would work to give Lao national unity and direction. The result was the "Committee for the Defense of the National Interests"—the CDNI. The CDNI described itself as a mass patriotic group rather than a political party; it favored various reforms, and in particular it advocated stern measures in dealing with the Communists. It was especially favored by army leaders, and it served as a ladder for the extraordinarily rapid rise of Phoumi Nosavan, the protégé of both the CIA and the Pentagon.

The most persuasive argument for helping the anti-Communist Lao create an organization like the CDNI was that North Vietnam, China, and the Soviet Union were helping the Pathet Lao in their effort to organize the countryside, and it seemed only prudent to help the anti-Communists in a countereffort. The other side of the argument was that such a policy gave up America's natural strengths in this kind of situation for the seemingly slicker techniques of the Communists. It was a policy, in a word, that had the weaknesses as well as the strengths of Allen Dulles' notion of fighting Communist fire with fire. In the first place, any organization with the professed aims of the CDNI would be a natural magnet for political opportunists in any country, for men whose only principle would be their own driving ambitions. In the second place, there is a profound difference between an organization espousing the goals of patriotism that is spontaneous and totally native and an organization which, while espousing such goals, still derives its impetus and its subsistence from interests that are, inescapably, foreign. In the end the American attempt to "play God" in Lao political life was hoist by its own petard.

The CIA's basic assumption seemed to be that Laos was sooner or later to become a major battleground in a military sense between the East and the West, and the programs they conceived and pushed through in Washington were based on this assumption. But it is one thing, for example, to train, arm, and direct the fighting of Kachin tribesmen in Burma, as the American OSS did in 1942–44, and quite another to arm and fight Meo tribesmen in Laos in 1960. The Kachins were armed in the midst of a world war in which American troops were fighting on a dozen fronts. In Laos, the United States was not directly engaged in fighting and might never be. The job of arming and training the Meo was well and efficiently done. The Meo were undoubtedly troublesome to the Communist Pathet Lao and their North Vietnamese cadre. And it should also be said that there were occasions of tension in 1962 and 1963 when it was useful to have the Meo blow up a bridge or occupy a mountaintop as a move in the deadly game of "signaling" that the United States had to play to deter the Communists from adventuring with the Geneva accords. But arming the tribesmen engendered an obligation not only to feed them when they were driven from their traditional homelands but also to protect them from vengeance. This was an obligation that in some circumstances could never really be discharged, and an obligation that might come to be a hindrance to implementing the Geneva accords and achieving a truly neutral Laos, which was in the longer-range interests of everyone concerned. Arming tribesmen sounds like a tough and realistic policy, even a generous one of helping brave fighters defend themselves. But it might in fact be not only unwise but unfair to the tribesmen themselves, those to whom it was seemingly designed to help.

INTERAGENCY RIVALRY

Each of the American agencies concerned with Laos—the State Department, the Pentagon, the Agency for International Development, (AID), and the CIA—sent people there to carry out their agency's programs, people with money to spend and influence and leverage to exert. Each had different interests and views on how to handle Laos as a foreign policy problem for the United States and each had its own private channels of communication to Washington, where the battles were carried on just as vigorously in the larger arena. In time, the differences between the agencies and departments became more marked and the exchanges sharper, with the CIA and the Pentagon generally on one side and the State Department and AID on the other. Each agency came to pursue its own programs and policies with less and less regard for the others, and with little relationship to an over-all American policy. The Ambassador, certainly, was not always right. One ambassador, a man who sided more often with the Pentagon, for example, became so blindly wedded to the policy of rigid anti-Communism that in congressional hearings much later he was still ascribing the rampant inflation of the time so obviously caused by the mismanagement of the United States aid program to Souvanna's negotiations with the Pathet Lao about a government of national union! Another ambassador became so thoroughly anti-CIA that he repeatedly informed the press not only of their actual gaffes but of his wildest suspicions. But the tragedy was that neither the Lao nor our allies could tell who really spoke for the United States—whether it was the CIA, the military, the AID officials, or the Ambassador. In the end there was open quarreling among the representatives of the different American agencies, and, to the shame of all Americans, the United States became the butt of jokes among both friend and foe.

THE ELECTIONS OF 1958

The elections called for in the November 1957 agreement between Souvanna and Souphanouvong were scheduled for May 4, 1958, and as the time neared, it became increasingly clear that the Communist NLHX would do well. Partly, this was because of the long list of negative factors described above—the repressive activities of the Royal Lao Army, the inflation and corruption caused by the mismanagement of the American aid program, the increasing gap between town and countryside, and so on. But there were also positive reasons that the Communists would do well—their excellent organization in the countryside and their efforts at the village level. Alarmed at all this, the American mission under the sponsorship of a new American ambassador, launched a crash program aimed at the villages, consisting of "more than 90 work projects," in the words of a congressional committee report, "including well digging, erection of small irrigation and flood control dams, repair of schools and temples, repair of roads and airfields, and construction of hospitals; and the dropping of some 1,300 tons of food, medical and construction supplies and other useful commodities."

But it was all too little and much, much too late. Nine NLHX candidates won out of thirteen running, and the leftist "Peace Party" led by Quinim Pholsena, who was at best a pro-Communist neutralist, won four seats. Souphanouvong himself won his seat by a larger majority than any other candidate in the whole country. There was much ineptness on the government side—they had run eighty-five candidates for the twenty-one seats at stake—but the significance of the election was clear.

Although not happy with the results of the elections, Souvanna apparently did not regard them as anything more than the beginning of the struggle he had always foreseen would follow the establishment of a government of national union. But that had been what he had always said was his purpose, to transform the struggle in Laos from the military to the political arenas. He announced that Laos had now "fully accomplished" the pledges made at Geneva to bring all elements into the national community and to hold elections, and he also renewed the declarations renouncing military alliances and military aid "except for the purpose of its effective territorial defense." On July 20, 1958, the International Control Commission adjourned *sine die,* in spite of the objections of the Polish representative and the loud protests from Hanoi and Peking.

EXIT SOUVANNA AND "TRUE" NEUTRALITY

But some factions in Laos were not prepared to accept either the election results or the circumscribed arena that Souvanna had in mind. Phoui Sananikone, although he occupied the post of Foreign Minister in Souvanna's government, was one who began to speak uneasily about Souvanna's form of neutrality, saying that "to be neutral means not to take part in any military alliance" and implying that neutrality therefore did not require a government of national union or preclude internal measures against the Communists.[2] Members of the CDNI, the "Committee for the Defense of the National Interests," which everyone knew that CIA had sponsored, were particularly active.

The United States Government was also concerned. J. Graham Parsons, the ambassador who had fought for "sixteen months to prevent a coalition," was now in Washington as Deputy Assistant Secretary of State for Far Eastern Affairs, and there were apparently many there who agreed with him. In any event, the United States Government reached a decision to hold up its monthly payment to the Lao Government—on the pretext that there was corruption in the commodity import program and a need for monetary reform. The CDNI and others made the most of the opportunity: a parliamentary crisis quickly flared up and on July 23, they succeeded in swinging enough votes to cause Souvanna to lose a vote of confidence in the National Assembly and resign.

ENTER PHOUI AND "PRO-WESTERN" NEUTRALITY

Souvanna was sent off to be ambassador to Paris, and Phoui Sanani-kone formed a government that excluded the two Communist ministers but did include four members of the CDNI who were not members of the National Assembly. He then embarked on the policy of "pro-Western" neutrality advocated by the United States Government and backed it up by putting an end to most of the abuses in the commodity import program, abolishing the license system, providing for American customs inspectors, and instituting an effective monetary reform.

The next seventeen months was the high water period of the policy of "pro-Western" neutrality. To most American government officials who had to deal with Laos, it seemed a sensible middle course. If Laos had been less remote or if its indigenous resources had not been so miserably inadequate, it might have made some sense to officials dealing with the problem to attempt to make an ally of Laos. If it had less strategic importance than it did, they would probably have been cheerfully willing to abandon it. Souvanna maintained that his policy of "true" neutrality was based on his knowledge of the Lao people and what they wanted, including the Pathet Lao. But the Communist record throughout the world had not been one to support the notion that they could be trusted to play by the rules in a coalition government, and to American officials familiar with that record Souvanna's policy seemed to be based on wishful thinking. In the circumstances, most of those who dealt with the problem therefore came to believe that the policy of pro-Western neutrality was the only chance for a solution that would keep Laos from becoming wholly Communist, yet not attempt the unattainable goal of making it an ally and a bastion.

But in retrospect, the Phoui policy itself seems to have been based partly on wishful thinking. One wonders whether the resources of Laos and its leaders were up to the precision, the steadiness of nerve, and the self-discipline demanded by a policy of pro-Western neutrality. Laos was situated on the front line of the Cold War and its territory was extraordinarily difficult to police, yet this policy required it to follow strict international neutrality with no implication of being used to threaten others and at the same time to maintain close ties with the West and the United States. It was a policy that would permit the Communists legitimate political activity yet keep them out of both the government and the army, with all the difficulty that implies.

Phoui and his policy also had the misfortune to come to the test just when Communist policy was changing away from the "peaceful coexistence" of the Bandung spirit to the hard line enunciated by Mao Tse-tung in his "East Wind Over West Wind" speech in Moscow in November 1957. It was during the next year that Hanoi, following this new hard line, reached the decision to begin the guerrilla war against the South. Preparations had been laid for this guerrilla warfare in the form of arms caches and trained cadres left behind after the cessation of hostilities in 1954 and by training additional cadres of southerners in the north for the day when they could be infiltrated back to their home territory. But the old Ho Chi Minh network of trails was essential to their plans for guerrilla warfare in the south, and the North Vietnamese in the mood then prevailing in the Communist world would not have let the legalities of the 1954 Geneva accords stand in their way, especially as those legalities applied to Laos. And they could in any event rationalize their action on the grounds that the 1954 Geneva accords were being frustrated by the failure to hold elections and proceed with reunification. The North Vietnamese might have been willing to go along with a form of neutrality for Laos that would have blinked at their use of the trails at levels slightly less than completely blatant. In retrospect, in fact, this capacity to blink at anything less than completely blatant use of the trails seems to have been the great strength of the Souvanna form of neutrality. But the Communist North Vietnamese could never have accommodated themselves to a form of neutrality, such as Phoui's, that would attempt to prevent them from using the trails. And this was underlined by their interpretation of the adjournment of the ICC. They saw its adjournment first and foremost as an undesirable precedent. "Peace in Indochina is indivisible . . ." their official protest said. "It is clear that the three international commissions should continue their activities as long as the political problems are not completely solved in the three countries [that is, until Vietnam is reunified]. In the present situation in Indochina, the winding up of the activities of the ICC in one country, Laos, for instance, without taking into account the settlement of the political problems in the other two countries, would have dangerous repercussions on the effective implementation of the Geneva agreements and on the activities of the ICC as a whole." But, second and just as important to the North Vietnamese, the adjournment of the ICC took away one of their principal means for limiting international inspection and other "interference" in Laos and hence one of the principal means the North Vietnamese had for obstructing attempts to prevent them from using the Ho Chi Minh trails. To North Vietnam, in fact, the course of events probably seemed still more ominous because Phoui, in accordance with his policy, had also established relations with the Nationalist Chinese Government on Taiwan and with South Vietnam—and permitted them both to have consulates in Vientiane.

Phoui had also made it clear that he regarded the Pathet Lao as agents of North Vietnam and implied that he would use the Royal Lao Army to reassert the government's control in Phong Saly and Sam Neua. North Vietnam responded by accusing Laos of violating their common border and by dispatching two companies of North Vietnamese regular troops to occupy the little town of Tchepone in Laos, just opposite the seventeenth parallel, which divided North and South Vietnam and was a junction of the Ho Chi Minh trails.

On January 15, 1959, the Lao National Assembly gave Phoui extraordinary powers for a year, and he embarked on a still harder policy line. He declared that he was exploring means of dismembering the NLHX on the grounds that it was a subversive organization (several NLHX deputies promptly left town), and on February 11, he accused North Vietnam of waging a campaign against Laos "by acts of intimidation of all sorts, including the violation and occupation of its territory."

In May, Phoui presented an ultimatum to the two Pathet Lao battalions, which had been stalling about being integrated into the Royal Lao Army, ordering them to integrate immediately or be forcibly disbanded. One battalion, stationed near Luang Prabang deep in government territory, agreed. But the other—taking the government forces completely by surprise—decamped to North Vietnam with all its equipment and dependents in a forced march from where it had been stationed on the Plain of Jars. In retaliation, Phoui arrested Souphanouvong and put him in jail in Vientiane.

The Pathet Lao, with Vietnamese help, then set about to drive out government forces and officials from the two provinces of Phong Saly and Sam Neua and to consolidate their control.

Phoui, in turn, asked for more American military aid and more American military technicians and advisers, and the United States agreed, announcing that it would send military technicians, who would wear civilian clothes in token deference to the Geneva accords, to help in expanding the Royal Lao Army from 25,000 to 29,000 men. And Phoui also appealed to the United Nations, charging on September 4, 1959, that North Vietnamese soldiers were fighting on Lao soil.

In response, the United Nations sent an investigatory subcommittee whose report stated that, according to practically all of the witnesses interviewed, "the hostile elements received support from the territory of the DRV [Democratic Republic of Vietnam] consisting mainly of equipment, arms, ammunition, supplies, and the help of political cadres."

Gradually the crisis subsided. One reason was apparently that the North Vietnamese were alarmed by all the publicity—the world's headlines had screamed crisis when Phoui appealed to the UN and fifty additional newsmen had arrived in Laos to report on the new "war." But in 1959 the North Vietnamese had just decided on launching the guerrilla warfare in the south and undue attention to Laos might well inhibit their use of the infiltration trails. But even more important, in all probability, was the fact that the Communists had what they needed and wanted for the immediate future. In many ways, in fact, the situation in Laos was better for them under Phoui than it would have been under a coalition government. For under Souvanna, the Communists would have had to permit the Vientiane government at least token representation in the provinces through which the trails passed and some political embarrassment would have been difficult to avoid, even though the Lao Government would try hard to look the other way. But in the new circumstances, the Communists could claim with considerable logic that the *de facto* partition of Laos had come about because of Phoui's pro-American policy and because of the United States "imperialist" policy of encouraging him in an anti-Communist posture. It was the Vientiane government that had brought about partition, the Communists could say, and what they, the Communists, did in their half of the country was their own business.

Still another aspect of the Phoui policy of "pro-Western" neutrality that seems to have been based on wishful thinking was internal. Phoui's policy depended on making use of a strong right wing in Lao politics and even of strengthening the right to do so. But at the same time the highly conservative Phoui could not command a center that would limit the growth of the right. And in the end it was this—the growth of the rightist CDNI and the rise of its leader, General Phoumi Nosavan—that brought about the downfall both of Phoui and his policy.

EXIT PHOUI

At the end of 1959, Phoui decided to reorganize his government and in the process to remove the CDNI ministers, including Phoumi Nosavan. Phoumi and the other generals moved against him in a bloodless coup within twenty-four hours, on December 31, 1959.

The British, French, and others feared that the establishment of a military dictatorship in Laos would mean the end of the Geneva ceasefire, and they were joined by the United States in exerting pressure on not only the generals but on the King as well. A compromise was finally reached in which a Lao elder statesman, Kou Abhay, from the south and thus apart from the Savannakhet-Vientiane regional factionalism, was chosen as an interim prime minister and new elections were set for April 1960.

ELECTIONS OF 1960

For the next three months Laos resembled nothing more than a Grade B spy-thriller movie, with the scurrying machinations of Chinese and Vietnamese agents rivaled only by those of the CIA. It was flatly alleged by Western newsmen that CIA agents were seen distributing money in an attempt to buy votes.[3] The Communist agents also distributed money, but they added terrorism, too, including assassination.

The government, however, controlled the tabulations and according to the final totals the Pathet Lao candidates were defeated by a landslide. In Sam Neua Province, for example, which was the home ground of the Pathet Lao and virtually inaccessible to the Lao Government, the Pathet Lao candidate was supposed to have received only thirteen votes out of over six thousand cast.

ENTER PHOUMI

With great satisfaction, General Phoumi and the other members of the CDNI proceeded to form a government that would be pledged to a strong anti-Communist, pro-Western position instead of one or another form of neutralism. Seeing the handwriting on the wall, Souphanouvong and the remaining Pathet Lao deputies being held under guard outside Vientiane escaped one night in the midst of a driving tropical storm. Or, perhaps in true Lao tradition, they were permitted to escape—for their guards went with them.

EXIT PHOUMI

But if Phoumi and the other "political" generals were bent on a hard policy of aligning themselves against the Communists in the Cold War, other members of the army were not. On August 9, 1960, Phoumi and the entire cabinet went to Luang Prabang for discussions with the King. Early the next morning troops of the Second Paratroop Battalion, by far the best and most combat-hardened in the Royal Lao Army, moved out from their temporary camp near Vientiane and occupied all the city's key points and government office buildings in a well-planned and fault-lessly executed *coup d'état*.

KONG LE

The commander of the Second Paratroop Battalion was a slightly built young captain, just over five feet tall, named Kong Le. I first met him some years later, at his command post in Khang Khay on the Plain of Jars and found him a dedicated nationalist whose most obvious trait was modesty, in spite of the fact that he had a flair for political leadership. An idealist, Kong Le had become more and more disturbed at the corruption in the army and Lao nation resulting from the mismanaged American aid program. He was also troubled by the turn away from Souvanna Phouma and his policy of neutralism, which Kong Le felt was the true desire of the Lao people. And he resented the increasing domination of Laos by foreigners, of which the most prominent were American. After Souvanna's ouster in 1958, the year when the Second Paratroop Battalion was formed, Kong Le began to recruit like-minded officers and men and to ready himself and the battalion for just such an opportunity as he had now seized.

Two days after the coup, at a public rally, Kong Le called for an end to the war of Lao against Lao; an end to corruption; and an end to foreign domination. "In my experience," he said, "many past Lao governments have told us they wished to follow a neutral course, but they never did so. My group and I decided to sacrifice everything, even our lives, in order to bring neutrality and peace to our nation." And he called on the King to appoint Souvanna Phouma as Prime Minister.

Souvanna was in Laos, on a visit from his post as ambassador to Paris, and consistent with his old policy of attempting to reunite all factions in Laos, immediately met with Phoumi and the King in an attempt to work out a compromise. As a result, the new situation was legalized: the former government resigned, and the King named Souvanna to form a new government with Phoumi as Deputy Prime Minister and Minister of Interior.

But Phoumi did not really intend to live up to the agreement, apparently having made it only to gain time. He went almost immediately to Savannakhet, his old home base, and began to seek support for a countercoup from his relative, Marshal Sarit of Thailand, and from among Americans who represented agencies likely to be sympathetic.

The normal passage of time had brought another change in American ambassadors, and just one week before the coup, the new Ambassador, Winthrop G. Brown, had arrived in Vientiane. After meeting and talking to Souvanna, Brown strongly recommended that the United States should back him and his policies. Washington, however, was locked in disagreement. The Assistant Secretary of State for Far Eastern Affairs was now the former Ambassador to Laos whom many Lao blamed for bringing down

Souvanna's government in 1958 by cutting off American financial support —J. Graham Parsons. And Parsons, certainly, was mistrustful of Souvanna, whom he thought of as naïve and even gullible. The CIA and the Pentagon were even stronger in their views. They were convinced that Souvanna's policy of attempting to bring about a government of national union would merely open the door to a Communist takeover.

But the decision was a compromise between the Ambassador's view and the Assistant Secretary's. Although there was some question as to how vigorously the representatives of the different agencies in the field would implement it and how much encouragement Phoumi might get in his intransigence unofficially and privately from the rival agencies, the policy decision was to urge Phoumi to return to Vientiane and take up his duties as Deputy Prime Minister in the new government. Souvanna would be supported, as head of the legally constituted government of Laos, but at the same time it would be United States policy to attempt to persuade him to abandon his policy of "true" neutralism and the effort to form a government of national union and to adopt instead the pro-Western neutralism so long advocated by Phoui Sananikone and the United States.

But Phoumi by now had had experience, not only in playing off one United States agency against another, but in playing the small power "puppet" game of manipulating the great power "puppeteer." On September 10, 1960, Phoumi formed a "Revolutionary Committee" chaired by Prince Boun Oum, head of an ancient family from Champassak in the south. Shortly thereafter, Thailand—through which supplies to Laos came —imposed an unofficial blockade on goods going to Vientiane. At the same time, air transports of a civilian American airline began a steady shuttle to Phoumi's base in Savannakhet.

Souvanna, on the other hand, opened negotiations with the Pathet Lao, looking toward the formation of a government of national union. He also permitted the Soviet Union to establish an embassy in Laos.

THE STRUGGLE IN WASHINGTON

In Washington, the fact that Souvanna was determined to pursue his attempt to form a coalition government brought a new crisis of decision. On October 7, it was announced that the United States had once again suspended its monthly payment to the Lao Government and Assistant Secretary Parsons was sent to Laos to confer with Souvanna.

Parsons came with three demands: (1) that Souvanna break off his negotiations with the Pathet Lao; (2) that he reopen negotiations with Phoumi; and (3) that the capital be moved to Luang Prabang, where the more conservative influence of the King would be felt. But Souvanna was determined and refused.

When Parsons went on to Bangkok, Ambassador Brown, who was still sympathetic to Souvanna, accompanied him and finally succeeded in persuading both Parsons and Washington to offer Souvanna a compromise. When he returned to Vientiane, Brown pointed out to Souvanna that while the non-Communist forces quarreled among themselves, Laos might well be lost to the Pathet Lao, who had followed their usual course of guerrilla nibbling while the negotiations were going on. The United States, Brown went on, would be willing to resume its financial payments to Souvanna if he in turn would not object to a resumption of U.S. deliveries of military equipment to Phoumi. The United States, Brown was able to say, had Phoumi's promise not to use the aid against Kong Le and the neutralist forces in an attempt to bring down Souvanna's government, but only against the Pathet Lao. Souvanna quickly agreed— hoping, for one thing, finally to convince the United States Government that he was not so naïve about the Communists as they believed.

But Phoumi violated the agreement. Over the next few weeks, as his military strength built up, it became increasingly clear that Phoumi was moving his forces into position for an attack on Vientiane. Ambassador Brown in late November was able to get a decision from Washington to stop military aid to Phoumi. But it was too late. His forces started north toward the capital. In desperation, Souvanna accepted an offer from the Soviet Ambassador to establish a Soviet-manned airlift of military equipment from Hanoi. But this also was too late. In early December 1960, Phoumi's forces reached the outskirts of Vientiane.

Souvanna made one last effort at negotiations, and then exiled himself to Phnom Penh in Cambodia. On December 13 the battle began. And on December 16, Kong Le's forces withdrew to the north, to fight beside the Communist Pathet Lao.

Souvanna did not resign, but the Lao National Assembly nevertheless endorsed the government Phoumi proposed, a government with Prince Boun Oum as Prime Minister and Phoumi himself as Deputy Prime Minister and Minister of Defense. In spite of the dubious legality of the new government, the United States and the Western powers duly recognized it. The Soviet Union and the Communist powers, on the other hand, continued to recognize Souvanna's government and increased their airlift of military supplies and equipment to both Kong Le's neutralist troops and to the Communist Pathet Lao.

A month later, on January 19, 1961, in Cambodia, Souvanna voiced his feelings to the press about both the United States and Assistant Secretary Parsons. Secretary Parsons, Souvanna went on to say, "understood nothing about Asia and nothing about Laos. The Assistant Secretary of State is the most nefarious and reprehensible of men. He is the ignominious architect of disastrous American policy toward Laos." Souvanna denied that he was anti-American, and said that he was only against the American policies of the moment. "What I shall never forgive the United States for, however," he said, "is the fact that it betrayed me, that it double-crossed me and my government."

And in Washington, final preparations were made for the inauguration of the Kennedy administration, which was to take place the very next day.

NOTES

[1] On this point see Arthur J. Dommen, *op. cit.*, p. 99.
[2] Dommen, *op. cit.*, p. 110.
[3] See Dommen, *op. cit.*, p. 133.

CHAPTER 11

The Crisis of 1961

KONG LE retreated rapidly from Vientiane and joined forces with the Pathet Lao in the mountains. Then, in a brilliant maneuver, their combined forces seized the strategic Plain of Jars, in the center of Laos. Phoumi's forces in the meantime, advanced with elaborate caution up Route 13 toward the junction where 13, heading north toward Luang Prabang, is joined by Route 7 coming west from Vietnam through the Plain of Jars. In early January 1961, the Eisenhower administration had attempted to bolster Phoumi's morale by giving him six AT-6 aircraft—fighter-bombers armed with rockets and bombs as machine guns—and they had also sent to Laos the so-called "White Star" teams of American military advisers, one team to each of Phoumi's battalions. But in spite of this "escalation," which although small still violated the Geneva agreements of 1954, Phoumi's forces proceeded with neither speed nor enthusiasm. It was not until late in February that they reached the junction, three-fourths of the way to Luang Prabang, where the Plain of Jars road joined 13. And they had reason to be cautious, for the Pathet Lao troops were built around cadres of North Vietnamese regulars, the highly motivated veterans of years of combat.

By the end of February 1961 the Pathet Lao and Kong Le forces had consolidated their hold on the Plain of Jars and on March 9 they struck at the key road junction with savage force. Phoumi's troops broke and ran, and within days the Communist and neutralist forces were threatening both Vientiane and Luang Prabang.

TO INTERVENE—OR NOT TO INTERVENE

There were long and agonizing meetings in the Secretary of State's office and conference room—with Rusk; McNamara; General Lyman Lemnitzer, then Chairman of the Joint Chiefs of Staff; Paul Nitze, Assistant Secretary of Defense for International Security Affairs; McGeorge Bundy from the White House; a representative of the CIA; J. Graham Parsons, still holding the position of Assistant Secretary for Far Eastern Affairs until a replacement could be found; and two or three of us representing other bureaus of the State Department. With the exception of Lemnitzer, Parsons, and the CIA representative, many of us were new not only to the convoluted problem of Laos but to any kind of politico-strategic problem. At the very first meeting, for example, McNamara seized on the idea of arming the Lao AT-6s with hundred-pound bombs. He was vigorous in his advocacy—which was followed by a somewhat embarrassed silence. Gently, the Secretary of State, addressing the room in general, recalled his own service in the China-Burma-India theater in the war and the experience with air power in that similar terrain of mountain and jungle. Air power had proved to be marvelously effective in supporting men on the ground but indecisive when used alone. Also, when one considered the size of Laos, or even of the Plain of Jars, and the number of Pathet Lao troops, it did not seem likely that six airplanes carrying two hundred-pound bombs apiece would be likely to do significant damage.

Another proposal was for a *coup de main* to seize the Plain of Jars itself—parachuting and airlifting up to a division of American Marines straight into the plain and holding it while Phoumi made his way across the mountains. "Can we get those troops into the plain all right?" General Lemnitzer was asked. "We can get them in all right," he said. "It's getting them out again that worries me." And when the idea was discussed with the President, he killed it completely by asking what would happen if the enemy attacked in the middle of the operation, before enough men had been put on the plain to defend the airfield.

Still another proposal was a plan that had long been on the books for an allied occupation of the southern panhandle of Laos and the Vientiane terrain compartment between the two great bends of the Mekong. The plan called for sixty thousand men and would require more American ground forces than were available. The Eisenhower "New Look" had reduced the ground forces in favor of air power, and it would have been impossible to put that many men into Laos without taking troops from the defense of Europe—right at a time when the Berlin crisis was daily becoming more acute. And the Joint Chiefs of Staff (JCS) had always been reluctant, not only about the plan itself, but also about the idea of any kind of limited intervention.

Most students of international politics think of the Korean War as a success—an overt aggression was stopped and the Communists brought to discipline their ambitions by a limited use of force which confined the war and prevented its spiraling to engulf the whole world. But to many of the higher-ranking American military, the Korean War was a frustrating humiliation. The American Army had been fought to a standstill by Asians, and by Asians whose arms and equipment were somewhat primitive by American standards. Air power, though freely used on the supply lines between the Yalu and the thirty-eighth parallel, had not succeeded in stopping the flow of men and equipment. The significance to the military of the limitations and restrictions put on a wider use of force—principally, bombing China north of the Yalu—was probably as much a rationalization as a frustration. But attitudes formed and hardened, and by 1961 it was a shibboleth among the Joint Chiefs of Staff that the United States ought never again to fight a limited war on the ground in Asia or perhaps never again to fight any kind of war on the ground in Asia. So often was the view expressed, in fact, that people in Washington began to speak of the "Never Again" Club. Some who held this view—among the staff of the JCS and even among the JCS themselves—seemed suspicious that even a show of force in Asia might be a White House or State Department plot to trap them into a situation where a limited war could not be avoided. And they did have reason for their fears. For even though there was no plot, neither the White House nor the State Department could guarantee that a frustrating, limited war could in the end be avoided. Everyone in Washington—civilian and military—dreaded the thought of getting bogged down in a niggling, harassing quagmire of a war in the jungles. But many among both civilians and the military were also convinced that the alternatives—either a very big war or the abandonment of Asia—would be worse. They were convinced that the Communists would probe our strength and determination with limited thrusts here and there. And they were also convinced that we would find it more difficult to avoid the black-and-white choice of war or withdrawal if we failed to meet these thrusts resolutely and with appropriately tailored responses—with just enough force to deter aggression but not so much as to cause the Communists to believe that we had ulterior designs of our own. But the "Never Again" view seemed to be that if force were to be used at all it should be used all-out—striking at the sources of enemy power. Not all of the Joint Chiefs fully subscribed to the "Never Again" view, but it seemed to the White House that they were at least determined to build a record that would protect their position and put the blame entirely on the President no matter what happened. The general thrust of their memoranda seemed to imply that they were demanding an advance commitment from the President that, if they agreed to the use of American force and there were any fighting at all, then there would be no holds barred whatsoever—including the use of nuclear weapons.

Over and over again the discussion each time came to the same dead ends. If Laos were abandoned, the Communists would hold the north-south road along the Mekong lowlands from which their pressure on South Vietnam, Cambodia, and Thailand would be mounted anew with even greater strength. An attempt to force the Communists to pull back—or even to deter them from further advances—by a less than all-out commitment of United States armed forces ran the risk of another Korean War, of a long, drawn-out, indecisive bloodletting. And a large-scale use of force, including, if necessary, atomic bombs as the "Never

Again" advocates seemed to desire, ran incalculable risks of spiraling into World War III.

In a corner of the office of the Secretary of State stood an old grandfather clock, one of a number of pieces of early American furniture that had been donated to the Department of State. To me, at least, the ticking of this old clock, which seemed slower and more deliberate than any I had ever heard, fixed the Laos crisis of 1961 in my memory. For each time the discussion again reached its dead end of hideous war or ignominious and far-reaching defeat, the silence was filled with that slow deliberate tick . . . tock . . . tick . . . tock . . . and with each silence the ticking seemed to me to be louder, slower, and even more deliberate.

A "POLITICAL" SOLUTION

What the President wished to explore was the possibility of a "political" solution. In his first press conference he had made it clear that in his mind United States goals in Laos were limited—that the United States wanted to see Laos as "a peaceful country—an independent country not dominated by either side." Abandoning Laos to the Communists would be dangerous. But at the same time the President found it difficult to see, as he wrestled with the problem of Castro and the upcoming Bay of Pigs, why the American people should be asked to fight in Laos, some five thousand miles away, and not in Cuba, only ninety miles away. A "political" solution offered a possible way around this black-and-white choice with the additional advantage that it did not close out the other alternatives. If the efforts to achieve a political solution failed, the options of giving up Laos or intervening still remained.

And at least some of the elements for a political solution seemed to be present. There was first of all a well-known political leader on whom a political solution could be based. Souvanna Phouma had embarked on a world tour to enlist support for an international conference to establish a neutralized Laos in which all factions had a voice in the government. Also, he commanded a measure of popular support as well as the support of Kong Le and his neutralist troops. The general neutralist attitude of the middle group of the Lao people, furthermore, was reinforced by the reluctance of Phoumi's forces to do much fighting, and there was evidence suggesting the Communist Pathet Lao would be almost as reluctant once the cadres of North Vietnamese were removed. The Soviet attitude was also a factor. Averell Harriman, reporting by cable from his first trip as roving ambassador, said that Khrushchev had made it plain that he did not want a war over Laos. Partly this was because he thought the Communists would get it anyway—"Why take risks over Laos?" he said to the then American Ambassador, Llewellyn E. Thompson. "It will fall into our laps like a ripe apple." And partly it was because the

Soviets felt there were so many more important matters on their agenda, such as Berlin.

The problem would be the Communist Chinese and North Vietnamese. Phoumi's forces could not stand up to the Pathet Lao and their Vietnamese cadres, and if the fighting continued, Laos would soon be theirs with no international strings attached to it at all. The only possible incentive for the Communists to go to the negotiating table was fear of an American intervention. And on this there could be no bluff. The United States had to be fully determined to intervene if it became necessary. This in turn meant that public statements and private communications about our determination had to be backed with concrete movements of American troops. At the same time, the nature of the troop movements had to be so limited that our willingness to settle for a truly neutral Laos would not be doubted and the military movements wrongly interpreted as a trick designed to retake Laos and expel the Communist forces entirely.

The Pentagon's objections—and the record of memoranda they were building—remained. But after National Security Council meetings on March 20 and 21, the President ordered *not* the movement of troops— not just yet—but the necessary steps preliminary to the movement of troops. A task force on Okinawa that had been especially formed and trained for fighting in Southeast Asia was put on alert. A Marine force in Japan was readied. The Seventh Fleet steamed at forced draft to the Gulf of Siam. A five-hundred man unit was dispatched to set up a helicopter repair base at Udorn, the airfield in Thailand nearest Laos, and an advance flight of helicopters arrived shortly thereafter. Stockpiles of supplies and equipment were sent to bases near the Laos border.

Then came the public announcement, described above, with the President appearing on nationwide television, the three maps of Laos behind him, and his warning that if the goal of a "truly neutral Laos" were frustrated by continued Communist attacks, the United States and its allies would have to "consider their response."

At the same time, the President voiced approval of a British proposal, put forward in their capacity as one of the co-chairmen of the 1954 Geneva agreements, to reintroduce the ICC into Laos and to convene a new conference in Geneva following the verification of a cease-fire.

The President flew to Florida on March 26 to meet with Prime Minister Macmillan. Reluctantly, Macmillan gave his support for a limited intervention in Laos if it became necessary, and they then jointly repeated the call for a cease-fire and a new Geneva conference. Rusk, in the meantime, attempted to enlist further support at the annual meeting of the SEATO Foreign Ministers in Bangkok—although with only limited success.

Publicly, the President asked Nehru to support a cease-fire and to exercise whatever influence he could on Moscow. Privately, he talked to the Soviets himself. While Gromyko was visiting Washington, he called at the White House. The President took him aside, and after remarking that miscalculation had been a frequent cause of war throughout history, the President quietly urged Gromyko to be certain that Moscow did not misjudge American intentions at this juncture of history.

THE COMMUNIST VIEW

What was happening on the Communist side can only be surmised. Harriman had reported that Khrushchev did not want a war in Southeast Asia, and his judgment was respected. But the test was whether or not the Communists were willing to agree to a cease-fire as a precondition for negotiations. The Soviet Union, Communist China, and North Vietnam probably all agreed that the goal was to make of Laos a Communist country. But as far as the Soviets were concerned the goal probably also included the secondary aim of making Laos a Communist country *without* running an excessively high risk of war. It also seems clear that the national interests of the three major Communist powers differed somewhat. The Soviets had other irons in the fire—Berlin, Europe, the Middle East, Africa. From the point of view of the Soviet Union's national interest, it was desirable to keep the risks of a blowup in Southeast Asia as low as possible. The Soviets undoubtedly wanted to concentrate on political means for bringing Laos into the Communist camp, even if this meant a rather long postponement of the goal and working toward it from within a "neutralized" Laos.

The Chinese Communists, on the other hand, although quite clearly wishing to avoid a war and fearing the consequences of an American intervention perhaps even more than the Soviets, apparently had a higher estimate than the Soviets of the risk that could be run before the United States would actually be provoked. But the Chinese still appeared willing to run high risks even when they recognized them as high.

The North Vietnamese seem to have had still other motives. It seems certain that they were the most impatient of all the Communist powers to see Laos brought into the Communist camp. But two factors motivated them toward caution. The first was the overriding goal of reunifying Vietnam itself on Communist terms. If the Communization of Laos interfered with the Communization of Vietnam, Hanoi was more than willing to postpone it. The second consideration was undoubtedly that Hanoi did not want to achieve the Communization of the successor states to Indochina and their subordination to Hanoi, which was clearly their long-range goal, if the cost was that a reunified, Communist Vietnam was in turn subordinated to Peking. Hanoi needed the help of both Moscow and Peking, and it could balance the one off against the other at

least to some extent. But a real blowup in Southeast Asia ran the risk to
Hanoi, not only of a Western take-over if the war went badly, but of a
repetition of what had happened to North Korea even if the war did not
go so badly. The Chinese intervention in Korea successfully repulsed the
UN forces, but it also left North Korea under Chinese domination for
several years.

President Kennedy considered that the Soviets were the key, and he
focused his efforts directly on Moscow. He wanted to convince the Kremlin that the alternatives to negotiations and a neutralized Laos would be
a struggle in which not only Communist interests would suffer, but Soviet
national interests as well.

A BREAK—AND DOMESTIC OPPOSITION

In any event, it was from the Soviets that the first break came—in an
unusual form, a broadcast on April 4, 1961, in *Vietnamese* beamed at
Southeast Asia. They repeated their opposition to the United States demand for a cease-fire as a precondition for negotiations, but then went
on to say that "cease-fire in Laos will help to create a favourable atmosphere for negotiations." The compromise the Soviets had in mind, it later
became clear, was that the proposal for a conference should be agreed
to *before* a cease-fire, but that the conference itself would not convene
until *after* the cease-fire went into effect.

But there things stalled. The Pathet Lao continued to nibble away at
Phoumi's positions, making steady ground. Backed by Harriman in his
cables from Laos, which he had by this time reached in his tour, the
State Department again proposed a limited commitment of American
troops to Thailand to underline both American determination and the
fact that it was holding back from a commitment of forces that would
be provocative. Again, the Pentagon insisted on all-out force or none—
they now talked of even more troops than the sixty thousand they had
earlier wanted and even more strongly of their opposition to any restrictions in terms of either territory or the weapons to be used. Although
they sometimes differed among themselves, the Joint Chiefs' position in
general was to oppose any intervention at all, as mentioned above, unless
they were given advance approval for the use of nuclear weapons if in
the judgment of the Joint Chiefs themselves nuclear weapons should
prove necessary—a condition which no President could ever accept.

This position stemmed primarily from the Pentagon's reaction to the
Korean War and from the natural reluctance of men whose responsibility
is basically technical to think in strategic terms, in the sense at least that
strategy at its vital center is inevitably political. But toward the end of
April, the position the Joint Chiefs took was also affected by the Bay of

Pigs failure—which came in the week of April 20. The President, too, reacted to the Bay of Pigs failure, but in the opposite direction. He had refused to use American troops to invade Cuba because he did not want to pay the political cost of using the overwhelming might of American power against a small nation that was not in fact a threat to American security. But it seemed possible that the Communists might see his decision as irresolution. Fearful of this, the President decided on at least a token introduction of American forces as a signal, and he instructed the American military advisers in Laos to take off their civilian clothes, put on uniforms, and quite openly accompany the Royal Army's battalions.

At home, Kennedy was assailed from all sides. He felt that the United States was overcommitted in Southeast Asia, but that it was his obligation to deal with the situation as he found it. He thought, perhaps wrongly, that doing nothing would earn the widest approval in America, but he understood the strategic importance of denying the Communists the north-south road and the political significance on the balance of world power of a "humiliation" over Laos. But he could hardly win. From both the press and Congress there was opposition to the commitment of American troops. But there was even more bitter criticism of the idea of negotiating with the Communists and a flat charge that a coalition government including the Communists, especially a government headed by Souvanna Phouma, would inevitably result in a "Communist take-over." Joseph Alsop, for example, was particularly scathing. Recalling that the White Queen in *Alice in Wonderland* had taught herself to believe as many as six impossible things before breakfast, he wrote that the leaders of the Western world did not really believe this impossible thing at Geneva, but that they were merely putting a polite face on what they recognized was defeat. "What the President is engaged in," wrote Keyes Beech in the *Saturday Evening Post,* "is a tactical retreat under cover of a show of American strength, which may save face but will not save Laos."

In the midst of the President's nicely balanced political and military moves on Laos, the Republican leadership in Congress chose to make a public statement opposing an agreement in Laos which would lead to a coalition government that included Communists. But when the President consulted the leaders of both parties, he found that they were also united in opposing any commitment of American troops to Laos.

The failure to transmit a much stronger signal of American intentions than putting our advisers in uniform probably cost the Lao troops fighting the Communists dearly. But the combination of Kennedy's moves, Moscow's interests, and the pressures of the in-between world typified by Nehru finally succeeded. The public announcement of the co-chairmen came on April 24. The cease-fire was to go into effect on May 3, and after some delay the newly reactivated ICC confirmed it. The Geneva conference opened on May 16, 1961. Averell Harriman was the United States representative, and G. M. Pushkin, a deputy foreign minister, represented the Soviet Union.

THE DECISION TO SUPPORT SOUVANNA

In the meantime, Harriman had seen Souvanna Phouma twice—once in New Delhi and once in Paris. Souvanna still wanted to try to reunite all factions of his country—including the Communists—in a government of national union under the umbrella of a new Geneva agreement guaranteeing its neutrality. The doubt in Harriman's mind was not about Souvanna's intentions, but about his ability to command the necessary political support within Laos to bring about a reunification successfully. Souvanna seemed to have more support than anyone else, but would that be enough in this faction-ridden land of Laos?

The other doubt was about the Communists. Thirty years of diplomatic experience at the top levels of government, including a tour as ambassador to Moscow itself, had given Harriman a sure knowledge of the Soviets, and they in turn respected him as a tough but trustworthy opponent. After his talks with their top people, as he told President Kennedy, he was convinced the Soviets did not want a war in Southeast Asia and were willing to seek an agreement. The Chinese and North Vietnamese, however, were another matter. About the most that could be said was that the United States must at least be sure that the blame for any failure to achieve a peace in Laos was theirs and not ours. By the time the talks began at Geneva, Harriman's advice was the government's decision.

But things did not go well at Geneva—or more accurately in Laos, where there were continued incidents of Communist violations of the cease-fire, most of which were attacks on Meo guerrilla bases in territory generally controlled by the Communists. Harriman at Geneva presented a list of thirty of these violations to the assemblage and assured them all that the United States would withdraw from the talks if an effective cease-fire were not achieved. In Washington, there was increasing skepticism of Harriman's judgment that the Communists really did want a settlement in Laos.

THE VIENNA MEETING

Then came the meeting between Kennedy and Khrushchev in Vienna. It took place on June 3 and 4, and it was harsh. They clashed over every subject that came up. Khrushchev responded with special ferocity when Kennedy referred, as he had done with Gromyko, to the possibility of "miscalculation." Khrushchev's response was so fierce, in fact, that when Khrushchev, a little later, told him that the decorations on his chest were Lenin Peace Medals, Kennedy could not help remarking, "Well, I hope you keep them."

The worst clash of all was over Berlin. Khrushchev insisted that the Soviets were determined to sign a treaty with East Germany and that following its signing if the United States tried to maintain its position in Berlin the action would violate East German sovereignty and would be met with force. Said Kennedy, "It will be a cold winter."

It was only on the subject of Laos that there was any agreement. They agreed that Laos should not become an issue between the two great powers. They agreed that the goal was a truly neutral Laos and that they would both use their influence to bring it about. Khrushchev spoke of locking the two foreign ministers in a room until they found a solution. Kennedy then raised the crucial question of a genuine cease-fire. And Khrushchev—in what amounted to a significant concession when one considers Soviet relations with the Communist Chinese and North Vietnamese at the time—agreed to give the cease-fire a high priority. The joint communiqué signed by both Kennedy and Khrushchev reiterated Soviet and American support for a neutral Laos and ended with the statement that "in this connection they have recognized the importance of an effective cease fire."

Not immediately but over time the Communist attacks lessened and the cease-fire became effective. But the Geneva conference still made painfully slow progress. Even the Soviets became impatient—"One cannot," Andrei Gromyko said, "sit indefinitely on the shores of Lake Geneva, counting swans."

"SATELLITE" TROUBLES

A problem was that both the Soviets and the Americans were having trouble with their allies and with the Lao faction they were supposed to represent. The Soviets were obviously having difficulties in getting the Communist Chinese and North Vietnamese to co-operate, but the details of their difficulties were hidden. The Americans' troubles were with Phoumi, and they were very public indeed.

As most of the great powers in history have discovered, a small and supposedly weak ally can be powerful in stubbornness. Several American administrations, for example, tried without success to persuade or pressure Chiang Kai-shek into withdrawing from Quemoy and Matsu. For when it came to the moment of truth, none was willing to use the ultimate and only really effective sanction, that of abandoning Taiwan and all the people on it. And the experience with Chiang has been repeated with

Syngman Rhee, with President Diem of Vietnam, and many others. It is sometimes difficult, most great powers discover, to avoid becoming the satellite of one's "satellites."

General Phoumi Nosavan was as clever in these matters as the others had been, and he understood the box in which the United States found itself. It was only the fear of American intervention that would convince the Communists that they should negotiate. But it was only the contrary fear that the United States might abandon Laos entirely that would convince Phoumi that a political solution was also the best hope for him. If the United States took too strong a stand against the Communists, and Phoumi decided there was no risk at all that the United States would abandon Laos, his course of action was obvious. He would adamantly refuse to negotiate with Souvanna for a coalition government and wait for an opportunity to provoke a Communist attack and so trigger an American intervention. On the other hand, if the United States took too strong a stand in pressuring Phoumi, it ran a risk that the Communists would believe that the Americans had already decided to abandon Laos, leaving nothing at all to deter them from breaking the cease-fire and returning to the tactic of nibbling away all along the line.

It is such dilemmas that are the source of much of the ambiguity of official statements on foreign policy, and American statements were properly ambiguous. In effect, they left the impression that what the United States would do depended very much on how we arrived at the moment of decision—that if it was Phoumi, for example, who broke the cease-fire in an attempt to provoke American intervention, the United States might well abandon Laos, but that if it was the Communists, the United States would probably intervene. But Phoumi was undeterred and promptly set about to resist all pressures to participate in a coalition government. For he had already had the experience in 1960 of forcing the United States to back down and bend to his will when he had marched on Souvanna's government after the Kong Le coup. And he undoubtedly also believed that this time, as in 1960, there would be a policy struggle in Washington in which he could count on the support of both the Pentagon and the CIA.

Phoumi had probably not reckoned on the differences between the Eisenhower and Kennedy administrations. President Kennedy was interested in foreign policy, especially Far Eastern policy, and he was knowledgeable about it. The old relationship between John Foster Dulles and Allen Dulles, which had given the CIA an especially potent position, no longer existed. CIA was still powerful, but it had lost much of the President's confidence in the Bay of Pigs fiasco, and the effects of the new administration's determination to reduce CIA's influence and achieve a better balance among the departments and agencies in Washington had already begun to be felt. So it was now the Pentagon that was the stronger of Phoumi's two allies, and the miserable performance of Phoumi's troops inevitably weakened their arguments in favor of supporting him.

PHOUMI VERSUS HARRIMAN

Another factor that Phoumi must not have counted on was Averell Harriman. The New Frontier, with its accent on youth, had put Harriman into the somewhat anomalous job of Roving Ambassador in spite of his great wealth of experience in foreign affairs. I remember chiding Richard Neustadt about this, since Neustadt had been a part of "Operation Talent Hunt" making recommendations on appointments at the very beginning of the Kennedy administration. "We thought he was a superannuated ex-Governor of New York," said Neustadt. "How could anyone know he would turn out to be both the wisest and most experienced of our diplomatists and at the same time the most youthful and vigorous?" But Harriman's sound advice and able execution of every assignment he was handed were rapidly winning the President's highest regard. It was in the midst of Phoumi's intransigence that Kennedy switched Harriman from Roving Ambassador to Assistant Secretary for Far Eastern Affairs. Phoumi now had to contend with someone of a quite different order. Harriman was tough as well as wise. He was brutally frank and he suffered no nonsense. At times he behaved like a curmudgeon—it was in this period that he earned the nickname "The Crocodile" from his colleagues in the Bureau of Far Eastern Affairs whose heads he bit off when their ideas were bad. But they loved it. When he was promoted to Under Secretary they gave him a silver crocodile inscribed "From his devoted victims."

Yet there was no stuffiness about him. He was completely at ease with people in spite of differences of station or of years. Most of his best friends in the new administration were thirty years younger than he. He recognized ability and he was not above being a little foxy in bringing people with ability to the fore. When he was first sent to Geneva, for example, he found a huge mission with over one hundred people in it. He soon discovered that one of these, William H. Sullivan, a Class Three officer then thirty-eight years old, was the ablest of the lot, and he promptly offered Sullivan the job of deputy. Sullivan replied that Harriman couldn't do it—there were several Class One and Class Two officers in the mission who ranked him. A few days later, Harriman called Sullivan in again. He had reduced the mission by half, and those sent home included all the officers senior to Sullivan.

Harriman also knew the feel and texture of power, and he had a towering prestige that dwarfed most of the other department and agency heads in Washington. He had also had more experience in the guerrilla warfare of interagency policy battles than anyone else. One anecdote will serve to illustrate. In London during the war when Harriman was running Lend-Lease he discovered that General J. C. H. Lee, who dealt in military supplies, had a separate channel of communications to Washington which was kept secret from Harriman. Something of General Lee's personality can be understood from the fact that although the C.H. in his initials stood for Court House, the soldiers under him swore that the whole batch of initials—J.C.H.—really stood for "Jesus Christ Himself." But Harriman knew how to handle the problem. "Look," he said, "you might succeed in getting me fired over this, but I will guarantee that I'll take you with me. Now, do I get to see the cables in advance or not?" Lee decided to co-operate, and thereafter they got along nicely. And Harriman carried this same toughness over into international affairs.

Harriman had seen Souvanna once more in September 1961, after which he again voiced the American hope that the three factions in Laos —Phoumi's conservative group, Souphanouvong's Pathet Lao, and Souvanna's neutralists—could be brought together in a government of national union. Harriman had also seen the King at Luang Prabang and Phoumi and Prince Boun Oum at Vientiane—and he made only a little effort to conceal his impatience with their arguments.

Intermittent negotiations among the three factions continued throughout the fall of 1961, but broke down because of Phoumi's intransigence. If a coalition government were to work, it seemed obvious that the posts of defense and interior would have to go to the neutralists. But Phoumi insisted on having them for himself.

But Harriman could be stubborn too. Back in Washington, he recommended that the cash payments Phoumi used to pay his troops be stopped, beginning in February, and the President backed him up. Then, Harriman insisted that each of the departments and agencies represented in Laos replace every American official who was a personal friend of Phoumi. There were some unforgettable battles about "interference in other agencies," but Harriman won.

Late in March 1962, Harriman made another trip to Laos, accompanied by William Sullivan, who was now his special assistant in Washington. He sent Sullivan up to the Plain of Jars to see Souvanna and Souphanouvong, and Sullivan reported back that both seemed willing to compromise. For his part, Harriman stopped off in Bangkok, where he persuaded Marshal Sarit, Phoumi's relative and mentor, to come with him to Nong Khai, in Thailand just across the river from Vientiane, to talk to Phoumi. Sarit urged Phoumi to co-operate in forming a government of national union, and there are some who were in Laos at the time who believe that Phoumi might have come around if given time and suitable opportunities for saving face. But Harriman lost patience with Phoumi's elliptical arguments. Phoumi, Harriman said emphatically, was a "soldier who was out of step" and that he was "leading his country to destruction."

THE BATTLE AT NAM THA

But trouble from the other direction was also brewing. The upper northwest corner of Laos, tucked in between Thailand, Burma, and Communist China, is the province of Nam Tha, and in late January 1962, Pathet Lao and North Vietnamese troops closed around the capital of the province, the town of Nam Tha itself, digging in on the surrounding heights.

The town lies in a dish-shaped valley that is reminiscent of Dienbienphu, and the notion that the Communists were preparing a trap for Phoumi similar to the trap they had prepared for the French was reinforced by the notation in a diary taken from a Vietnamese soldier that "Our troops, following the instructions of Uncle Ho, have come here to bring our contribution to the construction of a Dien Bien [sic]." Over the next few weeks, against American advice, Phoumi flew in more and more of his troops to reinforce the Nam Tha garrison. By the end of January five thousand of Phoumi's army, which by then totaled fifty thousand, were at Nam Tha, including important elements of his available artillery.

The pressure increased in February, with scattered Communist attacks on the Royal Army's outposts, and Phoumi reinforced the garrison again with paratroopers. Then, the pressure subsided, with both the Pathet Lao and the Vietnamese drawing back somewhat into the surrounding hills.

In Washington, we had been increasingly nervous over the possibility that the Communists might make a sudden lunge to test Phoumi's strength and to probe, as a minimum goal, United States determination to stand up for a neutralized Laos. Because of this nervousness, the specialists on the Soviet Union and on Asian Communism in the Bureau of Intelligence and Research scrutinized every move the United States took, looking for ways the Communist side might misinterpret it. Our pressure on Phoumi was one example, but even a routine letter from President Kennedy to the King of Laos assuring him that we did not intend to intervene militarily and promising to withdraw the American White Star teams worried us. The Communists would inevitably learn of the letter's contents, we argued, and they might regard it as evidence of a decision to disengage no matter what. Our fear was not so much that the Communists would launch an all-out offensive throughout Laos. Actually, such a blatant and dramatic assault would make our intervention almost inevitable. What we feared was a less dramatic, more ambiguous use of force—that they would "more or less automatically begin to place more emphasis on military means." We outlined all these considerations in a memorandum on April 24 to Harriman, which I asked Michael Forrestal to make a particular point of showing to the President, and the gist of which was cabled to our ambassador. Still another attempt was made to persuade Phoumi to withdraw from the trap, but without success.

On May 2, 1962, just 364 days after the cease-fire had been declared, one sector of the defense perimeter at Nam Tha received fire from the surrounding Pathet Lao and Vietnamese forces. The next day, twenty-five miles to the west, Communist forces attacked and captured the last remaining airfield in northern Laos, at Muong Sing. On May 4, they captured an outpost a mile and a half east of Nam Tha.

Then, at 3 A.M. on May 6, four Vietnamese battalions launched an assault on the northwest segment of the defense perimeter, and shortly thereafter other battalions attacked from the east, the northeast, and the southeast.

The twelve Americans on the White Star team with the defenders reported that first one sector, then another had been overrun. At 7:30 A.M. the team itself was evacuated by helicopter. By nine that morning, Nam Tha had fallen, and the survivors among the Royal Lao Army defenders were fleeing in disorganized panic down the road toward the Mekong and Thailand.

Over the next three days the intelligence reports showed no further troop movement. The attack had been a large-scale probe, a major although still-limited violation of the cease-fire, designed both to discredit Phoumi and his forces and to test American determination. Unless the United States responded promptly and effectively, the Communist side would be encouraged to step up their military effort. What we could expect was more of the same kind of nibbling tactics—a bite here and a bite there, intermittent but continuous, and so paced as to avoid presenting a single, clear-cut challenge that would make an American intervention seem justified. And as they went up the ladder, the pace of military encroachments would accelerate toward a military take-over of the whole country. It was the Laos crisis of 1961 all over again—only worse.

CHAPTER 12

Kennedy and the Neutralization of Laos

OVER the preceding few months an informal set of working relationships had developed to deal with Laos. Averell Harriman, William H. Sullivan, and the foreign service officers of the Bureau of Far Eastern Affairs were the central switchboard and conducted the whole operation. A group of us in the intelligence bureau, including specialists on Soviet and Asian Communism, served as a sort of intelligence and planning staff for Harriman and his bureau. Michael V. Forrestal, as special assistant to the President for Far Eastern matters on McGeorge Bundy's staff, kept the President informed and ensured co-ordination with the Pentagon and other agencies. And the President himself, through Forrestal and by telephone, kept day-by-day control, feeding his own ideas into both planning and operations. There was thus a more or less continuous interchange in which specialists at the planning and operating levels were kept informed of the President's strategic thinking, while their specialist knowledge and ideas at the same time flowed upward, informing and shaping that thinking.

In this instance what came out of the process was a paper pointing out the whole range of dangers, and particularly the danger that the Communists would further downgrade their estimate of the possible American reaction to further military advances. The minimum that the Communists probably wanted to achieve by the attack on Nam Tha was to discredit Phoumi and remove him as an obstacle to further Communist advances, even if these were entirely political and achieved through negotiations. But if there were no reaction and counterpressure from the United States, they would undoubtedly continue their military probing.

The paper recommended a series of diplomatic moves designed to make it clear that our goal was to re-establish the cease-fire and create a neutral Laos through the mechanism of a government of national union but that we would not tolerate a Communist military take-over. The Soviets and the British would be informed in their capacity as co-chairmen of the 1954 Geneva agreements; India in its capacity as chairman of the ICC; and Souvanna in his capacity as premier designate. But the paper also proposed that our ambassador seek out Souphanouvong and make sure the Communist Pathet Lao understood our intentions too.

The paper then went on to point out that none of this would be effective unless it was backed by concrete moves that would provide credible evidence that the United States meant what it said. What we needed was a package of moves that would signal to the Communists that if they continued on a military course, we would occupy the Mekong lowlands and the territory held by the Royal Lao Government up to the cease-fire line. But it should not be such a strong signal as to indicate that we had any intention of going beyond that cease-fire line. To accomplish this double purpose, the paper proposed a series of limited military moves: sending the Seventh Fleet to the Gulf of Siam; transferring a battle group of about a thousand men immediately to Thailand; ostentatiously moving a battle group already in Thailand on SEATO maneuvers right up to the Lao border opposite Vientiane; and, finally, taking immediate steps to improve the communications routes in northeast Thailand in case an occupation of Laos became actually necessary. Our estimate was that the Communists, including the Chinese, would prefer to continue negotiations toward a neutral Laos under a government of national union rather than run a high risk of American intervention. At the same time, we also calculated that the Communists, including the Chinese, would not be either provoked or frightened into further escalation by United States military moves that were clearly limited so as not to threaten their position in North Vietnam or Northern Laos but pointed only toward defending the portion of Laos still held by the Royal Lao Government.

The National Security Council (NSC) met in the cabinet room of the White House on Thursday, May 10, to consider these recommendations, and we were all braced for a battle between the "Never Again" view that either all-out force should be used in Asia or none at all versus the politically tailored recommendations that had been laid before the President. For even though many officers in the Pentagon did not share the "Never Again" view, it was clearly dominant at the very top. And the trouble was compounded by the fact that McNamara and Lemnitzer were both out of the country—although there was some comfort in this since they were returning via Thailand, where they would get a close view.

Harriman and I presented the case for the paper, and it was met by exactly the opposition from the Pentagon that had been expected: moving the fleet was all right, but not the troops. At one point, in the meeting, there was even a note of bitterness—an implication that the movement of troops the year before had not really been intended to bring about negotiations but to force the Communists to withdraw from Laos and that the President had backed down.

The counterproposal from the Pentagon was for a series of diplomatic protests, in addition to moving the fleet, for reversing our political pressures on Phoumi, and for embarking on another attempt to make a real army of Phoumi's forces by giving them still more arms and equipment combined with a crash training program.

But not even the advocates of this proposal took it seriously. Five

thousand of Phoumi's best troops had been at Nam Tha. Admittedly it
was veteran Vietnamese regulars that had defeated them, but their defeat,
nevertheless, had been very thorough. The latest reports from Laos were
that two thousand of the remnants had by this time reached the Mekong,
one hundred miles from Nam Tha, and had crossed over to Thailand,
where they had been interned. What the counterproposal really said was
—again—that the Pentagon's recommendation was to use military force
all-out or not at all.

In the face of such a split, a president has the legal power to decide.
But if the opposition was large enough, the price on other, equally vital
matters might be more than he would be willing to pay. At the very
least, a politically wise president would not want to make so far-reaching
a decision without considerable effort to bring as many key constituencies
along with him as he could, and certainly high members of the Executive
Branch like the absent McNamara. Since both proposals included sending
the fleet to the Gulf of Siam, the President approved this move. But
he decided to postpone his decision on all the rest until after another
NSC meeting, which he ordered for Saturday, immediately after Mc-
Namara and Lemnitzer were due to return. And he sent John McCone
and Michael Forrestal off to see President Eisenhower at Gettysburg.

Harriman and I rode back to the State Department together, and
the more we talked the more worried we were about the possibility
that the movement of the Seventh Fleet *alone* might lead the Communists to estimate our intentions wrongly. Fleets can be moved around
so easily that they do not constitute very much of a commitment,
especially in an age of nuclear power. If the Communists thought moving
the fleet was our only response, it might confirm them in an estimate
that we had written Laos off and encourage them to launch an offensive.
And if the President was unable to muster the support he needed and
felt that he had to decide against sending troops to Thailand, it would
be better not to involve American prestige even to the extent of sending
the fleet. In spite of Khrushchev's violent reaction at Vienna, what
Kennedy had said to him was true—most wars have arisen through
miscalculation. It might well be better not even to start the Seventh
Fleet in the direction of Thailand until the more fundamental decision
had been made.

Harriman was overdue at a public appearance, and it would arouse
suspicions if he was any later than he already was. But we should lose
no time in getting to the President—who was also overdue at a public
appearance—to give him a chance to consider this angle. So, acting in
Harriman's place, I called Bundy—who was just able to intercept the
President on his way out. The President's decision was to stop the fleet,
and the order was issued.

But within an hour the President called me back. He had just heard from McCone and Forrestal that Eisenhower was in favor of a very strong move, if necessary putting American troops into Laos itself. Unless McNamara and Lemnitzer came back with some new and extraordinarily persuasive information on the other side, which seemed unlikely, this support from Eisenhower would clearly make it easier to send the troops at least to Thailand. In view of this starting the fleet now might gain some time. What the President wanted to know was whether a Communist reaction was likely to materialize in the next two or three days. I did not think it likely. It would take a little time for the Communists to find out where the fleet was headed, unless there was a leak. It would take a little more time for them to ponder the meaning of the move. And it would take still more time for them to mount any sort of action if it was action they decided on. "Well," said the President, "let the fleet go ahead. But try to impress on everyone the importance of avoiding a leak to the press."

It was a quixotic hope. The next day the New York *Times* carried a story by Max Frankel that although the Kennedy administration had "written off" the right-wing forces under Phoumi as useless, the President would attempt to salvage some sort of peaceful settlement by ordering a "show of United States forces in Southeast Asian waters near Laos," which would probably start the coming weekend. The President was furious, particularly about the implication that all he intended was a "show of force." Max Frankel was a diplomatic correspondent, but using his byline on the story meant only that the *Times* had made a perfunctory effort to protect its sources. But the trial was clear both to the source and the motive. Among the hard-liners in the Pentagon there was obviously someone who was trying to turn the policy around—back to supporting Phoumi most probably, but possibly ahead to something more cataclysmic. What infuriated the President still more—insult added to injury—was the discovery that it had taken Jack Raymond, Pentagon correspondent of the *Times,* only three phone calls to get the entire story, only part of which the *Times,* with its usual sense of responsibility, had actually used.

THE DECISION

We met on Saturday morning, with McNamara and Lemnitzer right off the plane. McNamara was loaded with facts, figures, and statistics, and he somewhat brusquely interrupted the CIA briefing at the beginning of the meeting to run down the information he had brought back, which was only fifteen hours old and fresher than anything the CIA had on hand. Finishing up, he said that he and General Lemnitzer both supported the initial troop movements and most especially they supported the improvement of the communications and supply lines—

which had appalled McNamara as being totally inadequate for the needs of armed forces so highly developed technologically as the American. The meeting broke up quickly to permit the State and Defense departments to work out the details and met again that afternoon, when the President approved both the decisions and a guidance paper to be used in briefing the press.

The press guidance gave the picture. "We have been taking an increasingly grave view of the meaning of the situation in Laos over the past twenty-four hours," the guidance paper read. "The President has held two secret meetings with his senior advisors today, one this morning and one this afternoon." But the idea was not to heat up a crisis by alarming the public, but to cool one down by signaling the Communists. "In the meantime," the guidance paper continued calmly, "it is only prudent for the United States to take certain precautionary moves. . . . [However,] policy continues to be the reestablishment of a cease fire and negotiations toward a government of National Union." In response to a question as to whether the troops would eventually go into Laos, the answer would be that it depended on what the Communist side did next.

"MILITARY" VERSUS "POLITICAL"

So far, so good. But the troubles within the United States Government had only begun. The situation remained touch and go for weeks. This meant that planning had to go forward for the worst possible contingency, and it was in this planning that everyone concerned first realized how deep the cleavage between the political and the military approaches really was.

As I said, not all the officers in the Pentagon shared the "all-or-nothing" view. Neither did all the high officials in the State Department share the "political" view. Walt Rostow, head of the Policy Planning Council, for example, felt that serious consideration should be given to bombing North Vietnam. And some members of both the State Department and the Pentagon—the Secretary of State, for example—shifted their view. For the question was never simple, and there were legitimate and persuasive arguments on both sides. But although there were these layers of opinion —and shadings and shiftings—within each department and agency, the dominant view in the Pentagon was toward "all-or-nothing" and the dominant view in the State Department was toward the "political," that is, to limit and tailor the force used so that it would carry a political signal.

The specific and concrete issue was over what the United States should do if the Communist side again violated the cease-fire in a move that revealed that they were bent on a military take-over even though it was accomplished by a continuation of their usual, deliberately paced, ambiguous nibbling tactics. In a meeting in the White House on Sunday, May 13, and in subsequent meetings at the White House and between the State and Defense departments, it became apparent that Secretary McNamara had moved over to side with the dominant view among the military opposing the limited use of force for political purposes. The proposal was that if force had to be used, the first step should be a large-scale movement of troops to occupy the whole of the panhandle of Laos, right on over to North Vietnam, which borders the upper half of the panhandle. The advocates of this view, however, warned that the two hundred miles of mountains and jungles bordering North Vietnam would be impossible to defend. They recommended that unless the Communists, including the guerrillas in southern Laos, surrendered immediately, the next step should be an all-out attack on North Vietnam itself—land, sea, and air. What the United States would do if the Chinese Communists intervened was not spelled out, but the general impression was that the recommendation would be to retaliate on the mainland with nuclear weapons.

The "political" view began with the proposition that for international political reasons any use of force had to be tailored to our goal of a neutral Laos achieved through negotiations and a government of national union. If we were to have international support for our move, the intervention had to be to restore the cease-fire line and not encroach on the territory held by the Communists.

The cease-fire line, as it happened, divided the country at the foot-hills. The Communists held the mountains, and the Royal Lao Government held the Mekong lowlands. Thus, the "political" proposal came down to occupying the Mekong lowlands.

Here again, there was a political purpose to be served. Over half the people of Laos lived in the lowlands and almost all those who are ethnically Lao. Here were almost all the towns of Laos, the commerce, and most of the agricultural production. In the wider arena of Southeast Asia, the Mekong valley historically has always been an area of tension, and control of the valley has major psychological significance in the entire region. If the Communists gained control of the lowlands, the political shock effect would be severe.

But there were also military purposes to be served. Occupying the Mekong lowlands would not have much effect on the Communists' use of the Ho Chi Minh network of trails through the mountainous section of the panhandle, which they would continue to hold. But, given the ruggedness of the terrain, occupying the whole of the panhandle, including the mountains, would not do very much to keep the Communists from using the trails either, as everyone conceded. The more open lowlands were not so conducive to guerrilla warfare in our rear. And occupying the lowlands would deny the north-south road to the Communists—for with a road they could certainly increase the amount that could be in-filtrated into South Vietnam.

Then, too, if there was actually to be war, it would be much easier to defend Thailand at the line of the hills, *forward* of the Mekong, than from behind it. If the Communists held the lowlands and its north-south road, they could build up a force of several divisions—and choose their time and place of attack. The Mekong is not a very good military barrier; it is fordable at many points six months of the year. And the road network in northeast Thailand is east-west rather than north-south, which would make it difficult to shift reinforcements to meet attacks at different places along the line.

Forward of the Mekong, however, the north-south road would be be-hind the defenders, permitting them to shift reinforcements rapidly from point to point. But even more important was the nature of the terrain. The Communists would not be able to build up a front of several divisions, but would be compelled, both in their attack and in their build-up of their forward strength, to go through six or seven long, narrow defiles—fifty to one hundred miles long—passing through the Annamite chain of mountains. These steep-sided defiles would channel the heavy traffic needed for conventional war, and make it terribly vulnerable to bombardment from the air and guerrilla harassment from the ground. Thus the line of hills, forward of the Mekong, offered a near-perfect position for defense.

There was much sympathy for this view down the line in the military services. But there was very little at the top, and the case for the strategy of defending at the line of the hills, forward of the Mekong, had to be made pretty much by the State Department. To the disgust of some Air Force officers, however, the RAND Corporation—a quasi-governmental research organization supported mainly by Air Force contracts—gave the State Department some persuasive support. The RAND people had been engaged for some months on a logistics study of the routes through Laos, and they distributed their final report right in the middle of the debate. It turned out to be an eloquent statement of the case for de-fending at the hills and an alarming analysis of how many forces the Communists could put into the Mekong lowlands if they controlled the north-south road. The State Department made the most of it.

Also bearing on the decision was the estimate of the Communist re-sponse. The opinion of the "China watchers" and specialists on Asian Communism in the intelligence community was that if the United States introduced forces into the Mekong in response to further violations of the cease-fire and stopped at that, the Communists would introduce additional North Vietnamese forces and perhaps Chinese volunteers into northern Laos, but that they would *not* attempt to drive the American troops out. If the Americans attempted to take back territory already held by the

Communists, even in the southern panhandle, however, the estimate was that the Communists would strenuously resist. And if the American troops attempted to go north—to retake either northern Laos or to attack North Vietnam—the estimate was that the Chinese would undoubtedly intervene.

Thus the "political" argument, to sum up, was that for the United States the strategic objective was to *deny* the Mekong lowlands and the north-south road to the Communists, not to have it for ourselves. The least costly way of achieving this goal seemed to be a "political" solution achieved by "political" means—a neutral Laos through a government of national union. If the Communists compelled the United States to use force, it should be used for this same goal, to restore the cease-fire line and put negotiations back on the track. And if the Communists did not accept a neutral Laos and a government of national union as the way out, we would be holding the lowlands, denying them to the Communist side. This would put us in a sound international position politically, and militarily in a good position for defense, manning a line that we could hold at the least possible cost.

But none of this was disputed. The argument was about strategy only in the political sense of that word. The "military" approach started with grave doubts that Laos could be successfully neutralized through a government of national union and negotiations with the Communists. But what the advocates of the "military" approach really objected to was any course of action that might lead them to a limited war or a defensive position—no matter how good it was.

ACCOMMODATION OR FINAL SHOWDOWN

The debate was taut and tense, and some of the participants may have succumbed to feelings of vindictiveness. But nothing in it was petty. There was and is a great and fundamental issue here, born in the Korean War, finessed at the time of Dienbienphu, put off in the Laos crises of 1961 and 1962, and reopened by the struggle for Vietnam.

The issue is only partly that of subordinating military means to political goals; of the merits of the "defense" and the "offense"; of whether a limited, tailored response is better than "massive retaliation"; or whether we should adopt "win" or "no-win" strategies. The real issue is whether there is to be an accommodation, however painfully and slowly arrived at, between the Communist and especially the Chinese Communist world and the non-Communist world or a final showdown in which only one emerges dominant.

A final showdown would present a test of will and require a grim determination in picking the time and the place. An accommodation would take equally steady nerves and require a willingness to make the sacrifices and live with the frustrations of a limited use of force and political compromise. But the point is that the Korean War, Dienbienphu, the two Laos crises, and Vietnam are only the opening guns of what might well be a century-long struggle for Asia—and the choice of an over-all strategy is fundamental.

The meetings in the White House and between the State and Defense departments continued through the rest of May and into June with no result except a sharpening of the basic differences. The Secretary of State seemed reluctant to present the political case with as much forcefulness as the Secretary of Defense and the other able and vigorous spokesmen of the Pentagon presented the military case. Rusk, in fact, was uneasy that on one or two occasions the political case might already have been presented a little too forcefully in the rather free give-and-take that the President encouraged in the White House meetings.

In any case no decision need be made until the Communists moved, and the Secretary of State argued that the President ought not to make the decision in advance. If he decided that the United States should not intervene and the Communists learned of it, they would be encouraged to go ahead. If he decided that the United States should intervene and word got out, on the other hand, the public debate would inevitably become an obstacle to swift and effective action. But if there were no decision, there would be nothing to leak.

The result of this, however, was that the logistical planning papers slid by the intermediate phase of occupying the Mekong lowlands and defending at the line of hills and concentrated on bombing North Vietnam and the other phases near the top of the ladder of escalation favored by the military approach. Unless a start were made on the logistical problems of the intermediate phase, the President would never even have the option of choosing the political approach. The State Department finally did insist on a directive ordering the necessary logistical planning, but only after a delegation of presidential appointees had made a special plea to the Secretary of State to have their case presented to the President.

The announcement that the United States was sending the Seventh Fleet to the Gulf of Siam came on May 12 and that it was sending troops to Thailand came on May 15. On May 16, the Communist faction agreed to further negotiations—but they dragged their heels and actually launched another, smaller attack later on in May. Then on May 25, Khrushchev announced that the Soviet Union "continued" to support the establishment of a neutral Laos, although the American landings in Thailand had "hindered" a settlement. And the same day Souvanna agreed to return to Laos for the negotiations, setting a deadline of June 15 for either success or failure.

The American landings in Thailand apparently convinced the Communist side that, for the moment at least, the political course offered more opportunity and less risk than continued military nibbling. For Phoumi, on the other hand, the combination of Harriman's unrelenting pressure and the defeat at Nam Tha was too much; it broke his will. On June 11, 1962, Souvanna announced that an agreement had been reached on the composition of a government of national union.

The Geneva agreements neutralizing Laos were signed on July 23, 1962, almost fifteen months after negotiations had begun. The various provisions were complicated, and undoubtedly full of legal loopholes. But the essence of the accords were clear. Laos was to be truly neutral— Souvanna's first act, for example, was to declare that his government would "not recognize the protection of any alliance or military coalition, including SEATO," and his statement was incorporated into the Geneva agreements themselves. The International Control Commission was responsible for supervising the cease-fire, and implicitly empowered to act on the decision of a majority, which was an important change from the provisions of the Geneva agreements of 1954. All foreign troops were to be withdrawn within seventy-five days. In a special, although indirect reference to the use of the Ho Chi Minh trails as infiltration routes into South Vietnam, the parties to the agreement promised that they would "not use the territory of the Kingdom of Laos for interference in the internal affairs of other countries." Pushkin and Harriman, finally, had a verbal understanding that the Soviet Union and the United States would each accept responsibility for the continued good behavior of the Lao faction with which it was associated.

THE GENEVA AGREEMENTS IN PRACTICE

Just before the seventy-five-day deadline on troop withdrawal, the NSC met again with the President. There was evidence that substantial numbers of North Vietnamese troops would remain past the deadline, and pressure within the government had mounted to keep our own military advisers in Laos until the Vietnamese also withdrew. "How is it going?" Harriman was asked. "Just about as unsatisfactorily as we expected," was his reply.

We had put down what we expected in an informal "intelligence estimate" that Harriman and I used to brief the President. We felt, first, that the Communists continued to pursue their goal of gaining control of all of Laos, but that for the time being, at least, they intended to do so primarily through political means and generally within the terms of the Geneva agreements—the Geneva terms, that is, as conceived in very elastic "Communist" dimensions. But even though the Communists would probably rely mainly on political means, the North Vietnamese would undoubtedly insist on maintaining some military presence in Laos, both to backstop the Pathet Lao position and to maintain their hold on the infiltration routes into South Vietnam. But our judgment was that the Communists would make an effort to keep this military presence small and inconspicuous and would use the infiltration routes circumspectly. And by "circumspectly" we meant that they would continue to use the trails for infiltrating men on foot, cadres equipped with their own arms and whatever other, heavier equipment they could carry. We meant that they would use trucks where roads already existed and at the time of year that the roads were passable. But we also meant that they would probably not make any blatant or obvious effort to turn trails into roads or to improve the roads except at places and in circumstances where they were fairly sure they could get away with it without being seen. And our estimate, finally, was that the Communist side would stay at even this semicovert level only if there was continued evidence of an American determination to prevent their taking over the whole of Laos—by maintaining U.S. troops in Thailand or at least by continuing to improve the lines of communications and other installations that would facilitate their reintroduction.

Again, the policy to meet this situation had been worked out in the same informal process of exchanging guidance and specialist knowledge between the President, Harriman, Forrestal, and the State Department group of research intelligence specialists. Harriman, especially, felt strongly that the United States should comply with both the letter and the spirit of the agreements in every detail, that its record should be absolutely clean. Our military advisers should be withdrawn promptly, and thereafter there should be no violation of any kind by the United States, neither "black" reconnaissance flights to confirm whether the North Vietnamese had actually withdrawn nor cloak-and-dagger hanky-panky. The Lao themselves would inevitably find out what the Vietnamese were doing, and we could learn from them. Harriman wanted the political onus of any violations to fall on the Communists. If the Geneva agreements and the political solution failed in Laos, he wanted it to be the Communist side that had to pay the political cost, including the cost in terms of damaging their goals elsewhere in Asia and Africa, and not the United States. And he wanted the international political support that would come from a scrupulous observance of the Geneva agreements for still another reason. If the Communists broke the agreements and the United States had to intervene with force, he wanted to make sure we had all the international political support we could get.

Then, too, being absolutely meticulous in our support for the Geneva agreements and a government of national union under Souvanna would leave no doubt inside Laos where the blame for any breakup lay—and this would have its effects on relations between the three factions. "If Souvanna's government of national union breaks up," Harriman said more than once, "we must be sure the break comes between the Communists and the neutralists, rather than having the two of them teamed up as they were before." The point was that in our judgment it was by no means certain that it would be the Communists who won the political battle for control of a government of national union, especially if the non-Communists—the neutralists and the conservatives—worked together.

Suspicions about the Communists' intentions were voiced in the NSC meeting, but there was no serious opposition to the basic policy. "Well," said the President, swinging his chair around toward Harriman with a relaxed grin, "we'll go along with the Governor."

SUCCESS, FAILURE, OR STALEMATE?

The United States continued this basic policy during the rest of Harriman's tenure as Assistant Secretary for Far Eastern Affairs, and we continued to follow it when I replaced him after he became Under Secretary early in 1963. But the tests to which it was subjected were constant.

The Pathet Lao made their first move by attempting to take over Kong Le's neutralist forces. When he insisted on independence, they cut off the Soviet supplies coming to him overland from Hanoi. At Souvanna's request the United States stepped into the breach with a new flow of supplies through Vientiane.

The Pathet Lao then began a more subtle but also more vicious campaign, in which Quinim Pholsena, nominally a neutralist, was the central figure. Quinim directed a network of secret agents in an attempt to subvert the more susceptible officers under Kong Le and to assassinate those who were loyal. The Communists had some success in their attempts at subversion, but when they assassinated Colonel Ketsana, Kong Le's courageous chief of staff and old friend, the neutralists closed ranks. And they retaliated by assassinating Quinim himself.

The Communists then tried an out-and-out military offensive against the neutralists. They attacked Kong Le's position on the Plain of Jars, driving him back into the western half of the plain. But his men fought well, even against the Vietnamese regulars interspersed among the Pathet Lao, and there they held—while Harriman flew to Moscow to make it clear once more that we would not tolerate a military take-over.

Thus by the summer of 1963, the split was complete—and it had indeed come between the Pathet Lao and the neutralists. It was the Communists now who were isolated, and the non-Communist neutral and conservative factions who were joined in opposing them.

And then things settled down. Increasingly, it became clear that we had arrived at a tacit agreement—not on settlement of the Laos problem, but on its temporary postponement. The Communist North Vietnamese could easily put enough troops into Laos to take it over within two to four weeks, if they were willing to take the risk of an American intervention. But they were not willing to take that risk, mainly because the United States made sure that the risk was real. By using the more ambiguous guerrilla techniques they were applying to Vietnam, they could probably have taken Laos over on a longer time scale with even less risk. But they were unwilling to take even that level of risk over Laos, apparently because they felt the main arena was Vietnam. For this very reason, however, the Communists wanted to keep on using the infiltration routes through Laos into South Vietnam. But they were apparently willing to keep their use of the routes at guerrilla warfare levels; that is, to keep the use of the routes down to a level that was less than fully provocative. They had a small though important interest, in sum, in keeping open the option of a truly neutral Laos under a government of national union. What they did, in effect, was to follow a two-track policy. What the Communists seemed to be tacitly proposing was that for the time being both sides should respect a *de facto* partition of Laos along the Geneva cease-fire line. Until the matter of Vietnam was settled, there would be no progress toward a true government of national union, but the Communists would keep some token representation in Souvanna's government at Vientiane and thus avoid scuttling the Geneva agreements openly and irrevocably. Then, if the guerrilla struggle in Vietnam went *against* the Communists, Laos would quickly become the model for a truly neutral country in which the Communists participated in a coalition government without attempting to subvert it—at least for a while. But if the Communists *won* in Vietnam—they seemed to be saying—then they would regard Laos as part of the prize.

To those who felt that a showdown between Communist China and the United States was inevitable and believed that it was to the advantage of the United States that the showdown came sooner rather than later, any such tacit agreement to put the question of Laos to one side for a time seemed dangerous. And there is, of course, a respectable argument for this position. But to those who saw the long-run interest of the United States best served by an accommodation between Communist China and the United States and the goal in Southeast Asia as limited to denying the area to Communism rather than making it an American ally, a postponement seemed better than the obvious alternatives—a large-scale military intervention or surrendering it to the Communists. To those who sought this more limited goal, in other words, Laos was a victory— of sorts.

THE LESSONS

The lessons of the Laos crises are many—that agreements with the Communists can be kept by and large intact, for example, but only if one is willing to keep up the same level of commitment to keep the agreement as one was willing to use to obtain it in the first place. At one point, for example, Harriman was asked whether he was optimistic or pessimistic about the Geneva agreements on Laos. "Neither," he snapped. "I'm determined." For making successful agreements with the Communists—or, perhaps, anyone else—this is the correct attitude.

But in retrospect, it seems obvious that for President Kennedy, Laos was not so much a lesson as the crucible for the strategic concept that armed him for as great a test as any American president has yet faced—the Cuban missile crisis of 1962.

V

THE CUBAN MISSILE CRISIS

"At the height of the Cuban events, when the smell of burning hung in the air . . ."
—NIKITA KHRUSHCHEV, *December 12, 1962*

"And above all, while defending our own vital interests, nuclear powers must avert those confrontations which bring an adversary to a choice of either a humiliating retreat or a nuclear war. To adopt that kind of course in the nuclear age would be evidence only of the bankruptcy of our policy—or of a collective death-wish for the world."
—JOHN F. KENNEDY, *June 10, 1963*

V

THE CUBAN MISSILE CRISIS

"At the height of the Cuban event, when the smell of burning hung in the air..."

—Nikita Khrushchev, December 11, 1962

"And above all, while defending our own vital interests, nuclear powers must avert those confrontations which bring an adversary to a choice of either a humiliating retreat or a nuclear war. To adopt that kind of course in the nuclear age would be evidence only of the bankruptcy of our policy—or of a collective death-wish for the world."

—John F. Kennedy, June 10, 1963

CHAPTER 13

The Intelligence Story

THE SOVIET DECISION to deploy long-range nuclear missiles to Cuba must have been reached some time during the spring of 1962, and certainly no later than early summer.

As we now know, the Soviet plan was in two phases. In the first phase, Cuba was to be ringed with defenses—twenty-four batteries of surface-to-air antiaircraft missiles with a slant range of twenty-five miles; over one hundred MIG fighters; short-range (thirty-five to forty miles) harbor defense missiles; and coastal patrol boats armed with ship-to-ship missiles. The second phase was to bring in the offensive weapons, the IL 28 light bombers and the ballistic missiles. These would be accompanied by four battle groups of special ground troops armed with tactical nuclear weapons to give the missiles close-in protection—a formidable force of Soviet infantrymen that could, in fact, have defeated the whole Cuban army in very short order.

There were to be four ballistic missile complexes—at San Cristóbal and Guanajay, in western Cuba, and at Sagua la Grande and Remedios, in central Cuba. Three battalions of the thousand-mile Medium Range Ballistic Missiles (the MRBMs) were to be at San Cristóbal and three at Sagua la Grande. Two battalions of the two-thousand-mile Intermediate Range Ballistic Missiles (the IRBMs) were to be at Guanajay and two more battalions at Remedios. Thus San Cristóbal and Sagua la Grande would each have twelve launching pads and Guanajay and Remedios would each have eight—for a total of forty pads.

It was to be a major military deployment, in some ways as complicated to plan and carry out as a landing on a hostile shore. Each of the twenty-four antiaircraft sites had twenty-four missiles thirty feet long, and a variety of special trailers, fueling trucks, and radar vans. Each of the ten IRBM and MRBM missile battalions was to have eight missiles sixty feet long, and dozens of special vehicles per battalion—missile trailers, fueling trucks, radar vans, missile erectors, and personnel carriers. The grand total came to several thousand vehicles and over twenty thousand men. And it needed a sealift of more than a hundred shiploads.

Planning and co-ordinating a movement of this magnitude and re-scheduling and assembling the necessary shipping probably took several weeks. Since the first of the shipments began to arrive in Cuban ports at

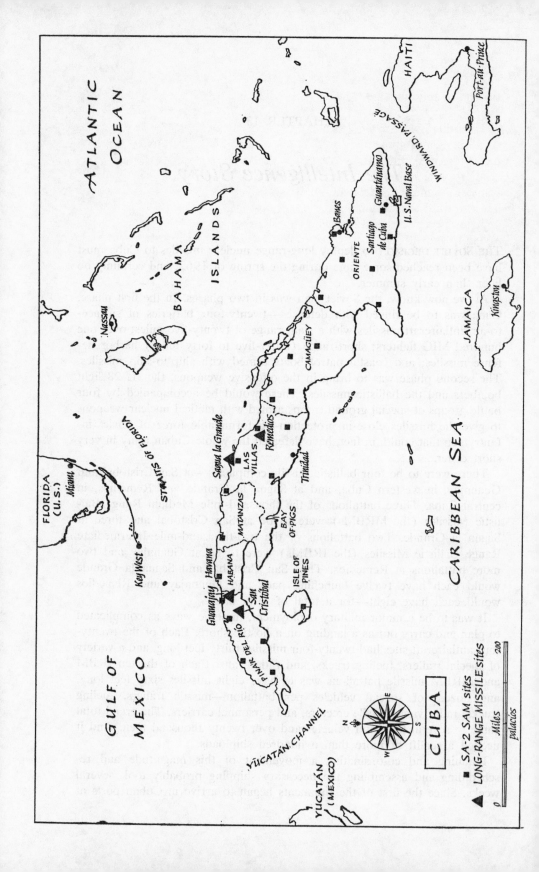

the end of July, the latest the decision could have been taken was probably June.

The other evidence available also points to June. Throughout the spring of 1962 Castro apparently pressed for commitments the Soviets were reluctant to give. In March, April, and May, the strains in Cuban-Soviet relations were severe, highlighted by the Escalente purges, which eliminated some of the more militant old-time Communists from Castro's government. Then, toward the end of June, the tension seemed to ease. Castro made a strange speech to some departing Soviet technicians, apologizing for the "poor treatment" they had received. Early in July, Fidel sent his brother, Raúl, on a flying visit to Moscow and following his return made a speech saying that neither internal uprisings nor exile landings were a threat but only an American invasion—which "we can now repel."

SOVIET MOTIVATIONS

What did the Soviets hope to accomplish by putting nuclear missiles in Cuba? As with the major policy decisions of all governments, whether dictatorial or democratic, different segments of the Soviet leadership undoubtedly saw particular advantages and disadvantages in putting missiles in Cuba according to their own parochial interests and responsibilities. But the Soviet government as a whole seems to have hit upon putting missiles in Cuba as a generalized, strategic response to a whole set of problems, military, economic, and political.[1]

Consider the view from Moscow eighteen months before the missiles decision, in January of 1961. In the Soviet Union, the domestic situation seemed good. Work was proceeding on the party program and on the twenty-year plan for increasing domestic production.

The world situation was also good. First and foremost, the Soviets were still basking in the afterglow of the Sputnik success, and the world generally assumed that the military and strategic balance had significantly shifted in the Soviets' favor. In the United States, a new, young, and presumably inexperienced president had just taken over the reins of government after an extremely close election, and he seemed to have few prospects except continued deadlock politically and recession economically. The Atlantic community had made little progress toward unity. The underdeveloped world was in ferment, offering exciting prospects for the Soviets: Africa, Latin America, and Southeast Asia all seemed full of opportunities. Finally, and most importantly, the Sino-Soviet dispute, although still disturbing, appeared to be contained for the moment. The eighty-one Communist parties had just met, and a *modus vivendi* with the Chinese still seemed possible.

Khrushchev expressed his satisfaction with all these favorable prospects in his speech of January 6, 1961. Confidently, he laid out an ambitious and aggressive program to extend Communist influence throughout the world—from Berlin, where he revived threats of an ultimatum, to the underdeveloped world, which he invited to embark on new and better "wars of national liberation."

But by the spring of 1962, things looked quite different from Moscow. President Kennedy and the West had stood firm on Berlin. There had been movement in the Atlantic community toward unity. The difficulties of dealing with the underdeveloped world had begun to sink in—the expense of foreign aid, the political instability of the emerging nations, their touchiness, their extremist nationalism, their inexperience, and also their instinct and skill in playing the great powers off against each other rather than being dominated by one of them.

And the Sino-Soviet dispute had gotten out of hand. In one sense, Communism is a doctrine of acquiring and using power. The trouble was that the Chinese were behaving like Communists, and the dispute had come to have a dynamism of its own.

Domestically, the Soviet leaders found that the demands they had themselves created with "de-Stalinization" and promises of consumers' goods had become a tiger that they were finding difficult to ride. There were just not enough resources to meet the whole long list of demands—a better life for consumers; the needs of the space program, prestigious though it was; the foreign aid required to play an active, worldwide role; and, above all, the effort to achieve military supremacy.

For the situation here, too, had changed—radically. And for the Soviet leaders this change probably caused the deepest anxiety of all. When the Soviets completed their first experiments with rockets and began to lay out their longer-run program, they apparently decided on a bold move. They elected to skip the logical next step—rockets of about 350,000 pounds thrust, like our Atlas—and to leap to giants of about 800,000 pounds. The successful result was the behemoth that gave the Soviets the Sputnik and the lift for their many other space achievements. But this rocket was also intended to serve as the work horse of the Soviet ICBM force, and American intelligence was rightly impressed. As the intelligence community looked at their estimates in 1958, 1959, and 1960, and even through the first half of 1961, they saw a missile gap developing that would come to a peak about 1963. Both the intelligence community and the Air Force made a major effort to win approval for a crash program through orthodox channels, but failed to change the Eisenhower administration's policies. Inevitably, the more convinced among the Air Force and intelligence people then tried an end run through leaks to senators and newspaper columnists who were favorably disposed. Reluctantly, the Eisenhower administration upped the American program. When Kennedy came in, he upped it again.

In the meantime, the Soviets began to deploy their giant rocket as an

ICBM near Plesetsk in the north. And this was apparently the fatal blow to their hopes of achieving a decisive advantage. For they discovered, one must assume, that this behemoth was just too big, too bulky to serve as a practical weapon. A newer, smaller, more streamlined missile had to be designed instead, and the Soviet ICBM program must have been set back many months.

The Soviets, of course, knew that their hopes of catching up with the United States had been set back, but so long as the Americans did not know the true situation the Soviets still enjoyed the immediate benefits of seeming to be about to catch up with the United States or even of having just surpassed it. When the Kennedy administration took office in 1961, the evidence on the Soviet missile deployment was still inconclusive. The U-2 flights had been discontinued after Gary Powers had been shot down on May 1, 1960, and even before that, there was great difficulty obtaining pictures of the deployment because of the almost constant clouds over the northern areas of the Soviet Union where the big missiles were being emplaced. Secretary McNamara became skeptical of the higher estimates when he saw them and pressed hard for better intelligence. But even as late as June 1961 the evidence was contradictory and the intelligence community continued to be split, with some Air Force estimates still going as high as three hundred Soviet missiles deployed and some Navy estimates as low as ten. It was not until the summer and fall of 1961 that the Americans discovered the true situation—and decided to tell the Soviets that they knew.

The first news of this came to the Soviets in a speech given in November 1961 by Roswell Gilpatric, Deputy Secretary of Defense. And it was confirmed in a variety of other ways in the weeks that followed.

The American decision to let the Soviets know that we knew was deliberate. But it was made only after much agonizing, since everyone involved recognized that telling the Soviets what we knew entailed considerable risk. Forewarned, the Soviets would undoubtedly speed up their ICBM program. They would do so anyway, of course, but this action to let them know what we knew meant the speed-up would be sooner rather than later. On the other hand, Khrushchev's several ultimatums on Berlin indicated that, if he were allowed to continue to assume that we still believed in the missile gap, he would very probably bring the world dangerously close to war. Thus the decision was reached to go ahead with telling the Soviets that we now knew. Gilpatric was chosen as the instrument because a speech by the Deputy Secretary of Defense was high enough to be convincing to the Soviets but not so high as to be threatening—whereas a speech by the President, the Secretary of State, or the Secretary of Defense might well have been. And the Gilpatric speech was followed by a round of briefings for our allies—deliberately including some whom we knew were penetrated, so as to reinforce and confirm through Soviet intelligence channels the message carried openly through the Gilpatric speech.

For the Soviets, the implications of the message were horrendous. It was not so much the fact that the Americans had military superiority—that was not news to the Soviets. What was bound to frighten them most was that the Americans *knew* that they had military superiority. For the Soviets quickly realized that to have reached this conclusion the Americans must have made an intelligence break-through and found a way to pinpoint the location of the Soviet missiles that had been deployed as well as to calculate the total numbers. A "soft" ICBM system with somewhat cumbersome launching techniques, which is what the Soviets had at this time, is an effective weapon for both a first strike, a surprise attack such as at Pearl Harbor, and a second, retaliatory strike so long as the location of the launching pads can be kept secret. However, if the enemy has a map with all the pads plotted, the system will retain some of its utility as a first-strike weapon, but almost none at all as a second-strike weapon. The whole Soviet ICBM system was suddenly obsolescent.

While the Soviet leaders fretted over these intractable problems, Castro clamored more and more insistently for military protection, magnifying the threat of an American invasion, and—in all probability—himself raising the subject of nuclear missiles. In any case, among the Soviet leadership all these problems, fears, and demands somehow converged on the thesis that at least a temporary and expedient solution to their several problems would be to install some of their older, more plentiful medium- and intermediate-range missiles in Cuba. It would give them a cheap and immediate substitute for the newer, more expensive ICBMs and let them stretch out the ICBM program to ease the pressure on resources. And it would meet Castro's demands and protect what had become, since Castro's self-proclaimed membership in the Communist bloc, not just another "war of national liberation" but the first opportunity to project Soviet power into the Western Hemisphere.

Thus the motive for the decision was strategic in the broad sense that a general improvement in the Soviet military position would affect the entire political context, strengthening their hand for dealing with the whole range of problems facing them—and unanticipated problems as well. But even though general rather than specific security and foreign policy goals were the principal motive, once the decision was made it did offer enticing prospects for specific gains in foreign policy as ancillary benefits. If the move in Cuba were successful and the over-all Soviet position strengthened, their leverage on Berlin would indeed be improved. NATO would surely be shaken and the chances of the U.S. successfully creating a multilateral nuclear force reduced. In Latin America, other potential "Castros" would be encouraged. American power would be less impressive and American protection less desirable, and some of the Latin American states would move in the Soviet direction even if their governments were not overthrown.

Then, too, a successful move in Cuba would cut the ground from under the Chinese Communists and go far toward convincing Communists everywhere that Soviet leadership was strong and Soviet methods in dealing with the "imperialists" effective.

THE INTELLIGENCE PROBLEM

The United States learned of the arms shipments to Cuba as soon as the first of them began to arrive, in late July 1962. But it was not until October 14 that American intelligence first learned that the decision included long-range nuclear missiles.

The Soviets cloaked the movement of both the defensive and the offensive arms with secrecy. Very few ports were used. Cubans living near the docks were evacuated. High fences were put up and guarded by Russians. Other Russians did much of the unloading. The equipment was landed at night, readied for transport by road, and moved out in night convoys to make room for the next shipment. Sites had been readied in remote areas, naturally screened by hills and woods, whose population had been evacuated. And once the equipment reached these sites, speed was added to security—no attempt was made to camouflage until after a weapon was operational. And the measures taken to ensure speed were extraordinary. Even the concrete arches in the buildings apparently intended to be used as nuclear storage magazines were prefabricated—cast in the Soviet Union and shipped the whole fantastic distance to Cuba.

Initially no public announcement was made even of the agreement to supply Cuba conventional arms. Then in late August, after the shipments had been going on for a month and the first newspaper stories had come out of Washington, "Che" Guevara visited Moscow, and this occasion was used to acknowledge, in a joint communiqué issued on September 22, that the Soviet Union had agreed to help Cuba meet the threats from "aggressive imperialist quarters" by delivering "armaments and sending technical specialists for training Cuban servicemen."

"COVER AND DECEPTION"

Thereafter, the Soviets' public and diplomatic stance was in effect what strategic planners would call a program for "cover and deception." In early September, Soviet Ambassador Anatoly Dobrynin on separate occasions told both Robert Kennedy and Theodore Sorensen, the President's special assistant, that the equipment they were sending to Cuba was "defensive in nature and did not represent any threat to the security of the United States." On September 11, 1962, in a public, official statement, the Soviets said that there was "no need for the Soviet Union to shift its weapons for the repulsion of aggression, for a retaliatory blow, to any other country, for instance Cuba. Our nuclear weapons are so powerful in their explosive force and the Soviet Union has so powerful rockets to carry these nuclear warheads, that there is no need to search for sites for them beyond the boundaries of the Soviet Union."

Georgi Bolshakov, a public information official in the Soviet Embassy in Washington, who had arranged for Aleksei Adzhubei, Khrushchev's son-in-law, to interview President Kennedy, was another instrument of deception. In Moscow in early October, Khrushchev told Bolshakov to tell the Americans that the arms the Soviets were sending to Cuba were "intended" only for defensive purposes. Mikoyan, Deputy Premier of the Soviet Union, was also present; and he went further still, making a special point that President Kennedy himself should understand that the Soviets were sending only antiaircraft missiles to Cuba, which could not reach American targets. To be sure he had it straight, Bolshakov took the conversation down in his notebook and diligently passed the word when he got back to Washington.

On October 13, Chester Bowles had a long conversation with Soviet Ambassador Dobrynin and pressed him very hard on the question of whether the Soviets intended to put "offensive weapons" in Cuba, and the Ambassador had convincingly and repeatedly denied any such intention.

A few days later, on October 16, Khrushchev repeated all this to the American Ambassador in Moscow, Foy D. Kohler. On September 25, Castro had announced an agreement with the Soviet Union to construct a fishing port in Cuba, and this had raised a storm of public suspicion in the United States that what was really being built was a submarine or naval base. Khrushchev was vacationing in the Crimea at the time, but shortly after he returned—on October 16—he told Kohler that he was furious at Castro for this premature announcement; that it would not have occurred if he had not been away; and that the last thing in the world that he, Khrushchev, wanted to do was to embarrass the President on the eve of elections. Soviet "purposes" in Cuba, he said, were wholly defensive.

Even as late as October 18, the Soviet foreign minister, Andrei Gromyko, personally assured President Kennedy that Soviet aid to Cuba "pursued solely the purpose of contributing to the defense capabilities of Cuba," that "training by Soviet specialists of Cuban nationals in handling defensive armaments was by no means offensive," and that "if it were otherwise, the Soviet government would never become involved in such assistance." Hearing this, Kennedy sent for and read to Gromyko the public statements he had made in September warning the Soviets against putting missiles into Cuba.

Analyzing this conversation the next day and comparing it with the earlier conversations, analysts in the State Department's Bureau of Intelligence and Research noticed something peculiar. On September 28, Navy planes watching Soviet ships at sea on their way to Cuba had taken pictures of some crates on the deck of one of the ships, crates of a peculiar size and shape that were similar to those the Soviets had used to ship IL 28 light bombers to Egypt and Indonesia. Unaccountably, the pictures had come to Washington through roundabout channels rather than direct and were not distributed until October 9. The reason that Bowles had pressed Dobrynin so hard on "offensive weapons" was that he had just seen the pictures of these crates and had uppermost in his mind the strong possibility that they contained IL 28s. What struck us in the bureau was that although Dobrynin seems to have had no knowledge of the decision to put missiles into Cuba, the people reading his cables in Moscow clearly did. Dobrynin would have reported his conversation with Bowles in full detail, and Moscow must have interpreted Bowles' comments as referring to missiles. Thus when he had his conversation with Kohler on October 16, Khrushchev must have assumed that the United States knew about the presence of the missiles—or at least considered that possibility. And even if Gromyko himself had not read the report of the Bowles conversation and reached the same conclusion before his talk with the President on October 18, the officials in Moscow who cleared his instructions must also have assumed that the United States knew about the missiles or at least must have provided for the possibility. And certainly any remaining doubts would have been dispelled when the President sent for and read to Gromyko his September warning, which specifically referred to missiles.

THE SOURCES OF INTELLIGENCE

The probability that the Soviets thought we knew about the missiles when Khrushchev talked to Kohler and Gromyko had his conversation with the President was vital to the decisions about how to handle the crisis, and I passed all this along to the White House. But all this came later. The Soviets did, in fact, draw a veil of secrecy and deception around their build-up of arms in Cuba—being just as secretive about the conventional arms as about the missiles. To pierce this veil of secrecy and deception, the United States had to rely on four major sources of intelligence. One was routine shipping intelligence. As a matter of course the United States knew what ships went to Cuba, whether from Communist or "free-world" ports. Second, there was a steady flow of reports from refugees. Third, there were the reports of actual intelligence agents within Cuba. And, finally, there were the photographs supplied by U-2 overflights.

Shipping intelligence did not reveal the contents of the ships. Refugee reports attempted to, but they varied widely in reliability—ranging from sober and accurate observations to the wildest kind of rumor. They also trailed events by days or even weeks, depending on how long it took a particular refugee to get out of Cuba to a place where he could be questioned. Another problem with refugee reports was simply one of mass. As the true colors of the Castro regime began to show, the hundreds of refugees became thousands. The CIA increased the staff of its interrogation center at Opa Locka, Florida, and of the research offices in Washington devoted to collating, comparing and studying the interrogation results. But the stream of refugees continued and processing frequently fell behind.

Agents' reports were of uniformly higher quality than the refugee reports, but they too suffered from a time lag. It took time for a subagent who had observed the loading of a ship or the movement of a convoy to make his way to the master agent, and it took still more time for the master agent to perform his part of the task. The result was usually a lag of ten days to two weeks between the time something was seen in Cuba and the time the report arrived in Washington.

By far the swiftest and most accurate intelligence came from the U-2 photography. As the world now knows, the whole system—the camera, the film, and the aircraft iself—was a marvel of design and engineering. At heights well over seventy thousand feet—almost fourteen miles—pictures were taken with a resolution of only two inches on a side, which means that the painted lines of a parking lot could be distinguished, for example, or the muzzle of a new kind of cannon peeping out of the wing of an airplane. In the hands of skilled photographic interpreters these pictures could produce an unbelievable amount of extremely accurate information.

These, then, were the sources of intelligence. But there was also the problem that Roberta Wohlstetter, in her analysis of the intelligence problem preceding the Pearl Harbor attack, called the "noise level"—the hubbub of rumors and false alarms.[2] To intelligence officers, of course, there is nothing new in the problem of having to separate intelligible bits of sound from a roar of background noise. Roberta Wohlstetter's story of Pearl Harbor "includes the alarm that fails to work, but also the alarm that has gone off so often it has been disconnected"—the command at Pearl Harbor had been alerted on June 17, 1940, on July 25, 1941, and again on October 16, 1941.

But the history of intelligence failures also includes the failure of believing false alarms. A notable example occurred in World War I. "On August 27," Barbara W. Tuchman writes in *The Guns of August,* "a seventeen-hour delay in the Liverpool-London railway service inspired the rumor that the trouble was due to the transport of Russian troops who were said to have landed in Scotland on their way to reinforce the Western Front." Fed by nothing more substantial than desperate hope, "the phantoms seen in Scotland took on body, gathering corroborative detail as the story spread." The reports were sometimes ridiculous, but in the end they turned out to be sufficiently plausible to sway German intelligence: "They stamped snow off their boots on station platforms—in August; a railway porter of Edinburgh was known who swept up the snow. 'Strange uniforms' were glimpsed in passing troop trains . . . Ten thousand were seen after midnight in London marching along the Embankment on their way to Victoria Station." For German intelligence one problem, as often happens, was that the reporters were frequently reliable and respected people. "An Oxford professor," Tuchman writes, "knew a colleague who had been summoned to interpret for them . . . A resident of Aberdeen, Sir Stuart Coats, wrote to his brother-in-law in America that 125,000 Cossacks had marched across his estate in Perthshire. An English army officer assured friends that 70,000 Russians had passed through England to the Western front in 'utmost secrecy.'"

The effect of these rumors on the Germans was almost as tangible as real Russian troops would have been. "Worry about a possible 70,000 Russians at their back was to be as real a factor at the Marne as the absence of the 70,000 men they had transferred to the Eastern Front."[3]

In the case of Cuba, refugee reports contained much accurate and useful information about the Soviet arms build-up, but the noise level was also unusually high. The normal spiraling of rumors was accelerated by a conflict of interest, for the interest of refugees from Cuba did not always coincide with the interest of the United States. The best if not the only hope of the Cuban refugees and especially of the refugee politicians was an American invasion. There was no need for anyone to manufacture reports, but only to believe and pass on the inevitable and completely spontaneous rumors voicing what all the refugees so desperately wanted to believe—that Castro and the Soviets were doing things that made an invasion necessary in the American interest and justifiable before the world.

There were, for example, persistent reports of thousands of uniformed Chinese Communists, none of which was ever confirmed. When the Congo crisis came into the headlines, some of the rumors from Cuba followed the lead: near Guantánamo, according to a number of reports, black African troops had been seen—with rings in their noses. And there were hundreds of reports of missiles in Cuba that were totally without substance.

For example, the file of reports devoted solely to missiles for the year *1959* is five inches thick—and in 1959 the Soviets had yet to send arms of any kind to Cuba. Yet some of these reports were full of persuasive detail: in this 1959 file there are twenty separate reports pinpointing a "missile installation" in the Ciénaga de Zapata area, including descriptions of concrete ramps typically associated with launching pads. Yet the area was in fact an empty swamp and remains so to this day.

But the stakes were too high for any rumor, no matter how fanciful, to be ignored. Every report containing anything specific that could be checked against photographs or other intelligence was in fact checked. And the U-2s were busy getting more.

THE SOVIET BUILD-UP

The sources of information available could not by their nature reveal what the Soviets planned to put in Cuba at some future date. But the sources did permit the United States Government to watch the build-up step by step as it proceeded.

The first arms were sent to Cuba in the summer of 1960. On November 18, 1960, the Eisenhower administration announced that at least twelve Soviet ships had delivered arms and ammunition to Cuba and that the total Soviet bloc military aid had so far amounted to about twenty-eight thousand tons. Shipments continued intermittently until early 1962, when there was a lull.

The shipments started again in late July 1962. During the third week in August, it was decided that we had enough information to merit giving the press a background briefing, and that, as Director of Intelligence of the State Department, I should be the one to give it.

The briefing was held on August 24 and catalogued what we knew of the arms build-up so far. It noted that the Soviets had resumed large-scale deliveries of arms to Cuba beginning late in July, after a lull since early 1962—that eight ships had arrived between July 26 and August 8 and that the total by August 24, the time I was speaking, may have reached twenty shiploads.

The cargoes, the briefing continued, included large quantities of transportation, electronic, and construction equipment, such as communication vans, radar vans, trucks, and mobile generator units. Although we did not yet know what was in the crates, we had some suspicions. "From what we have observed of this cargo," the transcript of the briefing reads, "it appears that much of it will go into the improvement of coastal and air defenses. It may include Surface-to-Air Missiles (SAMs), which the Soviets also supplied Iraq and Indonesia . . ."

The briefing noted the arrival of between three thousand and five thousand Soviet personnel, many of whom were clearly military technicians, although they did not appear to be in organized combat units but connected with installing the equipment we had seen coming in, and with training Cubans to operate it. None of the Soviets, for example, was in uniform. (None of the Soviet military personnel, in fact, was ever seen in uniform—their favorite dress was a sport shirt and a pair of slacks.)

Within ten days the crates had been opened, revealing surface-to-air missiles. On September 4, President Kennedy released a statement describing what we had seen—antiaircraft missiles similar to our Nike, the radar equipment to operate them, several motor torpedo boats with guided missiles having a range of fifteen miles, and 3500 Soviet military technicians. "There is no evidence," he went on to say, "of any organized combat force in Cuba from any Soviet bloc country; of military bases provided to Russia; of a violation of the 1934 treaty relating to Guantánamo; of the presence of offensive ground-to-ground missiles; or of other significant offensive capability either in Cuban hands or under Soviet direction and guidance. Were it to be otherwise, the gravest issues would arise."

On September 7, President Kennedy sent a request to Congress for standby authority to call up reserve troops; and on September 11, the Soviet Union in response stated that a United States attack on Cuba would mean nuclear war.

Then, on September 13, 1962, the President made a major public statement. Denying any intention to invade Cuba, he went on to issue a warning. "If at any time the Communist build-up in Cuba were to endanger or interfere with our security in any way," he said, "including our base at Guantánamo, our passage to the Panama Canal, our missile and space activities at Cape Canaveral, or the lives of American citizens in this country, or if Cuba should ever attempt to export its aggressive purposes by force or the threat of force against any nation on this hemisphere, or become an offensive military base of significant capacity for the Soviet Union, then this country will do whatever must be done to protect its own security and that of its allies."

In the meantime, the shuttle of Soviet cargo and passenger ships across the Atlantic continued. And so did American intelligence activities.

A U-2 had covered most of the island on August 29. Another was flown on September 5. The two flights gave an excellent mosaic of the western and central portions of the island, but only spotty coverage of the eastern portion. And what riveted attention, was a peculiar installation at the harbor town of Banes, on the northeastern coast. The installation was a ramp fitted with what seemed to be a robot airplane with swept-back, stubby wings. A second, special flight to look closer at this installation and to cover the rest of the eastern end of the island was delayed for several days by weather, but finally flew on September 17. With considerable relief, the intelligence community confirmed that the installation was a launching platform for a shore-to-ship, cruise-type missile having a range of thirty-five to forty miles.

The rest of the photographs of the missions of August 29, September 5, and September 17 showed surface-to-air missiles being erected around the perimeter of the island in the western and central portions; additional MIG fighters appearing at various airfields; additional vehicles and supplies for the Cuban ground forces; and several more of the patrol boats, armed with short-range missiles. But nothing more.

THE "SEPTEMBER ESTIMATE"

It was in this context that the United States Intelligence Board met on September 19 to consider the Soviet arms build-up in Cuba and to approve the "September estimate," which figured so prominently in the public debate following the crisis. The U-2 photographs revealed no activity except that described above. No agent reports had reached Washington of any activity except that already noted, and all refugee reports referring to specific locations had been checked against the available photography which showed either known activities, such as the installation of surface-to-air missiles, or no activity at all.

Addressing itself to the question of whether or not the Soviets would introduce offensive missiles into Cuba, the estimate concluded, in effect, that they would not. The reasoning behind this judgment was that the Soviets realized the Americans would be likely to discover the missiles and would probably react strongly—that, in other words, the likelihood of exposure was high and the probable consequences bad. When it came to nuclear matters, the reasoning went on, the Soviets were cautious. Never, for example, had they positioned strategic nuclear weapons outside the Soviet Union—even in Eastern Europe, where they would have been less provocative and much easier to defend than they would be in Cuba. Both air and sea communications between Cuba and the Soviet Union were long, hazardous, and peculiarly vulnerable to American interdiction. Castro was a self-elected member of the bloc—which runs counter to Soviet conceptions of themselves and their world—and the regime and Castro himself were unstable, hardly to be trusted either as the recipients of really dangerous weapons or as the hosts for weapons that remained under Soviet control. The estimate hedged, however, by noting that medium or intermediate range missiles in Cuba would significantly increase the Soviet capacity to strike at America's heartland and go far toward altering the strategic balance of power between East and West. It therefore urged the intelligence community to maintain a continuous alert.

After some discussion the Intelligence Board approved the estimate without dissent.

A month later it transpired that a day or two before the USIB meeting John McCone, the Director of Central Intelligence, had cabled from Europe, where he was on a wedding trip, to the CIA representatives working on the estimate to express doubts about its conclusions. We also learned that even earlier, in August, in speculating with the President about Soviet motives he had suggested that the purpose of the Surface-to-Air Missiles (SAMs) might be to hide the introduction of offensive missiles rather than to defend against possible invasions. McCone's reasoning was that the Soviets could not believe that antiaircraft missiles and the other equipment they were giving the Cubans would really stop the United States from invading Cuba if it wanted to, and that the Soviets must have more important motives—to shoot down our reconnaissance U-2s and to serve as a screen for the introduction of offensive missiles. The CIA estimators apparently argued in their return cable that the available facts also fitted a more conservative explanation: the Soviets had provided Surface-to-Air Missiles of the same type to both Iraq and Indonesia; and, given the Bay of Pigs affair of the year before, Castro's fear of invasion was certainly credible to the Soviets. The estimators pointed out, finally, that arms aid including antiaircraft missiles would at least guarantee that the U.S. could not pretend that exile groups were responsible for any future invasion but would have to take the public onus of doing the job itself. This was a persuasive argument, and McCone went along with it. No one knows how much doubt McCone really felt, for he often played the devil's advocate in arguing with his own estimators. In any case, whatever suspicions he had rested on deductive reasoning alone and he had no evidence, soft or hard, to support the notion that the Soviets intended to install missiles in Cuba. In the end, McCone decided against bringing his doubts to the attention of other members of the Intelligence Board or to the President, much less to insist on a change in the estimate, even though it was his legal right.

U-2 DIFFICULTIES

In the meantime, the intelligence-gathering effort was having difficulties. If the weather was right, a U-2 could cover the whole island of Cuba in a single flight. As a practical matter, however, there was usually some cloud cover, and for some time the routine had been to have two U-2 flights a month. As mentioned above, the first flight in September was on the fifth, going up one side of a line drawn down the middle of the island and down the other in the usual pattern designed to give a mosaic of the whole island in a single trip. As originally proposed, the second flight, which finally flew on September 17 over the eastern end of the island only, was to repeat this pattern. But the rapid deployment of the antiaircraft SAMs caused some second thoughts.

It was one of these same SAMs that the Soviets credited with shooting down the U-2 flown by Gary Powers over the Soviet Union on May 1, 1960. Many people in the Air Force and some in the CIA argued that a Soviet SAM could not shoot down a U-2 at full altitude—that Powers must have had engine trouble that brought him to a lower altitude within range. But there were solid doubts about this somewhat parochial thesis, and no one wanted to risk a man's life needlessly or to raise an international political storm that might restrict the flights in some way and thus limit our best source of intelligence.

Then, as if to underline both points, on September 9, 1962, a Chinese Nationalist U-2 was shot down over mainland China.

The next day the group that normally considered such matters, with the addition of the Secretary of State, met in McGeorge Bundy's office in the west basement of the White House. It was quickly agreed that the U-2 flights should continue, but it was also agreed that the usual flight pattern should be altered to minimize the risk of a shoot-down. The Secretary of State suggested, first, that rather than a single flight that would keep the U-2 over Cuba for a long period of time, there should be several flights that "dipped into" Cuban air space. In addition, he felt that these actual overflights should be obscured by a very large number of peripheral flights that looked into Cuba while remaining outside the three-mile limit. Everyone present thought the idea was an excellent solution to the problem, and it was this proposal that was adopted. A total of four actual overflights was authorized for the month.

For the remainder of September attention in the intelligence community continued to focus mainly on the eastern end of the island. As mentioned above, the special flight to look at Banes finally flew on September 17. It got a good look at the one installation at Banes, but clouds were still a problem over the rest of the eastern end of Cuba, and still another flight was scheduled. It was also delayed by the persisting cloud cover, but finally flew on September 26.[4]

Reports of "unusual activity" on the Isle of Pines and the old Bay of Pigs area caused a flurry in late September, and a U-2 was flown over both places on September 29. The activity was revealed as the installation of a surface-to-air missile and another of the short-range coastal defense missiles first identified at Banes. Following this, there was still some residual worry about the eastern end, and still another U-2 was sent there on October 5.

REFUGEES AND SECRET AGENTS

Throughout September the massive flow of refugee and agent reports had also continued. In the post-mortem of the crisis, with all the benefits of hindsight, four of these seem significant.

A subagent reported seeing on September 12 a middle-of-the-night truck convoy proceeding in a westerly direction from one of the secure port areas near Havana. Included in the convoy, the report continued, were trailers twenty meters (sixty feet) long whose contents were concealed by canvas stretched over what appeared to be a wooden framework. The

report was received in Washington on September 21 and distributed with
a CIA headquarters comment to the effect that what the subagent had
probably seen was a surface-to-air missile (which is thirty feet long).

A second report received in late September told of Castro's private
pilot boasting that Cuba had long-range missiles and no longer feared
the United States. The report was distributed without comment.

On October 3 and 4 two more reports were received in Washington—
one of "unusual activity probably connected with missiles" (type not
specified) in Pinar del Río, at the western end of Cuba, and a second
report, describing a second long-trailer convoy seen on September 17,
also heading west.

Suggestive though they now seem to be, these reports had neither
more nor less impact than similar reports received in the past. The intelligence community had been concerned about the possibility that the
Soviets might put missiles in Cuba from the beginning of the arms
build-up. But they were also worried about the possibility of a submarine
base there, installations that might interfere with our space work at Cape
Canaveral, and Cuban-based subversion. The intelligence community was
sensitive to all of these possibilities—and also to the possibility that the
Soviets might do something no one had even thought of. And so were the
policy-makers, as evidenced by President Kennedy's public warnings to
the Soviets of the consequences of the whole range of these possibilities.
Reports of this kind tended to increase everyone's sensitivity. In spite
of the CIA headquarters' comment downgrading the first report, for example, I had specifically called attention to the report in one of the
Secretary's large staff meetings. But such a vague allegation, suggestive
rather than conclusive, did not provide the basis for taking action against
Cuba, and as for sensitivity everyone's antennae were already quivering
and had been for weeks.

In late September, the specific worry had been about the portion of
the eastern end of the island still hidden under clouds. The first flight
in October, to repeat, was scheduled for and flew over the eastern and
not the western end of the island. Thin and tenuous as they were, these
reports triggered no special intelligence estimate. But they did focus
attention again on the western end of the island, where some kind of
activity, it now seemed clear, was going on, and it was to consider flights
over the western end of the island that a special meeting was held on
October 4. The agent reports described above were not mentioned at
the meeting, but McCone brought with him a map of Cuba showing
what areas had been covered by which flights and the CIA's estimate
as to which of the antiaircraft SAMs were most advanced in their construction. It showed a rhomboid-shaped area covering San Cristóbal
and Guanajay, which had not been covered since September 5 and in
which the SAMs were also most advanced. No mention was made at the

October 4 meeting of the possibility of missiles in the area, but it was perfectly obvious that if missiles had been deployed in Cuba they would have to be in this region.[5] The discussion focused on how soon the antiaircraft SAMs would be operational and the risk to the U-2 pilot and our continued use of the U-2 as an intelligence source. The dilemma between the need to continue intelligence surveillance of the island and the danger to the U-2 had led me several days earlier, late in September, to suggest using an alternative means for acquiring the information, but the idea was quickly discarded when we discovered it would mean a delay. The increasing danger of losing a U-2 also prompted a dispute between the Pentagon and CIA. On the grounds that it would be better to have the pilot a regular officer in uniform if a U-2 were shot down, McNamara succeeded in having the Air Force take over in spite of CIA's hotly argued protest.

At the October 4 meeting, it was decided to instruct those charged with U-2 operations to prepare for the group's further consideration a flight plan that would slice across the western end of the island coming near enough to the most advanced SAM site to photograph it effectively but not near enough to be shot down. On October 9, the special group met again and approved the plan that had been prepared.

THE POLITICAL PROBLEM

The rest of official Washington in the meantime was faced with a political problem—which they dealt with as best they could, continuing to make public the information on the build-up as it was confirmed. On October 3, the Under Secretary of State, George W. Ball, testified before a congressional committee in an open hearing on trade with Cuba. His statement, which was prepared from the daily CIA and Defense Intelligence Agency summaries and which I personally cleared with John McCone on October 2, gave the situation as we then knew it. Eighty-five shiploads had arrived; fifteen antiaircraft SAM sites had been established and a total of twenty-five was predicted. Four coastal defense missile sites; sixty older type MIGs and at least one advanced type MIG 21; sixteen missile patrol boats; and about 4500 Soviet technicians were now in Cuba.

When the committee chairman, Representative Kitchin, asked about the reliability of the intelligence and whether Cuba was becoming an offensive base, Ball replied that our information, we believed, was "quite complete." "Our intelligence," he went on to say, "is very good and very hard. All the indications are that this is equipment which is basically of a defensive capability, and that it does not offer any offensive capabilities to Cuba as against the United States or the other nations of the hemisphere."[6]

SENATOR KEATING'S INTERVENTION

Senator Kenneth B. Keating and Senator Barry Goldwater, both Republicans, had tried for some time to make whatever political hay they could out of the Cuba situation. Senator Keating was especially active. After the news stories based on my background briefing of the press on August 24, for example, Keating made a speech repeating the basic information with two differences—he called the Soviet personnel in Cuba "troops" rather than "technicians" and he said they were wearing uniforms. Since the Soviets had been seen only in sports clothes, the State Department denied that there was any information that the Soviet personnel were "troops" rather than technicians or that they were wearing uniforms (which gave Keating the opportunity after the crisis to imply that everything he had said had been denied).[7] Keating made several such speeches on the floor between August 31 and October 1, none of which ever went any further than the official State Department press backgrounders, except for such points as disagreement over whether the Soviets wore uniforms or whether they should correctly be called troops or technicians, and for calls for "action"—although he never specified just what that action was to be.

On October 9, just a few days after George Ball's testimony, Keating again took to the floor and again confined himself largely to what Ball had already made public.

Then, only twenty-four hours later, on October 10, Keating—in something of a rush—made another speech on Cuba. And this time he did say something different from what was in the backgrounders: he charged that six Intermediate Range Ballistic Missile bases were being constructed in Cuba.

After the crisis was over, Keating apparently began to fear that he was vulnerable to charges that he had either been peddling refugee rumors or that he had failed to give the government information vital to national security. For he began to insist, first, that the information he had was not mere refugee rumor and, second, that it was already known to the government—although suggesting at the same time that the information might not have been passed up to the highest levels of the government. In an interview on the NBC program *Monitor,* on Sunday November 4, he said, ". . . on the tenth day of October, I said that there were six intermediate missile sites under construction in Cuba . . . That was denied . . . And I want to say right here and now, that at every time when I spoke on this subject I either had it from official sources or I had it from others and confirmed by official sources before I ever said a word."

The senator elaborated on the theme in an interview with *U. S. News and World Report* published November 19, 1962:

Q. Senator, what were the sources of your information about Cuba?
A. The sources were either (a) sources in the U.S. government or (b) other sources—less than 5 per cent of which were Cuban refugees —all of which were verified through official sources of the U.S. government before I made any statement . . .
Q. What about the intermediate range missiles—those with a range of more than 2000 miles?
A. The intermediate missile launching sites came to my attention in early October. This information was verified officially on October 9, and I spoke on October 10.

With which official Senator Keating "verified" this information remained a mystery. The senator refused to name his source, other than to say it was an "American" who had "access to reliable information." "It was inconceivable to me that high officials would be in the dark over such a largescale and important development," Keating wrote much later, in 1964. "Yet it is clear now that they were."[8] But in spite of the implication that someone lower down in government was concealing security information from his superiors in the government, Senator Keating still did not name his informant.

Since no one in the intelligence community knew that there were missiles in Cuba until after October 14, it is difficult to see how the senator could have "verified" the information with anyone. In actuality, as soon as Senator Keating's charges began to come over the tickers on October 10, Thomas L. Hughes, the Deputy Director of Intelligence and Research in the Department of State, personally telephoned the chief of every intelligence agency in Washington or one of his deputies to ask if he had any reports to which Senator Keating might be referring. The answers were uniformly negative, and the State Department so informed the press.

If the first mystery is where Keating got his information, the second is just what information he had. He said there were six intermediate range missile sites in Cuba, but he did not say where they were located—which would have been most vital information. One of the most puzzling aspects of Keating's claim, in fact, is the use of this exact number—*six* sites, not "a number of sites" or "a site" but six. In fact, the Soviets intended to build *four* intermediate range sites and six *medium* range sites, but we now know that at the time Keating was speaking construction was not far enough along on several of the sites for an expert to have recognized them as missile sites, much less either a refugee or an ordinary secret agent. But the implication of an exact number, such as six, is that there was behind the information an intelligence research organization which received and compared different reports, checked one against the other, and reached a conclusion on the total of separate sites. Either that or someone wanted to lend authenticity to a deliberate plant of false information by making it appear that the story came from such an organization.

It might be argued that Keating got some refugee reports before official Washington did and served as his own intelligence research organization. But there were no reports either that came to the intelligence community later that reported "six intermediate-range missile sites" or that were available at the time that could have been totaled up to six sites. There seem to be, in fact, only two refugee reports of any significance that Keating might have gotten before official Washington did, but neither of these reports corresponds to Keating's allegations. One was a very suggestive refugee report accurately describing construction of what became the buildings the Soviets intended to use for nuclear storage at Remedios—the refugee had seen the construction work in mid-September and reported it to CIA officials at Opa Locka on September 20 but unaccountably the report was not forwarded to Washington until October 26, twelve days after the U-2 had discovered the missiles. A second report, also describing the Remedios site as of mid-September, was issued by an exile Cuban trade union group on October 18. This was actually four days after the missiles were discovered by the U-2, but the Cuban group might have had the information sooner even though they did not give it to the United States Government. Even so, both of these reports describe one site, not six.

One possible explanation is that Senator Keating let himself be rushed into peddling what were either rumors or a deliberate plant put out by Cuban exiles whose interest was to push the United States into an invasion. The other is that someone in the top levels of Castro's government was in disagreement with what Castro was doing and was trying to warn the United States. This may also be the explanation for a peculiarly elliptical statement by President Osvaldo Dorticós of Cuba in an address before the UN General Assembly. On October 8, 1962, Dorticós said, ". . . we have sufficient means with which to defend ourselves; we have indeed our unavoidable weapons, the weapons which we would have preferred not to acquire and which we do not wish to employ." For the Spanish word *inevitable,* which Dorticós used, may also be translated as "fatal" as well as "unavoidable." If this is the explanation, the choice of Senator Keating as the channel seems peculiar, although possible. But even so the mystery would still remain, not only why Keating refused even after the crisis to reveal his source, but also why he kept insisting that he had "confirmed" the information with sources inside the United States Government.

In any case responsible officials of the government had no information—

from intelligence or Senator Keating—that permitted them to conclude that the Soviets had put missiles in Cuba or were going to.

Thus it was that Presidential Assistant McGeorge Bundy appearing on ABC's *Issues and Answers* on Sunday, October 14, denied that the Soviets had any offensive weapons in Cuba just as a U-2 was taking the first pictures of them. Edward P. Morgan, the radio commentator, asked Bundy about the "interpretation of the military installations in Cuba which the administration emphasizes are defensive in nature and not offensive. Isn't it possible that these could be converted into offensive weapons virtually overnight?"

"Well," said Bundy, "I don't myself think that there is any present— I *know* there is no present evidence, and I think there is no present likelihood that the Cubans and the Cuban government and the Soviet government would in combination attempt to install a major offensive capability. It is true that the MIG fighters which have been put in Cuba for more than a year now, and any possible additions in the form of aircraft, might have a certain marginal capability for moving against the United States. But I think we have to bear in mind the relative magnitudes. The United States is not going to be placed in any position of major danger to its own security by Cuba, and we are not going to permit that situation to develop. . . . So far, everything that has been delivered in Cuba falls within the categories of aid which the Soviet Union has provided, for example, to neutral states like Egypt or Indonesia, and I should not be surprised to see additional military assistance of that sort."[9]

And while the argument raged on, the ubiquitous U-2 was about to lift the curtain. The flight approved at the special meeting of October 9 was readied on the tenth. It stood by, waiting for good weather on the eleventh, the twelfth, and the thirteenth. On the fourteenth, the flight was made as planned and without incident. Routinely, the package of films was flown to the processing laboratories Sunday night. Routinely, the processed film was flown to the photo-interpretation center Monday morning. Routinely, the photo interpreters began going over the pictures, frame by frame. Then, suddenly, routine stopped. At San Cristóbal, in western Cuba, the photographs clearly showed the erector-launchers, missile-carrying trailers, fueling trucks, and radar vans of a battalion of Soviet medium-range ballistic missiles.

NOTES

[1] This analysis of Soviet motivations owes much to the work, during and after the crisis, of Helmut Sonnenfeldt and Joseph W. Neubert, Soviet specialists of the Department of State.

2 Roberta Wohlstetter, *Pearl Harbor, Warning and Decision,* 1962.

3 Barbara W. Tuchman, *The Guns of August,* 1962, pp. 388–90.

4 In the aftermath of the Cuban crisis, some critics noted a discrepancy in delays attributed to cloud cover and the actual weather conditions over Cuba during the period. But it was not *actual* weather that determined whether a flight should or should not go, but the *predicted* weather. If the predicted weather was for less than 50 per cent clouds, the flight would go. If the predicted weather was for more than 50 per cent, the flight was usually delayed.

5 Colonel John Ralph Wright, Jr., of the Defense Intelligence Agency, was later given credit for first suggesting this area as a possible missile site.

6 *Hearings,* before the Select Committee on Export Control, H.R. 87th Congress, 2nd Session, Pursuant to House Resolution 403, Part 3, pp. 810–11.

7 The fact that there were four regimental combat teams of Soviet troops in Cuba was not discovered until low-level reconnaissance permitted their identification, and low-level reconnaissance was not authorized until after the crisis had become public. Even in President Kennedy's October 22 speech, he referred to "Soviet technicians" rather than "troops."

8 Senator Kenneth Keating, "My Advance View of the Cuban Crisis," *Look,* November 3, 1964.

9 In this remark and the one above about "any possible additions in the form of aircraft," Bundy seems to have had in mind the possibility—at the time he was speaking still unconfirmed—that IL 28 light bombers might be among the latest deliveries. Bundy had seen the same pictures of peculiarly shaped crates that Bowles had and read the same intelligence brief recalling the shipment of IL 28s to Egypt and Indonesia only a few days before this broadcast. It was not until the same October 14 flight that discovered the missiles that the contents of the crates were observed.

CHAPTER 14

The Intelligence Post-Mortem: Who Erred?

FROM the Soviet point of view, what had gone wrong? The first and ultimately the most serious error the Soviets made was in their estimate of the probable American response.[1] American attitudes toward Latin America, particularly Cuba, derive from an intimate history, which the Soviets seem not to have fully appreciated. Then, too, Americans came to nationhood behind the protective moat of two oceans, and the first major intrusion of foreign military power into this hemisphere was to have a shock power that the Soviets, growing up on the European Continent, could not easily understand. It may also be that American attitudes were so deeply held that the Americans themselves failed to recognize the need to articulate and explain them and thus from 1959 to 1962 sent out inadequate or even false signals that contributed to Soviet misunderstanding. And—clearly—Communist ideology distorts the Soviet view of the world and handicaps them in understanding others' attitudes and motivations, including American. In any event, of the whole range of possible American responses to their putting missiles in Cuba, the Soviets apparently thought that only two were likely: (1) that the United States would protest loudly, appeal to the United Nations, but ultimately acquiesce even though its strategic advantage had been sharply reduced; or (2) the United States would first threaten, but then sit down to negotiate—about U.S. missiles in Turkey as a starter and then, if the balance of forces was favorable to the Soviets, perhaps even about Berlin. This is not to say that the Soviets thought the Cuba venture was without risk. But it does indicate that they thought of it as an easily manageable risk. As it turned out, the risk was manageable; the error was thinking that it would be easy.

It could be argued, of course, that a second Soviet mistake was in getting caught—or at least in getting caught before their missile force was operational. For even if the United States response had been the same if the missiles had been discovered only after they were operational (as I personally believe both that it would and should have been), the Soviet bargaining position would have been much better with their missiles fully in place and ready to fire.

One possible explanation is that something went wrong. If one assumes that the antiaircraft SAMs were intended to screen the installation of the offensive missiles, then they should have been in place and operational— and if necessary used to shoot down U.S. planes—before the first of the long-range missiles or missile-associated equipment arrived. In fact, however, the SAMs and their associated radar nets did not become operational as a system until about October 27, when the U-2 was shot down, or at most a day or two earlier. We know that there were some technical difficulties—drainage problems apparently made it necessary to relocate at least some of the SAMs. But to screen the installation of the missiles, the SAMs would have to have been operational at the latest by October 1, as we shall see, and possibly as much as two weeks earlier, and it seems doubtful that technical difficulties could have caused a whole month's delay.

The Soviets relied on speed rather than camouflage when the missiles arrived at the sites, and the best explanation may be that they intended to substitute speed for screening by the SAMs too. Using the SAMs as a screen would have meant shooting down U.S. reconnaissance flights and thus heating up Soviet-American relations before the Soviets were ready for a confrontation. Recognizing this, the Soviets may have intended to use the SAMs not to screen the installation of the missiles but to remove any temptation the Americans might feel to try to take them out by selective air strikes if a confrontation actually came about. Our frequent background briefing of the press, and the accurate accounts in our newspapers day by day as the equipment went into Cuba would certainly have left them in no doubt that we were conducting reconnaissance, just as somewhat later, Bowles' hammering on "offensive weapons" in his conversation with Dobrynin and the President's pointedly reading Gromyko his earlier statements about missiles suggested that we had found out. What is possible is that the Soviets did not realize how good our reconnaissance was, or how frequent. If so, the Soviets may well have concluded that they didn't really need to make the effort to get the SAMs ready or, more importantly that they really didn't need to run the risk of shooting down U.S. reconnaissance planes prematurely, which using the SAMs as a screen implied. After all, if the combination of secrecy first and then speed did not work, the Americans were not expected to react violently anyway.

UNITED STATES INTELLIGENCE

What about the American intelligence effort? Was it a success or a failure? Could the missiles have been discovered any earlier than they were? The August 29 and September 5 flights, to repeat, showed nothing at all at San Cristóbal, Remedios, or Sagua la Grande, and only some unidentifiable scratchings of the earth at Guanajay. But the October 14 flight and others in the days immediately following October 14 showed some sites recognizable as ballistic missile installations in all four areas.

Survey work for the MRBM and IRBM sites must have been done in July or August. Construction work was apparently started on the Guanajay IRBM site in early September; on the San Cristóbal and Remedios sites work started sometime between September 15 and September 20; and on the Sagua la Grande site sometime between September 25 and September 30.

As to missiles and missile-related equipment, we now believe that the first missile shipment probably arrived in Cuba on September 8. The equipment was then moved out to the sites by night convoys—probably between September 9 and September 14, since the agent's sighting of the convoy was on September 12. And we believe that the second shipment probably arrived on September 15, again with the convoys moving out over the next few days.

From the time the decision was made in June until September 8, classic methods of intelligence—i.e., old-fashioned espionage—might have provided information of the Soviet intention to put missiles in Cuba if an agent had penetrated the inner circle of the Kremlin or Castro's immediate entourage. In the second stage—from September 8, when the missiles arrived at the ports, until the time they were installed at the sites— classic spying might have even revealed the actual presence of the missiles. An agent did in fact see the convoys and reported unusually long trailers, as we have seen. But he was not able to peek under the canvas concealing the missiles, which theoretically could have been done by an agent among the Soviet troops that unloaded the equipment and drove the convoys or among those few Cuban soldiers who were used as guides, guards, or liaison officers.

But notice, first, that the classic methods of espionage are extraordinarily difficult, time-consuming, and risky. Not obtaining information by classic means should not necessarily be counted a failure, while getting it would have been a lucky break. And notice, secondly, that to take the action the United States did in fact take and to mobilize public opinion in the United States and among our allies to support that action requires "harder" information than agent reports. It was only in the third stage—after missiles and supporting equipment had actually been installed at the launching sites—that the necessary "hard" information could be acquired. The "hardest" information of all were pictures, for example, and it was only in this third stage that the installations would be recognizable in aerial photography.

The United States, in other words, could not have reasonably expected to get the kind of information it needed until this third stage, when the missiles and related equipment began to appear at the sites. But when did this stage begin?

In the period following October 14, U-2s flew several times a day, and intelligence was able to watch the progress of construction on several of the sites almost hour by hour. The "before and after" pictures we were able to take of some of the sites of the thousand-mile MRBMs that were not started until after October 14 make it possible to construct an extremely accurate timetable. The MRBMs were a mobile, "field-type" missile. Designed for use by ground forces in combat, they are very similar to heavy artillery battalions in the way they are transported and put into position. They require no fixed installation, no concrete ramps, control bunkers, or launching pads. All they need is a dirt approach road and a flat piece of ground big enough to back together two vehicles—a missile erector to lift the missile to an upright position and a missile trailer to bring the missile to where it is to be erected. As Secretary McNamara testified, these highly mobile, thousand-mile *medium*-range missiles could be "deactivated, moved, reactivated on a new site, and ready for operations within a period of about six days." From the time the MRBMs arrived at a new location, in other words, they could in a pinch be put into operation within seventy-two hours. Working backward from this, CIA is reported to have concluded—and so testified before the Preparedness Subcommittee of the Senate's Armed Services Committee, chaired by Senator Stennis—that the earliest an MRBM site for launching the thousand-mile missile could have been identified from the air was October 8.

The two-thousand-mile IRBMs were different; they did require permanent construction. It was the four-slash "signature" of excavations for concrete revetments and associated equipment that revealed that the Soviets intended to put the two-thousand-mile *intermediate*-range missiles into Cuba, for so far as we know, no IRBM missiles ever arrived in Cuba—the missiles we actually saw at the sites inside Cuba and on the ships going out were MRBMs. In fact, the two-thousand-mile IRBM sites, which were not scheduled for completion until mid-November, never did reach a stage where they were ready to receive the missiles themselves. As I say, what permitted us to recognize the IRBM sites were the characteristic four slashes on the ground, the concrete bunkers going up, the concrete flash deflectors, the storage sites being constructed that were typical of those used for nuclear warheads, and other, associated equipment.

The truth of the matter is that no one really knows just when this construction could have first been recognized as an IRBM site. None of the missile sites was recognizable as such on the August 29 and September 5 U-2 flights; some were recognizable on the October 14 flight. The refugee whose report did not arrive in Washington until October 26 saw construction in mid-September that later, with the benefit of hindsight, seems suggestive. But whether the construction he saw would have been recognizable from the air as a missile site in mid-September is questionable.

It could reasonably be argued that the U-2 flight of October 14 found the missiles at just about the earliest possible date, especially considering the fact that the plane was standing by to fly on the eleventh, twelfth, and thirteenth and was delayed because of unfavorable weather predictions. On the other hand, it could also be argued that if the intelligence community had gotten suspicious of the western end of the island in late September and dispatched a U-2 to the right spot on say, October 2 or 3, it might have come back with photographic proof.

The question is whether it is reasonable to conclude that the intelligence community should have had its suspicions aroused about the western end of the island sooner than it did. There was no hint of location in the braggings of Castro's pilot, and therefore nothing to check. But even though it is understandable that intelligence was skeptical of a single man's estimate of the length of a moving trailer observed at night under difficult and probably nerve-racking circumstances, when viewed against the background noise and mass of similar reports that had been proved false, it is not unreasonable to say that the *first* report of the convoy *heading west* with exceptionally long trailers received in Washington on September 21 should have aroused more suspicion than it did. (The second report arrived in Washington only the day before the October 4 meeting that decided to send the U-2s to cover the western end of the island as soon as a reasonably safe flight plan could be developed.) I, for one, was even more willing to subscribe to this criticism when I later discovered that it was skepticism and skepticism alone that had prompted the CIA headquarters comment that what the agent had seen was probably a thirty-foot SAM antiaircraft missile. For I had assumed that the comment was put in for technical reasons—because, for example, the truck was not big enough to pull that kind of trailer, or some such.

Something else that was overlooked at the time, however, seems even more suggestive when one is armed with the benefit of hindsight. In going back over the reports, it was discovered that two of the Soviet cargo ships diverted from their normal tasks to carry arms to Cuba—the *Omsk* and the *Poltava*—had exceptionally large hatches. Looking back, the intelligence experts concluded that it was these large-hatch ships that had brought in the sixty-foot medium-range missiles in such secrecy. For what was significant was not only that they had large hatches but the fact that the intelligence reports also routinely noted that they were riding high in the water—indicating that they were carrying "space-consuming" cargo of low weight and high volume. But neither the fact that these ships had exceptionally large hatches nor that they were carrying space-consuming cargo was brought to the attention of either the policy-makers or the top levels of the intelligence agencies until after the missiles had been discovered in Cuba.

It is difficult to understand why the professional intelligence technicians down the line failed to see enough significance in these facts to bring them to the attention of the top levels. Of course, there was nothing new or startling about the ships themselves. One, the *Omsk,* had been built in Japan and both had been specially designed for the Soviet lumbering industry, where extra-large hatches are necessary and normal. Also, it was known that the Soviets had had some trouble finding the ships they needed to send their military aid to Cuba and the intelligence specialists on shipping presumably thought it understandable that lumbering ships could be more easily spared than some other kinds. Roberta Wohlstetter, pursuing her interest in the intelligence problem which she started with her analysis of the attack on Pearl Harbor, sees this failure to notice the possible significance of the large-hatch ships as an attempt to "save" a theory—that the Soviets would not put missiles into Cuba—by explaining away disturbing or unusual observations.[2] But the point here is just the opposite: the shipping intelligence specialists did not see the facts that the ships had large hatches and that they were riding high in the water as unusual or disturbing enough even to call attention to them, much less explain them away. The explanations came much later, when the discovery of the missiles caused a formal post-mortem to try to reconstruct what had happened and when. In any case, it was not until the September 19 estimate that the intelligence community addressed itself to the question of whether the Soviets would put missiles into Cuba and the shipping specialists did not know what the "Sovietologists" thought the Soviets would do until after that September 19 estimate was published, almost two weeks later. The fact that the shipping specialists did not call these facts to the special attention of their intelligence superiors was clearly a failure. But it was a failure not of rationalization, it seems to me, but of imagination—a failure to probe and speculate, to ask perceptive questions of the data, rather than of explaining away the obvious.

It has also been suggested that policy somehow inhibited intelligence. But there is no evidence of any attempt by the policy-makers to suppress information or to hamper intelligence-gathering activities. No request from the intelligence community to fly a U-2 over Cuba was ever refused. And the policy-makers were equally alert to the possibility that the Soviets might go against the September estimate. To ensure against leaks if intelligence ever did come in on offensive weapons and thus permit time to devise a policy for dealing with the problem, for example, President Kennedy in September ordered special security arrangements, which included a special code word, *Psalm,* that ensured that all those who would need to know would get intelligence on offensive weapons, but that no one else would get it. Such extraordinary measures would hardly have been taken if the policy-makers were complacently confident that the Soviets would stop short of introducing missiles into Cuba.

Afterward there were only two attempts by insiders to allege that policy interfered with intelligence, and both petered out. In the immediate wake of the crisis everyone in the intelligence community was understandably nervous that an unfair case might be made against them by the Senate investigating committee chaired by Senator Stennis. Reflecting this nervousness, a very high-ranking intelligence official testifying before a congressional committee seemed at first to deny the authenticity of George Ball's public testimony on October 3 and to suggest that Ball's confident assurances about the lack of evidence of offensive weapons in Cuba did not represent the intelligence community's view. But I had made a memorandum for the record noting that John McCone, the Director of Intelligence, had personally cleared and approved of Ball's statement—and that memorandum, let us say, clarified the problem. The second incident was a study that the Director of CIA instituted immediately after the crisis to determine if the missiles would have been discovered sooner if the Secretary of State had not requested on September 10 that the next flight be broken up into four separate flights. For a while there was some uneasiness at the possibility of some real alley fighting developing. But it was not difficult to show, first, that any delay caused by making four flights instead of one was negligible; and, second, that there had never been a turndown of any flight that intelligence had asked to be approved, but that on the contrary both the White House and the State Department had actually pushed for more intelligence all along. In such circumstances, the study was conveniently forgotten, all the more easily as it became increasingly clear that the congressional investigating committee was not going to make any sweeping accusations that the CIA and the intelligence community had failed.

It has also been argued that the intelligence community would have been more sensitive to possible indications like the large-hatch ships, the braggings of Castro's pilot, the report of long-trailer convoys, and the other subtle indications that seem significant in hindsight if the September 19 estimate had reached a different conclusion. The argument against this charge is, first, that none of these reports was before the estimators when the September estimate was made. None of the four agent and refugee reports that seem significant in hindsight arrived in Washington until after the estimate had been completed, and the information about the large-hatch ships and the fact that they were riding high in the water was not put before the estimators at all. Second, the estimate did warn that the military advantages of a successful deployment of missiles to Cuba would be so great that the intelligence operators should be particularly alert. What is more, the estimate reached the conclusion it did, not only because putting missiles in Cuba would be inconsistent with past

Soviet behavior, but because it would not be in the Soviet interests to do so, given the high risk of being discovered and the high probability of a strong American response. After all, intelligence estimators must assume that the opposition is acting in its own best interest or their job is completely hopeless. And certainly in this respect—the consequences of putting missiles in Cuba for the Soviets' best interests—it was the American estimators who were right and the Soviet estimators who were wrong. In this sense, to be correct, the American analysts would have had to estimate that the Soviets would misestimate.

Most of the reports that seem so significant in hindsight—large-hatch ships, riding high in the water, the braggings of Castro's pilot, and so on —did not provide any information that could have been the basis for further action, either in terms of targeting a U-2 or in terms of taking policy action. All that these reports could do, no matter how seriously they were taken, would be to increase sensitivity in Washington to the possibility that the Soviets would put missiles in Cuba. But the people in Washington, as even the public statements of the time show, were already sensitive to the point of nervousness. President Kennedy made several public statements warning the Soviets. He instituted special security precautions concerning intelligence on offensive weapons. Questions were asked on the subject in every congressional hearing that had even the remotest connection with Cuba. And everyone in official Washington talked about the possibility constantly.

The factors influencing the decision at the October 4 meeting to fly again over western Cuba were: (1) the need to check on the advanced state of the antiaircraft SAMs there; (2) the fact that there was an inland area that had not been covered since September 5, a whole month; (3) the report of "unusual activity probably connected with missiles" in Pinar del Río; and (4) the two reports of long-trailer convoys heading west. The report of "unusual activity" was distributed the day before the meeting, on October 3, and the second report of a long-trailer convoy was distributed the very morning of the meeting, on October 4. So the only report containing information on which at least intelligence action could be based, was the first report of a long-trailer convoy ("heading west"), which arrived in Washington on September 21. And this, it seems to me, could fairly be called a failure of intelligence—that is, not only should CIA headquarters have refrained from adding the comment that the agent had probably seen a thirty-foot SAM trailer rather than a sixty-foot MRBM trailer without some concrete evidence, but the intelligence community should have given more emphasis to this report and turned their attention to the western end of the island some ten days to two weeks sooner than it did.

For even though everyone in Washington was sensitive to the possibility that the Soviets might put missiles in Cuba, the over-all judgment that they would probably not undoubtedly led the people concerned to be more cautious about taking risks with the U-2 than they might otherwise have been. All through late September and early October, there was a determination to move slowly and deliberately. What was worrying both the intelligence and the policy people in Washington was the advancing state of readiness of the antiaircraft SAMs and the fact that these SAMs were more advanced models than we had seen before. In May 1960, Gary Powers's U-2 was shot down over the Soviet Union in circumstances that suggested that SAMs were effective at the U-2's top altitude, but the evidence was not conclusive. On September 9, 1962, right in the midst of the Cuban problem, a Chinese Nationalist U-2 was shot down over Communist China. It then seemed perfectly obvious that if we were not exceptionally careful a U-2 might be shot down over Cuba. No one wanted to risk a pilot's life unnecessarily, and there was also another consideration. If a U-2 were shot down, there would be a political storm in the UN and all over the world of sizable proportions, as was so vividly demonstrated when Powers's U-2 was shot down and the summit conference of 1960 wrecked. But it was not the certain political storm itself that caused the worry, but the possibility that the fuss might work to deny us any further use of the U-2. For without the U-2, intelligence was blind.

The caution was entirely justified, but there might have been a greater sense of urgency if the over-all judgment had been that the Soviets probably would put missiles into Cuba rather than that they probably would not.

But even so, as a practical matter, the difference at most would probably have been no more than three weeks. The soonest that the construction could have been recognized as missile sites was probably some time after September 15, and the decision to look again at the western end of the island was actually made on October 4. Given the vagaries of the weather, it would have been a fantastic stroke of luck if convincing photographs could have been obtained before September 21—and convincing photographs were essential to obtain support for the kind of action that would be necessary.

Given the inherent difficulties of espionage and the special circumstances, the laboriousness and risk in recruiting agents, the time lag in communicating secretly with an agent once recruited, the risk of a U-2 being shot down and the possible restrictions this might impose on our best source of information, the frustrations of cloud cover, the elaborate security precautions taken by the Soviets, their efforts at deception—given all these difficulties, it is probably something to be proud of that the missiles were discovered as early as they were. In sum, Cuba in 1962, it seems to me, must be marked down as a victory for American intelligence—and a victory of a very high order.

If a criticism is to be made of the intelligence effort, it is that, even though American intelligence had won a victory, it had also been—in one sense at least—a little lazy.

As the scientific instruments of information-gathering have become so marvelous, the intelligence community, having the normal American love of technical gadgetry, had neglected the time-consuming, tedious, but still essential methods of classical espionage. Recruiting, training, and planting an agent may take years, and it may be still more years before he reports anything of any significance. It is so much easier to send a U-2 or use some other scientific gadget. But there are some matters on which we need information that a U-2 camera cannot pick up. And in the case of missiles in Cuba, a U-2 could have been dispatched sooner, guided more directly to suspected sites, and routed on a safer track if there had been in Cuba a better network of traditional agents.

But the most important fact in the whole intelligence story is that the missiles were discovered before they were operational—and long enough before to permit the United States Government to assess the situation, develop a policy, and launch on a course of action.

None of the two-thousand-mile IRBM sites would have been able to launch any missiles at all until mid-November. On October 14, when the missiles were first discovered, the Soviets in an emergency could have launched at most one or two missiles from no more than two or three of the thousand-mile MRBM sites. By October 28, when Khrushchev agreed to withdraw, they might have been able to fire an initial salvo of between twelve and eighteen MRBMs. But by that time the American Strategic Air Command, polaris submarines, and ICBM forces were on full alert, ready to go—and so was an invasion force.

In the end, the Soviets were caught, as then Senator Hubert H. Humphrey said, "with their rockets down and their missiles showing"—and caught in time.

NOTES

[1] It has been suggested that the Soviets underestimated the United States response because they thought that the democracies were "too liberal to fight," as the poet Robert Frost reported Khrushchev as saying, or that Khrushchev concluded at the Vienna meeting with Kennedy and from Kennedy's refusal to use American troops at the Bay of Pigs that he was dealing with an inexperienced man who could be blackmailed. But the evidence is in the other direction. As Schlesinger points out (*A Thousand Days*, p. 821), Frost was interpreting an anecdote Khrushchev had quoted from Gorki, and he distorted Khrushchev's meaning in the process. Further-

more, both the Bay of Pigs and the Vienna meeting had come a year earlier, and since then Kennedy had done a number of things that would have demonstrated his toughness to Khrushchev, including standing firm on Berlin and putting troops in Thailand. It seems more likely that the Soviet decision depended on more than one man's estimate of another, and that the cause of their failure to foresee the level of the American reaction runs much deeper.

2 Roberta Wohlstetter, "Cuba and Pearl Harbor: Hindsight and Foresight," *Foreign Affairs,* July 1965, p. 700.

CHAPTER 15

"By This Time Tomorrow—A Flaming Crisis"

IT WAS late Monday afternoon, October 15, when the photographic interpreters found the first evidence of missiles on a U-2 picture of the San Cristóbal area in western Cuba. John McCone, Director of CIA, had been called out of town in the middle of the afternoon that same day—his stepson had been killed in an accident in California—and it was Lieutenant General Marshall S. Carter and Ray S. Cline, both deputy directors of CIA, who were the first to be informed. They each picked up a telephone and began to alert the government.

Carter called Lieutenant General Joseph F. Carroll, Director of the Defense Intelligence Agency, who in turn called Roswell Gilpatric, Deputy Secretary of Defense (Secretary of Defense McNamara was host that night for the "Hickory Hill University," an intellectual discussion group sponsored by Attorney General Robert F. Kennedy, and was not told until about midnight). Carroll, with two intelligence experts, then went to see General Maxwell D. Taylor, newly appointed as Chairman of the Joint Chiefs of Staff, who was giving a dinner party at his home. There, in a back room, certain of the guests were briefed—Taylor, Gilpatric, and U. Alexis Johnson, Deputy Under Secretary of State for Political Affairs.

As Carter was alerting the Defense Department, Cline was calling me, as Director of Intelligence and Research at the State Department, on my White House phone. Cautioning my children to keep the ordinary phone clear, I started trying to reach the Secretary of State. He was hosting a dinner for Gerhard Schroeder, the German Foreign Minister, in one of the formal dining rooms on the top floor of the State Department, and getting him to the phone without arousing suspicion took some doing.

I finally reached the security officer accompanying the Secretary and he managed to pass him a note to call me at home—urgently. At the first opportunity, Rusk excused himself for a moment and slipped out to use the phone in the pantry.

I "doubled-talked" the news. "Do you personally think this is it?" Rusk asked. "There has been time for only a preliminary analysis,"

I replied, "but from what I can get over the phone there doesn't seem to be much doubt."

Rusk asked me to meet him in his office first thing the next morning, and I continued with my phoning. George W. Ball, the Under Secretary of State, and Edwin M. Martin, Assistant Secretary for Latin American Affairs, both had to be informed, and I also had to get our own experts in the Bureau of Intelligence and Research started to work.

Martin was at the National Press Club giving a speech, the main theme of which, ironically, was that the evidence was that the military build-up in Cuba was "basically defensive in character." I reached one of his aides on the phone who explained that Martin was still on the platform and asked whether what I wanted to talk to him about was urgent enough to interrupt. "For God's sake, no," I said. "But have him call me when he's finished—so long as it doesn't attract attention." Martin called from a phone booth—ostensibly to tell his wife that he was on the way home.

McGeorge Bundy was also at home when Ray S. Cline's call reached him. After making sure that all the necessary wheels were in motion, Bundy decided not to disturb the President that night—he was going to need all the rest he could get. "At that point," Bundy later explained, "the President could only have fretted; and it seemed best to give the staff a chance to get rolling and get the intelligence materials in order, for the central requirement at that time was not haste, but the development of an effective plan of action."

The next morning—just before nine—Bundy briefed the President in his bedroom. The President, still in bathrobe and slippers, instructed Bundy to arrange for a meeting at eleven forty-five that morning of what became known as the ExCom, the Executive Committee of the National Security Council.

The ExCom met in the Cabinet room, in the low-lying west wing of the White House, and decided immediately to put Cuba under virtually constant air surveillance. From that time on, there was hardly an hour of daylight that did not see a U-2 over some part of Cuba.

In the discussion that followed almost all the major issues that had to be faced in the succeeding days were touched upon.

What had motivated the Soviets in their decision to put missiles in Cuba? What was behind the decision, and what did they hope to accomplish? Were the missiles in Cuba designed as an umbrella for a Soviet seizure of Berlin? Was this a sober decision, or an impetuous act similar to Khrushchev's shoe pounding at the UN? Was it Khrushchev's decision? Or did it mean that Khrushchev and his policy of peaceful coexistence were being superseded by a military take-over of the Kremlin? If so, were the missiles in Cuba only a preliminary to an attack on the United States itself?

Another issue was what this sudden jump in the nuclear megatonnage the Soviets could deliver on the American heartland would portend for the balance of power in the world. Secretary McNamara initially and for two or three days thereafter felt that Soviet missiles in Cuba made no real difference. He argued that their ICBMs could already reach the United States and that the Soviets would undoubtedly continue to build ICBMs no matter what happened in Cuba. Thus he concluded that putting medium and intermediate range missiles in Cuba merely permitted the Soviets to begin to close the gap in 1962 rather than a few years later. "A missile is a missile," was McNamara's argument, "It makes no great difference whether you are killed by a missile fired from the Soviet Union or from Cuba." The clear implication of McNamara's position was that the United States should do nothing, but simply accept the presence of Soviet missiles in Cuba and sit tight.

But several of the others disagreed with the proposition that Soviet missiles in Cuba made no difference. Such a sudden shift in the strategic balance, they felt, would give the Soviets untold political opportunities even if they did not intend to use the missiles in a purely military sense. And the political consequences of a sudden and dramatic closing of the gap were fundamentally different from a gradual evening out over a period of years.

Paul Nitze, then Assistant Secretary of Defense for International Security Affairs, also disagreed with McNamara on purely military grounds. The manned bomber force of the United States Strategic Air Command was based largely in the southern part of the United States, and it would be very vulnerable. There would be fifteen minutes' warning time from missiles based in the Soviet Union, but only two or three from missiles based in Cuba.

A third issue was what the American objective should be. Should our purpose be limited to getting the offensive weapons out? Or should we set a larger goal—removing the Soviet presence entirely and eliminating Castro and his regime?

A final issue was how this objective was to be accomplished. Realistically, what were the alternative courses of action open to the United States, and how effective would each of them be?

There were four major kinds of action the United States might take, each with several variants.

One was simply to do nothing. It was toward this alternative that McNamara's initial assessment would lead. If the missiles in Cuba made no real difference to the strategic balance and the world political stability resting on it, there would be no sense in running the risk of getting them out.

A second alternative was political and diplomatic action—to protest to Khrushchev, to go to the United Nations, to enlist the support of the Organization of American States, and so on.

A third alternative was to take out the missiles in a quick military move, with or without advance warning. Selective air strikes could be used to destroy the missile installations; parachute troops could be used to seize them in a *coup de main;* or the United States could launch a full-scale invasion by air, sea, and land.

The fourth alternative was blockade. And this, too, had several gradations. A blockade could apply to offensive weapons only, or to all armaments, or to all strategic goods, including POL—the petroleum, oil, and lubricants on which the Cuban economy was so dependent. Or the blockade could be total, denying the Cubans food and even medicine.

Various combinations of the latter three basic alternatives were also possible—a partial blockade could be imposed, for example, that would gradually increase in scope, eventually to be followed by either an air strike or a full-scale invasion if the Soviets did not reverse their course.

DOMESTIC POLITICAL PRESSURES

There was one special but peculiarly significant set of pressures bearing on the policy choices before the group that was not discussed at all in the ExCom meeting—although its presence must certainly have been felt. For behind the policy choices loomed domestic politics and an appalling array of rival interests and competing factions—beginning with those who had all along wanted nothing more than an invasion of Cuba and damn the risk of war and the cost to other American objectives.

The fact of the matter was that President Kennedy and his administration were peculiarly vulnerable on Cuba. He had used it in his own campaign against Nixon to great effect, asking over and over why a Communist regime had been permitted to come to power just ninety miles off our coast. Then came the Bay of Pigs, and now the Soviets were turning Cuba into an offensive military base.

Senator Keating, Senator Goldwater, and others had attacked the administration's posture toward Cuba and the Soviet program of arms aid as a "do-nothing" policy. These political pressures—and the administration's response to them—had already foreclosed some of the policy alternatives. The administration had not been able to say publicly that it was flying a U-2 over Cuba and that it was therefore absolutely certain that its information on what arms the Cubans had been getting was completely accurate. Indeed, there was some risk of exposure in merely acting confidently about the accuracy of official information. Thus in trying to meet the opposition's charges and to reassure the public without actually saying why it was so confident, the administration fell into the semantic trap of trying to distinguish between "offensive" and "defensive" weapons. In addition, Keating, Goldwater, and the others had beaten the drums so loudly that Kennedy had been forced not only to deny that "offensive" weapons were in Cuba but to put himself on the public record that his administration would not tolerate their being put there. At the time he made the statements, the President knew from incontrovertible evidence that there were no long-range missiles then in Cuba and he had the assurances of specialists on the Soviet Union that the Kremlin leaders were not likely to put them there in any case. Thus at the time they were made, the statements seemed both a necessary political response to opposition charges and a useful warning to the Soviets to reinforce their natural caution. On the other hand, if the missiles were not important enough strategically to justify a confrontation with the Soviet Union, as McNamara initially thought, yet were "offensive," then the United States might not be in mortal danger but the administration most certainly was. It would be damned if it failed to take action, but it would be equally damned if it did take action. And the greatest illusion of all would be for the President to think that the Capitol Hill advocates of a more belligerent policy would support him in such a policy once the chips were actually down. No one could forget that Senator Robert A. Taft, leader of the opposition during the Korean War, had praised President Truman's decision to fight in Korea in the twenty-four hours after it was made, but within weeks had begun to call it "Truman's War."

But since no one shared McNamara's view that the missiles were not important strategically and even he came to change it, the more important issue was at the other end of the spectrum. Not only had the political give-and-take led the administration into the "offensive" versus "defensive" dichotomy, but in responding to the charges of a "do-nothing" policy administration spokesmen had come dangerously close to ruling out one major alternative by several times saying that a blockade of Cuba would be an "act of war" against the Soviet Union.

What President Kennedy also had to remember was that his opposition was not all outside the administration and the Executive Branch. Charles G. Dawes's aphorism, that the members of the Cabinet are a President's natural enemies, quoted earlier, is relevant. Applied to the members of the ExCom in these particular circumstances, Dawes's aphorism was an exaggeration; applied more widely in the government, it was not. There had already been some mild attempts to push a more belligerent point of view by leaking slightly distorted information. Before George Ball had begun his congressional testimony on October 3 about the then current status of Soviet arms in Cuba, for example, all the information in Ball's statement had already been leaked to the congressmen and embellished to give the shore-to-ship harbor defense missiles Ball described a longer range than the thirty-five to forty miles the intelligence experts assigned to them. "Information has come to my hand . . ." said the Chairman, Congressman Kitchin, "that Cuba has received in recent days some air-breathing type offensive missiles with a range, with a booster effort, of some 130 nautical miles. If that is true, I would certainly think that would be an offensive weapon." This particular incident was unimportant; but it was a harbinger of much worse that was very likely to come, and soon.

There was, of course, no viciousness in the motives behind these seemingly disloyal efforts within the administration and the Executive Branch to block the administration from adopting one policy or to force it to adopt another, but only a normal and expected manifestation of the politics of policy-making. In every department of the government there were men not only with the "sincere convictions on policy" the British committee that was mentioned earlier had called stronger than pecuniary interests, but with passionate ones. One of President Kennedy's major problems in the Cuban missile crisis—as with all presidents facing crisis—was to free himself sufficiently from these political pressures, outside and inside his administration, so that he could deal effectively with the Soviets and Cuba.

THE NEED FOR SECRECY

None of this was discussed at the first meeting of the ExCom on October 16, as I said, although much of it must have been felt. But before the meeting broke up, the President did make one more decision—that we must avoid giving the Soviets any opportunity to grab the political initiative. The risk that Soviet radar would spot a U-2 had to be taken, but there should be no public disclosure of the fact that we knew of the Soviet missiles in Cuba until a course of action had been decided upon and readied. If at all possible, the two announcements—that we had discovered Soviet missiles in Cuba and what the United States intended to do about it—should be made simultaneously. Security was therefore essential, and the President made it clear that he was determined that for once in the history of Washington there should be no leaks whatsoever.

The decision to couple disclosure with an announcement of the United States response was not so inconsequential as it sounded—it expressed the President's determination not to be dragged along in the wake of events, but to control them.

It was also not so easy to carry out. Leaks are hard to stop—mainly, as we have seen, because of their usefulness to "inside opposition" as an instrument to block one policy or further another. But leaks are also hard to stop because of the normal human desire to look important, to impress friends and the press, to make people understand that one is really in the inner circle, privy to all sorts of vital state secrets. And probably no state secret of the whole century had been so vital as this one. Thus the decision to couple disclosure with an announcement of the

American response imposed a very tight deadline on analysis, on decision, and on the preparations to implement the decision.

One other consequence of the decision to delay disclosure was that the United States also needed a program of cover and deception. Life in Washington had to look normal over the next few days; and, by and large, it did. Between ExCom meetings the President sandwiched routine activities. On the morning of October 16, he kept a date with astronaut Walter N. Schirra, Mrs. Schirra, and their two children and showed them his daughter Caroline's pony while the ExCom was assembling in the Cabinet room. On Wednesday, October 17, he flew to Connecticut to keep some campaign speaking engagements. On Thursday, he presented some awards; met on domestic issues with the Cabinet; received a foreign visitor, Eifaku Sato, former finance minister of Japan; and, finally, had a long session with the visiting Soviet foreign minister, Andrei A. Gromyko.

Although the Soviets may have designed this grotesque meeting to serve their own purposes of cover and deception, it may have worked out to serve the American. Gromyko began by warning the United States that the Soviets were becoming impatient about Berlin and following the American elections would be compelled to sign a peace treaty with Communist East Germany. He then brought up the subject of Cuba, complaining of the resolution passed by Congress, the measure authorizing the call-up of reservists, and so on. Finally, he read from his notes the statement that Soviet arms aid to Cuba "was by no means offensive. If it were otherwise, the Soviet Government would have never become involved in rendering such assistance." It was then that Kennedy repeated his warnings of September 4 and 13, actually reading Gromyko the texts. As suggested above, the effect may well have been to add another indication that we probably had learned about the missiles. But if this is what happened, then the incident must also have reinforced the belief that we did not intend to do anything really drastic about it—at least until after elections—and so lulled the Soviets into a false sense of security.

On Friday, October 19, the President went to Cleveland and then on to Chicago to fill more commitments for campaign speeches. But on Saturday he canceled the rest of the trip and returned to Washington—ostensibly because of an "upper respiratory infection" and a slight temperature. Even on the day of the denouement, October 22, he chatted on and on with Prime Minister Milton Obote of Uganda while the entire Cabinet waited.

The rest of the government also kept up the pretense of "business as usual." A long-scheduled amphibious exercise permitted the Navy to concentrate several dozen ships and five thousand marines in the Caribbean without attracting undue attention. The Joint Chiefs of Staff were asked to remain in Washington for six weeks because of the urgencies of "budget planning." Everyone tried to keep up social engagements, although they sorely needed both the time and the rest that social engagements cost them. At one stage, nine members of the ExCom piled into a single limousine, sitting on each others' laps, to avoid attracting the attention that the whole fleet of long black cars would have done. A mock meeting was set up at the White House, ostentatiously attended by W. Averell Harriman, then Assistant Secretary of State for Far Eastern Affairs, and Phillips Talbot, Assistant Secretary for Near Eastern and South Asian Affairs.

Even so, there were some near misses. One afternoon someone looked out of a State Department window at the long line of black limousines drawn up at the diplomatic entrance, and thereafter high officials were driven into the basement and whisked upstairs by private elevator. After Gromyko's meeting with the President, there was a dinner for him at the State Department. Reporters saw McNamara and McCone arriving for a working session of the ExCom, which was held at the State Department in George Ball's conference room when the President did not attend, and wondered what the Secretary of Defense and especially the Director of Central Intelligence were doing at a dinner for Gromyko.

But without doubt the most important break of all for the United States was the failure of Soviet and Cuban radar. If the Soviets had concluded that we knew about the missiles but deduced from the seeming lack of activity that we did not intend to do very much about it, the heavy traffic of U-2s high in the Cuban sky would have been a dead giveaway. A U-2 at an altitude of 14 miles was beyond the vision of Cuban radar, but the radar the Soviets were putting in could easily pick it up. The only explanation seems to be that the new radar was not yet operational.

THE POLICY DECISION

On Wednesday, Thursday, Friday, and Saturday, the issues tentatively sketched out at the first meeting were explored more fully.

The United States Intelligence Board met to analyze the daily reports from the U-2 flights at least twice daily—not at the glossy new CIA building in Langley, Virginia, which was their usual meeting place, but in one of the old OSS-CIA buildings in Foggy Bottom. Construction on all the missile sites was proceeding rapidly. Although the IRBMs were some distance from completion, the MRBMs could be ready much sooner. There was not much time.

As to the effect of the Soviets putting missiles in Cuba on the world balance of power, the intelligence community had no doubts. When both the MRBMs and the IRBMs were fully operational they could deliver an initial salvo of forty missiles, each propelling a warhead of from three to four megatons. And this salvo could be followed by another within a few hours, the time it took to reload, unless the United States could get in a full retaliatory blow during the reloading time and completely destroy the launching pads. Both the MRBMs and the IRBMs were above ground and "soft"—vulnerable to attack themselves—and therefore useful mainly in a first strike. In such a first strike, the MRBMs could reach and take out most of our manned bomber bases in the Southern and Southwestern United States. The IRBMs could hit the ICBM bases in the north, in such places as Wyoming and Montana, and they could reach every major city in the country except Seattle. By stationing these missiles in Cuba the Soviets had increased the destructive power they could deliver on target in the United States by over 50 per cent. Even so, the intelligence community concluded, the deployment did not tip the balance so far that the Soviets would have an over-all advantage in total megatons on target. But almost as bad, what the Soviet increase in firepower did do was to give them enough to erode the American capacity to strike back—and hence to degrade the ultimate deterrent.

SOVIET MOTIVATIONS

As to the question of Khrushchev's position, with the benefit of hindsight it seems clear that the Soviet decision was arrived at "collectively," with Khrushchev in the chair and in full control throughout the crisis. At the time, of course, no one could be completely sure, but except for momentary doubts by one or two people during a particularly tense period at the height of the crisis, it was generally assumed in Washington that Khrushchev remained in charge.

Judgments about Soviet motives and purposes were inevitably a salient influence on judgments about policy, and even though no one analysis was singled out at the time for formal approval as authoritative, as time went on knowledgeable opinion tended to converge. Some of the initial, simpler explanations came apart on close examination. Berlin was undoubtedly in the minds of the Soviet leaders, for example, but under scrutiny their motives seemed to be more convoluted than either getting set, say, for a colossal trade of Cuba for Berlin, or strengthening their hand for a grand showdown. The Soviets did not put missiles in Cuba with the intent of using them in a military sense any more than the United States put Minuteman ICBMs in Montana with the intent of using them. On the contrary, as discussed above, the Soviet decision seems to have been an expedient, essentially temporary solution to a whole set of problems—the over-all U.S. strategic advantage and the "missile-gap-in-reverse," the exigencies of the Sino-Soviet dispute, and the impossible demands on their limited resources, ranging from defense and foreign aid to the newly created appetite in the Soviet citizenry for consumers' goods. The motive was strategic in a broad and general sense, based on the characteristic Soviet expectation that a general improvement in the Soviet military position would affect the entire political context, strengthening their hand for dealing with the whole range of problems facing them and unanticipated problems as well.

UNITED STATES OBJECTIVES

If the principal Soviet objective in putting missiles into Cuba was strategic in its broadest political sense, so was the American objective in getting them out. But beyond this, the discussion of American objectives in the ExCom meeting and throughout Washington inevitably merged with the discussion of the alternative means that might be used to accomplish these objectives. The United States could tolerate a gradual evening out of the strategic equation between the U.S. and the U.S.S.R., an evening out that would permit both political adjustments as it proceeded and at least tacit understandings, if not formal ones, on a whole range of matters, including arms control. But the United States could not accept a swift, sudden, and secret shifting of that balance. Thus, first and foremost, the American objective was to have the Soviet missiles removed from Cuba.

The United States, of course, would also have liked to see the end of the Soviet military presence in Cuba and the end of Castro's totalitarian Communist regime. But here is where the importance of means began to be felt. The full panoply of American military power was appropriate to getting the missiles out of Cuba—and it might be necessary. But at what point as one descends the ladder of objectives and they become less vital to American survival itself does military power begin to be inappropriate, entailing political costs greater than the possible political gains?

But the first step was the missiles, and the discussions focused mainly on them. One obvious suggestion was to trade the American missiles in Turkey for the Soviet missiles in Cuba. This idea was peculiarly ironic— and made the President especially angry when it was raised again at a later stage—because he had in fact instructed the State and Defense departments to arrange for the removal of the missiles in Turkey some time before the Cuban crisis had begun. The American missiles in Turkey, Britain, and Italy were obsolete, unreliable, inaccurate, and very vulnerable—they could be knocked out by a sniper with a rifle and telescopic sights. President Kennedy had raised the question of removing them at a National Security Council meeting shortly after his inauguration—if they were of little military value, why be provocative? But the Berlin crisis of 1961 made it politically difficult to go ahead. In May 1962 the Secretary of State was instructed to raise the question again with the Turks at the NATO meeting. But the Turks objected on political grounds, and there was a further delay. In the summer of 1962, Kennedy again raised the matter with George Ball, who was Acting Secretary in Rusk's absence, and after rejecting the State Department case for further delay, he ordered—in August 1962—that steps be taken immediately to remove the American missiles from Turkey.

Both the State Department and the Pentagon were slow, however, and the missiles were still there. But even though he had ordered them removed, the President rejected the idea of removing them under this kind of threat. American missiles had been deployed to Turkey, Britain, and Italy in response to the large-scale deployment of Soviet missiles in western Russia aimed at Western Europe; the decision had been openly debated for two years, with full and public agreement of the countries concerned; and the deployment had been publicly announced and carried out. Although Castro and the Soviets justified their action on the grounds of an American threat to Cuba, they never suggested that it was a nuclear threat requiring nuclear defenses. And both the decision and deployment were secret. If the Soviets wanted to talk about the removal of American missiles in Europe, the United States would be glad to do so —but only in the context of a disarmament agreement applying to both Eastern and Western Europe.

The discussions on Wednesday, October 17, examined the whole range of alternatives, but sentiment seemed to be strongest for an air strike or a *coup de main* by parachute forces, a "surgical operation" to eliminate the bases in a sudden, surprise attack. Of course, the risks of a surprise attack were high. No military commander would guarantee one hundred per cent success; and it was always possible that some local Soviet commander would panic, assume that the big war was on with the Soviet Union itself under attack, and take matters into his own hands. But just as importantly, a sudden attack without warning was morally reprehensible, in violation of American traditions and ideals. It was the Attorney General, Robert F. Kennedy, who argued most persuasively against a surprise attack, reminding the group of Pearl Harbor. "For the United States to attack a small country without warning," he said, "would irreparably hurt our reputation in the world—and our own conscience." And he added that he did not want to see John F. Kennedy go down in history as the American Tojo.

What both the President and Robert Kennedy had in mind was fundamental. They were acutely conscious that this was the first nuclear crisis the world had faced and that what they did to meet it would set precedents for future crises and perhaps an entire era.

The ExCom met almost continuously Wednesday, Thursday, and Friday, October 17, 18, and 19. On Thursday, the "surgical operation" to take the missiles out in a single blow by an air strike began to look less and less inviting. Even if it were successful, the United States would be left with a moral stigma, as the Attorney General said, and the Soviets would have solid evidence to support their propaganda that the United States would someday begin World War III by launching a surprise attack on the Soviet Union. The only way of lessening the moral stigma would be to give advance warning, and this would permit preparations and defensive measures that would make the attack less likely to succeed. Then, too, the Joint Chiefs of Staff insisted that the attack could not be limited to just the missile sites without risks that they regarded as unacceptable. Castro's planes, the artillery batteries opposite the American base at Guantánamo, the nuclear storage sites—all these would have to be eliminated in that first strike. Widespread destruction was unavoidable.

But even then the attack might not be completely successful—with or without advance warning. The United States would have to be fully prepared to follow immediately with an invasion, not only because it might be necessary to complete the destruction of the missile sites, but also because it might be necessary to head off the blood bath that would surely come in the political and military chaos that would follow.

There was also the question of the Soviet response. If the United States chose the sudden, violent course of knocking out the missiles, with or without warning, the Soviets would feel impelled to do something equally dramatic, and the most likely seemed to be retaliation on our bases in Turkey—a further widening and escalation of the confrontation.

To more and more of those involved, the trouble with an air strike was not only that there was no guarantee that it would be completely successful, but also that it set in train a series of events that would be extraordinarily difficult to manage and control.

The idea of an invasion alone was also discussed. But exactly the same criticisms that applied to an air strike also applied to an invasion. In addition, it would be extraordinarily difficult to keep the preparations for an invasion secret, and the element of surprise would probably be lacking. There would also be a delay, which meant that the missiles might become operational, for it would take time to assemble the necessary forces.

Thus by Thursday evening a consensus began to develop around the idea of a blockade against offensive weapons as a first step—in McNamara's phrase, maintaining the "options" of raising the level of the blockade, of launching an air strike, or of mounting an invasion as progressive increases in the level of force to be used if increases proved necessary. Before the day was over, the President had indicated his own preference for blockade.

It was not that a blockade was free of drawbacks. The first was what a number of administration spokesmen had said in the debate since August—that a blockade was contrary to international law, an act of war, although this would be altered somewhat if the Organization of American States, the OAS, voted in favor of it. Another trouble was that a blockade did not address itself directly to the question of Soviet missiles—it did not *remove* them, but only prevented a further build-up. And a blockade meant that American ships would oppose Soviet ships, stop them, and demand that they submit themselves to the humiliation of being boarded. If the Soviet ships refused to stop or submit to boarding, it would, like an air strike, put the Americans in the position of firing the first shot.

The great advantage of a blockade, on the other hand, was that it began at the very lowest level in the use of force and permitted a step by step progression up the ladder of coercion, giving the Soviets repeated opportunities to consider again the choice of withdrawing the missiles and making a settlement. It permitted events to be paced; it provided time—time between steps for each side to consider the next step and its full range of consequences. It kept at a minimum, in President Kennedy's phrase, the possibility of a "spasm reaction."

One major obstacle—not objection, but obstacle—to a blockade was that the JCS still wanted an air strike or an invasion. The President met with the Chiefs on Friday morning and came out of the meeting annoyed. He again repeated his preference for a blockade and at this time supplied the word *quarantine* to describe it. This was a phrase with obvious political advantages both at home, where it was reminiscent of President Roosevelt's "quarantining the aggressors" speech, and abroad, where it struck a less belligerent note than the word *blockade*. But before departing for a trip to Cleveland and Chicago, he also made it clear that his decision was still tentative.

It seems likely that the President was waiting to make his decision final mainly because of this continued opposition of the JCS to blockade and preference for more violent action. It was clear that some of the memoranda being written were not so much to present this or that case to the President—since he had already heard them all—but to build a record. If something went wrong, many of these papers would obviously begin to leak. Any alternative he chose was chancy, at best, and it is elementary prudence for a president to protect himself from the charge that he had overruled his military advisers on a "military" issue. Even as late as Saturday, he said that before making his decision on a blockade final he wanted to talk personally with the Air Force Tactical Bombing Command to make very sure that a limited air strike could not be successful.

In the circumstances, it was vital for the President to have a consensus or near-consensus in the ExCom in support of the course of action chosen. Yet that Friday, the near unanimity achieved on Thursday began to come apart. A high-ranking member of the ExCom, a hard-liner with experience in shipping, marshaled the arguments on the legal difficulties of a blockade, and all the other difficulties, objections, and obstacles to a blockade again came to the fore. It was at this meeting on Friday afternoon that the Attorney General argued so persuasively against a surprise attack, finally convincing the waverers that the wisest course might be the blockade even though it was the "slow agony" that Bundy called it.

On Saturday, after the President returned from Chicago with his "upper respiratory infection," those who still had misgivings about a quarantine had one final chance. Mindful of his need to have their support, even as the President decided on quarantine, he stressed to those who still advocated an air strike or an invasion that those choices were still open if the quarantine did not work and that they might well be needed. Those whose proposals were not chosen, he joked, were the lucky ones, for they could say, "I told you so."

The President then began to go over the "disclosure" speech Theodore Sorensen had been working on all through the night. The speech went through several drafts, and many different people were asked for their comments. It was at this point that the analysis, mentioned earlier, of the conversations between Bowles and Dobrynin, Khrushchev and Kohler, and Gromyko and President Kennedy became relevant. The analysis had concluded that Moscow must have interpreted Bowles's comments as referring to missiles and if this was so, then Gromyko had had remarkably little to say on the subject when he had his conversation with Kennedy on October 18. The best explanation for Gromyko's behavior seemed to be that the Soviets were hedging, trying to avoid a direct confrontation with the United States in the hope of leaving their hand free for negotiations or, if faced with extreme danger of war, for withdrawing the missiles with the least loss of face. It seemed wise to have our public statements take this into account—for us to take a firm and determined stance but one that still left the Soviets a way out. Both Harriman and Llewellyn Thompson, drawing on their experience as ambassadors to the Soviet Union, also stressed the importance of this. And it was the President's natural preference.[1]

The President had decided on Friday that Monday evening would be the time of disclosure, and the preparations were already in full swing. There was much to be done. Resolutions for the UN and the Organization of American States had to be drafted. Special arrangements had to be made to brief our major allies. Presidential letters had to be prepared for forty-three heads of government, and messages had to be sent to all our posts overseas, explaining our action. The congressional leadership had to be informed. The Pentagon had to alert the Strategic Air Command, assemble the quarantine forces, and prepare the troops needed for an invasion if that should become necessary.

At the State Department, U. Alexis Johnson, the Deputy Under Secretary for Political Affairs, was the man chosen to co-ordinate the "scenario"—a schedule of who was to do what and when, all keyed to "P-hour," seven o'clock Monday evening, when the President was to give his speech. ("P" for "Public" after someone discovered the original designation had a special meaning in nuclear war planning.) For Monday, October 22, the scenario read as follows:

9:00 A.M., Monday, October 22—ExCom meeting;

10:00—Lawrence O'Brien (Presidential Assistant for Congressional Relations) to notify congressional leadership;

12:00 noon—The President's press secretary, Pierre Salinger, to announce time of President's speech;

3:00 P.M.—National Security Council meeting, followed by Cabinet meeting;

5:00—The President, Rusk, McNamara, and McCone to brief congressional leadership;

6:00—Ambassador Dobrynin of the Soviet Union to see Secretary Rusk;

6:15—Under Secretary George Ball and Director of Intelligence Roger Hilsman to brief forty-six allied ambassadors;

7:00—The President's speech;

7:30—Assistant Secretary Edwin Martin to brief Latin American ambassadors;

8:00—Rusk and Hilsman to brief "neutral nations" ambassadors;

—Ball, Alexis Johnson, and Abram Chayes (the legal adviser of the State Department) to give first half of press briefing;

8:15—Hilsman to give second half of press briefing.

After checking over the preparations at a final meeting on Sunday, Rusk sighed wearily and suggested that everyone ought to get as much rest as he could. "By this time tomorrow, gentlemen," he said, "we will be in a flaming crisis."

All there was left to do was wait—and hope that nothing leaked that would give the Soviets a chance to take the initiative away from us.

Miraculously, the secret held—but just barely. All through the weekend Washington was taut with the sense of crisis. Too many high officials had canceled social engagements or were called away from them. Too many people were at the office too early and stayed too late. Too many lights were burning at the State Department and the Pentagon at odd hours.

By Saturday afternoon the Washington press corps knew something unusual was up and by Sunday they were frantic with curiosity. Most of the reporters accredited to the State Department and the Pentagon spent Sunday there, prowling the corridors looking for some lead.

Many reporters thought the Soviet Union might have delivered an ultimatum on Berlin; others thought the United States might have finally lost patience with Castro. A fluke question—were we planning an invasion of Cuba?—permitted Arthur Sylvester, Assistant Secretary of Public Affairs at the Pentagon, to justify a quibble, and he said "No" with some emphasis, since what was being planned was a quarantine. This turned attention away from Cuba and toward Berlin for a time and served as a useful smoke screen.

But by Sunday evening, several newspapers, including the New York *Times,* had most of the story. The President telephoned the publishers, asking them not to print it—which would give the Soviets warning and an opportunity to present the United States with an ultimatum. All of them promptly agreed, although the New York *Times* did publish a story about an "air of crisis" linked to a "new development in Cuba that cannot be disclosed at this point. . . ."

A few last-minute details had to be ironed out, and unscheduled meetings were sandwiched in. Legal details, details about military questions, details about Stevenson's speech at the UN—all needed to be checked with the President at one stage or another. My own problem was the intelligence briefing I was to give the ambassadors. It had to be convincing, for we would need support. We would be presenting our case to the Organization of American States at the outset, and we might soon need much more than political support from our allies. And it would be helpful if we had at least the sympathy of the "neutrals." But even so, there was considerable reluctance to let me use the U-2 pictures in briefing the ambassadors. The problem was not one of publicly admitting that we had been overflying Cuba, for we actually had some legal basis for the more recent U-2 surveillance. On October 3, a communiqué issued by the inter-American Foreign Ministers Conference had condemned secret military preparations in the hemisphere, and, pointing directly at Cuba, went on to say that it was "desirable to intensify individual and collective surveillance of the delivery of arms and implements of war and all other items of strategic importance to the Communist regime of Cuba. . . ." The objection came from the intelligence community, which was afraid of revealing too much about intelligence methods and techniques and especially the high quality of photography achieved by the U-2 camera systems. I met twice that day with the President to work it out, once at eleven in the morning in a very small meeting in his office at which Stevenson's presentation to the UN was also discussed, and again in the very large meeting at three in the afternoon that reviewed the whole scenario. The President decided that the pictures had to be used and within the next few days that they should be released to the general public.

There was a bad scare just six hours before the President's speech. The Soviet Mission to the United Nations announced early Monday afternoon that they would shortly have an important statement. Plans were quickly laid to announce the quarantine—but the "important statement" was merely Mr. Gromyko's departure speech.

FIVE P.M.——CONGRESSIONAL BRIEFING

The congressional meeting began with an intelligence briefing. After McCone and an aide had finished, the President began to talk. He explained why an air strike or an invasion would be unwise, emphasizing that the quarantine was only the first step. An invasion might soon become necessary, but it would take still another week to assemble the force and in the meantime it was essential to stop the Soviets from bringing in more equipment to make the missile bases fully operational. Senator Richard B. Russell of Georgia, Chairman of the Senate Armed Services Committee, urged an immediate invasion. A quarantine would take time and thus increase the risk. As for warning and striking the first blow, President Kennedy's speeches and the congressional resolution putting the Soviets on notice that the United States would not tolerate offensive bases in Cuba were ample warning. It was the Soviets who had struck the first blow by putting the missiles in Cuba. Surprisingly, J. William Fulbright, Chairman of the Senate Foreign Relations Committee, who had opposed the Bay of Pigs landings and who, a year earlier, in June 1961, had noted the possibility of Soviet missiles someday appearing in Cuba and had said that he doubted they would alter the balance of power in the world, supported Russell. It seemed to him that intercepting Soviet ships at sea was just as risky as taking out the bases themselves.

The President listened politely.

SIX P.M.——DOBRYNIN TO SEE RUSK

Ambassador Dobrynin was in New York seeing Gromyko off, when the State Department reached him to set up the six-o'clock appointment. He flew back to Washington and, going into Rusk's office, he seemed relaxed.

Twenty-five minutes later he came out—tense and, it seemed to reporters, shaken, clutching a copy of the President's speech in his hand. "Ask the Secretary," was the only reply he would give to questions.

SEVEN P.M.—THE PRESIDENT'S SPEECH

The President spoke to the nation and the world from his study. He began by describing United States surveillance and what it had discovered. He then pointed out the meaning of the missiles in Cuba. "This urgent transformation of Cuba into an important strategic base—by the presence of these large, long-range, and clearly offensive weapons of sudden mass destruction—constitutes an explicit threat to the peace and security of all the Americas. . . ." He talked about the necessity for new standards of international conduct on a small planet in a nuclear age: "Nuclear weapons are so destructive and ballistic missiles so swift that any substantially increased possibility of their use or any sudden change in their deployment may well be regarded as a definite threat to peace." The President went on to point out that for many years both the Soviet Union and the United States had recognized this fact and had deployed strategic nuclear weapons with great care, never upsetting the precarious *status quo,* which ensured that they would not be used in the absence of some vital challenge. "Our own strategic missiles," the President declared, "have never been transferred to the territory of any other nation under a cloak of secrecy and deception . . . this secret, swift, and extraordinary build-up of Communist missiles—in an area well known to have a special and historical relationship to the United States and the nations of the Western Hemisphere, in violation of Soviet assurances, and in defiance of American and hemispheric policy—this sudden, clandestine decision to station strategic weapons for the first time outside of Soviet soil—is a deliberately provocative and unjustified change in the status quo which cannot be accepted by this country if our courage and our commitments are ever to be trusted again by either friend or foe."

Finally, the President described what the United States intended to do about it:

"First: . . . a strict quarantine on all offensive military equipment under shipment to Cuba . . .

"Second: continued and increased close surveillance of Cuba . . .

"Third: It shall be the policy of this nation to regard any nuclear missile launched from Cuba against any nation in the Western Hemisphere as an attack by the Soviet Union on the United States, requiring a full retaliatory response upon the Soviet Union.

"Fourth: As a necessary military precaution I have reinforced our base at Guantánamo . . .

"Fifth: We are calling tonight for an immediate meeting of the Organ of Consultation, under the Organization of American States, to consider this threat to hemispheric security and to invoke articles six and eight of the Rio Treaty in support of all necessary action. . . .

"Sixth: Under the Charter of the United Nations, we are asking tonight that an emergency meeting of the Security Council be convoked without delay to take action against this latest Soviet threat to world peace. . . .

"Seventh and finally: I call upon Chairman Khrushchev to halt and eliminate this clandestine, reckless, and provocative threat to world peace . . ."

The world was witnessing its first crisis of the nuclear age, and the reaction was remarkable. In some parts of the United States, people stocked up on canned goods and dug bomb shelters. Some city dwellers evacuated. But most people in the United States and in all the other countries of the world recognized the futility of individual action and watched with breathless fascination the duel between the two greatest powers and the two lonely men who headed them.

The first Soviet reaction was a long propaganda statement, accusing the United States of violating international law, of provocative acts, of "piracy," and a vehement denial that the arms they were sending to Cuba were intended for anything but defensive purposes. The statement seemed designed to stall until the Soviets had time to decide on their response.

The Latin American reaction was crucial. The Organization of American States met on Tuesday and approved the proposed American resolution overwhelmingly—19 to 0—partly due to the hard and brilliant work of Assistant Secretary Edwin M. Martin and partly due to the courage of Latin American leaders who defied their leftist opposition and of such men as Emilio Sarmiento Carruncho, of Bolivia, who could not get through to his government for instructions but who at the risk of his political life still voted yes.

There was also in the speech an attempt, in the words of Abram Chayes, the State Department's legal adviser, "to make a little international law for the nuclear age." The speech took the position that "Nuclear weapons are so destructive, and ballistic missiles are so swift, that any substantially increased possibility of their use or any sudden change in their deployment may well be regarded as a definite threat to the peace."

The best of both worlds was not only to make such a contribution to international law, but also to have an airtight case in the context of the earlier treaty provisions and procedures of the OAS, which rested on the legitimacy of collective action by a regional organization qualifying under Chapter VIII of the UN charter. This is what the overwhelming endorsement of the OAS accomplished. What it also accomplished was a massive demonstration to Moscow of interAmerican solidarity.

Prompt support also came from our NATO allies. At first there had been some doubts expressed in the British press that there really were Soviet missiles in Cuba. But then President Kennedy authorized the release of the pictures, and all doubts were swept aside. (The same thing had happened when Rusk and I had briefed the ambassadors from the "unaligned" states, and many had stopped as they left the hall to wish the United States luck in the confrontation ahead.) Dean Acheson had briefed General de Gaulle, Chancellor Adenauer, and the NATO Council, and all of the NATO governments gave their support.

At the UN, the United States called for a meeting of the Security Council, and on Thursday Ambassador Adlai E. Stevenson presented the American case. He ended his speech by confronting the Soviet Ambassador, Valerian A. Zorin. "All right, sir," Stevenson said, "let me ask you one simple question. Do you, Ambassador Zorin, deny that the USSR has placed and is placing medium—and intermediate—range missiles and sites in Cuba? Yes or no—don't wait for the translation—yes or no?"

"I am not standing in the dock of an American court and I shall not answer at this stage," was Zorin's reply.

"I am prepared to wait for my answer until hell freezes over, if that is your decision," Governor Stevenson said, "and I am also prepared to present the evidence in this room."

And he turned to the enlargements of the U-2 photographs, convincing the world of Soviet guilt and mustering support for the action the United States was about to take.

NOTES

[1] A paper from the Bureau of Intelligence and Research also raised the possibility of putting as much blame on Castro for accepting the missiles as on the Soviets for supplying them—not only to make the most of Castro's reputation for intemperance and so attack a vulnerable target, but to lay the groundwork for bringing about a change of government in Cuba, if events during the crisis moved in such a way as to make that feasible. A corollary of this proposal would be to start the blockade somewhat higher on the ladder, specifically to include POL (petroleum, oil, and lubricants), which would put great pressure on the Castro regime. But the importance of giving the Soviets a clear and completely uncluttered warning that we held them totally responsible for any use of nuclear weapons based on Cuba was clearly overriding and the idea was dropped.

CHAPTER 16

"*Eyeball to Eyeball*"

PRESIDENT KENNEDY'S sensitivity to the precedents that would be set in this first nuclear crisis the world had faced was matched by a determination to pace and manage events so as to give the Soviet leaders time to think out the consequences of each move. His purpose was to avoid putting the Soviets in a position where their only response could be, as he said, a "spasm reaction."

Thus on Monday the President announced only his intention to impose a quarantine and waited until Tuesday, after he had OAS approval, to issue the actual proclamation. And the proclamation provided still another pause, making the quarantine effective twenty-four hours later, on Wednesday, October 24, at 10:00 A.M.

Even then, the President ordered the Navy screen not to intercept a Soviet ship until absolutely necessary—and had the order transmitted in the clear. Thus the first contact with a Soviet ship did not come until Thursday at 8:00 A.M. An oil tanker, the *Bucharest,* was deliberately chosen because it would obviously carry no arms. And it was hailed, but not boarded. The first boarding did not occur until Friday at 8:00 A.M.— and the ship boarded was not Soviet, but a Lebanese freighter under charter to the Soviets. In this way the President hoped to provide a series of carefully graduated steps, with ample time between each of them for the Soviets to weigh the consequences of going ahead with still another step or agreeing to a withdrawal.

The President was also determined to manage the crisis himself—and he did so, in all its exquisite detail. There was not going to be any possibility for someone down the line to push events any faster or further than he judged necessary. It was the President who decided what ships would be stopped and when, how the announcements would be made, what would be said publicly and privately. And there were very few slips. One, mentioned earlier, was Representative Van Zandt's violation of the secret briefing for congressmen when he revealed that the Soviet oil tanker *Bucharest* had been stopped, in which I came in the line of presidential fire. Another was a slip by Lincoln White, the official State Department spokesman. In making an announcement at the height of the crisis that work was still continuing on the missile sites at top speed, White went beyond his instructions and pointed to the phrase in the President's speech that "further action will be justified" if work on the missile sites did not stop. The result was to trigger headlines that an invasion was imminent and thus to raise the temperature to higher levels than the President intended. He made his displeasure known to the Secretary of State, the Assistant Secretary for Public Affairs, and Lincoln White himself, by direct phone calls and strong language— although he later joked that the whole incident might have helped the Soviets realize just how urgent the situation really was. Such incidents served to make everyone in Washington realize just how determined the President was to maintain a tight hand on events, and for once in a major crisis the many arms of the American government and all their multiple activities were directed through a single mind.

On Tuesday evening, the night before the quarantine went into effect, the latest intelligence reports from U-2 flights showed that work was going forward on the missile sites at full speed. Twenty-five Soviet ships were at sea proceeding toward Cuba on a direct course.

On Wednesday morning the Soviet government rejected the United States quarantine proclamation. Ominously, the Soviet ships heading toward Cuba were joined by six Soviet submarines.

Khrushchev apparently wanted to accompany his rejection of the quarantine with a threat, one that would be public but not official. He needed a foil and what he seems to have done was to scan the list of private American citizens visiting Moscow for a name that would suit his purpose. In any event, William Knox, President of Westinghouse International, who was in Moscow on business, suddenly got a call that Khrushchev wanted to see him at the Kremlin. Khrushchev admitted to Knox that Soviet missiles were present in Cuba and went on to say that the Soviet Union would use them if necessary. Attacking the quarantine proclamation, Khrushchev said that if the United States stopped Soviet ships, the Soviet submarines would be forced to sink a U.S. ship—all of which, he warned, would bring about World War III.

Also on Wednesday, the then Acting Secretary General of the United Nations, U Thant, proposed that the Soviet Union and the United States should enter into negotiations, during which period both the shipments of arms and the quarantine be suspended. The Soviet Union accepted the proposal promptly. But even though U Thant subsequently suggested that work on the missile bases should also be stopped during negotiations, the United States rejected the proposal, which would clearly blunt the American initiative and destroy its momentum. "As we made clear in the Security Council," President Kennedy wrote in reply, "the existing threat was created by the secret introduction of offensive weapons into Cuba, and the answer lies in the removal of such weapons."

The crucial question was how soon the Soviet missiles would become operational, and the President authorized the Navy to fly low-level reconnaissance missions, buzzing the missile sites themselves. The pictures the Navy brought back showed that work on the missile sites continued at full speed. It was these pictures that also revealed for the first time the presence of Soviet ground forces armed with tactical nuclear weapons.

Then, late Wednesday, came the first hint of a break—some of the Soviet ships heading toward Cuba, including five big-hatch ships, altered course and the rest of the dry cargo ships stopped dead in the water, wallowing while they waited for orders. It was apparently on this occasion that Secretary Rusk first made his remark that the "other fellow just blinked."

But as it turned out, this was not really a blink. At best it was only a sign that the Soviets realized what President Kennedy had been stressing all along to the ExCom—that in a nuclear confrontation neither side could afford precipitate action. A scribbled sign posted in a State Department briefing room made the same point in a wry attempt at humor: "In a Nuclear Age," it read, "nations must make war as porcupines make love—carefully." By stopping the ships, the Soviets were probably only being careful.

The Navy, in fact, had a more sinister interpretation. They suspected that the ships had altered course in order to pick up more Soviet submarines as escorts.

The President was determined to pace events, and issued orders that there was to be no shooting. The Soviet ships were to be kept in view but none was to be boarded until he issued the instructions. Although the Navy objected, he wanted the interception line to be drawn close in to Cuba—so that Khrushchev would have plenty of time for thought.

This led to a bitter clash between McNamara and Admiral George W. Anderson, Chief of Naval Operations. McNamara went to the Navy Flag Plot, the Navy's command center, and began to question Anderson sharply and in detail—who would make the first interception, were Russian speaking officers on board, and so on. Admiral Anderson apparently felt that Secretary McNamara's questioning constituted undue interference in the details of the Navy's work. McNamara, on the other hand, felt that he had a responsibility to make sure that the details of execution did not upset the President's carefully planned strategy. Both were probably right, and both were also under severe strain.

Only the dry cargo ships had stopped; the oil tankers continued on, and Thursday morning, as mentioned above, the *Bucharest* was hailed and then waved on. On Friday, the Lebanese freighter was stopped, boarded, and since there were no arms, allowed to proceed. U Thant, in the meantime, attempted to ease the tension by proposing that the Soviet Union keep Soviet vessels away from the quarantine zone and that the United States avoid intercepting them. Both Khrushchev and

Kennedy agreed, but the President pointed out again that work on the missile sites was still going on, stressing that this was "a matter of great urgency."

But at least the quarantine was working. Reports confirmed that twelve of the Soviet dry cargo ships—the ones suspected of carrying missile equipment—had turned around and were heading back toward the Soviet Union. The Soviets had decided against a confrontation at sea —at least for the moment.

But now came the real question: having prevented a further build-up of Soviet arms in Cuba, what could the United States do to bring *direct* pressure on them to withdraw? The President, presiding over the ExCom, considered again the whole range of choices, beginning with adding POL to the blockade list, which would squeeze the Cuban economy, and continuing up the ladder to an air strike and invasion.

By Friday, October 26, tensions began to come to a peak. Intelligence reports showed that work on all the missile sites was continuing at full speed. A White House announcement describing these activities concluded that the Soviets were trying to achieve "full operational capability as soon as possible." And no one on the American side could forget the consequences once all forty launching pads were operational.

Throughout Friday, the President communicated the American sense of urgency in a number of ways. He emphasized it in his message to U Thant. He had Executive Branch officials repeat it in their conversations at the UN, with the press, and with congressional leaders. On Friday, the general feeling in Washington, which was communicated to the Soviets, was that the United States could hold off its next step for no more than one or two days.

But this was the day, Friday, October 26, of the first real blink.

There are five basic channels of communication between the Soviet and American governments. One is by formal letter between the heads of government using embassy facilities. The mechanism is for the Soviets, for example, to deliver a letter from Khrushchev to the American embassy in Moscow, where it is translated and cabled to Washington. Usually, but not always, the Soviets will also cable the letter to their embassy in Washington, who will deliver a copy to the State Department.

Second, the Soviets—characteristically—maintain alternative sets of channels that by-pass their embassy in Washington and probably are handled in special ways at the Moscow end as well.

Third, views can be exchanged formally and officially by note or by letters between officials lesser than the heads of government.

Fourth, there can be an informal but still official exchange—orally, for example—between the ambassador and an official in the State Department or the White House.

Finally, the Soviets not infrequently use entirely unofficial channels. A special officer with a nominal title as a working-level official, or a Tass correspondent with unusual connections might be used to push a line or communicate a threat. Occasionally, the Soviets might use such an unofficial channel to try out a proposal or test a reaction in advance to avoid committing themselves prematurely.

In the Cuba crisis, all five channels were used—several formal letters were exchanged between Kennedy and Khrushchev; there were several less formal exchanges, as, for example, between Attorney General Robert F. Kennedy and Ambassador Dobrynin; and there were several entirely unofficial conversations, hints dropped by Tass correspondents at the UN, and the conversations with semiofficial Soviet citizens such as Georgi Bolshakov. But the decisive channels were probably the first, the letters between Kennedy and Khrushchev, and one very unusual channel of the last type, the very informal and unofficial. It was over this unofficial channel that the first hint of a blink came in.

At one-thirty Friday afternoon, John Scali, State Department correspondent for ABC and a man known to be trusted as a reliable and accurate reporter by the highest levels of the U. S. Government, received an urgent telephone call from a senior Soviet official, Aleksander Fomin, asking for an immediate appointment. Most Washington correspondents maintain a contact in the Soviet Embassy, and Scali had lunched with Fomin on several previous occasions, although never on such short and peremptory notice. What made this call so significant to Scali was not only the sense of urgency, but the fact that Fomin was known to be the senior Soviet intelligence officer in the United States—a man with his own direct channels of communication to the Kremlin.

They met at the Occidental Restaurant, and Fomin went straight to the point—and a very unusual point it was, too. He asked Scali to find out immediately from his "high-level friends in the State Department" whether the United States would be interested in a solution to the crisis along the following lines: (1) The Soviet Union would agree to dismantle and remove the offensive missiles in Cuba; (2) It would allow United Nations inspection to supervise and verify the removal; (3) The Soviet government would pledge not to reintroduce missiles, ever, to Cuba; and (4) In return, the United States would pledge publicly not to invade Cuba. He added that if Ambassador Stevenson pursued this approach at the United Nations, where U Thant was attempting to mediate, Mr. Zorin would be interested. And, after giving Scali his home phone number with instructions to call at any hour day or night, he emphasized that the matter was "of the greatest urgency."

Scali came directly to me and typed out the gist of his conversation with Fomin. The fact that the Soviets had chosen to communicate through Scali was not too unusual—as I mentioned, they frequently conveyed warnings or tried to set a mood through unofficial channels. What made this particular message unusual was its concreteness. Even so, there was some debate among the "Sovietologists" about how seriously to take it. I had copies of what Scali had typed out sent to the Secretary and the others concerned, and as the afternoon wore on, other little hints came in, originating mainly in the corridors of the UN, that made the Scali message look even more important. And later that night something came in that made everyone realize that it might be crucial.

But even before this, Rusk saw the possibilities in an entirely unofficial exchange of views with the Soviets, and after a short discussion with other members of the ExCom, he asked me to bring Scali up to see him in the private elevator.

Rusk told Scali that the approach made through him was the first direct word that the Soviets might be thinking of a deal and that it fitted in with some hints that had been dropped that afternoon at the UN. Rusk asked Scali to go back to the Soviet official and tell him the United States was interested, but that time was very, very short—no more than two days. Rusk had written what Scali was to say on a piece of yellow paper in his own handwriting:

"I have reason to believe that the USG [United States government] sees real possibilities and supposes that the representatives of the two governments in New York could work this matter out with U Thant and with each other. My impression is, however, that time is very urgent."

Rusk authorized Scali to tell the Soviet official that the statement came from the "highest levels in the government of the United States."

Scali then phoned Fomin and arranged to meet with him fifteen minutes later, at 7:35 P.M., in the coffee shop of the Statler Hotel, which is just a block from the Soviet Embassy.

Over coffee, Scali relayed his news. The one thing Fomin wanted to be certain of was that this in fact represented the views of the American government. Several times he asked if Scali's information on the U.S. reaction came from high sources and Scali replied that it came from *very* high sources.

Satisfied on this point, Fomin tried to do some dickering. Since there was to be inspection of Cuban bases, he said, why shouldn't there also be inspection of American bases in Florida from where an invasion of Cuba might originate?

This was a new element, Scali pointed out, and he had no information on how the United States Government might react. But, speaking as a reporter, he went on, he felt that this new element would raise a terrible complication. Since there were no American missiles pointed at Cuba, the situations were entirely different, and he felt President Kennedy would reject any such proposal. Scali again emphasized the urgency. If time were spent haggling over such a condition as Fomin's new proposal, there might be a disaster for Cuba, for the Soviet Union, and for the world.

Fomin thanked Scali, repeated with emphasis that Scali's information would be communicated immediately to the very highest levels in the Kremlin and simultaneously to Zorin at the UN. He departed in obvious haste—throwing down a five-dollar bill for a thirty-cent check.

Scali reported back to me and we both went again to see Secretary Rusk. In the meantime, a long, four-part cable began to come in—Khrushchev's letter to President Kennedy. This message has not been made public, but the key elements have been described in several magazine and newspaper articles. The letter was most emphatically not the "outcry of a frightened man," as some accounts would have it, but it was long and discursive, bearing the unmistakable stamp of Khrushchev himself. It contained no specific proposal or conditions, but the thrust of the whole message showed an appreciation of the risk of nuclear war and the need for reaching an agreement. One key passage, for example, likened the crisis to a rope with a knot in the middle, with President Kennedy pulling on one end and Khrushchev pulling on the other. The more they both pulled the more the knot tightened, until finally it could be cut only with a sword. But if they both stopped pulling, the knot could be untied.

This four-part cable must have been drafted at just about the same time as the instructions to Fomin. For the two communications were clearly related: the cable indicated a willingness to negotiate, and the unofficial approach through Scali suggested a formula for the negotiations.

"John," Rusk told Scali, "you have served your country well. Remember when you report this—that, eyeball to eyeball, they blinked first."

At the Secretary's request, a group of us in the Bureau of Intelligence and Research spent the rest of the night preparing an analysis of the Khrushchev cable and the Fomin approach—"to include any hookers in it"—to be ready for the members of the ExCom to read before the next morning's meeting.

Our judgment was that the Soviets had indeed blinked and that even though there were some possible hookers to be guarded against, the proposals should be taken seriously. On close examination, it seemed even clearer that Fomin's approach through Scali and the Khrushchev cable were really a single package. It was apparently Fomin's assignment to stimulate U.S. interest in Khrushchev's imprecise formulations by adding specifics—and especially on the question of inspection, which Moscow knew was central for the United States. There were hints of the other points scattered through the Khrushchev cable like "raisins in a cake," but the all-important offer of inspection had not appeared at all.

At the time the Khrushchev cable was sent and the approach made through Scali, we recalled, the Soviets had already (1) accepted the U Thant formula by which their ships avoided the quarantine zone and ours refrained from seeking them out; and (2) offered to withdraw their missiles, without attempting to link the withdrawal to anything but a "no-invasion" pledge. By these two moves, we reasoned, the Soviets had backed off from direct confrontation with the United States, had opened the way for talks, and had at least postponed a direct U.S. military effort to remove the missiles. And now there were the Khrushchev cable and the approach through Scali. From all the evidence, it seemed to us that Khrushchev had faced the prospect of an escalating confrontation squarely, that he was horrified at what he saw at the end of that road, and that he was sincerely searching for a way out. On the other hand, there was still the possibility that he was only playing for time until the missiles were fully operational, which would be about mid-November, only two or three weeks hence. Our judgment, therefore, was also that a precondition for further negotiations be that the Soviets stop work on the missile sites.

The ExCom met at ten o'clock on Saturday morning with hope running high. Then, at ten-seventeen, the news tickers cleared the first bulletin of a new note from Khrushchev then being broadcast by Radio Moscow. As the details came in, it was clear that the Soviets had reversed their position. What they offered now was to trade their missiles in Cuba for American missiles in Turkey.

News was also received that a single Soviet ship had detached itself from the others outside the quarantine line and was headed for Cuba. It looked very much as if the Soviets had decided to test our determination in a confrontation at sea after all or even to provoke an incident.

Worse news quickly followed. The SAM network of antiaircraft missiles had become operational. An American U-2 had been shot down, and the pilot, Major Rudolf Anderson, Jr., who had flown the U-2 that had originally discovered the missiles, was killed.

It was the blackest hour of the crisis. The ExCom had already considered what the American response should be if a U-2 were shot down. The decision was to take out the one antiaircraft SAM site responsible, and if a second U-2 were shot down to take out all the SAM sites on the island. In any case, Washington reasoned, the Soviets must have realized that shooting down U-2s would force the United States to take direct action against the SAMs, and their action therefore seemed to mean that they had decided on a showdown. There was speculation that the hard-liners in the Kremlin might be taking over, possibly backed by the military. Another explanation was that some of those meeting around the equivalent table in the Kremlin thought they could extract a higher price. Possibly encouraged by a newspaper column by Walter Lippmann suggesting that missiles in Turkey be traded for missiles in Cuba, they may have pushed the other members of the Soviet leadership to use this device to force Kennedy to compromise. But this did not really account for either the shoot-down of the U-2 or the fact that a Soviet ship was now heading for the interception line. If the Soviets were bargaining, it was a highly dangerous form. For it would not be possible in these circumstances to keep down the pace of events. Everything would be foreshortened, and an actual invasion of Cuba might be no later than forty-eight hours away.

THE "STRANGELOVE" INCIDENT

Then it was the American turn to make a slip. Early in the afternoon, Rusk had drafted me to carry a proposed reply to Khrushchev's Friday night cable over to the White House. I delivered it to McGeorge Bundy in the President's outer office, and after some discussion, left to return to the State Department.

As I passed the guard at the west executive entrance, he grabbed my arm to say that my office was calling me—urgently. I learned that another U-2, totally unrelated to the crisis, on a routine air-sampling mission from Alaska to the North Pole had picked the wrong star for its return flight and was at that moment over the Soviet Union. Soviet fighter planes had scrambled. The U-2 pilot had gone on the air—in the clear —to call for help, and American fighters in Alaska had also scrambled and were attempting to rendezvous with the U-2 to escort it home.

I ran upstairs and found the President, Bundy, and several others in Mrs. Lincoln's office.

The President knew at a glance that something was terribly wrong. Out of breath and shaky from over thirty hours without sleep, I told my story.

The implications were as obvious as they were horrendous: the Soviets might well regard this U-2 flight as a last-minute intelligence reconnaissance in preparation for nuclear war. It was just this sort of invitation to miscalculation that Kennedy's detailed instructions were designed to prevent. "One of your planes," Khrushchev himself later wrote, "violates our frontier during this anxious time we are both experiencing, when everything has been put into combat readiness. Is it not a fact that an intruding American plane could be easily taken for a nuclear bomber, which might push us to a fateful step . . . ?"

Ernest Hemingway once described true courage as "grace under pressure." The President gave a short, ironic laugh that broke the tension. "There is always some so-and-so," he said, "who doesn't get the word."[1]

It enraged the President to think that in spite of his earlier instructions to remove the missiles from Turkey they were still there, political albatrosses around his neck. The missiles in Turkey were obsolete, and removing them would not be any great problem in subsequent negotiations. But that did not help now. The immediate threat was that the Soviets were continuing construction on the offensive missile bases in Cuba at a rapid pace. There could be no negotiations while that rapid build-up continued. A statement to this effect, suggesting that the missiles in Turkey would be no problem in subsequent negotiations but that such negotiations could not take place while work continued on the Soviet bases in Cuba, was drafted as a response to the Soviet proposal and released as a public statement.

Some way had to be found to get back to the more promising proposals put forward on Friday—and quickly. Rusk called Scali to his office later that Saturday afternoon and suggested he see Fomin again and ask what had happened. Had the whole operation been a trap to divert attention while the Soviets planned a double cross? What was going on in the Kremlin?

Scali and Fomin met at four-fifteen in a deserted banquet hall off the mezzanine of the Statler Hotel. Fomin was puzzled and unhappy. Responding to Scali's challenge, he sought to explain the morning's message linking Cuba to Turkey and reneging on his formula of the night before as the result of bad communications—that the Saturday morning cable had been drafted before his report on the favorable American reaction had arrived.

Scali exploded. He said he couldn't believe Fomin's explanation. In his opinion, Scali said, it was all a "stinking double cross." And if this were so, Scali went on, it amounted to one of the most colossal misjudgments in history. The United States was absolutely determined to get the missiles out of Cuba, as the President had said. Time was now running out. A U-2 had been shot down and the United States had to conclude that the Soviet military people in Cuba had gotten new instructions.

Fomin said he was sure that there was no double cross, that the problem was a delay in communications. Lamely, he sought to defend the idea of swapping missiles in Cuba for missiles in Turkey. After all, the first such proposal had come from an American—Walter Lippmann, in his column three days earlier, on Thursday. Thumping the table, Scali said he didn't give a damn who had mentioned it unofficially. As a reporter who was well informed of United States Government thinking, he wanted Fomin to understand that it was completely, totally, and perpetually unacceptable. It had been unacceptable in the past, it was unacceptable today, and it would be unacceptable tomorrow and *ad infinitum*. If the Soviets wanted to talk about American missile bases in

Europe they should talk about it within the framework of general disarmament and not seek to inject it into the Cuban crisis.

They parted, Fomin assuring Scali that a reply would surely come soon and Scali repeating how critically short was time.

Scali went to the State Department to report and was whisked to the White House to stand by while the ExCom members read what he had dictated.

THE "TROLLOPE PLOY"

Then, with all the evidence on the table, the ExCom considered what to do next. And it was Robert Kennedy who conceived a brilliant diplomatic maneuver—later dubbed the "Trollope Ploy," after the recurrent scene in Anthony Trollope's novels in which the girl interprets a squeeze of her hand as a proposal of marriage. His suggestion was to deal only with Friday's package of signals—Khrushchev's cable and the approach through Scali—as if the conflicting message on Saturday, linking the missiles in Cuba with those in Turkey, simply did not exist. That message, in fact, had already been rejected in a public announcement. The thing to do now was to answer the Friday package of approaches and make the answer public—which would add a certain political pressure as well as increase the speed. Khrushchev's Friday-night cable had not mentioned or even hinted at inspection, but inspection had been a key element of the proposal put forward by Fomin. With certain items selected from the cable and others from the Scali-Fomin exchange, a reply was drafted for the President's signature: "I have read your letter of October 26th with great care and welcome the statement of your desire to seek a prompt solution to the problem," the President's letter read. "The first thing that needs to be done, however, is for work to cease on offensive missile bases in Cuba. . . . Assuming this is done promptly, I have given my representatives in New York instructions that will permit them to work out this weekend—in cooperation with the Acting Secretary General and your representative—an arrangement for the permanent solution to the Cuban problem."

Then came the "Trollope Ploy": "As I read your letter, the key elements of your proposals—which seem generally acceptable as I understand them—are as follows: (1) You would agree to remove these weapons systems from Cuba under appropriate United Nations observation and supervision [which had been mentioned only by Fomin]; and undertake, with suitable safeguards, to halt the further introduction of such weapons systems into Cuba. (2) We, on our part, would agree—upon the establishment of adequate arrangements through the United Nations to ensure the carrying out and continuation of these commitments

—(a) to remove promptly the quarantine measures now in effect and (b) to give assurances against an invasion of Cuba."

This message was released for broadcast to Moscow and the public. The President then personally dispatched Robert Kennedy to make crystal clear to Dobrynin the full sense of urgency and seriousness felt in Washington, the fact that the United States could wait no longer but would have to proceed toward an agreement and peace if the missiles were withdrawn or toward "strong and overwhelming retaliatory action." What the United States could not do, the Attorney General made clear, was remain any longer on dead center.

Again there was nothing to do but wait. As the meeting broke up, President Kennedy remarked that now it could "go either way."

Just before nine o'clock Sunday morning, October 28, Moscow radio announced that it would have an important statement to broadcast at nine sharp. It was a letter from Chairman Khrushchev: "In order to eliminate as rapidly as possible the conflict which endangers the cause of peace . . . the Soviet Government . . . has given a new order to dismantle the arms which you described as offensive, and to crate and return them to the Soviet Union."

To tie the final strings, a White House statement was quickly drafted confirming the agreement and just as quickly broadcast over the Voice of America. A fuller reply to the Chairman's letter was then prepared, and this, too, was released for publication and broadcast.

The two greatest powers in the world had avoided a clash, and the tension subsided. No one knows for sure what Khrushchev felt, but there are a few clues. In a speech in December reporting on the crisis, he spoke of a "smell of burning" and other things that indicate that he felt the world had come close indeed to a nuclear holocaust and that his own personal feeling was a sense of relief. Another hint came the same Sunday that the crisis ended. Late that day, October 28, Scali met with Fomin for the last time. "I have been instructed," Fomin said in the classic language of diplomacy, "to thank you and to tell you that the information you supplied was very valuable to the Chairman in helping him make up his mind quickly. And," he added, "that includes your 'explosion' Saturday."

As for Kennedy, he was naturally elated. Privately, with his brother, Robert, he expressed it with his typical wryness: "Maybe this is the night I should go to the theater"—thinking of Ford's. But publicly, he avoided any show of elation, and he cautioned the members of his administration against any tendency to gloat or claim a victory. For what President Kennedy really wanted was to use the crisis as a steppingstone to a lessening of tensions in the world and a *détente* with the Soviet Union.

AFTERMATH

In the aftermath of the crisis, there were long and delicate exchanges about what was really meant in the agreement. The first issue was whether the IL 28 light bombers were included. The range and pay load of these planes were too small to be a real threat to the United States, but for domestic political reasons it was important that *no* weapons that could be termed "offensive" remained. The Soviets came to understand this, and removed the IL 28s along with the missiles.

Another issue was Soviet troops and military technicians. Although not a specific part of the agreement, the United States certainly desired that the Soviet troops, too, be withdrawn. Khrushchev's response here was also politically sensitive. But it required that the United States be understanding of his political problem, too, which the Sino-Soviet dispute undoubtedly aggravated, and be patient about just how soon the Soviet troops would be withdrawn. The troops associated with the missiles apparently departed with the missiles. The rest, Khrushchev said, were in Cuba only to train the Cubans in operating the antiaircraft SAMs and other defensive equipment and would depart progressively as the training job was completed.

The third issue was inspection. This had been part of the agreement, but the Soviets had not obtained Castro's approval of the arrangement and he flatly refused to permit it—as he had earlier said, "whoever tries to inspect Cuba must come in battle array." On November 20, President Kennedy, announcing Khrushchev's agreement to remove the IL 28s and permit their departure to be observed from the air, said that, in view of the refusal of the Cuban Government to permit inspection or the setting up of lasting safeguards against the future introduction of offensive weapons into Cuba, the United States would continue its air reconnaissance activities.

In the meantime, the militantly uncompromising anti-Communists in the United States kept up a steady barrage of charges that the Soviets were cheating on the agreements. A particularly persistent charge, inspired by the Cuban refugees, was that the missiles were not really being taken out of Cuba, in spite of the photographs, but were being stored in caves. Some of the wilder charges, indeed, were not only that missiles were stored in caves, but that complete installations were underground—including "airfields, missile platforms, and rocket storage facilities," although no one explained how an airfield could be put underground.[2] Senators Barry Goldwater and Kenneth Keating were particularly active. Goldwater said that he was not convinced that the Soviets had removed their missiles and that he knew "some darned good military men who don't think so either," and said that he thought the President would have "to face up to the necessity of an invasion." On January 1, 1963, Senator Keating not only suggested that the Soviets had hidden the missiles in caves, but charged that new shipments of military equipment were arriving steadily and that the Soviets had not dismantled the missile sites but were maintaining and guarding them—and he continued to make the charges even after the Defense Department released low-level photographs showing that the concrete revetments had been broken up by air hammers.

In exasperation, President Kennedy asked a labor leader who was paying a call how he managed to persuade his membership that even as much as a 25-cent-an-hour raise was a victory if he'd used a 27-cent demand as a bargaining tactic. "It's my worst problem," was the reply.

But much more seriously, the speeches of Senator Keating and Senator Goldwater came very near to wrecking the agreement on troop withdrawal. Their charges and continual public emphasis on troop withdrawal so exacerbated the Soviet political position that the Soviets raised the question of reversing their decision on removing their troops. Eventually, they went through with it, but there is no doubt that the result of Goldwater's and Keating's intervention was to delay the withdrawal of Soviet troops for a considerable period of time.

But the evidence continued to mount that the Soviets had indeed pulled out their missiles and IL 28 bombers and that the Soviet troops and military technicians were also leaving. By March of 1963, the charges petered out. There really was no longer any doubt that President Kennedy had achieved a foreign policy victory of historical proportions.

SIGNIFICANCE

Why did the Soviets back down in Cuba? What are the lessons of the crisis? And what is its meaning for the future? Was it, indeed, a turning point in history?

The risks to both sides in the Cuban missile crisis were very real, very direct, and very high—as Dean Rusk said, a misstep might have meant the "incineration" of the entire Northern Hemisphere, including the North American Continent. Even so, it is not possible to say that it was a nuclear threat, as such, that caused the Soviets to back down. The Soviet leaders probably had considerable confidence in the judgment and sense of responsibility of the American leaders, and they undoubtedly assumed that the U.S. response would begin with conventional means and would continue to be confined to conventional means unless the Soviets themselves did something that raised the ante. On the other hand, it is also not possible to say that the Soviets backed down solely in the face of a threat to invade Cuba with conventional, non-nuclear forces, even though they knew that the troops they had in Cuba could not stand up to such an invasion. The Soviet leadership has often repeated, and not entirely with the intention of misleading us, that limited war always carries a risk of escalation to nuclear war. And certainly in the Cuban missile crisis there were a number of ways that events could have gotten out of hand.

On balance, in other words, the best judgment seems to be that the Soviets backed down in the face of a threat that combined both conventional and nuclear power. Cuba is close to the sources of American strength and distant from the sources of Soviet strength. With vastly shorter lines of communication, the United States could apply overwhelmingly preponderant conventional power at the point of contact—Cuba—and do so under an umbrella of nuclear power that foreclosed any possibility of the Soviets trying to use nuclear weapons to redress the imbalance at the contact point. It was this combination of overwhelming conventional power on the spot and adequate nuclear power overall that proved irresistible.

Let it also be said that the decision to withdraw required courage on the Soviet side and that although putting the missiles into Cuba was threatening and irresponsible, the Soviets handled the ensuing crisis with wisdom and restraint. All the MRBMs were operational by October 28, and although I believe the United States would and should have gone on to invasion if the Soviets had not agreed to withdraw their missiles, it is awesome to contemplate the situation of American ground and air forces attacking Soviet nuclear missiles poised on their pads and defended by Soviet ground combat forces equipped with tactical atomic weapons.

In any case, the first and most obvious lesson of the Cuban missile crisis is that of power. The United States decided to accept the Soviet challenge and U.S. strength and determination were sufficient to meet the challenge. The United States had both the power and the will, and the Soviet Union suffered a defeat.

But it would be a mistake to conclude that this same formula of will and power can be translated into success in every kind of confrontation —that it would necessarily have worked in Laos, for example, or Vietnam. The arena in the Cuba case was close to the sources of American power, as we have said, and far from the sources of Soviet power. But, more importantly, there was no doubt at all about the stakes: the threat from Cuba in October 1962 was nuclear, and it was directed at the American heartland.

It would also be a mistake to think that the formula of will and power is appropriate to all political objectives. The issue here is the relationship of means to ends—the appropriateness and acceptability both to world opinion and to the American conscience of using military force to accomplish particular objectives. It is acceptable and fitting that the United States use the full panoply of its military power to remove a threat to its survival. But at some point as one moves down the scale from national survival to progressively lesser objectives, the political cost of using raw military force begins to exceed the potential gain. When that point is reached, the wise nation shifts away from military force as the means to achieve its goals and adopts other instrumentalities. Reasonable men may quarrel at the wisdom of the exact point at which President Kennedy chose to make this shift in the Cuban missile crisis. He chose to shift just after the removal of the missiles and bombers but before the withdrawal of Soviet advisers and the elimination of the Castro regime. Reasonable men might argue for making shift at some slightly different point, but they would not question the principle itself.

We stand too close to the Cuban missile crisis to see its final meaning or to measure the full dimensions of its place in history. But surely any assessment of its significance must begin with the fact that it was the first nuclear crisis the world has ever known and that what President Kennedy and the United States did in meeting the crisis set precedents applicable to all the subsequent international crises of our time.

The keynote of the United States response was flexibility and self-disciplined restraint—a graduated effort which avoided trying to achieve too much and which stopped short of confronting an adversary with stark and imperative choices. Out of the basic policy flowed the precedents—restraint in the use of power; flexibility in developing a solution; the pacing of events to give the other side time to think and to obviate "spasm reactions"; the making of a "little international law" outlawing the secret and rapid deployment of nuclear weapons; the deliberate regard for precedent and the effect of present action on the longer future; and, finally, the relevancy to that longer future of moral integrity—a point on which both the President and the Attorney General so strongly insisted.

Whether the Cuban missile crisis marks a turning point in world history is as yet impossible to say. The Soviets put missiles into Cuba in an attempt to solve a set of problems—a strategic imbalance, the exigencies of the Sino-Soviet dispute, and the impossible combination of demands on their limited resources made by defense, their space program, their people's appetite for consumers' goods, and the drain of foreign aid needed to support their foreign policy. When the crisis was over, the missiles withdrawn, the same set of problems remained. The irony is that these same problems, which brought the world so near to nuclear war, later brought about the so-called *détente*—a relaxation of Cold War tensions. For it was the same pressures that led the Soviets to put missiles in Cuba that later led them to take up Kennedy's proposal for a treaty banning nuclear testing.

Following the crisis, the Soviets had only two alternatives. One was a crash ICBM program to redress the strategic balance. This would mean austerity at home, and a return to the coldest kind of Cold War abroad.

And, as a most unpalatable corollary, it would necessitate an immediate healing of the Sino-Soviet dispute—and on Chinese terms.

The other alternative was the one actually chosen—easing the tensions of the Cold War, with the Test Ban Treaty as the first concrete step. The ICBM program could then be stretched out, and the burdens lightened of competing so aggressively in the underdeveloped regions of the world. And this course of action also had a corollary for the Sino-Soviet dispute— a sharpening of the tension between Communist China and the Soviet Union.

In the Cuban missile crisis, the Soviets gazed down the gun barrel of nuclear war, as did we. They probed its awesome dimensions, and they drew back. This experience did not cause the Soviets to cease being Communists or to give up their goal of world domination. But for the moment, at least, they seemed to recognize that, on so small a planet as ours, nuclear war is certainly one means that would jeopardize their ends rather than serve them. For our part, we too learned something of the limitations of nuclear power and of the need of accommodation even in the midst of opposition.

The threat of nuclear war was not eliminated from the world by the events of October 1962, nor was there a reconciliation between East and West. But if either of these two objectives ever is attained, historians may well mark the Cuban missile crisis of 1962 as the beginning.

NOTES

1 The plane returned safely. The Soviets made no follow-up move, and the President decided to ignore the incident. Later, when Khrushchev protested, the President apologized.
2 The New York *Times,* November 28, 1962.

VI

THE CONGO CRISIS

"Call it nationalism, call it anti-colonialism, call it what you will, Africa is going through a revolution."
—SENATOR JOHN F. KENNEDY, *1959*

"The irony is that when the UN begins to be effective, it will also begin to have political interests of its own."
—AN AMERICAN DIPLOMAT, *1965*

CHAPTER 17

Crisis in the Congo

THE CONGO CRISIS was the Kennedy administration's first sustained test. It began before most of the others and lasted longer. And to a new American administration committed to vigor in foreign policy and to sympathy with the emerging nations, history could hardly have devised a more baffling and frustrating test. For the Congo crisis was like nothing else except, perhaps, the game of croquet in *Alice In Wonderland,* where the balls were hedgehogs that took every opportunity to unroll and creep away and the mallets were flamingos that interrupted every stroke by turning back their heads to argue with the players.

Dean Rusk, the new Secretary of State, Chester Bowles, the Under Secretary, and G. Mennen Williams, Assistant Secretary for African Affairs, had occupied temporary offices on the first floor of the State Department since shortly after their appointments were announced, and by the time they assumed responsibility, on January 20, they had been thoroughly briefed. And it was not long after January 20 that they found themselves in the midst of a howling crisis.

A United Nations force was supposedly occupying the Congo to restore and maintain law and order and prevent outside intervention, but it could operate freely only in the area around the capital, Léopoldville, and even in this area there were continual annoyances and clashes of jurisdiction. There were three separate centers of power in the Congo at the time, each eight hundred air miles from either of the other two, and each strong enough to repel invasion of its territory but not strong enough to extend its own control beyond the area immediately surrounding its home base.[1]

One of these centers of power was Léopoldville, situated in the western part of the country, controlled by President Joseph Kasavubu and General Mobutu. A second was Elisabethville and Katanga Province in the south, the center of the mining industry and the source of most of the Congo's wealth. It was controlled by Moïse Tshombe—a flamboyant personality who was not only closely allied with the Belgians and the mining interests but who had also hired white mercenaries and was therefore hated by the more radical nationalists all over Africa. The third center of power was Stanleyville, in the north, which was controlled by Patrice Lumumba and his lieutenant, Antoine Gizenga. At the time, how-

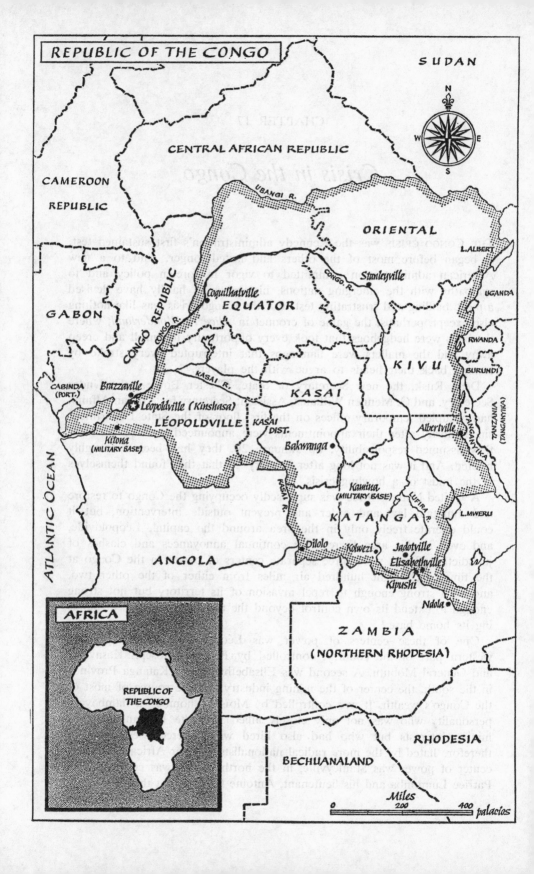

REPUBLIC OF THE CONGO

SUDAN

CENTRAL AFRICAN REPUBLIC

CAMEROON
REPUBLIC

UBANGI R.

ORIENTAL

L.ALBERT

Stanleyville

GABON

Coquilhatville

EQUATOR

CONGO R.

UGANDA

RWANDA

BURUNDI

KIVU

CABINDA
(PORT.)

Brazzaville

Léopoldville (Kinshasa)

LÉOPOLDVILLE

Kitona
(MILITARY BASE)

KASAI R.

KASAI

KASAI
DIST.

Bakwanga

Albertville

L.TANGANYIKA

TANZANIA
(TANGANYIKA)

ATLANTIC OCEAN

Kamina
(MILITARY BASE)

KATANGA

Dilolo

Kolwezi

Jadotville

Elisabethville

Kipushi

LUFIRA R.

L.MWERU

ANGOLA

Ndola

ZAMBIA
(NORTHERN RHODESIA)

AFRICA

REPUBLIC OF
THE CONGO

RHODESIA

BECHUANALAND

Miles

0   200   400

palacios

ever, late January 1961, Lumumba was supposedly being held in custody
by Tshombe in Katanga, and this was troublesome, for if there was a
hero type among the three major leaders of the Congo, it was clearly
Lumumba. A fiery orator who could play on the emotion of a crowd as
if it were a musical instrument, Lumumba was a fierce and uncompromising nationalist. His crowd appeal gained him followers within the
Congo and his leftist, bitter anticolonialism gained him support from the
other radical leaders in Africa.

And so the Congo smoldered the first week or two of the new administration. My own introduction to the problem came swiftly. On the
morning of February 11, 1961, just six days after taking office, I had
come in at seven forty-five to be briefed by the intelligence desk officers
in preparation for the Secretary's morning meeting with the Under
Secretaries and Assistant Secretaries. But it was only at the last minute
that the latest intelligence came in on the Congo, so I was late and out
of breath when I reported to the meeting that the Katanga government
had announced that Lumumba had escaped—but that intelligence suspected that he might really have been murdered.

The public storm broke two days later, on February 13, when Katanga
announced that Lumumba had indeed been killed—by "tribesmen," they
said, encountered during his "escape."[2] And his murder completed the
alienation of both the Communist bloc and the radicalist African and
Asian states from the UN's effort in the Congo. On February 14, the
Soviet Union presented a resolution to the Security Council calling for
Hammarskjöld's dismissal as Secretary General and the withdrawal of all
UN troops from the Congo, and coupled with the resolution was an
announcement that the Soviets were considering giving aid to Gizenga's
"lawful government" in Stanleyville. On February 14, the Stanleyville
government was recognized by the United Arab Republic and the next
day by East Germany, Yugoslavia, and Ghana. In the next few days
recognition came from Guinea, Mali, Morocco, the National Liberation
Front of Algeria, and the various Communist bloc countries. It looked
very much as if the Congo might become the arena for a major East-West
confrontation, and that there was a possibility that the struggle might
wreck the UN in the process.

It had all started on June 30, 1960, when the Belgian Congo became
a new nation, the Republic of the Congo, in independence ceremonies
attended by the Belgian king and dignitaries from all over the world.
Independence had come easily, with no more violence than a riot or two.
Nicknamed the "Happy Colony," the Belgian Congo had been quiet and
generally prosperous for fifty years. Its economy—based on the mining
industry of Katanga Province, which provided 60 per cent of the Congo's

total revenue—was unrivaled among the new states of Africa, and over 100,000 Belgian technicians and administrators were remaining to keep it going and to train replacements. Despite the lack of experienced Congolese, the prospects looked promising. Other colonies had become independent with far less and seemed to be making a go of it.

Then, three days later, everything began to come apart. Tribal fighting broke out almost immediately, which was probably not important. But, following some trouble at Camp Leopold II on July 4, Congolese soldiers of the Congo National Army, the former *Force Publique,* on July 5 and 6 refused to obey their Belgian officers and demanded immediate promotions and pay increases. By July 8 the *Force Publique* was a plundering mob, and disorder had spread over much of the country. Stories of rape and murder burgeoned through the Belgian community, and that night more than thirteen hundred women and children fled the country—to be followed by what was estimated to be three-fourths of the European population. On July 11 Katanga Province seceded from the republic, and Moïse Tshombe, the provincial president, proclaimed it an independent country. Joseph Kasavubu, President of the Congo, and Patrice Lumumba, then Premier, cabled the Secretary General of the United Nations requesting the "urgent dispatch of UN military assistance," and the Security Council, meeting during the night of July 13–14, 1960, authorized the Secretary General to take steps to provide it. On July 15, some sixteen days after the Congo's independence, the first troops of the UN forces, from Ghana and Tunisia, began to arrive in American planes.

There was, in fact, considerable ambiguity in the circumstances surrounding the Congolese request for UN military assistance. Belgian forces were available in the Congo; in accordance with the Treaty of Friendship signed on the eve of independence, Belgium held the military bases at Kamina and Kitona. As disorder spread following the army mutiny, the Belgians reinforced these troops with two and one half companies of paratroopers and tried to persuade Lumumba to ask for them to intervene to restore order. Lumumba continued to refuse, and on July 10 the Belgian Government went ahead anyway to protect the lives of Belgian nationals, even though it was a violation of the Treaty of Friendship for the Belgian soldiers to leave their bases without a request from the Congolese Government. It was the next day, July 11, that Tshombe proclaimed Katanga independent and Lumumba made the first request for UN military assistance—an oral request to Ralph J. Bunche, the Secretary General's representative, for UN assistance "to restore discipline in the Congolese army." But the formal cable to the Secretary General, signed by both Kasavubu and Lumumba and dispatched on July 12, requested UN military assistance not to restore order and discipline in the Congolese Army but to meet the Belgian "aggression." And this was followed on July 13 with a declaration that a "state of war" existed between Belgium and the Congo as a result of Belgian military intervention.

In the meantime, the Congo cabinet had also met on July 12 (in Lumumba's absence, Gizenga was in charge) and requested military aid not from the UN but from the United States. Although President Eisenhower refused and suggested that the request should go to the United Nations, Lumumba was disturbed and consulted the Soviet representatives in Léopoldville. Apparently acting on their advice, he persuaded Kasavubu to sign with him a cable to Khrushchev to the effect that the Congo "was occupied by Belgian troops and the lives of the Republic's President and Premier are in danger." The cable went on to say that "certain Western countries" were conspiring with Belgium against the Congo's independence and that the Congolese Government might "have to ask the Soviet Union's intervention should the Western camp not stop its aggression." Khrushchev promptly replied that if the Belgian troops were not withdrawn, the Soviet Union would not "shrink from resolute measures to curb the aggression."

THE SECURITY COUNCIL RESOLUTION

Given this confusion of multiple appeals with contradictory themes, it is something of a miracle that the interests of the members of the Security Council converged long enough to pass an enabling resolution. But the United States and the Soviet Union for the moment saw UN intervention as better for their interests than doing nothing—or at least not as bad. Argentina, Ecuador, and Italy went along with the United States, and Poland dutifully followed the Soviet Union. Both France and Britain were opposed to the idea, but neither felt strongly enough about the matter to do any more than express their distaste by abstaining. Only Tunisia and Ceylon were passionately in favor.

In the circumstances, it is not surprising that the keynote of the authorization given to the Secretary General was ambiguity. The Security Council resolution first called upon Belgium to withdraw its troops from the Congo. It then authorized the Secretary General to take the necessary steps in consultation with the Government of the Republic of the Congo to provide such military assistance as might be necessary "until, through the efforts of the Congolese Government with the technical assistance of the UN, the national security forces may be able, in the opinion of the Government, to meet their tasks . . ." The Security Council, clearly, did not know what they wanted the Secretary General to do in the Congo, but only that it wanted him to do something.[3]

THE STRUGGLE WITH LUMUMBA

Throughout the summer of 1960, Lumumba was increasingly at odds with the UN representative in the Congo and with some of his own colleagues in the Congolese Government. More and more openly he advocated violence in dealing with secessionist Katanga while at the same time asking Communist nations for arms and equipment, which they furnished in spite of the UN resolution. Then on September 5, 1960, Kasavubu moved against him. Exercising his constitutional prerogatives as President, Kasavubu dismissed Lumumba as Premier, accusing him of provoking discord within the government, depriving citizens of fundamental liberties, and "plunging the nation into fractricidal war." To be new Premier, Kasavubu appointed Joseph Ileo, then President of the Congo Senate. Having done his stolid duty, Kasavubu then went to bed.

But not Lumumba. He convened the Council of Ministers, and at four o'clock in the morning it voted to accuse Kasavubu of high treason, to declare him deprived of all functions, and to nullify his dismissal order. Lumumba himself went on the radio to declare that Kasavubu was no longer President, called on the army, people, and workers to "rise," and ordered the Soviet-equipped forces in Stanleyville and Kasai Province, most of whom were loyal to him personally, to come to Léopoldville by air—utilizing the Ilyushin 14 transports supplied unilaterally in violation of the July 14 resolution.

It was in these circumstances that the UN took the first of the decisions that brought it into the political arena of the Congo. Following Kasavubu's action in dismissing Lumumba, Andrew W. Cordier, the UN representative in Léopoldville, was visited by several delegations from tribal associations and smaller political factions begging for UN protection, and he quickly learned of Lumumba's call for reinforcements. It was clear that if he did not act to put a UN damper on the situation, there would be a slaughtering. On the other hand, it was also clear that putting a UN damper on the situation would have the effect of supporting Kasavubu at the expense of Lumumba.

Cordier moved. He seized the airport at Léopoldville and ordered the UN forces throughout the Congo to close airports where they were stationed. And to prevent any more inflammatory speeches, he also seized Léopoldville's radio station.

In what the Communist bloc and the Afro-Asian radicals also regarded as a political act, Hammarskjöld publicly demanded that member nations live up to the UN resolution by channeling all outside aid to the Congo through the UN. And he did so in such a way as to criticize, indirectly but unmistakably, the Soviet Union.

The African and Asian radicals were outraged that the UN had supported

Kasavubu against Lumumba, and the Soviets made the most of it. At the September 15 meeting of the Security Council, the Soviet delegate, Valerian Zorin, attacked Hammarskjöld personally and with bitter words. Zorin accused Hammarskjöld of "openly working to assist the colonizers," of "compromising in the eyes of the peoples the prestige of the organization of the United Nations," and of letting the West use "the organization of the United Nations as a screen to conceal their imperialist designs in Africa."

The Soviets vetoed a compromise resolution drafted by Tunisia and Ceylon, and over Soviet objections the Security Council then called for an emergency special session of the General Assembly. It met, and after impassioned debate, passed a resolution that directed the Secretary General to "continue to take vigorous action" in accordance with the earlier resolutions, appealed to the Congolese to seek a "speedy solution by peaceful means of all their internal conflicts for the unity and integrity of the Congo," and requested all member states to refrain from sending arms unilaterally to the Congo and "from any action which might tend to impede the restoration of law and order."

THE UN VERSUS THE U.S.S.R.

The Secretary General and the UN secretariat were thus upheld, but the cost was a constitutional crisis. On September 23, Khrushchev opened his own attack on the organization and on the Secretary General. He charged that the "colonialists" had been attempting to set up a "puppet government" in the Congo. "They have been doing this unseemly work," he went on to say, "through the United Nations Secretary General, Mr. Hammarskjöld and his staff." At the climax of the speech, Khrushchev announced that the time had come to abolish the post of Secretary General, and he put forward the so-called "troika" scheme to reorganize the secretariat to reflect the Cold War, dividing it among the East, the West, and the Neutralists. In this and subsequent speeches, Khrushchev delivered the fiercest, most vituperative attack on an individual that the body had ever seen. "To avoid misinterpretation," Khrushchev said on one occasion, for example, "I want to reaffirm that we do not trust Mr. Hammarskjöld and cannot trust him. If he himself does not muster up enough courage to resign, so to say, in a chivalrous manner, then we will draw the necessary conclusions . . . It is not proper for a man who has flouted elementary justice to hold such an important post as that of Secretary General." But it was when the Foreign Minister of the Philippines was speaking in Hammarskjöld's defense on September 26 that Khrushchev summed up the Soviet attitude most vividly, not in words but in a vulgar yet dramatic gesture—by taking off one of his shoes and using it to pound on the desk in front of him.

Throughout the fall of 1960, while the political battles raged in the UN, things remained about the same in the Congo itself. Ileo continued as Premier, and Lumumba was in house arrest in Léopoldville under the protection of UN troops. In late November, he escaped, only to be arrested by Mobutu's troops. On January 18, 1961, it was announced that Lumumba had been transferred to a prison in Katanga, whose premier was Lumumba's archenemy, Moïse Tshombe. Within a month, as related above, it transpired that he had been murdered.

The first thing the Kennedy administration did following the murder of Lumumba was to take a close look at all the different participants in the Congo crisis and at their motives—the Congolese leaders themselves, the other African states, our European allies, the Soviet Union, the UN, and last but not by any means least, the opposing groups within Washington itself.

THE CONGOLESE AND THE AFRO-ASIANS

The struggle among the different leaders of the Congo was in many ways simple competition for personal power, and mere opportunism is probably explanation enough for some of the moves of a Lumumba or a Tshombe. But the struggle also had its overtones of principle, of competing ideologies and rival visions of the Congo's future. It is a mistake to put precise labels on the different Congolese leaders and factions, for they were unformed in their ideology, feeling their way and shifting their stance as the circumstances shifted. But from the Washington point of view *at the time,* there seemed to be three main ideological camps among the Congolese, and each seemed to have a group of counterparts among the African and Asian members of the United Nations.[4]

THE RADICALS

The first group was the radicals, led first by Patrice Lumumba, and then Antoine Gizenga, with Ghana, Guinea, Mali, Morocco, and the United Arab Republic as their African and Asian allies. Having themselves struggled against alien masters, prejudice, and often brutal repression, they waved the bloody shirt of nationalism. Again, it is a mistake to think of them as having a well-formed ideology. They played with Marxist verbiage and a number were Communist sympathizers, but above all they were African nationalists. They were radical in their general inclinations, but malleable and inchoate in their doctrine. To the extent that they really did have a world view, it revolved around their fears of the old enslavement in a new guise—"neocolonialism." Since the "imperialists'" goal is to continue the old order—so ran the radicals' thinking—their method is to create states whose independence is a sham—"the practice," as Kwame

Nkrumah, President of Ghana, said, "of granting a sort of independence by the metropolitan power with the concealed intention of making the liberated country a client-state and controlling it effectively by means other than political ones."

A favorite tactic of the neocolonialists, in the radicals' view, is "Balkanization"—cutting up former colonies or encouraging secession, such as Katanga's, in order to create states too small to survive except through continued dependence on the metropolitan master. The leaders of such secessionist subunits, the argument runs, are not really spokesmen of genuine African interests but traitors, stooges of the imperialists.

Thus for these radical leaders and their African and Asian supporters, the question of the Congo was not either the danger of extending the Cold War to Africa or the breakdown of law and order but whether or not colonialism was truly at an end. The first test of this was not only the removal of Belgian troops but also the removal of Belgian influence, which was one of the reasons that Tshombe's white mercenaries became an issue. The second test was not only that the Congo be independent and governed by Africans but that it be a centralized state, headed by "true" nationalists; that is, radicals. Anything else, in their view, would be a neocolonialist sham. "For the radicals," as Robert C. Good, later Ambassador to Zambia, said, "the legitimacy of a postcolonial regime relates in part to its legal mandate . . . but even more, one supposes, legitimacy relates to the regime's credentials as a representative of genuine nationalism fighting against the intrigues of neocolonialism. This is why Lumumba was so extolled as the 'best son of Africa,' the 'Lincoln of the Congo,' the 'Black Messiah,' whose struggle was made noble by his unswerving demand for centralism against all forms of Balkanization and was rendered heroic by his unyielding resistance to the forces of neocolonialism that finally killed his body, but not his spirit."[5]

As far as the radicals were concerned, the purpose of the UN's presence in the Congo was to further these ends. The UN should remove the Belgians and their influence, and it should support without question the "legitimate" central government of the Congo—the radical nationalist government of Lumumba and Gizenga. Any other role or any policy of so-called neutrality regarding the different Congolese factions would, they felt, fall into the "neocolonialist" trap and perpetuate the trouble. If the UN could not be made to assume this, its "proper" role, they argued, then it should have no role at all and be forced to withdraw from the Congo entirely. Such was the view of the radicals.

THE CONSERVATIVES

Moïse Tshombe of Katanga was the symbol of the second group in the Congo, the conservatives. The conservative African states included most of the former French African states south of the Sahara, Cameroon,

Chad, Congo (Brazzaville), Dahomey, Gabon, the Ivory Coast, the Malagasy Republic, Niger, Senegal, the Central African Republic, and Upper Volta—which is an impressive list. These countries had only recently (and sometimes reluctantly) received their independence. Their leaders, for the most part weak and unsure, tended to follow de Gaulle's lead internationally, and he was adamantly opposed to any significant UN role in the Congo. But the relationship of the conservative African states to Tshombe was not so unequivocal as the relationship of the radical states to Stanleyville, and vague though the radicals' position was, the conservative position was even vaguer. More certain of what they were against than what they were for, the conservatives were against radicalism and Lumumba. But with the exception of Youlou in Brazzaville and Tsiranana in the Malagasy Republic, it is uncertain how many were in favor of Tshombe and his secession.[6] In general, the common ideology of the conservative states was tribalism, a preference for maintaining rather than cutting ties with the former metropole, continuing a close relationship with Europe, and accepting and legitimizing the state system inherited from the colonial era, while continuing to talk about African unity.[7] The implications of all this for their attitude toward the Congo was that, in addition to opposing a strong central government and favoring a loose federation, the conservative states regarded Belgium not so much as an aggressor, but as a friend to the Congo whose continuing help was vital. To the conservatives, in fact, there probably was no real aggressor. Thus the role of the UN in the conservative view was not only to maintain law and order, but also to hold the ring against any foreign intervention, whether it was Western or Communist. Beyond this role, the conservatives thought the UN should stay aloof. For the radicals the UN would not do enough in the Congo; for the conservatives, it was inclined to do too much.

THE MODERATES

The members of the third group were even less sharply defined in their views and less closely identified with each other than the conservatives. Inside the Congo, this third group included Kasavubu, Mobutu, Ileo, and Adoula. They seemed to Washington to be moderate and pragmatic nationalists, but more often than not they were merely inconsistent. Again, tribalism was a large factor. They came out in favor of a unified Congo, usually on a federalist pattern for tribal reasons, but at times some of them, especially Kasavubu and Albert Kalonji, seemed to prefer the same kind of *de facto* independence for their particular region that Tshombe wanted for Katanga. They were often critical of Belgium—as illustrated by Kasavubu's joining with Lumumba in the cable to Khrushchev—but they were willing to acknowledge Belgian contributions in the past and wanted Belgian assistance in the future. On the whole, the Congolese moderates wanted to co-operate with the UN, but there were many clashes on particulars, on personalities, and on the sensitivities of a new state unable to manage its own affairs.

Among the African and Asian nations, the moderates included Ceylon, Ethiopia, India, Liberia, Libya, Malaya, Nigeria, Somalia, the Sudan, Togo, and Tunisia. In general they had much the same orientation toward the nature of a future Congo state as the Congolese moderates. They wanted to see a unified Congo, but they were not agreed about its form. They were more interested in the restoration of order and stability in the Congo than in which faction came out on top. The very pragmatism of their attitude meant that the outside moderates divided on many issues— even splitting to some extent on whether to seat the delegates Lumumba and Gizenga sent to the UN, for example, or the ones that Kasavubu sent. What they shared was a general agreement on the role of the UN in the Congo and consistent support for its position there. The moderates wanted the UN to remain above the political battle in the Congo and to avoid the use of force if possible. What concerned them most in the beginning was disorder—tribal fighting, the rebellious troops, and the discredit that this reflected on the image of Africa and the developing world. In respect to the task of restoring order, at least, they favored enlarging the UN role and responsibility.

FRANCE, BRITAIN, AND BELGIUM

France in the Congo crisis maintained an Olympian aloofness. De Gaulle disapproved of any significant role for the "so-called United Nations" in the Congo, principally from a concern for the precedent it might set and his determination not to have outsiders involved in France's relations with its own former possessions, particularly Algeria. The French, accordingly, abstained from voting on the first UN resolution and refused to pay the special assessment. But the most significant French move of all was their refusal to permit UN planes to overfly French territory and to influence former French territories to do the same. This meant that a plane on a UN mission from an American base in Germany had to fly to the Mediterranean, then out over the Atlantic past Dakar, and then back in to Léopoldville.

Like France, Britain, too, disapproved of a large role for the UN but the British were not aloof. Britain was very much concerned about the prospect of continued disorder in the Congo and the possibility that the Communists might succeed in making it a political base for subversion all over Africa. It was particularly anxious that Katanga's industrial output not be interrupted. British businessmen and investors had large holdings in Katanga, and the "Katanga lobby" of Lord Liverpool and others was alarmed by the fighting and the possibility that Tshombe would adopt a scorched earth policy. Britain was also concerned about repercussions in Rhodesia and about the precedent all this would have and what it might portend for British investments elsewhere in the world.

Belgian motives were probably as complex as those of most of the other contenders in the Congo, but, except for the Congolese themselves, more intensely felt. Most of the money that had gone into the industrial and mining complex in Katanga was Belgian. The European technicians and administrators who had agreed to remain in the Congo were Belgian, and—again, second only to the Congolese—it was Belgians who were the victims of disorder, murder, and rape. And overall there hung the wounded pride of the former metropole.

THE SOVIET UNION

The motives of the Soviet Union in the Congo crisis were mixed. They saw in the Congo an opportunity first of all to make the position of the West as difficult as possible, for it is doubtful if they wanted to take over responsibility for the Congo. But they also saw an opportunity to extend their influence in Africa, a beckoning chance for a political base with enticing possibilities for the future. But as the Congo crisis built up, so did the crisis in the relations between the Soviet Union and Communist China, and Chinese rivalry in Africa spurred the Soviets on and complicated their purpose. The UN at first seemed a useful instrument to the Soviets, but as the drama unfolded, they came to see it as a threat. Ultimately, the Congo crisis prompted the Soviets to attack the UN itself and to raise for the first time the question of the U.S.S.R. continuing as a UN member.

THE UN SECRETARIAT

Throughout the Congo crisis, there was one other major political actor with motives and interests of its own—the UN Secretariat. As we have seen, the original UN mandate handed down to the Secretary General by the July 14 resolution was vague indeed—to provide military assistance until the national security forces of the Congo were able "to meet their tasks." Since the resolution also called on Belgium to withdraw its forces, it was presumably also the Security Council's intention that the UN force would prevent outside intervention by its mere presence in the Congo. Subsequent resolutions in those first few weeks were no different. The July 22 resolution called on Belgium "to implement speedily the Security Council resolution of 14 July 1960" on withdrawing its troops and authorized the Secretary General "to take all necessary action to this effect" without specifying what they thought the "necessary action" might be. The August 9 resolution repeated the call for Belgium to withdraw its troops speedily, declared that the "entry of the United Nations Force into the province of Katanga is necessary," but reaffirmed that the UN force should "not be a party to or in any way intervene in or be used to influence the outcome of any internal conflict, constitutional or otherwise." In such circumstances, Hammarskjöld and the UN Secretariat had to make some fundamental decisions of their own—decisions that inevitably had political consequences. In the beginning, among enthusiasts who saw the UN as a steppingstone to a world political order, there were those who saw in the Congo crisis an opportunity to extend the responsibility and power of the UN by enlarging its peace-keeping role. But as the Secretariat was forced to make more and more decisions with political consequences, it became itself a political contender and the center of a controversy that finally brought about a constitutional crisis for the UN itself. Under a political bludgeoning from several directions at once, the Secretariat before long found itself fighting to preserve its minimum power and influence and to salvage as much as it could of its reputation as a nonpartisan and impartial international civil service.

THE UNITED STATES

When the Congo crisis first began, in 1960, the Eisenhower administration's objective was to keep the Congo free of Communist domination, and to do so if possible without "bringing the Cold War into Africa"— by which was meant a direct confrontation in the Congo between the Soviet Union and the United States. But beyond this general objective, the story of the Congo crisis is the story, not only of trying to manipulate the rival Congolese factions, their outside supporters, and the UN itself, but of the struggle to get an agreement in the United States Government on the policy goal toward which they should be manipulated.

The battle raged all over Washington—in the press, on the floor of Congress, and within the State Department itself. One view started with the conviction that in Africa nationalism was the wave of the future, and the United States must put itself clearly and unmistakably on the "side of history." Belgian technicians and administrators were obviously essential in the Congo, but there could be no puppet states, such as Katanga. First, a rump Congo without Katanga would not be economically viable, and it would inevitably be the United States that would have to foot the bill. Second, if Katanga's secession was accepted, the moderates in Léopoldville would never recover from the defeat, and the Congo would become an easy prize for the Communists. A third danger was that disorder in the Congo, centrally placed in a volatile continent full of other states with potential secessionists, might have disastrous ramifications. But even if these risks could be tolerated, there was still a greater one. For in the view of those who saw the outlines of a "New Africa" emerging, if anything less than a unified Congo came out of the UN operation, the United States would get the blame. It would be on the wrong side of history in African eyes; our influence throughout black Africa would be all but destroyed; and the Congo would be only the first of many defeats.

It was the liberals of the new administration who were the core of the "New Africa" group—Chester Bowles, Adlai Stevenson, George Ball, G. Mennen Williams, and Harlan Cleveland. But Bowles could wield only marginal influence after he was shifted out of the Under Secretary's job. Stevenson, in New York, was too far away to exercise day-to-day leadership, although both his personal prestige and his position at the UN gave him powerful leverage on the over-all strategy. And George Ball was handicapped by his close identification with Western Europe and sympathy for the plight of the Belgians. Thus the main burden of leadership fell on Williams in his job as Assistant Secretary for African Affairs, on his deputy, Wayne Fredericks, and on Harlan Cleveland, Assistant Secretary for International Organization Affairs.

Cleveland had been dean of the Maxwell School at Syracuse and was well known among the active supporters of the UN. Wayne Fredericks was less well known publicly, but he had two very large assets. First, he had served with General Curtis LeMay during the war and understood the military problems well. Second, he had later been the principal officer of the Ford Foundation concerned with Africa, and his knowledge of the continent and its problems was intimate and detailed—as expert, in fact, as anyone in the United States. Williams, on the other hand, was not so expert on Africa, but he brought to the job the experience and knowledge of a professional politician, as well as the stature of a man who had been several times Governor of Michigan. A big, warm, friendly man, he knew the tricks a public figure must use to be remembered—his trademark was a green polka dot bow tie, which he wore with everything, including on occasion, a dinner suit. And he had a big enough reputation to command a public audience at will.

President Kennedy himself and his immediate aides in the White House tended to share the view of the "New Africa" group, at least to the extent of agreeing that a unified Congo should be the goal and that a failure to achieve it would put both the UN and the United States cross-legged with African nationalism. But a powerful section of opinion in Washington and within the State Department itself was intolerant even of the White House's pragmatic approach to the "New Africa" idea. The old-line career diplomats, who were Europe-oriented, were openly scornful. Although he was newly retired at the time, Robert Murphy, former Under Secretary and the senior and most eminent of the career men, was a spokesman for their disapproval of both the general policy of "encouraging the national aspirations of the people of Africa" and the "costly

United Nations expedition to Léopoldville . . . financed largely by the United States."[8] But most of the opposition to the "New Africa" view inside the State Department was not in favor of an independent Katanga. The difference was that the opposition group was inclined to take the whole matter much less seriously. New African states were proliferating rapidly anyway, and one more did not seem to make all that much difference. What the "Old Europe" people did take seriously, however, was any idea that we should push so hard for a particular solution that we would begin to alienate opinion among our NATO allies.

Thus as a practical matter, the differences came down to one of means, since a unified Congo under moderate leadership was what most of our NATO allies wanted to see. But even so, this left plenty of room for bitter battles. The "New Africa" advocates recognized that Belgian help and agreement were essential, but they were suspicious that if Belgium were put in the lead their policy would be too much influenced by the special interests of the *Union Minière du Haut Katanga,* the Belgian combine that controlled Katangan mining and industry. Even more important than the role of the Belgians was the question of risk. The "New Africa" group felt that the stakes were so high that in the crunches of the crisis the United States had to take very high risks and pay very high costs if necessary—that if using force was the only way to achieve the objective, then we had to use force even at the cost of alienating opinion among our NATO allies. And this the "Old Europe" group could not accept.

The press was divided along similar lines, except that the opposition to the "New Africa" view was more vituperative. One example will illustrate. "On the second level at the White House and in the State Department," William S. White, the columnist, wrote in the midst of the crisis, "are men so emotionally committed to anticolonialism that the President will need to show great force lest they carry his policies outside his own viable middling position by sheer evangelical zeal."[9] These men, he charged, are "seized with a holy mission, almost as zealous as the abolitionists who so plagued the fair and reasonable and practical Lincoln."

But the most vocal and active spokesman for Tshombe and Katanga and against the whole UN operation was Senator Thomas J. Dodd of Connecticut. In our Congo policy, Dodd charged, there were basic faults that plagued all of United States foreign policy. The first was to rely excessively on the United Nations. The second was "excessive deference to that fallen idol of liberalism, Nehru, and his neutralist companions." The United States, Dodd complained, was footing the bill for the UN operation, but it was Nehru who was determining policy—or, "To be more precise, it is being determined by Nehru's guiding genius in the field of foreign affairs, Mr. Krishna Menon, who has in my opinion justly come to be regarded as the personification of crypto-communism."[10]

This, then, was the line-up in the Congo, in the UN, and in Washington—a multiplicity of interests and an equal multiplicity of factions. The next problem for the new administration was to find a policy.

NOTES

[1] In fact, there was a fourth center—in the south Kasai, between Léopoldville and Elisabethville. Centered on Bakwanga, the so-called Mining State, under Albert Kalonji, was the world's principal source of industrial diamonds.

[2] Many UN officials later came to believe that Lumumba never reached Katanga alive, but that he had been beaten to death on the plane.

[3] See Ernest W. Lefever, *Crisis in the Congo, A UN Force in Action*, The Brookings Institution, 1965.

[4] See Robert C. Good, "The Congo Crisis: A Study of Post-Colonial Politics," in *Neutralism and Nonalignment, the New States in World Affairs*, edited by Laurence W. Martin, 1962.

[5] Robert C. Good, *op. cit.*, pp. 51–52.

[6] Even with Tshombe, secession was not really a matter of principle. Several years later, when it was all over, he became Premier of the unified Congo.

[7] Robert C. Good, "Changing Patterns of African International Relations," *The American Political Science Review*, September 1964.

[8] Robert Murphy, *Diplomat Among Warriors*, 1964, pp. 337–38.

[9] William S. White, "Which Friends Come First?," *Harper's*, March 1962.

[10] Thomas J. Dodd, "Congo: The Untold Story," *National Review*, August 28, 1962.

CHAPTER 18

Negotiations ... and Failure

THE POLICY toward the Congo crisis the new administration would have preferred and what it actually adopted were two different things. This was an administration committed to full involvement in world affairs, to vigor in the pursuit of foreign policy, to support for the UN, and especially to a new sympathy and understanding of the emerging peoples. All this pointed toward a policy of backing a stepped-up UN operation. But there were obstacles. Hammarskjöld and the UN Secretariat were bitter against Tshombe and the Katanga secessionists, but, having been burned once, they were determined to avoid giving anyone a pretext for accusing them again of either rashness or of failing to be impartial. Another obstacle to stepping up the UN operation was the UN representative in the Congo himself, Rajeshwar Dayal. Dayal was disliked intensely by the Congolese, who thought him arrogant and contemptuous, as only a Brahman can be. But Dayal was indeed a Brahman, and in one respect at least Senator Dodd had a point. For it was to India and Nehru that the Secretary General looked as the rallying point for neutralist support, just as it was to the United States that he looked for support from the West. Still another obstacle was the deep cleavage in the UN itself. The Security Council had been unable to agree on anything since it first met to consider Lumumba's arrest. The General Assembly had voted on two separate resolutions—both concerned with the release of political prisoners, with reconvening the Congo parliament, and with the hope for a special Round Table Conference to bring the dissident Congolese together—but failed to adopt either.

But for the new Kennedy administration, the biggest obstacle in trying to persuade the UN Secretariat and our friends to step up the UN operation was the division among our allies and the extension of that division to Washington itself. A Berlin crisis was shaping up; our NATO allies were distressed at the possible fallout from the Congo crisis on their own colonies and former colonies. Portugal presented an especially difficult problem. Angola was right next door to the Congo and the Portuguese colonial administration was not the most progressive in the world. A current Washington joke was that the Portuguese, having given three Angolans a University education were now about to embark on their second five-hundred-year plan. If our policy in the Congo went too sharply against what the Portuguese saw as their interests, it might well affect their attitude toward U.S. bases in the Azores, Portuguese possessions which were regarded as essential to European defense. In such circumstances, the Pentagon, which sided with our European allies, would quickly call up their friends in the Congress to do battle. For all these reasons, it was the better part of valor to go slow with any bold "New Africa" policy. A new attempt at reconciliation and negotiation had to be given a try.

The first step was to get a new resolution through the Security Council. Adlai Stevenson at the UN, and Harlan Cleveland, in Washington, worked on the Great Powers, with some adroit help from George Ball, who was highly respected by the French and others of our European allies, while Mennen Williams and Wayne Fredericks worked on the various African nations. After some maneuvering, a resolution was voted through on February 21, 1961. The vote was nine to zero with the Soviet Union and France abstaining. The prices paid to the various blocs among the UN membership were apparent in the provisions of the resolution—that Belgian and other military and paramilitary personnel be withdrawn, which was aimed directly at Tshombe's mercenaries; that the Congo parliament, in which Gizenga and the Lumumbist "radicals" could on most issues muster enough allies to command a majority, be convened; that the Congolese Army be reorganized; and, finally, that the UN should take "all appropriate measures" to prevent the occurrence of civil war and that these appropriate measures should include not only arranging for cease-fires, the halting of military operations, and the prevention of clashes, but also "the use of force if necessary in the last resort."

THE LONG TALKS

The second step was more time-consuming—to soothe the ruffled feelings, to bring in new faces, to bring the Congolese together by any kind of device in the hopes that out of discussion would come agreement and unity. Rajeshwar Dayal was persuaded to resign as the UN representative and was temporarily replaced by Sudan's Mekki Abbas—who was welcomed in Léopoldville by a brass band. Other new faces also appeared, including a new American ambassador, Edmund A. Gullion, the career foreign service officer who had impressed President Kennedy several years earlier during his visit to South Vietnam.

But nothing else seemed to happen. Again and again, the UN representative, or the American Ambassador, or the Belgian, or someone else would after long and painful effort succeed in getting a negotiating conference started—at Tananarive or Coquilhatville or Léopoldville or somewhere else. The talks would proceed, progress would be made on minor points. And then the talks would fail—with the visiting team frequently ending up in "custody." By June 1961 several attempts at a negotiated settlement between Kasavubu and the moderates in Léopoldville, on the one hand, and Tshombe and the conservatives in Katanga, on the other, had accomplished nothing.

But there was still some hope for a settlement on the left, between Kasavubu and Gizenga in Stanleyville. Under UN aegis, the Congolese parliamentarians agreed to meet in total isolation, on the campus of Lovanium University, outside Léopoldville, to negotiate a settlement, and the UN made what were probably the most elaborate arrangements in history to seal off the university buildings. Barbed wire was put up, searchlight towers built, soldiers with dogs patrolled the grounds. No money was allowed inside the grounds, not even blank checks; no liquor, weapons, or even women were permitted inside and none of the legislators were allowed to leave until after an agreement was reached. On August 1, they selected as Premier Cyrille Adoula, a moderate like Kasavubu who had been a friend of Patrice Lumumba's, although he was not of the same political complexion. Gizenga was chosen as Vice-Premier.

Tshombe refused to send his parliamentarians to the session, and success now depended on quickly reintegrating Katanga into the Congo. The need for speed increased the anxiety—and the willingness to take chances —both in the UN Secretariat and in Washington. Both the Secretariat and the "New Africa" group were convinced that what made Tshombe unwilling to negotiate meaningfully was his military strength and that this in turn rested not so much on his army of eight to ten thousand men as on the officer cadre—two hundred Belgian soldiers of fortune and the three hundred or so mercenaries Tshombe had hired mainly in South Africa, Rhodesia, and France. Now in September, 1961, the UN was ready to make an attempt to force the "immediate withdrawal" of the Belgian regulars and the mercenaries as called for six months earlier in the February 21 resolution. The result was an eight-day battle in Elisabethville, during which twenty UN soldiers, approximately fifty Katangan gendarmes, and several civilians were killed.

If it were not for the tragedy of these deaths, Round 1 of the Congo, as it came to be called, would have had its comic opera aspects. For one lone Katangan airplane, a Fouga Magister jet, dominated the skies and made the important difference. In Washington, frustration competed with disgust. At one of the endless meetings, Wayne Fredericks, recalling his days with General LeMay, Commander of the Strategic Air Command, put the feeling into simple words, "I always believed in air power," Fredericks said, "but I never thought I'd see the day when one plane would stop the United States and the whole United Nations." A frantic search for a small, preferably neutral power with enough airplanes to spare a few for the UN was immediately begun.

But the reaction elsewhere was sharper. The British were outraged at the UN use of force and in fact in the middle of the fighting refused refueling privileges in Uganda for Ethiopian fighters which the UN Secretariat had urgently requested. The French and the Belgians were just as angry as the British, while the Soviet Union, joined by the radicals, took the opposite position, accusing Hammarskjöld of holding back after the initial success in order to appease the "colonialists."

Secretary General Dag Hammarskjöld, apparently quite by accident, had arrived in Léopoldville on the morning it all began, September 13, and when events in Katanga got out of hand, he moved to arrange a cease-fire with Tshombe. They agreed to meet at Ndola, in the Federation of Rhodesia and Nyasaland, on September 17. That night, flying in darkness under a false flight plan to evade the pirate Fouga raider, Hammarskjöld's plane crashed as it neared Ndola airport—killing Hammarskjöld, the crew, and all the UN party. The world mourned a sensitive and humane man—an exceptional person and a great international public servant.

ROUND 2

Nothing at all had been settled, and in December, following an uneasy cease-fire, fighting broke out again between the Katanga gendarmerie and UN troops.

Acting Secretary General U Thant threatened to use force to restore order, but the next day one UN soldier was killed and two wounded by the Katanga forces, and the gendarmerie moved into position to block the road between UN headquarters and the airport. Then, on December 5, U Thant authorized "all counteraction—ground and aerial—deemed necessary" to restore freedom of movement for the UN forces. There was fighting at the roadblock on the way to the airport during the day, and that night Katangan planes bombed the airfield. But this time the UN was ready. In the period since Round 1, airplanes had been added to the UN forces and these now attacked the Kolwezi air bases and destroyed one of the jets and other planes on the ground.

In the meantime another battle was also raging, a less bloody battle, but no less bitter, between the United States and its close ally, Great Britain. On December 6, the United States announced that it would provide up to twenty-one additional transport planes to carry troops to Elisabethville—a clear implication that the United States and the UN Secretariat had agreed to carry out an offensive and end the Katangan secession. The British Government, on the other hand, the same day made a quite different announcement—a plea for conciliation followed by what in the language of diplomacy was a very sharp warning, both to the United States and to the UN. "The UN forces," the statement read, "are of course fully entitled to protect themselves when they are attacked, but they have not got a permit from the resolutions to try to impose a political solution by force."

Exactly the same battle was also going on inside the United States, and it was not going at all well for the "New Africa" group and the UN supporters. For Tshombe had intervened in the politics of American policy-making—and very effectively, too. Late in 1960, Michel Struelens, a Belgian public relations man, arrived in New York, where he set up the Katanga Information Center and began to make contact with prominent Americans, including members of Congress. Taking a leaf from the old China Lobby's book, the center was very helpful to anyone who needed information about the Congo—whether congressmen or editorial writers— and many, especially those of more conservative viewpoint, were happy to have the help. By the fall of 1961, Struelens had lined up a number of prominent people who were willing to form an "American Committee for Aid to Katanga Freedom Fighters" when the time was right—William F. Buckley, editor of the conservative *National Review,* retired generals such as Albert C. Wedemeyer, and so on. Senator Dodd of Connecticut was particularly helpful, and a variety of people were attempting to enlist the support of others. Herbert Hoover, although unwilling to join the committee, did in fact make a statement favorable to Katanga at a crucial moment. Senator Goldwater, too, found an occasion to accuse the State Department of "condoning aggression by international machinery and paving the way for a Communist takeover in the Congo." Congressman William Miller, Chairman of the Republican National Committee, and later, in the 1964 election, Goldwater's running mate, was also critical of Congo policy. Much of the support for Katanga and against the United States Government and the UN was undoubtedly spontaneous and would have arisen even if Struelens had not been around. But Struelens was around, and he made the most of whatever oppositionist sentiment he could find. As a political operation of persuasion, of enlisting support, and of making well-managed, telling use of that support, the Tshombe-Struelens effort on the American domestic scene was a slick and effective job —better by far, up to the end of December 1961, than the job done by the other side of the policy dispute, who were native Americans.

Struelens' activities on Tshombe's behalf were beginning to cut deeply by November 1961, and the noise from Capitol Hill was becoming more and more audible. State Department and White House officials did some heavy press "backgrounding"—anonymous, "not-for-attribution" sessions —in an attempt to explain why it was important to bring Katanga back into the Congo and all the other intricacies of a policy that had to bring along so many different allies and other contenders with such varied interests, but they had very little success. Something stronger than a backgrounder was clearly needed, and Rusk was persuaded to give one of his rare press conferences and to make a statement publicly supporting the

UN action. But to Williams, Cleveland, and the "New Africa" group, who felt that secession had to be ended quickly and decisively if the Western World were to avoid a defeat, Rusk's statement was a disappointment. For he seemed to pull back from full support to the UN. What the statement did, in fact, was to distinguish between the use of force in eliminating secession, which Rusk ruled out, and the use of force in maintaining the UN position in Katanga and restoring its freedom of movement, while peaceful negotiation and reconciliation went forward. "The primary mission of the UN force," his statement concluded, "is to protect themselves, to maintain their communications and to provide a situation in which the political processes among Congolese leaders can move on to a responsible and peaceful settlement. We fully subscribe to the UN program in that regard."

The British, on the other hand, pulled back even more sharply, at least for the moment. The Canberra bombers used by the Indian Air Force contingent had run out of bombs, and only Britain could supply new ones in time to be of any use. A wide section of British opinion was opposed to the UN operation in the Congo, including much of Prime Minister Macmillan's own Conservative Party and their natural allies among business interests in the City, to which was added the pressure from Sir Roy Welensky, Prime Minister of the Federation of Rhodesia and Nyasaland. Reluctantly, Macmillan gave in to American pressure and agreed to supply twenty-four bombs, but with the stipulation that they be used only "in preventive action against pirate aircraft on the ground and airstrips from which these aircraft are in operation."

In the meantime, the Belgians and the UN Secretariat were equally involved. Foreign Minister Paul-Henri Spaak in formal protests twice in one day accused the UN forces of brutality against civilians in Katanga. U Thant rejected both of these protests, warning that the UN forces might have to take action against *Union Minière* if it continued to help Katangan secession. He then went on with undiplomatic candor to voice the suspicions that had long been felt. "According to unimpeachable sources," U Thant wrote, "officials of the *Union Minière* have proudly admitted the manufacture of gendarmerie armored cars and of bombs which have been dropped on the airport and ONUC [the UN forces] headquarters in Elisabethville."

The United States continued the airlift that was bringing UN reinforcements to Elisabethville and by December 13 enough troops had arrived for the UN to take the offensive. But by this time, the shaky agreement with the British had come apart. On December 11, the British had reneged on their promise to send bombs to the UN forces, "until the UN clarifies its policy." Then, on December 13, Britain demanded that U Thant seek an immediate cease-fire in Katanga—which by implication was also a demand that the UN forces not launch their planned offensive.

U Thant's reaction was cool, but he needed support—which could come only from the United States.

Rusk was away, and the Acting Secretary was George W. Ball—the newly appointed Under Secretary following the "Thanksgiving Day" massacre that had removed Chester Bowles. In an unambiguous statement, Ball promptly announced that the United States was opposed to a cease-fire until the UN forces had achieved their "minimum objectives," which Ball defined as the need and right of the UN force "to protect itself, to maintain its freedom of movement and communications in order to discharge the mission given it by the Security Council and the General Assembly."

The counterattack was heavy. French Prime Minister Michel Debré had already gotten in the first blow by a speech attacking U.S. policy in the Congo the day before. This was followed by a French announcement barring overflight of French territory by any planes carrying men or supplies to the UN forces in the Congo. The NATO Council meeting in Paris was also mobilized, and for the first time in its history a majority of the foreign ministers were lined up against the United States. Senator Dodd was in the Congo, and made it clear in confidential cables sent over State Department channels that he would make trouble on Capitol Hill. At home, Struelens and his American allies decided that the time had come and, the same day that Ball spoke formally, they announced the formation of the "American Committee for Aid to Katanga Freedom Fighters," claiming Senator Dirksen of Illinois, Republican Minority Leader of the Senate, as a sponsor[1] and declaring that it would "vigorously protest illegal United Nations action against Katanga and United States air logistical support of this action."

On December 14, Tshombe followed up the counterattack by sending a cable directly to President Kennedy, expressing his desire to negotiate with Adoula and asking the President to intervene "to designate a suitable negotiator and to stop at once useless bloodshed."

While the United States considered how to respond to this concerted attack, the UN made the most of the time that Ball's statement had given them. The UN counteroffensive began on December 15, and continued on the sixteenth and seventeenth. Resisting pressure, U Thant said on the sixteenth that a cease-fire at that time would be a "serious setback" for the UN.

In Washington, the "Old Europe" sympathizers were alarmed, and so were those who merely feared the harm that a group of congressmen led by Senator Dodd could do on other matters, such as the purchase of bonds as a way of financing the UN. The "New Africa" people were generally still convinced that unless the UN offensive, which had been confined to Elisabethville, was extended to the rest of Katanga, Tshombe's power would remain unshaken, and he would be able to continue his secession. On the other hand, the UN's "freedom of movement" had supposedly been restored, which had been the publicly avowed "minimum objective." This meant that the political justification for continuing the offensive was weak. Also, there was at least a possibility that the action had shaken Tshombe sufficiently to permit economic and political pressures to have some influence, as well as the gentler pressures of persuasion. Then, too, the costs so far had been high. So far in Round 2 the casualties added up to twenty-one UN soldiers, 206 Katangan soldiers, and as many as fifty civilians. There were some among the President's advisers who were still convinced that sooner or later force would have to be used to end the Katangan secession and that the wiser course of action, and in the end perhaps the cheaper one, would be to do it now and get it over with. For what they feared was that delay would drive the moderate Congolese in Léopoldville into the arms of the Communists or, worse still, cause the moderates to collapse, leaving the way clear for the Communists to take over. But the threat of all this was distant, the political justification for continuing was bad, and a negotiated settlement with Tshombe, if not a sure thing, was at least conceivable. Caution prevailed.

President Kennedy responded to Tshombe's December 14 cable by sending messages to both Tshombe and Adoula in an effort to lay the groundwork for a meeting, and designated Ambassador Edmund A. Gullion as his personal representative. Arrangements were made for Gullion to pick up Tshombe in a U.S. airplane and escort him to the military base at Kitona, where his safety could be assured.

What came out of the meetings was the so-called Kitona agreement—signed on December 21—in which Tshombe agreed to recognize the *Loi Fondamentale* (the temporary constitution) and the "indissoluble unity" of the Congo, and to accept the authority of the central government and Kasavubu as President. But Tshombe never intended to abide by the Kitona agreements, and his stalling tactics were just as sophisticated as his intervention in American politics. He kept everyone concerned dangling on the hook for over six months. But neither the UN Secretariat nor their allies in the United States Government had the political leverage to force a change before the full skein of the policy of trying to integrate Katanga into the Congo through reconciliation had been played out.

In the State Department, Mennen Williams, Harlan Cleveland, Wayne Fredericks, and the others who had been convinced that more decisive action was necessary recognized in December, not only that they had been defeated, but that the cause of the defeat was their failure to lay the political groundwork at home—or, more accurately, that Tshombe and Struelens had played a better game of domestic American politics, of finding and using allies on Capitol Hill and in the press, than the Americans had. Mennen Williams, in particular, probably ought to have known better, given his experience in politics. But Williams had devoted himself to winning friends for the United States in Africa, where he had spent much of his time on good will missions. He had done an outstanding job at this, but only at the cost of neglecting to build support in Washington—and it was in Washington, not in Africa, that decisions about American policy were made. In a bitter speech at Detroit on December 27, Williams charged that the Katanga propaganda machine had been fabricating "horrendous lies of indiscriminate mayhem by the United Nations troops" that were totally false. Carl T. Rowan, who as Deputy Assistant Secretary for Public Affairs of the State Department was one of the highest-ranking Negroes in government, went even further. Pointing the finger directly at Struelens, "who operates out of some rather plush quarters in New York," Rowan said, "There has been a clever big-money campaign to convince Americans that they ought to support Katanga's secession." Hinting that *Union Minière* money was behind the whole affair, Rowan complained of the "extremely vocal help" that Struelens had gotten from some Americans "in dispensing a string of myths and a stream of misinformation about Katanga and the Congo."

But for the moment, at least, defeat for Williams and the entire "New Africa" group was total. On December 29, Williams had to issue a "correction" of his speech, changing "lies" to "tales." And on December 31, the new Under Secretary of State for Political Affairs, George C. McGhee, declared that neither of the two speeches had been "cleared at the highest levels of the Department."

THE UN LOSES PATIENCE

If the point that Tshombe did not really mean to integrate Katanga into the Congo needed driving home at this late date, the celebration in Elisabethville beginning July 11 of the "Second Anniversary" of Katangan independence did so. But what made the long delay so significant was the economic pressure on the central government. Almost no taxes were collected, except in the province of Léopoldville, but expenditures were astronomical. Katanga, on the other hand, keeping for itself the total revenue coming from *Union Minière,* was under no pressure at all.

The combination was more than U Thant could bear. In a news conference on July 20, he said, "Mr. Tshombe is a very unstable man, he is a very unpredictable man. I have tried to get Tshombe and the Central Government to negotiate but without any results." His exasperation with both Tshombe and his Ministers led the Secretary General to an extremely undiplomatic explosion. "I don't know what I can do," he said, "with such a bunch of clowns."

In the United States, those who wanted to use more forceful action were also strengthened. At his press conference on July 23, the President himself took a hand, describing the situation in the Congo as "very, very serious." For the first time, he named *Union Minière* as one source of the trouble.

The opposition also saw these signs of an approaching crossroads, and moved to try to head off any move toward a tougher line against Tshombe. Dodd took to the floor of the Senate on August 3 with a long review of everything that had happened in the Congo, accusing the State Department of dancing to Nehru's tune, and arguing that unity in the Congo would come naturally if only the UN would stop interfering. That same day, the American Committee for Aid to Katanga Freedom Fighters bought ads in major newspapers demanding immediate withdrawal of all UN troops, a bar on any sanctions against Katanga, and a suspension of congressional action on the bill to authorize the purchase of UN bonds. Arthur Krock joined the chorus, charging in the New York *Times* that the State Department was pursuing a "feud" with Tshombe—"a dogged policy whose conduct it has delegated to the UN."[2]

But there was an important difference in the situation in the summer of 1962 from what it had been six months earlier, in December. In December, strong measures to reintegrate Katanga into the Congo would have seemed unreasonable to the audience before which both the "New Africa" group and their opposition debated—the middle group of congressmen, newsmen, and all the others making up the interested publics for foreign affairs. But now, after all the months in which a patient and reasonable effort to bring Tshombe around had failed, these people, along with many of the contenders themselves, were beginning to share some of the frustration of the UN and the "New Africa" group.

A NEW PLAN AND A NEW POLICY

Emboldened by the evidence that the political situation would permit a new initiative, the "New Africa" people in the State Department—with Williams and Cleveland again in the lead—began to try out some ideas for a new plan and a new policy on selected members of the UN Secretariat. By mid-August their joint efforts had developed these ideas into a UN Plan for National Reconciliation, conceived as something U Thant could present to both Adoula and Tshombe. And it had been discussed with most of the interested member states, including the British and the Belgians.

Getting agreement on the plan, as opposed to the policy, was relatively easy. The plan proposed all the old compromises on all the old issues—adopting a federal constitution; sharing revenues on mining royalties and taxes between Katanga and the central government on a fifty-fifty basis; integrating Katangan forces into the Congo National Army; unifying the currency; granting a general amnesty; and reorganizing the central government to provide more provincial representation. What was new and what did require some maneuvering to get agreement was that the plan also included some deadlines—the constitution to be drafted within thirty days and agreement on sharing revenues, integrating the army, and so on within ninety days.

But agreement on the policy was something else again. For the policy called for pressure—not the use of force, but economic pressure, a boycott of *Union Minière* copper and cobalt ores, seizing Katanga assets in foreign countries; attempting to deny Katanga access to foreign exchange; and even closing the rail lines from Katanga to Rhodesia.

On August 12, 1962, the British Government formally notified the UN Secretariat that it was opposed to any form of sanctions against Katanga. But the British attitude had been clear much earlier, and U Thant had long since begun to appeal to the general membership of the UN and even to maneuver over the heads of government for public support. On August 1, he appealed to all UN members to bring economic pressure on the Katangese authorities if persuasion failed—economic pressure "of a kind that will bring home to them the realities of their situation and the fact that Katanga is not a sovereign state and is not recognized by any government of the world as such. In the last resort, and if all other efforts fail, this could justifiably go to the extent of barring all trade . . ." To this he added a direct appeal to *Union Minière*—declaring that the UN forces would protect *Union Minière* property from reprisals if the company stopped paying taxes to the Katanga government. By the time U Thant was ready to present the plan to the world, he was also ready at least to gamble that he had enough political support to sustain a threat. In presenting the plan, he also said that "the Katanga authorities must consider these proposals and respond to them within a quite brief period" or he would renew his appeal to UN members to apply economic sanctions.

Williams and Cleveland had also been busy within the administration, and on August 25 the U. S. Government gave its full support to the plan publicly, with the implication that it would also support the policy.

This statement reflected a tentative consensus within the United States Government that balanced off a number of different interests and fears which were shared at least in some degree by all the contenders, whether their sympathies were primarily with "Old Europe" or "New Africa." One set of fears primarily haunted the men who were concerned about the "new" Africa, although the others could see some of the danger—that a setback in the Congo would encourage resistance from the remaining old colonialists in Africa, give the new extremists a boost, and destroy everything that had so far been achieved by the painstaking efforts to encourage moderate African independence movements and so associate the United States with what seemed so clearly to be the tide of history. At the same time all this had to be balanced against the competing interests—harmony with our allies, the claims of whites in Africa, the claims of investors, and the conviction of the conservatives among the African states as well as within the United States itself that even a moderate pace toward fulfilling African demands would spiral out of hand and present the Communists with exactly the opportunity they were seeking. Thus the policy was a compromise, yet it represented a consensus—made possible partly by the fact that most of our European allies had been patiently nursed by hard work, especially by Mennen Williams and George McGhee, into agreeing with the plan if not the policy. The United States promised full co-operation in implementing the plan, especially with those states who had troops in the Congo, and on this basis most of the UN members, with the principal exception of the Soviet Union, were willing to go ahead.

On August 25, Adoula announced that the central government accepted the UN Plan for Reconciliation, and on September 3, Tshombe followed by announcing Katanga's "tentative" agreement. Three Tripartite Commissions, composed of representatives from Adoula, Tshombe, and the UN, were set up—for the military, the revenue, and the foreign exchange aspects of the plan. But then progress stopped.

Tension mounted. On September 12, a UN patrol clashed with a Katanga patrol on the outskirts of Elisabethville, and two gendarmes were killed. On September 20, a UN plane was shot down. On September 24, two UN soldiers were killed by mines laid by the Katanga gendarmerie near UN installations in Elisabethville.

In a desperate attempt at persuasion, McGhee was sent to the Congo. McGhee was known to be close to the Belgians, and he had been the one to administer the public rebuke to Williams and Rowan when they attacked Struelens, Tshombe, and *Union Minière* at the first of the year. If anyone could talk Tshombe into co-operating, surely he had the best chance. But even before McGhee had arrived back in the United States it was clear that he had had no effect.

In one last effort to break the impasse—or perhaps only to build a record—U Thant on November 1 and 2 addressed formal letters to both Adoula and Tshombe reviewing their commitments and assessing their performance. The replies were as expected—Adoula reiterating his support for the UN Plan for Reconciliation and Tshombe pointing to token concessions he had made and ignoring the major issues.

And so it stood. But as November wore on, Adoula's position became more and more precarious. In parliament, the radicals began to see their opportunity to push him to the left or even to bring him down and provide an opportunity for a radical like Gizenga. On November 27, 1962, a motion passed to revoke the state of emergency and release imprisoned opposition deputies. Encouraged, the radicals joined with Tshombe's representatives the next day to engineer a vote of censure—which Adoula just barely survived. If something effective and decisive were not done soon, it would all come apart: either Adoula would himself move into the pro-Soviet camp or he would be ousted in favor of those who were already there.

In Washington, there were urgent meetings to consider what to do next. George McGhee, fresh from his visit to Katanga, urged delay—postponing the imposition of sanctions to give Tshombe more time. But he cited no new evidence, and this time, unlike the year before, Williams, Cleveland, Fredericks, and the "New Africa" people had been busy laying the groundwork for political and public support. They had worked hard on our European allies, especially on the Belgians and Foreign Minister Spaak—who later in a public speech called Tshombe a "rebel" and went on to declare that Belgium would support the UN even in the use of force to end the secession. They had conducted an educational campaign on Capitol Hill and among the press. And they had also made some appeal for wider support in the general public. Early in November, for example, Williams had laid out in a public speech the problem they now faced in December—forecasting that if Katanga were not soon integrated into the Congo, Adoula's government would fall or seek help from radical sources, and predicting that not only would the United States and the UN both be discredited but that the resulting chaos in the Congo would invite Communist intervention.

There were even plans to silence the opposition—Michel Struelens's visa had expired and the immigration authorities were prepared to order him to leave the country or face deportation proceedings.

All this effort was given considerable extra impetus by the changing mood in Congress. For here, too, there were a mounting impatience and increasing signs of an unwillingness to go on footing the expensive bill for an operation that made no visible progress, and the expense was especially galling precisely because the Soviets refused to pay. Such a mood, of course, was a two-edged sword. Feeling the way it did, Congress would support vigorous action, but if the action failed it would turn completely away in disgust and leave no alternative but to withdraw.

The decision was to support U Thant in the application of economic sanctions, and the first step was a clever one designed to demonstrate that Tshombe had lost his most obvious potential ally. Paul-Henri Spaak, the Belgian Foreign Minister, was at that very moment visiting Washington, and he agreed to take advantage of the opportunity by joining President Kennedy in a statement reaffirming their support for the UN plan. The statement then went on to declare that their two governments had "up to this point directed their efforts toward accomplishment of the plan along the lines of voluntary discussions and actions of the parties concerned. This approach has not, however, produced the necessary results. If there is not substantial progress within a very short period of time, the United States Government and the Government of Belgium fully realize that it will be necessary to execute further phases under the United Nations Plan which include severe economic measures."

The statement was followed by mob action against the Belgian Consulate in Elisabethville, but no one was hurt. After several days of consultation, U Thant, on December 10, notified Tshombe that he had failed to carry out the provisions of the plan and that economic sanctions would be applied. The next day Adoula asked seventeen governments to embargo imports of Katangan copper and cobalt and U Thant followed by informing these same governments that Adoula's request was fully consistent with the UN plan and should be supported. U Thant also appealed to the Belgian Government to press *Union Minière* to stop remitting taxes to the Katangan government and began sending requests to other UN members to embargo trade.

On December 6, according to plan the United States immigration authorities published the order against Struelens, and, as expected, the Senate Internal Security Subcommittee, of which Senator Dodd was Chairman, condemned the State Department's "glaring abuse" of its visa power, declaring that the move to oust Struelens was intended to "silence a dissenting voice on US Congo policy."

On December 19—one year after the opening of the Kitona conference, on which so many hopes had been pinned—Tshombe announced that rather than have Katanga rejoin the Congo he would adopt a "scorched earth" policy. "We would," he said, "destroy everything." There was no longer even a pretense that Katanga could be reintegrated by policies of persuasion.

NOTES

[1] Dirksen later denied that he was a sponsor, but then went on to express his sympathy and to urge a cease-fire.

[2] A low point was reached in September, when Senator Strom Thurmond called for a congressional investigation after reading into the Congressional Record two articles from the Richmond *News-Leader* (allegedly based on information supplied by Struelens) accusing Under Secretary George Ball, Fowler Hamilton, Administrator of the Agency for International Development, and Dag Hammarskjöld's brother of being involved in a syndicate which would profit enormously if the Katanga copper mines were put out of business—charges that were quickly and easily refuted.

CHAPTER 19

Military Force ... and Success

THERE WERE a number of people in the White House and the State Department among those of both the "New Africa" and the "Old Europe" persuasion who had long thought that economic sanctions would not work. And President Kennedy himself was one of the skeptics. The mood in Congress had convinced the President that they would revolt against a continuation of the past year's squirming on dead center. He was also acutely aware that the UN authority to maintain military forces in the Congo would expire on December 31 and that the debate to renew the authority would give the congressional opposition to our Congo policy the opportunity to raise a fuss and perhaps to gain more allies. He was also concerned that India, whose troops were now the mainstay of the UN operation, would need all its forces at home to meet the threat from Communist China following the Chinese attack on India in October 1962. In any case, the Indian troops were scheduled to depart in February 1963, and since they had proved to be the most effective fighters in both Round 1 and Round 2, it was apparent to the President—and Tshombe, too—that with their departure the possibility of serious UN military action would be drastically reduced. Disturbed, the President telephoned George Ball to talk about the need to get some new thinking going on what came next—pointing out that the only alternative, given the mood on Capitol Hill, India's troubles, and so on, seemed to be either using force to end the secession of Katanga or pulling out of the Congo entirely.

Major changes in policy about continuing problems can usually be made only when a number of the participants in Congress, the press, and the various agencies and departments in the Executive have abandoned hope that current policy will succeed and the rest of the participants have at least come to have doubts. Thus the President and Ball had two tasks before them, the analytical task of developing a new policy and the political task of selling it to enough of the undecided to carry the day. The old policy was a compromise between two well-identified groups— "Old Europe" and "New Africa," both battle-scarred, and it was unlikely that either would be capable of much new thinking at this stage. But even if they were, their scars alone would make it hard to sell their new thoughts. It would be helpful if the new ideas came from a new group, and it was probably for this reason that the President and Ball turned to the State Department's Bureau of Intelligence and Research. Standing on the edge of Congo policy, the bureau had been one of the first of the doubters. In mid-August, we had written a paper questioning the underlying assumptions of Congo policy that had attracted the President's attention. Pointing out that Katangan autonomy was based on independent power, the paper had argued that its integration was not likely to be achieved by threats, but only by changes in Tshombe's position or changes in the sources of his strength. The paper had concluded that, although the alternative of using military action to reduce Katanga remained, it would not be easy and if the efforts to achieve unification through negotiation failed, as we believed they would, it might be wise to consider whether a partial withdrawal might not be a practical contingency.

In any case, on Friday, December 9, Ball asked me to come to his office and to bring along Robert C. Good, who was Director of the Office of Research and Analysis for Africa in the Bureau. Relating what the President had said, Ball went on to say that as far as he could see we were getting nowhere in the Congo and that it was dead certain that we could not go on like this any longer. What was needed—on a crash basis, to be ready for the President Monday morning—was a careful and thorough analysis of the situation and of the policy alternatives now facing the United States, including our judgment of the outcome of each of these alternatives. For his part, Ball said, he would be frank to confess that he was beginning to think that withdrawal might be the thing to do.

The group of analysts under Good worked all through the weekend and gathered for the last time Sunday afternoon to go over the final draft. And this final draft was not what any of us expected it would be when we had first started to work Friday night. For over the weekend as we wrestled with the problem and argued with each other, we had come to see things differently than we had before.

We still concluded that the present policy was failing. Tshombe was getting stronger. Adoula's future was uncertain. There was evidence that the Communist bloc was making headway and a Communist military presence in Léopoldville was now a distinct possibility. The UN could not field an effective force in Katanga much longer.

We had carefully explored and rejected several alternatives. One was to turn the whole problem over to the African states—but we concluded that the African states could not handle it by themselves, since they had neither the power nor the sense of unity. Another was to try to buy Léopoldville's acquiescence to Tshombe's secession by increasing foreign aid—but we concluded that Léopoldville could not be "bought" so long as it had the alternative of Soviet aid. A third was to back Tshombe as the "unifier of the Congo"—but although we could visualize Tshombe coming to power after the Congo was unified, we could see no prospect that Tshombe, working from Katanga, could win enough support in the rest of the Congo to make it a realistic possibility that *he* could do the unifying.

Thus we concluded that the real choices were only two—using military force to bring about integration or disengaging the United States from the Congo entirely and working to get the UN out as well.

Tshombe preferred being the President of a *de facto* independent Katanga to subordinating himself to the central government, and the only effective inducement was to make secession less palatable to Tshombe than association with the central government. Our present policy was to try to make secession unpalatable by means of economic pressure applied through *Union Minière,* and also to imply a threat of worse to come if Tshombe did not accede. The trouble was, first, that Tshombe saw through the threat and recognized our reluctance to use force if the bluff was called. Second, Tshombe also seemed to sense the weakness in our attempt to use *Union Minière* as a weapon of economic pressure— that a business concern's first loyalty is to its stockholders and employees and so is a poor instrument of political reform. It seemed to us questionable that Belgium would in the end implement *meaningful* economic sanctions and, which was more important, even more questionable that Tshombe would believe they would. Our conclusion was that the only thing that would move Tshombe was a *credible* threat of military coercion, and that the only way to make the threat credible was actually to decide to do it.

If such a decision was made, we asked ourselves, what would have to be done to make it work? Five requirements seemed necessary. First, the decision would have to be made immediately, for any further delay would only complicate the task. Second, the preparations would have to be completed very quickly, including not only further concentration of UN military contingents in Katanga but also provision of transport and building up equipment and prepositioning sufficient fighter aircraft to neutralize Katanga air power. Third, an attempt should be made in consultations with the UN and the Belgians to arrive at an agreed and detailed course of action. It seemed to us that the evidence of rising Soviet influence in the Congo might well sway the Belgians—as it was swaying us—but if the Belgians were not able to go along, we would have to go ahead without them, bearing the full onus of the operation. Fourth, if Tshombe did not come around when he saw that we did indeed mean business, and it became necessary to use military force then we must be prepared to move very swiftly, for the political costs would rise steeply if the fighting dragged out. Whether by conquest or negotiated agreement, the Katanga gendarmerie must be dismantled as an organized fighting force. Finally, if the decision were to apply military force, opportunities should be given Tshombe to back down on reasonable terms under UN guarantees for his safety and his position as the leader of

Katanga Province. Being leader of Katanga would be no attraction in a highly centralized Congo, so the UN must also be sure to extract from the central government an agreement to establish a loose federal organization.

We felt that among the several risks in forcing the integration of Katanga the greatest of all was that the UN military action would have to run its full and probably destructive course with a high cost in lives, especially Congolese and Belgian lives. If this risk was felt to be too great, we concluded that the only alternative for the United States was disengagement.

But we also felt that disengagement contained even greater risks. In the first place, a complete and immediate disengagement was just not possible. As a practical matter, disengagement meant disengaging from the UN military operation—no longer taking initiatives in mobilizing support for the UN action, and so on—all leading to a gradual reduction in UN strength in the Congo. But, given the increasing signs of Soviet activities, including attempts to woo even the moderates in Léopoldville, we estimated that the Communists would parlay our disengagement into a position of considerable influence, through a military aid program, including Soviet technicians to train the Congo army, a program which their representatives in Léopoldville were offering anyone who would listen. One could easily foresee that from a base in the Congo, the Communists could play hell with affairs in much of Central and Southern Africa. Ironically, the greatest risk we foresaw in a policy of disengagement was that we could not make it permanent, but would be dragged back into full engagement on much less favorable terms than we now had, unpleasant though these often seemed.

When we had finished, Good sank back in his chair, shaking his head. "I never would have believed," he said, "that I would ever reach a conclusion that the best thing to do in the Congo was to use military force."

George Ball felt much the same—the notion of getting out was tempting, he said, but when you thought it all through the risk was just too great. Those of the "Old Europe" persuasion were, of course, most reluctant of all to abandon the current policy. But it was that same day, December 11, 1962, that Foreign Minister Spaak came out with his statement that Belgium would support the UN and the central government if they were to resort to force to end Katangan secession—and Spaak's statement carried the day so far as the State Department was concerned.

Preliminary soundings with the UN Secretariat and among member nations supporting the UN operation revealed that they had been thinking on similar lines, and the next step was to turn the general strategy into a concrete plan. Working in a day-long meeting in George Ball's conference room, Mennen Williams, Wayne Fredericks, Harlan Cleveland, and specialists from the Bureau of African Affairs, the Bureau of

International Organization Affairs, and the Bureau of Intelligence and Research, developed the original suggestions further. The idea of a U.S. military mission that would signal our intentions effectively to Tshombe, for example, was added at this time.

The President, about to depart for the "Skybolt" conference with the British at Nassau, considered the proposals at a meeting of the National Security Council. For once there was a consensus on a vigorous, positive course of action, and after weighing the arguments, the President approved the basic recommendation—provided there was close co-ordination with our allies and provided also there was a special effort to brief the press and key congressmen on the evidence that had been accumulating of renewed Soviet activities in the Congo and the long-run danger of a Communist take-over in Léopoldville from which they could subvert not only Katanga but all the neighboring African states as well.

ACTION

A joint effort by the UN Secretariat, the United States, and the foreign offices and UN missions of the member states supporting the UN operation in the Congo turned all this—and related thinking that had been going on in the Secretariat and among other UN members—into an operational plan. In the meantime, the press backgrounding in both Washington and Nassau on the evidence of Soviet activities produced a raft of stories. These were useful in explaining the United States motives in supporting the action the UN forces were about to take, but not very helpful so far as the Secretariat and some of the other UN members were concerned. And there were some red faces in Washington a little later when it turned out that excessive enthusiasm in Washington and especially in Léopoldville had blown up the stories to quite unjustified proportions—that the staff of the Soviet Embassy, for example, had increased in a few weeks from 10 to 100 persons. But the Soviet staff had increased considerably, and the significance of the increase was underlined by the Soviet offers to supply military aid if anyone would request it.

Negotiations moved rapidly, but in the meantime, events also moved. On December 17, the UN Congo headquarters protested that Katangan air operations "seriously and immediately threaten" to spiral into armed clashes with the UN forces. On December 18, Adoula issued a white paper that reviewed his discussion with Tshombe and declared his willingness to "greet with favor all attempts of the Elisabethville leaders to truly resolve the Katanga crisis." And on December 19, Tshombe made his statement that he would scorch the earth rather than be forced to rejoin the Congo.

This set the stage nicely, and on December 20, the State Department announced that the United States was sending an eight-man military mission to the Congo under Lieutenant General Louis Truman "in co-operation with the United Nations to determine what additional forms of assistance the United States could provide to ensure the ability of the United Nations to maintain peace in the Congo."

On December 21, the U. S. Consulate in Elisabethville was stormed by about a hundred students, both African and white, while Katanga police stood by; and, at the UN, Soviet Ambassador Zorin denounced the mission as "arbitrary unilateral action" and "direct subversion."

On Christmas Eve a UN helicopter was shot down and the crew captured and beaten, one of whom, an Indian lieutenant, died after being left wounded and unattended. On the night of December 27, small-arms fire on UN positions in Elisabethville increased and continued on through the next day in spite of efforts to stop it by Tshombe, who seemed to be losing control of the gendarmerie. After formally notifying Tshombe that it would take action if the firing did not cease, the UN moved to the attack and quickly gained control of the Elisabethville area. Tshombe and several of his ministers fled to Kipushi, near the Rhodesian border.

The UN forces continued their advance on December 29. They bombed the airfield at Kolwezi, where Tshombe's mercenary-operated airplanes were based, and ground columns moved on Kipushi, which fell the next day without firing a shot. Tshombe fled again, to Kolwezi, issuing another statement threatening "total destruction" if the UN advance did not cease. On the same day, the British Foreign Office declared its opposition to the UN move, stating that it had repeatedly emphasized to U Thant the "futility of trying to impose a political settlement on the Congo by force."

UN forces entered Kamina, in central Katanga, on December 30, and proceeded toward Jadotville, where there were important *Union Minière* installations. The Secretary General's representative for the Congo, Robert Gardiner, a Ghanaian, announced in Léopoldville that the UN was "not going to make the mistake of stopping short this time," and in New York, U Thant himself made it equally clear that no action would be taken against Tshombe if he returned to Elisabethville.

But a number of people in both Washington and Brussels began to lose their nerve. Stories appeared in newspapers that "United States officials manifested second thoughts . . ." when they considered the "political chaos and economic paralysis" that would result if the fighting were prolonged and especially if Tshombe carried out his scorched earth threat. From Belgium came an official—and public—appeal to the UN to halt the military operations. On December 31, U Thant announced that he would delay further action "a short period, perhaps a fortnight or so."

What happened next has provided food for controversy ever since. The UN column under Brigadier Reginald S. Noronha heading toward

Jadotville was approaching the Lufira River. UN headquarters issued orders on January 2 for them to halt at the river pending further instructions. The next news from the Congo was that the column had not only crossed the river, but had taken Jadotville—where they were warmly welcomed by "large African crowds." And the next news was that the UN troops had killed two Belgian women and wounded a man.

All the suspicions of the conservative African states, Senator Dodd, and those in the press who shared their views were inflamed. After statements like Gardiner's that the UN wasn't going to stop short this time, it seemed only logical that either the Secretary General himself or his field representatives were trying to pull a fast one. U Thant dispatched Ralph Bunche to the Congo to conduct an investigation and give the UN something with which to quell the public outcry.

What Bunche found out was that before the order got to Brigadier Noronha he had already reached the river, found the bridges out, crossed two of his companies on the debris, and established an eight-hundred-yard bridgehead. When he got the order to halt at the river, he was already straddling it, and under sporadic fire. Withdrawing in such circumstances would have been military insanity, so Noronha advanced. Resistance evaporated—there was not even any attempt to carry out the "scorched earth" threats—and the brigade proceeded into Jadotville unopposed. There, tragically, a car driving toward a UN checkpoint suddenly speeded up, and one or more of the UN soldiers, edgy as they were, opened fire, killing the two Belgian women and wounding the man.

RACE TO THE FINISH

Tshombe was now in Kolwezi, a major site of *Union Minière* operations, reorganizing his forces and preparing for further operations. The gendarmerie had begun to blow up the bridges between Jadotville and Kolwezi. In addition to Kolwezi, Tshombe's forces still held Dilolo, Sakania, and the four main hydroelectric plants in south Katanga, two near Kolwezi, and two at the northern end of Lufira reservoir, near Jadotville.

Thus U Thant and the "New Africa" group in the State Department who backed him were still faced with a difficult choice. The UN forces had gained control of almost three-quarters of the productive facilities of *Union Minière* and done so without either heavy casualties or the destruction that was so feared. But the one-fourth of the productive facilities that Tshombe still held was a trump card. The Congo was bankrupt and the destruction of even one-fourth of Katanga's precious industry would so tarnish the victory that neither U Thant nor any of the others concerned would be likely to survive the political backlash. On the other hand, another cease-fire and more "negotiations" would only give Tshombe an opportunity to stall for time to consolidate his position and defenses in Kolwezi, and to mobilize support abroad and especially in the United States. And mobilizing this support would probably not be very difficult. Senator Dodd, for example, had already branded the UN advance a "flagrant, inhuman act of aggression." Calling for an international investigation in an appeal to the International Commission of Jurists, he had said that it was "an unspeakable tragedy that the world organization which was set up to prevent war and preserve the peace should now be starting wars and massacring innocent civilians at the behest of an extremist war faction within the UN . . ." U Thant decided to go ahead, provide Tshombe every possible opportunity to surrender with face, but at the same time push the UN columns on as fast as possible. It was a gamble, but speed seemed the only way out.

On January 3, 1963, a spokesman for U Thant, responding to an appeal from Tshombe for a cease-fire and "negotiations," made a blunt statement: "It is now too late for negotiations. . . . Past experience with cease-fire agreements with the Katanga gendarmerie indicates their futility, since they are not respected. Indeed, in the light of last week's events in Elisabethville it may be questioned whether there is any responsibility and effective control over that force."

The United States followed this statement with an announcement that trucks, armored personnel carriers, mine-clearing equipment, transport aircraft, and other United States military equipment would begin arriving in the Congo within a week. On January 4, the State Department called on Tshombe to end Katanga's secession, and promised him a place in the future political life of the Congo, the people willing, if he recognized his "heavy responsibility not to persist in action which he has threatened—a scorched earth and a fight to the finish."

In Léopoldville, Ralph Bunche announced that the "UN forces will continue operations to restore freedom of movement through secessionist Katanga province both in the south and the north. Freedom of movement will be achieved, I hope, without further resistance, but it will be achieved."

Others were at work attempting to persuade Tshombe, and he finally agreed to come to Elisabethville under the escort of the Belgian consul—but all he did when he got there was to announce at a press conference that it was the firm decision of the Katanga government to carry out the scorched earth policy if the UN forces continued toward Kolwezi. The UN first put Tshombe under house arrest in Elisabethville, but then released him and he returned to Kolwezi.

The UN columns continued their advance. On January 11, they entered Sakania. On January 15, the column heading toward Kolwezi reached the Kikiluwe River, where they clashed with Katangan forces and drove them back. The UN troops crossed the river and continued toward Tshombe's stronghold at Kolwezi.

The next day, January 16, 1963, Tshombe informed the UN that he was ready to end Katanga's secession. Skeptical, the UN authorities agreed to a meeting in Elisabethville the next day. There, Tshombe signed a joint communiqué that authorized the UN forces to enter Kolwezi and agreeing to methods for disarming the Katanga gendarmerie.

Cautiously, the UN forces approached Kolwezi—and entered without difficulty, finding Tshombe there to welcome them. After two and a half years, Katanga's secession was ended.

VII

THE UNITED STATES AND COMMUNIST CHINA

"And, as the 20th Century moves toward the 21st, long-range missiles will probably also come into the range of Chinese production. Then, if not by stupidity or mischance sooner, the United States will have with China a great nuclear war, unless far-reaching accommodations have been worked out sooner, with accompanying changes of spirit.

"It is perhaps a noble illusion that an honorable peace will come if only we rectify *our* errors. But it is nevertheless an illusion, and one that can bring death. The continuance of peace between China and the United States, during the rest of the 20th century, depends on changes in China as well as in the United States. And we cannot be confident that those changes will occur."

—OSCAR GASS, *"China and the*
United States," Commentary,
November 1962

"I would like to see a lessening of . . . tension. That is our hope from the beginning. But we are not prepared to surrender in order to get a relaxation of tension."

—PRESIDENT JOHN F. KENNEDY,
News conference, March 8, 1961

CHAPTER 20

Communist China: Power plus Ambition

In 1834, Alexis de Tocqueville predicted that two countries would dominate the twentieth century—the United States and Russia. Both had extensive territory and natural resources; both had large, hard-working populations; and both had the promise, visible beyond their immediate problems, of the kind of national unity and political organization necessary to direct their populations and resources to the achievement of national goals. It was presumably for lack of this third ingredient—effective political organization and direction—that de Tocqueville left China off his list. But by the time John F. Kennedy became President of the United States, it had long been clear to anyone with eyes to see that China would have to be included in any such prediction made today. For the portentous fact was that for the first time since the decline of the Confucian imperial system the teeming millions and vast territory of China were directed by a single, effective political will—the Chinese Communist party.

THE STRUGGLE FOR POWER

The Communist Party of China was founded in 1921. For a time they co-operated with Sun Yat-sen's Kuomintang party that had overthrown the Manchu dynasty, but then in 1927 they prematurely attempted to seize power. The long struggle had begun, a struggle in which even the adversaries remained unchanged. For it was Chiang Kai-shek who crushed the uprising and Mao Tse-tung who led a thousand of the survivors to Chingkanshan, a mountain on the border of the provinces of Hunan and Kiangsi.

Mao spent seven years on Chingkanshan, where he developed his theories of guerrilla warfare and his strategic concept that the Chinese must turn orthodox Communist doctrine upside down and base their bid for power on the peasants and the countryside rather than on the proletariat and the cities. But even though the Communists succeeded in expanding their control over most of Kiangsi Province and into parts of Fukien, the area was too near the sources of the Nationalists' power to be an effective base, and the Communist forces suffered successive defeats. In October of 1934, they started on their famed Long March—

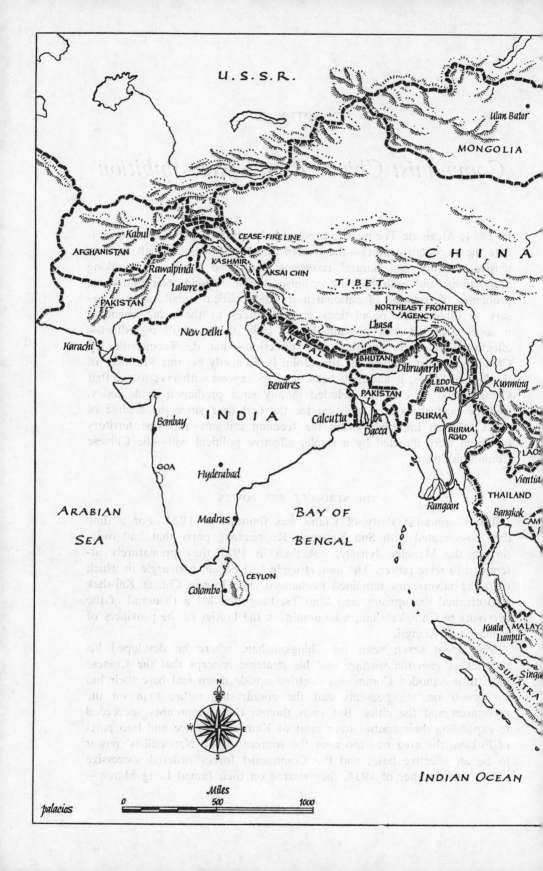

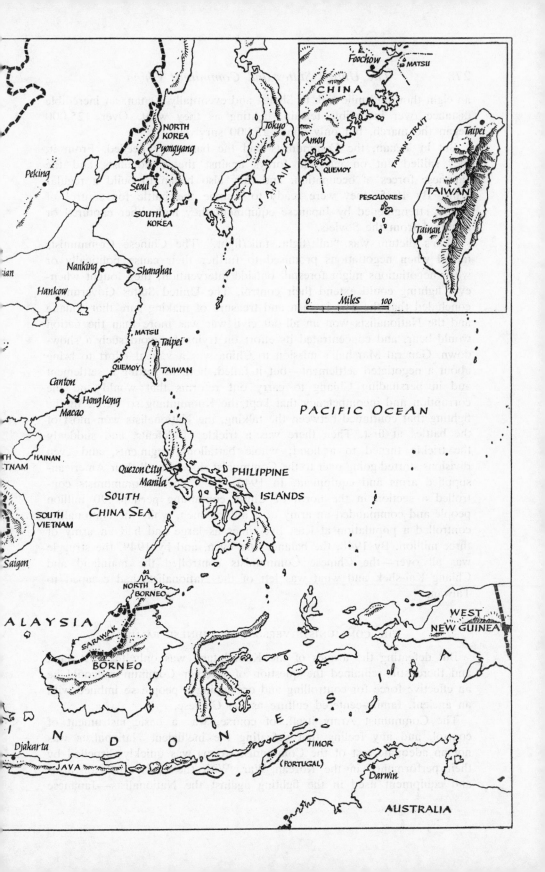

an eight-thousand-mile trek to Shensi and eventually Yenan, an incredible distance over incredible terrain, fighting as they went. Over 125,000 began the march, but only about 25,000 survived.

But in Yenan, the Communists had the base they needed. From it, they sallied out on guerrilla forays against the Nationalists and the Japanese forces of occupation, and they also began to build a regular army. By 1945, they were ready to resume the battle for control of China, strengthened by Japanese equipment they had either captured or acquired from the Soviets.

Mao's dictum was "talk/fight, talk/fight." The Chinese Communists talked when negotiations promised to further their cause politically or when negotiations might forestall outside intervention; they fought whenever fighting could extend their control. The United States Government concluded that the cost in men and treasure of making sure that Chiang and the Nationalists won an all-out civil war was more than the nation would bear, and concentrated its effort on trying to avoid such a showdown. General Marshall's mission to China was a valiant effort to bring about a negotiated settlement—but it failed, both in getting a settlement and in persuading Chiang to carry out reforms that would end the corruption and incompetency that kept the Kuomintang so weak. In the fighting that continued between the talking, the Nationalists won most of the battles at first. Then there was a trickle of defeats, and suddenly the trickle turned to a flood: whole battalions, regiments, and even divisions started going over to the Communist side with all their American-supplied arms and equipment. In 1945, the Chinese Communists controlled a section in the north of China containing perhaps 90 million people and commanded an army of a million men, while the Nationalists controlled a population at least five times as large and had an army of three million. By 1948, the balance was even, and by 1949, the struggle was all over—the Chinese Communists controlled the mainland and Chiang Kai-shek and what was left of the Nationalists had escaped to Taiwan.

THE COMMUNISTS VERSUS THE CHINESE FAMILY

But defeating the armies of the Kuomintang was only the first step, and there still remained the question of whether Communism could be an effective force for controlling and organizing a people so imbued with an ancient, family-centered culture as the Chinese.

The Communist Army itself, of course, was a basic instrument of control, and any feeling that defeating the inefficient Nationalists was not an adequate test of the Communist troops was quickly dispelled by their performance in the Korean War. With the basic stock of arms and equipment used in the fighting against the Nationalists—Japanese equipment of World War II vintage and American equipment captured from Chiang—and with only supplemental supplies from the Soviets, the Chinese Communist troops in Korea fought with stubborn discipline, inflicting heavy casualties and receiving even heavier without breaking. "Political power," Mao had said, "grows out of the barrel of a gun . . ." and the Chinese Communists used the army as the main instrument of direct control—brutally crushing any show of armed opposition wherever it appeared. By the end of the Korean War, even the intermittent guerrilla outbreaks that flared here and there during the first two or three years after the Communist take-over had petered out.

But purely military control and effective political organization are different, and in the latter task it was the unity of Communist Party leadership and the personal qualities of Mao himself that were most significant. There seems to have been no serious disagreements within the top echelon of the Party at this time, and Mao's leadership was apparently unquestioned.[1] Certainly Mao was well suited to the tasks that lay ahead. Puritanical, determined, ruthless, yet sensitive and idealistic—a poet without pity—Mao was also a theoretician and an ideological leader. Paradoxically, there are some instructive similarities between the godless Mao and Martin Luther, who was also an effective revolutionary. Like Luther, Mao was an avid reader when young—Mao said of himself that he read "greedily, like an ox that has rushed into a vegetable garden . . ." Also like Luther, Mao writes with an earthiness that appeals to men of the soil. Luther, for example, compares mankind to a sow wallowing happily in manure—and this is one of his least vulgar vulgarities—while Mao once described the Party's economic work as being "like the footbandages of a slut, long as well as smelly."[2] Luther hated his father, and so did Mao. Luther's father-hate took the form of a profound doubt of divine righteousness, and it led him to use his gifts of language and leadership to bring about a massive revolution against the Church of Rome.[3] Mao's father-hate was no less far-reaching, for it seems to have armed him in the monumental task of destroying the Chinese family system—a system whose central ethic was the Confucian ideal of filial loyalty.

The attack on the family system began in earnest on February 21, 1951, with the so-called "Regulations for the Punishment of Counter-revolutionaries" and the land reform program which was carried out at the same time. Mass trials were held in every village, the peasants were encouraged to denounce landlords and former officials and their families for past crimes and "exploitations," and the crowds themselves were urged to judge and condemn. Shouts of "Kill! Kill!" were followed by execution on the spot.

This wave of terror continued all through 1951 and 1952 and was renewed in 1955. No one knows how many people were killed all told, but it must have been many millions.[4] Its effect, in any case, was to eliminate from Chinese rural life both the landlord and the rich peasant.

The next step in establishing control over the countryside was to set up collective farms on the Soviet model, and this was completed in one spectacular rush in the winter of 1955–56. In these few months, five hundred million people were grouped together into collective farming units—destroying completely a traditional pattern of small-scale individual farms and village life that had endured for two thousand years.

In the cities the same results were achieved with the "Three Anti" and "Five Anti" campaigns against evils that were charged to the business community, such as tax evasion and bribery, and with the nationalization of factories and businesses. By the end of 1956, business and commercial activities throughout China were conducted through state-owned or semisocialized enterprises, and the traditionally shrewd and energetic entrepreneurs of China no longer existed as a class.

Thus by the end of 1956, all possible focal points for opposition within the Chinese population had been eliminated. In the countryside, many among the landlords and rich peasants had been killed. In the cities, among the intellectual and business communities, they had been dispersed and integrated into tightly supervised organizations of control. Politically, the results were the same.

THE QUESTION OF CONTROL

Borrowed from the Soviets, these organizations for supervision and control began with the Communist Party itself. The Party hierarchy demands total loyalty, and comes close to achieving it through a combination of indoctrination and surveillance by secret police. Party membership increased from less than one and one half million in 1946 to four and one half million in 1949, but careful recruitment, training, indoctrination, and periodic purges ensured Communist purity.

The Party members, in turn, became the cadre to fill key control positions in nonparty organizations. Beginning with residents' units in the cities and work groups in the rural collectives or communes, up through district and province, the government was staffed almost entirely with Communist Party members. Beyond this, Party members infiltrated the Army, police, workers' organizations, youth groups, factories, businesses, art, theater, sports, education—every conceivable kind of group covering every aspect of human life.

The purpose of this fantastic network that blankets China is not merely the police function of discovering antiregime sentiment or activity, but the positive function of indoctrination and direction. The Chinese Communists will not tolerate apathy or self-isolation; individuals are brought into organizations of all kinds and deliberately caught up in

Communist controlled and directed "political" activity. The ultimate effect of this combination of organization and positive direction was to "politicize" the entire Chinese population, and to give the Communist regime the "ability to mobilize the mass of the people for purposes which it chooses."[5]

Certainly events inside China have demonstrated the Communist regime's total command of the Chinese population and its ability to direct their energies toward what the regime wants, no matter how frequent the zigs and zags in policy or whether or not the policy goals are popular. Confident of their control in 1956, for example, the Communists deliberately decided to permit discussion, and in May, Mao proclaimed the slogan "Let a Hundred Flowers Bloom Together; Let Diverse Schools of Thought Contend." Cautiously, a few intellectuals spoke of minor things. Then, after the Hungarian Revolution and the Soviet intervention to put it down—events which had been followed with wonder by both people and Party in China—the Communist leadership decided in May 1957 to go even further and take the lid off entirely, inviting criticism as well as "discussion." The motive behind this loosening of controls may have been to try to head off the kind of discontent that had led to the revolt in Hungary and to stimulate initiative and co-operation. But the results were astounding. Some of China's most respected intellectuals spoke out bluntly, and there followed a flood of public criticism—of Communism, of police-state methods, of economic policies, of relations with the Soviet Union, and of almost every other aspect of the regime and its policies. To those who were present at the time, it was apparently almost unbelievable. As a Chinese intellectual and diplomat who later defected said in a television interview, "I think the Hundred Flowers Campaign was the most amazing campaign during the past fifteen years of Chinese Communist history. The people really pour [sic] their heart out and the criticism and the condemnation against the Communists were just incredible. People like me in Communist China were amazed to see that the people had so much grievance against the Communist regime. I did believe Mao Tse-tung was sincere in launching that Hundred Flowers Campaign. Obviously he was quite confident that his regime gained the support of the Chinese people, so the Chinese Communists can afford to be a little lenient and liberalize a little bit of their regime. . . ."

This outpouring of criticism was an amazing display of how much disaffection the Communist regime had created. But in a peculiar twist it also revealed a certain amount of support for the regime in an unexpected place—among intellectuals. For much of the criticism from intellectuals was of means and on occasion specific policies for achieving particular goals and purposes were accepted, either explicitly or implicitly. As A. Doak Barnett says in his study of Communist China, ". . . despite the disaffection which came into the open in 1957, it is clear that many intellectuals in China, for reasons of nationalism and ideology, continue to give the regime strong backing in its basic aims."[6]

For exactly one month, the outpouring continued. Then, brutally and effectively, the Communists reversed the "Hundred Flowers" policy and launched on a "rectification" program to root out opposition, leading eventually to a purge in the Party itself and the transfer of over a million government and Party bureaucrats from the cities to the villages.

This capacity to open the floodgates of criticism and just as quickly turn them completely off again was an impressive demonstration of the Chinese Communists' system of control. But the commune program and the Great Leap Forward of 1958 were even more impressive. The seriousness of the economic problems China faced—population growth, as well as some of the results of collectivization—became more apparent to the regime in 1957, and after an internal debate the advocates of boldness won out. Early in 1958, the so-called Great Leap Forward was announced—a plan to mobilize the entire population in a vast development scheme to build small- and medium-sized factories all over China (including the highly publicized "backyard steel furnaces") and to increase the rate of economic growth at a fantastic pace. Coupled with the Great Leap was the commune program, which in one year merged over 700,000 collective farms into 26,000 communes. The idea, which was rarely realized, was to have the tasks of cooking and caring for the children done in mess halls and nursery schools, and so free the women for work in the fields.

The Great Leap Forward was a failure in economic terms, and the Communists were forced at least to modify their notions about the communes. But the implications of what these two programs demonstrate about the Communists' control over the Chinese population and their capacity to whip the masses up to frantic activity is worthy of reflection. The family system was eliminated entirely among many peasants and further weakened elsewhere, and the Communists' ability to control the people still further enhanced. But more significantly and ominously, considering Chinese Communist goals and purposes, the regime had demonstrated a capacity to evoke a release of almost frenetic energy from the nation's masses—a release of human energy unlike anything seen in the world since the burst of religious fervor that brought the hundred-year spurt of cathedral building in the Middle Ages.

The failure of the Great Leap Forward shows that the Communists will not be able to work a miracle of economic development in China. But it also demonstrates a capacity to control and direct the Chinese population that the Communist regime can and will use to keep the peasant's standard of living down and so permit both human energy and material resources to go into making China a formidable military power—and soon.

THE POTENTIAL FOR MILITARY POWER

Certainly China has the resources for such a goal. Its manpower, of course, is the greatest in the world: the population of mainland China will reach one billion, in all probability, by 1980. Although lacking sufficient oil and the higher grades of coal, China apparently has among the world's largest reserves of both iron and coal of lower quality, as well as fully adequate reserves of such essential metals for industrialization as aluminum, antimony, tin, copper, tungsten, lead, zinc, manganese, and mercury. The potential of water power for producing electricity is huge.

And in spite of resounding failures, the Chinese Communists have done more with their potential than many other nations attempting industrialization have done with theirs. A key element was Soviet aid, which at least up to 1960 supplied about two billion dollars' worth of machinery and equipment and over ten thousand technicians for almost 300 projects that occupied strategic spots in the Chinese plan of industrial development. Building on these key projects handled by the Soviets, the Chinese were able to achieve a rate of growth in gross national product that has been estimated by Western economists at the impressive figure of 7 or 8 per cent a year for the period from 1952 to 1957. In 1958, during the Great Leap Forward, there is reason to believe that growth reached the truly extraordinary rate of 17 or 18 per cent, dropping to 12 per cent in 1959 and to a more familiar 3 or 4 per cent in 1960 and 1961 in the period of aftermath. Subsequently, the Chinese Communists turned to building a more substantial agricultural base, rather than giving overwhelming priority to industry. But in spite of this and in spite of all the spectacular failures, it seemed possible by 1961 that the Chinese Communists might yet achieve their old boast, later abandoned, that they would soon overtake Great Britain in production from basic industries. And a nation with the manpower of China and the industrial capacity of Great Britain would make a formidable military power, indeed.

POWER FOR WHAT? THE GOALS OF COMMUNIST CHINA

The purposes for which Communist China would use her new-found unity and strength were clear. "Our nation," Mao Tse-tung said in September of 1949, "will never again be an insulted nation. We have stood up." Events over the next few years showed that the Chinese Communists were committed to policies of national power and prestige, that they were determined to be a Great Power with a large voice in the affairs of the world, and that they intended to make an attempt to dominate the whole of Asia.

It was probably the Soviet Union that planned and engineered the attack on South Korea, although they undoubtedly consulted the Chinese. But the Chinese decision to intervene in the Korean War was most likely an independent decision, taken from national considerations as much as from Communist.[7] At the outset of the Korean War, President Truman ordered the Seventh Fleet to "neutralize" the Taiwan Strait and declared that the legal status of Taiwan was an open question, subject to determination by a peace treaty with Japan or by the United Nations. The Chinese Communists reacted violently to these actions, which they regarded as intervention and "armed aggression against the territory of China." Over the first few months of the war, in fact, they seemed to be more preoccupied with Taiwan than with what was happening in Korea.[8]

Following the successful counterattack by the UN forces at Inchon and especially as they approached the thirty-eighth parallel, the Chinese became more agitated. Chou En-lai, the Chinese Foreign Minister, said on September 30, 1950, that "the Chinese people will not tolerate foreign aggression, nor will they supinely tolerate seeing their neighbors being savagely invaded by the imperialists." Even stronger reactions and warnings were expressed to K. M. Panikkar, the Indian Ambassador to Peking, culminating in a specific and formal warning in a dramatic midnight meeting on the night of October 2–3, that if the American forces crossed the thirty-eighth parallel, the Chinese would intervene in the war.

The General Assembly had been debating the issue of crossing the parallel and unifying Korea by force in one form or another since the Inchon landings on September 15. Soviet attempts to obtain Chinese Communist participation in the debate failed, and so did Indian efforts at a compromise. On October 7, the General Assembly passed a resolution endorsing "all appropriate steps to ensure conditions of stability throughout Korea," and the United States First Cavalry Division crossed the thirty-eighth parallel that same day. On October 16, a few Chinese Communist "volunteers" entered Korea secretly, followed in late October and early November by forces that totaled over three hundred thousand.

The Chinese Communists also took the opportunity to seize Tibet. On October 24, 1950, they announced that their troops had been ordered to "liberate" the country. The Tibetans were quickly defeated, and when the Chinese offered a treaty—the so-called "Agreement on Peaceful Measures with China"—that seemed to permit Tibet some degree of autonomy under Chinese sovereignty, they accepted.

But if the Korean War demonstrated Chinese Communist determination, it also demonstrated that they could make a realistic assessment of the situation and respond flexibly to it. By June of 1951, it had become clear that neither side could win in Korea without risking a world war and the pattern of limited war in which the Communists had a sanctuary in Manchuria and the UN forces had a sanctuary in Japan had become well established. It was at this time that the Soviets arranged for negotiations on a cease-fire—clearly with the approval of the Chinese and perhaps on their initiative.[9] As the cease-fire talks dragged on, the Chinese were also negotiating with the Soviet Union for economic aid, and the fact that it was not until after Stalin's death in early 1953 that the Soviet aid agreement was announced and that the Chinese brought the cease-fire negotiations to a conclusion may be indicative of a divergence in Chinese and Soviet interests at the time.

Still another sign of the development of more sophistication in Communist China's foreign policies came at an "Asian and Pacific Peace Conference" held in Peking in October 1952. The Chinese had made enormous efforts to see that the conference was well attended, and they then used it to launch a policy of "peaceful coexistence," calling on the United Nations both to end the fighting in Vietnam and Malaya and to "bring about just and reasonable settlements through negotiations." It was a dramatic departure from their usual dogmatic preachments of violence, revolution, and irreconcilable hostility between East and West.

Clearly, the Chinese Communists were about to embark on a new course in foreign policy, but one untidiness still remained. In the period from 1949 to 1953, the Chinese had also been the sponsors of aggression in other places than Korea and of a different kind. Immediately following World War II, the Communist Parties of Southeast Asia—in Burma, Thailand, Malaya, the Philippines, and French Indochina—had launched on campaigns of terror, using weapons left over from the war. In most places, these insurrections were crude and unsophisticated campaigns of indiscriminate killing, and they alienated more people than they enlisted. But once the Chinese Communists had succeeded in their revolution, they took the lead in putting the insurrections on a more effective, politically sophisticated course. But even so, by the time the Korean truce was signed in June 1953, only one of these—in Indochina against the French —was anywhere near success.

The Chinese stepped up their aid to the Communist-led Viet Minh throughout the rest of 1953, and by the spring of 1954, as related in an earlier chapter, the French had agreed to the Geneva Conference. And the Chinese came to Geneva as equals with the Great Powers, a symbol of status and prestige which was itself a Chinese Communist goal. When the French defeat at Dienbienphu came, the Communist North Vietnamese apparently wanted to keep on fighting until they controlled all of Vietnam, but they were persuaded to settle for less by both the Soviets and the Chinese. The Soviet national interest would not be served by further fighting in Asia, and there may also have been a link between Soviet pressure on Hanoi to end the war and the French decision to reject the proposed European Defense Community. But it was the Chinese whose influence was undoubtedly the greatest in engineering the compromise that created two Vietnams and permitted the separate settlements for Laos and Cambodia. Whether because they were convinced that the United States would intervene rather than permit the whole of Vietnam to be lost or because they wanted a pause in the fighting on their border areas so they could concentrate their resources on internal development, the Chinese Communists decided to compromise. But the important fact is that it was the Chinese who made the decision, not the Vietnamese. And this state of affairs, too, was undoubtedly a Chinese Communist goal.

THE NEW CHINESE FOREIGN POLICY

With the signing of the Geneva agreements in July 1954, the stage was set for the new Chinese Communist line, and they were not long in unfolding it. In June, even before all the details in the Geneva agreements had been worked out, Chou En-lai had taken time off from what was ostensibly a trip home to pay formal visits to India and Burma, and in both places joint communiqués had been issued which laid down the so-called *panch shila*—the five principles of peaceful coexistence. First mentioned as what seemed to be an incidental part of the treaty signed in April by which India recognized China's sovereignty over Tibet, the *panch shila* called for mutual respect for sovereignty and territorial integrity, for nonaggression, for noninterference in each other's domestic affairs, for mutual benefit and equality, and for peaceful coexistence. At the ceremonies marking the signature of the Geneva accords, Chou made the *panch shila* the keynote of his speech—as it was to become the keynote of the next phase of Chinese foreign policy.

At first, most of the foreign offices in the West thought of the "Five Principles" as a vague and rather simplistic propaganda gimmick. But they misunderstood the appeal in Asia. The shadow of China had always been long in Asia, and any sign of Chinese willingness to move toward accommodation was bound to be welcomed and encouraged. The "Five Principles" also reflected an essentially Asian attitude and approach—Asians are not only anticolonial, but they are suspicious of alliances and bases and they are powerfully attracted by such ideas as neutrality and nonalignment. Armed with the "Five Principles," the Chinese Communists launched on a wide-ranging diplomatic offensive throughout the world to reassure the weaker nations about China's intentions, to separate the Asian states from the West, and to counter the pull of SEATO—the Southeast Asia Treaty Organization, which the United States was in the process of forming. The results were impressive. From 1950 to 1953, Communist China had established diplomatic relations with only two countries, Finland and Pakistan. But from 1954 to 1957, it established relations with fourteen.

Even as early as the fall of 1954, this diplomatic campaign to improve relations and seek friendships had made enough progress to permit the Chinese to take some risks. Reminding the world and especially its new-found friends that Taiwan and the offshore islands, which the Nationalists still controlled, were part of China even in the Nationalists' view, and making a distinction between the use of force to regain control in one's own territory and the use of force for external aggression, the Chinese Communists began the bombardment of Quemoy and Matsu, the largest of the offshore islands. In a carefully paced and politically disciplined program of bombardment and military probes, the Chinese tested American determination to support the Nationalists—combining diplomatic and political pressures with bombardment and the threat of invasion, but stopping short of full-scale military involvement. The crisis reached a peak in early 1955—but then began to subside, partly because the American response had been firm and partly because the Chinese Communists apparently felt there was more to be gained politically by continuing their diplomatic peace offensive.

The first opportunity came in April 1955 at a nongovernmental conference in New Delhi attended mostly by Communists. Here the Chinese were able to lay the groundwork for a new and appealing theme—"Asian solidarity." But the really significant opportunity came at the historic conference at Bandung, in Indonesia.

THE BANDUNG CONFERENCE

The 1955 Bandung Conference had been called by the "Colombo" powers—India, Burma, Indonesia, Pakistan, and Ceylon—as a formal meeting of the governmental leaders of Asian and African countries only. For the first time, it brought together in one place, with no Western powers present, such Asian and African leaders as Nehru of India, Chou En-lai of Communist China, U Nu of Burma, Mohammad Ali of Pakistan, Kotelawala of Ceylon, Sihanouk of Cambodia, Romulo of the Philippines, Nasser of Egypt, and Nkrumah of what became Ghana—leaders from a total of twenty-nine Asian and African countries.

Nehru and Chou dominated the conference, but it was clearly Chou who profited most. Repeating that "revolution is not for export," Chou adopted a stance of reasonableness and accommodation. Outside the conference, he took advantage of the occasion to sign a treaty with Indonesia on the status of overseas Chinese and to offer to negotiate with the United States on "relaxing tension in the Taiwan area." Inside the conference, Chou refrained from pushing obviously Communist lines—"We do not hide the fact that we believe in Communism," he said, but then went on to say that there was no need to "publicize one's ideology" at Bandung, for the Chinese had come to the conference "to seek unity and not to quarrel." He hit all the reassuring themes—speaking in his opening speech, for example, of the respect that Chinese Communists had for religion, even though they were themselves atheists. But above all he repeated over and over again at every opportunity, whether private dinner party or public occasion, that Communist China was devoted to peace and that it wished "to establish normal relations with all Asian and African countries, with all the countries of the world, and first of all with our neighboring countries."

In the next two years, the Chinese Communists exploited the theme of "Asian solidarity" to the full. The Chinese sent high-level, high-prestige visitors, including Madame Sun Yat-sen, wherever an invitation could be wangled, and in turn, arranged for a whole string of visits to Peking—Prime Minister Suhrawardy of Pakistan, U Nu of Burma, Sukarno of Indonesia, Sihanouk of Cambodia, and Souvanna Phouma of Laos. And they also embarked on an aid program, modest in actual value but important in terms of impact. Prince Sihanouk of Cambodia, for example, was given a radio station—with one of the most powerful transmitters in all of Southeast Asia.

RETURN TO THE "HARD" LINE

But those among Asian leaders who hoped that "peaceful coexistence" and "Asian solidarity" were something more than just a tactic in Chinese Communist policy were doomed to disappointment. In the autumn of 1957, the Soviet Union launched the first sputnik, a feat which gave the Communist world enormous prestige, not only as the leader in space science, but also in military and strategic terms, as the first nation to achieve a workable intercontinental ballistic missile. Launching the world's first man-made satellite undoubtedly gave the Communist leaders confidence that they could risk stepping up the pressure on the free world. But it may also be that tensions internal to the Communist nations had created a need for external hostility, especially in the case of Communist China, which had just experienced the "Hundred Flowers" outpouring of criticism. In any case, Mao Tse-tung declared a shift back to a harsher, more hostile policy in a dramatic speech on November 18,

1957, at the celebrations in Moscow of the fortieth anniversary of the Bolshevik Revolution. "I consider," Mao said, "that the present world situation has reached a new turning point." Re-emphasizing the Cold War between the Communist and non-Communist worlds, he went on to say that there were "now two winds in the world: the east wind and the west wind. . . . I think the characteristic of the current situation is that the east wind prevails over the west wind; that is, the strength of socialism exceeds the strength of imperialism."

The first concrete manifestation of the new policy came in Chinese relations with Japan. The Kishi government had hoped to increase trade with Communist China and had made important concessions to that end. But early in 1958, the Chinese stepped up their pressures on the Japanese. When Kishi said that, since Japan did not recognize Communist China, the Chinese trade mission would not be permitted to fly its flag, the Chinese Communists reacted violently, first by breaking off negotiations and then, following an incident involving an insult to the Communist flag, by canceling all existing contracts and cutting off trade entirely.

A more serious and risky manifestation of the new policy came in the late summer, when the Chinese Communists moved large numbers of troops into position opposite the offshore islands and, as in 1954–55, threatened to invade. The threat was combined with subtleties—publicly and privately, through agents in Hong Kong, the Communists appealed to Nationalist leaders to make a deal. But it also ran a high level of risk—Communist China and the United States, in the words of Secretary of State John Foster Dulles, came to the "brink of war" before the Chinese decided to let the crisis taper off.

One of the ironies of the new Chinese policy was that it produced a growing hostility toward India, which had long pursued policies of friendship and accommodation with China, and even toward Nehru himself, who had sponsored Chou En-lai's introduction to Asian and African leaders at the Bandung Conference. The immediate cause was Tibet. Following their occupation of Tibet in 1950–51, the Chinese Communists had begun to build a network of roads permitting truck traffic between the different segments of Tibet and three main highways linking the central Tibetan plateau with Sinkiang and China proper. These roads in some cases crossed Indian territory or territory in dispute, but the real trouble was political. The roads permitted the Chinese to consolidate their hold on Tibet, and they began to use this control to eliminate the Buddhist religion and remake Tibetan society. The methods included every instrument that conquerors have used on an alien population, including torture and degradation of the Buddhist monks and the mass removal of children to China for re-education and to break the influence of parents. In 1959, the Tibetans revolted, and the Communists put down the revolt with savage brutality. The Dalai Lama, traditional leader of the Tibetan people, fled, and the Indians gave him refuge. Their motive may have been simple humanitarianism, for they were sensitive enough on the policy implications for their relations with China to keep him in one of the most inaccessible places in all India and to refuse permission for journalists and others to see him. But the Chinese nevertheless reacted with vehement hatred and promptly precipitated the first of the Sino-Indian border crises.

But it was in Southeast Asia that the new Chinese Communist policy of increasing hostility had its greatest impact—by encouraging the local Communists in a direct use of military force, first in Laos and then in South Vietnam. In both Laos and Vietnam, the Chinese Communists could stand behind the Pathet Lao and the Viet Cong with aid and encouragement, but with very little risk to themselves so long as the level of force used was kept low and the pace controlled. In effect, a major attack was launched, but it was by indirect aggression—by encouraging and supporting a civil war through the guerrilla tactics and political techniques of "internal war."

NOTES

[1] The first serious dissension among the top leadership was apparently later, in the purge of Kao Kang and Jao Shu-shih in 1954–55 for attempting to usurp positions second only to Mao himself, and the purge in 1959 of Marshal P'eng Te-huai, the Defense Minister, for machinations with Moscow in connection with the Sino-Soviet dispute. Both of these were dwarfed by the great internal struggle which became public in 1966 with the purge of P'eng Chen, Mayor of Peking.

[2] Denis Warner, *Hurricane From China*, 1961, p. 3.

[3] Erik H. Erikson, *Young Man Luther, A Study in Psychoanalysis and History*, 1962.

[4] Mao himself admitted to 800,000 killings up to 1954 in a speech he gave on February 27, 1957.

[5] A. Doak Barnett, *Communist China and Asia, Challenge to American Policy*, 1960, p. 18.

[6] A. Doak Barnett, *op. cit.*, p. 32.

[7] Allen S. Whiting, *China Crosses the Yalu, the Decision to Enter the Korean War*, 1960.

[8] Whiting, *op. cit.*, p. 53.

[9] A. Doak Barnett, *op. cit.*, p. 95.

CHAPTER 21

The Development of United States Policy

THUS THE THREAT of Communist China as it had unfolded since 1949—
and as it appeared to the Kennedy administration in 1961—was formidable. There could be no doubt that the Chinese Communists were in full
control of the mainland. They had, in addition, demonstrated a positive
capacity to mobilize the energies of the Chinese people and to direct
these and China's considerable economic resources toward the development of military power and the achievement of national goals. It was
already clear in 1961, for example, that in spite of natural disasters and
widespread hunger in China, the work on an atomic bomb was going
forward and that the first explosion would undoubtedly take place sometime between 1963 and 1965. Their foreign policy had clearly demonstrated a determination to play a big role in the world, to have a large
voice in world affairs, and, more ominously, to make an attempt to
dominate all of Asia. But even as the acts of the Chinese Communists
exposed how ruthlessly they would pursue their ambitions, these same
acts had also demonstrated their cautiousness and realism. They had
made realistic appraisals of their military capabilities and had taken
risks in direct relationship to their own conception of China's vital
interests. Their acts had also shown that ambition was combined with
subtlety and sophistication in technique. They had the discipline to limit
demands for long-term political purposes when the going was good, as at
Geneva after Dienbienphu, or to cut losses when the going was not so
good, as in Korea. And they had shown the flexibility to shift from hard
to soft tactics and back again to fit the changing situation—or even to
pursue both hard and soft policies simultaneously.

UNITED STATES POLICY

Successfully meeting such a formidable and subtle opponent requires
policies not only of equal determination but of equal subtlety and
flexibility. But United States policy toward China developed in circumstances and under pressures, domestic as well as foreign, that made not
for flexibility but rigidity.

In 1948, the United States Government became so thoroughly dis-
illusioned with the corruption and stubborn incompetency of the Nation-

alist Kuomintang that it saw no hope in continuing to support it. Europe in 1948 was also in danger. The crisis over the Berlin blockade was at its height. Greece was under attack by guerrillas based in Communist Yugoslavia and Bulgaria. And all of Europe was in an economic crisis, resulting from World War II, that offered the Communists in France and Italy, especially, what was clearly a decisive opportunity. General George C. Marshall was Secretary of State, and, as a result of the mission he had just completed to China, he was convinced both that the Nationalists would not reform in time to save China without the full-scale use of American troops and that in these circumstances the United States could not save both Europe and China and would therefore have to make a choice. The decision was to continue only limited assistance to the Nationalists.

On January 21, 1949, Dean Acheson became Secretary of State in the second Truman administration, just as the Chinese Communists reached the Yangtze River, and there were renewed pleas from the Nationalists for American help in defending this natural barrier—pleas that were strongly supported by the Republicans in Congress. But Acheson stuck to the established policy, and at a background meeting with a group of Republican congressmen said that he could not foretell the outcome of events in China "until the dust settled."

Over the next few weeks—in a portent of things to come—the Republicans made more and more of an issue of China policy. Senator Styles Bridges called for a "full dress investigation by Congress of the State Department's position toward China." Senator William F. Knowland offered a resolution calling for a joint committee to do the same. A Democrat, the isolationist Senator Pat McCarran of Nevada, introduced a bill to provide over a billion dollars in loans to Nationalist China.

The Communists easily swept past the Yangtze barrier on April 21, 1949. When the Nationalists soon thereafter fled to Taiwan, the thesis that aid alone could have saved China looked somewhat ridiculous—but after a short lull the partisan attacks on Acheson and the State Department were renewed with increased vehemence.

Although Communist control was a fact, the State Department did not seriously consider an early recognition of Communist China in spite of its conviction that the Nationalists had no real prospect of going back. On the contrary, the United States sought to discourage other nations from acting very promptly. The motive for this policy was in large part the need to make concessions to congressional sentiment to gain support for the all-important Marshall Plan for European recovery. But in part the policy also stemmed from Chinese Communist moves that made any consideration of recognition increasingly difficult. Edmund O. Clubb, and other American foreign service officers stationed in China, had pinned down the true Leninist hue of the Chinese Communists in their dispatches of the early thirties, but if anyone really did believe the "agrarian reformer" myth, Mao Tse-tung dispelled any doubt on July 1, 1949. In a policy statement captioned "leaning to one side," he flatly rejected neutralism on the "Titoist" model in the Cold War between East and West and declared that Communist China was an ally of the Soviet Union and an enemy of the United States and "imperialism."

Mao's own isolationism and fear and hatred of the outside world led him not only to go slow in seeking recognition but in some ways to discourage it. His policy was to destroy every vestige of the "imperialist domination of China" and to deny legal status to any foreign diplomatic establishments until all such vestiges were removed. The imperialists, he argued, had always been hostile to the Chinese people and would "definitely not be in a hurry to treat us as equals." The policy Mao laid down was that "as long as the imperialist countries do not change their hostile attitude, we shall not grant them legal status in China." Shortly thereafter an American vice-consul was arrested and beaten in Shanghai. The American Consul General in Mukden, Angus Ward, and his staff, who had been in house arrest for a year, were now jailed.

Thus the combination of pressure from Congress and difficulties posed by the Chinese Communists themselves closed any possibility that the United States could respond favorably when the Chinese proclaimed their new government on October 1, 1949, and invited recognition. The State Department announced that the United States Government would take no action without consulting Congress.

On December 30, 1949, India recognized Communist China. Britain followed on January 6, 1950, and was quickly joined by Norway, Ceylon, Denmark, Israel, Afghanistan, Finland, Sweden, and Switzerland. Then, on January 14, the Chinese Communists seized official American properties in Peking. The State Department recalled all American officials in China and closed all American government establishments.

But the decisive question for the future of United States policy was not so much whether or not to recognize Communist China as whether or not to defend Taiwan. Taiwan would undoubtedly fall to the Communists if the United States stood aside, and, once it did, such questions as recognition and admission to the United Nations would become politically academic.[1] The Secretary of State notified the National Security Council in August of 1949 that political and economic measures could not prevent the Communists from taking over Taiwan and that its fall could be expected shortly. Also in August, the Joint Chiefs of Staff reaffirmed their view that direct United States military action to protect Taiwan would not be justified on military and strategic grounds.

In the meantime, there was a steady drumfire of support for the Nationalists from the Republicans, inside and outside of Congress.

Senator H. Alexander Smith, of New Jersey, proposed that the United States occupy Taiwan with American troops. Senator Knowland suggested a U.S. military mission. Senator Robert A. Taft, of Ohio, argued that Taiwan should be kept out of Communist hands even if it took the United States fleet to do it. Former President Herbert Hoover, in response to a letter from Senator Knowland, came out for U.S. naval protection of Taiwan, the Pescadores, and possibly Hainan.

But the administration stuck to its policy. On January 5, 1950, in a statement released by the White House, President Truman declared that the United States had no desire "to obtain special rights or privileges or to establish military bases on Formosa . . . ." Stressing that the wartime Cairo Declaration had specified that Taiwan would be returned to China, the statement went on to say that the "United States will not pursue a course which will lead to involvement in the civil conflict in China. Similarly, the United States Government will not provide military aid or advice to Chinese forces on Formosa." And on January 12, 1950, Secretary Acheson in his controversial speech before the National Press Club drew a defense perimeter from the Aleutians to Japan, to the Ryukyus, and then to the Philippines that left Korea outside but even more pointedly omitted Taiwan.

Republicans in the Congress retaliated by opposing an administration bill providing economic aid for South Korea, on the grounds that aid to Korea made no sense in the "absence of an overall policy for the Far East." The administration got its aid to Korea only by agreeing to extend the deadline for spending the money granted to the Nationalist regime under the China Aid Act. The struggle between the administration and its opponents on policy toward Taiwan had reached a stalemate.

THE ATTACK ON KOREA

Then, on June 25, 1950, the matter was settled by the Communist North Korean surprise attack against South Korea. In a public statement on June 27, President Truman announced that he had ordered the Seventh Fleet to neutralize the Taiwan Strait, permitting neither side to attack. "The attack on Korea," his statement said, "makes it plain beyond all doubts that Communism has passed beyond the use of subversion to conquer independent nations and will now use armed invasion and war. . . . In these circumstances the occupation of Formosa [Taiwan] by Communist forces would be a direct threat to the security of the Pacific area." And, as mentioned above, he also declared that the United States now regarded the legal status of Taiwan as an open question.

In September 1950, UN forces landed at Inchon, defeating the North Korean Army. In early October, the UN authorized the unification of

Korea by force, U.S. forces crossed the thirty-eighth parallel, and by November the Chinese Communists had intervened.

It was not long after this that the State Department finally became the captive of its critics and swung over to the position that the Nationalist regime on Taiwan was still the government of all of China. On May 18, 1951, Dean Rusk, then Assistant Secretary of State for Far Eastern Affairs, speaking before the China Institute, said that we could "tell our friends in China that the United States will not acquiesce in the degradation which is being forced upon them. We do not recognize the authorities in Peiping for what they pretend to be. The Peiping regime may be a colonial Russian government—a Slavic Manchukuo on a larger scale. It is not the Government of China. It does not pass the first test. It is not Chinese. It is not entitled to speak for China in the community of nations."

CONGRESS, THE CHINA LOBBY, AND THE CLIMATE OF OPINION

As many nations have learned to do, the Chinese Nationalists had been active participants in the American policy-making process, not only through public relations activities typified by the so-called China Lobby but by paying special attention to the American Congress. In the Congress it was Representative Walter H. Judd, a Republican from Minnesota and a former missionary to China, and Senator William F. Knowland— the "Senator from Formosa"—who were most prominent. But there were many others.

The whole question of China policy was enflamed by the hearings following Truman's dismissal of MacArthur in 1951, and it became a major issue in the election of 1952, with the Republicans charging that the Democrats had "substituted on our Pacific flank a murderous enemy for an ally and friend."

Prominent in the public debate on China policy from the beginning had been the so-called "China Lobby." Alfred Kohlberg, an importer who headed the American China Policy Association, William Loeb, a publisher, and Frederick C. McKee, an industrialist who headed the China Emergency Committee, along with Congressman Judd and Senator Knowland, were the focal points of its activity. They pressed at every opportunity for greater support and commitment to Chiang Kai-shek and the Nationalists and never failed to attack those who were skeptical of the Nationalists' ability to return to the mainland. In 1953, after the election of Eisenhower, the group formed the "Committee of One Million Against the Admission of Communist China to the United Nations" to collect a million signatures in opposition to seating the Communists. In 1955, the committee announced that since there had been "a series of oblique declarations from several major internationally-minded American groups hinting at the need to recognize Communist China and to admit that regime to the UN for the sake of 'peace,' " the committee had been reorganized as simply the "Committee of One Million" to fight this possibility. In a review of its own accomplishments from 1957 to 1960, the committee took credit for having helped to kill proposed Senate hearings on trade with Communist China by means of a nationwide postcard campaign, for having organized a letter-writing campaign in support of Dulles' "brinkmanship" policy during the offshore islands crisis of 1958, of having helped nullify in 1959 the effects of the Conlon report (which had recommended a series of steps to implement a "two-Chinas" policy by which Communist China would be seated in the UN but the Nationalists would also retain a seat), and of having worked "closely with all candidates" in the 1960 campaign, when "those few candidates who openly supported the admission of Communist China to the UN were defeated."

MCCARTHYISM AND CHINA POLICY

But the peak of passion came when China policy became a major target of McCarthyism. It was probably inevitable that the witch hunt launched by Senator Joseph McCarthy of Wisconsin would come to focus on the loss of China. The fear engendered by an implacable, ruthless foe, the bewilderment engendered by problems so endlessly tangled in complexity, the exasperation in dealing with foreign friends who were corrupt and incompetent, the frustration of insufficient power or outright impotency—all of these typified our experience in China and all were equally typical of the McCarthyite attempt to explain all our troubles in terms of a Communist conspiracy.

The first such charge of conspiracy had come early, in November of 1945, when Patrick J. Hurley, the prominent Republican whom Roosevelt had appointed as Ambassador to China, resigned with a blast at the State Department and the career "Old China Hands" who, Hurley charged, had "sided with the Chinese Communist armed party" and had sabotaged United States policy. In 1949, when the State Department published a white paper on China—which was designed to show, in the words used by Acheson in his letter of transmittal, that "the ominous result of the civil war in China was beyond the control of the government of the United States."—General Hurley repeated his charges. He called the white paper "a smooth alibi for the pro-Communists in the State Department who had engineered the overthrow of our ally, the Nationalist Government of the Republic of China and aided in the Communist conquest of China." Walter Judd joined in by charging that the State Department had omitted sixteen facts and documents which would have supported the critics of China policy, and Senators Knowland, Bridges,

McCarran, and Wherry called the white paper a "whitewash of a wishful, do-nothing policy which has succeeded only in placing Asia in danger of Soviet conquest."

Senator McCarthy had hit on the "Communism in government" theme almost accidentally in a speech at Wheeling, West Virginia, on February 9, 1950, in what had been up to that time a stumbling search for an issue to use in the upcoming 1952 elections. Although the month before McCarthy had characterized John S. Service as a man "who as a representative of the State Department said that the only hope in Asia was Communism," as his sole contribution to a debate on aid to Taiwan, he did not at first center his attack on those who had been connected with China policy. But several of the "Old China Hands" were on his original list of eighty-one "cases" of Communist sympathizers in the State Department. Then, shortly after his Wheeling speech, McCarthy met Alfred Kohlberg for the first time and heard Kohlberg expound his thesis that the Institute of Pacific Relations was the instrument of Communist penetration of the State Department.[2] In front of the Tydings Subcommittee, convened to investigate the charges against the State Department, McCarthy accused Ambassador Philip C. Jessup of having an "unusual affinity for Communist causes." He named Owen Lattimore, a professor at the Johns Hopkins University and sometime consultant to the State Department, as "one of the principal architects of our far eastern policy" and went on to accuse him of being "an extremely bad security risk." And he repeated the accusations against John S. Service.

When Jessup, who flew back from Asia to face his accuser, successfully refuted the charges against himself, McCarthy staked his whole attack on the one case of Owen Lattimore—whom he now accused of being the top Soviet espionage agent in the United States.

The focus of the whole McCarthy attack therefore became China policy and the people connected with it. And many others joined the McCarthy band wagon. On March 27, Senator Bridges delivered a bitter personal attack on Secretary of State Acheson, declaring that our trouble in both Europe and Asia was no accident—that "Stalin had help from inside our ranks." On April 5, Senator Knowland joined the attack with a speech comparing Lattimore's writings with the resolutions adopted by the Sixth World Congress of the Communist International and other Communist publications.

And so it went. Before the McCarthy madness had run its course, the twenty-some China specialists in the Foreign Service had either resigned, retired, or run to cover in jobs dealing with other parts of the world. Even outside scholars had been affected, and to some extent excluded from influence. A group of authors associated with the Institute of Pacific Relations, for example, reviewed twenty-two of thirty books on China for the New York *Times* in the period from 1945 to 1950 and thirty of thirty-five books for the *Herald Tribune,* but none for either paper in the period from 1952 to 1956.[3] Both career officers in the State Department and men in public and political life were intimidated. And the effects persisted long after McCarthy's downfall and death, for the Committee of One Million continued to muster as many as 339 congressional signatures for their newspaper ads and to dissect every public speech for hints of deviation from their rigid orthodoxy.

THE EISENHOWER ADMINISTRATION

Such was the situation the Eisenhower administration inherited when it took office in 1953, and the dilemmas it faced were cruel. Domestically, the trouble was partly of the Republicans own making. The Republicans had used the United States' failure in China and the Korean War as steppingstones to office, and they could not be less uncompromising toward the Chinese Communists after the election than they were before. Abroad, the dilemmas were more complicated. It was a fiction to maintain that the Communists did not control the mainland of China, but it certainly served no useful purpose for the United States to reward aggression by recognizing Communist China or by encouraging their being seated in the United Nations. The "hate America" propaganda which poured from the Chinese press and radio may have had some of its origins in the overly rigid American policies, but the campaign was, nevertheless, no help. Neither side seemed capable of sustained reasonableness. The Chinese Communists proposed an exchange of newsmen in 1956, and the United States refused it. The United States came around in 1957 and reopened the question, but by this time the Chinese were in an uncompromising mood. Still another set of dilemmas were posed in U.S. relations with the Nationalist regime on Taiwan. Politically, reports of Chiang Kai-shek's continued dictatorship and the oppression of Taiwanese by the "mainlanders" made the Nationalists no asset to the United States in Asia or elsewhere in the world. Strategically, Taiwan was not essential to the security of the American position in Asia, though it would, of course, be useful under certain circumstances if the Chinese Communists embarked on a military rampage. For humanitarian reasons alone, the United States would be reluctant to see the Communists take over Taiwan, and each new act of aggressiveness by the Communists— Korea, Tibet, the sponsorship of guerrilla insurrection in Malaya, the Philippines, and Vietnam—increased the American commitment to protect Taiwan. But it was certainly not in the United States' interest to become involved in a Chinese Nationalist attempt to retake the mainland, much less to permit Chiang to maneuver us into a war to restore him to power. Yet his determination to hang on to the offshore islands could have just this effect. The islands had some military and political utility for the Nationalists, but they were certainly not essential for the defense of Taiwan. As one former ambassador has written, "The loss of offshore islands as such undoubtedly would be less important to President Chiang than the danger of the two Chinas idea which he considers implicit in drawing a line down the Formosa [Taiwan] strait."[4] But here again each time the Chinese Communists increased the pressure on the offshore islands the United States' dilemma was posed anew. If the United States made it clear that it would *not* help defend the offshore islands, the Communists would be encouraged in their belligerency. If the United States indicated only that it *might* help in their defense, some deterrent effect was maintained without a total commitment of United States prestige—but even a policy of ambiguity could not avoid some measure of increased commitment and the companion risk of becoming involved in some future spiral into war.

The Eisenhower administration's response to these multiple dilemmas was to continue the trend begun under Truman of making policy in reaction to pressure—from domestic interests, from allies, from the Nationalist Chinese, and from Communist China. One of the new administration's first acts was to respond to domestic pressures by "unleashing" Chiang Kai-shek—declaring that the Seventh Fleet's mission, which had been to neutralize the Taiwan Strait, no longer included shielding the mainland. But there were counterpressures, too. As the then United States Ambassador wrote, "Our position in Formosa remained basically unchanged, owing to the tangible factors which continued to govern; but the Chinese, not unnaturally, interpreted our step as suggesting the possibility of American support for offensive action on their part."[5] Responding in turn to this pressure, the administration instructed the ambassador to ask President Chiang that no such action be initiated without consulting the United States, and Chiang agreed. The Nationalists had been "unleashed" and promptly "leashed" again.

The new administration also appointed Walter S. Robertson as Assistant Secretary of State for Far Eastern Affairs, reportedly at the instance of Senator Knowland, Representative Judd, and others who had advocated full United States support for Chiang Kai-shek and the Nationalists. And Robertson pursued a vigorous policy of trade embargo, travel restrictions, and so on, designed as much as possible to isolate Communist China from the non-Communist world.

The administration's response to the aggressiveness of Communist China was to attempt to forge a coalition of allies and to increase support for the Nationalist regime on Taiwan. The Manila pact, creating the Southeast Asia Treaty Organization, was signed in 1954 with Britain, France, Australia, New Zealand, the Philippines, Thailand, and Pakistan, and a series of mutual aid pacts were signed with Korea, Japan, and several others. Under the Mutual Defense Treaty of 1954 with the

Republic of China, the Nationalist Government on Taiwan received large amounts of military and economic aid.

When the Chinese Communists stepped up their pressure on the off-shore islands in 1954–55, the United States increased its support to the Nationalists and also its public commitment. President Eisenhower requested the Congress to pass a resolution authorizing him to use American forces to defend Taiwan and the Pescadores, leaving the question of using American forces to defend the offshore islands deliberately ambiguous. Dulles used the occasion to persuade the Nationalists to evacuate Tachen, an island in the north that was peculiarly difficult to defend, but the Nationalists in turn used the occasion to strengthen their own defensive position on Quemoy and Matsu and to commit themselves even more strongly to their defense. The 1958 offshore islands crisis—when Dulles went to the "brink" of war—had the same effects.

But there were opposite pressures to which the Eisenhower administration also responded. At the end of the civil war several thousand Nationalist troops had retreated into the wilds of northern Burma, where they settled down to a life reminiscent of the warlord period in China. The Burmese at first were preoccupied with their internal strife, but as the Burmese Government was able to extend its control outward, the presence of the Nationalist troops became a problem. The problem burgeoned when the Nationalists, having received additional ammunition and equipment by air, undertook a large-scale raid into Yunnan. The raid was a colossal failure, but the protest from the Chinese Communists was more than enough to make the Burmese determined to end the situation. The Burmese, most of Asia, and many Americans were by this time convinced that the CIA had sponsored the idea of keeping a Nationalist army-in-being in Burma and had made all the arrangements and furnished the equipment to rearm and resupply these troops by air. In any event, in 1952, the new Eisenhower administration wanted peace in the area and, seeing the Kuomintang troops as a possible spark, requested Chiang Kai-shek to evacuate them to Taiwan. But Chiang wanted to leave the troops in place—the possible threat to peace was of less concern to him, since in certain circumstances war would be the best opportunity for the Nationalists to return to the mainland. In any case, Chiang felt that having troops in Burma might be very useful on occasion. In the end, however, American pressure prevailed, and in late spring, 1953, over seven thousand Chinese—most but not all of the Kuomintang troops—were flown out of Burma to Taiwan.

Another example of a United States response to pressures against isolating Communist China was the development of what became regular talks between the American and Chinese ambassadors in Warsaw—conversations which as a practical matter served as a partial substitute for recognition. The first negotiations between the United States and the

Chinese Communists were at Panmunjom in connection with the cease-fire in the Korean War. These were followed by an approach to the Chinese through the American Consul General in Geneva, seeking information about Americans held prisoner in Communist China. The Chinese Communists, possibly as a political and propaganda gambit to imply *de facto* recognition, proposed that these talks be raised to the ambassadorial level and transferred to Warsaw. There were obvious advantages to having a place to talk with the Chinese Communists about a number of very practical matters, such as the repatriation of Americans imprisoned in China, as well as a place to probe for the Chinese attitude on more general questions, and the United States Government agreed—insisting only that the talks in no way implied diplomatic recognition.

SAN FRANCISCO SPEECH, 1957

But the resultant of all the multiple pressures was still a policy stance composed more of myth and rigidity than of realism and flexibility. The policy with both its myths and rigidity was summed up by Secretary of State John Foster Dulles in a speech at San Francisco on June 28, 1957. The key phrase in the speech—and the basic assumption of the policy—was that the United States Government regarded the Chinese Communist regime as "a passing and not a perpetual phase." It was from this assumption that policy flowed. "We owe it to ourselves, our allies, and the Chinese people," the Secretary went on to say, "to do all that we can to contribute to that passing." Accordingly, United States policy was so to act and speak as to encourage Chinese overseas and on the mainland to look to the Nationalists on Taiwan as the government of all of China. The policy, moreover, was to abstain "from any act to encourage the Communist regime, morally, politically, or materially," and this included refusing to extend diplomatic recognition, opposing the seating of Communist China in the UN, putting an embargo on any trade or cultural exchanges, and encouraging our friends and allies to follow suit.

NOTES

1 Tang Tsou, *America's Failure in China, 1941–50,* 1963, p. 527.
2 Philip Horton, "The China Lobby," *Reporter,* April 29, 1952.
3 Robert P. Newman, *Recognition of Communist China,* 1961, pp. 11–12.
4 Karl Lott Rankin, *China Assignment,* 1964, p. 226.
5 Rankin, *op. cit.,* pp. 154–55.

CHAPTER 22

The Policy Struggle: "Two Chinas" or the "Year of the Tiger"?

It was the TV debates with Nixon that won Kennedy the Presidency—not because of any particular issue they debated but because seventy million Americans saw for themselves that Kennedy was Nixon's equal and not the immature and inexperienced rich boy that Nixon had been saying he was. But one issue, the issue on which the two had in fact spent most of their time, had resounding implications for foreign policy. In their initial answers to a question on the little offshore islands of Quemoy and Matsu, before the qualifications added in later debating blurred the distinction between their positions, they were, in Theodore H. White's phrase, "tentatively fingering at one of the supreme problems of American statecraft, our relation with the revolution in Asia."[1]

Kennedy said that the two islands were strategically indefensible—referring to the fact that Quemoy, for example, lay only five miles off the mainland shore in the mouth of the harbor of Amoy—that they were not essential to the defense of Taiwan, and that he was in favor of persuading the Chinese Nationalists to pull out. Nixon took the opposite view, that the islands were in the "area of freedom" and that no part of the free world should be given up to the Communists.

The debate focused on the islands, but the real issue was our attitude toward the Chinese civil war and the question of whether or not Communism was the "passing phase" that Dulles had said it was. In 1955, Chiang Kai-shek had quite readily given up the Tachen islands, another group of offshore islands farther north. But he had strengthened the garrisons on Quemoy and Matsu—not because he really felt they were of any military importance, but, as mentioned above, because of the "danger of the two Chinas idea which he considers implicit in drawing a line down the Formosa Strait."

In this sense, the Chinese Communists also had a stake in the Nationalists continuing to hold the offshore islands. For they were just as vehemently opposed to the "two Chinas" policy as the Nationalists, and the islands served not only as an obstacle to that policy but also to keep the civil war alive. The Formosa Resolution of 1955 had specified that the United States would defend Taiwan and the Pescadores, and had included Quemoy and Matsu only if the President at the time decided that the attack on them was a prelude to an attack on Taiwan itself. What this did was to put the President on a political spot. The China Lobby and its friends would naturally interpret any major fighting on the offshore islands as a prelude to an attack on Taiwan, and call for full support even if it meant war. The opposition, on the other hand, would just as inevitably charge that the Nationalists had provoked the fighting to embroil the United States in Chiang's war to get back into power on the mainland. But the real irony was that if the United States took steps to end the civil war—which would inevitably lead to a "two Chinas" policy whether or not that was intended—not only might it drive the Nationalists to an act of desperation, but it might lead the Chinese Communists to attack the islands without any provocation other than the mere attempt to end the civil war. For both the Nationalists and the Communists, in sum, Quemoy and Matsu were as useful as a lever on the Americans as on each other.

For the same reason, Quemoy and Matsu were a lever in the policy debate in the United States. If Communism on the mainland was a "passing phase" or if a military showdown with the Chinese Communists was inevitable, as some of the extreme hard-liners thought it was, then it would be wise to stick to the "one China" policy and to keep the civil war going. Quemoy and Matsu served both purposes.

Thus by going on the record that he was in favor of persuading the Chinese Nationalists to give up Quemoy and Matsu, Kennedy aligned himself with those who felt that Communism was now well entrenched on the mainland, regrettable though that might be, and that the longer-range interests of the United States lay in easing the risks of continuing the civil war and in looking toward some change in our policy of regarding the government in Taiwan as the true government of all of China.

Given his pragmatic approach to foreign policy, however, Kennedy was more likely to move slowly and tentatively in this direction than to rush. But there were clearly men in the new administration who might rush, and it was on these, and especially on Chester Bowles, that the China Lobby and its friends focused attention. Bowles had written an article for *Foreign Affairs* on China policy that had been published in April of 1960. In it he had dismissed the idea of immediate recognition of Communist China and seating it in the UN as problems that were "not at the moment solvable." But he had called for what amounted to an end to the civil war and the beginning of a "two Chinas" policy, urging the "neutralization of the offshore islands" and the evolution of "an independent Sino-Formosan nation." As the new appointees—Rusk and Bowles—came up for their confirmation hearings, the administration braced itself for a rough time.

In his testimony, Rusk ruled out any thought of recognizing Communist China. "I see no prospect at the present time," he said, "that normal relations can be considered or established with the authorities in Peking because they seem to think that abandonment of the people on Formosa would be a prerequisite." But he then went on to say that it would be very difficult to consider progress on world disarmament without taking into account the forces on the Chinese mainland. When Bowles' turn came, he said that recognition of Communist China was, for the time being, out of the question, and added a vigorous statement of United States determination to defend Taiwan whatever the risks and costs. Pressed on the "two Chinas" question, Bowles said that since both the Nationalists and the Communists opposed the idea, it would be pointless for the United States to pursue it.

These were standard answers, not expected to forestall a long and vigorous attack that read into the record everything that at least Bowles had ever said or written on the subject. But, amazingly, the attack never came.

Encouraged, the administration considered some very modest and tentative initiatives. On March 7, 1961, in one of the regular meetings between the Chinese Communist and American ambassadors in Warsaw, the United States proposed once again that the two countries agree to exchange newspaper correspondents. But the Chinese refused even to discuss the matter until the United States agreed to end its "occupation" of Taiwan. If this were not convincing enough proof that the Chinese Communists would rebuff any direct approaches, the continuation and even step-up of their "hate America" propaganda was. It almost seemed that the Communists feared a change in U.S. policy toward China as much as the China Lobby did. Before Kennedy had even assumed office, Communist propaganda belabored him incessantly, and Mao himself declared to a group of Africans and Asians that Kennedy was "worse than Eisenhower."

But there were, conceivably, steps that could damp down the civil war and put some international political pressure on the Chinese. The first of these, an attempt to reduce still further the Chinese Nationalist troops in Burma, was not really new and more of a reaction than an initiative. But it was a step toward "ending the civil war."

In the years since 1953, when seven thousand of the Nationalists in Burma, including women and children, had been evacuated, the Burmese had again become convinced that the groups of armed men still in the area were not "bandits and renegade Chinese soldiers intermarried with tribespeople," but a hard core of Nationalist troops deliberately left behind and whom the Nationalists continued to support by air. The Burmese had conducted an offensive against these forces in 1960, and announced another offensive on January 12, 1961. Then, in the middle of February 1961, a Chinese Nationalist B-24 was surprised while dropping supplies to "Kuomintang irregulars" in a Burmese village. The B-24 shot down a Burmese fighter plane, and was itself shot down in turn, crashing over the border in Thailand. Again the United States put pressure on the Nationalists, and again President Chiang agreed to evacuate any of what he called Nationalist army "hold-outs" who would now come voluntarily. This time a little over four thousand were brought out, although the Burmese found this less than fully satisfactory, since the Nationalists' insistence that the evacuation be voluntary meant that a few bands of irregulars continued to roam the wilds where Burma, Thailand, and Laos come together.

A second, true initiative toward "ending the civil war" was the proposal to recognize Mongolia. A Soviet-sponsored Communist state of ten million people, Mongolia had been under Chinese control only intermittently throughout the history of modern China and not at all for at least thirty years. President Chiang had given up any claim to Mongolia for China in the Chinese-Soviet Treaty of 1945, although he had not gone so far as to recognize it.

The Chinese Communists, under Soviet pressure, did recognize Mongolia when they came to power in 1949—although Mao was not satisfied, for he raised the question of Chinese suzerainty or at least greater influence with Khrushchev in 1954. In 1955, the Soviets attempted to get Mongolia into the UN through a package deal which would have brought in eighteen new members, including Italy, Spain, and Japan, which the U.S. wanted badly. Despite heavy pressure from the United States, Chiang held out on a point of "face"—refusing to acknowledge that Mongolia was a state until the Soviets had negotiated the matter with *his* government rather than the Communists. The Nationalists vetoed the admission of Mongolia, and the Soviets vetoed Japan (which finally gained admission a year later). Now the question was up again. On April 19, 1961, the General Assembly voted to recommend to the Security Council the admission of both Mauritania and Mongolia.

Linking the admission of Mongolia to that of a new African state put the United States and Nationalist China in a difficult position. If the Nationalists vetoed Mongolia this time, Mauritania would also be blocked, and enough of the African states might blame the Nationalists to tip the balance in favor of admitting Communist China to the UN when it came up again in the fall.

But Chester Bowles and others saw an opportunity here for taking an initiative that would have repercussions on the whole of our policy in Asia, including policy toward Communist China itself. There were only four Asian Communist countries: China, North Vietnam, North Korea, and Mongolia. We did not regard the half-countries of North Korea and North Vietnam as true states, but we did acknowledge that Mongolia was in fact a state even if we did not recognize its government. Since Mongolia was Soviet-oriented, by recognizing it we could make a distinction between the more aggressive, Stalinist policies of Communist China and the more moderate Soviet policy under Khrushchev, to which Mongolia also subscribed. Another political advantage was that recognition would also demonstrate to other Asians that our policy was not so completely rigid as it was accused of being and that it did not slavishly follow the dictates of President Chiang Kai-shek, as was also frequently charged. Finally, recognition of Mongolia, situated as it was on the far border of China next to the Soviet Union, would give us, through an embassy in the capital, Ulan Bator, a "window" on a part of the world to which we had little access, and a source of much-needed information on what was going on. And if we took this kind of initiative, which would ensure the admission of Mongolia to the UN and hence Mauritania as well, it would be easier to persuade the African states to continue to side with us on the question of seating Communist China.

The idea made sense, and a feeler was extended to the Mongolian Ambassador in Moscow to determine whether his government would be receptive to an exchange of ambassadors and willing to provide facilities and guarantees for a meaningful and effective embassy in Ulan Bator. On June 29, 1961, the State Department announced that the response to the diplomatic gestures was "such that it was possible to continue the discussions."

Then the storm broke. The Nationalist Government on Taiwan did not like it, but the China Lobby in the United States liked it even less. Marvin Liebman, Secretary of the Committee of One Million, launched an angry attack, arguing that Mongolia was not an independent state, and charging that recognizing it was a move "motivated by pressure from Communist states." Congressional sympathizers quickly followed suit. Representative Walter Judd, the long-time Republican spokesman on Asian affairs, for example, denounced the move as "incredible." His statement went on to say that "The gains will be insignificant, but the losses are likely to be catastrophic." Everett Dirksen, Republican leader in the Senate, proposed an amendment to the foreign aid bill opposing recognition of both Communist China and Mongolia. Most of the congressional critics, in fact, saw the move as a preliminary to the recognition of Communist China itself. An example was Senator Keating's statement. "What I suspect is really meant," he said, "is a U.S. mission in Outer Mongolia would be the thin end of a wedge designed ultimately to push Red China into the United Nations." Even the merits of Mongolia as a listening post were challenged. Senator Styles Bridges said that the only thing the mission would hear was "the bleating of sheep, the whinnying of vast herds of wild Mongolian ponies, the lowing of cattle and whatever musical notes yaks may emit."

The press reported—quite accurately—that the State Department was actually split on the wisdom of the move, and identified Chester Bowles as the leader of the group advocating it. President Kennedy, the stories went on, supported Bowles even though Rusk was "somewhat luke-warm" about the whole idea and had finally gone along when it became obvious that he was "outgunned" at the White House.[2] Following the press lead, the congressional opponents of recognition attacked Bowles, who was already embattled in the aftermath of the Bay of Pigs, as at least an "appeaser" and hinted at something worse. For it was not long before some of the ghosts of McCarthyism were invoked. Owen Latti-more, McCarthy's principal target, had written extensively about Mon-golia, and the critics in Congress made the most of it. Representative Pelly, for example, said that it could be assumed that Lattimore was again advising the Department of State.

Then, with almost fictional irony, someone discovered that Owen Lat-timore was at that very moment on a visit to Mongolia. "I do not think it is an accident," said Senator Dodd, "that, at the very moment when there is a big drive on to persuade the State Department to grant recog-nition to Outer Mongolia, Owen Lattimore should have arrived in the so-called People's Republic as a VIP visitor." Representative John Ash-brook, jumping on the band wagon, inserted in the Congressional Record an article by Alice Widener charging that "Informed sources at the UN say it is highly probable that Lattimore's real mission to Mongolia during the summer will be to work with Mongolian Reds conducting negotiations for the setting up of an official U.S. diplomatic mission at Ulan Bator . . ." Dodd called for an official congressional investigation, and wrote the Secretary of State demanding to know whether or not Lattimore was on an official mission.

In Congress, the stalwarts of the China Lobby, including members of both parties, mustered their forces and quietly let it be known that they intended to destroy Kennedy's foreign aid program with crippling amend-ments unless the administration abandoned its plan to recognize Mon-golia. A few days later, Lincoln White, the official State Department spokesman, announced that negotiations to establish relations with Mon-golia had been suspended. "We believe," White said, "that, in view of the existing world situation, it is in the best interests of the United States to suspend further exploration of that matter at this time."

Defeated in its attempts at taking an initiative, the new administration soon found itself fighting desperately to maintain the Nationalists' posi-tion in the United Nations. For ten years there had been a "moratorium" on the question of seating Communist China. Each year, when the Gen-eral Assembly met, the Soviets had introduced a resolution to seat Com-munist China. And each year the General Assembly had voted to postpone considering the question. But the margin had grown smaller and smaller each year as more and more of the new African and Asian states became independent and obtained UN membership. In 1951, the vote had been 37 to postpone discussion of the Soviet resolution and 11 against, with 4 abstentions. By 1960, the vote was 42 to postpone, 34 to take the question up, and 22 abstentions. And following the 1960 vote, three important countries that had sided with the United States in the past—Canada, Great Britain, and Brazil—had informed the United States that in 1961 they would vote to go ahead. The "moratorium" formula, clearly, would work no longer.

The parliamentary situation was simple. The question was not one of admitting a new state to the United Nations, for "China" was already a member. It was merely a question of whose claim to represent China would be accepted—the Nationalists or the Chinese Communists—and this required only a simple majority in the General Assembly, rather than a veto-free vote in the Security Council.

There was in fact a rather large majority of the members of the General Assembly who favored seating the Chinese Communists—provided a seat could be retained for the Nationalists. But both the Communists and the Nationalists flatly rejected this "two Chinas" policy. So far, there had also been a majority against unseating the Chinese Nationalists, but it would not last long. There was simply no possibility of avoiding a debate on the question in 1961, and if a majority to seat Communist China and expel the Nationalists did not develop this year, it would in the next. Such a resounding defeat of a long-standing American policy would obviously be damaging internationally. And the repercussions domestically, in the general public and in Congress, would be horrendous.

One possibility was for the United States to agree to a debate, and then propose that the question of seating Communist China be declared an "important question," which, according to the charter, required a majority of two-thirds. It would be several years before two-thirds of the General Assembly would agree to seat Communist China at the cost of expelling the Nationalists—but the idea was still a gamble, for if it failed, the Communists would probably get their seat immediately. The President, Rusk, Stevenson, Bowles, and all the rest agonized, and then decided on a somewhat less risky compromise, a plan to stretch the whole procedure out. The decision was to try to persuade the General Assembly to postpone the issue for a year while a special committee studied the question not only of seating Communist China but also of enlarging the Security Council and the Economic and Social Council.

But to the Committee of One Million, such subtle tactics were an anathema; only total and unyielding opposition would do. Throughout the summer, the committee and its allies in Congress kept up a steady barrage. In June, Senator Mansfield had questioned the need for another resolution opposing recognition of Communist China and seating it in the UN, since there had been one almost every year, and all were still valid. But Senator Dirksen said the State Department had been playing "Russian roulette" with China policy and insisted that a resolution was needed to "mobilize public opinion." If the Democrats did not agree to a resolution, he threatened, he would attach one to the embattled foreign aid bill. In July, Representative Judd and Senator Hruska went on TV to say that "when we have criminals in a city, we don't invite them into the FBI to help deal with the situation." Senator Dodd also joined the fray, accusing Communist China of playing the principal role in international narcotics traffic. The Senate passed its resolution in July, and the House followed with its on September 1—by a vote of 395 to 0.

On September 21, 1961, the Committee of One Million sponsored a rally in Carnegie Hall, where Senator Dodd gave voice to what the State Department feared would be the result if Communist China won a seat in the UN—that the Committee of One Million would lead a campaign to take the United States out of the organization. "If the UN goes over this precipice, I do not believe anything can save it," Dodd said. "It shall by its own act," he continued, "forfeit the respect and confidence of honest men everywhere. It shall by its own will swallow the poison which shall destroy its heart and soul and leave only an empty shell."

On September 25, with the United States abstaining, the General Assembly voted to inscribe the question of Chinese representation on the agenda and to debate it.

There followed an intense diplomatic effort focused on the Asian and African nations. But the most important effort of all was to persuade Chiang Kai-shek and the Nationalists how important it was that they not veto the admission of Mongolia and provoke the African states into voting against them.

In the midst of all this activity, the Chinese Communists decided on a little political warfare. Marshal Chen Yi, Foreign Minister of Communist China, in October announced that he would be willing to have a conference with the United States "at the Foreign Minister level"—if the United States proposed it. "China's attitude," he said in an attempt to make the United States look rigid and Communist China reasonable, "is that the United States must take the initiative in any new moves because we have done all we can." Somewhat lamely, Rusk and Kennedy could only point to the fact that we were already talking to the Chinese Communists in Warsaw and at the Geneva Conference on Laos—which had been going on since spring.

But President Chiang finally agreed to abstain rather than veto Mongolia's application for membership, and on October 25, the Security Council approved both Mongolia and Mauritania.

On December 2, Stevenson made a full-dress speech on the question of seating Communist China before the General Assembly. One point in what was an exhaustive cataloguing was that letting Communist China in would shake public confidence in the UN. The reference seemed to be to the activities of the Committee of One Million and their allies in the Congress, and if noisy and unrelenting opposition had done nothing else, it had demonstrated that the seating of Communist China was an "important question" if in no other sense at least in its repercussions on United States participation and role in the UN. On December 15, the General Assembly went beyond the proposal for a special committee and a year's study and voted 61 to 34 with 7 abstentions to make Chinese representation an "important question," requiring a two-thirds majority. On the same day, shortly afterward, they defeated the Soviet resolution to seat Communist China by a vote of 48 against, 37 for, with 19 abstentions.

THE YEAR OF THE TIGER

And now it was the turn of the hard-liners. In the Chinese calendar, as President Chiang Kai-shek began to remind visitors, 1962 was the "year of the tiger," a good omen for the long-awaited return to the mainland. The Nationalists were realistic enough to acknowledge that Taiwan's eleven million could not defeat the mainland's seven hundred million in a military showdown, and this is not what Chiang advocated. His argument was that the mass of the Chinese people were ripe for revolt. The harshness of the regime, the failure of the Great Leap Forward and the commune system, the natural disasters that had caused crop failures for three years running—all these, he argued, meant that just a little push, the landing of a division, say, would trigger a rebellion and topple the regime. In a public statement, early in 1962, President Chiang said that his army might invade the Chinese mainland at any time, that it *must* invade to save the world from certain disaster. "Either subjectively or objectively we can no longer vacillate or hesitate to perform our duty to deliver our people, our nation and the whole world from catastrophe. . . . The situation, both at home and abroad, is such that we can no longer passively wait and see if something will happen." He said that the mass uprising against the Communists that he had been predicting and his "holy expedition from Taiwan to save our people and punish the traitors" might come at any time. "There is no doubt," he said, "that we can annihilate the Communists, reunify our country, and restore freedom to the people on the mainland in the nearest future."[3] Officially and unofficially, privately and publicly, the pressure from Taipei continued to mount.

And the Nationalists had allies in the United States, not only in the Committee of One Million and the Republican opposition in the Congress, but in the Executive Branch itself. Bowles's influence had been reduced after his ouster in the "Thanksgiving Day Massacre," and there were plenty of people who felt that the thesis that the Communist regime could be toppled should be tested. There were a few in the Pentagon and CIA, in fact, who believed that a direct confrontation with Communist China was inevitable and that the best thing for the United States to do was to choose the time and place. Everyone in the administration, from the President on down, of course, would have liked to see the end of Chinese Communist foreign ambition and repression of its own people. But there was a natural affinity between the intelligence services, say, and the Chinese Nationalist view. Communist China was a self-proclaimed enemy of the United States, and it had drawn a veil of secrecy around itself that screened its activities even from the fellow-Communist Soviet Union. The fact of the civil war gave the Nationalists every reason to conduct the aggressive intelligence activities appropriate to wartime, and the American intelligence services benefited. It was only human for some of those most intimately concerned to view the Nationalist case with more sympathy than cold objectivity might support.

Cynics felt that what was really intended in the idea of landing a division or two on the mainland was not so much to trigger a revolt as to trigger American intervention—to create a situation in which the United States would be forced to come to the aid of beleaguered Nationalist troops on a mainland beachhead and so precipitate a major war between the United States and Communist China that would put the Nationalists back in power. But there was in fact some merit to President Chiang's case, as well as sympathizers for it. The basic argument for an invasion was that the Chinese peasantry on the mainland were miserable and dissatisfied with the Communist regime. They might not spontaneously rise against the massive strength of the Communist armies and police, but an invasion of a division or two, if it could seize and hold a beachhead, could act as a match to ignite a spreading revolt. The second argument was that the growing Sino-Soviet dispute would make the Soviets reluctant to come to China's aid, even if it were defeated.

For the Kennedy administration, the dilemma was clear. If the United States encouraged Chiang, and it turned out that the Communist regime was not ready to topple, it would be the Bay of Pigs all over again, only much, much worse. For American support of an invasion would lead to a major war between the United States and the Chinese Communists, and possibly with the Soviet Union. On the other hand, if the Communist regime was really ready to topple and the United States failed to support the Nationalists, the Democrats would stand accused of being the only party in history that lost China twice. There was danger, in truth, that this charge would be made even if the administration did nothing more than be energetic in discouraging the Nationalists from making the landings in the first place. For the arguments for an invasion began appearing in the columns of American newspapermen who were sympathetic to the Nationalists—and so did the intelligence information that tended to support those arguments.

As Director of Intelligence at the State Department, I had followed carefully what little information there was on conditions and attitudes inside Communist China, and although there seemed to be much discontent on the mainland, I was most skeptical of the notion that it was great enough to drive an unarmed people into bloody rebellion against such a strong and ruthless regime. But just at this time I had a chance to discuss the whole problem with one of the most powerful and well-informed men in the Chinese Nationalist Government, Generalissimo Chiang's elder son, Chiang Ching-kuo.

Averell Harriman, then Assistant Secretary for Far Eastern Affairs, was having a meeting of all our ambassadors in the Far East at the mountain resort of Baguio in the Philippines. On the way home he was to see President Chiang, and in preparation he wanted me to visit Taiwan to meet and talk to Ching-kuo, who was not only Chiang's most likely successor but who also headed the Chinese Nationalist intelligence services. I arrived in Taipei on March 8 and went directly to the office where I was to see Ching-kuo.

Chiang Ching-kuo is the elder of two sons born to the Generalissimo by his first wife. She was killed in a Japanese bombing raid in 1939, but the marriage had come to an end after the birth of a second son— ten or fifteen years before the Generalissimo's marriage in 1927 to Soong Mayling, one of whose famous sisters married Dr. Sun Yat-sen and later became a deputy chairman in Communist China. Ching-kuo was born in Fenghwa, Chekiang Province, in 1909, but there was much mystery surrounding his early life—which he seemed to find useful, for he did nothing to dispel it. When Chiang Kai-shek joined the Kuomintang in 1925, he sent Ching-kuo to the military academy at Leningrad which he had himself attended, but there are conflicting stories about what happened next. One is that Ching-kuo was expelled from the academy for "anti-Stalinist" activity, and was imprisoned in Siberia. The other is that he asked to leave in order to take a job in a Soviet factory to learn modern industrial methods and that he rose to become the factory manager. In any event, when Chiang and Stalin signed a nonaggression pact in 1937, Ching-kuo returned to China with his Russian wife. The Generalissimo welcomed him warmly and gave him a tough and important job—governorship of Kiangsi, the province that had been under Communist control until they abandoned it to begin the "Long March" to Yenan. Ching-kuo did well in re-educating the peasants and re-establishing Kuomintang control, and had held progressively higher posts in the period since then.

Five feet six inches tall and weighing about 170 pounds, Ching-kuo was chunky and tough. Friendly but dignified and somewhat reserved, he gave an impression of being shrewd and hard in his judgments of people. Occasionally showing wit, he loved the ancient Chinese finger game—in which two players chanting in rhythm each try to guess the total number of fingers they both show. It is a game of cunning at which Ching-kuo was very good—as I learned to my sorrow that evening at a dinner party, for the penalty for guessing wrong is to drain a glass of rice wine.

In our afternoon meeting, Ching-kuo gave me a large and impressive number of arguments for choosing the Year of the Tiger, and the information the Chinese Nationalists had to support them. The problem, however, was tricky. For mere discontent is not enough. An army can continue to fight effectively with a fairly large percentage of men who are not really loyal. One out of four of the fortress troops that garrisoned the Nazi defenses in Normandy during the D-Day landings and fought so well, for example, was not German but Ukrainian or Uzbek—Soviet soldiers who had gone over to the Germans and whose dependability was questionable. Actually, the cadre of loyal people need not be too large in most circumstances. Miro Cardona, the exiled Cuban leader, for example, once said that only 20 per cent of Castro's militia was loyal—but that 20 per cent was enough to ensure that the militia would fight in at least a defensive role. And whether discontent among the mass of people is sufficient to cause them to rise is even harder to measure. The United States Government, for example, supposedly had hard evidence at one time in the form of letters or other communications indicating discontent from one out of seven adults in Cuba, and it was a fair supposition that even more were equally discontented but were either afraid to communicate or had had no opportunity. Yet it is not a valid deduction to conclude that these people were so desperate that they would rise against the Castro regime, even if an opportunity presented itself, as the United States had learned at the time of the Bay of Pigs. And even if the discontent is great enough to make people willing to risk death, in a police state a successful revolt is most unlikely. The most significant aid that Castro got from the Soviet Union was not arms, but technical instruction in police-state methods. Within the twenty-four hours following the Bay of Pigs landing, Castro had arrested almost a quarter of a million people.

What is more, they were by and large the *right* quarter of a million, the leaders and even the potential leaders of the opposition to Castro. Identifying these people, watching and keeping track of them, and then sweeping in to arrest them in a period when they would be dangerous was an impressive demonstration of just how effective modern police-state techniques can be.

In the case of the mainland of China, furthermore, there was the additional question of whether it would be to the Nationalist regime and the old, discredited Kuomintang to whom the Chinese people would rally even if they did rise. An exiled leader has great difficulty keeping himself in the eyes of his people from a distance, and the Nationalists had been gone from the mainland for thirteen years.

Chiang Ching-kuo did a masterful job of marshaling his arguments and evidence, but much as I would have liked to believe that the Chinese Communist regime was about to topple, I could not conclude that the evidence was there. But it also seemed to me that the wiser attitude for the United States would be to temporize while the Nationalists developed more and better intelligence. Although it seemed extremely remote, there was always some possibility that new evidence would support the notion that the mass of the people would revolt and no one wanted to overlook such a possibility. On the other hand, if new evidence indicated the opposite conclusion, as I believed it would, then it would be better for the Nationalists to reach that conclusion themselves on the basis of the evidence than for the United States to try to force it on them. The only disadvantage was that increased intelligence activity would go against easing the civil war and might even give the appearance of stepping it up. But this was hardly significant, since the Nationalists' propaganda and repeated public statements about the Year of the Tiger had raised the temperature as high as anything could, short of an actual invasion.

I reported to Harriman at Camp John Hay at Baguio in the Philippines, which I was amused to find unchanged from my boyhood days there when my father was stationed at Manila thirty years before. When the ambassadorial meetings were over, Harriman went on to Taiwan and repeated the discussion with President Chiang. He reached the same conclusion that I had.

But the pressures continued. Shortly thereafter someone came up with an idea for a "covert" but large-scale landing on the mainland—a sort of even grander Bay of Pigs—and the senior CIA man in Taiwan came flying back to Washington to try to sell the idea. The only time I ever saw Rusk speak with feeling in a meeting was on this occasion. He felt that the idea that a large-scale landing could be made to look as if it were really a spontaneous uprising of the people on the mainland was utter nonsense, and it was even greater nonsense to suppose that the United

States could escape responsibility. We agreed that what the Nationalists ought to do was acquire more and better intelligence on what conditions really were, but everyone should also understand that we would be astounded if that intelligence would show that a rebellion was imminent.

And just then, in April of 1962, a new and puzzling factor entered the equation. For years there had been a steady trickle of escapees from Communist China into the tiny British Crown Colony of Hong Kong. In the early months of 1962, for example, the British had apprehended an average of two hundred Chinese a month who had succeeded in eluding the Chinese Communist border guards and entered Hong Kong illegally. Then, inexplicably, in April of 1962, the Chinese Communists lifted their restrictions. For the month of April, the total refugees jumped from the usual two hundred to fifteen hundred. By May 5, the flow had reached a thousand a day; by May 14, four thousand a day were crossing; and by May 19, five thousand a day. Hong Kong contained only 391 square miles in its entire area. It was so chronically short of fresh water that the pipes were turned off for all but a few hours each day. Almost the entire food supply had to be imported. If the refugee flow continued to increase at this stupendous rate, Hong Kong seemed likely to sink quietly into the sea under the sheer weight of the human tide that was engulfing it.

In the Bureau of Intelligence and Research, we concluded that the Chinese Communists' original reason for lifting the travel restrictions was probably related to the complaints of the overseas Chinese that relatives had not been allowed to emigrate. By lifting restrictions, the Communists probably hoped to curry favor with the overseas Chinese, whose support was important to the Communists, while at the same time anticipating that the British would find the additional refugees too great a burden and take it upon themselves to bar further emigration through Hong Kong. But the whole thing had apparently gotten out of hand because of a quite unrelated Chinese Communist decree transferring "useless" citizens from the cities back to the countryside in anticipation of food shortages in the upcoming winter. Taking advantage of the fact that the Communist regime had lifted the ban on travel to Hong Kong, the refugees going back to the villages had turned instead to Hong Kong, and the Communists were hesitating about using the amount of force it would take to stop them and so confessing publicly both to the level of peasant discontent and the extent of the food shortages.

But even though there was no intelligence to support the notion that the flood of refugees indicated widespread famine or imminent rebellion, the policy battle in Washington quickly revived. Supreme Court Justice William O. Douglas and others had frequently suggested raising trade barriers or extending aid in the form of surplus foods as a way of reversing Communist hostility and splitting China and the Soviet Union. On March 15, 1961, Senator Humphrey had renewed this suggestion, and by April, stories were coming out of Washington, attributed to high administration officials, suggesting that the choice facing the United States was between letting the Chinese sink further into famine and risking a possibility of a desperate Chinese move into the rich and underpopulated peninsula of Southeast Asia or providing avenues through both trade and aid through which it could get the food it needed to feed its people—a thesis Chester Bowles had frequently expounded. What gave the notion renewed impetus was that Harriman, McGhee, and others felt that, even though the flood of refugees did not indicate a rebellion on the mainland, the situation might still provide an opportunity for a political initiative. The opposite view was that any relaxation of our policy would make it easier for the Communists to survive the strains and that, if anything, ways should be found to step up the pressure. The battle was quickly joined.

And it soon spilled over into the press. Joseph Alsop, analyzing the refugee flood to Hong Kong and the economic troubles on the mainland, concluded that the alternatives on the mainland were narrowing to a change in leadership or a violent convulsion. "Sentimentalists in this city and elsewhere in the United States are meanwhile beginning to talk of feeding starving China," Alsop went on to say, "which would simply mean getting Mao Tse-tung off his self-created hook. There is considerable solid evidence that the Russian Communist revolution was saved from foundering in famine by former President Herbert Hoover and his Quaker relief. It will be past bearing if the same role is played in China by Justice William O. Douglas and others of his kidney."[4] Outraged, the editors of the Washington *Post* responded in a long and passionate editorial. "The consequences of the cataclysm about to descend upon the Asian continent," they wrote, "may be so vast and terrifying that it is hardly within the competence of human prophecy to foresee its limitless possibilities for good and evil. In any case, it would not be easy to make the American people the silent spectators of suffering that it is within their power to relieve. The noble impulses that led the people of this country to feed the Russian people in the 20s will not be denied just by dubbing the humanitarian intervention as sentimental Quaker folly."[5] Beyond the humanitarianism, the *Post* editors also saw policy. "A great storm is arising in Asia . . ." the editorial concluded. "This country must be ready for that storm. . . . The nation must be prepared to pursue a course that will utilize its power to minimize the suffering of China's hapless millions, and that will, at the same time, safeguard the security and protect the good name of the people of the United States."

Inside the administration, Harriman and most of us concerned with the problem had concluded that lifting trade barriers would not accomplish any very far-reaching political results by itself. The Chinese Communists would probably reject out of hand the idea of either buying or accepting food from the United States, and the only political advantage of offering food would be that the onus would fall on Communist China rather than the United States. By this time, the second year of the Kennedy administration, it was clear that a more flexible China policy could not be accomplished by a policy gimmick. It was obvious that more flexibility was needed, but it was also obvious that firmness, and a willingness to face Chinese threats would also continue to be needed. For before the Chinese Communists would be responsive to policy initiatives from the United States, they had to be convinced that continued hostility had failed and that they had come up against an unyielding wall of resistance. Isolated initiatives, like lifting trade restrictions, would accomplish nothing and might even run counter to the goal. Until the advocates of the Year of the Tiger had their arguments fully explored and considered, initiatives in flexibility, in fact, might trigger the very disaster that the initiatives sought to avoid.

The decision was a compromise—to escape the onus of refusing to lift trade restrictions on food but not to launch on anything resembling a political offensive. At his press conference on May 23, 1962, when asked if he would consider it in the national interest to offer surplus grains to China, President Kennedy replied that the United States had not been asked—implying that although we would not offer, neither would we refuse. A few weeks later, Chen Yi, the Chinese Communist Foreign Minister, said that China would not accept aid. "We do not," he said stiffly, "need to be a beggar."

In the spring and summer of 1962, the real danger was probably not that the United States would miss some great opportunity to embark on a new and more rational China policy, but that our attitude toward the problems of the Year of the Tiger would be misread by one side or the other with disastrous consequences for the whole world. One danger was that the Nationalists would begin to think that the United States was about to abandon them and plunge into an act of desperation. The other was that the Chinese Communists would either feel that the United States was sponsoring an invasion that they could successfully meet only by pre-empting and attacking themselves, or that the United States was ready to abandon the Nationalists and would stand to one side while the Communists seized first the offshore islands and then Taiwan.

All through the spring of 1962, American policy was on tenterhooks while the Nationalists made more and more threatening statements and speeches, while the Communist radios blared back, and while the Committee of One Million and Republican hard-liners in Congress exchanged bitternesses with their domestic opponents. Then, in the middle of June 1962, intelligence reports began to come in of an enormous build-up of Chinese Communist troops along the mainland coast opposite Taiwan and at Amoy, facing Quemoy. Combat divisions from Manchuria, North China, and Central China began to stream down toward this so-called "invasion coast," pre-empting the railroads and bringing civilian railway traffic to a complete halt for several days. Within a week, the troop concentrations opposite Taiwan had been increased by half a million men, with all their planes, tanks, and other equipment.

In the intelligence community the three possible explanations that seemed most likely were: (1) that the Chinese Communists had built up their forces as a defensive move, a precaution against the thinking of the Year of the Tiger, and an effort at deterrence, to give the Nationalists and the United States pause; (2) that the Chinese Communists were preparing a new politico-military Quemoy-Matsu crisis along the lines of the crisis of 1958; and (3) that the Chinese Communists were getting into position for an onslaught on Quemoy-Matsu and Taiwan, either because they thought the United States would not stand by the Nationalists or because they thought an invasion with United States backing was imminent and that their best chance was to pre-empt and attack first. In the Bureau of Intelligence at the State Department, we initially felt that No. 3 (preparation for an all-out assault) was the least likely; that No. 2 (preparation for a new politico-military Quemoy-Matsu crisis) was possible; but that the most likely was No. 1 (that the moves were principally defensive). But as the build-up continued until the total seemed greater than what would be necessary for pure defense, we shifted our view slightly. We continued to feel that the primary purpose of the troop movement was to deter the Nationalists from attacking, but we also began to feel that the Communists might have decided to exploit the troop movements politically by creating a new offshore island crisis.

The intelligence community as a whole, however, possibly influenced by John McCone's somewhat apocalyptic view that sooner or later a showdown with the Chinese Communists was inevitable, thought that the possibilities of No. 3, that the moves were preliminary to a major assault, were somewhat higher.

When we met in the Cabinet room of the White House on June 20, 1962, it was McNamara who spoke not only with passion against No. 3, the idea that the Chinese Communists had decided on a major attack, but with contempt. Statistics were his business, and he thoroughly demolished the notion that the build-up was a preliminary to an attack—at least up to that moment—by showing that the landing equipment available to the Chinese Communists, landing boats, motorized junks, and so on, in Amoy and along the coast was totally inadequate even to launch an effective invasion force against the offshore islands, much less Taiwan.

But the policy problem was to see that the move *continued* to be defensive. To make sure that the Chinese Communists had not wrongly concluded that we were encouraging the Nationalists, our ambassador in Warsaw was instructed to meet with the Chinese Communist ambassador on June 26, and inform him that no United States support would be given to any Nationalist attempt to invade the mainland, and the nature of the instructions was then made public. And, to make sure that the Communists would not also wrongly conclude that the United States would abandon Taiwan, the Seventh Fleet was ostentatiously reinforced and the President, at his press conference on June 27, issued a public warning. Reiterating that U.S. policy continued to be opposed to the use of force by either side in the Taiwan Strait, he went on to declare that "The United States will take the action necessary to assure the defense of Formosa and the Pescadores." Under this policy, he continued, any threat to the offshore islands would be judged in relation to its wider meaning for the safety of Taiwan and the peace of the area. "Exactly what action would be necessary in the event of any such act of force," he said, "would depend on the situation as it developed. But there must be no doubt that our policy, specifically including our readiness to take necessary action in the face of force, remains just what it has been on this matter since 1955."

The summer and fall wore on with no change in the situation in the Taiwan Strait. In September a Chinese Nationalist U-2 was shot down over Communist China, and when the U-2 pictures of Cuba were released in the missile crisis of October 1962, the world had a measure of the kind of intelligence the Nationalists were getting.[6] And throughout the autumn there was a steady stream of announcements from Peking of raids on the mainland by small commando forces and landings by Nationalist guerrillas—all of whom, the Chinese Communists announced, had been either killed or captured.

The frequency of the Nationalist commando and intelligence raids on the mainland had clearly been stepped up. But the fact that the Communist forces had been so successful in mopping them up so soon after they landed just as clearly indicated that the peasantry was not in the rebellious mood the Nationalists had hoped.

In September 1963, Chiang Ching-kuo visited the United States at the invitation of the Kennedy administration. After his return, there were a number of press stories out of Taiwan that the Nationalists believed that the Communists were growing weaker all the time and that the best strategy for the Nationalists was simply to wait. Other Asians interpreted this to mean that the Nationalists had finally abandoned hope of retaking the mainland. The Chinese Communist armies massed on the invasion coast were gradually returned to their regular stations. The Year of the Tiger was ended.

NOTES

1 Theodore H. White, *The Making of the President, 1960*, 1961, p. 351.
2 The Washington *Post*, July 7, 1961.
3 New York *Times*, March 30, 1962.
4 Joseph Alsop, the Washington *Post*, June 18, 1962.
5 The Washington *Post*, June 24, 1962.
6 The official State Department spokesman on October 10, 1962, stated that two U-2s had been sold by Lockheed to the Chinese Nationalists just at the end of the Eisenhower administration on a private commercial contract for which the United States Government had issued export licenses.

CHAPTER 23

The Chinese Attack on India and the Harriman Mission

BY THE FALL OF 1962, it was already clear that the heavy concentrations of Chinese Communist troops assembled opposite Taiwan and the offshore islands were not going to be used in an assault. But this in no sense meant that Mao Tse-tung and the Communist leaders in Peking had given up their aggressive tactics or their ambitions.

In October 1962 the Soviet Union and the United States were locked in history's first nuclear confrontation, the Cuban missile crisis, totally absorbed and preoccupied. And it was at this precise moment that Communist China chose to lunge—not at Taiwan but at India, over the top of what had so long been considered the impassable military barrier of the Himalayas.

Heavy skirmishing on the border had begun in late October, and the Indians thought it was nothing more than that. But on November 15, the Chinese launched what was quickly revealed to be a major offensive. By November 18, the Indian forces were reeling backward in full retreat, and on November 19—just as the Kennedy administration was pausing to draw breath after the missile crisis, Nehru went on the air to appeal for help from both the United States and Britain. Early the next morning, Rusk called me to his office: "Can you be ready to go to New Delhi with Averell Harriman by five this afternoon?" As it turned out, a delay in making the necessary diplomatic arrangements prevented us from leaving that afternoon. But within twenty-four hours, the Harriman mission was on its way.

The first hint of trouble between China and India had occurred, as mentioned earlier, when the road-building program the Chinese had started in order to consolidate their hold on Tibet brought the Chinese to the poorly defined border areas that the Indians considered their own territory. And it flared unmistakably when the Indians gave refuge to the Dalai Lama after his flight following the Tibetan uprising in 1959.

The two major areas in dispute lay at opposite ends of the Himalayas. In the east, the Chinese had vague claims to the North East Frontier Agency—the NEFA—a heavily forested strip of steep, mountainous terrain along the India-Tibetan border between Burma and Bhutan that was inhabited mainly by tribesmen. The MacMahon Line, which the Indians recognized, followed the "natural boundary" along the crest of the major ridge, while the Chinese claim put the border well forward on the Indian side of the crest, down to where the foothills rise from the great Indian plain. The other trouble spot was at the extreme northwest of India, in the Ladakh area of Kashmir, where the Chinese occupied the Aksai Chin, a bleak, eighteen-thousand-foot plateau of rock and sand and snow. The Chinese did not have the same historic claim to the Aksai Chin, but here it was Indian territory that jutted forward of the crest of the "natural" ridge line. For the plateau lay precisely in the path of the easiest and most direct route for the strategic road the Chinese were building to link Tibet with the province of Sinkiang.

Relations between India and China had worsened considerably since the border skirmishes first broke out in 1959 and the Chinese had occupied not only the Aksai Chin, where they had proceeded to build their road, but also a number of minor border posts in other parts of Ladakh. A long string of vituperative notes was exchanged about the border incidents, and China attempted to seduce Nepal away from India's tutelage. In the heady political climate following India's successful seizure of the Portuguese enclave of Goa in December of 1961, V. K. Krishna Menon, the controversial, caustically anti-Western Defense Minister, said publicly that India would reclaim her border areas "one way or another"—a gratuitous insult to the Chinese. The Sino-Soviet dispute was worsening by this time, and, to the annoyance of the Chinese, Indian diplomacy was designed to enlist the support of the Soviets. What was worse, it was having some success, for the Soviets announced that they hoped the Chinese and the Indians would come to a "peaceful accommodation," implying that the Soviets were at least neutral. The Indians also attempted some crude pressure tactics. They notified China that the 1954 Trade Agreement between the two countries would be allowed to lapse unless the Chinese evacuated the disputed territories. At the same time, the Indians unwisely provided the Chinese ample provocation by adopting a "forward strategy"—establishing isolated outposts *behind* the Chinese outposts that India felt had encroached on what they considered their rightful territory—and Prime Minister Nehru, in the early fall of 1962, announced publicly that the Indian Army had been ordered to clear India's territory of the Chinese aggressors. But none of this seemed to provide a satisfactory explanation for the sudden and savage Chinese onslaught.

CHINESE MOTIVES

The Chinese motives, in fact, were probably complex. As we analyzed the situation in the Bureau of Intelligence and Research, three seemed to be basic. One—and probably the least important—was simply geographic; that is, ease of communications. The Chinese were determined to consolidate their hold on Tibet, and, to do so, they had carried out an impressive program of road-building through some of the most difficult terrain in the world. They had a genuine need for the Aksai Chin, while its value to India seemed to be mainly symbolic of national prestige and sentiment—part of the "sacred soil" of Kashmir. The very least gain the Chinese could hope for probably was that their claims in the NEFA could be traded for the Aksai Chin.

A second motivation for the attack was undoubtedly related to Communist China's relations with the Soviet Union and the growing Sino-Soviet dispute. The quarrel between the two Communist giants had several facets, but one of the arguments was over how the Communist bloc should deal with the in-between nations. The Soviet Union had encouraged India's neutralism and poured huge amounts of economic aid into the country and much political and diplomatic effort. India, which aspired to leadership of the Asian and African neutrals, had become a symbol of the Soviet policy of "peaceful coexistence" to which the Chinese so violently objected. Thus the Chinese attack was also an effort to force Moscow to choose between Peking and Delhi, and a slap not only in the face of India, but in the face of the Soviet Union as well.

The third—and probably most important—motive seemed to stem not so much from China's Communism as from her nationalism, from the Chinese leadership's vision of China's place in Asia and in the world. If the Indians had not been provocative, no motives beyond the geographic could have been engaged, and the Chinese may well have had to fall back on conceding their claims in the NEFA and elsewhere in exchange for the Aksai Chin. But a touch of arrogance in the manner of India's bid for leadership of the in-between world had caused some resentment on which the Chinese could capitalize, and the Indian policy of "forward strategy" and the public threat to clear their territory of "aggressors" provided provocation the Chinese could use to justify military action in the eyes of the in-between world. And this opened possibilities for political gains that were even more enticing.

India's bid for leadership of the in-between world was based on a policy of neutralism abroad and a program of economic development through basically democratic procedures of parliamentary socialism at home. The world had identified Communist China as India's true rival, and China's bid for leadership was based on militant hostility to the old Western powers abroad and forced development through authoritarian Communism at home. A sharp military defeat humiliating India would undermine her bid for leadership and discredit her policy and program. And the risk was relatively low. Britain and the United States might well intervene if China attempted to conquer and occupy India, but a carefully limited, quickly administered attack could be precisely managed and controlled, and the risks of outside intervention and escalation minimized. If Britain and the United States moved to intervene, the troops could be pulled back and the price for peace lowered. And if Britain and the United States hesitated, the attack could be pressed and the demands raised.

But beyond all this beckoned something even more alluring. The Himalayas and Tibet had been regarded by all the world as an impassable military barrier, effectively sealing off the subcontinent and its teeming millions from the main Eurasian land mass. But although the world did not yet realize it, the Himalayas and Tibet were now in fact not so much an obstacle as a forward base for Chinese power. Defeating the Indians would project that power into the subcontinent itself, in a convincing demonstration that China was now a force to be reckoned with. Never again would anyone in the world be able to think about the subcontinent without considering the interests of China and the fact of its power.

THE U.S.S.R., PAKISTAN, AND U.S. POLICY

The first skirmishing came on October 20, mainly in the NEFA, but also in Ladakh.[1] That night, Prime Minister Nehru on a nationwide radio announced what had happened and spoke sorrowfully of a cruel awakening to the harsh realities of world politics. After the initial push, the Chinese paused for a political gambit in their talk-fight, talk-fight tactics and offered an armistice on condition that both sides withdraw twelve and one half miles from the *lines they actually controlled*. Nehru refused, declaring a state of emergency on October 26. The Chinese, in turn, renewed their probing in both Ladakh and the NEFA, where military engineers and huge gangs of workers followed immediately after the troops, carving roads out of the sides of the steep ravines.

Nehru asked Britain and the United States for a modest amount of emergency help, largely small items of military equipment in short supply. Both responded promptly, but the larger question of U.S. policy remained. In our analysis, policy would turn on how we estimated the intentions and probable reactions of not only the Chinese and the Indians, but of both the Soviets and Pakistanis as well.

Pakistan's position was equivocal. The depth of emotion symbolized by the confrontation of Indian and Pakistani troops in divided Kashmir is hard to exaggerate. But some measure of it can be felt in the fact that in the bloody aftermath of partition, when the British departed, over half a million people, Muslim and Hindu, were killed and untold millions more lost everything they owned, land and belongings, as they fled the carnage. Thus the Pakistanis had little sympathy for an India under attack by the Chinese. Privately, they were delighted at her humiliation, and they hoped there would be enough military pressure from the Chinese to induce India to come to terms with Pakistan on Kashmir. But as a practical matter, they also hoped that the pressure would not be enough to endanger the security of the subcontinent as a whole. Although the Indians continually voiced their fear and suspicion that Pakistan would take advantage of the situation to seize Kashmir and the United States had to reassure them that it was exercising its right of inspection to see that no U.S. arms aid would be used in military adventures, Ayub Khan, the President of Pakistan, was careful to avoid giving the Indians any cause for alarm. But Pakistan bitterly protested U.S. arms aid to India on the same grounds that India had protested it when Pakistan joined SEATO—that the balance of power on the subcontinent was being upset and that U.S. guarantees could not prevent the arms from eventually being used against Pakistan rather than Communist China. And the Pakistan press began questioning the wisdom of the policy that had aligned Pakistan with the United States in the first place.

The Soviet Union found itself in an even more awkward position: its largest Communist ally was in armed conflict with its greatest friend in the in-between world, and Moscow's effort to assume a neutral posture in the dispute was both a result of its rift with the Chinese and a cause of greater cleavage. And United States emergency military aid to the Indians intensified the Soviet dilemma—for Peking would charge that Moscow was now being neutral between its Communist ally and a country supported by "U.S. imperialism." We concluded that Moscow's overriding concern would be to avoid making an ultimate choice between Peking and New Delhi, and they would push at every opportunity for negotiations between the two antagonists. But the Soviet Union's fatal shortcoming was that it lacked sufficient leverage on either the Indians or the Chinese to persuade them to scale down their demands and conditions to a point where such negotiations would become possible. Moscow was unwilling either to threaten China with the ultimate sanction of a total split or to tempt it with total support. On the other hand, Moscow would find it impossible to back India's claim with full support, and the limited help it was willing to supply India was insignificant if Britain and the United States would fill the breach. Thus the only response an offer from the United States for large-scale military aid would probably evoke from the Soviets would be renewed efforts at bringing the disputants to negotiations. The only two contingencies that would lead the Soviets to veer sharply toward the Chinese would seem to be if India should renounce her nonalignment policy and become fully and openly allied with the West or if military developments—events in the Taiwan Strait as well as those in India—took such a turn as to threaten Communist China's survival. And in those circumstances, it seemed clear that Moscow would, however grudgingly, feel impelled to protect the integrity of the Communist world.

As far as the Chinese Communists were concerned, the main question was whether or not they could be effectively deterred. Our estimate was that their intentions were limited, more political than military, but it was also possible that their appetite would grow with the eating. The Chinese Communists had been essentially cautious in their policies over the past decade, and especially in confronting American power. They were willing to take risks, but they had taken extraordinary precautions to see that those risks remained manageable. In this situation, they probably calculated that our alliance with Pakistan through the Southeast Asia Treaty, our friendship for India, and the incompatibility of the two in view of the Kashmir dispute—the whole triangle, in fact, of the India-United States-Pakistan relationship—would so complicate our problem that our response was likely to be minimal. Thus we would have to take care that our actions and words made the signals to the Chinese Communists clear. For if their attack on India was in any way in the nature of a probe, they would go ahead or draw back, depending on the vigor of the United States response.

THE REACTION IN INDIA

In India, the shock had been profound. Reports from the front of lack of ammunition and equipment exposed the miserable state of the Indian armed forces. Krishna Menon's policies were given the blame, even though Nehru and the entire cabinet were also responsible, and he was quickly forced to resign—in part, no doubt, as a gesture toward the West. The opposition in parliament attacked the nonalignment policy as a failure and urged a restoration of defense relations with the West. But Nehru hoped to take advantage of the Sino-Soviet dispute to continue a new form of nonalignment, and he asked the Soviet Union for military aid at the same time as he did Britain and the United States. The successful military defense of the subcontinent from an outside threat quite obviously was possible only if Pakistan and India resolved their differences over Kashmir and made some joint arrangements. But it was clear that, shocked and humiliated though his country was, Nehru, being himself a Kashmiri Brahman, would attempt to use British, American, and Soviet aid and power as a substitute to deter the Chinese Communists rather than settle with Pakistan. What no one yet knew was the attitude of the men in the government below Nehru and just how long he could continue to impose his policy views while the Chinese attack continued.

And the Chinese attack did continue. In Ladakh, the offensive beginning on November 15 captured forty-three Indian posts, pushing the Indians back all along the line. In the NEFA, on the first day the Chinese captured a strategic pass, flanking the Indian defenders and cutting off the line of retreat for many of the forces defending the western portion. Twenty-four hours later, on November 16, at the little town of Walong, in the eastern portion of the NEFA near Burma, the Chinese destroyed the brigade defending the most direct route into India from China proper and captured the brigadier commanding. What was left of the NEFA corps, which was less substantial than its name suggests, virtually disintegrated, and its individual soldiers who survived made their way back as refugees over side trails.

By November 18, the Chinese Communists were within thirty miles of the plains of Assam—where the American airplanes were based that flew the "hump" of the Himalayas in World War II to supply China and whose oil fields and tea plantations earned much of India's foreign exchange. And there was no effective Indian fighting force standing in the way.

It was on November 19 that Nehru called on Britain and the United States. The Kennedy administration was just looking up from the Cuban missile crisis—the blockade was lifted on the twentieth—and in consultation with the British it was decided that both countries would send high-level missions to determine how we could help. In the meantime, the United States dispatched a squadron of turbo-jet C-130s, whose large cargo capacity, high speed, and short landing characteristics made them invaluable in supplying the troops at the high altitudes of Ladakh and in shifting both forces and equipment to the NEFA from Kashmir, where the troops had been facing Pakistan.

THE HARRIMAN MISSION

The American mission consisted of Averell Harriman, Assistant Secretary for Far Eastern Affairs; Paul Nitze, Assistant Secretary of Defense for International Security Affairs; General Paul Adams, Commander in Chief of the so-called Strike Command, a mobile force of corps strength that would be called upon if United States ground forces should ever be needed in the defense of India; Carl Kaysen, of the White House staff; and me, as Director of Intelligence at the State Department along with a half-dozen staff experts. We met with the President for a last-minute briefing—I remember Rusk mentioning that four of us there, Rusk, McNamara, Phillips Talbot, the Assistant Secretary for Near Eastern Affairs, and I had all served in the China-Burma-India theater during the war and found the battle place names in this new war all too familiar.

But the Chinese Communists were engaged in political as well as military warfare, and a full twenty-four hours before the mission left—in fact, only a few hours after Nehru's appeal for help and just minutes before President Kennedy had announced the composition of the team—the Chinese Communists had declared a "unilateral cease fire." They then went on to say that beginning in December they would withdraw their forces, also unilaterally, to positions twelve and one half miles back from what they had held before the November offensive—conditional on an armistice,

Indian acceptance of the cease-fire, and a prohibition against any Indian attempt to re-establish any of the forty-three posts in Ladakh.

In the questioning following his announcement of the mission at his news conference, President Kennedy called the fighting "a very serious struggle which may lead to a full-scale war if it hasn't already." Mentioning the Chinese cease-fire move, he indicated that the administration viewed it with caution. None of us in fact was sure it would be wise for the Indians to accept it, and the next morning the President sent me a personal memorandum so hastily dictated and typed that he had corrected one typographical error himself and missed another—asking me to have a memorandum sent to him "on what the implications are on [corrected to of] the Chinese Communists offer of [a] cease fire. If it were genuine would it be a good thing for the Indians to accept it or would it be better for them to refuse it in spite of their military difficulties." I had just time enough to speak briefly about the President's request with Thomas Hughes, who would be acting head of the bureau in my absence.

Before the TV cameras at the airport, Harriman recalled that just over twenty years before, President Roosevelt had sent him on a similar mission in somewhat different circumstances—to Moscow, when Nazi Germany had attacked the Soviet Union. And then we departed.

THE "MCNAMARA SPECIAL"

The airplane was a "McNamara Special." The Secretary of Defense was disturbed at the number of generals and admirals who had plush airplanes, wastefully standing by for use only in VIP travel, and he was trying to set an example. Instead of a private plane, the top civilians in the Defense Department had only a kit of eight portable bunks and twenty-two portable seats which could be quickly installed in the empty top half of a KC-135 jet tanker. The KC-135 was a four-engine Boeing 707 jet fitted out for refueling B-52 bombers in flight, and using the kit of portable bunks and seats did accomplish a large saving. For any tanker that happened to be in the vicinity could be fitted out in hours, and after dropping its party on the other side of the world, it could go on about its refueling business. But cheap though a "McNamara Special" was, it was also vastly uncomfortable. There were no windows at all, and the passengers could never tell whether it was daylight or dark. The cabin did not have an inner shell, as civilian airliners do, and the noise level was impossible—a steady, blasting roar that turned a policy discussion into a shouting contest. One irony, however, was that the frequency range of Harriman's slight deafness apparently coincided with the frequency of the airplane's noise, and for him it was quieter than for the rest of us. More than once he fussed at us for shouting.

The lack of an inner shell also meant that the temperature was hard to regulate. Your feet might freeze while your head steamed. Even worse, it might be ninety degrees when we were trying to sleep and forty when we were trying to work. There was a grueling job ahead of us, and we worried about the effects of starting out this way on Harriman, who was then seventy-one. Then, to make matters worse, he caught a cold.

We flew eighteen hours from Washington to New Delhi in that vibrating roar and fluctuating temperature, at six hundred miles an hour, with only a brief fueling stop at Adana, Turkey. We spent ten hectic days in India and Pakistan, conferring with officials, seeing conditions firsthand, traveling, working, talking all of each day and most of each night. We flew back from Karachi to Washington—another eighteen hours in the roar, with a fueling stop in Spain—drafting our report to the President by outshouting the jets and bracing ourselves for the maelstrom of meetings that awaited us in Washington. Two of us on the mission were in our early forties, and when we got off the plane at Andrews Air Force Base in Washington, the strain showed in our drawn faces and weary step. But to Harriman, high policy and diplomatic trouble-shooting were an elixir, and he came off the plane grinning that it was all just the thing for a cold—from which he had completely recovered.

In the shouted analysis of our instructions on the way to New Delhi, it seemed to us that whether the Chinese actually carried out their unilateral withdrawal and kept to the cease-fire or the whole proposal was merely a trick, our problem remained the same. Part of our mission was merely to demonstrate United States support for India and so to send the Chinese Communists a signal of deterrence. I remember teasing Harriman that if it worked the United States would have discovered the most economical deterrent of modern times—his name and our titles. But beyond this immediate emergency, future Chinese behavior would depend on whether or not an effective deterrent could be created in the subcontinent. And, to determine this, we needed to know whether the Indian people were calm and resolved or in panic; whether the Indian Government was functioning effectively or disorganized; whether the defeated Indian Army still had a disciplined cadre around which it could be rebuilt or needed a complete revamping, and, finally, just what kind of help would be required from Britain and the United States to accomplish this. Then, we had to put it all in a general political context, just how India and Pakistan each assessed the nature of the threat from Communist China in both the short and long term, and whether they were willing to modify their hostility toward each other. For, in the long run, a subcontinent divided by its own rivalry and bitterness would be vulnerable to almost any outside threat and certainly one so powerful as Communist China. The only effective defense of the subcontinent against such a threat would be a joint defense by both India and Pakistan standing together. And we could not in conscience recommend that the American people make the sacrifice required to help rebuild India's strength if that strength were to continue to be dissipated in a quarrel with Pakistan, who was also a friend to whose defense the United States contributed.

INDIA AND NEHRU

We touched down at New Delhi just after dark on November 22, Thanksgiving Day. As we came out of the raised hatch of our windowless plane we saw a wild scene of TV camera lights, newspapermen, Indian and American, a long line of limousines, our "long-legged ambassador," as Harriman called his old friend, the six-foot-seven J. Kenneth Galbraith, and the senior members of the American Embassy. The crowd of Indians behind them was warm, and friends I had known in Washington pressed forward to speak in choked tones of India's gratitude for Britain and America's generous response in their time of need.

With only a pause to wash, we went straight to the Prime Minister's residence, gathering in a long reception room just left of the entrance, and I thought it ironic to see the walls lined with the pictures of the militant neutralists whom Nehru had aspired to lead, including Nkrumah, who had sided with China and denounced British and American aid as nefarious.

Once assembled, we were led up stately stairs to another, smaller reception room. Shortly thereafter, Nehru came in, accompanied to my utter surprise by an acquaintance, the economist and writer Barbara Ward. Miss Ward had been touring some of the Indian villages when the attack came and she was paying a call on Nehru, an old friend, to report her impression of their reaction. In village after village, she said, the young maidens had come up to the Indian officials accompanying her to press on them the gold necklaces and bracelets that were to have been their dowries as contributions to the Indian Defense Fund. After a few minutes talk, Miss Ward excused herself, and the Prime Minister led us back to a sitting room, where we were joined by his sister, Madame Pandit.

Dressed in the traditional tight-fitting trousers and high-collared tunic of North India, with his personal trademark, a red rosebud, tucked in a buttonhole, Nehru looked tired and strained. To so proud a Brahman as Nehru, a man of great achievements in his own country but of frustrated ambition on the world stage, it must have been difficult to greet Americans over the ruins of his long-pursued policy of neutralism. And the very fact that we were determined there would be from us no hint or gesture of "I told you so" probably made it even more difficult. Though cordial in his greeting, he did not express any of the sentiments of the crowd at the airport. He listened distantly as Harriman recalled America's association with India in World War II and the magnificent performance that Indian troops had given in the Middle East and Burma campaigns. He listened even more distantly as Harriman said that we were pleased to be able to come to discuss how the United States might help India in the present circumstances. His letters to Kennedy asking for help had painted a desperate picture, but face to face Nehru seemed to want to avoid talking about it all. I remember having a feeling of unreality, as if our long journey and dramatic arrival were just an incongruous prelude to a social call. Harriman asked what Nehru knew from the latest reports from the two fronts, and Nehru, still distantly, said that the cease-fire was so far holding, but that even though they welcomed a cease-fire, they were suspicious of its true purpose. He asked, more from politeness, it seemed, than from interest, of our judgment of Chinese motives, and I outlined the analysis given above. Harriman wanted to know if the Indians had communicated with the Soviets, and was told—also distantly—that they had earlier let the Soviets know of their intention to ask the West for arms aid, and the Soviets had replied that they understood both the request and the need for it. And, most distantly of all, Nehru listened silently while Harriman with exquisite delicacy hinted of the need for a settlement of the Kashmir dispute and for taking measures of joint defense with Pakistan. With neither wise insight nor quotable quote to record for history, we rose to go.

Ambassador Galbraith had arranged a turkey dinner at the embassy, and after a rather solemn Thanksgiving meal, we talked of the procedures we would follow the next few days, and especially how we would coordinate our activities with the British team, under Duncan Sandys, which was to arrive the next morning. And we agreed that it would be best if each team went about its own business separately, coming together toward the end to compare our findings and co-ordinate our recommendations to our respective governments.

The next day the mission split into two main groups. Paul Nitze and General Adams began briefings on the military situation, including trips to the two fronts, while Harriman, the Ambassador, Kaysen, and I called on the various ministers on the civilian side. Each of us also undertook to see special groups—I, for example, concentrated on learning as much as I could of the Indian intelligence estimates—and to sample the opinions of people in industry, business, the press, and so on.

In his conversations with the principal ministers of the Indian Government Harriman repeated the same, essentially simple policy themes he expressed to Nehru. The United States wanted to help, but India would have to be realistic about the cost and complexity of modern defenses. A full defense capability, air as well as ground, was not only astronomically expensive, but it took time. The most important thing was to get the Indian ground forces into shape. For the time being, air defense, if needed, would have to come from friends. On the political side, however, the United States had no desire to persuade India to join SEATO or any other form of alliance. On the contrary, the United States was inclined to think such a move unwise, and it seemed best for India, if at all possible, to continue to maintain its good relations with the Soviet Union. Finally, Harriman suggested, it should be obvious that no American president could recommend to Congress that it should appropriate large amounts of military aid to two friends—and we counted both India and Pakistan as friends—who used a portion of it to glower at each other across their common border while failing to co-operate in facing the common enemy. But the main purpose of our visit was not to enunciate U.S. policy, but to listen, to observe, and to learn.

What we learned was, first, that as Barbara Ward had reported the people of India were responding well. The only real worry was that in the cities the fear of bombing was frighteningly high, and since India had almost no air defenses at all, this could be dangerous. Everyone recalled that hundreds of people had been killed in Calcutta in World War II during a token raid by the Japanese—not from bombs, but by being trampled and crushed by panicky hordes of refugees.

The government, too, though hard-pressed, was functioning well and effectively. The civil service was carrying on, and the top ministers were in control and giving direction, especially Chavan, who had taken over the defense portfolio from Krishna Menon.

But it was on the military side that what we learned was most encouraging of all. The Armed Services were in a sorry state in terms of equipment, ammunition, supplies, and, to some extent, in training—for which condition the Indians blamed Krishna Menon, probably unfairly. But the basic cadre of the Armed Services was intact, their courage and discipline unshaken. In spite of their very thorough defeat, there was no panic. General Adams reported that the command system was working well, and that at the front line airfields, supplies were being received and stored properly for protection against the weather, with efficiency and dispatch. The Indian Army would need a great deal of arms and equipment, and air defenses would pose a particular problem. But the basic sinews—the command structure, the trained cadre, the discipline, and the morale—on which to rebuild were there.

On the political side and the need for an accommodation with Pakistan, it seemed that the people were ahead of the government and the government was ahead of Nehru. Many influential Indians in industry, business, and the press offered the view that an adjustment should be made and some even went so far as to speak of India's giving up Kashmir entirely. But when one considered the depth of feeling and the communal strife during partition, caution did seem wise. Even though the people might seem willing to accept an adjustment in the first flush of defeat and desperation, would they think later that a settlement had taken advantage of their misfortune and be even more bitter? But even though Nehru was still very much the national leader, one had the impression that the defeat had shaken his grip on the government, so that his ministers had a bigger voice than they once had and that Nehru had to consider and accommodate to their views more than he formerly did. In any event, Harriman and Sandys together were able to extract his promise to enter into negotiations with Pakistan, if Pakistan would agree.

Our attention, in fact, had already been focused on Pakistan. Two days before the agreement was reached with Nehru, Harriman had asked me to go to Karachi to talk to Brigadier Riaz Hussein, the head of Pakistan intelligence, and to see, in preparation for Harriman's talks with President Ayub, how Pakistan viewed the Chinese threat. The constantly strained relations between Pakistan and India had practical results, and there was almost no commercial air service between New Delhi and Karachi. Luckily, an American Air Force plane, one of those assigned to the Air Attaché, was being ferried to the Middle East, and I was able to get myself and some stranded American newsmen aboard. The plane was a bucket-seat C-47, one of the type that had been the work horse of World War II, and seeing it took me back eighteen years. As soon as we were airborne, my behavior was instinctive—arranging some parachute packs at the rear, I promptly went to sleep.

INTERLUDE

It turned out that Riaz was on a swing through West Pakistan but could meet me in Lahore—which provided me with a bright and lovely interlude. For when our talks were over, I had twenty-four hours in one of the oldest and most fascinating of Asia's cities.

Several hundred miles northeast of Karachi, beyond some of the harshest desert in the world, Lahore is a garden city, the center of a rich region of farming and horse breeding—both its chrysanthemums and its horses are world famous. A sports center in a sports-minded nation, Lahore makes two of the three finest of the world's tennis rackets. But Lahore, in fact, is not one city but three. The first is the ancient Asian city, seemingly as old as mankind, with twisting streets, sometimes so narrow that two men can pass only by turning sideways—little streets of a single trade, like the Tinsmiths', where pots and pans festoon the fronts of shops no bigger than a packing case. This is the Lahore of bazaars and spicy smells and teeming people.

The second Lahore is a city of ancient monuments and stately palaces and mausoleums. It had been a Mogul capital, and its tombs and fortresses rival those of Delhi.

The third Lahore is nineteenth-century British, for it was once the capital of all the Punjab. Here, there is a square where the administrative offices stood and where the Zam Zam gun still stands—the great brass cannon, cast in the 1600s, on which Kipling's Kim played "king of the castle." And here, too, are the stately homes, grouped around the palace and gardens of the Governor General, the flowers and hedges and lawns, watered by canals, of a transplanted England.

There are only three seasons in South and Southeast Asia—hot-dry; hot-wet; and "simply lovely." November in Lahore is the best of "simply lovely"—clear, sunny days and crisp, cool nights with just a light touch of frost by morning. I stayed with the American Consul General, David M. Bane, and his wife, and since they knew what these trouble-shooting missions were like, they made the arrangements accordingly. When independence came to Pakistan, it seemed likely that Lahore would be the capital city, and the United States grabbed up a lovely house for what it thought was to be the embassy, the elegant former home of a prince, complete with its own prize-winning collection of chrysanthemums. The Banes put me up in the guest room of this most comfortable house, overlooking the garden of chrysanthemums, fed me a dinner without other guests, and let me go off to bed immediately afterward. The next day, they had arranged a late-morning sightseeing trip to see the old city and the Mogul ruins, shepherded by the consulate's long-time chauffeur, an old Punjabi soldier who had served in Burma at the battle of Mandalay, where I, too, had been. He was right out of Kipling: "Ah, sahib, sir!" he said, beaming at finding something close to a comrade at arms, "That was good fighting!" We lunched with the Governor General of West Pakistan, the Nawab of Kalabagh, a giant of a man with huge handle-bar mustaches, who presided over a magnificent curry, in the grand style of emperors and viceroys with a liveried servant behind each guest and a bearer for each new dish. And I rode around the fantastic gardens in a tiny pony cart—miniature in every respect, tiny wheels, tiny little ponies, and driven by a tiny man, a fierce looking Northwest Frontier tribesman not quite four feet tall. But in all this delightful interlude that the Banes had arranged the most thoughtful of all was the shopping tour. "You have children," Mrs. Bane said the first evening. "They will expect something from a trip like this, and I know you couldn't have found a chance to do any shopping at all." It turned out to be the best shopping tour of my life, for she had arranged to have two merchants come to the house, and I sat in the Banes' living room by a fire, sipping a drink, while buying my older son a tennis racket, the younger a brass model of the Zam Zam gun, and various more feminine items for the girls.

RENDEZVOUS IN KARACHI

The interlude was over, and I flew to meet Harriman and the others in Karachi. After Harriman and Sandys had finally obtained Nehru's agreement to enter negotiations on Kashmir with Pakistan, Duncan Sandys, on November 27, had flown to Rawalpindi to confer with President Ayub Khan, and Harriman had followed the next day. The sessions had gone well, and although he was skeptical of Nehru's intentions, Ayub had quickly agreed to the proposal for negotiations. Ayub, Harriman, and Sandys had worked out the text of a joint announcement at a dinner meeting on the twenty-eighth, and on the twenty-ninth Sandys had flown back to New Delhi to obtain Nehru's approval. Although it was not mentioned in the communiqué, Pakistan's assurances that it would not take advantage of India's transferring its troops from Kashmir to the NEFA was a factor influencing Nehru just as the vulnerability of East Pakistan if Assam, right on its northern border, fell to the Communists was a factor influencing Ayub. On November 30, in both Rawalpindi and New Delhi, the joint communiqué was issued—and it seemed to offer more hope for settling the dispute between India and Pakistan than anything in its fifteen-year history. "The President of Pakistan and the Prime Minister of India," the communiqué read, "have agreed to resolve the outstanding differences between their two countries on Kashmir and other related matters so as to enable Pakistan and India to live side by side in peace and friendship. In consequence, they have decided to start discussions at an early date with the object of reaching an honorable and equitable settlement."

That evening, November 30, 1962, in a hopeful, almost gay mood, the members of the Harriman mission all gathered at Ambassador Walter P. McConaughy's residence in Karachi for a formal and leisurely dinner that was intended as a respite from work and something of a celebration. Then, as we gathered for drinks on the stone-floored veranda just outside the high-ceilinged dining room, an aide from the embassy came rushing in waving a piece of paper. The Foreign Minister of Pakistan, Mr. Dehlavi, had just telephoned from Rawalpindi and asked that the text, which he dictated, of an all-India radio broadcast the government of Pakistan had monitored be given to Harriman. "Mr. Nehru," the text of the broadcast read, "told the Lok Sabha [the Indian Parliament] this morning that anything which involved upsetting the present arrangements in Kashmir would be harmful to the people of Kashmir and the future relations between India and Pakistan. But, he said, he was always prepared to discuss these and other matters with the representatives of Pakistan. . . . Mr. Nehru added that he had explained to Sandys and Harriman that it would not be possible for India to bypass or ignore certain basic principles. In reply to a question, Mr. Nehru said that the reported broadcast by BBC this morning giving possible bases for a settlement for the Kashmir issue had no foundation whatsoever." The Foreign Minister in his telephone call had said, diplomatically, that he was relaying this message for our information and nothing else, but he did think that the one sentence in particular should be brought to Harriman's attention—that "anything which involved upsetting the present arrangements in Kashmir would be harmful" and so on, since the "present arrangements" that could not be upset presumably meant the current cease-fire line between India and Pakistan in Kashmir. What had been intended as a somewhat formal dinner celebration promptly became a scene of confusion. Harriman, naturally, was outraged. If it was true that Nehru had so blatantly disavowed any intention to negotiate meaningfully it would not only make it impossible for us to recommend any substantial aid to India, but it would be, in fact, an insult to our whole effort. By dint of much long-distance telephoning, it was finally established that Sandys, equally disturbed, had flown immediately to New Delhi.

Between bites of what was left of dinner, Harriman began drafting his own public statement, conferring with each of us across the big table. Mr. Nehru, the statement said, had "made it quite clear" that India "was prepared to enter discussions to resolve the differences between India and Pakistan on Kashmir without preconditions." "I feel sure," Harriman's statement concluded, "that he intends to carry out this undertaking." The statement was released as we left for the airport and the eighteen hours of pummeling ahead of us on the "McNamara Special."

Under pressure from Sandys, Nehru issued a "clarification" of his earlier statement—denying that he had intended any "restrictions or preconditions" on the talks.

This incident was hardly an encouraging finale to our mission, but the night's work had just begun. Aboard the plane, we sat down to draft our report to the President.

The problem, it seemed clear, was not now one of immediate, large-scale war, but of creating an effective long-term deterrent power on the subcontinent. India had rejected the conditions set out in the Chinese Communist proposal for a cease-fire, but would at the same time avoid upsetting the cease-fire so long as the Chinese Communists continued it. The Chinese, on the other hand, were clearly being cautious, partly, as mentioned earlier, because of the prompt dispatch of the Harriman and Sandys missions, which served as a signal of American and British support. So long as the Indians did not give them an excuse, it seemed clear that the Chinese Communists would not launch a major attack. And if they in fact pulled back twelve and one half miles in a unilateral withdrawal, so much the better.

Also, as mentioned above, the basic sinews of the Indian Army and Government were sound. The Indians recognized Communist China as a threat, and they were determined to build and maintain a larger defense establishment. Inevitably, there would be changes in Indian foreign policy and view of the world that would make it more sympathetic to our own position.

It seemed obvious that it was in the interests of the United States to help India in the task of building its strength. There was now a power vacuum where it was in our interests to have a balance. But it seemed equally clear that it would be a mistake to require formal ties or association in any sort of alliance structure as a condition for that help. On the contrary, it also seemed in the United States' interest not only that India remain outside such formal alliances as SEATO, but that she maintain her friendly relations with the Soviet Union.

Emergency aid should obviously continue as long as the emergency was acute. But beyond that there would be two major problems. One was purely technical. The Indians feared the effects on the urban population if their cities were bombed, and what they really wanted was not only to re-equip their armies, but to provide a complete air defense system of the latest and most sophisticated type. But the cost of this would be astronomical, and for the immediate future, the best that could be hoped for was that aid and India's own efforts could combine to build a "ground environment" for air defense—the radar installations, airfields, and other items of infrastructure—so that in the event of a major attack, American and British air forces could come into India and operate effectively.

The other problem was political—the old bugaboo of Kashmir and the relations between India and Pakistan. It was of course clear that the United States could not adopt as policy the crude bludgeon of making military aid conditional on a settlement between India and Pakistan. Much as we might want to see a settlement in the interests of a rational and economical defense of both countries, the United States could not and would not let either India or Pakistan be conquered by the Chinese Communists. As a practical political matter, if the threat from Communist China went up, so would military aid—whether or not there was progress toward a settlement. But it was equally clear, also as a practical political matter, that there would be less aid in the absence of a settlement and co-operation in defense of the subcontinent. Quite apart from the question of rationality and efficiency, the more the United States gave India aid in the absence of a settlement, the more Pakistan would move toward an accommodation with Communist China, and there clearly was a limit to what the United States could give India and still maintain friendly relations with Pakistan.

There are fleeting moments when history gives statesmen an opportunity to get ahead of events, an opportunity for an act of creative imagination that turns war toward peace, or enmity to friendship. The Chinese attack on India might well have been one of these, for Nehru's countrymen were deeply shocked, and to those of us who were there, they seemed ready for a few short days to respond to leadership armed with both perception and resolution. But Nehru was so deeply entangled in the past of the Kashmir dispute that perception was clouded, and he was apparently so weary and discouraged at the failure of his policy of neutralism that his resolution was also impaired. On December 16, 1962, Harriman dared to speak of the matter more bluntly and in public for the press. "It is going to be difficult," he said, "for the United States to give military aid both to Pakistan and India if a considerable part of it is used to defend against each other. Some agreement must be reached to disengage these forces." Nehru could stand no more. Lashing out at "pressure tactics," he was painfully and publicly frank about what he intended. "So far as we are concerned," he said, "while we are prepared for greater contacts and greater trade between Kashmir and Pakistan and for adjustments in the present cease fire line which is not a very sensible one, we are persuaded that any major change would be the ruin of the vale." If history had indeed presented Nehru with an opportunity, it had now been spurned.

THE LESSON

But the most portentous lesson of all in the 1962 attack on India was the skill and sophistication demonstrated by the Chinese Communists. Their attack had been a masterpiece of orchestrating military, political, and psychological instrumentalities as a single, limited, disciplined and controlled operation directed toward and subordinated to a political end. In their propaganda and political moves, they had made skillful use of the provocation the Indians supplied, and succeeded in taking much of the sting out of the charge of aggression. They had launched a military attack over what had always been considered the world's most difficult terrain barrier, accomplishing feats of logistics and road-building as they went; and they inflicted a convincing defeat on the Indian Army, humiliating a principal rival for Asian leadership and projecting Chinese power into the subcontinent for the first time in history. Throughout the whole affair, they had also retained the political initiative, calling for cease-fires and negotiations at every politically sensitive turn, and succeeding in putting the onus for rejection on India. And in early December, they enhanced their posture of "peaceful intent" still further by going ahead and withdrawing their troops twelve and one half miles, unilaterally, as they said they would and in spite of the Indian rejection of the proposal. "There is no doubt who is in control over there," said one Kennedy aide in grudging admiration of a formidable enemy. "Can you imagine the difficulty we would have with the Pentagon in pulling back and giving up territory that had cost that many casualties, no matter how great the political end it served?" It was perfectly obvious that Communist China was becoming not only a powerful enemy but a politically skillful one— which might in the end be just as ominous.

It was also perfectly obvious that the United States would have to consider again its policy toward Communist China. "I would regard that combination . . ." President Kennedy said a few months later in regard to Communist China and the probability that it would soon have nuclear weapons, "of weak countries around it, seven hundred million people, a Stalinist internal regime, and nuclear powers, and a government determined on war as a means of bringing about its ultimate success, as potentially a more dangerous situation than any we faced since the end of the Second [World] War. . . ." And the implications for the United States were clear. "As you say," the President said on the same occasion, "it may take some years, maybe a decade, before they become a full-fledged nuclear power, but we are going to be around in the 1970s, and we would like to take some steps now which would lessen that prospect that a future President might have to deal with."[2]

NOTES

[1] For a fuller account of these events, see Wayne A. Wilcox, *India, Pakistan, and the Rise of China,* 1964.

[2] Press conference, August 1, 1963.

CHAPTER 24

Policy for the Second Kennedy Administration

ANY SHIFT in United States policy toward Communist China would have to proceed slowly, tentatively, and incrementally—a step at a time. But it would also have to take into account a series of events that had been taking place within the Communist bloc itself that was so momentous, it now seemed clear, that future historians might well regard it as the single most significant international political fact of our day—the Sino-Soviet dispute.

THE SINO-SOVIET DISPUTE

The dispute between China and the Soviet Union, certainly, was fundamental in all the rich connotations of the word. It was concerned, first of all, with ideology, with the true meaning of the sacred texts of the Communist world and the Communist vision of the future. It also was concerned with power, with who should have power within that world, with who should lead and who should follow. In a very real sense, Communism is a doctrine for getting and holding power, and in their bid for leadership of the Communist world, the Chinese were really just behaving like Communists. The dispute was also concerned with the organization of decision-making within the Communist world and the nature of the relationship among the different parties. The key words in this aspect of the debate were "centrism" and "polycentrism"—the tags for whether Russia's *national* interests should be synonymous with the interests of the *whole* of the Communist world or whether the *national* interests of the other parties should also be considered in determining policy. The differences also extended to policy toward the in-between world, whether the friendship of the Communist world should be extended to "national-bourgeois" regimes, as in India, or only to the radical nationalists and "national liberation movements." The Soviets, as we have seen, chose friendship with such states as India and encouraged them in a policy of "neutralism," while China advocated support only for the militant, and went so far as to attack India with military force partly as a deliberate affront to the Soviet Union. And the dispute was also concerned with grand strategy, with the question of how aggressive the Communist world should be in its dealings with the West and how much risk should be run of nuclear war. This difference was symbolized by the exchange between Mao and Khrushchev at the time of the Cuban missile crisis, with Mao saying that the West was only a "paper tiger" and Khrushchev's replying that this particular paper tiger had "nuclear teeth."

All of these different aspects and themes appeared and reappeared as the dispute unfolded. It apparently had begun in 1956 at the 20th Congress of the Communist Party of the Soviet Union—the congress at which Khrushchev finally felt strong enough to attack the memory of Stalin and begin the process of "de-Stalinization."[1] In a published statement in April 1956, the Chinese offered a "balanced"—i.e., rival—analysis of Stalin's "serious mistakes" and his merits, concluding that his contribution outweighed his errors and that the errors, which reflected contradictions between the "individual and the collective in a socialist society," could be minimized if Communist leaders exercised "sufficient prudence." The Chinese followed up this statement, they later revealed, with conversations with Soviet leaders in which they maintained that the basic policy line during the Stalin period had been correct, and that the Soviets were at fault in failing "to consult with the fraternal parties in advance" of their attack on Stalin.

The Chinese carried their bid for a larger voice in policy one step further later in 1956, during the Polish and Hungarian crises. The Polish Communist leadership had demanded greater autonomy, and the Soviets met the demand by moving up "troops in an attempt to subdue the Polish comrades by armed force"—an act, the Chinese charged, of "great power chauvinism" that the Chinese opposed at the time. The situation was reversed in the Hungarian crisis. This was not a bid for greater autonomy by a Communist leadership, but a mass revolt that both the Soviets and the Chinese regarded as "counterrevolutionary." But the Soviets were slow to intervene, the Chinese charged, and did so only after the Chinese had insisted on "the taking of all necessary measures to smash the counterrevolutionary rebellion . . ."

Both sides recognized the dangers to the Communist world of a split, and they intermittently made efforts to heal it. The Soviet government, for example, issued a declaration on October 30, 1956, recognizing the need for "mutual respect" in the relations between "fraternal countries," and Peking responded with a statement supporting the Soviet declaration —although it also expressed approval for the Polish position and warned against "great power chauvinism." Much more importantly, we now know that sometime in 1957 the Soviets signed an agreement to assist Communist China in the area of "new technology for national defense"— nuclear weapons.

It was undoubtedly the signing of this agreement that led Mao to make two important concessions. The first was his public bow to the Soviet leadership in his speech in Moscow on November 17, 1957, in which he declared that "the socialist camp must have a head; and this head is the U.S.S.R." and that "the Communist parties of all countries must have a head; and this head is the C.P.S.U. [Communist Party of the Soviet Union]." The second, and more significant concession was that Mao dropped Gomulka—the reality that the phrase about the U.S.S.R. being head of the socialist camp reflects. Mao got a nuclear commitment, in other words, in exchange for helping Moscow restore discipline in Eastern Europe.

But the Chinese continued to push their more militant line. It was also in late 1957 that Mao expounded the thesis, in the wake of the Sputnik success, that the "East wind prevails over the West wind." And there were other irritants. The extravagant claims the Chinese made for the Commune program and the Great Leap Forward, which were launched in 1958, carried an implication that only the Chinese had found the true road to Communism. For their part, the Soviets felt that they had tried and discarded such radical measures, and that they should have been consulted.

But it was in military and international affairs that the difficulties were sharpest. During the 1958 Quemoy-Matsu crisis, the Soviets were extremely cautious and no more than lukewarm in their support of the Chinese. In its exposé of September 1963, Peking said that the Soviets had withheld a commitment of support the Chinese needed to face down the United States until Moscow was sure no risk remained—by which time it was too late for the commitment to be of any help. And from the Chinese point of view, Soviet behavior was even worse in the political sphere. They implied that in his talks with Mao Tse-tung, when he visited Peking in October of 1959, Khrushchev sought to end the civil war with the Nationalists and to institute a policy of "two Chinas."

On top of all this, there were disagreement and misunderstanding about just how much the Soviets had promised to do in helping Communist China develop nuclear weapons. In their later statements the Chinese suggest that it was no misunderstanding but a Soviet decision to renege on what had been a commitment to help them build a nuclear capability. But what may really have happened was that the Chinese asked for the weapons themselves and Khrushchev countered with conditions that the Chinese found unacceptable—for the Chinese alleged that the Soviets "put forward unreasonable demands designed to bring China under Soviet military control." In any event, it was immediately after this episode that the Chinese publicly reasserted that the atomic bomb was a "paper tiger."

In June, according to the Chinese, the Soviet Union finally rejected

Peking's request for a "sample" atomic bomb. Moscow, furthermore, apparently dabbled in subversion by encouraging Marshal P'eng Te-huai, the Chinese Defense Minister, in opposing the rest of the Chinese party— but unsuccessfully, for he was promptly purged. The Khrushchev visit to the United States in September of 1959 and the "Camp David spirit" that came out of it apparently brought all these developments into crisis, for Khrushchev found it necessary to make a sudden trip to Peking, immediately following his visit to the United States. But it seems only to have made matters worse. Not only did the ebullient Khrushchev use the occasion to push the "two-Chinas" policy, as mentioned earlier, but he also warned the Chinese in a public speech against "testing by force the stability of the capitalist system."

Throughout 1960, there were more and more virulent exchanges of propaganda. Much of the Soviet output was aimed at Albania, but everyone in the world knew that the real target was Albania's mentor, Communist China. Then, in July of 1960, in Peking's words, Moscow "suddenly took a unilateral decision recalling all Soviet experts in China within one month"—a most serious blow to the developing Chinese economy.

In 1961, Khrushchev forced the Albanian issue to a crisis, breaking diplomatic relations, withdrawing Soviet naval units from the base at Vlorë, and ending all Soviet aid. The Chinese stepped in with aid to replace what the Soviets had stopped, and at the 22nd Congress of the Communist Party, Chou En-lai made a speech attacking Khrushchev for his Albanian policy. Then he left the congress early—ostentatiously laying a wreath on Stalin's tomb as he departed.

There were outbreaks of actual fighting on the border between China and the Soviet Union in 1962, and what was apparently a Soviet attempt at large-scale subversion in the Chinese province of Sinkiang. In retaliation, the Chinese closed Soviet consulates throughout the country.

There then began a fierce competition for the allegiance of the Communist parties of every country in the world. And the debate grew hotter still—with each side publishing more and more of the formerly secret correspondence in an effort to bolster its own case. By early 1963, Peking was denouncing the Soviet Communist Party leaders as betrayers of the revolution, arguing that the underdeveloped areas of the world were the real focus of the "struggle against imperialism" and that the real leader of the struggle was the Chinese Party. Moscow, in turn, was attempting to show that the Chinese were indifferent to the risks of nuclear war and bent on dividing the Communist world along "racist" lines. In the summer of 1963, the Chinese distributed, first in Moscow and then throughout the world, a letter, dated June 14, 1963, declaring that they intended to split every Communist Party whose leaders sided with the Soviet Union. By the fall of 1963, when the opportunity had come for the Kennedy administration to devote some serious thought to the problem of China policy, the dispute had progressed to a stage that amounted to an open declaration of hostilities.

U.S. POLICY

Given the background of American policy toward China, the bitterness and the ruined careers, it is not surprising that the American government approached the related problem of policy toward the Sino-Soviet dispute gingerly. And there was also considerable puzzlement about just exactly what the consequences would be for the United States and what a wise policy would consist of. The Eisenhower administration's public policy toward the dispute was simply to ignore it, and for the first year and a half the Kennedy administration followed suit. On July 10, 1961, for example, in answering a question following a talk at the National Press Club, Secretary Rusk said there was credible evidence of a split, but that he did not think that "the prospect of such divisions would be a sound basis for policy for the free world."

But as the Sino-Soviet dispute loomed larger and larger, it simply had to be faced. And, slowly, the State Department did come to face it. "I recall a Secretary's Planning Meeting in January, 1962," a letter from James C. Thomson, Jr., says, "at which all the powers of State appeared to focus for the first time on the reality of a permanent Sino-Soviet split. The impact on the minds around the table that morning was dramatic, and you could hear the ice of 12 years begin to snap and crackle as an intellectual thaw set in. I kept careful notes on that meeting and regard it as something of a turning point. One after another State's operators and planners toyed with the new world of possibilities that non-monolithic communism might offer to U.S. policies."

But as so often happens, it was pressure from the public press that really drove the State Department to face the issue, for under the constant questioning of the press the policy of simply ignoring the Sino-Soviet dispute became increasingly embarrassing. Robert J. Manning, Assistant Secretary for Public Affairs, and his deputy, James L. Greenfield, particularly felt the pressure. They were both fighting a battle to be more forthcoming with the press, which was against all the instincts of the State Department, and this was an example of their problem. There were many complaints from on high about leaks or simply about damaging newspaper stories that were damaging precisely because they were based on incomplete information, and Manning and Greenfield argued that the best way to meet these problems was not by tighter and tighter restrictions on dealing with the press, but by a positive program taking the initiative in giving them information. In this particular instance, they had an ally in

William J. Jorden, who had been recently named Special Assistant to the Under Secretary to deal with the psychological and informational aspects of policy questions and who had made a more rational treatment of the Sino-Soviet dispute his first priority. Enunciating a public policy toward the dispute would, of course, be exceedingly delicate, and Secretary Rusk, especially, was reluctant to see it even attempted. The compromise was a decision to comment "factually" on the dispute as a first step—that is, to describe what had actually been taking place—second, to analyze the causes of the dispute as we saw it at that time, and finally, to offer our view of the probable future course of Sino-Soviet relations, but to avoid speculation about the consequences for the United States or a full statement of policy. In these circumstances, it seemed appropriate that I should be the one to give this basic speech, in my capacity as Director of Intelligence and Research.

It was agreed in the early fall that I would give the speech at a Foreign Affairs Council meeting in Texas on November 8—not knowing that the Cuban missile crisis, which itself became a factor in the Sino-Soviet dispute, would intervene. But we decided to go ahead.

Relating the highlights in the history of the dispute, the speech went on to an analysis that saw the dispute as fundamental—concerned with ideology and power and grand strategy as well as being a bid for leadership by the Chinese Communists. The speech rejected the two extremist explanations—that the dispute was a hoax designed to blind us to the Communist conspiracy or that it marked a complete end to the alliance between China and the Soviet Union. "Communist ideology," the speech went on to say, "with its goal of world revolution, still provides an overall basis for unity between Peiping and Moscow. So long as both partners see the United States as the greatest obstacle to the attainment of this goal, they will try to patch over their differences and unite against the common enemy."

But even though our analysis saw the reasons against a complete and final break as compelling, it also recognized that the antagonisms were so deep-seated that "we cannot foresee any genuine reconciliation of the dispute . . ." The dispute, the speech concluded, would continue to be with us for some time—it would not proceed rapidly either to a complete and final break or to a complete and final healing.

IMPLICATIONS OF THE DISPUTE

As time went on, it became increasingly clear, not only that this prediction was correct, but that the attention of the leadership in both China and the Soviet Union was fixed hypnotically on each other. Thus the dispute itself began to be the single strongest influence on both the

Chinese and the Soviets, and their moves on the international scene increasingly came to be made principally in terms of the effect, not on the United States and the non-Communist world, but on each other and the dispute itself. A very obvious implication, for example, was that the Chinese Communists would welcome recognition from any Western nation *except* the United States; and that any direct initiative from the United States toward regularizing relations would be thoroughly rebuffed. China clearly needed an outside enemy to point to in her attempt to win the allegiance of the other Communist parties and to enlist support for her hard line within the Soviet Party itself, which she was also doing. The United States, as the single most powerful nation in the world, and the principal obstacle to further Communist expansion, was the obvious and only candidate. United States policy had been to refuse to recognize Communist China and to oppose her being seated in the United Nations, and some liberals argued that all we had to do was to offer recognition and Chinese hostility would disappear. The truth was that the Chinese—precisely because of the dispute—would not only reject any such move but would use it as proof of the efficacy of their hard line. Although it was certainly true that United States policy needed to be more flexible than it had been in the past, what everyone had to understand was that before increased flexibility would work there probably also had to be more firmness. So long as the Chinese felt that aggression and their policy of hard-line intransigence were successful, they would hardly turn to "peaceful coexistence." Basically, it was this policy that combined firmness with flexibility that had not only checked the expansionism of the Soviet Union but had done so without war. NATO, United States rearmament, troops to Europe, and so on had been just as essential as recognition, the United Nations, and continued negotiations.

RE-EXAMINATION

This public recognition symbolized by the speech on the Sino-Soviet dispute was a far cry from the fundamental re-examination of our China policy that was really needed, but it was at least an indication that the government was doing some thinking about the subject. But nothing much more could be done for the moment.

There then came the Chinese Communist attack on India, and a few months later, in March of 1963, Harriman was promoted to Under Secretary of State, and I to his old post as Assistant Secretary for Far Eastern Affairs.

Harriman turned over the responsibilities of the office of Far Eastern Affairs with characteristic verve. "It's one of the best jobs in Washington," he said. "The problems there are really tough." But then he turned to the problems themselves, and he stressed above all else the problem of relations with Communist China. "You must immediately," he charged me, "begin to think about laying the groundwork for what the President might do about China policy in his second administration." Communist China would be the big problem of foreign policy in the future, Harriman went on to say, and it was going to be trouble no matter what we did. We would have to be tough, but if we were wise enough and big enough to be farsighted and flexible as well as tough, we might be able to get sufficiently ahead of events to keep the trouble manageable.

The President's thinking was in the same direction. In the spring of 1963, following the peaceful solution of the Cuban missile crisis, Kennedy sought to move toward a *détente* with the Communist world and especially the Soviet Union. In what historians will undoubtedly regard as one of his greatest speeches, that on the "Strategy of Peace" given at the American University on June 10, 1963, Kennedy sought to assure the Communist world that the United States rejected any idea of a "Pax Americana." He appealed to the American people to re-examine their attitudes toward peace, toward the Soviet Union, and toward the Cold War—asking Americans "not to see only a distorted and desperate view of the other side, not to see conflict as inevitable, accommodation as impossible and communication as nothing more than an exchange of threats." Calling for a nuclear test ban and measures to halt the arms race, he appealed to both sides to take concrete and realistic steps toward peace. "So," he said, "let us not be blind to our differences—but let us also direct attention to our common interests and the means by which those differences can be resolved. And if we cannot end now our differences, at least we can help make the world safe for diversity."

The American University speech was aimed in the first instance at furthering a possible *détente* with the Soviet Union, but President Kennedy would have liked to see progress in the same direction with Communist China. In his debates with Nixon, he had aligned himself with those who wanted to move toward ending the civil war. Then, again, in 1961 he had spoken of his desire to see a "lessening of tension"—so long as it did not require surrender in order to achieve that lessening of tension. And it was after the American University speech, in August of 1963, that Kennedy spoke in the words quoted above of the ominous prospect of a Communist China, Stalinist in orientation, bent on aggressive war, and armed with nuclear weapons, and of his desire "to take some steps now which would lessen that prospect that a future President might have to deal with."

In the last press conference of his life, on November 14, 1963, Kennedy, in answering a question, gave in microcosm an outline of the policy of "firmness and flexibility" we were developing. Asked about prerequisites or conditions for resumption of trade with Red China, the President replied: "We are not planning to trade with Red China in view of the policy that Red China pursues. When the Red Chinese indicate a desire to live at peace with the United States, with other countries surrounding it, then quite obviously the United States would reappraise its policies. We are not wedded to a policy of hostility to Red China. It seems to me Red China's policies are what create the tension between not only the United States and Red China but between Red China and India, between Red China and her immediate neighbors to the south, and even between Red China and other Communist countries."

Although he never scheduled a formal discussion devoted primarily to the question of China policy, the President had on several occasions commented on the need for some rethinking—to Harriman, to Forrestal, and to me. Thus without there being a full-dress review and discussion both a program and a policy began to take shape in the minds of those of us concerned with the Far East.

INITIATIVES

We would need, of course, to find an occasion to enunciate the basic policy of firmness and flexibility and to develop public support for it. Then, we would need a series of actions that would get the United States off the hook of rigidity on which it was impaled—that would demonstrate to the world that it was not the United States that was "isolating" Communist China but Communist China that was isolating itself, through its pariah policies.

The moves we had in mind were simple, but they had solid political leverage. One was to lift the restrictions on Americans traveling to Communist China. We had proposed an exchange of newsmen, for example, but the Chinese could reject this and still argue that the United States was attempting to isolate China because of the ban on the travel of American citizens. Lifting these restrictions might seem a small step, but it would deny the Chinese an argument and give our friends among the African and Asian nations a lever in their future discussions with the Chinese.

Second, we could recognize Mongolia. Here all the same arguments used in 1961 were still pertinent. Our policy toward Communist China sometimes looked more anti-Asian than anti-Chinese Communist, and we needed something that would make the point that we were not against either Asians or Communists as such, but the aggressive policies the Chinese had been following. While we did not regard either of the half countries, North Korea or North Vietnam, as states, we had long acknowledged that Mongolia was a state, and had not opposed its membership in the UN. Since Mongolia was pro-Soviet, recognizing it would not only demonstrate a new flexibility in United States policy and be a political asset with the other Asian nations, it would also distinguish between an Asian Communist country committed to policies of "peaceful coexistence" and the more belligerent Chinese Communists and their policies. Our recognizing Mongolia would not please Peking. And it would give us a window on the other side of China and a source of information about a part of the world of which we were far too ignorant.

All of these arguments, to repeat, were the same as in 1961, except for the implications of the Sino-Soviet dispute and the additional displeasure our recognizing Mongolia would cause Peking on this account. But by 1963 one other argument could also be added. Mongolia was the only Asian Communist country that had signed the nuclear test ban treaty, and this made it even more ideal as an instrument for demonstrating that we judged Communist nations neither by their ideology nor by their race (European Communists as opposed to Asian Communists), but by their behavior and policies.

Both of these proposals had been quite thoroughly discussed within the administration and several times postponed. But the President had indicated that we should raise the subject again after the turn of the year.

In addition, I had two further ideas. One was to find some way of bringing Communist China into the disarmament talks at Geneva—or at least of putting her in the position of refusing invitations to participate, publicly and repeatedly. It was perfectly clear from our intelligence that Communist China was working furiously on an atomic bomb and that she would probably succeed in exploding one by mid-1964. It seemed wise to get the United States at least a little ahead of events by trying to bring Communist China into the disarmament talks *before* she exploded the bomb. Disarmament, of course, could not be truly accomplished without Communist China's participation, and although I had little confidence that China would in fact come to the Geneva talks, much less sign a treaty, here again it seemed politically essential that the world understood that it was Communist China herself that kept her from participating and not the United States. And it would be ideal if we could drive the point home by finding ways to have the invitation continuously renewed.

The second idea was for the United States to re-examine its restrictions on trade with Communist China—and for all the same reasons. Here again, I did not think that the Chinese would be willing to trade with the United States. But I thought it would be wise politically if the world understood that it was the Chinese themselves and not the United States that was blocking further trade. And here, too, it would be ideal if these pressures could be continuously reiterated by repeated offers.

None of us thought that any of these moves would bring about a great thaw in the coldly aggressive policies of Communist China. The roots of their policies lay too deep in the continued existence of an independent Taiwan supported by the United States and in the value to the Chinese of having the United States as a whipping boy in their obviously paramount conflict with the Soviet Union. Our guess, to repeat, was that the

Chinese Communists would not permit any Americans to travel in their country except those who would write what the Chinese Communists wanted them to write. We expected no increase in trade. Nor did we expect that the Chinese—at least for some time—would come to Geneva for the disarmament talks. What we did expect was, first, that the other countries in Asia would more and more come to see that it was the Chinese who were the cause of their own isolation and not United States policy, as I have said. Second, we expected that over time there would be subtle and steady political pressure on the Chinese at least to pretend to be more forthcoming as they tried to line up African and Asian opinion and found the questions about who was isolating whom more and more difficult to answer. Finally, we expected one other, still more subtle effect. There were many signs that the upcoming "second echelon" of Chinese Communist leaders was dissatisfied with the rigid, primitive, and doctrinaire policies of the old veterans of the "Long March" who were still in power, and there were many more signs that the old leaders were anxious about this dissatisfaction and fearful that when the second echelon came to power they would turn against the old doctrines both at home and abroad. We did not expect these second-echelon leaders to be any less Communist than the old veterans, but only that they would see that the world was more complicated and that they would adopt more pragmatic policies, just as the second echelon who followed Stalin in the Soviet Union had done. It seemed wise, not only to point up this tension, but also to lay the groundwork for the kind of flexibility that could meet the opportunities that would come later.

SAN FRANCISCO SPEECH, 1963

In the fall of 1963, the time seemed more than ripe for at least the beginnings of this groundwork for a new flexibility. As I said, the Chinese were expected to explode their first nuclear device sometime in mid-1964, and it would be wise to get ahead of that event. Things were generally quiet in the world, the test ban treaty had been signed, the "peace initiative" was progressing, and a *détente* seemed to be developing with the Soviet Union. The "Year of the Tiger" talk had subsided, and the Chinese Nationalists and their allies on the American domestic scene seemed to be more and more reconciled to adjusting to the situation. And just about that time, the Commonwealth Club of San Francisco invited me to speak on Friday, December 13, preferably on China policy. There were a couple of wisecracks about the date, but San Francisco was the traditional place for major speeches on China policy—it was in San Francisco that Dulles had made the last full statement on the subject in 1957—and I decided to accept. If anything happened to make a statement at that time inadvisable, I could always fall back on repeating once again the now tired and routine themes the State Department had been following since Dulles' speech of six years before.

James C. Thomson, Jr., then Special Assistant in the Bureau of Far Eastern Affairs; Lindsey Grant, Officer in Charge of Mainland China Affairs; Allen S. Whiting, Director of the Office of Research for Far Eastern Affairs; Joseph W. Neubert, also a special assistant in Far Eastern Affairs; Abram Manell, Public Affairs Adviser for Far Eastern Affairs; and I worked and reworked the basic speech, with some additional help from Robert W. Barnett, Deputy for Economic Affairs. The key difference between this speech and the policy it outlined and Secretary Dulles' 1957 speech and the policy it outlined lay in the basic assumption on the question of Chinese Communist control. Dulles' speech assumed that the Chinese Communist regime was a "passing and not a perpetual phase." And, as mentioned earlier, it was from this assumption that policy flowed. "We owe it to ourselves, our allies and the Chinese people," to repeat Dulles' conclusion, "to do all that we can to contribute to that passing." This assumption, of course, was no longer valid, and although there had been no public statement announcing the fact, the United States had long since ceased to base its policy on that assumption—a fact which had often been explained to our friends on Taiwan. We felt that in fairness to ourselves, our allies, and the American people, there should be a public acknowledgment of this changed assumption and an analysis of its implications for United States policy. And this was the first point that the final draft of the speech made. Recounting the history of the Great Leap Forward, the commune program, and so on, it pointed out that, although the mainland economy had collapsed, the Communist regime had not. "Nor was its authority effectively challenged. It retained firm command of the instruments of control." Although we might not like it, realistically we must recognize the true situation: "We have no reason to believe," the speech bluntly continued, "that there is a present likelihood that the Communist regime will be overthrown."

The speech then went on to outline a policy of firmness, flexibility, and dispassion. By firmness, we meant firmness in our support for our friends and allies, including the people and government of the Republic of China on Taiwan; firmness in our determination to maintain our strength in Asia and firmness in our determination to meet aggression wherever it occurred. By flexibility, we meant a willingness to seek and carry out initiatives that seemed promising and to negotiate with anyone who sincerely wanted to negotiate, including the Chinese Communists. And by dispassion, we meant analyzing our problems and our policies coolly, without emotion, to discover our own best interests—appealing to the American people to substitute rationality in China policy for the emotionalism of which, God knows, there had been too much. In all three aspects, the policy was basically what President Kennedy had followed so successfully in dealing with the Soviet Union—when the Soviets put missiles in Cuba he dealt with them very firmly indeed; but he had the flexibility to leave them a way out and the dispassion to negotiate a test ban treaty a few months later without letting the emotion of the past cloud his vision of what was good for both the United States and the world.

The speech went on to analyze the differences between the first and second echelons in the Chinese Communist leadership, to point to the tension between them, and to hold out some hope for an evolutionary process similar to what had gone on in the Soviet Union—which might "erode the present simple view with which the leadership regards the world" even though they would undoubtedly remain Communists. Reiterating United States determination to stand by our friends, including the people and government of the Republic of China on Taiwan, and its determination to frustrate any attempt by Communist China to "subvert or commit aggression against its free world neighbors," the speech ended on the point of flexibility. "We do not know what changes may occur in the attitudes of future Chinese leaders, but if I may paraphrase a classic canon of our past, we pursue today towards Communist China a policy of the Open Door: We are determined to keep the door open to the possibility of change, and not to slam it shut against any development which might advance our national good, serve the free world, and benefit the people of China. . . . We hope that, confronted with firmness which will make foreign adventure unprofitable, and yet offered a prospect that the way back into the community of man is not closed to it, the Chinese Communist regime will eventually forsake its venomous hatreds which spring from a rigid class view of society. We hope that they will rediscover the Chinese virtue of tolerance for a multitude of beliefs and faiths; and that they will accept again a world of diversity, in place of the gray monolith which seems to be Communism's goal for human society."

The speech was carefully phrased to avoid providing labels and slogans to those who would oppose it. But it clearly acknowledged that the policy of the Kennedy administration was based on a willingness to reach an accommodation with the Chinese Communist regime—provided only that the Chinese Communist regime was willing to modify its hostility in the same direction.

On Friday, November 22, 1963, I was host at a luncheon in the Secretary of State's private dining room on the eighth floor of the State Department Building honoring Senator Raul S. Manglapus, Chairman of the Foreign Relations Committee of the Philippine Senate, with Averell Harriman and Senator Frank Church, among others, as guests. Senator Church was called to the phone toward the end of the meal, and just as the waiters were serving dessert, he threw open the door. Swaying and pallid in the doorway, he called out, "The President has been shot—and is dead." Harriman and I jumped up and started downstairs, turning back in confusion to excuse ourselves from our guest of honor. Rusk was in mid-air on his way to Tokyo with several other members of the Cabinet, and we gathered in George Ball's office, to wait for the news and the confirmation. When it came, I went on down to my own office, to be alone to grieve for a man who was not only a leader, but who had become a friend.

A PERSONAL DILEMMA

The next few days of hectic grief permitted no time for thought. But once the funeral was over, we had to face the question of whether to go on with the China policy speech or to cancel it. One thing was perfectly clear: the program of initiatives—recognizing Mongolia, lifting travel restrictions, attempting to bring Communist China into the disarmament talks at Geneva, and re-examining trade restrictions—the program with which we had thought to follow up the speech would have to be postponed. President Johnson had a major task of getting a firm grip on the government and establishing himself in the eyes of the American people and the world as the effective leader of the United States, and he could not afford these concrete actions until that task was accomplished. The program of initiatives would clearly have to wait until after the 1964 elections, at the least. On the other hand, giving the speech at this time might be very useful, not only from the President's point of view, but from the point of view of furthering the policy it espoused. If the public reaction was bad and a howl for blood came up from Congress, the President could disavow the policy and me along with it on the perfectly valid grounds that this was really an initiative of the previous administration. If the public reaction were favorable, on the other hand, it would set the scene for him to take up the concrete program whenever he judged the timing was right. From the Johnson administration's point of view it seemed a good thing to go ahead with the speech—so long as the President himself was not too closely and personally identified with the decision to make it.

But this very fact highlighted my personal problem of whether it was wise for me to make the speech in the altered circumstances. I was closely identified with President Kennedy, and since I had known President Johnson only slightly, I would be peculiarly vulnerable to attack. At one stage, James Thomson, Abram Manell, and Joseph Neubert out of loyal friendship came to me in a body to say that even though they thought it was in the interests of the United States that the speech be given, their judgment was that I would be taking considerable personal risk. The China Lobby would undoubtedly raise a howl, and if they succeeded in getting support in Congress and the public, it would be I who would have to take the rap. And rightly so. For no matter who okayed making the speech, it was I who would deliver it and I who was recommending the policy. The only way around that would be for the President to make the speech himself, which he could not do for the same reason that he would not be able to follow it up with the program of initiatives we had designed.

The office of the Assistant Secretary of State for Far Eastern Affairs is on the sixth floor of the State Department Building, at the southwest corner, looking out over the Lincoln Memorial, the Memorial Bridge across the Potomac, and on past to Arlington National Cemetery and Lee Mansion. It is just below Lee Mansion, at exactly the level of the State Department's sixth floor that President Kennedy is buried, and whenever I turned my chair to ponder out the window, my eyes fell naturally on his grave and, if it was dusk, on the flame flickering above it. But it was not sentimentality to want to see his aspirations for Asia furthered. The world was changing rapidly, and it seemed obvious that in the interests of its own future and of mankind, the United States should lay the groundwork for a less emotional, more rational policy toward the China question. This particular speech at this particular time would test the public reaction at almost no risk to the Johnson administration's future choices about the question. I was, after all, the natural spokesman for an approach that called for more firmness as well as more flexibility. In the first place, I held the office of Assistant Secretary for Far Eastern Affairs, which is responsible for relations with China. But there were other reasons. As an academic and former professor, I had some credentials that would tend to blunt the criticism of the more ardent liberals—criticism some liberals would surely make that the speech called for too much firmness and not enough flexibility. At the same time I also had some credentials that would tend to blunt the criticism from the right. I was the son of a Regular Army officer, and myself a graduate of West Point; I had served ten years in the Regular Army; in World War II, I had fought with Merrill's Marauders and been decorated as well as being severely wounded, and later had led an OSS guerrilla group operating behind the enemy lines in Burma; and I had had a long background in such places as Princeton's Center of International Studies as an advocate of tough policies for dealing with the strategic problems of an age that encompassed both missiles and limited wars. If the China Lobby or a new generation of McCarthyites tried to charge me with being soft on Communism, they would have some difficulty in making it stick.

When Averell Harriman had been promoted to Under Secretary and I to his old post as Assistant Secretary, Sidney Hyman, the writer and authority on the presidency, expressing his pleasure, had said that Harriman's wealth and my alternative career as a professor gave us something particularly precious in government service—the freedom to speak up, to stand on principle. "You are both free men," Hyman said, "and in my opinion free men is what these two hot jobs most need!" I decided that if the administration decided to go ahead and clear the speech, then I was ready to deliver it and to take the responsibility for recommending it.

We updated the speech, to include the fact of President Kennedy's death, and sent it around for clearance. The White House staff cleared it, although the President himself did not read it. Governor Harriman's office also cleared the speech—although Harriman himself did not read it until after it had been mimeographed for release. He also approved, although he told me later he would have changed one or two sentences, particularly a reference to a Chinese comment on President Kennedy's assassination, if he had seen it earlier. And the speech was also cleared with the Defense Department and with various offices within the State Department.

I also took a copy up to the Secretary of State. Describing what was in the speech, I warned him that the China Lobby would probably raise a fuss, along with the Chinese Nationalists and probably some congressmen. We discussed the implications of an intelligence report that the French were about to recognize Communist China. Finally, I asked if he wanted to go over the speech himself. He saw no need for it—and that was that.

Advance copies of the speech were distributed in the State Department, and the next morning I departed for San Francisco. At a stopover in Denver, I telephoned my office to discover that there had been even more clearance. At the Secretary's staff meeting that morning, Phillips Talbot, Assistant Secretary for Near Eastern Affairs, had raised a question about the speech. George Ball, who was Acting Secretary since Rusk had left town for the weekend, had then read it through and had given it his approval.

At noon at the Commonwealth Club, in a blaze of TV lights, I began: "I am honored to be invited to this distinguished forum. . . ." And when it was finished I went to the home of my parents, who were retired in San Francisco, to wait to see if the roof would fall in.

Concerned that the initial news play be an accurate account of just how the speech differed from the Dulles policy, Allen Whiting, on his own initiative, had taken the precaution of briefing the press very fully, especially the New York *Times,* the two wire services, and the two local Washington papers. Due to his efforts, the press play was as accurate and as balanced as we could have wished. Also, undoubtedly due to his efforts, which communicated some of his own conviction that the speech represented a departure of historical significance, the press coverage was also big and prominent. By and large, the speech got front-page treatment from coast to coast.

We had to wait a while for the reaction from the so-called China Lobby, but it came. Timing it to coincide with the return of Congress, the Committee of One Million issued an elaborate statement charging that the speech was "soft on Communism." It argued that what the speech advocated was a "Two Chinas" policy and devoted much of its space to attacking that policy, asserting that the Chinese Civil War "must still be decided, as almost all Chinese agree, by a final victory of one side or the other." And it maintained that the United States was involved in that civil war. "These acts of help on our part," the statement argued, "however 'defensive' they are intended to be, can never be 'peaceable.'" But the statement did not stop at this. By a clever use of quotation marks around common expressions such as "live and let live," and "understanding" and "respect" for your enemies, the statement implied without saying so that these were the words of the speech—and so made it appear to advocate, not a policy of firmness combined with flexibility, but a policy of softness and cowardly accommodation. And the threat was unequivocal: ". . . when Government representatives publicly present views contrary to announced policy," the statement read, "such action must either be considered irresponsible or an indication of a change in policy. Either way, the American people and their Congress must take whatever action is appropriate."

The *National Review* and other right-wing publications joined the attack. The New York *Daily News,* for example, said that President Chiang had a huge army ready to "go roaring back to mainland China, whence he was driven in 1949 by the Reds with important help from U. S. State Department stupes-if-nothing-worse. Why not let Chiang get going?" From the left some of the more ardent liberals were also critical —as was also expected. Advocating the immediate recognition of Communist China, they objected that the speech had not gone far enough.

But most of the editorial opinion was favorable. "Wholly realistic," said the *Arkansas Gazette;* "lucid and thoughtful" from Edward P. Morgan of ABC; "sound policy" from the St. Louis *Post Dispatch;* "wise and useful" from the Des Moines *Register;* and "refreshing" were typical comments. The conservative Boston *Herald* said the China problem was "brilliantly set forth" and that the policy was "clearly the right position." Other conservative papers with favorable comments were the Toledo *Blade,* the Chicago *American,* and the Philadelphia *Bulletin.* By January 24, we had counted twenty-one editorials from papers throughout the country—fifteen praising the speech, three attacking it from the right, and three attacking it from the left.

J. Kenneth Galbraith summed up the domestic reaction very neatly in a single comment. Popping into my office one day, he said, "I've been reading stacks of editorials and I want you to know that I represent a committee of *ten* million. It was a great speech." And he was out the door.

Abroad, quite naturally, the editorials from the newspapers of our friends and allies were overwhelmingly favorable—almost unanimously so. There were, in fact, only two countries from which the editorial comment was uniformly bad—Communist China and Nationalist China, neither of which wanted to see any easing of the civil war.

There were three comments we particularly valued. One was from Harriman when de Gaulle recognized Communist China. "Thank God for that statesmanlike speech," he said. "It got us a little bit off the rug before de Gaulle jerked it from under us entirely." Another was from Joseph Kraft, who referred to the speech in one of his columns as "an opening to the future." The third was a letter from Theodore H. White, author of *Thunder out of China.* "Off and on for the past twenty years, as you know," White wrote, "China has been my central interest in foreign policy; I've read all the statements going back beyond the days of Stanley K. Hornbeck [head of Far Eastern Affairs in the thirties]. This one is not only good. It will pick up an echo with the years . . ."

But gratifying though all this was, it was only the beginning of the beginning. Max Freedman summed it up as an "effort to break through old taboos and to discuss relations with China in the same responsible spirit that marks the discussion of other problems." And he went on to express the hope we all shared, that "slowly a debate on China can take place . . ." For Communist China and the United States in the years since World War II had somehow gotten on a collision course that could bring disaster to both. In the words of the quotation that began these chapters on China, "And, as the 20th Century moves toward the 21st . . . the United States will have with China a great nuclear war, unless far-reaching accommodations have been worked out sooner . . ."

NOTES

[1] See Harry Gelman, "The Sino-Soviet Conflict: A Survey," in *Problems of Communism,* March–April 1964, Vol. XIII; and Donald S. Zagoria, *The Sino-Soviet Conflict, 1956–1961;* Princeton, 1962, on both of which I have drawn heavily.

VIII

INDONESIA, MALAYSIA, AND CONFRONTATION

"The weak who know how to play on their weakness are strong. This is the secret of women, and of the developing nations."

—MAURICE COUVE DE MURVILLE,
Foreign Minister of France

CHAPTER 25

Indonesia and the New Nationalism

THE LAST TIME I saw President Kennedy was the evening of November 20, 1963; he left the next morning for Texas. That meeting was on Cambodia, which had just terminated the American aid program; the evening before we had met on Indonesia and its "confrontation" with Malaysia. In looking back, it seems symbolic that President Kennedy's attention those last few days of his life was focused not on Communism and the Cold War, but on the looming problems of the new nationalisms, which both Sukarno's Indonesia and Sihanouk's Cambodia typified. For beyond the immediate threat of Communist expansionism the most portentous development of our time is probably the direction which the new nationalisms will take, especially in Asia. And of all Americans, President Kennedy had acquired a stature with the peoples of the emerging nations that was unique.

Certainly there could be no doubt by 1961 of the importance of these developments for the United States. Asia is a great arc—from Japan and Korea in the north, down through China, the salient of Southeast Asia and the great islands of the Philippines and Indonesia lying across the routes from the China Sea to the Indian Ocean, and on down to the subcontinent of India and Pakistan. In that great arc live one-half of the world's peoples. In terms of population, two of the nations in this arc of Asia, India and China, are the world's largest. Three others—Indonesia, Pakistan, and Japan—rank fifth, sixth, and seventh. In economic terms, the potential at least is comparable. Indonesia alone, when its resources are developed, will become the third or fourth richest nation in the world. Writing of the American character in 1834, Alexis de Tocqueville said of Americans that "the better to look after what they call their business they neglect their chief business, which is to remain their own masters." There could be no doubt that in every way—strategic, economic, and political—Asia would be an arena of decisions shaping America's fate and that part of America's chief business should be to continue to have a voice there.

When Kennedy took over it was clear that the events in Asia affecting our fate in the first instance would revolve around Communist China. But even as the Chinese Communist threat was rising, the force of the new nationalisms was also taking shape. The emerging peoples were stirring, and their achievement of national identity would release human energies so vast that the mind boggled at the attempt to imagine them. The teeming millions of Asia had been dormant, turned inward on themselves for millenniums. But the new nationalisms were calling forth their energies and organizing them. "More energy is released by the awakening of these new nations," President Kennedy said in his acceptance speech at Los Angeles, "than by the fission of the atom itself." But toward what goal these forces would be directed was in doubt.

If the new nationalisms took an aggressive turn, as German nationalism had done under Hitler or Japanese nationalism under the militarists, the world would face dreadful times. But if the new nationalisms moved into constructive channels, and these surging human energies were directed toward the tasks of development and peace, their potential for good was unlimited. For they were ample to build a world.

All this was apart from the Cold War, but the new nationalisms quite clearly had implications for the struggle with Communism. For the aspirations of the emerging world, President Kennedy pointed out, do not fit the Communist idea of world order.[1] The Communist vision, he went on to say, is of a monolithic world—"where all knowledge has a single pattern, all societies move toward a single model, and all problems and roads have a single solution and a single destination." The Communists see a world of gray uniformity, all nations with the same economic system, the same political system, the same political party. "No one can doubt," the President concluded, "that the wave of the future is not the conquest of the world by a single dogmatic creed but the liberation of the diverse energies of free nations and free men."

But the new nationalisms, clearly, had a hypnotic fascination for the Communists. The Communists seemed to understand that the new nationalisms were the mortal enemy of any ideology that aimed to make the world all the same and in its own image. They also understood that if the new nationalisms did move into constructive channels it would mark the end of Communist ambitions. For the Communists, the choices were only two. One choice was to capture the leadership of the new nationalism, as Ho Chi Minh and the Communists captured the leadership of the nationalist revolt against the French in Indochina. The other would be to steer the nationalist movements that they could not capture into collision with the West and the United States—as they tried to steer Indonesia into such a collision, first over the West New Guinea dispute and then through "confrontation" with Malaysia.

KENNEDY AND ASIA

If there could be no doubt of the importance of Asia to America's future, neither, by 1963, could there be any doubt that Kennedy had acquired impressive stature among Asians. It is difficult to convey the appeal that Kennedy had to the emerging peoples. But anyone who knew these peoples was conscious that his popularity was unrivaled in recent times by any other American since Roosevelt. I have often puzzled about how this had come about—trying, without sentimentality, to see how President Kennedy had managed it and how one might advise another President to go about building up a similar stature in the emerging countries. Partly, of course, it was the same sense of style and grace that appealed to so many Americans. Partly it was his youth. Partly it was his "New Frontier" call to get "America moving again," with its suggestion of revolutionary change. And both the youth of the Kennedy administration and its image of movement and change were confirmed in Asian eyes by Robert F. Kennedy's trip to Japan and Indonesia in early 1962, which was hugely successful. But although all these events contributed to the growth of President Kennedy's appeal in Asia, each reinforcing and accentuating the other, I think the principal source of his appeal was that he genuinely *cared* about the emerging peoples and that he had come truly to understand them and their aspirations.

His speech in 1957 on Algeria that criticized the French for not granting independence and the United States Government for its support of France probably marked the beginning. The speech reverberated around the world. It brought Kennedy much criticism from the administration and the State Department, accusations that he had irresponsibly attacked an ally and weakened the NATO alliance. But in the emerging countries there was at first surprise that there was a foreign policy voice, even an opposition senator, who really understood their deepest yearnings— and then a surge of hope. And each speech thereafter piled up fresh evidence of his understanding.

Seemingly little things also made their contribution. Before President Sukarno's visit to Washington in 1961, Kennedy remarked in conversation that when you considered things like CIA's support to the 1958 rebellion, Sukarno's frequently anti-American attitude was understandable. This remark seems somehow to have worked its way back to Sukarno, who found the generosity and understanding that prompted it confirmed when he met the President himself.

But most important of all in the growth of Kennedy's stature among the emerging peoples was that his action in foreign policy generally supported the words both of understanding and of peace—the Alliance for Progress, the 1962 Geneva agreement on Laos, the Cuban missile crisis, and the nuclear test ban treaty.

THE NEW NATIONALISM—AN ANALYSIS

The unique factor in Kennedy's appeal to the emerging peoples, in sum, was his understanding of them. But understanding was not easy.

Their leaders were tempestuous; they made violent speeches full of insulting remarks; and their demands were all too often preposterous. But understanding was possible, and it affected the kind of policies the United States pursued.

In Africa, as we saw in the Congo crisis, the leaders of the new nationalism—the radical nationalists—saw their greatest threat in "neocolonialism." The fear was shared in Asia. Most of the leaders in both Africa and Asia had had personally humiliating experiences in their young manhood. They all flinched under memories of discrimination or worse, and there was undoubtedly a genuine fear that their old colonial adversaries, clever as they were, might contrive some subtle way of continuing their domination. Many of these leaders were uneasy, for example, about the consequences of economic aid and the use of foreign technicians and even more uneasy about large-scale private investment. There was a genuine fear in Africa that the secession of Katanga, for example, was an attempt at "Balkanization" sparked by *Union Minière* and the Belgian colonists to break up the Congo into pieces too small to exist except as dependencies. In Indonesia, there was some measure of equally genuine fear that the new Malaysia was really a cloak for a continued British and Western presence and an instrument for Western domination of the area. Sukarno and the Indonesians, be it remembered, had incontrovertible proof that the 1958 rebellion had received air drops of equipment from planes based in Malaya and the Philippines, and that the CIA was behind this support. But even though some measure of fear was present in the assault on "neocolonialism," fear was probably less important than a determination to stand tall in the world, to be the equal of the old colonial masters in every way. It was, after all, the pride of nationalism that suffered the greatest humiliation from colonialism, the humiliation of a people being subjugated and treated as inferiors. True independence meant not only political self-government, but eradicating every last vestige of foreign presence and starting anew.

The need for a purging to achieve true independence is why the idea of struggle is so central to the new nationalism. Sukarno, for example, in his speeches endlessly repeated the theme of the necessity for struggle. "If, for example, at this moment," he said in one speech, "an angel were to descend from the heavens and say to me: . . . 'I shall grant you a miracle, to give the Indonesian people a just and prosperous society as a gift, as a present,' then I would reply: 'I don't want to be granted such a miracle, I want the just and prosperous society to be the result of the struggle of the Indonesian people.'" Ahmed Ben Bella, to give another example, is reported to have argued that Britain consciously and deliberately betrayed Nigeria by giving it independence on easy terms, knowing that this would preserve Nigeria's Englishness.[2]

All of this is also related to a search for identity, for nationhood, and the need these people have to feel that they are more than just a collection of tribes and villages. Basically the need is emotional, but it is also very practical. One of the fundamental problems of the emerging nations is to overcome the localism, the isolation of the different regions and provinces, the inward focus of the villages, the differences between tribes and regions. Ways must be found to concentrate power at the center to permit them to make and carry out decisions as a nation.[3] And nationalism provides the unifying identity.

There is an aspiration to see their countries developed economically—but not so much for what they would call materialistic reasons, a high standard of living and high consumption, as for reasons, again, of national prestige. It is not really automobiles and television sets they want, but the steel plants, factories, jet airlines, and all the rest that make a country strong and powerful and modern. They will more often than not sacrifice a project that contributes toward development for a short-term addition to prestige. The Indonesians in 1962, for example, signed a nineteen-million-dollar contract for jet airliners just a few months before they were forced to ask the United States for an emergency loan of seventeen million dollars for things that kept them alive. The jets were for the Garuda Indonesian Airways and were essential if Garuda was to stop losing money and meet the competition who had moved on from propeller type aircraft. But it was not economics that really made the jets so vital to the Indonesians—or that made having the Garuda airline itself so important—but nationalism.

For it is fundamental to these peoples' nationalisms, their fierce independence, their determination to look the rest of the world in the eye as equals, that they have the power and the prestige to give them a voice in the affairs of the world, a hand on the steering wheel of the planet.

"TROUBLESOME" DIPLOMACY

All of this makes the new nations noisy and troublesome. Their demands are strident, as we have said, and their methods reckless. Sukarno, a master practitioner of "troublesome" diplomacy, once argued that reckless measures are the only means that a new and weak nation has for attracting the attention of the great powers and making its needs and demands felt, and there is a point to his argument. I remember on one occasion I completely lost patience at what seemed one of Sukarno's more outrageous moves—banning trade with Singapore, trade which earned Indonesia the foreign exchange it had to have. Averell Harriman's reaction was different. He recalled that in the nineteenth century Britain would send a cruiser around to stand offshore whenever particularly difficult negotiations were in progress. "It may seem like cutting off your nose to spite your face," Harriman said, "but that's the only 'cruiser' the new nations have."

The leaders of the new nationalisms are themselves men of a different breed, men with a capacity for reaching and exciting the mass of the peoples that neither Asia nor Africa has seen before. In Asia, the traditional mandarin-type leader—a man like Chiang Kai-shek, or Ngo Dinh Diem, or Syngman Rhee—still commands respect and thus can hold tenaciously on to power. But the mandarin kind of leader stands above the mass of the people, aloof whether benevolent or tyrannical. Men like Sukarno or Sihanouk, on the other hand, reach out to the mass of the people with the doctrines of nationalism to excite and arouse. Sihanouk's own life, in fact, symbolizes the change. He was born a prince and ascended the throne. But he later abdicated to become an elected leader, basing his strength on the people. By the 1960s, what opposition he had was primarily within the old aristocracy and his own royal family.

Again, understanding this kind of leader is not easy. The United States, for example, hoped for such a leader in Vietnam—a man like Magsaysay of the Philippines, who defeated the Communist Hukbalahap guerrilla rebellion, a man who could fire the peasants against the Communist Viet Cong guerrillas. But it was clear that if such a leader did arise in Vietnam recognizing him would take not only insight and wisdom on the part of the United States but a great deal of forebearance as well. For such a leader would undoubtedly come out of one of the movements that caused so much turmoil in Saigon, from the Buddhists, the students, or the "young Turks" in the army, all of which were representative of the new nationalism. Thus the new leader would necessarily be antiforeign, and he would talk and act as anti-American as he could without actually denying himself American support. His policies would necessarily be reminiscent of "neutralism" in the sense that they would be designed to rid Vietnam of *all* foreign influence, non-Communist as well as Communist. The new leader, in fact, would in all probability have most of the attributes that so many Americans found disquieting in the militant political priest, Tri Quang, who—significantly—made a point of understanding no language at all except Vietnamese.

U.S. POLICY

There was always a danger that the Communists could capture the leadership of one or another of these new nationalisms. But there was an even greater danger that the Communists could lead the new nationalisms into a grand alliance with the Communists against the West even though they failed to convert them to Communism. Kennedy was not sentimental about these peoples or their flamboyant leaders. He recognized that they would be troublesome, that their ambitions would get out of bounds, and that there would be times of tension in which policies of stringent firmness would be inevitable. But he spoke of a "world of diversity" in which each nation could develop its own full potential peaceably, preserving and cultivating the essence of its own culture and way of life. Those of us who were dealing with these problems in his administration understood these to be his general guidelines. The effort to project oneself into the other fellow's position, to develop an understanding of the new nationalisms should be made. The United States, where it could without injury to other interests and with regard to our own friends and obligations, should try to find a way to provide the new nationalisms all the help we could in developing economically, in assuming the responsibility that was rightfully theirs for maintaining peace in their own region, and in finding the voice in world affairs to which they were entitled. Our purpose, in a word, was to help them achieve their legitimate aspirations. But it was also recognized that this would be a difficult and long road, testing patience and understanding again and again. For these were tempestuous movements and demanding leaders, as I say, and they would inevitably experiment with troublesome methods and excessive demands—which would require policies of firmness as well as understanding.

But it was clearly worth all the effort. If the West and the United States did develop the necessary understanding and succeeded in helping the new nationalisms into constructive channels, the benefits would be overwhelming. It would mark the end of Communist ambitions, as President Kennedy said. It would mark the beginning of the end of poverty in the world and the start of a bright new life for all the world's oppressed. It would mark the beginning of an era in which the emerging peoples came to assume more and more of the responsibilities for peace in their own regions and in the world.

INDONESIA AND SUKARNO

In Indonesia by 1961, when the Kennedy administration came in, Sukarno was firmly in the saddle. A colorful figure of boundless energy, Sukarno like other revolutionary leaders had a vivid, earthy command of the vernacular and could arouse crowds to peaks of emotion. He had a fondness for coining words like *"nekolim"*—for "neocolonialist imperialism." But he also had a talent for expressing ideology in terms a villager could understand—dismissing Jeffersonian democracy, for example, as "fifty percent plus one" and holding up his own concept of "guided democracy" as an extension of the traditional village decision-making process of discussion and consensus which achieved not "fifty percent plus one" but unanimity. Sukarno also delighted his crowds, clowning with accompanying dignitaries, and joking with them from the platform—even making somewhat vulgar references to his international reputation as a lady-killer. On one occasion, for example, he announced that he had "gone to bed early last night, but not to sleep."

But Sukarno was more than a speech-maker and rabble-rouser. He, more than any other single leader, could take credit for helping to bring about Indonesian independence and for welding the disparate elements of Indonesia into one nation. And the nation was disparate. The hundred million Indonesians are of Malay stock, but there are wide differences in language and customs, and even in skin color, as, for example, between the lighter Javanese and the darker Sumatrans. Buddhism had once been strong in Indonesia, and so had Hinduism. Then came Islam, which had already begun its conversion of Indonesia by the time of Marco Polo's visit in 1292; and since that time it has spread to cover the whole of the nation with only a few exceptions, such as Bali.

In his sixties at the time of the Kennedy administration, Sukarno had been one of the organizers of the Indonesian Nationalist Party in the 1920s and a principal in the struggle for independence. The Dutch had arrived in the sixteenth century, and, except for a brief period in the early 1800s when the British occupied Java, they had steadily expanded their occupation throughout the islands, including Bali, which they occupied in 1906. The Communist Party of Indonesia was organized following World War I, and it staged a rebellion in the 1920s, which the Dutch put down with savage brutality. It was in the wake of this rebellion that a group of young students, including Sukarno, organized the Nationalist Party.

The Japanese occupation during World War II gave the Nationalists their real opportunity, and they saw it early. An ancient prediction, dating from the period of Kadiri, an early kingdom, was revived and repeated endlessly throughout World War II—that "a white buffalo will come to rule Java, and will remain for a long time; he will be supplanted by a yellow monkey, who will remain only for the lifetime of the maize plant; then, after a period of chaos, Java will come back to its own people."[4] Sukarno and the others of the Nationalist movement co-operated with the Japanese and used the opportunity to become known to the Indonesian public and to create the political organization that was used after the war to fight the Dutch. This included an army which was recruited and trained by the Japanese for their own purposes but was converted to the cause of nationalism. Even before the war was over, Sukarno had made his famous speech laying out the ideological foundations for an independent Indonesian nation. These were the *Pantja Sila,* or "five principles"—nationalism; internationalism or "world familyhood"; *Mufakat,* a sort of town-meeting democracy through discussion and consensus; social justice; and belief in God. Although a Westerner might find these five principles a rather meaningless collection of abstractions, they had an electrifying effect on the Nationalist movement. "Probably in no other exposition of principle," one authority wrote, "can one find a better example of the synthesis of Western democrat, modernist Islamic, Marxist, and indigenous-village democratic and communalistic ideas which forms the general basis of the social thought of so large a part of the post-war Indonesian political elite."[5] A measure of the Indonesian's attitude is that they thought it completely appropriate that in 1960 during an address to the General Assembly, Sukarno should quite seriously propose that the *Pantja Sila* be incorporated into the Charter of the United Nations.

Independence was proclaimed on August 17, 1945, after an all-night meeting at Sukarno's house in Djakarta, and there followed a chaotic four years of fighting interspersed with negotiations until 1949, when the Dutch agreed to transfer sovereignty over all of the Dutch East Indies— except West New Guinea.

Next came a period of experimentation with parliamentary democracy, with Sukarno as President.[6] Government succeeded government with bewildering rapidity. None dealt effectively with the problems facing the new country or moved toward the goal of true nationhood, and Sukarno intervened whenever he could do so successfully from his position as President. By 1957, Sukarno was openly advocating constitutional changes to bring about presidential government and what he later called "guided democracy." Then, in 1958 came the rebellion. And what gave the issue its politically cutting edge was the threat that the rebellion really signaled the return of the "colonial imperialists." For soon the rebels began to get outside help parachuted in by planes based in Malaya and the Philippines, and shortly after that the Indonesians acquired evidence that one source of the help was the CIA.

When the army, under Nasution, put down the rebellion successfully, its prestige and political power rose accordingly. Meanwhile, the Communists, too, increased their influence. Pursuing a "national front" strategy, they demonstrated in the elections of 1957 their capacity to give Sukarno the organized mass support which he needed and which he could not himself provide, since he had neither a political organization of his own nor the stomach for the long, tedious work it would take to build one.

And so there came a new political balance in Indonesia. The army needed Sukarno, with his towering appeal to the mass of the people, as a leader and as a symbol of national unity. The Communist Party also needed Sukarno, not as a leader and symbol, but as a protection against the army and to give them the legitimacy they required and the time to perfect their organization in the provinces and the villages. Sukarno, at the apex, needed the army to balance the Communists, and he needed the Communists to organize his mass following and to balance the army. Thus in 1959, the arrangement was formalized: Sukarno proclaimed the establishment of "guided democracy" and reintroduced the Constitution of 1945, providing for presidential rather than parliamentary government.

Sukarno was now firmly in the saddle. But he was not a dictator in the usual sense, even though in some matters he had dictatorial powers. His mass appeal was in the Southeast Asia tradition of the "just prince" or "God-king," although based on the ideology of the new nationalism. He did not have a party organization through which control could be exercised nor, as mentioned above, the stomach for the labor of creating one. Yet each of the two other major political forces, the army and the Communist Party, did have hierarchical organizations of control. The one balanced the other, and Sukarno, the army, and the Communist Party became what one observer called a "coalition of mutually dependent but antagonistic partners."[7]

Thus in Indonesia, the problem of political stability and the more fundamental problem of concentrating and focusing sufficient power at the center to achieve nationhood and to make and carry out national decisions had been solved for the immediate future in the form of a flamboyant personality who was both mass leader and consummate politician, believing in the new nationalism but at the same time manipulating all its symbols—the determination to be truly independent, to be powerful, to have a voice in world affairs. But although Sukarno will probably never be surpassed for sheer skill in manipulating these forces, it was the new nationalism itself that was the driving force of Indonesia, the source of its internal political organization and stability, of its view of itself, of its mass appeal to its own people, and of the compromise among the centers of power and the disparate regions.

The implications for policy are obvious. Sukarno's personality, his notoriously blatant pursuit of women, his vanity, his Marxist verbiage, his troublesome policies, his anti-Westernism and anti-Americanism, even his disregard for balanced budgets—all these traits were offensive to people in the West (as well as to many Indonesians), and no other Asian leader aroused so much personal animosity with the possible exception of the coldly arrogant Krishna Menon. Many people in the West and in Indonesia longed for Sukarno's departure, thinking that Indonesia would itself then change and no longer be a problem to the world. If it was indeed Sukarno, the man, who was the principal driving and unifying force, then once he departed Indonesia might well turn to other goals. But if the true driving force was the new nationalism, and Sukarno expressed that nationalism truly even though he was to many of his fellow Indonesians a flamboyant, egocentric exaggeration of it, then the change would not be as fundamental as his opponents in the West hoped. Sukarno would be replaced by men who shared the values of nationalism, even though they might be wiser and less dramatic, and the basic thrust of Indonesian aspirations would remain the same even though the methods became more responsible and less troublesome.

WEST NEW GUINEA

The Indonesians had never ceased clamoring for the transfer of West New Guinea—or West Irian, as they called it—and now that political unity and purpose had been at least temporarily established, they set about to force the Dutch to turn over this last piece of the old Netherlands East Indies to the new Indonesia. On August 17, 1960, the fifteenth anniversary of the 1945 declaration of independence, Sukarno announced that Indonesia was breaking off diplomatic relations with the Netherlands.

The motive, again, was pride of nationalism, the determination to be recognized as a power in the world, and, especially, "to complete the revolution," to tie the last bow on true nationhood. Some Westerners assumed that Sukarno needed a foreign adventure to attract attention away from economic difficulties at home and to permit him to take repressive measures against his domestic political enemies. Others thought the motive was simply Indonesian imperialism, or Sukarno's own grandiose dreams of empire, especially since the Papuans, the inhabitants of New Guinea, are a black people not even kin to the Indonesians. Some Asians, on the other hand, suggested that Indonesian motives sprang from the need to deny the Dutch a base from which they could launch an attack and re-establish their old colony. But none of these theories is very persuasive. There was no doubt that administering a defeat to the old colonial masters would be immensely satisfying to the Indonesian nationalists, and Sukarno would of course make the most of any victory he could achieve. But it is wishful thinking to believe that the principal motive was Sukarno's need to attract attention away from domestic difficulties. Although this effect was not unwelcome, it was not the cause. It is also true that Indonesian territorial ambitions could feed on success until they became grandiose beyond imagination, but there is no evidence that such ambitions were a principal motive at that time. And although there may have been some fear of the Dutch using West New Guinea as a base among less sophisticated Indonesians, the leaders certainly no longer feared that the Dutch could successfully return. All the evidence, in sum, points to the pride of nationalism. West New Guinea had been a part of the Netherlands East Indies, to which Indonesia was the successor state, and if the Indonesians failed to wrest every remnant of the old Indies from the colonialists, then they had failed in nationhood.

Breaking relations accomplished nothing but to dramatize Indonesian determination to secure the transfer of West New Guinea and to emphasize that Indonesia had decided the time had come to begin its campaign. What they needed now was international political support and concrete help in building up their military strength. Sukarno planned a world tour to garner political support, and, in the meantime, General Abdul Haris Nasution, a hero of the revolution and head of the Indonesian armed forces, visited Washington in a search for arms aid. His visit was fruitless, and he then went on to Moscow, where he found the Soviets more forthcoming. They signed a 400-million-dollar agreement with Indonesia in January of 1961, just before Kennedy took office—an installment on credit for arms that eventually came to a total of over one billion dollars. The Dutch countermove was to announce a ten-year program to prepare West New Guinea for self-government, and the battle was joined.

KENNEDY AND SUKARNO

The Kennedy administration in the months following its inauguration remained aloof from the West New Guinea dispute, but began a series of modest steps toward improving Indonesian-American relations. In 1958, the United States had changed ambassadors. It is not clear whether the change was merely coincidental or was related to the failure of the 1958 revolt, which was becoming obvious, and the evidence the Indonesians were acquiring that the CIA had given it support. In any case, the new man, Howard P. Jones, decided that the nature of Indonesian nationalism had not been correctly understood. He recommended a change in policy, of which the key element was supplying arms to the Indonesian armed forces, designed both to head off the Communists and to strengthen the responsible elements of the new Indonesian society. The Eisenhower administration had accepted this recommendation, and in the intervening two years Jones had been hugely successful in establishing a warm personal relationship with Sukarno, who regarded Jones as one of the few Westerners who really understood him and Indonesia. Washington, however, was less responsive to Jones' subsequent recommendations, and something had to be done to convince the Indonesians that the new administration sincerely wanted to improve relations.

But there were obstacles. The biggest was Allen Pope, an American pilot who had been shot down on May 18, 1958, flying a B-26 bomber for the rebels, for the Indonesians had evidence that Pope was an employee of the CIA. In the days immediately following Pope's capture the Eisenhower administration had taken several steps that worked to give Indonesia an incentive to play down the Pope case—authorizing the sale of rice for Indonesian currency, for example, and lifting an embargo on shipment of small arms and other military equipment. Although the Indonesian military authorities still held a press conference exhibiting the evidence of Pope's connection with the CIA, they postponed his trial for nineteen months. When it was finally held, in April of 1960, Pope was charged with bombing a village as well as military targets, and the sentence was death. But the sentence had not yet been carried out when Kennedy came into office and clearly the first step in improving relations was to convince Sukarno and the Indonesians that something would have to be done about Pope. For the public outcry in the United States if he was executed would make any real improvement in relations extremely difficult.

Ambassador Jones pointed out that Sukarno was a personal leader who had often said that personal relations were as vital in international politics as in domestic. He had made a state visit to meet Eisenhower in 1956 and had been hurt and outraged at the snub when Eisenhower pointedly omitted a return visit to Indonesia during his tour of the Far East in 1960. Jones strongly advised that Kennedy invite Sukarno to visit the United States, and within a month of taking office, he did so.

The meeting went well. Kennedy recognized the politician and dedicated nationalist in Sukarno, while Sukarno came away with a growing sense of Kennedy's statesmanship and his empathy for the striving peoples of the world. Nothing concrete was accomplished, but the meeting did make Kennedy feel that although it would be difficult to steer Sukarno and Indonesian nationalism into constructive channels it was not impossible.

Accordingly, Kennedy found an opportunity to praise the new Indonesian eight-year economic development plan. He then appointed a team of economists under Professor D. D. Humphrey, of Tufts University, to study how the United States might help—a clear indication both that the United States thought that Indonesian nationalism could be nudged into constructive channels and that the United States was willing to help with economic aid. And plans were laid for Attorney General Robert F. Kennedy to include Indonesia on the trip he was planning to make to the Far East in early 1962—for the Indonesians would not miss the significance of a visit by the President's brother and close adviser.

THE THRUST FOR WEST NEW GUINEA

In the meantime, Sukarno was making his effort to gain international political support for his claim to West New Guinea. Chou En-lai visited Indonesia in March 1961, and on April 1 he signed an amity agreement backing the Indonesian claims. Sukarno, on his world tour, signed another pact in Moscow on June 10, which provided the Indonesians more credits for Soviet arms, and two days later the Soviet Union announced that it, too, backed the Indonesian claim. Sukarno went on to Belgrade, where he negotiated still another agreement for military equipment.

And on his return to Indonesia, Sukarno watched the shipments of arms arrive and made increasingly belligerent speeches. "For years," he said, "we practiced a policy of 'friendly persuasion' toward the Dutch . . ." but now, he went on, Indonesia was turning toward "another method."

And things began to go the Indonesians' way. The original trouble over West Irian started during the negotiations for Indonesia's independence in 1949, when a last-minute disagreement over its status developed. Rather than endanger the whole agreement, since all the other major issues had been settled, both sides agreed to take up the problem of West New Guinea separately, with both sides also committed to settling it within one year. But the Dutch stubbornly resisted all pressures—from every quarter—even to begin negotiations. Actually, there is reason to believe that Dutch public opinion had long since begun to shift away from this intransigence, but Dr. Joseph Luns, long-time foreign minister of the Netherlands, was on this issue the most stubborn Dutchman of them all. And he kept his government in line. It was not until 1960, eleven years after the original agreement, that Luns came up with an alternative to continuing West New Guinea as a colony—and this was for transferring it to a UN trusteeship looking toward an eventual goal of independence. It was concerning this plan that the Indonesians got their first break, and things began to go in their direction. For in the autumn of 1961, the UN General Assembly rejected the Luns Plan and the whole idea of UN trusteeship as a possible solution to the problem.

The Netherlands were now faced with a distasteful dilemma. It was clear even to foreign observers that the Dutch public would not support a war in the jungles to preserve a colony in New Guinea. On the other hand, both the government and people of the Netherlands detested Sukarno and recoiled from giving in to his demands. What Sukarno needed to push the Dutch into negotiations was pressure from friends and world opinion, and he devised a cunning scheme to conjure it up. On December 19, 1961, Sukarno issued a proclamation of national mobilization—calling it with typical rhetoric the "People's Triple Command for the liberation of West Irian" or "Trikora" for short. And he followed it up, not only with the bustle of mobilization, but by sending out patrol boats and air transports to land and parachute token guerrilla groups inside West Irian itself.

It was a shrewd move. United States policy was to preserve its friendly relations with both the Netherlands and Indonesia by maintaining a passive neutrality. President Kennedy, for example, in response to a question in April 1961, had said that it was "difficult" for the United States even to offer its good offices unless it was asked by both parties.[8] Yet passive neutrality on the part of the United States—and this was also true of the United Nations—inevitably favored the *status quo* and thus the Dutch. The spectacle of the Soviet Union and the other Communist countries supplying Indonesia with a billion dollars of military arms and equipment and the increasing Communist influence that was the logical resultant of this aid had given the United States cause to worry about the wisdom of continuing this policy of passive neutrality. But the prospect of war between Indonesia and the Netherlands made it even worse. And although the possibility of increased Communist domination might not worry some members of the UN, the possibility of war most certainly did.

Both the Secretary General and President Kennedy appealed to Sukarno for moderation and urged both Indonesia and the Netherlands to turn to negotiations. In replying to President Kennedy, Sukarno begged the United States, in effect, to abandon its policy of passive neutrality and to take positive measures to bring the Dutch to accept negotiations. And he repeated that, given the long history of the West Irian dispute and the political position he now found himself in, he could not long avoid the use of force. The Indonesian Ambassador to Washington, in fact, stepped out of diplomatic channels by urging reporters to carry the word that the United States should step in to mediate before it was too late.[9]

It is true enough that Sukarno found himself in a difficult political position. But he had deliberately created it, and he now took one more step to put himself on the brink and burn the bridges on the road that took him there: he announced to the Indonesian people that West Irian would be returned before the end of the new year, 1962.

U.S. POLICY

But a shift in policy from passive neutrality to one of pressing actively for negotiations was not easy for the United States. The Kennedy administration took pride in its sympathy and understanding for the emerging nations, but the American friendship for the Netherlands was old and treasured. It was also intimately interconnected with the problems of NATO and the defense of Europe, and this was at a time when the Soviet Union was renewing its threats on Berlin. Thus the power line-up in the United States and Washington was tricky. As far as the general public was concerned, the principal fact was a massive lack of knowledge or understanding of either Indonesia or its peculiar brand of the new nationalism, and this lack of knowledge was covered over with a thick crust of understandable indifference. Indonesia is a long way away from the United States, and many much more severe problems were practically on our doorstep. About all that came through to the mass of the American public were the anti-American barbs in Sukarno's more flamboyant speeches. The net result was a vague impression among most Americans that Sukarno's Indonesia was an anti-American, Communist or crypto-Communist dictatorship.

Even among the "attentive publics" and the well informed, in the press, in the academic world, and in Congress, knowledge of Indonesia was superficial at best. The hard-liners in the press and Congress, thinking back over the experience with Castro, were inclined to take Sukarno's pro-Communist statements as an indication that he might willingly take his country into the Communist orbit. As a minimum, they saw Sukarno as a belligerent adventurer who had to be taught a sharp lesson quickly, before his appetite grew gargantuan. Arthur Krock, for example, called the idea of a transfer of West New Guinea to Indonesia "a triumph of annexation by aggression." And Senator Dodd at the height of the crisis said that those who favored ceding West New Guinea to Indonesia did not appreciate the "strategic significance" of the territory and "that in turning over control of this territory to President Sukarno we are turning it over to a government which, of all the governments in the non-Communist world, risks, perhaps, the greatest chance of falling to Communism before the decade is out." Congressman William S. Broomfield, a member of the House Foreign Affairs Committee who aspired to the position of foreign policy leadership among Republicans so long occupied by Representative Walter Judd of Minnesota, thought that in opposition to Indonesia he had an issue that might give him that leadership. In Broomfield's view, Sukarno was a power-mad dictator, and at one time or another Broomfield, speaking on the floor of the House, called Sukarno a "despot," a "bully," a "Hitler," and an "international juvenile delinquent." Broomfield's goal in time became to cut American aid down to the barest minimum and to press for a hard line of policy that would stop just short of forcing a break in diplomatic relations.

The Republicans on Capitol Hill, in fact, were easy enough to recruit to the hard line. Although there had been a traditional interest in Asia among congressional Republicans, the identification had been, not with revolutionary movements, but with the mandarin-type leaders—Chiang Kai-shek and Syngman Rhee. Opposition also came from those who saw Europe as the center, not only congressmen but newspaper columnists like Krock and William S. White. And Europe was under immediate threat—Soviet pressure on Berlin was at a peak. In addition, those who saw Europe as the center also saw NATO as the bulwark against these pressures. The policy implication was that dissension within NATO should be avoided even at the cost of supporting the Dutch in their most intransigent posture and alienating Indonesia completely.

Within the Executive Branch itself, the line-up was unusual and interesting. What was most unusual was the position of the Pentagon. In colonial questions concerning Africa, the Pentagon would usually side with the "Old Europe" view. The Azores base was vital to the logistical support of NATO, and Portugal was so sensitive about the implications for their own colony of Angola of any anticolonial stance by the United States that the Pentagon feared the Azores base would be jeopardized. But when it came to Indonesia, the Pentagon's attitude was different. Indonesia did not represent any direct military threat: it simply did not have the military power in being. Its geographic location, off the salient of Southeast Asia, also removed it from the arena of East-West confrontation. To the extent that the Pentagon exercised its influence, in fact, it tended to be on the side of emphasizing the friendliness side in a policy of "firm friendliness." The reason was that the Pentagon had an opportunity to develop an understanding of Indonesia through two major aid projects.

One of these projects was a civic action program designed to use Indonesian military units on civic projects—rehabilitating canals, draining swampland to create new rice paddies, building bridges and roads, and so on. This civic action program was particularly important to the Indonesian military, for it enabled them to justify maintaining a large army in peacetime and also to develop popular support among the peasantry —both of which the army would need when the showdown with the Communists finally came, as they all fully expected would be inevitable.

The second project was a training program which had gone on for a number of years. It had gone on long enough, in fact, so that one-third of the Indonesian general staff had had some sort of training from Americans and almost half of the officer corps. As a result of both the civic action project and the training program, the American and Indonesian military had come to know each other rather well. Bonds of personal respect and even affection existed, as a matter of fact, that gave the Pentagon an understanding of Indonesian motives and aspirations that was better than any other agency in Washington.

Thus paradoxically, opposition to a shift from passive neutrality in the West New Guinea dispute centered in the State Department. On the question of Indonesia, the "Old Europe" group, supported by strong voices inside the CIA, were decisive. Chester Bowles, Mennen Williams, and others who were fighting for a more sympathetic policy toward the emerging nations, thought of India, Africa, and Latin America as having higher priority, and they had their hands full in any case. And the Far Eastern Bureau, weakened in the McCarthy era, lacked the strong leadership that it would have to have to carry weight in Washington.

And so matters stood throughout the spring, summer, and early fall of 1961. Then came the "Thanksgiving Day Massacre" that shifted Bowles to Ambassador at Large, promoted George Ball to Under Secretary, brought Walt Rostow, Frederick Dutton, and Richard Goodwin over from the White House—and put Averell Harriman into the job of Assistant Secretary of State for Far Eastern Affairs.

Vigorous, tough, wise, experienced, exercising political power in his own right as already described, Harriman was just what the Far Eastern Bureau most needed. At seventy, he put youth and vigor into the bureau —he demanded new ideas and bit off the heads of old ones with cantankerous impatience. He had personal prestige and power; he knew how to use it; and he understood the new nationalisms intuitively, both the need for firmness when their ambitions soared and the equal need to provide them an honorable alternative. Shortly after he took over someone on a TV show asked him something about "that Communist, Sukarno." At his crocodile best, Harriman snorted back, "He is *not* a Communist, he's a nationalist!" and earned the respect of half of Asia. The balance of power in the State Department promptly shifted, and United States policy began to move from "passive neutrality" to a more active role in trying to head off actual hostilities and in bringing the two disputants into face-to-face negotiations.

ENTER ROBERT F. KENNEDY

And so it was that Robert F. Kennedy's trip to Japan, Indonesia, and Berlin took on a new meaning, and at least one additional stop—The Hague—was added.

Robert F. Kennedy carried a private message to President Sukarno (in the form of a letter from President Kennedy) and a public message to the people of Indonesia. The contents of both were about the same. In front of the students at the University of Indonesia in Djakarta, for example, when he was questioned about West Irian, Kennedy said, "We have been a friend of the Dutch for a long time and we have no apology to make for it. The Dutch were among the first to come and settle our country. They founded our biggest city, New York City, then called New Amsterdam . . .

"At the same time," he continued, "we have also had a close relationship with the people of Indonesia. We vigorously supported Indonesia's struggle for independence during the late 1940s . . . We feel that our best role can be played in trying to bring the government of Indonesia and the government of Holland—two close friends of the United States—together so that they can resolve this problem peacefully. That is the policy of the United States."

The students pushed Kennedy again, trying to get him to say that if Indonesia's demands were not met and it went ahead and used force the United States would side with the Dutch. Kennedy replied that he was hopeful negotiations would not break down but if they did the United States position would be determined by who was responsible for the breakdown. But by this time he had become impatient: "There is a good deal of criticism in Indonesia about the United States position on this matter. We have allies throughout the world, and we don't agree with everything that they do, and they don't agree with everything that we do. . . . You have disagreements among the various people that live here in Indonesia. But you don't suddenly say that they are disloyal, or that that shows that they are not for democracy, because you disagree with them. . . .

"There was a good deal of feeling in the United States," he continued, "that as Attorney General I shouldn't have come to Indonesia because of the incidents that have occurred here. But the President and the Administration and the vast majority of the American people felt that we should come and that we should try to make a greater effort to understand one another. And that is part of the role that I am playing here. But I also ask for some understanding on your part. This is not a one-way street, ladies and gentlemen."

There was a vigorous ovation; Kennedy's directness, his candor, and his obvious sincerity had won through.

And he did equally well with President Sukarno. They had several meetings and long hours of discussion, and they made real progress. Sukarno came to recognize in Robert Kennedy the same tough integrity and loyalty that he had seen in his brother, the President, combined with a true understanding of what the new nationalisms were really all about. Before Kennedy left Djakarta, President Sukarno and the Indonesian cabinet had agreed to drop their most onerous preconditions for negotiations.

Kennedy went on to Berlin, and then, finally, to The Hague, where, as he said, he "came up against a number of Dutch leaders who were as intransigent in their position regarding West New Guinea as were some of their opposite numbers in Indonesia."

But negotiations were finally started under UN auspices, with Ellsworth Bunker, one of the most experienced of American career diplomats and negotiators acting as mediator on loan to the UN for the purpose. They dragged on for months—the United Nations tried to increase its pressure on both sides. The United States did the same, and also offered carrots —in different forms—to each. But the Dutch were adamant, both in their refusal to compromise and their unwillingness to make the sacrifices necessary to maintain a "Dutch New Guinea." The Indonesians, on the other hand, were apparently willing to make sacrifices—in July they moved their forces into position for an invasion.

The threat of immediate invasion had an effect and a face-saving compromise was agreed upon, an arrangement under which West New Guinea was transferred first to UN jurisdiction and then to Indonesian, seven months later in May of 1963.

The Dutch were publicly unhappy. The Prime Minister himself in a speech to the nation said of the agreement, "We were forced into it against our will and against everything we honor." He did not mention the United States by name, but the implication was clear. "The Netherlands could not count on the support of its allies, and for that reason we had to sign."[10]

The Soviets—who had put up credits for a billion dollars' worth of arms in hopes of a war from which the Communists would benefit—were equally unhappy.

Even the Indonesians were not as happy as one might have expected. Although they had finally been able to "complete the revolution," there was some bitterness that it had cost them so much struggle to get what they regarded as rightfully theirs in the first place. They were disappointed that the United States had kept to the middle ground of calling for negotiations rather than openly forcing the Dutch to give in— although they did release the B-26 flyer, Allen Pope, as a good-will gesture. And they were generally confirmed in their suspicions that the "Old Established Forces" were still addicted to "colonialist imperialism." Sukarno himself was at least slightly disappointed that the agreement did not provide for the transfer of territory until after his deadline of the end of 1962. But he was able to announce that the agreement had been reached on the August 17 anniversary of the original Indonesian declaration of independence, and he added that with the completion of revolution, Indonesia's territorial aspirations had been fulfilled.

As for the United States, it had been castigated by both sides—by the Dutch for pushing them too hard and by the Indonesians for holding them back. The whole affair was dreary and disheartening. "We were not," as the Attorney General said wearily, "dealing with completely reasonable men on either side of this controversy."[11] But President Kennedy was convinced that avoiding war was "in the long-range interest of the free world, of our allies . . . [of] the Dutch and the Indonesians." "So the role of the mediator," the President went on to say, "is not a happy one, and we're prepared to have everybody mad, if it makes some progress."[12]

NOTES

[1] Charter Day Speech, University of California, Berkeley, California, March 23, 1962.
[2] Russell Warren Howe, "Would-Be Leader of the 'Third World,' " June 19, 1965.
[3] W. Howard Wriggins, "Political Development: Varieties of Political Change and U. S. Policy" in Roger Hilsman and Robert C. Good, eds., *Foreign Policy in the Sixties,* 1965.
[4] Bruce Grant, *Indonesia,* Melbourne, 1964, p. 6.
[5] George McT. Kahin, *Nationalism and Revolution in Indonesia,* 1952, p. 123.

6 For an account of this period, see Herbert Feith, *The Decline of Constitutional Democracy in Indonesia,* 1962.

7 Frederick P. Bunnell, "Indonesia's Foreign Policy in the 1960s: President Sukarno Moves from Non-Alignment to Confrontation," a paper prepared for the Asia Society's conference on "The Foreign Policies of the Southeast Asian States," May 14–15, 1965, and Herbert Feith, "Dynamics of 'Guided Democracy,'" in Ruth T. McVey, ed., *Indonesia,* 1963.

8 Press Conference, April 12, 1961.

9 Warren Unna, the Washington *Post,* December 20, 1961.

10 The New York *Times,* August 17, 1962.

11 Robert F. Kennedy, *Just Friends and Brave Enemies,* 1962, p. 134.

12 Press Conference, April 11, 1962.

CHAPTER 26

Confronttaion

INDONESIA was now at a crossroads. It had used the noisy techniques of "confrontation diplomacy," the forces of its nationalism, and the opportunities presented by the Cold War to play off the Great Powers against each other with impressive skill. It had brought about the transfer of West Irian and "completed the revolution." But even though its leaders had denied that Indonesia had any more territorial ambitions, there were still the other aspirations of its "new nationalism"—to be taken seriously, to have a voice in both regional and world affairs, to carve out a position in which they were respected for their power and their ability to influence events. They were skeptical that the "Old Established Forces" would be willing to accommodate to these aspirations unless they were forced to it—which is what the Indonesians felt they had learned in the West Irian business. They were now familiar with the techniques of "confrontation diplomacy," and those techniques had worked. Indonesia could continue down that path—waving the bloody shirt of nationalism. It could attempt to steer the "New Emerging Forces" into radical opposition to the "Old Established Forces," and, by showing the emerging nations the pathway to the fulfillment of their aspirations, it might even earn for Indonesia a position of leadership. The growing split between the Soviet Union and Communist China offered even more temptation—for the split presented Indonesia with an opportunity to play, not only the East off against the West, but Moscow against Peking, which lessened the risk of an association with Communist China.

But, as the Americans and others pointed out, there was an alternative. Indonesia, the American argument repeated, was the fifth largest nation in the world, and, if its natural resources were developed, the third or fourth richest. If Indonesia turned its attention and energies to economic development and began to realize this potential, its power and influence would rest on the solid basis of economic strength—and be unquestioned. With the forces of its nationalism channeled into constructive paths, Indonesia could be one of the principal architects of "Asian solutions" for Asian problems and a leading voice in regional associations which would soon acquire basic responsibility for the affairs of the region.

The first step in this alternative path would be an economic stabilization program. World War II, the struggle against the Dutch, the political instability and rebellions that followed, and the West Irian dispute had all taken their toll of the Indonesian economy. It was a shambles.[1] Roads, docks, and other elements of the transportation system were in need of repair. Only 50 per cent of the busses and trucks in Java were operational because of a lack of spare parts. The weaving industry was operating at half its capacity due to a shortage of yarn. In the whole nonagricultural sector of the economy, according to an official Indonesian report to the nation, production was running generally only between 25 and 35 per cent of capacity. Inflation was spiraling—by 1963 the amount of money in circulation had doubled over the previous year.

In a modern, industrialized state operating on a true money economy, these statistics would have spelled economic collapse. But not in Indonesia. All this had happened before. "But somehow," in the words of one observer, "the economy went on with sufficient ramshackle strength to maintain a population of 100 million."[2] The land is rich; rice grows well and bananas and other tropical fruit need only to be picked. Starvation is almost unknown, and few clothes are needed in such a balmy land. And so, when the economic statistics go down, people go back more and more to a barter economy. They eat less rice and more fruit. The nonmonetized, barter-type, village-based half of Indonesia's dual economy grows larger, and the monetized half, based on trade and manufacture, shrinks.

It was for all these reasons that Sukarno felt so little pressure to adopt an economic stabilization program—and it was for all these reasons that economic sanctions have had such slight effect in forcing Indonesia to abandon foreign policies of "confrontation." Thus the only incentive to adopt an economic stabilization program was the lure of development, of becoming a modern, industrialized, and powerful state.

The Indonesians had developed in early 1961 a grand plan for economic development covering an eight-year period and costing over five billion dollars, and they had applied to the International Monetary Fund for a loan of this basis. The Fund, in turn, laid down conditions that amounted to a program of economic stabilization. Then came the report of Professor D. D. Humphrey's mission, which President Kennedy had sent out. The Humphrey report was basically optimistic—concluding that, if Indonesia took the necessary steps toward stabilization, an aid program should be developed of between $325 million and $390 million over a five-year period, with $125 to $155 million being raised multi-nationally and $200 to $235 million coming from the United States.

The United States Government was under no illusions that the Indonesians thought of "noisy diplomacy" and economic stabilization as black and white alternatives. Any Indonesian nationalist, much less President Sukarno, would use the techniques of "noisy diplomacy" whenever those techniques best suited the goals at issue. And this would be especially true if a Western nation were opposing Indonesian aspirations in a situation that could be made to appear to be an issue of "neocolonialism" —in which one of the "Old Established Forces" seemed to be denying the rights of one of the "New Emerging Forces." For the Indonesians, quite clearly, the problem was not going to be whether they pursued one policy or the other, but just how they would mix the two policies. And from the United States point of view, the important thing was to get the Indonesians *started* on a program of economic stabilization and development and to try to persuade them to keep their "noisy diplomacy" at least a notch or two below the level that would make it impossible for the United States and the others to continue the program.

ENTER "MALAYSIA"

Sukarno had little taste for economic problems and even less interest in solving them. But under pressure from some of his principal ministers, he agreed that Indonesia should begin to move in the direction of economic stabilization and development. Then an accident of history presented a glittering opportunity for another adventure in "noisy diplomacy"—the formation of Malaysia.

Malaya had become independent on August 31, 1957, following the defeat of the postwar Communist guerrilla movement—but what was left out of the Malayan Federation was the 225-square-mile island of Singapore, a city of over one and a half million people and the natural center of trade and commerce for the whole Malayan peninsula. The problem was ethnic. The energetic, hard-working Chinese comprise over 35 per cent of the population of Malaya, while the easygoing Malays were 40 per cent. And in Singapore the Chinese numbered 75 per cent of the population. Singapore needed a hinterland just as much as Malaya needed a port, but if the two were combined the Chinese population would comprise 42 per cent of the new nation and the Malay population only 39 per cent. Pressed by their overcommitments around the world and especially east of Suez, the British came up with the idea of adding to the merger their three Borneo territories—North Borneo, Sarawak, and Brunei. This would swing the population balance back to give the Malays 41.5 per cent and the Chinese 38 per cent, with the rest divided among Indians, Pakistani, Ceylonese, Europeans, and tribal peoples. The Moslem extremists in Malaya were violently opposed to this scheme, and even the moderates had misgivings about the feasibility of incorporating into a new nation territories across so many hundreds of miles of ocean. But the Tunku Abdul Rahman agreed—in what has been suggested was in part an act of gratitude to the British. On May 27, 1961, he proposed that steps be taken to bring Malaya, Singapore, North Borneo,

Brunei, and Sarawak "closer together in political and economic cooperation."

In August of 1961, the British Commissioner General for Southeast Asia, Lord Selkirk, visited Indonesia to inform them of the plans for the new Malaysia, and the Indonesians seem to have accepted the notification without comment. The United States, too, was kept informed, although it was not until the fall of 1962 that United States support was actively sought and given. Shortly thereafter, in February 1963, President Kennedy, in response to a question at one of his news conferences, said, "We have supported the Malaysia Confederation, and it's under pressure from several areas. But I'm hopeful it will sustain itself, because it's the best hope of security for that very vital part of the world."

One of the pressures to which President Kennedy referred was from the Philippines. Macapagal, then President of the Philippines, had been pushing the Philippine claim to part of North Borneo since he had been a congressman. In the eighteenth century, the Sultan of Brunei had ceded part of his territory to the Sultan of Sulu, whose sovereign rights ultimately descended to the Republic of the Philippines. Although the British had indeed made payments to the Sultan of Sulu and his successors until 1936, the Philippine claim was tenuous at best. Most Philippine opinion, in fact, would probably have been satisfied with almost any procedure that indicated at least that the British were making an effort to placate Philippine nationalism. But the British treated the matter as an annoyance, unworthy of anything but an impatient rebuff.

ENTER DUNCAN SANDYS

In the opinion of some observers, much of the blame for this "bull-in-the-China-shop" treatment of the Philippines belonged to Great Britain's Minister of Commonwealth Relations, Duncan Sandys—as well as much of the credit for bringing Malaysia into being. Commenting on his appointment, the London *Economist* wrote on August 1, 1960, "His qualifications for handling the reputedly delicate if routine relations between Britain and the countries of the former empire are not obvious. Mr. Sandys is good where mountains of administrative work have to be moved, unpopular decisions fought through, complex legislation mastered, and brought to the statute book. He denationalized steel, radically reformed the Armed Services, induced the aircraft firms to merge. In no case did he become popular with the civil servants or those he dealt with; though if he inspired little love, he won respect. He worked till all hours, he made up his own mind; he thereafter proved immovable by argument or criticism. Is this what the Commonwealth needs?"

Sandys's reputation was that of an international "tough guy." He was not of the same intellectual caliber as his colleagues; he lacked in tolerance for others; and he had a notoriously quick temper.[3] "His countrymen," the London Sunday *Times* said on one occasion, "probably have many reasons to be grateful, but gratitude, warm and spontaneous, is rarely accorded to and probably not even expected by someone with the personality of Duncan Sandys." But Sandys did have a reputation for success in negotiations, although his methods, according to outside observers, were not to rely so much on persuasion as on battering away at his opposite numbers until the parties agreed out of "sheer weariness." In the talks leading to the plan for the formation of Malaysia, which Sandys conducted, for example, "He kept the delegates up all night, again and again, until they finally slumped together in blinking unity."[4] Perhaps the most charitable thing that can be said of Duncan Sandys's performance in the crisis of Indonesia's "confrontation" with Malaysia is that he lived up to his reputation.

But up to this point in time, the Indonesians saw neither the opportunity for a policy of confrontation nor any reason to cavil about the formation of Malaysia. On November 20, 1961, for example, when the Indonesian Foreign Minister, Dr. Subandrio, was presenting the Indonesian case for West Irian before the General Assembly, he said that the Indonesians were "not only disclaiming the territories outside the former Netherlands East Indies, though they are of the same island [New Guinea] but—more than that—when Malaya told us of her intentions to merge with the three British Crown Colonies of Sarawak, Brunei and British North Borneo, we told them that we have no objections and that we wish them success. . . . Naturally, ethnologically and geographically speaking, this British part [of Borneo] is closer to Indonesia than, let us say, to Malaya. But we still told Malaya that we have no objections to such a merger based upon the will for freedom of the peoples concerned."

THE BRUNEI REVOLT

But then there was a sudden revolt in Brunei, in North Borneo. Ironically, the Sultan of Brunei in the end refused to join the Malaysia federation, as the result of a dispute about oil revenues and about his relative rank among the other sultans of the new federation. But the revolt was really not related to the question of Malaysia. It was sparked by an exile rebel leader, Azahari, who had undoubtedly obtained some covert support from the Indonesians—partly, in all probability, to test the mood of the population in the British Borneo territories and partly in gratitude for the fact that Azahari and his group had supplied volunteers to help the Indonesians in their struggle for independence. The British put down the revolt in a matter of days, but it illustrated to the Indonesians that there was a revolutionary potential in the North Borneo territories that might make a policy of "confrontation diplomacy" a success.

There were some indiscreet statements from Kuala Lumpur about Indonesian involvement in the Brunei revolt that gave the Indonesians an excuse, and then an exchange of notes and protests. On January 8, 1963, President Sukarno denounced the concept of Malaysia; on January 21, Subandrio, the Indonesian Foreign Minister, declared a policy of "confrontation"; and on February 1, General Jani, Chief of the Army, said that the Indonesian armed forces were ready, awaiting only the order to move.

ECONOMIC STABILIZATION AND THE OIL AGREEMENTS OF 1963

But no order came—as yet—and under nudging from his own ministers and friendly ambassadors, Sukarno agreed to begin at least to move toward economic stabilization and development. In March, the government issued an "Economic Declaration," which was a serious effort to meet the conditions laid down by the International Monetary Fund and to outline a strategy of short-term stabilization so as to permit long-run development.

Indonesia needed foreign exchange; $225 million a year was required just to service the foreign debt piled up for arms and economic aid during both the independence fight and the struggle for West Irian—although the Indonesians were able to persuade Moscow and others to ease the terms and extend the time. The foreign exchange needs for development could only be met after this first $225 million was paid. Much of the foreign exchange earned went into imports that could probably be described as luxuries, but this, too, presented a dilemma. One of the peculiar problems of the developing countries is that inadequate administrative and tax-collecting techniques make it difficult for them to rely on income taxes or sales taxes and hence make them dependent for state revenue on taxes on imports. The vicious circle is that to get the revenue to start economic reforms, a country like Indonesia needs a high flow of imports. This means obtaining foreign exchange in the short run, which in turn interferes with the reinvestment needed to build up domestic industries and manufactures.

In May, the regulations implementing the Economic Declaration were put into effect. The amount of rice and other food that had been distributed at subsidized prices was sharply reduced, and the costs of various public services were increased. Bus fares, for example, were doubled; rail fares trebled; and postal, telegraph, and telephone charges quadrupled. The measures were naturally unpopular, and the PKI—the Communist Party of Indonesia—made the most of it, charging in particular that the regulations were really a monetary juggling demanded by the Americans as a condition for American aid. But the Indonesian Government seemed willing to take the pressure and push on.

Another key element in the whole economic equation was the foreign oil companies and the need for some sort of agreement that would permit them to continue to operate. Rubber was the biggest single earner of foreign exchange but oil was a close second, and Indonesia could not manage without the refining facilities and sales organization these companies provided. The three big oil companies, two American and one British, were Caltex, Stanvac, and Shell. Caltex alone took 230,000 barrels a day from the Sumatran oil fields, which are large even by the standards set by the fields of the Middle East. The total investment of the American oil companies since the war amounted to almost $500 million, and Shell's investment was even larger than this total. But it was not the investment, which had apparently been largely written off, that mattered most to the companies, but workable arrangements by which they could continue to handle the world marketing and continue to explore for further deposits.

Negotiations had been dragging on since 1960, when the Indonesian Government decreed that oil was "wealth which is controlled by the State" and transformed the oil companies into contractors working for the Indonesian Government. The oil companies had gone along, but there were much misunderstanding and suspicion on both sides and the negotiations had become more and more embittered. The Indonesians wanted a 60-40 split of the profits, to which the companies did not object. But the Indonesians demanded that this be on the posted price, which was usually higher than the realized price, and the companies would have none of that. Another aspect was whether the companies would pay Indonesian taxes and duties out of their remaining 40 per cent or *before* the 60-40 split. And there were also problems about the price the Indonesians would pay for the marketing and refining facilities they would acquire, and about how much hard currency the Indonesians would need—and the companies would supply—to permit them to operate the facilities once they were taken over.

In April of 1963, the Indonesians accused the companies of procrastinating and set a deadline of June 15—either negotiations would be completed or foreign oil operations would end. Shortly thereafter representatives of the oil companies paid a personal visit to Averell Harriman, as Under Secretary, and me, as Assistant Secretary for Far Eastern Affairs, to ask for advice and assistance. They underlined their sense of desperation by saying that they would rather close down in Indonesia than agree to the Indonesian demands, under which they felt they could not operate.

We wanted to do all we could to protect American investments in Indonesia. At the same time, viewed against the issues of war and peace, the possible loss of a major country to Communism, or the channeling of the new nationalisms into violence, even such large investments as these dwindled in importance. But there was also the other side of the coin—without the foreign exchange earned by oil exports, economic stabilization and development would be impossible for years, and the Indonesians could not sell in the non-Communist world without the help of the companies and their sales organization and distributing facilities. The only alternative would be the Communists, and specifically the Chinese. The Chinese were heavily dependent on Soviet oil, and as the Sino-Soviet dispute went to new heights of bitterness the thought of an alternative source for oil must have been tempting for the Chinese even though the high wax content of Indonesian oil would pose problems for their refining facilities. For all these reasons, political and strategic as well as economic, President Kennedy, Harriman, and I were determined to do all we could to bring about a successful conclusion to the oil negotiations.

It was obvious that some special effort had to be made to impress on President Sukarno and the Indonesians the seriousness of the situation and the many implications that would flow from a failure to reach an amicable settlement. But the point had to be made without any sense of threat, for if anything would make the sensitive Indonesians gladly bear the sacrifices of a failure of the oil negotiations, it would be an attempt to bully or threaten them. Harriman suggested that a special representative of the President be named to meet with Sukarno in Tokyo, where Sukarno would be visiting. This was important. For it was peculiarly relaxing for Sukarno to be in Tokyo, with its gaiety and personal associations and its freedom from the kind of pressures that the PKI were able to mount in Djakarta.

Kennedy agreed and named Wilson Wyatt, Lieutenant Governor of Kentucky and Stevenson's campaign manager in 1952, to be his representative. Ambassador Howard P. Jones was brought up from Indonesia to handle the high-level discussions with the Indonesians when the going got rough or key points needed clearance at high levels on the Indonesian side. Walter Levy, a professional consultant on oil matters and an old friend of Harriman's, Abram Chayes, legal adviser to the State Department; and Michael V. Forrestal, White House aide for Far Eastern Affairs, went along as members of the mission. It was an exercise in "preventive diplomacy." Abram Chayes later said, "We wanted not so much to make history, but to keep history from being made."

Wyatt handled his task superbly, with tact and sympathy, explaining the importance of an amicable settlement for the many other Indonesian aspirations. And Sukarno responded. Walter Levy served as an adviser to the Indonesian delegation with the same loyalty to their interests that a lawyer has to his client, for which the Indonesians were at first unbelieving and then profoundly grateful. "For years," one Indonesian representative said later, "the American oil people were exploiting us, but now we are exploiting at least one American oil man!" Under Levy's sympathetic guidance they came to see where their benefits could be increased and where they had misunderstood and made demands that would make a viable enterprise impossible. In the end, both sides made concessions—the oil companies, for example, agreed to a 60-40 split, time payments for their assets, and so on, while the Indonesians agreed that the split should be on actual rather than posted price, that taxes should be paid before, not after, the split, and that the assessment of the value of the facilities being taken over should be realistic. Most important of all, the companies got, not only the right to market Indonesian oil under profitable arrangements, but the right to conduct exploration for new deposits subject to the same arrangements for a period of twenty-five years. The oil companies were delighted—not only with the agreement, but with the active co-operation of the United States Government. "Both sides have good reason to be gratified by the settlement," was the comment by *Fortune* magazine. "It has given the Indonesians a chance to display a semblance of economic responsibility at a time when they are seeking a large loan from the International Monetary Fund and more aid from the U.S. As for the oil companies, the agreement makes it possible for the oil companies to stay on in Indonesia, and to do a profitable export and domestic business for some years to come. . . . Last, but not least, they have won unexpected support from the United States government."

A SUMMIT MEETING AND "MAPHILINDO"

The Australian Foreign Minister, Sir Garfield Barwick, an able and perceptive jurist, in the meantime had been at work trying to bring about a meeting of Indonesia, Malaya, and the Philippines, on the assumption that more progress might be made in a meeting unhampered by the presence of Western sponsors. Sir Garfield's efforts took place in March at a Manila meeting of ECAFE—the Economic Commission for Asia and the Far East. It was agreed that the Tunku and Sukarno would meet in Tokyo toward the end of May and that in the meantime both sides should observe a truce in the propaganda war between them. In Washington, we held our breath—but the lull continued.

And when the Tunku and Sukarno did meet, it went very well. Their joint press statement reaffirmed the old 1959 Malaya-Indonesia friendship treaty, and, with a fanfare of publicity, laid the groundwork for a meeting of the Filipino, Indonesian, and Malayan foreign ministers to take place early in June.

They met in Manila on June 7, and the negotiations again went better than anyone had dared hope. The three foreign ministers agreed to "welcome" the formation of Malaysia, provided some way could be found to confirm that the peoples of the Borneo territories supported the concept of Malaysia. The British would certainly reject the idea of a plebiscite as presenting many too many problems for the present stage of events. For one thing, it would be impossible to mount a plebiscite before August 31, the date on which Malaysia was scheduled to come into being, and the political repercussions of a long delay would be severe. But the ministers worked out a brilliant compromise. They agreed that an "independent and impartial authority, the Secretary General of the United Nations or his representative," should endeavor to "ascertain" whether the concept of Malaysia had been an issue in the last election held in the Borneo territories and whether or not the results of the election had reflected a decision by the people to support the concept of Malaysia. The second major proposal the foreign ministers put forward was for "Maphilindo"—a permanent consultative organization of Malaysia, the Philippines, and Indonesia that would lead eventually to some form of confederation. Arrangements were then made for a "summit" meeting of Sukarno, the Tunku, and Macapagal on July 30 in Manila to ratify the "ascertainment" proposal and the meeting broke up in the friendliest and most hopeful atmosphere yet.

A WALK ON EGGS

Again in Washington we held our breath. I think we all recognized that, if lasting good relations were established among Indonesia, the Philippines, and Malaysia and if Indonesian nationalism were finally steered safely into constructive channels, there would still be many ups and downs, near disasters, and breath-taking rescues—reminiscent, perhaps, of one of the old-time movies of the *Perils of Pauline,* if it were not for the somber consequences of war and destruction. We felt we were walking on eggs. Sukarno and the Tunku were both volatile and free-wheeling personalities who made speeches on every possible occasion, responding emotionally to the crowd in front of them and frequently forgetting that modern news media carried their words beyond their immediate raptly attentive audience. And there was also Duncan Sandys.

But we were encouraged by the progress the foreign ministers had made. For something like Maphilindo—arrived at in just this way, by the Asians themselves—was what we meant by the phrase an "Asian solution." It seemed to us to be the only true and lasting answer to the problem, not only of settling the dispute over Malaysia, but of providing Indonesia a peaceable and constructive share of responsibility for regional affairs.

THE ANZUS TREATY

On the other hand, there was also another side to the coin of United States policy, which also had to be shown. There is little to be gained by threats and posturing in international affairs, but it was important that everyone understand the consequences if matters really got out of hand. A regular meeting of the ANZUS Pact countries—Australia, New Zealand, and the United States—was scheduled for June 5 and 6 in Wellington, New Zealand, and Averell Harriman was the American delegate. Meeting with the press in Australia on his way to the meeting, Harriman took the opportunity to reassure the Australian public that he did not believe Indonesia had any designs on the Australian half of New Guinea, but also to say that the ANZUS Pact would be operable in the event of trouble there—the three ANZUS countries would be "in it together." The official communiqué following the meeting made the same point. "Anything which happens in the Pacific area is of vital concern to all three," it said, "and . . . a threat to any of the partners in the area, metropolitan and island territories alike, is equally a threat to the others. The ANZUS treaty declares in simple and direct terms that in matters of defense Australia, New Zealand, and the United States stand as one."

All this was a firm warning. In fact, it was such a firm warning and captured so many headlines in the United States and Asia as well as in Australia that President Kennedy called me to ask whether Averell had not gone a little farther than the treaty provided. But he had not. The treaty provides that an attack on the territory of any of the signatories or an *attack on the forces of any of the signatories in the treaty area* would bring the treaty into force. The treaty had been negotiated by John Foster Dulles when he undertook the Japanese Peace Treaty assignment for President Truman as part of the permanent security arrangements for Australia and New Zealand accompanying the Japanese Peace Treaty. Ironically, the provision about an attack on troops in the treaty area had envisioned an attack on *American* troops, since the United States no longer had territories in the area but still did have troops there.

The treaty, of course, did not specify what action the signatories would take when it became applicable, but only that each would consult and take such actions, in accordance with its own constitutional practices as it deemed appropriate. But the treaty would be in force and all concerned understood that, as a practical political matter, the level of the United States' response would at the very minimum be appropriate to the level of the threat. The President's concern was that this be clear to all, and he directed me to see that our instructions reflected his concern.

For the rest, we bent our efforts to urge restraint and patience on all concerned. Over and over, we pointed out to the Indonesians that the surest path to achieving their ambition of playing an important role and exercising their rightful influence was to develop their resources and utilize the opportunity being provided for responsible negotiations. And to the British and Malayans, we repeated that, although no one could guarantee that the Indonesians would not in the end take the trouble-making path, the point was to avoid doing anything they could inter-pret as a provocation, which would create a political opportunity and tempt them to take that path. At every turn, it should be clear to the world that there was a sincere desire to meet Indonesia's legitimate needs and desires. If the Indonesians chose troublemaking, in other words, they should also have to accept the onus for it in the eyes of the entire world.

THE MANILA MEETINGS

But the British insisted on going ahead with the scheduled meeting in London to put the final touches on the Malaysia agreement between the UK, Malaya, Singapore, North Borneo, and Sarawak, in spite of what this implied; i.e. that they would go ahead with Malaysia no matter which way the UN "ascertainment" went. It was signed on July 9, and Sukarno's reaction was to accuse the Tunku of a breach of faith. "I declare to the world," he shouted, "that Tunku Abdul Rahman is a man who does not keep his word . . . I declare here openly that we Indo-nesian people not only disagree with Malaysia but we oppose it at all costs . . . Now I have my doubts about the coming Maphilindo summit conference." Even more violent speeches followed—"To crush Malaysia we must launch a confrontation in all fields. We cannot talk sweetly to the imperialists" and "We'll crunch up Malaysia and spit out the pieces" are two examples. The Philippines appealed to both sides to resolve their differences at the Manila summit conference, and not in public speeches. And American, Australian, and Filipino diplomats spent their time urg-ing circumspection, restraint, and calm. Nobody was taking bets on whether there really would be a Manila summit conference, and hopes went up and down like a Yo-Yo on a string. When a cable from Am-bassador Howard Jones finally arrived in Washington saying that Sukarno had boarded the plane for Manila and was actually on his way, there was an almost audible sigh of relief.

But no one knew what would happen when Sukarno got to Manila and hopes had begun to dim. The reason was not only the British un-willingness to make concessions in the Malaysia timetable toward "as-certainment," but the credibility of United States policy and intentions. For we were being seriously undercut by opposition at home, in Congress and elsewhere.

DOMESTIC CONSIDERATIONS

Each year the American aid program seemed to be having more trouble in Congress. One basic reason was that the liberals, who had always been the strongest supporters of the idea of aid, were beginning to show signs of becoming disenchanted. They had hoped that aid would bring economic development to the emerging, poverty-ridden nations of the world, and that development in turn would bring responsibility, stability, and peace. But it was turning out to be so much more complicated than this. Development took longer than the liberals had assumed, and it took a lot more than aid—education, organization, administrative skills and techniques, and even a change in social attitudes. What was particularly hard for the liberals to stomach was that the exigencies of both the Cold War and rival nationalisms often made it necessary to use aid for its political leverage, and this seemed an almost intolerable corruption. For all these reasons, liberal support for foreign aid was beginning to wane, and the long-time opponents of it or those who supported aid only if it was more or less directly related to building up the non-Communist world's military defenses had renewed their efforts to cut the program down.

In an effort to head off these moves, President Kennedy—after much debate inside the administration—had appointed Lucius D. Clay to head a "Committee to Strengthen the Security of the Free World" to review both the economic and military aid programs "to determine whether the level and distribution of these programs is contributing materially to the security of the United States and is directed to specific and attainable goals of economic and political stability in the free world." Appointing a committee of distinguished citizens is a familiar ploy in the politics of policy-making. If the committee is not to be a transparent attempt to sugar-coat what an administration intended to do all along, the committee's mandate must have some cutting edge. But if it does have a cutting edge, there will then be a struggle over who will be appointed to the committee, convinced opponents or convinced supporters. Or, if the fight is heavy, the struggle will be over appointing people who do not appear to be convinced opponents or supporters but who one or the other side hopes will turn out to be. Everyone in Washington thought that the Clay Committee was an attempt by the President to head off opposition to his aid program and in trying to counter cynicism he was pushed into giving the committee a sharper mandate and to appoint members whom the opponents of aid found credible. As a result, the whole exercise backfired. The report was carping and critical. It did come to the conclusion that a continuing aid program was necessary for the nation's security, but this admission was so grudging and so much ammunition was supplied to the opposition in the process of reaching that conclusion that the aid bill suffered its largest cut from Congress in history, from $4.9 billion requested to $3.2 billion actually appropriated.

And the report contained a number of statements that were damaging to relations with particular countries. The report was issued in March 1963, right in the midst of the effort to inveigle Indonesia into more constructive channels, and its specific comments on Indonesia, although not unsound, were not very helpful as a public statement. "We do not see," the document said, "how external assistance can be granted to this nation by free-world countries unless it puts its internal house in order, provides fair treatment to foreign creditors and enterprises, and refrains from international adventures." As several Indonesian officials said, they could accept such a statement as a reasonable assessment of political realities if the statement was made privately, but that when it was made publicly it became a gratuitous insult.

THE BROOMFIELD AMENDMENT

But worse was to come. Right in the midst of the delicate negotiations on the oil agreements Representative Broomfield, in a speech on the floor of the House, attacked Indonesia and United States policy toward it, demanding an immediate suspension of "all further economic and military assistance to Indonesia." He also decided that the vehicle for his opposition to Indonesia would be an amendment to the foreign aid bill prohibiting military aid to Indonesia of any kind and requiring a special presidential determination that economic aid to Indonesia was vital to American security before it could be continued. In my capacity as Assistant Secretary, I went to Broomfield to beg him not to tie our hands with this amendment, which would make our task with Sukarno and Indonesia so much more difficult, and so did many others of the administration. Secretary Rusk publicly deplored "the tendency in the Congress to legislate foreign policy as it might apply to specific situations or specific countries." But Broomfield was adamant.

Broomfield took the formal step of introducing his amendment in early July, just as the Filipino, Indonesian, and Malayan foreign ministers were hammering out the agreement in Manila that gave us so much hope. On July 26, just four days before the "summit" meeting was due to open in Manila, it was announced that the Foreign Affairs Committee had adopted the amendment. Broomfield himself told the press that the vote "wasn't even close" and that it was "definitely bipartisan"—thereby rubbing salt into the Indonesian wounds.

The task for United States diplomacy was to use whatever influence it could muster to steer Indonesian nationalism into constructive channels.

Its influence was marginal in any case, for it was not just a question of persuading the Indonesians, but of persuading allies, such as Great Britain, as well. What the Broomfield amendment did was to strengthen the hand of the hard-liners in both the British Government and in the Indonesian.

NOTES

[1] For a summary of the state of the Indonesian economy in 1962, see Bruce Grant, *Indonesia,* Melbourne, 1962, Chapter 6.
[2] Bruce Grant, *op. cit.,* p. 83.
[3] *Newsweek,* February 3, 1964.
[4] *Newsweek, loc. cit.*

CHAPTER 27

The Summit, Maphilindo, and Burning Embassies

THE MANILA CONFERENCE opened on schedule July 30, 1963. Macapagal, as President of the host country, gave the opening speech of welcome, but just as he was saying, "The question in the minds of many is, 'Will this conference succeed . . . ?'" the electricity failed, killing lights, microphones, and air-conditioning. It seemed a sign.

But the next day, Sukarno, the Tunku, and Macapagal all seemed in a jovial mood—with Sukarno making appreciative remarks about the pretty Filipino girls and his qualifications as a judge—and the working meetings began.

In Washington, we were eager for any scrap of news about how things were going. The time difference between Manila and Washington meant that the people in Manila were going to bed just as we were getting up —so we expected to have a cabled report of their past day's happenings just as our new day started. But it didn't always work out that way, and Ambassador William E. Stevenson and I often found ourselves shouting double-talk over a bad long-distance phone link either in the middle of his night or the middle of mine. An able and sensitive envoy, Stevenson was plagued by a less than adequate staff, and he had not had full support from Washington in his attempts to improve it. Much to our annoyance and frustration, for example, on one or two occasions, the embassy staff apparently went home at the normal end of the workday rather than staying around to buttonhole delegates and find out what had happened at important evening meetings. It was not very likely that we could have done much about it if a snag developed, for whatever influence of either carrot or stick we possessed had already been used. But it would have been intolerable to think that the conference had foundered on something we could have unsnarled if we had only known about it.

The negotiations continued, and it seemed to us that the Tunku was managing them brilliantly. As the outlines of an agreement began to emerge, it seemed clear that he was trading concessions on the *form* of bringing Malaysia into existence for concessions on *substance*. The Tunku was willing, for example, to postpone the date that Malaysia would come into being, which had been set for August 31, so that the Indonesians

could say that it had not come into being until *after* it had been confirmed
that the wishes of the people had been "ascertained." And he agreed to
let the UN teams be accompanied by Indonesian and Filipino "observers." In return, Indonesia and the Philippines agreed that instead of a
plebiscite, on which Sukarno had been so insistent, the UN teams would
survey the last election in the North Borneo territories to determine if
the concept of Malaysia was an issue, if the electoral rolls were fair and
proper, if the elections were free, and so on—all of which seemed to
mean that a positive finding in favor of Malaysia was virtually guaranteed. Some among those most hostile to Indonesia argued that Sukarno
might still refuse to welcome Malaysia, in spite of a favorable finding by
the Secretary General. But the point remained that if an agreement of
this kind were achieved and carried out scrupulously to avoid any act
that could be interpreted as a provocation, the Indonesians would have
to pay a high political cost among Asians and Africans if they nevertheless decided to go ahead with the "confrontation" policy. So the Manila
accords, signed and scrupulously implemented, would not only be a deterrent to the Indonesians' continuing "confrontation," but would make
the measures necessary to meet "confrontation" politically easier to carry
out if the Indonesians still went ahead with it.

The final agreement was issued on August 5, 1963, in the form of an
Accord, a *Statement,* and a *Declaration.* The *Accord* was the agreement
of the foreign ministers as ratified by the three heads of government. It
provided that Indonesia and the Philippines would "welcome" the formation of Malaysia if the Secretary General of the United Nations "ascertained" that the wishes of the peoples of North Borneo favored Malaysia; that the incorporation of North Borneo into Malaysia would not
prejudice the Philippines' right to pursue its claim in North Borneo in
accordance with international law and the principle of the pacific settlement of disputes; and that the three nations would establish "machinery
for frequent and regular consultation"—Maphilindo.

The *Statement* spelled out the manner of the Secretary General's
ascertainment—that it would be done by examining the recent elections.
It provided for observers from Indonesia and the Philippines and repeated the assurances concerning the Philippine claim. It confirmed the
setting up of Maphilindo and provided for national secretariats to be
established which would develop the necessary machinery for Maphilindo. And it contained a statement of Asian solidarity and independence with an implied dig at both Britain and the United States and a
hint at Indonesia's charge that they had covertly supported the 1958
rebellion with aid routed through their military bases in Malaya and the
Philippines. "The three Heads of Government," the statement read, "further agreed that foreign bases—temporary in nature—should not be
allowed to be used directly or indirectly to subvert the national inde-

pendence of any of the three countries. In accordance with the principle enunciated in the Bandung Declaration, the three countries will abstain from the use of arrangements of collective defense to serve the particular interests of any of the big powers."

The *Declaration* reaffirmed the three nations' adherence to the principle of self-determination; expressed their determination to promote economic progress and social well-being; confirmed their opposition to colonialism and imperialism in all its forms; identified themselves as "new emerging forces" pledged to co-operate in building a better world based on national freedom; and expressed again their determination to move forward with Maphilindo through frequent and regular consultations.

REACTION—IN BRITAIN, INDONESIA, AND THE U. S. CONGRESS

The British were visibly unhappy about the Manila accords, and the Colonial Office and Duncan Sandys were furious. The North Borneo territories were British colonies, and what Britain did with its own colonies was, in Sandys's view, her own business. He disliked postponing the date for the formation of Malaysia and its implication that the approval of Indonesia and the Philippines was necessary. Lord Home, the Foreign Minister, asked U Thant to complete the survey by August 31, but the best that U Thant could promise was two weeks later, September 15. Sandys also disliked the idea of observers from Indonesia and the Philippines, and its similar implications. And he disliked the whole idea of the UN inspecting elections in a British colony—and especially as a concession to a nation like Indonesia.

The Tunku's signature on the Manila accords had to be conditional on British approval—since the North Borneo territories would continue under British sovereignty until after Malaysia came into being—and Sandys and the Colonial Office apparently wanted to withhold that approval. But the Foreign Office prevailed. Reluctantly, the British agreed.

But the British press—apparently inspired by leaks—accused the Tunku of having conceded too much, implying that he was a babe in the woods, an innocent incapable of standing on his own feet. And all this seemed to demonstrate that the Indonesians had a point about the "neocolonialist" attitude of the British, that they regarded the Tunku as a rather incompetent little brown brother who had to be protected from himself.

In Indonesia, the Manila accords seemed a switch away from the traditions of the revolution, but the British criticism of the Tunku probably helped in earning popular support. The comment was generally favorable, but not enthusiastically so. Ali Sastroamidjojo, Chairman of the Indonesian Nationalist Party, for example, said cautiously that he thought

Maphilindo was at least not contrary to Indonesia's "free and active" foreign policy and that the results of the summit meeting were closer to Indonesia's ideas than the results of the earlier meeting of the Foreign Ministers. The Communists, on the other hand, did not approve and urged that the policy of "confrontation" and "crush Malaysia" be continued.

In the United States, I was called before the Far East Subcommittee, chaired by Clement Zablocki, to explain the implications of the reference to the "temporary nature" of foreign bases for the American installations in the Philippines; the significance of the citation to the Bandung Declaration; and the pledge to abstain from the use of collective defense arrangements "to serve the particular interests of the big powers." The congressmen were also distressed about rumors then current in Washington concerning the economic stabilization program for Indonesia and just what the United States had or had not promised concerning the "$250 million" of aid the stabilization program was supposed to require.

In response to our queries President Macapagal and the Philippine Government had given us all the assurances one could wish about the future of the bases. As one Filipino said, "Even the Indonesians understand the need. Pointing to the Chinese, one said to me 'Thank God for the U. S. Seventh Fleet.' And another said, 'For you Filipinos the threat is the Chinese Reds. For us Indonesians it is the Chinese—Red or Yellow.'" And the references to not using the bases for subversion, to the "new emerging forces," and to their determined opposition to colonialism and the "particular interests of the big powers," were all understandable.

As far as the economic stabilization program was concerned, it was quite obvious that it could not be pursued unless there were peace and stability in the region; if the Manila accords and Maphilindo succeeded in creating the requisite peace and stability, it was certainly in the United States' national interest to support it. If the Manila accords—or subsequent negotiations—failed to produce the requisite peace and stability, on the other hand, then there was no sense to go ahead with aid that was keyed to economic stabilization and development.

Our policy so far in the Kennedy administration had been to try to encourage Indonesia to steer the forces of its nationalism into constructive channels, to turn toward economic development and toward picking up some of the responsibility for peace and security in the region. In the meantime, we had continued with a minimal aid program of two different kinds and serving two different purposes. One kept open our channels of communication and stood as a constant reminder of what was possible while at the same time serving humanitarian purposes. Through the Food for Peace surplus food program—Public Law 480—we were sending Indonesia several million dollars a year of surplus rice and other foodstuffs. Quite apart from its humanitarian aspects, this program served as an example to encourage steps toward economic development and also as some small deterrent to moves in the wrong direction. We also had a small technical assistance program which, with its university contacts, was an important element on the civilian side. The second type of aid was designed to support those elements in Indonesia who opposed the growing strength of the Communists and who would have to fight the Communists if they attempted to take over control in a *coup d'état* and it came to an armed struggle. We continued to sponsor training for officers in the Indonesian armed services, as described above, and to support civic action by the armed services—the well- and canal-digging, bridge- and road-building program that helped the army develop popular support in the villages, support they would need in any future struggle with the Communists. We helped equip and train Mobile Police Brigades (Mobrigs), whom the Communist rioters came to fear.

In general, we felt the Manila accords were a hopeful development and should be encouraged. But we also felt that it would be a mistake to pin all our hopes of persuading the Indonesians to steer their nationalism into constructive channels on the Manila accords. For even if the accords were by and large successful, there would still be troubles ahead and many disheartening ups and downs before Indonesia really settled on a steady course. Economic development was going to be much more difficult and take longer than the Indonesians realized. Even if they started on development, they would become discouraged at times and backslide for a while. Also, it seemed clear that we all had to understand the depth of emotion in this new nationalism, their fierce independence, and the fact that there were some things they would put ahead of economic development which might seem to us to be no more than a matter of prestige but which were to the Indonesians symbolic of their nationhood. The Indonesians, for example, would probably give up any amount of aid and cut themselves off completely from even trade rather than appear to buckle under pressure. They felt they had a right to be consulted in a decision to create a new nation in their own backyard, and they were determined to exercise it. The internal political situation in Indonesia would also have its effects. The army could not let the Communists have a monopoly of nationalistic fervor, for example, or the whole internal balance would be upset. Then, finally, there was the personality of Sukarno himself. An ardent patriot, a great leader in the independence movement, Sukarno was also a born politician. He had pride and vanity and was inordinately sensitive to slights and insults. He was not likely to distinguish in all cases between what the American press or an American congressman said about him and the official position of the United States Government. He, too, on occasion would be tempted to stray from the straight and narrow path the Clay Committee had insisted upon of "putting its internal house in order" and abstaining from "international adventures."

Our conclusion was that the Manila accords were a hopeful development, but that for all these reasons, there was going to be trouble intermittently no matter how well things seemed to go in the immediate future. But we also felt that if we accepted all these complexities, maintained a basic sympathy and understanding for the new nationalisms as well as a policy of firmness against their unwarranted demands, and were willing to keep plugging away in spite of the occasional setback, then it was still possible that Indonesia would turn into constructive and peaceful channels. The United States was trying to do what it could to save a major country from falling into Communism—or from joining into a grand alliance with the Communists against us even though they did not become Communists themselves.

All these arguments were the theme of our pleas to the House Foreign Affairs Committee both in testimony and in private conversations. In effect, we asked that the committee avoid taking away the administration's flexibility, our ability to increase or decrease our aid according to the circumstances—not, in a word, to take the political weapons out of our hands.

The committee as a whole seemed reassured and willing to go along with the policy we were pursuing. But Congressman Broomfield was still determined to go ahead with the amendment cutting off military aid of any kind, even though this would include equipment for the Mobile Police Brigades and civic action which were so important in strengthening the army for any future struggle with the Communists. And he also insisted on going ahead with the requirement that the President would have to make a special determination that aid was necessary for the United States' national interest before we could continue even the minimum of economic aid.

THE UN "ASCERTAINMENT"

U Thant had promised to try to complete the UN survey by September 15, and it was August 16 before they could even begin. The British had rather glumly agreed to at least the letter of the Manila accords, and Duncan Sandys himself went to Malaya to keep a tight rein on matters. The Indonesians, for their part, continued to make belligerent statements coupled with seemingly inconsistent pledges expressing willingness to accept the UN verdict. On August 28, for example, President Sukarno said that if the people of Borneo wanted to join Malaysia, "We will have to bow our head and obey," but that Indonesia would still oppose the federation. General Nasution admitted in another speech that Indonesia had trained more than six thousand anti-British, anti-Malaysian rebels in

North Borneo and spoke somewhat threateningly about Indonesia's capacity to do even more. But he then went on to say that Indonesia had no territorial ambitions and if popular support for Malaysia were proved, Indonesia would be "legally bound to halt its assistance to the underground movement." Yet clashes between "Indonesia-based" guerrillas and Gurkha Rifles units occurred in the territories even as the UN teams began their work. The signs were not auspicious.

First, there was trouble about the procedure the UN teams planned to follow, and then even greater trouble about the Indonesian and Filipino observers. The Indonesians and Filipinos wanted thirty observers, which Sandys, with considerable justice, thought was excessive. Both sides finally agreed to four observers and four assistant observers from each country.

Then, when the observers actually showed up, Sandys objected that the Indonesian team included intelligence experts—which we had all expected anyway—and refused to let them accompany the UN teams. He finally gave in, after the United States protested to the Foreign Office. But much of the damage had already been done. The Indonesian and Filipino observers had not been present for three of the total of six days the UN teams had spent touring the North Borneo territories. "It is a matter of regret," U Thant later wrote, "that this understanding [on observers] could not have been reached earlier, so that all observers could have been present in the territories for the entire period of the inquiries and that questions of detail pertaining to the status of the observers unnecessarily delayed even further their arrival. A more congenial atmosphere would have been achieved if the necessary facilities had been granted more promptly by the Administering Authority." In fact, it was more than a matter for regret. In one fell swoop, Sandys had handed the Indonesians what the in-between world would regard as a provocation, a "neocolonialist" violation of the Manila accords with which to beat both the British and the Malayans, and a plausible excuse to deny the validity of the Secretary General's findings if they favored Malaysia.

But worse was yet to come. Under what was apparently heavy pressure from Sandys, the Tunku on August 29 announced that the scheduled date for the establishment of Malaysia was being postponed from August 31 until September 16 so as to permit the UN survey to be completed. And then, gratuitously, he added that Malaysia would be established on that date whether or not the UN findings were favorable. Duncan Sandys made a similar statement.

This announcement, U Thant wrote stiffly in his final report, "led to misunderstanding and confusion and even resentment among other parties to the Manila agreement, which could have been avoided if the date could have been fixed after my conclusions had been reached and made known." Others saw a more ominous meaning: "Given the widespread expectation in all quarters that the UN review would conclude in favor of Malaysia, the premature announcement constituted an unwarranted provocation. And, given the well-known sensitivity of Sukarno, it was a grave tactical error—if the British, in fact, wanted the Manila Agreements to stand."[1]

For my part, I did not see how such a blatant insult could be ignored by the Indonesians and Filipinos. "You know," I remember saying to one of the most senior of my British friends, "I knew that some of the people I would have to deal with in this job were going to be emotional. But I never dreamed that among the most emotional of all would be some Anglo-Saxons."

"John Bull is the national symbol," he replied, shaking his head sadly, "but there are a few Englishmen who are more like the one in the china shop."

Everyone did their best to try to pick up the pieces, but the Indonesian reaction was predictable. "This highhanded announcement," Sukarno said, "made while the ascertainment of the people's wishes was only in the opening stages, is ludicrous. . . . Indonesia has been duped and humiliated in the eyes of the whole world. This affront to my country is a personal hurt."

This was followed by a formal note on September 3 protesting this "reckless and premature decision" as a "unilateral act contravening the letter and spirit of the Manila Summit agreements." The decision, the note charged, "forestalls the outcome" of the UN inquiry.

On September 14, the UN survey was completed and the findings were for Malaysia. "I have come to the conclusion," U Thant wrote in his final report, "that the majority of the peoples of Sabah (North Borneo) and of Sarawak, have given serious and thoughtful consideration to their future, and to the implications for them of participation in a Federation of Malaysia. I believe that the majority of them have concluded that they wish . . . to engage, with the peoples of the Federation of Malaya and Singapore, in an enlarged Federation of Malaysia . . ."

On September 15, the Indonesian Cabinet met and decided that Malaysia was illegal and could not be recognized. Dr. Subandrio, the Indonesian Foreign Minister, said that the UN survey was not conducted in accord with the Manila agreements and that Indonesia would withhold recognition of Malaysia until corrections were made to the UN report. The Philippines also informed Malaysia it would defer recognition.

On September 16, Malaysia was formally established in elaborate ceremonies. Malaysian crowds stoned the Indonesian Embassy in Kuala Lumpur, and in Djakarta Indonesian crowds stoned both the Malaysian and British embassies. Gilchrist, the British Ambassador, a blunt, imperious Scotsman with a spade beard and a reputation for "tough" diplomacy, met with a delegation of the rioters. He explained that the Secretary

General's report had sanctioned Malaysia and then shouted at the crowd in Indonesian—*"Hid up* [Long live] *U Thant!"* Moreover, he sent out his military attaché, Major Roderick "Red Rory" Walker, to march up and down playing the pipes to show the rioters that there would "always be an England." Properly goaded, the rioters turned over the Ambassador's car and set it on fire.

On September 17, Malaysia broke relations with Indonesia. On the eighteenth, mobs attacked the British Embassy in Djakarta and burned it to the ground, while police stood by making no effort to stop them. On the nineteenth, mobs in Kuala Lumpur attacked the Indonesian Embassy, and tore down the *garuda*—the national crest in the form of an eagle. They dragged the *garuda* through the streets to the Tunku's residence, and then lifted up the Tunku himself on their shoulders so that he could put his feet on it. On September 20, Indonesia announced the take-over of all British companies and on September 21 cut off all trade with Malaysia, including the entrepôt trade with Singapore, on which Indonesia depended so much for vital foreign exchange.

The United States announced that it had suspended all shipments of arms and ammunition to Indonesia. It also announced that since the economic stabilization program was obviously infeasible in the circumstances the economic aid contemplated in support of that program would be held in abeyance.

PICKING UP THE PIECES

And then we set about to pick up the pieces. There were clearly some second thoughts in Djakarta about what had happened, and Sukarno quickly agreed to pay for rebuilding the British Embassy. Then, too, Sukarno had not so much turned his back on economic stabilization as he had leaped at the opportunity for political gain that the British had given him in the way they had handled the formation of Malaysia. What we had to do was to create a political opportunity in the opposite direction—and we thought it was at least possible.

The previous July, Forrestal and I, with Harriman's warm endorsement, had started a campaign to persuade the President to take a trip to the Far East, an idea he had toyed with for some time. I had laid out the rationale in a memorandum on July 8. The argument was, first, that there were two halves to the Communist world and thus two halves to the problem of peace—symbolized by the Sino-Soviet dispute. The second argument was the need to steer the emerging nations into constructive channels as the means for achieving their aspirations. "The President's American University speech, his trip to Europe, Harriman's follow-up mission to Moscow [which culminated in the nuclear test ban treaty] are having their effects on the Atlantic side of this equation," the memorandum argued. "What is needed now are steps to consolidate the Pacific arena—most of all to prevent the Chinese Communists from misunderstanding the nature of our commitments to the free Asian world, and to encourage the non-Communist Asians themselves. . . . What is needed now is a dramatic affirmation of America's presence and commitment to Asia. This affirmation should be related primarily to the new forces of Asian unity and economic strength. Its cast should be fresh, positive, not merely a restatement of the old, essentially military and defensive commitment. To achieve these results, there is no substitute for a Presidential visit. . . ."

This memorandum was written before the Manila meetings, when things looked more hopeful. The issues at that time were the economic stabilization program for Indonesia, the formation of Malaysia, and the potentialities for co-operation in the idea of Maphilindo. We felt that Indonesia was teetering on the verge of a fundamental decision whether to turn toward co-operation with the Communist nations or toward more peaceable channels for achieving the goals of nationalism, and the evidence at that time was that the decision was in the direction of the peaceable. "This decision, inevitably, is tentative," the memorandum went on to say, "not only in the sense that Sukarno will waver in the face of difficulties, but also that he will have trouble bringing the disparate elements of the Indonesian population along with him in this decision. The President's trip will go far towards making the decision stick. At the same time, the Malaysians are embarking upon a great enterprise of consolidating diverse peoples into a new nation—and they will need encouragement. Moreover, the Malaysians, the Indonesians, and the Filipinos have taken the first tentative steps toward a federation of Malay peoples [Maphilindo] with the implied suggestion that it is to lay the groundwork of a defense against Chinese Communist aggression."

The President had mulled over the idea of this trip in his mind and had virtually decided to go. Sukarno had repeatedly raised the question of a trip by President Kennedy—as mentioned earlier, he had been hurt and angry when President Eisenhower had deliberately omitted Indonesia from the itinerary of his Far East trip, and he was eager to have that slight erased. In addition, a visit from Kennedy, who so excited the Asians, would fit well with Sukarno's hunger for prestige and recognition outside of Indonesia. And he would put a visit from Kennedy to good political use inside of Indonesia as well. But Sukarno understood as well as everyone else that President Kennedy could not visit Indonesia in the circumstances of "confrontation" and that if the dispute had not been settled, Kennedy, too, would have to omit Indonesia from the itinerary. Drumming up a presidential visit would have been out of the question in the altered circumstances of full "confrontation," but since one had already been planned, we might be able to build a "political opportunity" around it.

We developed a "package" of recommendations. Ambassador Jones would return to Indonesia with an offer of about $11 million of Public Law 480 surplus rice, which Indonesia sorely needed. He would mention the trip—and also the need for speed in getting negotiations going, since the trip would have to be made early enough in 1964 to avoid becoming entangled with presidential elections. And if all this went well, I would follow Jones in a week or so, going first to Djakarta, and then on to Kuala Lumpur and Manila.

We met with the President at nine in the evening on November 19, 1963, and he approved the approach. Then came the disaster in Dallas, only three days later.

PRESIDENT JOHNSON AND INDONESIA

One of the first pieces of paper to come across President Johnson's desk was the presidential determination called for by the Broomfield amendment, by which the President had to certify that continuing even economic aid was essential to the national interest. Since everyone down the line had known that President Kennedy would have signed the determination routinely, we were all surprised when President Johnson refused. Instead, he asked Secretary McNamara for a detailed list of just what the Indonesians were actually getting under the remaining aid programs—whether it was trucks and tires and things that could be useful in a military campaign even if they weren't arms. McNamara turned the Pentagon upside down in a fury of accounting, and he came up with not only a definitive list, but a proposal by which he, as Secretary of Defense, would decide on progressive cuts to bring increasing pressure on Indonesia. There were some mutterings in the White House as well as the State Department at what seemed a large-scale transfer of responsibility for essentially political matters to the Secretary of Defense, but the center of the President's concern remained the determination required by the Broomfield amendment.

It came to a head in a meeting of the National Security Council on January 7, 1964. The President was unwilling to sign the determination. But he did agree to have the United States undertake one last effort at peace-making. There was a faint hope that if the three Asian leaders could be persuaded to resume negotiations, some solution could still be found. The Manila summit meeting, after all, had come up with what everyone had thought was a miracle.

But it was obvious that a cease-fire would have to come first. Sukarno had to be persuaded that it was unreasonable to expect the Tunku to negotiate with a gun at his head, and the Tunku had to be persuaded that negotiations were worth while if a cease-fire was arranged. A high-level presidential emissary would have to visit all three leaders—Sukarno, the Tunku, and Macapagal—and then go on to London.

All of us closely involved felt that if anyone could bring it off, it would be the Attorney General, Robert F. Kennedy. He had, of course, the very considerable asset of the Kennedy name. But there were other reasons that were equally important. Kennedy knew Sukarno from his previous trip, and got along well with him. Kennedy also was very familiar with the problems involved. But most important of all, he had demonstrated in several similar situations a skill and understanding, in articulation and in negotiations, that was outstanding.

And among his friends, there was also the feeling that if he would undertake the assignment it would be a good thing for the Attorney General himself. Although his sorrow still weighed heavily, Kennedy had shaken off the preoccupation of grieving—grief, he had remarked, is a form of self-pity—and an important mission might help.

President Johnson agreed to a peace-making mission with Kennedy at its head—although he continued to decide against signing the determination. In a grueling trip, Kennedy visited each of the four capitals. And he did succeed. After reporting to President Johnson, Kennedy described the agreement to the press. "I have reported to the President . . ." he said, "that the Philippines have agreed to sit down at a conference. . . . During that period of time a cease fire will take place in that part of the world. President Sukarno has issued a cease-fire order in Indonesia, and already the regular military units of Indonesia have been called off . . . It is a step forward. There are obviously great problems still ahead. . . . But I think with good will and with genuine effort that the conference has a chance of success. The alternative, really, of the conference is the continued war in the jungle."

The conference did take place—but somehow nothing happened. It would have been helpful if steps could have been taken to create the right kind of atmosphere for the meeting, to put pressures at one point and inducements at another. But this was not done. The presidential determination continued to be an obstacle. The British, too, continued to urge a hard-line policy—particularly Douglas-Home, the new Prime Minister, when he visited Washington in early February.

Robert Kennedy seems to have felt that he had been let down. "Kennedy had taken the mission seriously," Theodore H. White reported, "but when he had returned to tell the President his findings, he had been received just once in the Oval Office—to find himself required to brief a clutch of congressmen in the new Presidential presence. Thereafter—no contact with the President nor any solicitation of his findings from the State Department. Johnson had tried to give Kennedy a sense of participation, but Kennedy had participated in nothing after this exertion, and felt he had been used as a decoration to paste the Kennedy name over the politics of another man."[2]

Over the next few months, the United States cut the remaining items of aid and the level of hostility and mutual recrimination between the United States and Indonesia rose. The United States, in fact, had made a major shift in its policy. It had abandoned its effort to steer the new nationalism of Indonesia into constructive channels, and moved to a hard line in support of the British effort to isolate Indonesia politically and contain it militarily.

United States policy had been to discriminate, to be firm against bad policies but to maintain sufficient influence to encourage good ones. It had also been to discriminate between the different segments of Indonesian society, specifically to continue aid programs that strengthened the nationalist elements, such as the army. For a battle was clearly coming between the nationalist elements and the Communists, and it was not at all certain which would prove to be the stronger. The army and the nationalist elements might still win, but the United States could no longer take credit for having strengthened them for the battle.

NOTES

[1] Frederick P. Bunnell, *op. cit.*
[2] Theodore H. White, *The Making of the President, 1964,* 1965, p. 261.

IX

VIETNAM

"Gentlemen, let's not talk about this matter too much in military terms; to do so might make it a military problem."
—GENERAL GEORGE C. MARSHALL,
as reported by Dean Rusk

"This is another type of war, new in its intensity, ancient in its origin—war by guerrillas, subversives, insurgents, assassins, war by ambush instead of by combat; by infiltration, instead of aggression, seeking victory by eroding and exhausting the enemy instead of engaging him. . . . It requires a whole new kind of strategy, a wholly different kind of military training."
—JOHN F. KENNEDY, *June 6, 1962*

"Every quantitative measurement we have shows we're winning this war."
—ROBERT S. MCNAMARA, *May 1962*

"Experience has taught us that no one nation has the power or the wisdom to solve all the problems of the world or manage its revolutionary tides; that extending our commitments does not always increase our security . . ."
—JOHN F. KENNEDY, *May 25, 1961*

"There are those that say you ought to go north and drop bombs, to try to wipe out the supply lines. . . . We don't want our American boys to do the fighting for Asian boys. We don't want to get involved in a nation with 700 million people and get tied down in a land war in Asia."
—LYNDON B. JOHNSON, *September 25, 1964*

CHAPTER 28

Subterranean War

"WHAT ARE WE DOING about guerrilla warfare?" was one of the first questions Kennedy asked his aides when he became President. What he had on his hands, he went on to say, was not nuclear war or large-scale conventional war, both of which we were equipped to fight, but guerrilla war, which we were apparently not equipped to fight. The President meant Vietnam, but he was convinced that what was happening there had wider implications—that guerrilla warfare was a new form of aggression for which we needed a new strategy. The story of Vietnam is the story of the struggle over what that strategy should be. And it was, as McGeorge Bundy said, the most divisive issue in the Kennedy administration.

FISH IN THE SEA

By 1961, the great debate on nuclear strategy and on the implications of the limited, conventional war in Korea had clarified the requirements for deterring both. In the meantime, however, the Chinese Communists had become the advocates of a more subtle use of force, a way under and around our defenses. It was more than the ancient tactics of the guerrilla, for it combined these with terrorism and political subversion. "Revolutionary warfare equals guerrilla tactics plus political action" ran one slogan. It was a more sophisticated and ambiguous threat than nuclear or conventional war, slipping past the definitions of aggression embodied in international law, whose roots went back to an earlier age. It was a way of using military force, not across national boundaries, but inside them—a new kind of "internal" war, or, as President Kennedy used to say, a "subterranean" war.

The theoretician of Communist revolutionary warfare was Mao Tsetung, and his first principle was the famous phrase that guerrillas were fish swimming in the sea of the people: "Guerrillas are fish, and the people are the water in which they swim. If the temperature of the water is right, the fish will thrive and multiply." In Mao's doctrine, the guerrilla warfare that the fish wage has three stages. The first is largely political, with the cadre building support among the people, propagandizing, and recruiting. The second stage is active guerrilla warfare, with bands of guerrillas ambushing government forces, raiding, and harassing, but avoiding pitched battles. All this is combined with discriminating terrorism, assassination, sabotage, and blowing up bridges and power plants. The second stage, in a word, is a systematic effort to destroy the people's confidence in the government's ability to protect them and to make the government suspicious of the people—turning government and people against each other. It might be that power can be seized in the turmoil that follows this second stage. If not, the third and final stage is to establish "liberated areas"—base areas in which not only can supplies and recruits be obtained, but in which the efforts of the entire people can be directed to the support of the war. In these base areas, the guerrillas can be transformed into regular forces and so turn guerrilla terrorism into a civil war in which the government troops ". . . can be engaged directly in conventional combat and destroyed."

Mao and his closest disciples, such as Lin Piao, consistently argued then and later that "revolutionary wars" cannot be either initiated from outside or sustained by outside help, but that virtually the entire burden must be carried by the people of the country fighting for its "national liberation." And experience, certainly, has shown that a revolutionary group can come at least close to doing the job by itself. In the first stage—if the temperature of the people is right—all that is needed is a trained and dedicated cadre and a doctrine to guide their efforts. Food, money, and supplies can be obtained from the people, and the fact of their making the contribution commits them to the cause. Even in the second stage, outside help is not really essential. Money and supplies come from the people; weapons and ammunition can be taken from the government forces through ambush or surprise attack. Building the political base must still be the first priority, and too many arms too soon from outside might actually interfere with that task. In most guerrilla movements the most useful outside help at this stage has been in highly specialized equipment—radios, codes, and medical supplies. It is only in the third and final stage that outside help might make a decisive difference, after the struggle had been transformed into a regular civil war. At that time, two conventional armies are locked in sustained combat, and the need for ammunition, weapons, and supplies assumes really large-scale proportions. But even at this stage, the need for outside help might not be great if the "liberated areas" are large enough and if there is no large-scale outside assistance going to the government side.

All this was Mao. But on January 6, 1961, Khrushchev and the Soviet Union declared the same kind of war, in a speech laying down Soviet determination to support and encourage "wars of national liberation." Seeing its significance, President Kennedy directed that all the members of his new administration read the speech and consider what it portended.

KENNEDY'S RESPONSE

Kennedy had read Mao on guerrilla warfare and Che Guevara and the others. He let us all know of his interest in the subject and started us thinking about it. From the beginning of his administration, the President was convinced that the techniques of "revolutionary warfare" constituted a special kind of threat. As early as May 1961, he broke tradition by delivering in person a "Special Message to the Congress on Urgent National Needs" in which his concern about the concealed aggression of guerrilla warfare was prominent. "They have fired no missiles; and their troops are seldom seen. They send arms, agitators, aid, technicians and propaganda to every troubled area. But where fighting is required, it is usually done by others—by guerrillas striking at night, by assassins striking alone . . . by subversives and saboteurs and insurrectionists, who in some cases control whole areas inside of independent nations." And he hammered on the point that guerrilla warfare was different from any other kind and that it required new tactics and doctrines. "This is another type of war," he told the graduating class of West Point in 1962, "new in its intensity, ancient in its origins—war by guerrillas, subversives, insurgents, assassins; war by ambush instead of by combat; by infiltration, instead of aggression, seeking victory by eroding and exhausting the enemy instead of engaging him. . . . It requires in those situations where we must counter it . . . a whole new kind of strategy, a wholly different kind of force, and therefore a new and wholly different kind of military training."

He pushed the Pentagon to do more, and when he discovered that the results of his pushing had been marginal, he had a session with the Joint Chiefs of Staff that led to a sharp upgrading of the Special Forces training program at Fort Bragg and more support for General William P. Yarborough, its commander. He wanted the Special Forces, who were to be the experts both in guerrilla and counterguerrilla warfare, to be an elite corps, and over the objections of the JCS he directed that they wear the green beret as a symbol of their elite status. He set up an interdepartmental "counterinsurgency" committee under General Maxwell D. Taylor, with Robert F. Kennedy as his own special representative. And he pushed the State Department into establishing a special "counterinsurgency" course of instruction which everyone who was going to the vulnerable underdeveloped countries had to attend, no matter what department they came from or how high they ranked. Henry Cabot Lodge, for example, attended such a course before he departed for his post as Ambassador to South Vietnam.

But resistance to these ideas continued. On April 18, 1961, for example, the newspapers carried a story that General Lyman Lemnitzer, Chairman of the Joint Chiefs of Staff, after a recent trip to Vietnam felt that the new administration was "oversold" on the importance of guerrilla warfare and that too much emphasis on counterguerrilla measures would impair the ability of the South Vietnamese Army to meet a conventional assault like the attack on South Korea by the ten or more regular North Vietnamese divisions. No one thought that General Lemnitzer himself had leaked the story. But it was clear that it was an accurate reflection of his views as well as those of the other chiefs.

VIETNAM: 1954–60

The specific point of guerrilla attack was South Vietnam, and the peculiar circumstances of Vietnam inevitably shaped the policy response to that attack.* Soon after the Geneva agreements of 1954 divided Vietnam at the seventeenth parallel, the Emperor Bao Dai appointed Ngo Dinh Diem as Premier. The Ngos were an ancient mandarin family who had served the Emperor of Annam at Hué from the sixteenth century. The family was converted to Catholicism sometime in the seventeenth century, and in the 1870s over one hundred of its members were massacred by an anti-Catholic mob. Diem's father, who escaped, also served the Emperor, rising eventually to be the chief mandarin at the court. Diem himself was an extraordinarily devout Catholic, a celibate, perhaps even a religious mystic. And he was also a patriot. He passed the mandarin examinations and rose rapidly in the career of public service until the French appointed him, at the age of thirty-two, Minister of the Interior under the new Emperor, Bao Dai. But the French reneged on their promise of reforms, and Diem resigned in protest. It was this act of resignation that established him as an anti-French nationalist, and he maintained the reputation by steadfastly refusing to accept further appointments. He spent the next twenty years living obscurely in Vietnam or in exile—some of this with the Maryknoll fathers in the United States—but his reputation as a nationalist and a patriot continued to grow. By the time of the Geneva agreements of 1954, he was one of the few Vietnamese public figures who were free of any taint of being either pro-French or pro-Communist. (As a province chief, he had broken up an early Communist network, and the Communists had murdered his revered older brother, Ngo Dinh Khoi.) He was the logical choice for the premiership.

The problems that Diem faced as the Premier of half of a war-torn country were overwhelming. Destruction was everywhere, and the economy was in chaos. The people were war-weary and discouraged, and there was the additional burden of almost a million Catholic refugees who had fled to the south. The Communists, on the other hand, had left behind a network of agents, guerrilla cadres, and caches of arms when they had gone north. Two powerful religious sects, the Cao Dai and the

* Maps of Vietnam and Southeast Asia can be found on p. 92 and pp. 276–77.

Hoa Hao, maintained private armies that were in semirevolt, and Saigon and its Chinese-populated twin, Cholon, were dominated by still another private army, belonging to a gangster sect, the Binh Xuyen. Diem had some support from the Americans—mainly from Edward Lansdale, an Air Force colonel on loan to CIA. Lansdale was an imaginative, controversial officer who had helped Magsaysay defeat the Communist Hukbalahap guerrillas in the Philippines and who became the model for the sympathetic "Colonel Hillendale" in the novel *The Ugly American*. But Diem had little help from anyone else except his own family. For Vietnam itself was terribly short of trained men of any kind, and most of those who were trained were discredited by their past service to the French. And what authority Diem had was diluted by the power still held by the Emperor, Bao Dai. No one who knew the situation in Vietnam gave Diem more than a very slight chance of coming out alive, much less of bringing the country under his control.

But somehow he did it. There was a lull in outside pressure that gave him an opportunity, for the Chinese Communists were in the "Bandung" phase following the Korean War. For the time being they were pursuing a peace offensive based on the *panch shila*—a peace offensive of which the Geneva agreements of 1954 were, in fact, one result. Diem took full advantage of the lull, and in a series of battles interspersed with political maneuverings he succeeded in breaking the power of the sects, disarming their troops or incorporating them into the regular Vietnamese forces. By the fall of 1955, he was able to hold a referendum unseating Bao Dai as Emperor and establishing himself as President and Chief of State.

Thus by 1956, the political opposition had been eliminated and Saigon's authority had been established over the provincial capitals and —apparently at least—over the countryside as well. The internal threat was seemingly in hand, and the external threat from the north was on the way to being met—by a new, 150,000-man army that an American Military Assistance Advisory Group was training and equipping to meet conventional war as the Americans had known it in Korea.

The Geneva accords had called for elections leading to the unification of North and South Vietnam in 1956, but Diem announced that he would have none of it. Pointing out that South Vietnam had never signed the Geneva agreements, Diem went on to say that, since the Communists would not permit free electioneering in the north, he would not permit free elections in the south. And the United States concurred.

In the years immediately following 1954, Diem accomplished much good for his country. The refugees were settled, many on new lands. Agriculture was vastly improved—rice production almost doubled, rubber production increased by a fifth, new fiber crops like kenaf were introduced, and pig production was so greatly increased that it became a foreign exchange earner second only to rice and rubber. And many of these improvements were directly attributable to a land reform program instituted by President Diem. It was far from perfect, but it still had considerable success.

With American help, Diem's government made a beginning on a health and sanitation program for the villages, and substantial progress on a program to eradicate malaria. Education made even greater strides. The number of elementary school students doubled; the number of secondary-school students trebled; and the number of university students quadrupled.

At first Diem was popular. But by 1957, his popularity had begun to wane. Increasingly, his regime became more dictatorial, and he ruled more and more by decree. His greatest mistake, many of his advisers thought, was in abolishing elections for village headmen and municipal councils in 1956 in favor of direct appointments. Village elections had been an ancient and traditional part of Vietnamese life, and this act did more than anything else to convince the Vietnamese that Diem was "antidemocratic." The great influence of the northerners in his regime was also resented. So was the predominance of Catholics. But what was resented even more was the influence of the Ngo family and Diem's brothers—Archbishop Thuc; Ngo Dinh Can, who ruled central Vietnam with an iron hand and feudal methods from Hué; and most especially the arrogant and supercilious Ngo Dinh Nhu and his acid-tongued, flamboyant, man-hating, termagant of a wife, the beautiful but vicious Madame Nhu. Diem, however, behaved like a mandarin. The more criticism there was of his regime and family, the more he bore down on the opposition, moving more and more toward a police state and more and more toward policies of repression in denying any form of political activity or expression.

In February of 1957, an attempt was made to assassinate Diem, and from that time on reports and rumors of coup-plotting became an endemic part of life in Saigon. In November of 1960, there was a major coup attempt by the elite parachutists—which revealed that disaffection had spread beyond politicians and intellectuals to government officials and military officers, the very center of the anti-Communist elements of society on which the struggle against the Communist guerrillas depended. Diem continued in power, but only at the cost of continued repression and the debilitating practice of appointing generals and other officers not on the basis of ability but of personal loyalty.

THE GUERRILLA WAR BEGINS

It was in November 1957, following the Soviet Sputnik success, that Mao proclaimed that the "East Wind prevails over the West Wind" and so heralded the shift from the "Bandung" policy of peaceful coexistence back to a hard line. In South Vietnam incidents of guerrilla terrorism and assassination began to mount. By 1958, for example, as many as twenty-five village officials were assassinated in a single month. And then, sometime in 1958, trained cadres began coming over the old Ho Chi Minh trails, officers and noncommissioned recruited from among the ninety thousand Communist sympathizers who had gone north in 1954. These cadres had since been trained as guerrilla leaders and political agitators and were now being sent back to their own villages and districts to make contact with the agents left behind and to organize and recruit. They carried radios, code books, medical supplies, their own arms, and certain specialized arms and equipment such as machine guns and booby traps. A major attack was being launched. It was indirect, but still it was aggression—through the guerrilla tactics and techniques of "internal war."

There was some problem on the part of Western military men in recognizing that there was a threat. General Samuel L. Myers, deputy chief of the American military mission in testimony before the Senate Foreign Relations Committee, as late as April 1959, for example, said that the guerrillas in South Vietnam had been "gradually nibbled away until they ceased to be a major menace to the Government." But if any doubt remained, it was dispelled in May of 1959, when the Communist Party of North Vietnam called for the unification of Vietnam through all "appropriate means" and a few months later publicly assumed responsibility for the "liberation" of the south. In 1960, Ho Chi Minh, speaking to the Communist Party Congress, emphasized the need to "step up the national democratic people's revolution of the south," and in December 1960 the National Liberation Front of South Vietnam was duly formed.

KENNEDY'S FIRST MOVE

By 1961, when President Kennedy came to office, Vietnam was approaching a crisis. The Viet Cong had increased their strength to about five thousand regular guerrillas, and they more or less controlled a considerable portion of the countryside. Lansdale, by now a General, had just returned from a secret trip to Vietnam ordered by the previous administration and his report shocked President Kennedy when he saw it.

The new President all but decided to send Lansdale himself as the new American Ambassador, but the suggestion raised a storm in the Pentagon, where Lansdale was viewed as an officer who through his service with CIA had become too "political." Since there was, of course, a certain amount of truth in the charge, McNamara was persuaded and Lansdale was put aside.[1]

Elbridge Durbrow, the incumbent ambassador, however, clearly had to be relieved. He had been required to bear so many messages of disapproval from the United States that he had not been welcome at the presidential palace in Saigon for several months. Following the November 1960 coup attempt, things had gotten even worse, since Diem believed, wrongly, that Durbrow had known of the plans for the coup in advance but had not warned the regime. In the end, President Kennedy chose Frederick E. Nolting, a career foreign service officer from an old Virginia family. Nolting was a big, soft-spoken man who was so comfortable to be with that almost everyone used his nickname, Fritz. He was ideal for the job of restoring good relations with Diem and attempting to influence him toward concessions that would bring his regime wider support from within Vietnam and make it politically easier for the United States to give him the aid he requested.

President Kennedy grumbled occasionally about the United States being "overcommitted" in Vietnam and Southeast Asia, but he could not go back on the commitments already made. He might avoid a qualitative change in the United States involvement—for example, raising our commitment to the level of a war like that in Korea. But he could not refuse to give more of the same kind of assistance that had been given in the past so long as the recipients could use it effectively. Or at least he could not refuse to give more of the same kind of assistance without disrupting the whole balance of power and fabric of the security structure of the region, where so many countries had based their policy on continued American involvement.

VICE-PRESIDENT JOHNSON'S TOUR

A set of recommendations prepared during the previous administration to increase the number of American advisers in Vietnam and to step up the economic and military aid programs was approved in April. Then, in May, the President sent Vice-President Johnson on a tour of the Far East to reassure our allies in Asia about the intentions of the new administration. The Vice-President found Diem "remote from the people" and "surrounded by persons less admirable than he"—but he felt it necessary to hail him publicly as the "Winston Churchill of Southeast Asia." But more important, the Vice-President recommended a fundamental decision to "move forward promptly with a major effort to help these countries defend themselves." Time was running out, he felt, and the United States had to "pull back our defenses to San Francisco and a 'Fortress America' concept" or go ahead with a full, forward strategy.

Both Johnson and Nolting urged reforms on Diem, and he reluctantly agreed to move in that direction. The United States then sent an economic mission to Vietnam under Eugene Staley, and it came back with a detailed plan for managing and developing the economy and for determining the nature and role of American aid.

THE TAYLOR-ROSTOW MISSION

But the Viet Cong made still more gains. By this time intelligence was estimating that the full-time, regular guerrilla troops numbered about twelve thousand men. With these and their several thousand more irregulars, the Viet Cong were able to bring together several different guerrilla bands at one time, totaling as many as a thousand men for a single attack. The pace of the guerrilla war had also intensified, and both government and Viet Cong casualties were running between seven hundred and twelve hundred a month. In a dramatic demonstration of what they could do when they chose to, the Viet Cong on September 18, 1961, overran a provincial capital over fifty-five miles from Saigon. They beheaded the province chief, loaded up the arms and ammunition they had captured, and departed before a relief force arrived. President Diem was convinced that the Communists intended to try to cut the country in half, isolating Hué from Saigon, and that they might well succeed if he did not get help quickly. He requested an increase of aid from the United States, and on October 11, 1961, President Kennedy announced that he was sending General Maxwell Taylor and a small team of advisers from the different agencies and departments to see how the United States might assist further.

Taylor was accompanied by Walt W. Rostow, then McGeorge Bundy's deputy on the White House staff, but there was no one of anywhere near comparable rank from the State Department. Secretary Rusk had recently acceded to pressure from below to try to get the chairmanship of the Vietnam Task Force returned to the State Department, and had been successful. But he did not want the State Department to play a prominent role in the upcoming decisions on Vietnam. For he regarded Vietnam as essentially a military problem even though a number of his colleagues in the State Department disagreed.

In any event, it was on the military aspects that the Taylor mission focused. General Lansdale, for example, was a member of the mission, and his experience with the political undercurrents in Vietnam was probably greater than any other American's, as were his sources of information. But much to his disgust, he was put to work estimating the costs and number of men required to "seal off" the 250-mile borders of jungle and mountains through which the infiltrators came—a question that he thought itself revealed a misunderstanding of guerrilla warfare. Lansdale did in fact see Diem and Nhu while he was in Vietnam, and he noted that some of the disturbing signs that he had noticed on his January trip were aggravated. Diem's unwillingness to delegate authority to anyone but Nhu was having its consequences in overwork for themselves and inefficiency in the operation of the government. Both were defensive and increasingly isolated. Diem seemed especially cut off, since he apparently got his information only through Nhu.

Even Rostow, on whom the main burden of making the political assessment fell, was preoccupied with the problem of the infiltration routes. His argument was that these routes of access made the situation different from the guerrilla terrorism that had been defeated in Malaya and the Philippines. He noted that the guerrillas in Greece had been beaten only after the Yugoslavs closed the border, and he argued that unless a way could be found to close the Vietnamese border political reforms would do nothing but buy a little time. This view, in fact, was a basic premise in Rostow's thinking. In a major speech analyzing the Communist use of guerrilla warfare and its relationship to the modernization process in developing countries, delivered that spring of 1961 at the Fort Bragg Special Forces School, Rostow had called the "sending of men and arms across international boundaries and the direction of guerrilla war from outside a sovereign nation" a new form of aggression. He had also warned that "this is a fact which the whole international community must confront and whose consequent responsibilities it must accept. Without such international action those against whom aggression is mounted will be driven inevitably to seek out and engage the ultimate source of the aggression they confront." This of course was an argument for bombing North Vietnam, a course of action for which Rostow was a responsible advocate on this and subsequent occasions.

The final report contained three sets of recommendations. The first was in effect a series of demands for political, governmental, and administrative reforms by the Diem government. The second set of recommendations was that the United States should provide the sinews of material aid and the technical advisers required for a broadly conceived counterguerrilla program—including economic measures; village-level civic, social, and political action. The United States would also furnish arms and equipment for self-defense corps and the specialized equipment, helicopters and so on, to free the Vietnamese military from static defense and to give them the mobility to seek out the guerrillas in their own territory. The program would include helicopter pilots, mechanics, and other highly trained technicians who would operate the equipment while training Vietnamese to take over. In addition, the Taylor report also recommended the sending of some special Air Force squadrons— with the code name "Farmgate"—of slow-flying, propeller-driven B-26s and T-28s. These were Air Force units especially designed and put together for the purposes of small-scale, guerrilla warfare.

With the exception of "Farmgate," these first two of the three sets of recommendations in the Taylor report were merely more of the same kind of assistance that had been given in the past—even fifteen thousand advisers, the level reached in 1963, in a nation of fourteen million people is still support for what would continue to be a Vietnamese struggle. But the third set of recommendations was for a qualitative change in the nature of the United States commitment—for the Taylor report also proposed the introduction into Vietnam of over ten thousand regular American ground troops, initially, and accepting the possibility that as many as six full divisions might eventually be required. The mission of these American troops—revealing the continued focus in General Taylor's mind on the possibility of a conventional, Korea-type attack—would be to hold the ring against invasion from the north by regular North Vietnamese divisions and to man the northern borders against infiltrators, while the South Vietnamese dealt with the guerrillas in the rear.

Thus what General Taylor was advocating was essentially the same large-scale American commitment that Vice-President Johnson had recommended. But this did not accord with President Kennedy's own analysis of the nature of what was happening in Southeast Asia. He had read deeply after his tour of the area in 1951, and his comments on the Indochina crisis when he returned had revealed his conviction that if Communism were to be defeated in Asia it could be done only by the force of nationalism. "Without the support of the native population," he said, "there is no hope of success in any of the countries of Southeast Asia." To try to oppose Communist advances "apart from and in defiance of innately nationalistic aims spells foredoomed failure."

There were few alternatives to the Taylor-Johnson policy that was offered. None of the factors that seemed to make it possible to neutralize Laos existed so far as South Vietnam was concerned. In Laos, all the different factions, including the Communists, seemed to want peace and to be left alone. But the Communist North Vietnamese were clearly determined to try the "internal war" technique as an instrument for gaining control over the south. Both the Soviet Union and Communist China seemed willing at least to put Laos aside for the time being, but Communist China was clearly determined to support the North Vietnamese effort in the south and openly downgraded the risk that the action would provoke the United States into retaliating by an attack on either North Vietnam or mainland China. In Laos, finally, there was a major political figure on whom a policy of neutralization could be based, a figure whose advocacy of neutrality over the years had made him its symbol, a figure who had a measure of popular appeal in the country. But there was no Souvanna Phouma in either North or South Vietnam.

There was one imaginative proposal—a notion put foward by Chester Bowles to enlarge the area of neutrality far beyond both Laos and Vietnam, to include Burma, Thailand, Malaya, in fact the whole of Southeast Asia. So far as I know, President Kennedy did not make any specific comment on this suggestion, but my sense of his attitude is that he accepted the concept as a farseeing expression of the ultimate goal for

Southeast Asia toward which we should work, but that its time had not yet come. I think he would have said that our policy should lead toward the goal of a neutral Southeast Asia and avoid getting United States prestige so thoroughly pinned to "victory" in Vietnam as to preclude that goal, but that until Communist ambitions had been blunted against the realities of native resistance from within Southeast Asia we could not do much more than continue to support that resistance.

The President's decision, at any rate, was along these lines. He approved of the effort to bring about reforms in the Diem government by persuasion and of the step-up in military and economic aid and the increase of American advisers, technicians, and helicopter pilots, including the "Farmgate" B-26s and T-28s with their pilots and mechanics. But he did not approve the commitment of American ground troops.

In an interesting example of one type of gambit in the politics of Washington policy-making, the President avoided a direct "no" to the proposal for introducing troops to Vietnam. He merely let the decision slide, at the same time ordering the government to set in motion all the preparatory steps for introducing troops.

For their part, Diem and Nhu again reacted in typically mandarin fashion. They resented the American insistence on the need for reform and reacted with a flurry of anti-American stories in Vietnam's controlled press and sharp treatment of American officials in Saigon. But over the following months, Diem and Nhu responded to Nolting's tactful reminders by making some quiet changes—not by any means everything the United States requested, but changes at least in the direction of reform.

THE SEARCH FOR A STRATEGIC CONCEPT

In Washington in the meantime, the search for a strategic concept to meet the "subterranean" technique of guerrilla warfare had been continuing. Rostow's speech at Fort Bragg had analyzed the relationship between guerrilla warfare and the "modernization process" taking place in the nations toward which the Communists were directing their attack. Rostow saw the modernization process as true revolution, containing its own dynamics. Like all revolutions, modernization was disturbing, upsetting the old ways and producing the vulnerabilities of transition on which the Communists could prey. The Communists, Rostow pointed out, were the "scavengers of the modernization process."

Rostow's conclusion was that the best way to win a guerrilla war was to prevent it from happening, and his analysis of the strains of modernization led to valuable insights of how this could be done in the villages and countryside of the emerging nations.

His conclusion was that the task for the United States was not only to hasten the process of modernization, to get a country past the vulnerable period of transition, but also to protect its independence during that vulnerable period. And it was the difficulty of this task of protection at the period of greatest vulnerability that led Rostow to the conclusion that it might be necessary to "seek out and engage the ultimate source of aggression." The vulnerabilities of a nation in transition were so many and the task of defeating guerrilla terrorism so great that he saw no other alternative. He was particularly impressed by the fact that historically—in Malaya, the Philippines, and other places where guerrilla terrorism had been defeated—it had taken ten to twenty soldiers to each guerrilla.

Other pioneering work was going on in the Pentagon, in CIA, in the Agency for International Development, and particularly at Fort Bragg. In the State Department's Bureau of Intelligence and Research, we set to work analyzing the political questions involved, and I began to mull and ponder over my personal experiences as an OSS guerrilla leader operating behind the Japanese lines in the neighboring terrain of Burma.

Our analysis was delivered as a speech in August and then released.[2] One section analyzed the military aspects of guerrilla warfare in terms of the need for popular support. The danger of large-scale military operations was that their very destructiveness would alienate the people. What is more, the argument ran, regular forces, although essential for the task of deterring conventional aggression, were unsuited by both training and equipment for the task of fighting guerrillas. Regular forces were road-bound, unwieldy, and cumbersome, inevitably telegraphing their movements to the elusive guerrilla. Drawing on our historical experience as a young nation in Indian fighting, on the jungle experience of the Philippine Insurrection at the turn of the century, and on OSS experience in World War II, we argued that the way to fight the guerrilla was to adopt the tactics of the guerrilla. Small bands should be spotted at intervals throughout the area to be pacified. Using guerrilla tactics, they would harass and ambush, while central reserves would be used to reinforce and to ambush on escape trails leading from the point of contact. As the guerrillas in an area were slowly worn down, government control could be extended and the people given the means to protect themselves. And when the area was cleared and secured, the security forces could move on to the next.

The other part of our analysis of guerrilla warfare focused on the political aspects of the problem. Having stressed the vital importance of gaining popular support, our analysis went on to argue that "it would be mistaken to think that guerrillas cannot thrive where governments are popular and where modernization, economic development, and reform are going forward." The point of the argument was that the existence of a guerrilla movement did not mean that a government was either popular or unpopular, and that modernization, reform, and measures to make the government popular could not alone defeat an established guerrilla group, but had to be combined with military and police measures to provide physical security.

But the approach was essentially political. What was needed to meet the guerrilla threat successfully, we felt, were reformers to organize mass parties and social and political programs that could become the basis for modernization.

In the Special Forces School at Fort Bragg, in the war colleges, and elsewhere in the armed services, there was a serious and systematic study of guerrilla warfare as it was known in the Philippines, Greece, Malaya, and so on. Out of this effort of study and debate came general agreement on the nature of guerrilla warfare and on the idea that meeting it successfully would require an emphasis on political, economic, and social action into which very carefully calibrated military measures were interwoven. But an important segment of the military did not accept the emphasis on political warfare. In a speech at Fordham University on November 7, 1962, for example, General Earle G. Wheeler—who was later Army Chief of Staff and then, in the Johnson administration, Chairman of the Joint Chiefs—said that what the United States was committed to support in Vietnam was "military action . . . Despite the fact that the conflict is conducted as guerrilla warfare," Wheeler went on to say, "it is nonetheless a military action . . . It is fashionable in some quarters to say that the problems in Southeast Asia are primarily political and economic rather than military. I do not agree. The essence of the problem in Vietnam is military."

The top American general in Vietnam, General McGarr, was finishing his tour of duty, and there would, quite obviously, be enormous advantages if his replacement could be chosen from among the younger officers who shared the conviction that guerrilla warfare was as much a political as a military problem. The ideal choice, in fact, would be a Special Forces officer, like Brigadier General William P. Yarborough, or someone who had had OSS guerrilla experience in World War II, like Colonel William R. Peers. Both suggestions were made, but only as suggestions and not as a matter of policy principle. Reaching down so far for the top man in Vietnam would arouse antagonism in the top brass of the Pentagon, and so would the appointment of an officer from among the ranks of the somewhat unorthodox Special Forces. If the State Department had made an issue of the matter, the President might have had more freedom for maneuver. But the Secretary of State felt that the question of choosing the senior American military officer in Vietnam was strictly a Pentagon affair. In the end, the President accepted General Taylor's suggestion of General Paul D. Harkins, who had been with Taylor in Korea and who was now Commander in Chief of the army's forces in the Pacific.

A TRIP TO VIETNAM

The *Marine Corps Gazette* devoted its entire issue of January 1962 to the subject of guerrilla warfare, as mentioned above, including both Rostow's speech and mine. The President read the issue "from cover to cover," as he wrote the editor, and discussed the whole problem with me on the occasion described in an earlier chapter. Then, within two or three days, General Maxwell D. Taylor, then Special Military Representative to the President, called to say that the President wanted me to go with Secretary McNamara to Honolulu for the second of what became a long series of monthly meetings between the top Americans in Saigon and those in Washington. The President had two special tasks in mind for me. First, he wanted me to pass on the thinking about guerrilla warfare that had been going on in various places in the United States to General Harkins, who would be taking up his duties in Vietnam in a very few weeks. Then, he wanted me to go on to Saigon with Ambassador Nolting to look over the situation and report back.

Honolulu was routine, but Saigon was not. Although I had spent a lot of time in Southeast Asia, I had never been to Vietnam before. I found Saigon itself a charming combination of France and Asia, and the Vietnamese people as bright and attractive as any in the world. The women are delicate and lissome, and their wraithlike beauty is accentuated by their traditional costume, the *ao dai,* which is the most feminine in the world. The *ao dai* is a blouse and translucent silk trousers, snug around their slimly rounded hips and falling loosely to the ankles, topped by a diaphanous tunic of some bright pastel shade with a high neck and split at the waist so that both halves are free to wave in the breeze. Even in the mass the result is charming. When the young girls crowd the streets of Saigon, hurrying by on foot and bicycle, they flutter like a cloud of butterflies.

The senior helicopter commander in Vietnam at the time was a West Point classmate of mine, and his special knowledge was a vivid supplement to the usual round of formal briefings and high-level conversations. He took me on special flights over the delta region, with its dense population, canals, and endless stretches of rice paddies; over the narrow, but also heavily populated coastal strip; over the solid jungle and mountain of War Zone D, a long-time Communist hide-out immediately northeast of Saigon; and over the piedmont terrain to the north bordering on Cambodia. Everywhere we could see the signs of Viet Cong terrorism—

bridges blown up, ditches dug across the roads, and wrecked trucks beside them. In each province, the evidence of damage went right up to the gates of the provincial capital—and this was true even for Saigon itself. The only safe way to go the eighteen miles from Saigon, for example, to Bien Hoa, where an American air force unit was stationed, was by air or arrange to be escorted by a company of soldiers.

American and Vietnamese intelligence as of January 1962 was estimating that there were about sixteen thousand regular Viet Cong guerrilla forces operating in South Vietnam and that they had about one hundred thousand sympathizers and supporters.[3] Both troops and supporters were concentrated mainly in the less populated central provinces of South Vietnam with two notable exceptions—two heavy concentrations in the Mekong River Delta, the very center of the South Vietnamese population.

The Ho Chi Minh trails through Laos were being used to infiltrate cadres—trained officers and noncommissioned officers—from North Vietnam. These, of course, provided the vital skeleton of leadership, men who were trained for "internal war," in its political as well as military techniques and who were the vehicle of Hanoi's direction of the warfare and the act of their aggression. But they were not numerous, only a few thousand a year—for the rank and file of the guerrillas were being recruited *inside* South Vietnam. It took about three months to walk over these trails from North Vietnam to the delta region in the south, about half the distance inside South Vietnam itself. The men were able to carry their own arms, personal equipment, and food for the journey. But they were not able to carry much else, except radios, code books, medical supplies, and some specialized equipment. Food for the Viet Cong, like the rank and file recruits, came from the villages of South Vietnam. Many of the weapons the Viet Cong used were made by hand inside South Vietnam—like the zip guns of New York City's teenage gangs— and so was much of the ammunition. Other weapons were French, left over from the Indochina war, and an increasingly high proportion were American, captured from the South Vietnamese. One of the most significant facts of all about the use of the infiltration routes was that the cadres that were being sent over them were all *South Vietnamese.* Ninety thousand Communist or pro-Communist southerners had taken the opportunity afforded by the Geneva accords of 1954 to go north, and it was from among these that the infiltrating cadres were picked. The reason, it seemed clear, was partly the need in guerrilla warfare for an intimate knowledge of local terrain and people. But an even more important reason seemed to be the international political advantage to be gained by maintaining the fiction that the Viet Cong was a genuine revolutionary movement arising spontaneously from within South Vietnam. If only southerners were used to fight in South Vietnam, it made it difficult to justify an attack against North Vietnam as retaliation for the guerrilla warfare in the south. And, most importantly of all, by using only southerners in the south, Hanoi seemed to be sending a signal that it wished to establish rules that limited the game, permitting them to save face and salvage prestige if the "internal war" in the south failed.

To meet this threat, the South Vietnamese Government had 175,000 regular soldiers, trained and equipped by the Americans to fight a conventional, Korean-type war, a civil guard of 67,000, and a self-defense corps of 54,000. This was a ratio of eight to one in favor of the government, but past experience had shown that defeating a guerrilla movement requires a ratio more like fifteen to one. The reason is obvious—the government must protect vital installations, bridges, power plants, and so on while the guerrilla seeks only to destroy, and this means that the government must put many of its troops on simple guard duty or the whole economy could be brought to a halt. Even a very few completely desperate men can immobilize thousands, as the handful of gunmen in the Dillinger mob demonstrated in the 1930s when they terrorized the Middle West with their bank robberies.

The measures recommended by General Taylor and adopted by the President would raise the level of Vietnamese strength. In addition, it was General Taylor's hope that the "Farmgate" squadrons of fighter-bombers would give the Vietnamese a decisive edge in firepower and that the helicopter squadrons would give them a decisive edge in mobility. Taylor thought, in fact, that the helicopters might well permit a ratio of soldiers to guerrillas more like ten to one, since they would make it possible for a battalion to fight one day in one province and the next day in another. But what was still needed was a strategic concept based on a true understanding of the nature of "internal war."

It turned out, however, that important work on such a concept was well advanced in Saigon itself, principally by the head of the British Advisory Mission, Robert K. G. Thompson. Thompson was a career officer of the British colonial service, and he had spent most of his life in Malaya. He had occupied responsible office there during the Communist guerrilla terrorism of 1948 to 1959—and from 1957 to 1961 he was successively Deputy Secretary and Secretary for Defence, before taking over the British Advisory Mission in Saigon in 1961.

In Malaya, the British had at first dealt with the guerrilla terrorism as if it were a purely military problem, relying on large-scale military operations, bombing jungle hideouts, and so on, but after two years they were worse off than when they started. It was then that they developed the "new village" program that finally won. Thompson had been at work in South Vietnam applying this experience to the situation there and had come up with what he called the "strategic hamlet" plan.

Thompson pointed out that the Viet Cong's main effort was not in fighting the regular troops—they could have done much more of that than they were actually doing—but in attempting to gain *administrative* control over the sixteen thousand hamlets of South Vietnam.[4] Winning battles against regular Viet Cong units in the field would not really affect the struggle for the villages either way. It was exactly the technique the Communists had used against the French.[5] The French forces established an "iron triangle" of forts around the Red River Delta and Hanoi, and they won every engagement along the battle line. But in the villages *inside* the triangle, Communist agents were at the same time extending and consolidating their administrative control over more and more villages by alternating propaganda and political persuasion with assassination and terror. And the villages gave them a base for both taxation and recruitment. Some villages had two "governments"—a French colonial government by day and a Communist one by night. But it made no difference even if French troops occupied a village for a time. Everyone in the village knew the French would leave sooner or later and whoever had given them information on Communist agents would be executed in the most dramatic fashion. In one case, for example, the Communists woke a whole village in the middle of the night and forced them to watch while three offending youths had their heads hacked off—and the heads were then nailed on the bridge leading to the village as a reminder.

Thompson argued that it was a classic axiom that guerrillas could maintain themselves indefinitely so long as they had support from the population in the area where they operated. The support could be voluntary, motivated by, say, patriotism, as was the support given the French *maquis* effort against the German occupation in World War II. Or it could be given reluctantly, because the guerrillas so ruthlessly dominate the population that the forces of law and order cannot give the people protection from terroristic retaliation on those who help the government. Where a guerrilla force enjoys support from the people, whether willing or forced, it can never be defeated by military means. However much it is harassed and attacked, shelled, mortared, and bombed by superior forces of infantry and artillery, air and sea power, Thompson argued, it is the essence of the guerrilla force that it avoids combat except in conditions of its own choosing. It retains the initiative and selects its own targets. It pursues this policy through all the stages of Mao's "People's Revolutionary War."

The only way to defeat a guerrilla force operating in this way, Thompson was convinced, was systematically to cut it off from its true base of support—the people. For this, obviously, the first step had to be to find a way to give the people physical security. For if they were not protected from the marauding bands of guerrillas and their retaliation, they could not exercise a free choice between supporting the guerrilla forces or supporting the government. And what he proposed as the instrument to provide this physical security was the "strategic hamlet."

STRATEGIC HAMLETS

The strategic hamlet program was, simply, a way of arming the villages of Vietnam so that they could defend themselves if they were attacked by a small band of marauding guerrillas and at least hold out until reinforcements came if they were attacked by a large band. Setting up a strategic hamlet, however, would require political skill, care, and time. Civic action teams would have to be trained to go into each village, to provide simple government services, agricultural extension loans, a school and a teacher, wells, good village and district administration, and effective police protection, as well as training in the use of weapons for self-defense. The role of the police, of course, would be vital—for they would have to win enough people over to the government side to identify the Communist agents before it would be safe to distribute arms to a village militia. And during the weeks and months that all this was going on, regular military forces would have to be stationed in the region to protect both the civic action teams and the villagers until the hamlet was ready to defend itself.

A task that would require especially delicate handling would be consolidating the inhabitants into a compact, defensible unit which could be surrounded by a moat and barbed wire. Most hamlets in Vietnam are a cluster of huts, with a few individual huts scattered out from the main cluster at distances of anywhere from a hundred yards to a mile or so. The outlying houses would have to be dismantled and moved inside the hamlet defenses. Inevitably, there would be opposition to being moved from the traditional homesite, away from family graves, away from family fields, even if it were only a few hundred yards. Later on in the program, as the area covered by strategic hamlets increased, in some cases whole villages would have to be moved, as had happened in Malaya, if they were isolated or particularly accessible to a nearby guerrilla unit. In these cases, the opposition would be even greater.

The essence of the program, however, was that it was to be a program—one lone strategic hamlet could not effectively defend itself. There had to be hedgehogs of strategic hamlets, slowly spreading out like an oil blot from the sea toward the mountains and jungle. Plastic identity cards had to be issued, curfews established, and provincial forces trained to set up checkpoints and ambushes during curfew hours. An iron grid of security had to be established to control the movement of both goods and people, of rice and recruits. A solid bloc of these hamlets, firmly established and consolidated, had to be extended outward to make a zone of security. The people in them had to be armed for their own protection and supported by military and paramilitary forces serving as reinforcements and ensuring the security of their rear areas and their lateral communications with each other. A strategic hamlet program of this kind, Thompson argued, could create the physical security the villager must have before he could make a free choice between the Viet Cong and the government. The primary role of the strategic hamlet was to provide that free choice.

But even though security is the first requirement in fighting guerrilla warfare, it would not be enough by itself to make the villager choose the government side. He could only be brought to choose the government side if the government could show him that what it had to offer him was something better than what the enemy could offer him.

And this, Thompson said, was the second role of the strategic hamlet. He saw the hamlet scheme and the bureaucratic apparatus that would be created to run it as the means for a revolutionary change in the peasant's lot—economically, politically, socially, and culturally. The election of village officials, which Diem had abolished, would be reinstituted. Land reform would be pushed forward, better medical services would be provided, and so would schools, teachers, agricultural credit and extension work, and so on. A governmental structure would be set up for the first time in the history of Vietnam in which information about villagers' needs would go up the ladder, and simple government services would go down.

All this, Thompson argued, should be looked upon as a war measure more important than defeating the Viet Cong in actual battle. If the program were successful, if the peasant in the strategic hamlet really did see that he was better off than under the Viet Cong or than his counterpart was in North Vietnam and if he was also free of the fear of retaliation, then he would finally commit himself to the government's side. He would give government forces information about the location and movement of Viet Cong units and individuals; he would deny the Viet Cong the food and funds and supplies they needed; he would fight against their raids on his village and deny them the opportunity to acquire recruits, whether by persuasion or impressment. The peasant, in effect, would be the one who defeated the Viet Cong, not by killing them but by reducing them to hungry, marauding bands of outlaws devoting all their energies to remaining alive. It would take years of slow, painstaking work, but once this turning point was reached, Thompson was convinced, once the majority of the population had taken the vital decision to throw in their lot with the government, the struggle against the guerrillas would be won. From there on only mopping-up operations would remain.

Thompson proposed that the program should begin with the heavily populated delta, and he offered a phased, fully developed plan to accomplish it.

It seemed to Ambassador Nolting and others in the embassy that Thompson's ideas made a great deal of sense—as they certainly did to me when I heard it all from Thompson himself. And his recommendations jibed completely with the results of the studies we had been conducting in the Bureau of Intelligence and Research. Our analysis of past guerrilla wars seemed to indicate that guerrilla techniques were successful in only two sets of circumstances. One was when the main body of the enemy was fully engaged. The French *maquis,* for example, enjoyed the support of virtually the entire population of France against the German occupation; they were well supplied by air drops from the United Kingdom; and they were well organized. Yet they were not successful until after D-day, when the main body of the enemy was tied down in Normandy. The other set of circumstances was that to be found in Southeast Asia, as well as parts of Africa and Latin America. In Southeast Asia, most peasants lived in villages, in a culture that turns each village inward on itself. The people have little or no identification with the national government. More often than not, the government is remote and little felt, except at tax collection time, and it is usually incapable of giving the villagers day-by-day protection. The villagers are politically and psychologically isolated, by culture, by distance, and by lack of modern transportation systems. In such circumstances, it is not difficult for a trained and disciplined cadre of organizers to recruit an effective guerrilla force. In Burma in World War II, for example, several hundred officers and noncommissioned officers of the American OSS succeeded in building a guerrilla force of thirty thousand men behind the Japanese lines—and they did it with white faces, too.

The State Department analysis also argued that the idea that government existed for the benefit of the people, that a government could really *care,* was as revolutionary in most of Asia as anything the Communists had to offer. The program had at least a chance to win over the allegiance of the people, we felt—if only they could be given physical security for a long enough period of time for the appeal to begin to work.

There were also advantages on the military side of the equation. It is an axiom of war that a primary objective is to cut the enemy's supply lines and to destroy the main body of his strength. The mistake so far had been to conceive the infiltration routes as the enemy's supply line and the regular Viet Cong guerrilla as the main body of his strength. But the true supply lines in a guerrilla war were the thousands of roads and trails radiating out like spokes of a wheel from each of the sixteen thousand hamlets of South Vietnam. And the main body of the enemy's strength was the people of South Vietnam—at least potentially. What the strategic hamlet program was designed to do was to cut those true lines of supply and destroy the guerrilla's access to the main source of strength, the food and potential recruits in the villages.

And the plan had one other strategic advantage of special moment—it would force the guerrilla to fight on the government's terms rather than the guerrilla's. Cut off from its normal flow of supplies from the villages, the guerrillas would have to come out from their mountain and jungle fastnesses to find food and recruits. If a guerrilla band ventured into an established zone of strategic hamlets, it would be entering a meat grinder. Sooner or later it would run into a civil guard patrol or ambush, which would trigger the dispatch of regular troops as reinforcements and further ambushes on the escape routes. If the group went deeper into the zone, it would get hungrier, starved by the controls on the movement of food and people. Eventually the guerrilla group would be forced to attack a strategic hamlet, announcing its presence and triggering more reinforcements and more ambushes. Once solid blocs of strategic hamlets were established, in other words, the whole war could be turned around. Instead of the government forces seeking out the guerrilla and being ambushed, the guerrillas would be forced to come to the government forces and themselves be ambushed.

The more I reflected on my own experience as a guerrilla in Burma and imagined what it would have been like if we had been facing strategic hamlets during World War II, the more I was persuaded. At one stage when I was a guerrilla leader, for example, the Japanese put a whole regiment of almost three thousand men against our guerrilla battalion of not quite three hundred. They conceived of their task as one in conventional warfare, of trying to force our group into a set-piece battle, and they operated in large, unwieldy units that were easy to follow as they moved to set up the trap. As reports came in from our agents and from friendly peasants, we could see their battalions moving into position to form a great half-circle in the north. Thinking in conventional terms, they assumed that a guerrilla unit in trouble would run toward its own lines, in this case north. But actually the concentration of troops is heaviest of all near the front lines and the safer thing for a guerrilla force to do would be to go south, to go deeper into enemy territory where there would be fewer regulars. Then, a Japanese battalion appeared to the south, to chivy us into the trap. We dutifully went north, deeper into the trap until nightfall. Then we broke up into smaller groups and slipped away south to a rendezvous two days' march away—but leaving ambushes on all the trails.

Our Burmese guerrillas were half-sick, undernourished, and poorly trained. The Japanese were regulars, superb fighters, who could walk faster than we and for greater distances. Yet because of the inappropriateness of the conventional tactics they used against our guerrillas they suffered over one hundred dead in a month of chasing us, while we lost only two.

The lesson to be drawn from these experiences was that large-scale, conventional military operations were not effective against guerrillas and that "the way to fight the guerrilla is to adopt the tactics of the guerrilla." What we envisioned was a grid, made up of squares thirty to fifty miles on a side, with a counterguerrilla band in each square behaving like guerrillas, never sleeping two nights in the same place, ambushing and patrolling. Then, highly mobile reinforcements could be held centrally, ready to come in when contact was made and to lay ambushes on all escape routes. The object in this scheme was to wear down the guerrilla by using his own tactics, but what I now saw was that this method would have to be combined with something like Thompson's strategic hamlet plan if the guerrillas were to be prevented from recruiting replacements to offset the attrition.

It seemed more and more possible that an effective strategic concept could be developed by combining Thompson's strategic hamlet plan with the work in Washington and Fort Bragg on both the military tactics to be pursued and the measures to combat the strains of modernization with which Rostow was concerned.

What was clear above all else was that the single most important principle of all—as the British had discovered in Malaya—was that civic, police, social, and military measures had to be combined and carefully co-ordinated in an over-all counterguerrilla program and that there had to be a unified civilian, police, and military system of command and control.

The political and civic action effort at the village level had to be given central emphasis, as in Thompson's plan, and so did police work. If military measures were effectively meshed in, the orthodox military priorities would have to be turned around. But this would be difficult for the Pentagon to accept. Orthodox military doctrine demands that a commander seek out the main body of the enemy and destroy him. The emphasis is on mobility, for in conventional war there is great danger in tying forces down in static defense where they can be defeated piecemeal. For conventional war this is sound doctrine, forged in the fire of combat through many wars. But if the analysis of the nature and requirements of guerrilla warfare was correct, the military priorities would have to be quite different.

THE MILITARY TASKS

Essentially, there would be five separate military tasks. The first was static defense, but it was unavoidable. Forces would have to guard bridges, power plants, communications centers, and other installations essential to keep the economy functioning.

The second task would also tie forces down in static defense. But it was the guts of the strategic hamlet program. This was the "clear and hold" task of pushing regular Viet Cong out of a district or at least holding them at bay so the civic action teams could go to work in the hamlets and of providing the teams and hamlets protection for the weeks or months it took to turn the area into a solid bloc of strategic hamlets capable of defending themselves.

The third task was only partly mobile. This was to serve as reinforcements for strategic hamlets or civil guard units under attack and to set up ambushes on the escape routes.

Only the fourth and fifth tasks would resemble conventional tactics, emphasizing true mobility in seeking out the enemy. But even these would require a guerrilla rather than conventional approach. For the fourth task would be to keep jabbing at the regular Viet Cong forces to keep them off balance as much as possible so they could not concentrate in large enough force to move into a zone of strategic hamlets and destroy enough of them to discredit the program. But here again, this could not be construed as seeking out and destroying the enemy, for the bulk of the government forces would have to be used to concentrate on the first three tasks, and for a long time there would simply not be enough troops available. In the very last stages of the program, when the allegiance of the population had been won and the guerrillas were completely isolated in the mountains, when the whole rural population was protected by strategic hamlets, and when the regular forces were freed from the first three tasks—then and only then would it be possible to shift to a "seek-and-destroy" strategy.

And the fifth task was even more particular, for it would be purely guerrilla. "Sealing off" the borders of South Vietnam and cutting the infiltration routes in any absolute sense would take a million men. But progovernment guerrilla forces operating in the mountains and jungles of South Vietnam through which the infiltration routes passed—and possibly inside Laos as well—could chew up the bands of infiltrators. Laying ambushes, raiding, and patrolling as guerrillas themselves, units of the South Vietnamese Special Forces, for example, could make it much more difficult for the infiltrating Viet Cong, forcing them to fight their way down the trails, to carry more food, more ammunition, and more equipment. Progovernment guerrillas could not cut the Ho Chi Minh network of trails, but they could choke down the flow of traffic over it.

THE OPERATION AT BINH HOA, JANUARY 21, 1962

As it happened, President Diem gave Ambassador Nolting and me an opportunity to see just how much a reorientation in the military priorities was needed almost immediately—he invited us both to observe one of the largest operations so far mounted. On January 21, 1962, an attack was undertaken against the Viet Cong at Binh Hoa, some seventeen miles west of Saigon where a "peninsula" of Cambodian territory juts outward into Vietnam. According to intelligence reports, there were three hundred Viet Cong at a point about two miles from the Cambodian border and a full Viet Cong battalion three or four miles southeast, toward Saigon, at the edge of the only suitable area for a parachute drop. The reports were five days old, but air photos showed an installation that appeared to be a place where the guerrillas were manufacturing munitions, and the decision was to attack.

The plan was prepared by the senior American adviser to the Vietnamese Third Corps. It called for prepositioning four battalions on boats in the river the night before the operation. At 0755 hours the next morning, B-26s from the "Farmgate" squadron were to bomb and strafe the cluster of huts near the Cambodian border where the three hundred Viet Cong were reported to be encamped—but through a tragic error in map-reading, they in fact attacked a Cambodian village just over the border, killing and wounding a number of villagers.

At 0800 hours B-26s attacked the installation suspected of munitions manufacture near the drop zone with five-hundred-pound bombs, and T-28s attacked the huts bordering the drop zone with rockets.

The explosion of the first bomb was the signal for the four battalions to disembark and set up blocking positions along the river and a canal, east and south of the area supposedly sheltering the Viet Cong battalion.

The bombing and strafing continued for forty-five minutes. There was then a fifteen-minute lull.

At 0900 an airborne battalion parachuted into the drop zone and immediately attacked. Two of the four battalions in blocking positions also attacked, forming a pincers.

Except for the error that led to bombing the Cambodian village, the plan was well and efficiently executed—but it was more appropriate to the European fronts of World War II than it was to guerrilla warfare. The prepositioning of troops in boats on the river inevitably gave the guerrillas warning—and if they had failed to heed that warning, the preparatory bombing gave them another. In any case, such elaborate traps will rarely work against guerrillas; the only way to "trap" them is to make contact by blanketing an area with a large number of guerrilla-size patrols, and then follow the contact by reinforcements and ambushes along the escape routes. The greatest problem is that bombing huts and villages will kill civilians and push the population still further toward active support for the Viet Cong.

And so it was at Binh Hoa on January 21, 1962. Villagers reported that there were in fact about two hundred Viet Cong in the area—but that they had moved out one hour before the air strike began. As a result, no contact was made with the Viet Cong that day. No one knows exactly how many Cambodians were killed because of the map-reading error, but in the strafing and bombing around the drop zone five civilians were killed and eleven wounded. A *Life* magazine photographer, Howard Sochurek, who followed the parachutists in by helicopter reported that among the five civilians killed were a two-year-old boy, a five-year-old girl, and a seven-year-old boy.

In fairness, no one should forget that guerrilla warfare was a new and radically different military experience for all military men, requiring them to unlearn old lessons as well as to learn new ones. It would be unfair and unreasonable to expect the military to abandon overnight the principles learned the hard way in bloody and honorable combat in World War II and Korea. The fact that this is precisely what is needed if the subterranean attack of guerrilla warfare is to be met in no way condemns the military or excuses those who do so. Yet it seems obvious that an operation like that at Binh Hoa was not only fruitless but that it helped to recruit more Viet Cong than it could possibly have killed.

REPORT TO THE PRESIDENT

Ambassador Nolting and the embassy had concluded some time before that Thompson was on the right track and had recommended that the United States exert its influence with President Diem to urge that he adopt Thompson's plan, and they were pleased to have support.

I had taken careful notes on R. K. G. Thompson's plan, my conversations with President Diem, the briefings, the Binh Hoa operation, and so on—the pages above are, in fact, drawn from those notes—and had organized them for an oral report to the President. But first I went to General Taylor, who was then Special Military Representative to the President. After going through the whole thing from start to finish, I suggested that there might be portions of it that he would prefer to give the President himself. "No sir!" General Taylor said. "The President should get the full story straight from you, not secondhand. And don't pull any punches, either."

When I got to the Binh Hoa operation in the report, the President shook his head. "I've been President over a year, how can things like this go on happening?" Turning to General Taylor, he asked him to find out why this was still going on—and then they both laughed to see my anguished look. "And try to do it without making the author of the report too unpopular with the Joint Chiefs of Staff," the President added.

The President was impressed with Thompson's ideas and agreed that this was the direction we should go in developing a strategic concept for Vietnam. He told me to write the whole thing up as a formal report under that title—"A Strategic Concept for Vietnam"—and over the next few weeks kept me busy giving the oral version to different people—his brother, the Attorney General; the heads of CIA and AID; and the Vice-President, who was unfortunately in the midst of a Texas political crisis which kept him preoccupied on the telephone during most of the briefing. But what was almost too much, even from a President, was when he thought of General Harkins—for Harkins was by that time in Saigon, and I had to make a special trip.

But I was able to stall that for a few weeks, and before I left the President made one remark that turned out to be painfully prophetic for both himself and his successor. Recalling my statement that it would be impossible to cut off the infiltration routes completely, no matter what draconian measures were taken, the President said that it was really worse than that. Even if the flow was choked down to a trickle, he went on to say, we would still have to carry a political burden. It was not that anyone would actually lie, but every time things went badly in the future, there would be more reports about an increased use of the trails, and people in Saigon and Washington would take them more seriously. "No matter what goes wrong or whose fault it really is, the argument will be that the Communists have stepped up their infiltration and we can't win unless we hit the north. Those trails are a built-in excuse for failure, and a built-in argument for escalation."

NOTES

[1] On three subsequent occasions recommendations were made, largely by the State Department, to assign Lansdale to Vietnam in one or another capacity, but these were also vetoed by the Pentagon until Ambassador Henry Cabot Lodge succeeded in overcoming their objections in 1965.

[2] Both Rostow's speech and mine were subsequently published in anthologies on guerrilla warfare. One of these was under the sponsorship of the *Marine Corps Gazette* and contained a foreword by President Kennedy. See Lieutenant Colonel T. N. Greene, ed., *The Guerrilla—and How to Fight Him,* Frederick A. Praeger, New York, 1962. The other was *Modern Guerrilla Warfare,* Franklin Mark Osanka, ed., the Free Press, 1962.

[3] By 1966, with the benefit of both hindsight and additional information, this estimate had been raised to 23,000 regulars.

[4] Thompson has given an account of his analysis and proposals in his *Defeating Communist Insurgency,* London, 1966.

[5] See Bernard B. Fall, *Street Without Joy,* 1961, and *The Two Vietnams,* 1963.

CHAPTER 29

"And How Do You Know If You're Winning?"

THE SOCIOLOGIST David Riesman once pointed out that the autonomous personality of the nineteenth century differed from the autonomous personality of the twentieth century mainly because of the differences in the obstacles that he had to overcome. In the nineteenth century, the obstacles were hard and solid—symbolized by the stern and unbending Victorian father. In the twentieth century, they were soft, enfolding, and resilient. Overcoming them was like pushing your way through cobwebs. The United States had a strategic concept for overcoming the guerrilla warfare in Vietnam, but implementing it was more and more reminiscent of Riesman's cobwebs.

The American Military Advisory Headquarters in Saigon had become interested in the strategic hamlet idea and had come up with a proposal to build some strategic hamlets along the road from Saigon to Tay Ninh Province in the Ben Cat region—a proposal they dubbed "Operation Sunrise." Unfortunately, it represented a total misunderstanding of what the program should try to do. The motive behind the Sunrise proposal was the American military headquarters' concern about the flow of recruits—which were sent from Tay Ninh Province for training in War Zone D, the Communist jungle base immediately northeast of Saigon. The trouble was that the Sunrise operation, first of all, would require that *all* the hamlets in the region be moved bodily to new locations, not just one or two houses that would have to be brought into an already existing central cluster. We all knew that moving whole hamlets was a politically hot potato, in both Vietnam and the United States, and although it would have to be done on occasion, those occasions should be kept to an absolute minimum and certainly not attempted at the very outset of the strategic hamlet program. Secondly, the absolutely fundamental principle that the program should proceed outward from a secure base, like a spreading oil blot, was completely ignored. For the Ben Cat road was not next to a secure area but at the outer periphery, running through the empty piedmont bordering Zone D's jungle fastness that sheltered the strongest of the Viet Cong's strongholds. Operation Sunrise, in other words, handed the Viet Cong a perfect opportunity to discredit the whole strategic hamlet program.

When I made my second trip to Saigon, on March 17, 1962, as the President had directed, both Harkins and Nolting agreed with our uneasiness about Operation Sunrise. Both had in fact pressed Diem and Nhu to cancel the operation, although they were handicapped by the fact that it was Harkins' predecessor who had first suggested it. In any case, Diem and Nhu were insistent, and both Nolting and Harkins felt that if we pressed them too hard it would jeopardize the whole strategic hamlet program, which Diem had not yet finally approved. All we could do was to try to see that enough troops were assigned to guard duty to deter the Viet Cong from making an example of these four hamlets and then hope.[1] We could not, of course, tell the press that we had been trying to get Sunrise called off. But they saw its flaws immediately and the whole thing cost us heavily in adverse publicity. Homer Bigart of the New York *Times,* particularly, belabored the point—identifying "Operation Sunrise" as an American program and labeling the strategic hamlets as a form of concentration camps.

What was even more disturbing in my talk with Harkins and Nolting was the information that Nhu had become an advocate of the strategic hamlet program and that there were signs that he intended to adapt it to his own purposes and attempt to blanket the whole country with "strategic hamlets" all at the same time, with no regard for the "oil blot" principle or the strength of the individual hamlets. It had been clear for some time that Nhu was going to be a source of trouble, an *éminence grise* isolating Diem from his people and from reality. Harriman, who was at this time Assistant Secretary, had in fact been exploring the idea that Diem might be persuaded to send Nhu to Paris as Ambassador. But Nolting had spoken to Nhu about the dangers of going too fast on the strategic hamlet program, and he was hopeful that Nhu would come around. The way to do this, Nolting said, was with the carrot and not the stick, and Harriman should abandon the idea that Nhu should be shelved. But Nolting's able deputy, William Trueheart, was discouraged and pessimistic, fearful that Nhu would so corrupt the program as to destroy it. On March 19, 1962, President Diem approved the proposal for a strategic hamlet program, with Thompson's delta plan as the first priority, and appointed Nhu to be its head.

Back in Washington that same day, March 19, 1962, I wrote several memoranda reporting my impressions from the trip. In addition to the concern about what Nhu would do to the strategic hamlet program, there were several other problems that caused misgivings.

One went back to the fact that the Taylor mission had not had high-level representation from the political side, and to the Secretary of State's reluctance to have the State Department take the lead in decisions about

Vietnam. The decision to appoint Harkins and the directive setting out his responsibilities and authority had been decided just prior to the Honolulu meetings. Nolting had been in Washington at the time and there, in conversations with Rusk and later in Honolulu with McNamara, he had tried to have the relationship between the Ambassador and the senior American military adviser clarified. Like everyone else, Nolting hoped not only that Vietnam could be saved but that it could be saved without the intervention of United States combat forces. But he, particularly, knew that the margin was not great. He was convinced that the task was essentially political, and he was concerned to have that clearly understood. But he failed to get either concessions from the Secretary of Defense or support from the Secretary of State. He and Harkins did manage to maintain excellent personal relations, but the cost was a mutual forbearance that probably foredoomed the two halves of the American effort to proceed independently of each other. A civilian inter-agency committee, chaired by Trueheart, the Deputy Chief of Mission, for example, pursued the strategic hamlet program with full co-operation from the military in terms of logistical support, the provision of barbed wire and other supplies that came through the military pipe line. But the military at the same time proceeded to fight the "shooting war" quite independently, with little or no attention paid to co-ordinating the military effort with the "oil blot" principle of establishing hamlets. From the beginning, the United States effort lacked both the "unified civilian, police, and military system of command and control" and the "subordination of civic, police, social, and military measures to an over-all counter-guerrilla program" that were the first principles of the strategic concept that had been worked out.

Another cause of concern was the pressure from the military, both Vietnamese and American, to gain the President's approval for the use of military devices that had political disadvantages—such as napalm and defoliants. The battle over napalm—jellied gasoline used in incendiary bombs that burned horribly—had long since been lost. It was a standard item of issue, and the Vietnamese Air Force already had ample stockpiles. Diem and Nhu were enthusiastic about the effectiveness of napalm, and so was the military high command. When General Harkins was asked about the political consequences when villages were hit with napalm, he replied that it "really puts the fear of God into the Viet Cong"—forgetting that in theory at least they were Communist and therefore atheists. "And that," he said, "is what counts." Defoliants, however were new. They were chemical weed killers, which had been highly developed in the United States and were widely used, for example, to kill vegetation along the rights of way of power lines. The military headquarters in Saigon thought that these defoliants would be ideal for clearing the underbrush along the sides of roads where the Viet Cong laid their ambushes and for destroying crops in areas under Viet Cong domination, and General Taylor and the Joint Chiefs of Staff agreed. The State Department view, on the other hand, was that the political repercussions would outweigh any possible gains. Defoliation was just too reminiscent of gas warfare. It would cost us international political support, and the Viet Cong would use it to good propaganda advantage as an example of the Americans making war on the peasants. My own feeling was that at a much, much later stage, when the Viet Cong had been isolated from the population and were attempting to grow their own food in the mountains, the advantages might be significant. But there were certainly no advantages at the present stage when the same rice might be used by both the peasants and the Viet Cong. And as for removing the cover for ambushes, while in Vietnam I had flown down a stretch of road that had been used for a test and found that the results were not very impressive. The leaves were gone, but the branches and trunks remained. Even if they had not, it was not leaves and trunks that guerrillas used for cover, but the curves in the road and the hills and valleys. Later, the senior Australian military representative in Saigon, Colonel Serong, also pointed out that defoliation actually aided the ambushers—if the vegetation was close to the road those who were ambushed could take cover quickly; when it was removed the guerrillas had a better field of fire. But the National Security Council spent tense sessions debating the matter.

Another issue of tension was "interdiction" bombing. Everyone agreed that the T-28s and B-26s of the "Farmgate" units were a very useful addition to the firepower of a South Vietnamese unit actually locked in combat with a Viet Cong unit in the field. What was debatable was whether it was on balance a gain or a loss to bomb huts, "structures," and villages that had been reported to be Viet Cong. The issue was not just of the reliability of the intelligence reports, which was questionable. The real issue went to the heart of Air Force doctrine. And in this, the ground force officers tended to be sympathetic. They and the South Vietnamese troops with whom they served as advisers were being shot at, and they naturally wanted all the help they could get in shooting back. Everyone also agreed that indiscriminate bombing, or even carelessness in bombing, would turn the people toward the Viet Cong, and that intelligence was often faulty. As one American expert put it, the best weapon for fighting guerrillas was a knife, and the worst was a bomber. The second best was a rifle, and the second worst was artillery. But neither the American nor the Vietnamese military were willing to give up "interdiction" bombing entirely—which brought them into opposition to the counterguerrilla strategic concept and its insistence on subordinating military measures to a political program. The result, as usual, was a compromise that in some ways brought the worst of both worlds: interdiction bombing was continued but under stringent intelligence criteria and elaborate centralized controls that limited its use. The military fretted under the limitations, citing incidents in which they took casualties that might have been avoided with more thorough preparatory bombing. And the rest of us fretted about the opposite kind of incidents and the use the Viet Cong were making of them. For they made a practice of removing their own dead, but laying out in the middle of the street the old men, women, and children killed in air strikes.

The two greatest worries, however, were that the "shooting war" would proceed without sufficient co-ordination with the strategic hamlet program and that Nhu's implementation of the hamlet program itself would be too slapdash and try to do too much too soon.

THE SHOOTING WAR

But in spite of the worries, there was a noticeable improvement throughout the spring and early summer of 1962. The influx of United States military aid and advisers boosted the morale of the war-weary South Vietnamese troops, and they showed more *élan* and offensive spirit than they had since the very early days. And the helicopters were grand. They gave the government forces a fantastic mobility, sweeping down out of the sky to set down a battalion here, another there. Roaring in over the treetops, they were a terrifying sight to the superstitious Viet Cong peasants. In those first few months, the Viet Cong simply turned and ran— and, flushed from their foxholes and hiding places, and running in the open, they were easy targets. Success gave still another boost to morale, and the government troops became even more offensive minded. The American advisers, for example, had had great difficulty getting the government troops to go on night operations—"the night belongs to the Viet Cong" was the saying. But by July 1962 even this began to change. The night of July 20 in the largest helicopter attack so far in the war, day or night, government troops put down right smack on top of a Viet Cong battalion and killed 141, losing less than thirty of their own.

AND STATISTICS

Secretary McNamara, with his knowledge of the techniques of statistical control in industry, had set up a number of statistical criteria to help us know how the war was going. By the late summer of 1962, all these statistical indicators had significantly improved. The number of actions initiated by the government troops, a measure of their offensive-mindedness, was up. The number of Viet Cong killed was up, and so was the ratio of Viet Cong killed to government killed. The number of government desertions was down, and the number of Viet Cong captured or defecting was up. Another, even more important statistic was also favorable. About a third of Viet Cong weapons were home made, crude one-shot "zip" guns. Another third were old French weapons, left over from the Indochina war. Another third, but steadily increasing in proportion were American, captured from the government forces. It was therefore particularly encouraging when in September and October of 1962 the government forces for the first time in the war captured more Viet Cong weapons than they lost.*

But even though the statistics were encouraging, there were here and there little signs beginning to appear that were not so encouraging. Sometime in late July 1962 the Viet Cong began to understand that the strategic hamlets were the key to the war—that it was the hamlets that would cut their true lines of communication, their access to rice and recruits. In the delta, especially, the Viet Cong began to attack the strategic hamlets. Nhu's failure to honor the "oil blot" principle and the military's failure to provide an adequate system of rapid reinforcement or otherwise co-ordinate military measures with the political program began to tell. For the hamlets were terribly vulnerable.

Also sometime in late July 1962 the Viet Cong began to develop better tactics against the helicopters. Instead of running when the 'copters showed up, the Viet Cong took cover and learned how to shoot at a helicopter and where. More and more helicopters began to come back with bullet holes in them, and with increasing frequency helicopters were actually shot down. The helicopters first sent to Vietnam were the old banana-shaped transports, with two machine guns added for nominal protection. But by the late fall of 1962, Viet Cong tactics were so good that new, heavily armed helicopters, with four big machine guns and

---

* The question of statistics, their accuracy, reliability, and meaning, was troublesome throughout the Vietnam struggle. Reports of enemy casualties and of the number of engagements initiated by government troops (designed to show offensive-mindedness) were the least reliable of all. On the theory that the number of weapons captured and lost could be subjected to some sort of check if challenged, the figures on this ratio were regarded as more trustworthy. In addition, they were also regarded as more significant. If the people continue to support the guerrillas, whether through conviction or fear, the supply of manpower available to the guerrillas is virtually unlimited. This accounts for the frequently noted phenomena that as the guerrilla struggle increases in intensity and the casualty rates mount, the numbers of guerrillas in the field also increase. The reason is that the proportion of guerrillas to total population is usually very low and that it is easy for the guerrillas to recruit more men if the people support them. When a man is killed, he is quickly replaced. Furthermore, as the intensity of the fighting increases, the guerrillas tend to capture more weapons, and hence to be able to use more men, whom they promptly recruit. (On this point, see R. K. G. Thompson, *op. cit.*, pp. 39–41.) Hence the figures on the ratio of weapons captured to weapons lost tend both to be more reliable than the other statistics, and more significant. In Vietnam it is revealing that these figures always permitted much less optimism than any of the other figures.

sixteen rocket pads, had to be sent out to serve as escorts for the transport 'copters.

Another related sign was a slight stiffening in Viet Cong resistance, a
return, really, of their old aggressiveness. Like the French, the American
military kept hoping that the Viet Cong would someday, someplace,
stand and fight, although they knew full well that guerrillas avoid pitched
battle except at times and places that they are convinced that they can
win. This was why a seemingly insignificant incident in early October was
worrisome to the men in the field—and, as it happened because of President Diem's reaction to it, this particular incident was much more
significant than even the men in the field realized at the time. Elements
of the Seventh Division, stationed in the delta in the region around the
town of My Tho, were on a routine sweep, when suddenly one of the
Viet Cong units chose to turn and fight. It wiped out a whole platoon of
Rangers, among the best troops the government had.

As a sign of stiffening Viet Cong resistance, the incident was bad.
But it had even longer-range repercussions when President Diem heard
about it. For a few days later, Diem called the Seventh Division commander to Saigon and rebuked him for his high rate of casualties and,
intentionally or not, discouraged him from undertaking too many offensive operations.

No one knows what Diem's reasons for this action were. It could be
argued that he sensed that defeating the guerrillas would be a long, slow
process and that it would be better to husband the strength of the government forces rather than dissipate it in too much American "gung ho"
offensive-mindedness. The basic idea of the strategic hamlet program was
consistent with a slow approach in its stress on the "oil blot" principle.
But he never raised this question with either General Harkins or Ambassador Nolting, who did not learn of Diem's "go slow" instructions until
much, much later. And this gives credibility to the rival explanation,
which a few of the military advisers in the field adopted as well as most
of the American press, particularly David Halberstam of the New York
Times and Neil Sheehan of the United Press International.

THE PRESS VIEW

Halberstam and Sheehan started with the conviction that the struggle
against the guerrillas could not be won with Ngo Dinh Diem and his
regime. Diem, they felt, was an unpopular dictator, hearing and believing nothing but what his baleful brother, Ngo Dinh Nhu, and Madame
Nhu told him. Because of its unpopularity, the regime adopted more and
more repressive measures, and this made it inefficient as well. Province
chiefs, corps commanders, division and regimental commanders, and
even battalion commanders, were promoted, according to this thesis, not

because of their effectiveness as soldiers but as a result of personal loyalty to the Ngos. This made for inefficient, cowardly leadership—it led, the argument concluded, to "political" generals who would not fight and who falsified the records.

Halberstam and Sheehan made friends with Lieutenant Colonel John Paul Vann, senior American adviser to the Seventh Division, an energetic, idealistic, dynamic officer with strong convictions about the need for a more aggressive and efficient conduct of the war and a willingness, in order to achieve it, to tread on the toes of either his Vietnamese counterparts or his own American superiors. The town of My Tho and the Seventh Division headquarters were only forty kilometers by road from Saigon—a quick and easy drive—and Vann became a major source for Halberstam and Sheehan and served as their litmus paper to test the progress of the "shooting war." In the weeks following Diem's admonition to the Seventh Division commander, Colonel Vann—and through him Halberstam and Sheehan—became convinced that the Seventh Division was conducting operations against places that intelligence indicated were *free* of Viet Cong. This would inflate General Harkins' statistics on offensive operations, but avoid casualties. And when operations were mounted against areas where the Viet Cong really were, Vann and the newsmen were also convinced, the battle plans left a gap through which the Viet Cong might escape—again as a device for keeping government casualties low.

The evidence to support this interpretation of what was happening in the fall of 1962 in Vietnam is laid out in Halberstam's book, *The Making of a Quagmire.* In it, for example, he argues that in the end the helicopters did more harm than good, for they permitted the government forces to conduct operations on regular "office hours"—out in the field in the morning and back at base by cocktail hour. But Colonel Vann and the two or three other military advisers who were convinced that the "shooting war" was not going well were not able to convince the American military headquarters in Saigon of the merit of their view, nor were Halberstam and Sheehan doing much better in gaining adherents in Washington. Neither did very well, that is, until the battle of Ap Bac, which was a village near My Tho.

THE BATTLE OF AP BAC

Regular troops and conventional tactics are not effective against the guerrilla, and the more they are used the more frustration mounts. As late as October 1964, for example, a senior military spokesman in Saigon, speaking of ambushes, said, "Our fervent hope is that they'll stick their neck out with about six battalions around here some day and try to hold something, because as of that time, they've had it. . . . The VC are excellent at ambushes, but that's kind of a coward's way of fighting the war . . ."

The trouble, of course, is that if the guerrilla knows his job he will avoid a set-piece battle unless the cards are stacked in his favor. Very occasionally, however, a trap will work, and the guerrilla will be forced into a set-piece battle. This is what happened at Ap Bac.

Good intelligence was received in the last few days of December 1962 that a battalion of Viet Cong numbering about two hundred men were at the little village of Ap Bac. The government plan called for landing one battalion of regular forces by helicopter just north of the village to pin the Viet Cong down, while two battalions of civil guard troops would come up on foot from the south. Air and artillery support were also available, but most important of all was a company of armored and amphibious personnel carriers mounting a fifty caliber machine gun and recoilless rifles. Called 113s, these vehicles were the nearest thing to a tank in Vietnam, and their role at Ap Bac was to assault the Viet Cong position from the west. There was also a reserve force standing by with helicopters to fly them to whatever spot they were needed as the battle developed.

The first of the government battalions was landed without much trouble—the Viet Cong held their fire to avoid giving away their positions, while they probed for a way out to the south. Their probe met the first of the civil guard battalions, and they shifted their probe to the west. Here they ran into the second civil guard battalion and apparently saw the armored personnel carriers coming up still farther to the west. So the Viet Cong commander decided to return to the prepared positions at Ap Bac and give battle—"It is better," he wrote in his after-action report, which was later captured, "to stand and die than run and be slaughtered."

Back in their foxholes, the Viet Cong quickly pinned down the government troops advancing from the north through the flat paddy fields. The government commander and Colonel Vann then decided to land the reserve force by helicopter just west of the village. The Viet Cong had a clear field of fire on the helicopters as they came in with their troops. Five helicopters were shot down, three Americans were killed along with a large number of the Vietnamese troops as they left the helicopters and spread out toward the village.

Urgent orders went to the armored 113s to attack and relieve the situation—but the commander, whom Halberstam in his account calls a "key Diem appointee," refused to take his vehicles through the network of canals and paddy fields. The American adviser to the 113 unit finally scouted a route through the paddy fields himself, but it took the force four hours to cover it, although they took only fifteen minutes coming back over the same route. And when they finally did get to the scene of the battle, they still hung back, firing their machine guns and recoilless rifles blind, crouched down behind the armor.

The two civil guard battalions to the south came under the command of the province chief, rather than the Seventh Division—an arrangement, Halberstam says, that Diem and Nhu used in order to play province chiefs and division commanders off against each other. In any case, this particular province chief refused several requests to attack and relieve the two regular battalions. One of the civil guard battalion commanders, in fact, saw the opportunity in front of him and himself requested permission to attack. But the province chief insisted that his troops were there to form a blocking position, not to attack.

That night the Viet Cong slipped away, carrying their own dead, but leaving behind the government casualties—sixty-one dead and over one hundred wounded. It was a stunning defeat for the government forces. They had outnumbered the Viet Cong at least four to one. They had the mobility of helicopters. They had the superior firepower of artillery. They had support from the air. They had the awesome might of the armored personnel carriers. Yet they had been badly beaten.

What Colonel Vann and Halberstam had been saying about the inefficiency, bad leadership, and lack of aggressiveness of the government forces seemed to be confirmed—if not their conclusion that the cause of it all was the corruption and unpopularity of the Diem regime. The Diem government, naturally, tried to put the battle in the most optimistic light by arguing that the Viet Cong had suffered even more heavily than the government. It disgusted the American reporters that the American military headquarters did not deny this interpretation. It disgusted them even more when American headquarters actually seemed to agree with that interpretation. Then, a few days later, General Harkins himself called Ap Bac a "Vietnamese victory," because it had "taken the objective"— and their disgust was complete.

Halberstam, in fact, became vehemently convinced that General Harkins was misleading his own government. At times he seemed to suggest that information being sent to Washington was deliberately distorted. Generally, however, he argued more charitably that it was the result of a vicious circle. The Americans were so wedded to a policy of supporting Diem that they were blind to plain facts. They were so saddled with a policy of optimism that they stupidly misled themselves. They believed the false statistics which Diem and Nhu passed over to them, even if Diem and Nhu did not believe the false statistics with which they were being supplied by accommodating generals and province chiefs they had appointed solely for reasons of politics.

DETERIORATION OF THE "SHOOTING WAR"

Halberstam probably overstates his case, but the evidence does support the conclusion that the initial momentum had gone out of the "shooting war" some time in the summer or fall of 1962, and that the military situation had actually begun to deteriorate. Ap Bac was not the only sign of a renewed initiative, confidence, and aggressiveness on the part of the Viet Cong. They fought their way into a heavily defended Special Forces camp at Plei Mrong in the central highlands, breaking the perimeter. The Americans were finally able to rally the defenders, but over 39 were killed and 114 weapons captured. They overran a strategic hamlet in Phu Yen, in the central coastal region, again capturing a substantial number of weapons. Throughout the country, more and more isolated posts were being overrun, and the defenders' weapons captured. Diem and Nhu insisted on continuing to show the flag at these untenable outposts deep in Viet Cong territory or near the jungle far from reinforcement, in spite of the fact that they obviously served the Viet Cong as storehouses for American weapons which they could take whenever they chose. The fact that they now chose was a sign that the guerrillas had expanded their numbers and needed additional weapons. The statistics were also down somewhat. The ratio of weapons captured to weapons lost turned unfavorable again in November 1962 and stayed that way.[2] The kill and desertion ratios were also less favorable. The number of Viet Cong-initiated incidents was over a thousand in February 1963, the highest for a single month in the whole war. But the statistics on government-initiated operations continued high, and this was particularly encouraging to the American military command at Saigon, because of their emphasis on aggressiveness. There were some misgivings about the fact that there was no way for Americans to gather the statistics or really to check on them and that we were therefore completely dependent on the hierarchy appointed by Diem and Nhu. But the policy continued to be one of "cautious optimism."

AND IN THE HAMLET PROGRAM

This, then, was the "shooting war." The political and social side of the equation, the strategic hamlet program, was also worrisome. The trouble was that enemy strength continued to go up. Intelligence credited the Viet Cong with actually increasing their regular unit strength in 1962, from about sixteen thousand to twenty-three thousand, in spite of having suffered, according to government claims, losses of twenty thousand. At the same time, captured documents, interrogation of prisoners, and other intelligence indicated that *at the most* only three to four thousand infiltrators had come down the Ho Chi Minh trails. The explanation in Saigon was that the increase in Viet Cong strength was partly due to better intelligence methods; that is, that there had really been more Viet Cong all along than previous estimates had allowed. And there were also suggestions—as President Kennedy had foreseen—that the last month of 1962, for which the reports were not in, might show a "vast increase" in infiltration. But what seemed most likely was that the Viet Cong continued to maintain and even improve their access to the villages, their source of recruits as well as food. And this meant that the strategic hamlet program might also be in trouble.

On December 19, 1962, I sent the results of a study we had been making in the Bureau of Intelligence and Research to Governor Harriman, with copies to the President and other members of the National Security Council. The strategic concept, we recalled, specified a combination of military, political, economic, and social action on such a scale and so co-ordinated as to constitute a national response to the Viet Cong challenge. Broadly speaking, the program required: (1) developing military and paramilitary counterguerrilla capabilities; (2) separating and protecting the population from the Viet Cong; and (3) applying the political and economic and social measures that are necessary to convert military successes into political gains. Looking at the evidence available, we concluded that there "appears to be no reason as yet to question the soundness of the concept, but there is a very real question as to how well and whole-heartedly it is being put into effect."

In the first category—developing military and paramilitary capabilities—the logistics part of the problem was rapidly being overcome. Weapons, helicopters, radios, ammunition were all flowing to South Vietnam at an impressive rate. But the evidence also indicated that the increased capabilities were not being exploited as effectively as they might be. "First, GVN [Government of Vietnam] military forces continue to rely heavily on large-scale operations and conventional tactics. Second, excessive use of air strikes in the absence of ground contact with the enemy continues to kill a lot of innocent peasants. Third, inadequate delegation of authority and political interference by the leadership has restricted initiative in the field. Independent and offensive deployment of civil guard and Self-Defense Corps units has weakened strategic hamlet defenses and produced heavy casualties."

The second category—isolating the Viet Cong and winning the peasants—was concerned with the strategic hamlets themselves. According to the government of Vietnam more than 3500 hamlets had been completed and 2000 more were under construction. What was not certain was how much of the program of social, political, and economic measures was actually being carried out inside the hamlets that had been declared completed. "In many," the memorandum related, "nothing seems to have been done but to construct a bamboo or barbed wire fence. The hamlets have become a major Viet Cong target, which suggests that the Viet Cong feel the hamlets do threaten their access to the people. However, we cannot generalize about the success with which the hamlets have withstood Viet Cong attacks."

The third category was "pacification"—the point at which military and social action meet. "Establishing strategic hamlets," we said, "and systematic military-political pacification are distinct but necessarily integrated phases of the strategic concept. The purpose of these measures is to isolate and protect the peasants from the Communists, to gain their support in the counterguerrilla effort, and ultimately to produce lasting political, social, and economic reform at the local level." But even though the Vietnamese Government had given high priority to the concept, the "hamlet program on the whole has been precipitous and uncoordinated, and the pacification plans [i.e. Thompson's delta plan] slow to be implemented:

"—Vietnamese leadership looks on the strategic hamlet program as a panacea, and there is still considerable confusion among local officials as to the objectives of the program and the procedures for implementing it.

"—strategic hamlets have been, and still are, being thrown together in the absence of a coordinated pacification effort, such as conceived in the Delta plan, and with only perfunctory attention to defense and socio-economic administrative improvements.

"—pacification operations have been only applied to six of South Vietnam's forty-one provinces, and have been completed in none. Although Diem formally assigned top priority to the Delta plan provinces in August, he has failed, probably for political reasons, to support the strategic hamlet program essential to the Delta plan or indeed the general pacification effort itself."

Our over-all assessment and conclusion were not encouraging: "The GVN has developed an effective strategic concept for counter-insurgency and has, in fact, mounted a national effort to implement it. The principal defects appear to arise mainly from improper emphasis applied to various aspects of the concept:

"—the Army has overemphasized large-scale actions and the use of artillery and air power as compared with small unit actions and intelligence collection. Although emphasis on patrols and on ambushes appears to be increasing, continued and excessive use of air power and crop destruction [with defoliants] however well controlled may well develop a militant opposition from the peasants and their positive identification with the Viet Cong.

"—the GVN has overemphasized the establishment of strategic hamlets per se, and has only begun to fit them into an integrated political-military pacification effort.

"—GVN failure to emphasize political, social, and economic reform at the outset may deprive the entire effort of much of its impact. Much depends on the ability of the Government to show convincing evidence of its intent to improve the lot of the peasants. Instead, Government efforts appear to be aimed largely at increasing Government control over the peasants."

A PRESIDENTIAL MISSION

The President asked Michael Forrestal and me to take a quiet trip to Saigon to see if there was anything more that might be done, and we arrived on December 31, 1962—just in time for the debacle at Ap Bac.

But we found that in spite of Ap Bac, General Harkins and Ambassador Nolting were strongly and quite genuinely optimistic. They had several reasons. First the flow of American military aid—helicopters, armored personnel carriers, weapons, and ammunition—was at full volume, and it was impressive. The mere sight of all that hardware was good for Vietnamese morale. Aid for the civilian side of the program, especially the strategic hamlets, was just beginning to come in, and Ambassador Nolting and his deputy, Trueheart, both felt that once it, too, reached full volume the results might be dramatic. They were impressed with the drive that Nhu had put into the strategic hamlet program. He claimed, for example, that four thousand had already been established and that new ones were being set up at the rate of three hundred to four hundred a month. And they were impressed with the vigor with which the military side was being pushed, the new aggressiveness displayed by the government troops as demonstrated by the statistics on the number of operations mounted at their initiative.

It was truly encouraging, they felt, but there were also disturbing aspects. A memorandum for the record that I dictated at the time reads as follows:

At this point, some 36 hours after having arrived in Saigon, I have the impression that things are going much better than they were a year ago, but that they are not going nearly so well as the people here in Saigon, both military and civilian, think they are. They have a sound concept in the strategic hamlet program; they have aid; and they have lots of people. All this gives them a sense of movement and of progress. The trouble is, however, that the progress and movement is highly uneven. One would wish that this was the fault of the Vietnamese, and to a considerable extent, it is. But I am afraid that a great share of the responsibility belongs to the Americans. We have the impression that any one of these programs, such as the strategic hamlet program . . . requires precise and efficient coordination of the activities of many different American agencies; and you also have the impression that this coordination is not really being accomplished. The failure to provide a police program that is even remotely phased in with the provision of barbed wire and radios for the strategic hamlets is one example. Thus you have strategic hamlets going up enclosing Communists inside their boundaries with no provision for winkling out those Communists.

Other things are similar. You also have the impression that the military is still too heavily oriented toward "sweep" type operations. There is also still the same emphasis on air power as there was before. Almost every operation, so far as I can tell, still begins with an air strike which inevitably kills innocent people and warns the Viet Cong that they should get moving for the troops will be coming soon. I think all this indicates that the Americans are just as much to blame as the Vietnamese.

A GENERAL'S OPINION

The most disturbing analysis on the military side came from an old friend of mine, a West Pointer who was now one of the youngest generals in the army and clearly destined for the top. He had been several months on a special mission to Vietnam connected with the development of new tactics and equipment. Since he was not in the chain of command, he was free of any commitment to any particular policy line or interpretation, yet he had been an observer on dozens of operations. He described a typical operation in the following words.

"Intelligence reports that a Viet Cong battalion is at a certain village. An operation is mounted for, say, eight o'clock in the morning, following close on the heels of an air strike. But there is usually a delay before the troops move out—while they wait for confirmation that the air strike has in fact taken place.

"The helicopters then move out, and the troops are landed by the village. They move forward. Suddenly, there is a scurrying on the right flank, and someone drags a peasant out of a rice paddy, where he has been hiding. He is bound and taken back as a suspected Viet Cong.

"The troops proceed. A black-clad man jumps up from a paddy field on the left and runs toward the jungle. He is shot and killed—presumed to be Viet Cong, since he ran.

"When the troops arrive at the village it is deserted, except for a senile old man or perhaps an addled young girl—an 'Ophelia' type. Under interrogation, the 'Ophelia' points toward a cellar or a spot in the nearby jungle and the troops drag out and bind another suspected Viet Cong.

"It is now noon. Cookpots are brought out of packs; perhaps a chicken is captured; and a meal is cooked and eaten.

"In the afternoon there is more patrolling, and the helicopters return to fly the troops back to their base."

This able young general had been an observer on so many operations that had proceeded in just this way that he had begun to think that the purpose of the bombing at the beginning of an operation was to give any

Viet Cong that happened to be in the neighborhood sufficient warning so that battle—and casualties—could be avoided. And he, like Halberstam, put it down to Diem's policy.

He had three other criticisms. One was of a recent decision by the Pentagon to take the responsibility for administering the Special Forces' work with the *montagnards,* the hill peoples, away from the CIA and turn it over to the regular army headquarters in Saigon. "What this will mean," he said, "is a further step away from using guerrilla techniques against the guerrillas and another step toward regular, conventional tactics." His second criticism was that nothing at all had been done along the lines of the recommendation of a year earlier to use Vietnamese Special Forces to act as guerrillas in both Laos and the mountains of South Vietnam to ambush, harass, and chew up the groups of infiltrators coming down the Ho Chi Minh trails—making them fight their way south. The blame for this failure he put mainly on Nhu, who controlled the Special Forces and used them to further his own personal political aims. But he also blamed our own military high command. For here, again, there was a group that felt that long-range, guerrilla patrolling inside Laos would be a precedent for limited warfare. It was basically the same issue that had caused the policy battles during the Laos crisis. The group in the military who were determined that there should "never again" be a limited ground war in Asia were willing to go into Laos only if they were permitted to go in full force and with advance permission to use air power—which raised the question of "escalation" and our commitment to the 1962 Geneva agreements on Laos.

"And what is your third criticism?" I asked. "Well, we have a huge headquarters here in Saigon, so big it has twenty-two generals. My third criticism," he said ruefully, glancing down at the stars on his shoulder, "is that there are too many American generals in Vietnam."*

Coming from one of the most promising young generals in the United States Army, all this was most disturbing. But, as the general said, he could not be sure about any of his criticisms. The government forces seemed to be staging operations that were either not intended to close with the enemy or were designed to leave the enemy an escape route, but no one could be certain. Guerrillas were elusive and counter-guerrilla operations traditionally had a low rate of contact. Battles did occasionally take place between the government forces and the Viet Cong. Many were Viet Cong ambushes or Viet Cong attacks against outposts and strategic hamlets. But some were the result of offensive action by the government forces and Viet Cong were being killed in all types of engagement. A final judgment was difficult to make.

* None of the twenty-two, incidentally, had had Special Forces training, and none was concerned with the strategic hamlet program. In the whole headquarters, in fact, only two lieutenant colonels were assigned to that particular program.

STRATEGIC HAMLETS IN THE COASTAL STRIP

The real test of the strategic hamlet program was in the delta, which Forrestal and I would visit with R. K. G. Thompson. But in the meantime we looked at several hamlets in the narrow coastal strip between Saigon and Hué. Two or three looked good. The outlying houses had been taken down and rebuilt inside a compact perimeter. There were good defenses, good fields of fire, and the self-defense units seemed to know their weapons and how to use them. There were signs of political and social action programs—cement pigstys, a good well, a new schoolhouse, and so on. But two or three of the other strategic hamlets we saw were pitiful. The defenses were a sham—a moat and a wall, topped by barbed wire and bamboo spikes, meandering around fields and outlying houses for so many miles that a whole division would be needed to defend it. But the defenders were only a few old men, armed with swords, a flintlock, and half a dozen American carbines. One wondered where the young men were, and which of the many gaps in the wall they used when they came back at night to collect food and see their wives.

One very large question was what could be done to improve the police work inside the strategic hamlets. For it seemed obvious that putting up defenses around a village would do no good if the defenses enclosed Viet Cong agents—no matter how much political and social action took place. Another large question was what could be done to improve the time it took to get reinforcements to a village under attack. "Flare ships"—aircraft equipped to drop parachute flares that lit up the countryside—were a great help to a village or outpost under attack, but other reinforcements seemed to be much too slow. While Forrestal and I were in Vietnam a strategic hamlet in the central coastal region was attacked and the defenders held off the Viet Cong for twenty-four hours before they were overrun—but the reinforcements arrived only after the Viet Cong had killed the defenders, captured their weapons, executed the village officials, and departed.

So again the evidence was mixed. Impressive progress on the strategic hamlet program in the narrow coastal strip was counterbalanced by obvious failures, and here, too, a final judgment was difficult.

THE PRESS PROBLEM

If we learned nothing else, we learned that in guerrilla warfare it is not easy to know whether you are winning or losing. We had official briefings from the Vietnamese and from the Americans. We had long, confidential talks with our top people. We consulted friends at any place we could find them. We went out in the field to see whatever we could ourselves. We talked to newsmen privately. President Kennedy himself, in fact, had made a point of this. He had asked me to meet *alone* with the American reporters in Saigon to see what we in Washington might do to help improve their difficult situation—and also, he had made a point of saying, "Find out how they think the war is going."

Relations with the press in Vietnam were troubled. Partly, the source was the same as within the American government—a difference of opinion over the way to meet the guerrilla attack and, increasingly, over the policy of supporting Ngo Dinh Diem. This difference of opinion, in fact, eventually came to split the press itself. At one stage, for example, Joseph Alsop accused the American press in Vietnam of conducting a crusade against the government, of painting a "dark, indignant picture," and of sticking to Saigon and not visiting the "front." Marguerite Higgins went so far as to say that the American reporters "would like to see us lose the war to prove they're right." Some articles attacked Halberstam and Sheehan by name. Probably the most unusual event of all was an unprecedented editorial in *Time* magazine that accused the American press corps in Vietnam of "helping to compound the very confusion that it should be untangling for its readers at home. . . . They have covered a complex situation from only one angle, as if their own conclusions offered all the necessary illumination"—which led to several resignations, including that of Charles Mohr, chief of *Time*'s Southeast Asia Bureau.

The American press permanently stationed in Vietnam were almost all convinced that the struggle against the Viet Cong could not be won so long as Diem and his family remained in power, and their conviction was reinforced by Diem's policy of making life difficult for reporters who wrote things he did not like or even having them expelled from Vietnam entirely. The United States policy of supporting Diem irritated them. And the policy, under Nolting, of attempting to bring about reforms through friendly persuasion irritated them even more. But what infuriated them—and justifiably so—was when the policy of trying to get along with Diem resulted in the mission failing to protest effectively when Diem did something outrageous like expelling an American newsman when he wrote an unfavorable story.

All this was worsened by ineptness on the part of both the embassy and the American military headquarters in the way they handled the press. Ambassador Nolting argued with the press, usually accepting Diem's side of a controversy, and rarely if ever gave them a story. General Harkins gave the appearance of distrusting them. He refused, for example, to give American newsmen advance notice of operations because of the danger of leaks to the Viet Cong—a position which seemed to question the reporters' patriotism. In general, the attitude among high American military officers made the reporters feel that they were expected to write just what the military wanted them to write. The reporters frequently cited the remark Admiral Felt, Commander in Chief in the Pacific, made on first meeting Neil Sheehan—"So you're Sheehan. Why don't you get on the team?"

But even with the most skillful and sympathetic treatment, relations with the press would still have been troubled, for the government and the press had fundamentally different interests. The United States Government, for example, had introduced aircraft with the "Farmgate" units that were not provided for under the Geneva agreements and had increased the number of American advisers far past the six hundred permitted under those agreements. The American government believed that these moves were fully justified by the fact that it was the North Vietnamese that had started the guerrilla aggression in South Vietnam in violation of the Geneva agreements, but at the same time the American government did not want what they were doing highly publicized. The interest of the American press on the other hand—even their duty, as they saw it—was to inform the American public fully on what their government was doing. And I must confess that my own instincts in this case were on the side of the reporters. In March of 1962, after returning from my second trip to Vietnam, what seemed to me most urgently in need of revision was the policy of trying to keep "Farmgate" and the extent of American Air Force participation secret. We in the State Department had made too much of the political costs of a violation of the Geneva accords that was in truth fully justified by Communist aggression, and the President had made too much of adverse press reaction. In this early period, at least, it was a fair criticism to say that, whereas Eisenhower had read the newspapers too little, Kennedy was reading them too much.

In late November 1962, American reporters had been excluded by the Vietnamese Government from an operation that had involved forty-five American helicopters, the largest so far, on the grounds, they later said, that they were afraid one might be killed. This made the reporters angry and what made them even angrier was that the American mission took it lying down. But this had now been corrected—American reporters could go where American soldiers went—so the reporters with whom I met had no complaints about the co-operativeness of the American authorities. As for the Vietnamese authorities things had not improved, but the reporters seemed to feel that recently, at least, the mission had supported the newsmen better than they had in the past. As for the war, they seemed to agree that the influx of military aid and helicopters had helped—but most of them emphatically did not agree that the optimism of Harkins and the American military headquarters was justified. One reporter, Charles Mohr, told me something that seemed particularly significant—that from the beginning of his tour in Vietnam he had driven regularly the forty miles to My Tho, in the Seventh Division area, but that the road was no longer safe. Mohr felt that the basic trouble was that the Ngo family, and particularly Nhu, were unalterably hostile to the United States. The only difference of opinion between us was that it seemed to me that our objective was not to be liked, but to get a job done.

So once again the judgment was mixed. Most of the reporters in Vietnam could agree both that Diem had obvious and serious flaws and that he also had impressive strengths. But they differed on whether it would be strengths or weaknesses that tipped the balance in the struggle with the Communists.

POLITICAL ATTITUDES AND THE "NATIONAL CADRE"

Actually, the issue was bigger than just the personality of Diem, his dictatorial regime, or his family. The issue was the political viability of the country and whether or not even the potential existed in South Vietnam to carry out the kind of tightly disciplined, precisely co-ordinated political, social, and military program that would be needed to defeat the guerrillas. On the plane going out Forrestal and I had decided that this would be the central judgment. We had since discovered that making a judgment on any aspect of guerrilla warfare was difficult—but this, clearly, was the most difficult.

No one really knew what the peasants thought. But the evidence available, again, seemed to indicate that they were turned inward on themselves—pro-Viet Cong if they lived in safe Viet Cong territory; pro-government if they lived in safe government territory; and wishing that both sides would go away if they lived in an area of contention. This only meant that the political situation was fluid in so far as the peasants were concerned—that the peasants were at least in theory persuadable and that something like the strategic hamlet program was the right approach. But what was the attitude of the people who would have to implement the strategic concept in all its aspects? These were the people who might be called the "national cadre" of Vietnam—the officers and noncommissioned officers of the armed services, the government bureaucrats, the functionaries at province and district level, the teachers, the tiny strata of business entrepreneurs and labor leaders, and the small number of professional men. These were the people who would have to run a counterguerrilla program. American help was needed, for there were too few of these people with too little training for them to do the job all by themselves. But without them it would be impossible.

It was not so much a question of these people being anti-Communist or of how deeply they wanted to resist Communist domination and preserve their half of Vietnam. There was a hard core of Catholics at all levels of the national cadre who were bitterly anti-Communist, of course. And the leadership of the sects, such as the Hoa Hao, were almost as staunch in their anti-Communism as the Catholics, although they were far from enthusiastic followers when it was Diem who led the fight against the Communists. As far as the rest were concerned, however, the Confucian and Buddhist members of the national cadre, they seemed to want at least to *try* to prevent a Communist take-over, but without the same passion. Although there were inchoate stirrings of Vietnamese nationalism always present, the opposition of the national cadre to Communism was clearly not an ideological commitment.

A dictatorial, ascetic mandarin who was at the same time a devout Catholic was hardly the one to call forth the passionate dedication inherent in the latent nationalism of such a national cadre. It was perfectly clear by this stage in history, certainly, that no one was going to persuade Diem to become a popular democratic leader, even though he might grudgingly go along with making enough reforms to make his regime more responsive to the people and their needs. But precisely as a mandarin, Diem might well be able to serve as a symbol that would suffice to organize the efforts of the national cadre—if he could give them enough executive leadership to produce practical successes. No matter how one twisted and turned the problem in other words, it always came back to Ngo Dinh Diem.

THE PERSONALITY OF DIEM

I had met Diem in January of 1962, on the occasion of my first visit to Vietnam. Ambassador Nolting and I had spent six hours with him. Diem was a compulsive talker, and he used the occasion of meeting a foreign visitor as a bridge enthusiast would an evening at cards. He had welcomed me as a former guerrilla fighter whose views he wanted to hear, and had then talked without permitting an interruption for the whole six hours. On that occasion all the qualities of asceticism and ability and patriotism had come out very strongly. But so had the qualities of self-isolation, of distrust of everyone around him, and of his inability to delegate authority to anyone but Nhu. To Ambassador Nolting's distress, for example, Diem had volunteered some disparaging remarks about his Vice-President, the old and revered Nguyen Ngoc Tho. And he spent much of the time relating how he had discovered on a captured map vital information that his intelligence people had overlooked and how this had convinced him that he would have to set up an independent intelligence agency in the palace which he himself would head. In January of 1962, Diem had seemed distraught, disorganized, and cut off from his own people.

When Forrestal and I saw him in January of 1963, however, he was calmer, more self-possessed, and more statesmanlike. He still talked compulsively and interminably—but what he said was more to the point and showed a deep concern for the welfare and future of all his people. Forrestal and I had just visited the American Special Forces camp at Plei Mrong, which had only a few days before been overrun by the Viet Cong with the loss of over sixty of the *montagnards* being trained and 114 weapons, and this had started off our conversation. Diem drew us a remarkably detailed sketch of the defenses of the camp and accompanied it with a devastatingly correct and completely fair critique of the mistakes in siting weapons, in cutting fields of fire, and so on made by the West Point commander of the camp. It made me squirm, particularly when Diem recalled that I, too, was a West Pointer. He then went on to talk of the *montagnard* people, giving us an analysis of the history and tribal differences among them that was masterful. And he followed this with a boldly stroked picture of his vision of the future development of the *montagnard* peoples that was both magnanimous and moving.

"Well, what do you think?" I asked Forrestal after we left. "Will we 'sink or swim Ngo Dinh Diem?'" quoting the popular phrase coined by Homer Bigart. "You told me he was impressive," Forrestal said, "and he is. Both Chiang Kai-shek and Syngman Rhee were able to lead their nations successfully—in certain circumstances. Diem could too, if the circumstances are right. But only if it were he who really led it."

What Forrestal clearly had in mind was Diem's brother, Nhu, and Nhu, able and vigorous though he clearly was, seemed to be an influence leading to disaster. He had a paranoiac suspiciousness in his make-up and a grandiose, even apocalyptic view of himself and his family that hinted of madness. Talking to him at a dinner given by Nguyen Dinh Thuan, the able and levelheaded Secretary of State, for example, I was reminded that Nhu had visited Algeria for a few days at the height of the Algerian crisis and had then gone to Paris to offer his services to de Gaulle—assuring him that he, Nhu, could solve the Algerian problem in a week or two at most. Now, at the dinner, Nhu was telling us that he had conceived a grand strategy to defeat world Communism for once and for all—by having the United States lure Communist China into a war in Laos, which was "an ideal theater and battleground." It made me shudder.

Here again, on the question of the political viability of Vietnam, the commitment of the national cadre and their capacity to carry out a disciplined and co-ordinated counterguerrilla program, the judgment was mixed. There were assets and there were liabilities, inextricably entangled.

R. K. G. THOMPSON AND THE DELTA

There were some people in Vietnam at this time who argued that Diem, the political morass in Saigon, and the slow-moving incompetency of the central government would not be decisive obstacles if the province and district officers were good and if they were given full support in their effort to carry out the strategic hamlet program, especially in the delta. It was, of course, R. K. G. Thompson who was the most respected authority on this problem and who would be the man to talk to.

And Thompson, who a year earlier when I had seen him had been rather gloomy, was now the most optimistic of them all. What he told us and what he showed us in a tour of the delta—hopping from one little airfield to another and flying low over roads and hamlets—offered the most solid basis we had yet seen for believing that at least a beginning was being made. I had expected Thompson to be worried over the too rapid proliferation of strategic hamlets. He was. Many were being established in exposed areas, in violation of the "oil blot" principle, and many more were nothing but a shell, a strand of barbed wire with nothing inside—no police work to eliminate Viet Cong agents, no defenses worthy of the name, no positive benefits to win the allegiance of the people. But he showed us a nucleus of hamlets that were good, and he felt that if our luck held this nucleus could be expanded to cover the bulk of the population in the delta. There were a lot of "ifs" in this judgment—*if* the Viet Cong reaction to the strategic hamlets did not get any more violent than it was, *if* the military would keep the Viet Cong off balance by "clear and hold" operations that would permit the nucleus area to be expanded, and *if* nothing else happened to put the program off stride.

But in spite of the "ifs" Thompson's judgment was optimistic. After agonizing delays, President Diem had adopted Thompson's delta plan without damaging changes. The program had then had a very shaky start, but now it was proceeding well. Thompson also had reason to believe that Diem would soon adopt an amnesty program of the kind that had been so effective in Malaya. American aid for the hamlet program was beginning to arrive in impressive quantities. Social and economic benefits were beginning to reach the hamlets—materials for school construction, cement for pigstys, fertilizers, poison to use against the rats that destroyed so much of the rice, and even occasionally a generator for electric lights. The training programs for local troops, the civil guard and the self-defense corps, were beginning to pay off. And the Viet Cong reaction to the hamlet program had been slow, and so far not effective.

The only caveats Thompson had beyond those mentioned above were two. The first caveat was against being impatient and wanting to complete the strategic hamlet program too rapidly. It would be particularly bad to go fast now that the program was entering areas that were more heavily penetrated by the Viet Cong. The aim, he felt, must be to establish a solid advancing framework, leaving no salients or pockets under Viet Cong control behind. If the government tried to go into the bad areas too quickly it would merely overreach itself and commit too many forces to the static defense of new strategic hamlets while the rear was still insecure and vulnerable. "If we plan for a long haul, we may get quick results," Thompson said. "But if we go for quick results, we may at best get a long haul."

Thompson's second caveat was against being unprepared for the inevitable Viet Cong reaction. Viet Cong policy, he felt, would probably be to reinforce the guerrilla units in any salients and pockets left behind and to try to subvert and reinfiltrate nearby strategic hamlets. In this respect, it would be most important to watch hamlets where there *ought* to be a lot of Viet Cong activity. If there weren't any, it would be a strong indication that the Viet Cong had succeeded in maintaining their contacts inside the hamlet and were playing it quiet.

But all these were—so far—only potential dangers. The concrete results up to date, Thompson felt, were solid ground for optimism. All this was persuasive—and it was even more so when Thompson took us up to inspect the delta from the air. The ditches cut across the road that had been so striking the year before were filled in, and the traffic was moving. Bridges had been repaired. Radiating out from a provincial capital established strategic hamlets could be seen close in to the capital and farther out people working on the defenses of new ones. The improvement was visible; it was incontrovertible; and it was convincing—at least that a beginning had been made.

REPORT TO THE PRESIDENT

Our report to the President began with the flat statement that "The war in South Vietnam is clearly going better than it was a year ago." And it then went on to recite the facts described above of American aid received, statistics on the military side, operations launched at government initiative, strategic hamlets established, and so on.

On the negative side, it was again the fact that the Viet Cong had increased its strength in spite of the claim that twenty thousand had been killed that impressed us most and the clear implication that this meant that the Viet Cong continued to maintain their access to the villages where they got both food and recruits.

"The question that this conclusion raises—and the basic question of the whole war—is again the attitude of the villagers. It is difficult if not impossible to assess how the villagers really feel, and the only straws in the wind point in different directions. The village defenders in many of the strategic hamlets that have been attacked resisted bravely. But in an unknown but probably large number of strategic hamlets the villagers have merely let the Viet Cong in or supplied what they wanted without reporting the incident to the authorities. There is apparently some resentment against the Viet Cong about the 'taxes' they collect and suspicion based on the stories the villagers hear about what is going on in North Vietnam. But there may be just as much resentment and suspicion directed towards the government. No one really knows, for example, how many of the 20,000 Viet Cong killed last year were only innocent or at least persuadable villagers. Whether the strategic hamlet program is providing enough government services to counteract the sacrifices it requires or how the mute mass of the villagers react to the charges against Diem of dictatorship and nepotism simply cannot be determined. At the very least, the figures on Viet Cong strength imply a continuing flow of recruits and supplies from these same villages and indicate that a substantial proportion of the population is still cooperating with the enemy— although it is impossible to tell how much of this cooperation stems from fear and how much from conviction. Thus on the vital question of villagers' attitudes, the net impression is one of some encouragement at the progress in establishing strategic hamlets and the numbers that resist when attacked, but encouragement overlayed by a shadow of uneasiness."

Our final conclusion, like the judgments on which it depended, was mixed:

"Our overall judgment, in sum, is that we are probably winning, but certainly more slowly than we had hoped. At the rate it is now going, the war will probably last longer than we would like, cost more in terms of both lives and money than we had anticipated, and prolong the period in which a sudden and dramatic event could upset the gains already made."

As diplomatically as possible—since the sensitivities of so many different services and agencies were involved—our report went on to make its criticisms:

"The most serious lack is that of an overall plan keyed to the strategic concept . . ."

This was delicate, for there actually were two plans. The trouble was that neither one of the two was "keyed to the strategic concept and through which priorities can be set and the coordination of military and civilian activities accomplished." One of the over-all plans was simply logistical, detailing the supplies needed for each province. And the other was a "national explosion" plan proposed by General Harkins. This was to have every Vietnamese military unit in the country suddenly and simultaneously take the offensive—a "national explosion." It was this kind of purely military effort that Thompson presumably had in mind when he warned that "If we plan for a long haul, we may get quick results, but if we go for quick results, we may at best get a long haul."

"One result of the lack of an overall plan is the proliferation of strategic hamlets that are inadequately equipped and defended or established prematurely in exposed areas.

"A second result of the lack of an overall plan is that essential aspects of the strategic concept are neglected. The police program is an example— an effective police system is vital to guard against Communist agents remaining inside the strategic hamlets and to man the checkpoints and patrols that are essential in controlling the movement of goods and people. The present police system is clearly inadequate . . ."

"Still another result of the lack of a plan is the difficulty of coordinating military and civilian activities. One example is the proportion of 'clear and hold' as opposed to 'hit and withdraw' [or, more familiarly, "seek and destroy"] operations. There are no statistics available, but a number of American military advisers feel that the proportion of 'clear and hold' operations in which troops clear an area and then remain to protect the civic action teams while they build strategic hamlets is too low in proportion to the 'hit and withdraw' operation designed to destroy regular Viet Cong units. The latter type of operation is essential to keep the Viet Cong off balance and to prevent their concentrating for a large-scale attack. But it should be subordinate to the systematic expansion of secure areas."

There was too much emphasis on ". . . elaborate, set-piece operations. These large-scale operations provide insurance against defeat, but they are expensive, cumbersome, and difficult to keep secret. From a political point of view, they have the additional disadvantage for the Vietnamese of maximizing the chances of killing civilians . . ."

"On the use of air power and the danger of adverse political effects, our impression is that the controls on air strikes and the procedures for checking intelligence against all sources are excellent. In spite of this, however, it is difficult to be sure that air power is being used in a way that minimizes the adverse political effects . . . and the use of air power is going up enormously."

THE "EYES ONLY" ANNEX

The President's copy of our report had an annex for his eyes alone. "(1) There is no overall planning effort that effectively ties together the civilian and military effort. (2) There is little or no long-range thinking about the kind of country that should come out of a victory and about what we do now to contribute to this longer-range goal. . . . (3) Among both civilians and military there is still some confusion over the way to conduct a counter-guerrilla war. Many of the lower-ranking people out in the field in actual contact with the problems seem fully conscious of the importance of the civil and political aspects, but in the middle and higher levels understanding is far from perfect. The American military mission must share some of the blame for the excessive emphasis on large-scale operations and air interdiction which have the bad political and useless military effects described in our report. . . . (4) In general, we don't use all the leverage we have to persuade Diem to adopt policies which we espouse. . . .

"The real trouble, however, is that the rather large U.S. effort in South Vietnam is managed by a multitude of independent U.S. agencies and people with little or no overall direction. No one man is in charge. What coordination there is results mainly from the sort of treaty arrangements that are arrived at in the country team meetings . . . The result is that the U.S. effort, although massive is fragmented and duplicative. . . .

"What is needed ideally is to give authority to a single strong executive, a man perhaps with a military background but who understands that this war is essentially a struggle to build a nation out of the chaos of revolution. One possibility would be to appoint the right kind of general as Ambassador. A better alternative would be to appoint as ambassador a civilian public figure whose character and reputation would permit him to dominate the representatives of all other departments and agencies.

"There are, of course, some formidable political and bureaucratic problems in taking either of these steps. What is more, we cannot say that the matter is urgent or that disaster would inevitably or immediately follow if things remain as they are.

"Progress toward winning the war is being made under the present set-up—although as we have said, it will take longer than expected, cost more, and prolong the period in which a dramatic event could wipe out the gains already made. On balance, our recommendation would be *not* to make any sudden and dramatic change but to keep the problem in mind when changes are to be made in the normal course of events."

Summing it all up, it seemed to us that the word for the situation in Vietnam was *fragile*. "It's like a man carrying an oversize porcelain vase over piles of gravel—tricky walking, and one slip and the vase is shattered," I said at one point. "Well, it would be even more like it if you added that the gravel pit was also inhabited by a bunch of unruly boys—rocks at hand."

In March 1963, Averell Harriman was moved up to be Under Secretary for Political Affairs, and I took over his former job as Assistant Secretary for Far Eastern Affairs. And in April, I found myself once again at the monthly Honolulu meeting, with Secretary McNamara and General Earle Wheeler, then Chief of Staff of the Army, from Washington, and Ambassador Nolting and General Harkins from Saigon. General Harkins gave us all the facts and figures—the number of strategic hamlets established, number of Viet Cong killed, operations initiated by government forces, and so on. He could not of course, he said, give any guarantees, but he thought he could say that by Christmas it would be all over. The Secretary of Defense was elated. He reminded me that I had attended one of the very first of these meetings, when it had all looked so black—and that had been only a year and a half ago.

A moment later, a State Department aide passed me a note, and I wordlessly passed it on to Ambassador Nolting. It contained only two words, in an attempt at Latin—*cave statisticus.*

NOTES

[1] By dint of these efforts, these four hamlets did survive until 1964, when they were lost to the Viet Cong.

[2] The statistics given here were those made available to the Department of State *at the time.* State Department files show that more Viet Cong weapons were reported captured than lost for the first time in the period September–October 1962, and that the ratio turned unfavorable again in November and stayed that way throughout 1963 and into 1964. R. K. G. Thompson, however (*op. cit.,* p. 40), reports that the ratio turned favorable in August–September and remained favorable through March 1963, turning down again coincident with the Buddhist crisis.

I am unable to explain this difference, except to repeat what was said before, that statistics were a source of trouble throughout the Vietnam struggle. In addition to the trouble due to doubt about the accuracy, reliability, and meaning of the statistics, there was also trouble because they were so frequently revised. Sometimes these revisions were on the basis of later and better information. Sometimes, they represented the effort of a higher headquarters to tone down what they considered either wishful thinking or undue pessimism on the part of a lower headquarters. And, inevitably, there were allegations, especially in the more hostile press, that some of the revisions were attempts to cover up bad judgments or to justify a policy position after the fact.

In later years, for example, the estimates on Viet Cong strength for 1960–64 were revised upward (see footnote, page 529). Although these revisions do have the effect of putting the military failure to deal with such small numbers of guerrillas in a more favorable light, the fact is that enemy personnel and documents captured months and even years later did bring in new information showing that the previous estimates were too low. What is troublesome about the statistics on the ratio of weapons captured to weapons lost is that these figures were not estimates, but supposedly hard facts on which information acquired through captured personnel and documents would not be likely to have any bearing. It is, certainly, difficult to see how later information could improve upon a count, even if it was an inaccurate count, of weapons lost during a battle, or on the number of enemy weapons gathered up after a battle, counted, and turned in.

CHAPTER 30

The Buddhist Crisis

FORRESTAL and I thought that the struggle against the Viet Cong guerrillas was being won, as described above, but that it would "take longer than expected, cost more, and prolong the period in which a dramatic event could wipe out the gains already made." The event came sooner than we expected, and it was more dramatic than we had ever dreamed.[1]

May 8, 1963, was celebrated in Vietnam as the 2527th anniversary of the birth of Gautama Buddha. In Hué, ancient capital of Annam and the site of the greatest flowering of Vietnamese Buddhism, priests and their followers chose that day to parade in protest of government orders forbidding them to fly the Buddhist flag or to use the local radio station to broadcast a statement by one of their younger leaders, Thich (Venerable) Tri Quang. They massed in front of the radio station, and refused to disperse. Government troops in armored cars were then brought in, under command of a major, the deputy province chief.

What happened next is confused. The Buddhists claimed that the major ordered his troops to fire without any provocation whatsoever. The major claimed that he gave the order only after he heard an explosion which he said he assumed to be a Viet Cong grenade. In any case, the armored vehicles did open fire, killing nine people, according to most reports, and crushing some of the bodies under their wheels.

The origin of the incident was ironical. Some days before, Diem had attended celebrations in Hué marking the twenty-fifth anniversary of the appointment of his older brother, Ngo Dinh Thuc, as bishop. There was a profusion of Catholic flags in the procession, and when Diem saw them he reminded the local officials of a long-standing ordinance, intended to foster patriotism, forbidding the flying of any but the national flag. He directed that thereafter the ordinance should be enforced.

A more politically sensitive regime might have delayed enforcing the ordinance until another Catholic occasion. Or it might never have promulgated such an ordinance in the first place. Certainly a more politically sensitive regime would have handled the crisis that followed the killings in a different way. But in the mandarin view, the ruler should never make concessions under pressure or admit to a mistake. A concession to a grievance or compensation for loss of life or property can be made only as the ruler's act of unsolicited magnanimity. Diem was mandarin to the core, and his family name and prestige were also in-volved—Hué was not only Thuc's diocese, but the capital of the semi-autonomous political region run by his brother, Ngo Dinh Can. The more the Buddhists protested, the outside world was outraged, and American embassy officials counseled conciliation, the more imperious he became.

The government's initial position was that the troops had not fired at all—the Viet Cong had thrown a grenade, the crowd had panicked, and people had been trampled. This made the Buddhists even angrier, and the next day several thousand people demonstrated, although peaceably, in front of the province chief's house. The government responded by banning all further demonstrations—which angered the Buddhists still more.

The more militant group of Buddhist monks centered around Tri Quang apparently saw an opportunity to rally wider support for their cause in Hué and perhaps an opportunity to better the Buddhist po-sition and increase their power throughout Vietnam. For the most promi-nent of their number at the time, Thich Tam Chau, next published a letter addressed to "all Buddhists in Vietnam" appealing for support and action "to protect our religion in an orderly, peaceful, nonviolent man-ner" and asking Buddhists to be "ready to march the road to martyrdom." But the government stuck to their story of a Viet Cong grenade, re-treating only to the extent of promising an investigation of what had happened.

On May 13 the Hué group submitted five "aspirations" to the govern-ment: (1) that the ban on religious flags be lifted; (2) that Buddhism and Buddhists have the same legal status as Catholicism and Catholics; (3) that Buddhists be free to preach their religion; (4) that the victims and relatives of victims of the May 8 riots be compensated; and (5) that the officials responsible for the May 8 incident be punished.

BUDDHISM IN VIETNAM

The population of South Vietnam is about fourteen million people. Of these, about a million and a half are Catholics. Another two million are members of one or another of the sects, such as the Hoa Hao. The rest of the population is Buddhist, but many are only nominally so. Confucian-ism lies deep in the culture, and many of the villagers practice a form of ancestor worship. The Vietnamese Ambassador to the United States, Tran Van Chuong, for example, once explained that for purposes of ceremonies at birth, marriage, and death, he would call himself a Bud-dhist, but for all the other purposes that Westerners associate with religion—ethics and spiritual meaning—he would call himself Confucian. The number of active, practicing Buddhists in Vietnam was probably more like four million.

It also should be said that it would be a mistake to think of Buddhism in Vietnam as a religion or a church in the Western sense or to think of Buddhist bonzes, or monks, as the equivalent of, say, Catholic priests. Buddhism in Vietnam partakes in some measure of what a Westerner thinks of as religion, but it also partakes of philosophy and ethics and tradition. There is no Buddhist hierarchy of the kind found in Western churches, and only rather casual training and procedures for becoming a bonze. In most of the countries of Southeast Asia, a variety of people —including soldiers and politicians—might several times in their lives don a saffron robe and spend a year or two as a Buddhist monk. And those who spend their lives as monks are usually devout but very simple men. Most are uneducated, and only a very few have any knowledge of the outside world.

The Buddhist crisis in Vietnam was not in fact caused by religious persecution. The truth of the matter is that there was not really any significant amount of persecution of the Buddhist religion in Vietnam. But there was discrimination against the Buddhists and in favor of the Catholics. Laws left over from French days, for example, treated the Catholic church as a religion and the Buddhists as an "association"— which gave the Catholic church rights in acquiring property denied to the Buddhist pagodas. Catholics also got ahead in the government, probably not so much because they were Catholics as because they had had an education, which was available mainly if one could attend the French Catholic schools. Catholic villagers were frequently excused from labor on the roads or, later, in constructing strategic hamlets.

The only true persecution of Buddhists was local. Here and there a zealous Catholic priest combined with an equally zealous Catholic official and the result was occasionally that whole villages decided to convert to Catholicism.

But even though there was no persecution of Buddhists by the central government, the discrimination and pressure had by 1963 created a bitter resentment among many of the Buddhist priests.

Both the fact that the issue was not really one of religious persecution and the fact that Buddhism was not an organized religion in the Western sense were important to the Buddhist crisis. But, for understanding the events of 1963, the most significant aspect of Buddhism in Vietnam was probably that it was Vietnamese. The Diem regime was unpopular, and it was dominated by French-educated Catholics. The Viet Cong were Communists, professing a foreign ideology and, people said, doing strange things to the old way of life in the villages of the north. Even the old mandarin system of governance, still so much a part of life in South Vietnam, was essentially Chinese. The stirrings of nationalism in Vietnam were still only stirrings, inchoate and formless. But they were there. The Vietnamese could not look back to a period when Vietnam had been a single, united nation. But there had been an empire with its capital at Hué that controlled what is now central Vietnam, an empire that had expelled the Chinese overlords. It was in this same period that Buddhism, as mentioned above, had its greatest flowering in Vietnam, a flowering which was again centered in Hué. Buddhism in Vietnam had an umbilical tie with nationalism; and in a land where political expression had been denied for generations, it became the vehicle for all kinds of political aspirations, including these nationalistic yearnings.

Vietnam, in truth, was in the midst of two struggles, not one. The guerrilla warfare was not a spontaneous revolution, as Communist propaganda would have it, but a contrived, deliberate campaign directed and managed from Hanoi. But Vietnam was also in the throes of a true revolution, a social and nationalistic revolution very much akin to the "new nationalisms" that pervaded both the Congo crisis and Indonesia's confrontation with Malaysia. Even while the struggle went on against the Viet Cong, power was in the process of passing from the French-educated mandarin class to representatives of the new nationalism, the Buddhists, the students, and the "young Turks" in the military.[2] These groups were ill-formed, emotional, xenophobic, inchoate—hence the turbulence.

About the only political group in Vietnam that did not ally itself with the Buddhists was the Viet Cong. The Communists had apparently overlooked the Buddhists or written them off for doctrinaire reasons. In any case, they did not have the cadre of agents inside the Buddhist movement that would have permitted them to make effective use of the situation. The Viet Cong were very slow to react to the Buddhist crisis, and when they did their efforts were inept. They made one or two attempts to turn demonstrations into riots, but with negligible results, and they made only a stab at making common cause with the Buddhists in the field of propaganda. The only explanation that seems plausible is that the Buddhist phenomenon was apparently so foreign to what Communist dogma pictures as the true nature of politics that the Viet Cong were simply nonplussed. Actually, the Viet Cong had every reason to fear the Buddhists—for they represented nationalism and as in Indonesia and the other emerging countries, if the "new nationalism" in Vietnam found itself in time, it would mark the end of Communist ambitions.

The Buddhists bit on an issue not so much of religious persecution as religious discrimination. They tasted political blood, and they bit harder. And for a time they became a rallying point for all the discontent in a discontented society.

In their five "aspirations," which the Hué leaders issued on May 13, there was already something more than the original issue of discrimination against the Buddhists and in favor of Catholics. The third "aspiration," implying by its demand for freedom to preach Buddhism that there was religious persecution in Vietnam, really began to raise the Buddhist goals past the purely religious to the political. And as the crisis went on and Diem and Nhu continued to be intransigent, the political came more and more to dominate.

THE PROTEST GROWS

At first, the Buddhist effort was tentative and groping. But over the few weeks following May 8, it became surer and more self-confident. The Buddhist leadership was unworldly at times, and naïvely cynical at others. But they developed an excellent organization, capable of making politically strategic decisions, of planning demonstrations to further their cause, and of mounting demonstrations and bringing them off with almost military precision. The pagodas in the big cities—especially Xa Loi pagoda, in Saigon, and Tu Dam, in Hué—became headquarters, with mimeograph machines grinding out propaganda leaflets and press releases by the ream.

As time went on, the Buddhist ranks were swelled by supporters from all the many segments of society disaffected with the Diem regime for whatever reason. Between these voluntary sympathizers and their own Buddhist supporters, the monks found that they had amateur intelligence agents at every level of the Diem government passing them information on the government's plans and countermoves, and the Buddhists used it to good advantage, in planning demonstrations and in their relations with the Western press. They never did learn the niceties of press relations—they would hold a press conference, for example, to denounce a reporter who wrote a story they considered unsympathetic. But they quickly learned how the Western press could be used and manipulated to serve their purposes. They began to carry signs in English, as well as in Vietnamese, for example, for the benefit of the Western photographers. They learned the practice of putting out press releases in advance, and of tipping the press off so they could be on hand when a demonstration began. They even learned to call the press for other purposes—they were timid and frightened of what Nhu's secret police might do, and they understood that there was some measure of protection in just having the Western press around.

The Diem regime, to repeat, had retreated from the position that the damage on May 8 had been caused by a Viet Cong grenade only to that of promising an investigation. Their response to the five "aspirations" was to reiterate that an investigation was in progress. In Hué, the Buddhists began experimenting with hunger strikes by nuns and bonzes —within the confines of the pagodas. On May 21, they held a protest meeting in Hué, and found it attracted more attention. On May 28, several hundred monks demonstrated in front of the opera house in Saigon to dramatize the beginning of a two-day hunger strike in Saigon. On May 30, bonzes massed in front of the National Assembly building.

Late in May, Diem met with the more moderate Buddhist leadership, and there were hopes that he would move to a reconciliation and head off the rise of the more militant priests. But after the meeting, he authorized a statement that the Buddhists were "damned fools" because the constitution guaranteed religious freedom.

This gave the militants the edge within Buddhist councils, and they mounted a silent procession of several thousand in Hué. The next day, there was violence—rioting which was finally broken up by troops. Over sixty people were injured, some of whom suffered burns, and the press throughout the world was filled with headlines about "blister gas." It finally transpired, but too late to help the Diem regime, that the grenades were tear gas of an old French type activated by acid. Some of the grenades had failed to work, but they did splash acid. But all this came out later. Diem, at long last, began to grasp that the protest had become a crisis. He dismissed three officials in Hué, including the major who had commanded the troops on May 8, and set up a committee headed by Vice-President Tho, who was himself a Buddhist, to negotiate a settlement.

THE POLITICS OF SELF-IMMOLATION

The Nhus continued to press the hard line. On June 8, for example, Madame Nhu issued a statement charging that the Buddhists were infiltrated with Communist agents and threatening strong action by the government. Even so, Diem's actions might have sufficed if they had been taken at the outset, but now the Buddhists had really begun to taste political blood. Late on Monday, June 10, a Buddhist spokesman tipped off the American reporters to "something important" that was to happen the next morning. Several reporters paid no attention—it was the last time they ignored a tip from the Buddhists—but Malcolm W. Browne, of the Associated Press, was on hand.[3] At eight on the morning of June 11, at a pagoda near downtown Saigon, about 350 nuns and monks began a hypnotic chant, accompanied by a rhythmic drumming and the burning of incense. Promptly at nine, according to Browne's report, the chanting stopped. Banners were unfurled calling on the government to meet the Buddhist demands, a procession was formed up in two ranks, and moved out—preceded by an automobile, which Browne remarked upon as unusual for Buddhist processions. The procession moved in a slow and orderly march until it reached the intersection of two of the largest of Saigon's boulevards, where the automobile seemed to stall.

The marchers flowed on around the stalled car—but suddenly, they turned and stopped, forming a ring about thirty feet in diameter in the very center of the intersection. The monks in the car got out. One ceremoniously placed a small cushion in the center of the ring. A second monk then came forward, later identified as the Venerable Quang Duc, a dignified, straight-backed man in his seventies who had been a Buddhist priest all his life. He seated himself on the cushion and assumed the "lotus posture" of contemplation, cross-legged with hands folded in the lap, head slightly bowed. A third monk then poured gasoline over Quang Duc's bowed head and shoulders and stepped back. There was a slight movement of Quang Duc's folded hands—and he was engulfed in a towering column of flame.

The ring of monks and nuns moaned in anguish; many prostrated themselves toward the leaping flames. There was a stench of gasoline and burning flesh. For nearly ten minutes Quang Duc maintained the lotus posture, his eyes closed and his hands calmly folded, as his face blackened and the flesh burned from his shaven head and body. Finally, he toppled over, dead.

A shudder of horror spread over Vietnam and out across the world. Malcolm Browne had taken pictures of the burning monk, which appeared everywhere. Self-immolation is an emphatically persuasive argument that one believes in his cause, and self-immolation by burning is more emphatic still. The facts of whether or not there had been religious persecution in Vietnam instantly became irrelevant—the world believed that there must have been.

Within Vietnam, the effect was awesome. Quang Duc's body was cremated, but the heart, according to the bonzes, would not burn. It was put in a glass chalice at Xa Loi pagoda, where thousands came to view it in awe. His ashes were distributed to all the pagodas in the land; the remains of his charred clothing were cut into tiny pieces and distributed to the faithful for their miraculous healing power. It was, the people believed, a time of miracles. At sunset in Saigon thousands claimed to see the weeping face of Buddha in the evening sky.

Madame Nhu sneered that all the Buddhists had done was to "barbecue a monk." And she made other outrageous comments over the following weeks. She suggested that Quang Duc's death was murder, not suicide, and accused the Buddhists of drugging him. She charged that Malcolm Browne had bribed the Buddhists to set up the burning so that he could get a dramatic picture. She said that she "gaily clapped her hands" at the Buddhist self-immolations, and suggested that some of the American newsmen, particularly David Halberstam, should follow the example—offering to furnish the gasoline and a match. And her callousness shocked Western opinion even more.

President Diem went on the radio to repeat that the constitution guaranteed religious freedom and to add the enigmatic statement, as if to reassure those who were skeptical, that he, President Diem was the constitution.

During the rest of June 1963 and on into July, Buddhist demonstrations were more and more frequent. Inevitably, the police were increasingly repressive. The demonstrations were broken up by force, Buddhist monks and nuns were beaten and dragged off to jail. The second fiery self-immolation occurred in August, and there were still more in the fall. A young bonze got out of a cab at the central market in Saigon, doused himself in gasoline—and went up in flames. Another did the same thing a few days later outside the Saigon Cathedral, just as people were emerging from mass. A young nun failed in an attempt to take her life by slashing her wrists, but another nun succeeded with fire. All in all there were seven self-immolations in Vietnam that summer and fall of 1963. One or two of these seven may have been carried out without the prior knowledge of the Buddhist leadership, but the rest were part of a planned campaign.

WASHINGTON AND THE POLICY PROBLEM

In Washington the frustration with Diem's reluctance and general ineptness in handling the Buddhist protest was shared in all agencies. There was really no lack of public and political support for aiding the Vietnamese in the struggle against the Communist Viet Cong at that time, but there was considerable distaste about the corollary that supporting Vietnam also meant supporting Diem and his regime. And as sympathy for the Buddhists spread over the world, the United States paid an increasingly high political price abroad as well as at home. But about all that we could do was to instruct the American Embassy in Saigon to keep prodding Diem to move promptly along a path of reconciliation and offer suggestions as to how it might be accomplished.

The task fell to William Trueheart, the Deputy Chief of Mission—for Nolting had departed on a much-needed holiday with his family just before the crisis developed. (Nolting had asked for purely personal reasons to be replaced at the end of his two-year tour, although he offered to stay over until a replacement could be found. It was agreed that he should take his holiday, a cruise in the Aegean, and then stop off in Washington for consultations before returning to Saigon for a month or two until his successor had been named.) Trueheart was an old friend of Nolting's—he had gone to Saigon as deputy, in fact, at Nolting's special request—and he fully agreed with Nolting's policy of getting along with Diem. But over the next few weeks, Diem's paranoiac stubbornness in resisting concessions to the Buddhists and his blindly suicidal policies of repression came to convince Trueheart that at least so long as Nhu, the *éminence grise,* remained in his dominating position of power and influence, Diem was hopeless. The issue was not really one of making concessions to the Buddhists or whether or not they could be appeased. By this time the Buddhists had probably upped their goal to that of trying to bring down the Diem regime itself. The issue was handling the Buddhist crisis in a politically sensitive way that would make further Buddhist demonstrations and immolations appear unjustified and so lose them support both abroad and inside Vietnam itself. If the Buddhists did succeed in toppling Diem, someone remarked, it would be through a sort of political jujitsu—defeating him by using the blind rushes of his own strength. All we need to do, one of the militant young Buddhists said of Diem and Nhu is to "throw down the banana peel for them to fall on."

Disarming the Buddhist movement was not impossible. As Trueheart, under instructions, repeated endlessly, all Diem had to do was to wipe out the old discriminatory laws, punish the officials responsible for the May 8 incident, and indemnify the victims, preferably in a dramatic personal gesture, such as a visit to the scene at Hué. Diem's paranoiac pride and mandarin stubbornness may have made such concessions more difficult than they would have been for a different type of leader, but not impossible. In the end Diem behaved so as to get the worst of both worlds. He made concessions, but he made them grudgingly and too late—losing his mandarin dignity by appearing to do so only under pressure as well as losing the political gain that would have come if the concessions had been timely.

THE JUNE 16 AGREEMENT

On June 16, Vice-President Tho and the Buddhists succeeded in producing a joint communiqué that attempted to meet the five "aspirations" by a series of assertions—that religious freedom should be respected, and so on—although it only promised, again, that the Hué incident would be "investigated." Under pressure from the United States, Diem signed it. But he added a special notation saying that the government had always believed in the points of the communiqué, which implied that concessions were neither needed nor being made. Nothing to implement the communiqué did in fact happen over the next few days, and there were renewed threats in the *Times of Vietnam,* the mouthpiece of the Nhus. The Buddhists, for their part, went back to the streets in new demonstrations—and the regime charged that they had broken the agreement.

Madame Nhu repeated her sneers about the Buddhist "barbecues," and announced that if she had her way the priests would be "beaten ten times more." In interviews with foreign correspondents, she began to charge that the Buddhists were out-and-out Communists. Nhu began to suggest that there were too many Americans in Vietnam—that our aid should continue, but that Vietnam would be better off if the advisers and the others were sent home.

And the Buddhists responded with still more demonstrations. The Diem police broke up the demonstrations with clubs, and the Western press was filled with photographs of frail, passive little priests, with shaven heads and saffron robes, empty-handed and unresisting, being beaten by military police and carted off to jail in an American truck marked with the "clasped hands" symbol of American aid.

As far as the United States was concerned, Diem's policies were not only alienating him from his own people and the outside world, they were alienating the United States Government from *its* people and *its* international support. The pictures in the press, the editorials, the grumblings on Capitol Hill, the polite but worried queries from allies, all began to mount. It was decided that Trueheart should be instructed to point all this out to President Diem and give him a formal warning that if the repressive policies against the Buddhists were continued, the United States would be forced to "dissociate" itself from them in a public statement.

If a public statement "dissociating" the United States from Vietnamese actions against the Buddhists were in fact made, of course, it would be a most serious step. Diem would regard it as an insult and a humiliation, almost an invitation to those who opposed him to attempt a *coup d'état*. But we were not making such a statement—yet. What we were doing was to point out to Diem that his actions were generating pressures on us and to warn him that the logic of what he was doing would inevitably lead to a situation where we would no longer have any choice. Diem's actions were affecting the American reputation and position in the world, and it was not unreasonable to ask an ally to make allowances for our situation as we had so often been asked to make allowances for his.

Diem's response was cold and uncompromising. In effect, he simply turned his back on Trueheart—and on the United States.

Early in July, Vice-President Tho announced that the investigation of the Hué incident had confirmed what the government had contended from the beginning—that it was the Viet Cong who were responsible. Since no one really believed this, inside or outside the Vietnamese Government, the announcement was interpreted—correctly—as an Asian way of saying that the government had rejected a policy of reconciliation with the Buddhists and decided on one of further repressions.

The regime also had begun to realize to what great advantage the Buddhists were using the foreign press. The press, of course, was a subject on which Diem and the Nhus had always been rabid, and they returned to their hatred with vehement relish. Diem himself resurrected Madame Nhu's charge that Browne had bribed the Buddhists to arrange Quang Duc's burning. On July 7, some of Nhu's plainclothes secret police surrounded a group of American newsmen, and roughed them up, particularly Malcolm Browne and Peter Arnett. When the embassy protested, the police merely called in Browne and Arnett and subjected them to interrogations on the charge that it was the newsmen who attacked the secret police.

CHOOSING A NEW AMBASSADOR

In Washington, the decision about a new ambassador had finally been made. The name most prominent in the discussions was Edmund Gullion, who was finishing up his tour as Ambassador to the Congo, but the Secretary of State made it clear that he did not want him. The recommendation that Forrestal and I had made "to appoint as ambassador a civilian public figure whose character and reputation would permit him to dominate the representatives of all other departments and agencies" had stimulated thinking in this direction, and someone came up with the name of Henry Cabot Lodge.

Lodge, for his part, was unhappy out of government and had indicated that he would be willing to take on an assignment. He spoke French with native fluency, which was an important asset for an ambassador to a country that had been a French colony. In 1962, as a reserve officer on a two-week tour of active duty in the Pentagon, Lodge had written a paper on Vietnam and had developed such an interest in it that he asked if there would be any objection to his doing his 1963 tour of active duty in Vietnam itself.

Some of Lodge's political enemies have accused him of seeking the post as a steppingstone, but I am convinced it was not true. After Lodge had been appointed, but while he was still in Washington, he and I had a long talk—alone. "I am sixty-one," he said, "I will never run for elective office again. A Republican administration is too far away for me to hope for a high appointive office. I want you to know that if it will serve the United States, I am expendable. Just don't do it for unimportant reasons." I nodded in agreement and admiration.

As for President Kennedy's part, I think that he was intrigued at the thought of having his old opponent in the Senate race of 1952 and Nixon's running mate in 1960 as his ambassador to such a hot spot. There were extraordinary political dangers in having a prominent Republican as ambassador—but there were also some interesting political advantages. The appointment was announced on June 27.

By this time, there was dismay in Washington, not only about the course on which Diem had embarked, which seemed so suicidal, but also over the failure in communications. Diem would neither listen to what we had to say nor offer any explanation for the policy his government was following. We decided to go ahead with the original plan to have Nolting return for a time to Saigon. It was remotely possible that he could draw upon the two years of patiently trying to see things Diem's way and of doing everything possible to go along with his demands. If there was any American to whom Diem and Nhu owed a personal debt of loyalty, it was "Fritz" Nolting. The idea was that Nolting would return immediately to Saigon, that he would stay until mid-August, and that we would all attend the next meeting in Honolulu—on August 21—which would be a convenient time for making the shift in ambassadors.

Nolting arrived back in Saigon on July 11, a sweltering, humid day, typical of Vietnam in the monsoon. He met with the press at the airport and managed to express American support for religious freedom and at the same time deplore "internal dissension"—and to do so without mentioning Diem's name.

NOLTING AND DIEM

Nolting was deeply angry at Trueheart, not so much because of what had happened, but because Trueheart had changed his mind about Diem and was now convinced that the Viet Cong would never be beaten by the Diem regime. Nolting had staked his whole career and future on getting along with Diem and building up credit with him that could be drawn upon during difficult periods. His tour in Vietnam had cost him and his family much personal sacrifice, financially and in terms of the well-being of his children, two of whom he had had to leave back in the United States at a crucial time in their lives. Yet he had followed the policy with gentle skill and loyalty. To him, the whole justification for his past work and sacrifice as well as for his future in the foreign service depended on how Diem and Nhu now responded.

Nolting, at least, could talk to Diem, and he did so constantly. The first task was to get the charges against Browne and Arnett dropped, and Diem finally did drop them—but only after delivering a diatribe against the whole of the American press in Vietnam, who were, he said, "low-caliber" and "insulting."

But beyond that, Nolting made little headway. Nhu and Madame Nhu and their newspaper kept up a steady stream of invective. The Buddhists continued their demonstrations. And the police increased the level of repression—on July 17, for example, almost a week after Nolting's return, they surrounded the Xa Loi pagoda with barbed wire and for a while allowed no one either to leave or enter.

What Nolting was trying to persuade Diem to do was to adopt a true policy of conciliation and to announce it in some dramatic way—by a personal appearance coupled with a nationwide broadcast. But the most Diem would do, and even this with the implication that it was a personal favor to Nolting, was to make a short radio broadcast on July 19, announcing a more liberal policy toward the flying of Buddhist flags and the formation of a special committee to investigate Buddhist complaints. The statement was inadequate and accomplished nothing.

Many of the people in the American mission felt that Diem might have been more forthcoming if it had not been for the influence of Nhu, who was behaving more and more strangely. John Mecklin, head of the United States Information Service in Saigon, reports that at a dinner party in front of high-ranking Vietnamese and Americans, including Ambassador Nolting himself, Nhu attacked his own brother, saying that "Diem was inept and 'weak,' an incompetent leader because he tried to compromise with the Buddhists. He, Nhu, was ready to quit the government if Diem failed to be tough, and indeed he had already submitted his resignation if Diem wanted to accept it."[4] And he rambled on in this vein for five hours. Saigon was full of rumors that Nhu was planning a coup against his own brother, and one newspaperman was so bold as to confront Nhu with the story. Nhu denied that he intended a coup, but he went on to say that if the Buddhist question were not solved, it would indeed lead to a coup, a coup which would be anti-American, anti-Buddhist, and anti-weak government.[5] Secretary Thuan, for whom we all had great respect, later told American friends that Nhu was taking opium at this time and this helped push him toward his states of extremism.[6] "You could begin to see the madness in his face," Thuan said, "a sort of somnambulistic stare, always with that cold smile." And there were repeated intelligence reports that Nhu had some notion, reminiscent of his offer to de Gaulle to settle the Algerian war, that he could negotiate an end to the war and that he had been attempting to set up a secret channel of communications with Hanoi.

NOLTING'S LAST DAYS

Shortly thereafter, Nolting, in what he thought was a casual aside to an interviewer, remarked that there had been no persecution of the Buddhists in Vietnam and that the Buddhist crisis was a side issue distracting time and energy from the important thing, which was to win the war. The statement that there had been no persecution of the Buddhists was, of course, basically true, but following the weeks of lurid pictures of priests being beaten a public statement to that effect was inept. And to call the Buddhist crisis a side issue was provocative. The Buddhists seized on Nolting's remark, charging that Nolting had never been inside a pagoda and knew nothing of Buddhism, and that his remark must be only a "last gift to Ngo Dinh Diem." And the Nhus also seized on it, hailing Nolting in the *Times of Vietnam* and playing the story to bring out the implication that the United States was siding with the government and against the Buddhists.

Everything that happened to Nolting those last few weeks went sour, as if all the fates of Asia were conspiring against him. Diem and Nhu decided to name a strategic hamlet after him, and trapped him into agreeing by saying that the ceremony would be held on any day convenient for him. The poor hamlet would immediately become a target for the Viet Cong, but there was no way out. Nolting asked that the ceremony be kept secret, but the press found out all about it days in advance. The day before the ceremony, an American helicopter accidentally machine gunned the village, wounding several people—and the press played it big. The very day of the ceremony, a Vietnamese army jeep knocked down and injured a small boy in the hamlet—and the garbled news stories reported that it was the Ambassador's car that had struck the boy and that he was killed.

The second suicide by burning came on August 5, and Nolting, who was scheduled to depart on August 15, tried again with Diem. As a last favor to Nolting, Diem finally agreed to make a public statement calling for reconciliation with the Buddhists, choosing as his vehicle an interview with Marguerite Higgins. What Diem actually said to Miss Higgins, however, was that conciliation had been his policy all along—and, somewhat ominously, that this policy he had been following all along was "irreversible." Nevertheless, the statement seemed to be a concession, even if it had been made in a somewhat "Asian" fashion, and the United States Information Service played it up around the world.

Diem's private assurances to Nolting, however, had contained somewhat more solid comfort. There had been rumors in Saigon that the regime was planning a thorough crackdown on the Buddhists, and certainly the Nhus were quite openly arguing for a crackdown. Nolting sought and received assurances from Diem that no such action would be taken.

With this assurance as his final accomplishment, Nolting on August 15 said his farewells to the embassy staff at the airport and departed. The very next morning, in Hué, still another priest burned himself to death.

DENOUEMENT

Lodge, Nolting, and I were together in Honolulu on August 21 when the tickers began to clack out the news. Early in the predawn hours, all telephones to United States offices and residences in Saigon had been cut, except for one line to the American military headquarters. At just about the same time, Vietnamese military units had attacked the major pagodas in Saigon, in Hué, and several other cities. At some pagodas in Saigon, the bonzes had resisted, and they were shot down and grenaded. Religious statues and holy relics were desecrated. American reporters arrived at Xa Loi in time to see the end of the action there, and they reported that many of the monks were wounded and some presumedly killed. A

few escaped—two took refuge in the compound of the United States
Agency for International Development, which was just next door, and Tri
Quang himself, after hiding two days, made it into the American Embassy
with the secret police right behind him.

I remember someone cursing softly as we read the tickers. The assault, timed for the period between ambassadors, was a deliberate affront. Diem had callously broken his word. He had made no gesture to
salvage the dignity of the United States. He was presenting us with a
fait accompli that he knew violated our deepest sense of decency and
fair play, and he was doing it with a disdainful arrogance, contemptuously confident that we would swallow this just as we had swallowed
so much in the past. There was a stricken look on Nolting's face.

"Thus the Diem regime's final gesture to 'Fritz' Nolting," John Mecklin
later wrote: "flagrant abrogation of its solemn last word to this fine man
who had staked his career on the regime's defense."[7]

NOTES

[1] The following account of events in Vietnam draws on John Mecklin, *Mission in
Torment*, 1965; David Halberstam, *The Making of a Quagmire*, 1964–65; Malcolm
Browne, *The New Face of War*, 1965; and Marguerite Higgins, *Our Vietnam Nightmare*, 1965.
[2] For an analysis of this social revolution in Vietnam, see George A. Carver, Jr.,
"The Real Revolution in South Viet Nam," *Foreign Affairs*, April 1965. Carver
served in Vietnam with CIA on political intelligence.
[3] The following account is based on that given in Browne's book, *The New Face
of War*, 1965.
[4] John Mecklin, *Mission in Torment*, 1965, pp. 177–78.
[5] David Halberstam, *The Making of a Quagmire*, p. 227.
[6] Robert Shaplen, *The Lost Revolution*, p. 189.
[7] Mecklin, *Mission in Torment*, p. 181.

CHAPTER 31

The Cable of August 24

IN WASHINGTON, Harriman and Forrestal drafted a stiff public statement labeling the assault on the pagodas a "direct violation by the Vietnamese Government of assurances that it was pursuing a policy of reconciliation with the Buddhists." The note dissociated the United States from the Vietnamese actions, and condemned them. It was promptly cleared with the Secretary of State and the President and released. This statement marked the severance of relations between the United States and the Diem regime; but it was only the epitaph, the actual severance had been the Diem regime's act of desecration in violation of its pledged word.

Diem and Nhu's act of desecration also severed the relations between their regime and the Vietnamese people. The Vietnamese Ambassador in Washington, Tran Van Chuong, who was Madame Nhu's father, resigned with a passionate denunciation of his own child. All but one member of the embassy staff followed suit. Vu Van Mau, the Foreign Minister of Vietnam, also resigned—and in a dramatic gesture of courageous defiance, he shaved his head like a monk. There were more and bigger Buddhist demonstrations, and, for what was the first time in memory, the traditionally apathetic students at the University of Saigon began to riot. Soon thereafter, the secondary-school students also began to stage demonstrations.

Lodge had been ordered to fly directly to Saigon, and he arrived in the late evening on August 22, just thirty-six hours after the assault on the pagodas. The next morning, his first act was to pay a visit to the two Buddhist monks who had taken refuge in the compound of the Agency for International Development, (AID), dramatically underlining United States disapproval of what the Diem regime had done. The visit was Lodge's own idea, carried out on his own authority, but it was perfectly consistent with our condemnation of the assault on the pagodas and communicated that condemnation to the Vietnamese people much more effectively than the formal phrases uttered in Washington.

That same day, Friday, August 23, Lodge in Saigon and those of us on the other end, in Washington, began to be faced with still another problem. The first press reports out of Saigon had said that the attacks on the pagodas had been carried out by "troops" as well as police, and airborne units were specifically mentioned. Martial law was imposed early in the morning following the attacks, and this, too, was picked up in news dispatches and linked with the army. The Voice of America, as was its routine custom, reported all these news stories in its regular Vietnamese broadcasts as they were received. Embassy and CIA reports for the first day or two continued to assume that it was army units that had carried out the attack, and officials in Washington briefed the press accordingly. And the Voice broadcast the stories resulting from the briefings —that it was army troops that had carried out the attacks.

But by Thursday we began to get reports pointing in the other direction, that it was not the army that had carried out the assaults. The whole affair, according to these reports, had been planned by Nhu and carried out by his secret police, some of whom were disguised as airborne troops, and by the notorious Colonel Tung and his Special Forces, which came directly under Nhu and served as his private little army. Certain newsmen, notably Halberstam and Sheehan, also began to get out stories denying that the army had been involved and putting the blame on Nhu and Tung. At the same time, we began to get reports that a number of high-ranking officers were distressed at the effect of the Voice of America broadcasts on ordinary soldiers, who were more likely to be Buddhist than anything else, and on the relations between the army and the Vietnamese people. The Voice was the one sure source of accurate news in Vietnam, and it had an enormous audience.

Then, two of the most senior and highly respected of the Vietnamese generals, at considerable personal risk, contacted American officials in two separate but apparently related approaches.

What these two generals said added up to three major points. They denied that the army had had anything to do with the attacks on the pagodas or that they, the generals, had even known about it. Diem and Nhu had proposed a plan to establish martial law. The army leaders thought of this plan as an opportunity to increase their own influence in turning the government toward a policy of conciliation, and they had agreed to it, but nothing else. They invited us to investigate for ourselves —it was not the army, but Nhu, the secret police, and Colonel Tung's Special Forces that had violated the pagodas.

The second point was really a demand. If the Voice of America broadcast blaming the army was allowed to stand, the effects on morale within the army and on relations between the army and the people would be serious. They felt that when the United States had satisfied itself that it was not the army that was responsible, the Voice of America should broadcast that fact.

Finally, these two generals had a request. The attack on the pagodas was evidence of the lengths to which Nhu was prepared to go. The generals said that they had reason to believe that his plotting included their own executions. Also, they continued, they had reason to believe that

Nhu might attempt to make a deal with Hanoi and sell out the whole country. If at some point they and their fellow generals felt compelled to move against Nhu and the regime, what would be the attitude of the United States Government? And the two generals said that they needed to know very quickly.

All this arrived in Washington on Saturday morning, August 24, and a decision had to be made. The evidence by this time was overwhelming. It was clear that the army had had nothing to do with the assault on the pagodas. It had been planned by Nhu and carried out by his secret police and Special Forces. It seemed perfectly obvious that in justice and honor the Voice of America should correct itself and cleanse the army and the generals of the charges against them.

A second issue was Nhu. As the discussions proceeded in Washington that morning, it seemed more and more clear that if Nhu continued in power the regime would continue to follow the suicidal policies that were not only dragging Vietnam down to ignominy and disaster but the United States as well. And powerful support for that view came in a long-distance telephone call from one of the most senior of the American officers holding direct responsibility for Vietnam, Admiral Harry Donald Felt, Commander in Chief of the Pacific. Felt was a man of courage and high integrity. Later, when criticism in the more conservative press began to mount, some of those involved tried, in their background talks with pressmen, to blur their own responsibility and shift it to others. But Felt stood up: he volunteered to newsmen that he had talked to Washington while the policy was being formulated and that his opinion was embodied in it.

More reports also arrived from Saigon. The airborne troops resented the attempt to put the blame on them for the attack on the pagodas. In other units, junior officers and noncommissioned officers were especially upset, and there was talk of a coup from below. But perhaps the most convincing judgment of all came from one of the highest-ranking civilians in the Vietnamese Government, a man who was loyal to Diem and on whom Diem heavily depended, and at the same time a man who was held in the highest respect by the Americans. He had sought out an American official to say that he would remain loyal to Diem, even though he felt the end was near, but that he wanted to urge that "under no circumstances should the United States acquiesce in what the Nhus had done." Nhu was now in a dangerously triumphant mood, bragging contemptuously that he had "taught the Buddhists and the Americans a lesson." Nhu had moved into a commanding position, the official said, and if he continued in it the result would be disaster for both the war and the country. If Nhu continued in power, he concluded, the Communists would control all of Vietnam within six months.

The third issue was Diem himself. For all our troubles with Diem in the past, most American officials still regarded him highly. He had increasingly withdrawn and turned inward on himself. He had permitted his government to become a "liar and a criminal," as one very high-ranking American later put it. Yet we hoped against hope that we might still be able to continue if somehow he could be persuaded to remove Nhu from direct power and take charge himself.

A fourth issue was the question of political stability in Vietnam. The Vietnamese were fighting a Communist insurgency and could ill afford political warfare among themselves. If the generals moved against the regime to get rid of Nhu, they might try to save Diem and they might not. The decision would probably be against Diem, but it had to be Vietnamese, not American. And Diem might refuse to be saved. In that case, who would come after Diem? There was no candidate of proven ability and stature. Vice-President Tho was too old and lacked the will and determination. The generals would put General Duong Van Minh —"Big" Minh—at their head, because he was the most senior general and because he was likable. His role would be like General Naguib's had been when the Egyptian Army ousted the King—a nominal head only. Minh did not have the talent or appetite for political power, and someone else was bound to replace him soon. The picture was not a happy one. There might well be a series of coups, and the political turmoil in Saigon would inevitably hurt the war effort. The best that could be hoped for if the Diem regime was removed would be that, like Egypt, Vietnam would find her Nasser the second time around—or the third—or the fourth.

But there would be even more political instability if the Diem-Nhu regime continued as it was. Ever since 1957, more and more of the national cadre had become disaffected. And now, there were reports that some were beginning to think that anything might be preferable to a Diem regime with Nhu in a domineering position—even the Viet Cong. The intellectuals and the sects had long been against the regime. In 1960, there had been the coup attempt by the parachutists, who stopped fighting only on the promise of reforms that never came. In 1962, there had been the bombing of the palace by air force pilots—and Diem still continued to forbid the use of five-hundred-pound bombs without his written permission! Diem's fear of this discontent in the army had led him to put political loyalty higher than military ability in making so many appointments that some observers felt the war effort had already been damaged beyond recovery. And now there were the Buddhist crisis and the outrage against the pagodas, which had driven whole new segments of the national cadre into opposition. Diem and Nhu seemed remorseless, determined to meet further opposition with still further repression, which would drive still more segments into opposition. But even if they did not, there was a question whether they had already gone too far to recover no matter what they did. It was a choice between lesser evils, a high probability of political instability if the generals moved against the regime, and more or less certain disaster if the Diem-Nhu regime continued as it was.

Two cables to Saigon were drafted. One was an unclassified press guidance, giving the straight facts as we understood them—that American officials now had overwhelming evidence that it was the secret police and the Vietnamese Special Forces under Nhu who were responsible for the attacks on the pagodas and the mass arrests of monks and students; that some had been disguised as army troops or members of the youth corps; that the military leaders had agreed to martial law in the hope that it would lead to a peaceful settlement, but that they did not know of the plans to attack the Buddhists.

The exact text of the second cable has never been published, but its contents have long since been revealed.[1] The United States Government could not accept the actions taken by Nhu against the Buddhists, the cable said, nor could it, in view of what had happened, tolerate a situation in which power lay in Nhu's hands. Diem should be given every chance to rid himself of Nhu and to correct the situation himself, and the United States representatives should press for the necessary measures at every level of the Vietnamese Government. But if Diem remained obdurate, the United States would have to face the possibility that the regime could not be preserved.

The military leaders, the cable continued, should be told of the above, that we would find it difficult to support the regime economically and militarily unless the Nhus were removed from power and steps taken to redress the wrongs against the Buddhists. We wished to give Diem every opportunity to do this, but if he refused we were prepared to accept the obvious implications. Any decisions would have to be Vietnamese, including the decision whether or not to try to retain Diem even though they had to use force to remove Nhu. We would certainly be prepared to work with Diem without the Nhus, but that was up to the Vietnamese. We could take no part in any planning or action. But if action were taken, an interim, anti-Communist military government could expect that American support for the war effort would continue.

The cable also recognized the need for removing the taint on the Vietnamese Army. It proposed having the Voice of America broadcast a statement along the lines contained in the "press guidance" cable as soon as the Ambassador gave the word.

George Ball, Averell Harriman, Michael Forrestal, and I all participated in the drafting, but the fact that it was Saturday made the problem of further clearance difficult. It was made more difficult still by the fact that so many members of the cabinet were out of town. The President was at Hyannis Port; Rusk was in New York; and both McNamara and McCone were on vacation.

There was no problem so far as the President and Rusk were concerned. Wherever the President went, secure communications went too, and Rusk used the facilities at our mission to the UN. Both were sent early drafts of the cable and through several telephone conversations both participated in the revisions. Rusk, for example, added an important provision for continuing to furnish the Vietnamese war supplies if there were a breakdown in central government communications for any reason. Roswell Gilpatric was Acting Secretary of Defense, and he cleared the cable for the civilian side of the Defense Department, apparently concluding that it was not necessary to disturb McNamara's vacation. The Acting Director of CIA also went over the draft, and he too decided to approve without disturbing his chief's vacation—adding the comment that the time had clearly come to take a stand. For the military, the job of obtaining clearance fell to General Victor Krulak, the head of the staff section responsible for the Far East on the staff of the Joint Chiefs. Krulak was an intelligent and very ambitious Marine Corps general who stood no more than five foot six—and, naturally, was nicknamed "Brute" by his Marine Corps colleagues. Krulak was personable and fair-minded, and he was very sophisticated and knowledgeable about the Far East. But he knew where his natural allies lay, and he hewed closely to the views of the senior officers in the Pentagon. His relations with the conservative press, especially Marguerite Higgins, were intimate, but Krulak and Halberstam were enemies.

Krulak located General Maxwell Taylor at a restaurant, and Taylor cleared the August 24 cable for the military side of the Defense Department. Although Taylor did not know it at the time he cleared the cable, Forrestal had already released it. General Krulak had telephoned that he had located Taylor and that everything was all right—from which Forrestal had assumed that Krulak had already obtained Taylor's approval, which he did not actually get for another hour and a half. But it made no difference, for Taylor approved the cable without question.

Lodge responded within twenty-four hours. He agreed enthusiastically with what was proposed—except that he felt strongly that he should not go to President Diem with an ultimatum. An ultimatum would make Diem more intransigent, not less. He might feel impelled to do something desperate—kill all the top military leaders, or order the United States out of the country and appeal to Hanoi. Besides, it was neither right nor fitting that the United States should go to Diem. Diem and the whole world knew the depth of our disapproval of his acts against the pagodas, and Diem and the whole world also knew what we felt was necessary to make amends and correct the situation. It was Diem who had broken his word; it was Diem who had sullied the good name of the United States— and it was Diem who should come to us.

This was a question that could be postponed until after we learned whether or not the generals did intend to move. So, on Sunday, after a quick check of the responsible top officials in Washington, it was agreed to defer a direct approach to Diem until we knew more about the situation.

Lodge had also agreed with the plan to arrange for a Voice of America broadcast that would remove the taint from the Vietnamese Army. The mechanics of this were based on the practice of the Voice to report what was in the American press rather than be an original source of official United States Government news. I called the duty officer at the United States Information Agency, and we worked it out that I would brief AP, UPI, and the New York *Times* from the first, "press guidance" telegram. Since it was likely that the reporters would go beyond the briefing and speculate on further United States policy moves, we also agreed that the Voice would take from the AP and UPI ticker stories *only what was already in the press guidance telegram,* a copy of which was in their hands.

I called John Hightower, senior AP State Department correspondent—only to find that he would not be available for another two hours. And the man from the *Times* was also temporarily out of touch. But I found Stewart Hensley of UPI at his home, and he took down what I read to him from the unclassified guidance cable. He immediately wanted to know what the United States was going to do next—what Nhu had done to the Buddhists and to us was a traitorous act against an ally, would the United States cut aid to the Diem regime as an expression of our disapproval? Hensley was an old friend. I suggested that since we had not yet decided on anything like cutting aid, maybe it would be better if he didn't speculate on what the United States would do next. Hensley—rightly, I must confess—expostulated with me on this. As a reporter covering the State Department, he had a duty to interpret, to speculate in a responsible way on what the United States *might* do next—so long as he clearly labeled it as speculation. And I had to agree.

It would be a little while before I could reach Hightower and the *Times,* so I called the duty officer at USIA to tell him this. Again, I cautioned him to be sure that the people on duty at the Voice used *only* that part of Hensley's story that came from the press guidance telegram, and none of the speculation that followed. And then I went home.

But something went wrong. The people who actually made the broadcast did *not* check it against the press guidance telegram. At eight o'clock Monday morning Saigon time, the Voice broadcast the whole of Hensley's report in both English and Vietnamese—not only that the United States had proof that the Vietnamese Army was innocent of the assault on the pagodas and that Nhu's secret police and Special Forces were to blame, but the flat statement that "the U.S. may sharply reduce its aid to Vietnam unless President Diem gets rid of secret police officials responsible for the attacks."

Understandably, Lodge was upset. He was due to present his credentials to Diem at the palace at eleven that morning, and, given the mood of both Diem and his brother, Lodge feared there was a possibility they might do something insane. Harkins had been scheduled to go along, but Lodge decided that it would be better if he did not. "If they try any funny business," he said, "it might be better if one of us were on the outside."[2]

The Secretary sent Lodge a personal cable apologizing on behalf of both the State Department and USIA for the failure of the machinery over the weekend to carry out exact instructions, and the Voice carried the State Department's public denial that any decision had been made to cut aid to Vietnam. For a few hours, all of Vietnam had apparently thought that the United States had decided to sever relations with Diem and his regime and held its breath to see who would attack first, Nhu or the generals. But the prompt denial settled the matter. The slip increased the disgust of both Vietnamese and Americans, like Halberstam, who were convinced that the whole Diem regime was rotten and the United States should long since have severed all support of it. And it intensified their conviction that the United States Government was not only blind to the disaster Diem and Nhu were bringing down on Vietnam and the United States, but indecisive as well. The slip also confirmed the Vietnamese military in their natural inclination to proceed very, very slowly, if at all, and to be very, very sure of what they were doing if they decided to do anything—trusting no one at all with their plans, Vietnamese or American.

Back in Washington, General Taylor began to have misgivings. He communicated them to McNamara when he returned, and McNamara shared them. So did John McCone. By Monday morning, when the National Security Council met, the President had learned of these views through the Attorney General, and was annoyed both at the possibility that the government might have moved too fast and at the signs of disagreement among his advisers. He opened the meeting by saying that he wanted a full discussion including assurances that this was not a repetition of Herbert Matthews and Cuba (Herbert Matthews, reporting for the New York *Times* from Havana, was credited with influencing the Eisenhower administration to support Castro's bid for power against Batista). Second, he wanted to know how everyone stood. It was not too late to back off. The response to the generals' request was not due to be made for a few hours yet, and even if it had already been made there was plenty of time for us to tell them we had changed our minds and wanted to continue to support Diem and Nhu.

The discussion was an analysis of the growing disaffection in Vietnam among the non-Communist elements of society whose support was essential if the war against the Viet Cong was to be pursued successfully. And it was a prediction of the probable effects of the act of desecration against the pagodas, the Diem regime's continued policy of repression, and the continued dominance of Nhu. A new element was a report that had come in just that morning that posters with Nhu's picture were being put up all over Vietnam—a symbol of his increased power. What Rusk, Ball, Harriman, Forrestal, and I feared was not only that there would be worldwide political repercussions if the situation continued as it was but that the heart would go out of the war effort. If the younger officers and noncoms, who were likely to be Buddhists, did not revolt, they might just drift away. McNamara, Taylor, and Krulak conceded this, but wanted to try to find a way to get Diem to return to his old position and his old policies. With all his faults, they argued, Diem had once been a strong leader and had once been able to command enough support to pursue the war effort. But they also agreed that in the circumstances we had to tell the generals that, although we would prefer to see Diem remain—without Nhu—if the Vietnamese decided otherwise, an interim, anti-Communist military government could expect that American support would continue.

The consensus was that even though the present course of action was dangerous, doing nothing was even more dangerous, and the President went around the table one by one to make sure. The Secretary of State summed it up by saying that if we acquiesced in what had happened and the present situation in Vietnam continued, we would be on an inevitable road to disaster. The decision would then be whether to get out and let the country go to the Communists or move United States combat forces into Vietnam and take over.

The unresolved question was the approach to Diem himself. McNamara insisted on it; Lodge was doubtful whether it should be made at all; and the rest of us thought that it was really a question of when and how. The President directed that the NSC meet again the next day, and that Ambassador Nolting, who was now back in Washington, be asked to attend this meeting and all future meetings on the subject.

At the next meeting, the President queried Nolting at great length. Asked about the assurances he had had from Diem, Nolting brought out a long hand-written memorandum detailing assurances from both Diem and Nhu that they would not adopt this policy of "brutal surgery" against the Buddhists. But he held no animus, and he gave a dignified defense of Diem and his past record. Nolting speculated pessimistically on the possibility of persuading Diem to send Nhu away: Ambassador Durbrow had tried to do just that, under instructions, but it had been Durbrow who had left Vietnam, not Nhu. The President laughed at this, "The way things are going we may be forced to have Lodge tell Diem just that. If you're right Lodge's tour will be the shortest round trip in history!"

Nolting was pessimistic about the capacity of the generals to lead the country, and his recommendation was not to jump until we were sure there was some place to jump to. It might well be that the events of the past few weeks had made it impossible both for the Diem-Nhu government to succeed and for the United States to continue to support them. But he recommended taking it very slow and easy and making an attempt to try to live with Diem and Nhu—even though it meant that the United States would have to take its lumps around the world.

The Secretary of State commented wryly that world reaction to the desecration of the pagodas meant something more than just taking our lumps. And even more important was the reaction among the Viet-namese people, which should not be underestimated. The evidence coming in raised doubts that the war could ever be prosecuted successfully by a Diem-Nhu government.

The President decided to ask both Lodge and Harkins for their view on the central question, whether the turmoil would spread beyond Saigon, Hué, and the cities to the countryside and so affect the prospects for a military success.

August 28 was marred by two unhappy episodes. One was a sharp exchange between the State Department representatives in the middle of the NSC meeting. George Ball expressed the view that the consequences of going along with the Diem-Nhu government in view of what they had done would be that the war against the Viet Cong could not be won. Nolting, struggling still to retrieve the effort of two and a half years, said that he felt that a decision *not* to go along with Diem and Nhu would be to renege on past commitments. Ball responded that he had no sympathy for that view, for Diem and Nhu had been the ones to violate commitments—and massively. Harriman, somewhat testily, said that he had disagreed with Nolting's views for many months. He was sorry to have to be so blunt, but he felt that Nolting had been profoundly wrong all along in his advice to "go along" with Diem. And for my part, I sided with Ball and Harriman.

The second episode was different. A telegram had been sent by private Pentagon channels, unbeknown to the rest of us, which seemed to suggest to Harkins how he should answer the questions posed to him in the cable following the NSC meeting on August 27. The existence of this private telegram was discovered by accident, and the President had a private talk with those responsible—all too reminiscent of small boys being taken to the woodshed. The only redemption was that the episode did become the source of some relief from the tension. At a later meeting that same day, Harriman, who had not known of the President's private talk, archly remarked that he "had been very puzzled by the response from General Harkins until he had read the outgoing cable from the Pentagon." The President had some difficulty containing himself until the meeting had dispersed—whereupon he burst into laughter. "Averell Harriman," he said, "is one smart cookie."

The result was that a new set of cables had to be sent to Lodge and Harkins, asking again for their frank and personal assessment. Both responded that they did not believe that the war would be won if the United States acquiesced in what Diem and Nhu had done and continued to support a Diem-Nhu government. The only disagreement was that General Harkins thought that we should make one last-ditch effort to try to persuade Diem to get rid of Nhu, and Lodge felt that presenting Diem with such an ultimatum would be useless and very dangerous to the generals.

The same disagreement continued between the Pentagon and the State Department in the National Security Council. The Secretary of State was skeptical of an approach to Diem, unless it was postponed to the very last minute. Diem and Nhu had more than once demonstrated that they were capable of irrational acts. Now they were facing a truly desperate situation—the end of their regime and perhaps the end of their family. Presented with an ultimatum, they might institute a blood bath of both Vietnamese and Americans. Diem and Nhu might even appeal to Communist North Vietnam to intervene with their divisions. The Secretary of Defense, on the other hand, was in favor of an approach to Diem because he doubted whether anyone else could run the country. "And who," the President asked, "is running it now? It is certainly not being run very well."

The President again polled the meeting, going the rounds one by one—was there anyone who favored backing off? There was not.

But it was all an exercise in futility. By August 31, it was clear that the generals had stopped their actual planning and that they were not going to move. Many months later, someone asked the generals what had happened in those last days of August. They said that the key to their planning was General Dinh, the officer in command of the forces in the immediate area of Saigon. He was a highly erratic personality with the kind of soaring ambitions and opportunism that made him Nhu's willing collaborator. When the other generals approached him with their plans, he held back, and this meant that a bloodless coup would be impossible. John Mecklin reports that he asked Lodge why the generals had failed to carry through and that Lodge replied, "Perhaps they're afraid to die, like everyone else." This was undoubtedly part of the explanation, but there were other facets, too. The generals themselves indicated that they did not trust the assurances that the United States would remain aloof. Later, they said that a few of their number believed Nhu's braggings that the CIA had told him that he had President Kennedy's personal approval. They noted that John Richardson, the head of CIA in Vietnam, worked closely with Nhu in the development of the Special

Forces and in the Vietnamese intelligence effort, and they were known to
be friends. In any case, the generals indicated at the time that past
history had shown that "certain elements" of the United States Government had always sided with Nhu in all instances. None of this was true,
but these generals apparently were afraid of being betrayed unless the
United States would take an active part—and this the United States
should never do. The United States could and should dissociate itself
from a regime which had turned against both the United States and its
own people, and the United States could promise to support an anti-
Communist regime that replaced it. But the United States should not
participate in the decision to replace the regime or in action to carry out
that decision.

One other factor seems to have been paramount. Among both Americans and Vietnamese, the greatest concern of all was that a *coup d'état*
might result in a civil war between pro-Diem and anti-Diem forces that
would give the Viet Cong an opportunity. The military leaders wanted to
avoid this. In addition, they wanted to be sure that the decision to replace the Diem regime, if it were made, came as close to being a "national" decision as they could make it, reflecting unanimity among the
key military and civilian leadership. Much later, we learned that in this
period immediately following the attack on the pagodas and throughout
the early autumn of 1963, both civilian and military leaders were, in
effect, taking a highly dangerous poll on the question of this decision. It
was only when they were convinced that the decision was virtually unanimous, that the national cadre, so to speak, agreed that the war could
not be won with the Diem-Nhu regime and that the regime should be
replaced—it was only then that the actual plans for a coup were laid and
the decision sealed by a "blood oath" of the senior generals of the armed
forces.

NOTES

[1] E.g., Arthur M. Schlesinger, Jr., *A Thousand Days*, p. 991, which gives a basically
accurate version. Partial and sometimes distorted versions appear in Mecklin, *Mission
in Torment*, and Higgins, *Our Vietnam Nightmare*, pp. 192–99.
[2] John Mecklin, *Mission in Torment*, p. 194.

CHAPTER 32

The Agonies of Decision

THE PROBLEM of United States policy still remained. The Vietnamese might or might not decide to replace the Diem regime. But the United States still had to decide on how to handle its relations with that regime. All the elements of the problem remained the same. We could not acquiesce in what Diem and Nhu had done. We could not continue to support a regime that had gone back on its word and refused to make any amends whatsoever. We could not win a war with a regime that had turned against both its own people and its ally and continued to insist on following the policies that had brought about that confrontation.

In the meantime, the situation in Vietnam had severely worsened. Well over a thousand Buddhist priests were in jail, and the principal leader, Tri Quang, was still enjoying asylum in the American Embassy. But enough of the Buddhist leaders had survived to set up an underground which began distributing leaflets. To the Buddhist demonstrations were added those of the university students. Many of these had also been jailed, and the regime closed the universities at both Hué and Saigon. The secondary-school students then took up the torch of demonstrations, and they too were jailed. To the despair of the regime, the grade-school students then began to demonstrate. In its paranoia, the Diem regime had only one answer to any opposition—and they arrested the grade-school students, hauling them off by the hundreds to jail in trucks. For days, the children's bicycles stood in their racks outside the closed schools, rusting in the monsoon rains.

The regime did not descend to reprisals against the children, but there were sickening stories of them being forced to witness the torture of older prisoners. But the real significance of both the demonstrations by secondary- and grade-school students and their arrest came with a moment's reflection about who the parents of these children were. What little opportunity there was for education in Vietnam came to the sons and daughters of military officers, civil servants, and professional men— the national cadre again, on whom the war effort depended. There were several reports on high-ranking military officers visiting prisons in uniform trying to locate and obtain the release of sons and daughters, including one report that the commander of the Vietnamese Marine

Corps had spent the whole day searching before he found his younger brother.

Worldwide, too, the Diem regime had lost most of what little sympathy that remained for it. And in the United States we were having real trouble. McGeorge Bundy called me on August 31 to point out that the New York *Times* that morning had put two stories side by side on the front page—one on the Vietnamese Government's repression of the Buddhists and our disapproval, and the other on the death of two more Americans in Vietnam. Diem would have to be made to understand that this could not go on. The foreign aid bill had just suffered the worst cut in its history, and the President felt it was largely due to the sense of disillusionment about the whole effort in Vietnam. There were also reports that an amendment might be put forward to forbid any aid at all to Vietnam unless the regime changed its policies.

THE NSC MEETING OF AUGUST 31

The President was in Hyannis Port, and the NSC met on Saturday, August 31, at the State Department to consider what to do next. The State Department recommendation was to continue our posture of public disapproval and open negotiations with Diem to try to force a change in his policies. We could not and should not abandon Vietnam, but we could not and should not continue our support under the present conditions, which made it impossible to continue.

The Secretary of State said that in his opinion the disaffection had not yet spilled over from the cities to affect the war effort. But Harriman and I and the working-level officers on the Vietnam task force felt that the war effort really had been affected, even if the statistics did not yet reveal it. We felt, indeed, that the war effort had not been going nearly so well at any time as we had been led to believe. And this was the heart of the issue. The judgment shared by Harriman, Ball, Forrestal, and me, with the Secretary of State in general agreement, was that the war was not really going well, that it had never been really going well except for one short period in the first half of 1962, and that the continuation of Diem's and Nhu's repressive policies would affect it even more.

McNamara, Taylor, and the Joint Chiefs of Staff were not so convinced as we that guerrilla warfare was fundamentally political. They were less worried about the consequences of a continuation of Diem's and Nhu's policies of repression, and they were more sympathetic to the argument that Vietnam really needed a certain amount of authoritarianism if it was to beat the Viet Cong. But it was the question of how the war was going that stirred up the most emotion. McNamara and Taylor, especially, had made so many public statements that we were winning that they interpreted any suggestion that we were not as a criticism of their judgment and of the whole Pentagon effort. And their sensitivity was increased by the fact that under General Harkins the military effort in Vietnam had concentrated on the "shooting war" and brushed past the political side of the "counterinsurgency" concept.

Since the President was absent, the Secretary of State had been acting as chairman of the meeting. At the end, he pointedly invited the Vice-President, Lyndon B. Johnson, to give his views—the first time such an invitation had been issued in these meetings. In substance, the Vice-President tended to agree with the Pentagon. The meeting ended inconclusively. The only decision was to ask Lodge's views on the wisdom of an approach to Diem and what might be said.

TV FORCES A DECISION

The dynamics of a democratic society operating in an age of modern, electronic communications, however, turned out to be what public administration experts call "action forcing." It happened that the major TV networks were at this time inaugurating early evening news programs of a full half hour, and the President had long ago promised to help get them off to a good start with an interview. The first was with Walter Cronkite of CBS on September 2 at Hyannis Port, and the subject of Vietnam and the Buddhist crisis was an inevitable question. The President had to answer—and whatever answer he gave would be a policy decision. The White House staff, sensitive to the struggle within the administration and the widening rift, prepared a proposed response that was as innocuous as possible—and so tended to favor the military's view to go along with Diem. But the President tossed it aside and bit the bullet. "I don't think," the President said, "that unless a greater effort is made to win popular support that the war can be won out there. In the final analysis, it is their war. They are the ones who have to win it or lose it. We can help them, we can give them equipment, we can send our men out there as advisers, but they have to win it, the people of Vietnam, against the Communists.

"We are prepared to continue to assist them," he continued, "but I don't think the war can be won unless the people support the effort and, in my opinion, in the last two months, the government has gotten out of touch with the people. . . ."

Mr. Cronkite then asked if the Diem government had time to regain the support of the people, and the President said he thought it did. "With changes in policy and perhaps with personnel I think it can. If it doesn't make those changes, I would think that the chances of winning it would not be very good."

The meaning of this reference to the need for "changes in policy and personnel" was that the President had decided that the tension between the United States and the Diem regime would continue until the policy of repression against the Buddhists and the students had been abandoned and some arrangement made to lessen the dominant position in the government occupied by Ngo Dinh Nhu.

That evening, my wife asked me what would happen next, and my response was that I thought it meant there was a long and difficult period ahead. We had embarked on a policy that avoided the extremes both of withdrawing from Vietnam or of actually taking part in direct action to change the government. The policy was one of trying to discriminate by continuing to support those Vietnamese who were struggling against the Communists but maintaining the tension of our disapproval of Diem's and Nhu's repressive policies. It would be frustrating to those who preferred simple, black-and-white answers and it would require very steady nerves.

In Vietnam, the demonstrations continued, and so did the arrests. On September 7, eight hundred students were arrested. On September 10, the secret police rounded up one hundred more students, whom they had identified as leaders, and closed four more high schools.

NHU'S ANTI-AMERICAN CAMPAIGN

Nhu began a campaign of intimidation against the Americans. Every day there were stories in the Nhus' *Times of Vietnam* accusing CIA or the USIS mission of some fantastic plot. On September 2, for example, there was a four-column front-page story of how the CIA was supposed to have spent twenty-four million dollars *in co-operation with the Viet Cong,* to try to organize a *coup d'état.* Rumors were circulated that Nhu had prepared an "assassination list," and samples were distributed around Saigon. For some unknown reason, John Mecklin, the USIS chief, was at the top of every list, and Lodge finally called to ask if he would like to be transferred. Mecklin said he would stay. Nhu planted rumors that mobs would attack this or that United States installation. The Americans had to lay in stocks of arms and food and maintain guard duty. Their nerves were taut. On one occasion, Nhu told a Western newsman in an interview that his recommendation was that the Americans should all be sent home, helicopters and all—they did not know how to fight this kind of war. And by mid-September there were a number of intelligence reports that Nhu was in touch with Hanoi in an attempt to cook up some kind of a deal—which was possible, although we suspected that it was Nhu who was disseminating the reports in an attempt to frighten us.

THE DIVIDED MISSION

Within the American mission to Saigon—and within the wider American community there, including the press—there were the same divisions as in Washington. John Richardson, the head of the CIA mission to

Vietnam, argued persistently that the United States should continue to support Diem and Nhu. But most of his staff disagreed with him, and emotions reached such a pitch that some members of the CIA staff felt that the only way their views could reach Washington was through leaks to the press. The disagreement in the CIA mission became such common knowledge that the *Times of Vietnam* had a story on it—headlined "CIA, Your Split is Showing." But the same split went through the whole mission and every agency. The top military headquarters was convinced that the war was going well and that it remained unaffected by the Buddhist crisis. Yet many officers serving as advisers in the field disagreed. It was reported, for example, that at one official briefing that General Harkins arranged for General Krulak, on one of Krulak's visits from the JCS in Washington, the Vietnamese briefer said that there were 123 strategic hamlets in the Seventh Divison area. Later, when only Americans were present, Lieutenant Colonel Fred Ladd, a West Pointer and the Seventh Division adviser, said that there were really only eight hamlets worthy of the name—and General Harkins rebuked him for doubting the Vietnamese statistics.

The press was equally divided, although the hard core of the resident press—Halberstam, Browne, and Sheehan—was convinced that the war could not be won with the Diem regime. And the whole thing had a dynamism of its own. Every faction was so passionately convinced of the rightness of its cause that leaking to the press became a patriotic act. An officer in a particular agency would leak something to the press, thinking this would force "them" to see the truth—"them" being his colleagues, or his boss, or, more likely, Washington over his boss's head. Both factions played the game. Those who were convinced that we were losing the war and that it would get worse if we continued to support Diem leaked to Halberstam, Browne, or Sheehan. Those who felt we were winning, or had a stake in feeling we were winning, and wanted to go on supporting Diem leaked to Marguerite Higgins on her visits, or to Alsop, or to one of the Hearst reporters. The newspapers would play it big, and the rift between the factions would widen still more.

Among the American government agencies, it was CIA and the CIA station chief, John Richardson, that got the worst of it—probably because CIA's general aura of secrecy and mystery made it the most vulnerable. The notion that they took policy into their own hands against the policy of Washington made its way into almost every paper in the United States. But in fact Richardson and the agency were meticulous in clearing even routine matters they thought might have political repercussions. They took a particular beating in the United States press, for example, over a payment to the notorious Colonel Tung, Nhu's hatchet man who headed the Special Forces. CIA had helped develop the Vietnamese Special Forces so they could be used on commando-type raids against the Viet Cong, and CIA paid a monthly subsidy to help cover their salaries. When the September payment was made, the first one after the Special Forces had been used to attack the pagodas, some outraged junior officer in CIA leaked it to the press. CIA was accused of pushing its own pro-Diem policy behind Washington's back. But the truth was that Richardson and CIA had sought and obtained approval to go ahead from both the White House and me to make the payment. The United States Government had not yet faced up to the whole problem of what it would do to obtain its publicly announced goal of "changes in policy and perhaps personnel," and until it had faced the whole problem our decision was that piecemeal steps should be avoided and routine continued.

There was an NSC meeting scheduled for September 6, and that morning the President telephoned to ask if I had done any thinking about "selective cuts in aid that would not hurt the war effort but still make Diem and Nhu understand that we meant business." One, of course, was to cut the payments to Colonel Tung's Special Forces—for they were surely not being used in the war effort. Another was to cut the so-called commodity imports program. This, like the one in Laos described earlier, was designed to soak up excess purchasing power to keep down inflation. With so many men in uniform and out of production, too much money was chasing too few goods. In the commodity imports program, the United States sent to Vietnam such commodities as tobacco, condensed milk, and so on. These goods would be sold on the open market for piastres, which were simply withdrawn from circulation. Cutting this program would not hurt the war effort directly. It would permit a growing inflation, but that would take time. The trouble with these selective cuts, of course, was that they had no real leverage. Nhu could find other sources of income for his Special Forces and continue to use them against domestic opposition rather than the Viet Cong. The commodity import cuts would mean a sacrifice in semiluxuries, and eventually inflation—although here, too, there were other ways to attack the problem of inflation. Selective cuts that did not hurt the war effort, in other words, would not exert enough pressure to force Diem to change. But they did have considerable symbolic and psychological impact. Although Diem already knew that we disapproved of his policies, selective cuts would show him more vividly than anything else that this disapproval ran deeper than our several disagreements in the past. And they would tell the world, the Vietnamese people, and the military leadership in Vietnam that our public statements of disapproval were more than just words.

At the NSC meeting of September 6 the discussion at first centered on Lodge reopening "tough negotiations" with Diem. Lodge had called on Diem and Nhu and had made known to them what we thought should be done. But he did not want to take the initiative in reopening negotiations, even "tough" ones. He felt that if he went to Diem for this purpose it would be interpreted throughout Asia as surrender. But even worse, the best that could be hoped from such negotiations would be token reforms, putting a façade over what had happened and nothing more. We needed concrete and fundamental changes, and the only possible way to get them, in Lodge's view, was to make Diem come to him. But there were people at the NSC meeting who thought Lodge should be ordered to go to Diem, and the discussion became an exercise in meandering frustration.

During the Cuban missile crisis, it had been the Attorney General who had asked some of the more fundamental and wiser questions, and he did so again at this meeting. The first and fundamental question, he felt, was what we were doing in Vietnam. As he understood it, we were there to help the people resisting a Communist take-over. The first question was whether a Communist take-over could be successfully resisted with any government. If it could not, now was the time to get out of Vietnam entirely, rather than waiting. If the answer was that it could, but not with a Diem-Nhu government as it was now constituted, we owed it to the people resisting Communism in Vietnam to give Lodge enough sanctions to bring changes that would permit successful resistance. But the basic question of whether a Communist take-over could be successfully resisted with any government had not been answered, and he was not sure that anyone had enough information *to* answer it.

The ensuing debate on whether or not we were winning the war or had ever been winning it produced no agreement. But McNamara leaped on the Attorney General's question as to whether anyone had enough information to answer the basic question and proposed still another mission to Vietnam to "get the facts." One might ask what questions could be put to the harassed officials in Vietnam that had not already been put to them, or whom a Washington delegation might see that had not already been seen or what a Washington delegation could do that our mission in Saigon could not do better. But a proposal to send a mission to "get the facts" is hard to combat, and the result was a decision to send General Krulak once again to check on the military situation. There was no counterproposal from the Secretary of State, but there were no objections when I suggested that a State Department man ought to be included to check on the political situation—although McNamara directed Krulak to depart within ninety minutes and it took a personal phone call from me to get the departure delayed until the State Department representative arrived at the airfield.

I chose Joseph A. Mendenhall to be the State Department representative. He was a senior foreign service officer with long experience in Vietnam who was then head of the planning office in the Bureau of Far Eastern Affairs. In addition, it was agreed that Krulak and Mendenhall would bring back with them two key officials of the American mission in

Vietnam to give additional reports. The first was John Mecklin, head of the USIS in Vietnam, and the second was Rufus Phillips—who had worked for Lansdale in the early days of our involvement in Vietnam and who now headed the section of the American aid mission that was responsible for supporting the strategic hamlet program.

THE KRULAK-MENDENHALL REPORT

Krulak and Mendenhall flew out in a "McNamara Special." They traveled twenty-four thousand miles, visited centers all over Vietnam, and returned—all between September 6 and September 10. And on September 10, the NSC met once more. General Krulak reported that he had talked with eighty-seven members of the American advisory system, although not with any Vietnamese. His general conclusion was that the "shooting war" was still going ahead at an impressive pace. It had been affected by the political crisis, but not greatly. Vietnamese officers were, of course, aware of the Buddhist crisis, but most had viewed it with detachment and had not permitted religious differences to affect their relationships. American advisers reported some dissent and dissatisfaction among Vietnamese officers with the regime, although it focused more on Nhu than on Diem. Nhu's departure would be hailed, but the advisers doubted that the Vietnamese military were willing to stick their necks out to accomplish it. The war was going well and would be won if current programs were pursued, irrespective of the defects of the regime.

Mendenhall had visited Saigon, Hué, and several of the provincial cities and towns where he talked mainly to Vietnamese he had known in his earlier years in Vietnam. He reported that he had found a virtual breakdown of the civil government in Saigon as well as a pervasive atmosphere of fear and hate arising from the police reign of terror and the arrests of students. The war against the Viet Cong had become secondary to the war against the regime. There was danger of an outbreak of a religious war between Buddhists and Catholics if the oppression did not cease. Nhu was held principally responsible, but increasingly Diem and Nhu were viewed as sharing responsibility. He had found a similar atmosphere of fear and hate in Hué and Danang. In the northern coastal areas, the Viet Cong had recently made advances. It was not clear whether this was directly attributable to the Buddhist crisis, but it was clear that Buddhist agitation had extended to the rural areas in the coastal regions. Students in Hué and Saigon were also talking openly of the possibility that the Viet Cong might be a better alternative than Diem. Mendenhall concluded that the war could not be won unless, as a minimum, Nhu withdrew or was removed from the government.

President Kennedy looked quizzically from one to the other. "You two did visit the same country, didn't you?"

General Krulak volunteered to explain the difference—Mendenhall had gone to the cities and towns; he, Krulak, had gone to the countryside. The war was being fought in the countryside. Yes, someone replied, but it was being managed and directed by the people who live in the cities.*

Nolting discounted Mendenhall's report. He said it was well known that Mendenhall had for several years believed we could not win with Diem. It might be true that there was a paralysis in the civilian government, as Mendenhall reported. There were fear and paralysis in 1961, too, and we had overcome that.

McGeorge Bundy said that in 1961 the fear and paralysis had been caused by the Viet Cong and we had overcome it by strengthening the war against the Viet Cong. Now it was the government itself that was causing the fear and paralysis, and it was a little difficult to strengthen a war against the government.

When John Mecklin's turn came he reported that in his judgment the "regime's action against the Buddhists had decisively alienated such a large portion of the population that it could no longer hope to win a war in which popular support was vital."[1] Even if the Pentagon was right that the military effort had not yet been weakened, the rot was so widespread it would eventually weaken it disastrously. In Mecklin's judgment, the time had come for the United States to apply direct pressure to bring about a change of government, however distasteful such action might be. This would be dangerous—there might be a civil war. For this reason

---

* The State Department intelligence bureau picked up these remarks in a paper written shortly afterward to take issue with the idea that anyone had really reported on the "countryside." The questions being asked, the paper argued, were about whether the army's morale had been affected by recent political events. Yet morale in a disciplined organization was always less concerned with fundamental purposes than it was with more immediate affairs. Troops were less concerned with the basic purpose of a war than with their own competency and that of their immediate commanders, whether they received support from higher echelons, and success or failure in their own local battles. Bad morale in an army would not be the *first* symptom of a disintegration of the war effort, but the final and irretrievable result. As the paper said, the significant question was the attitude of the true "countryside." What was the attitude of the population from which the Viet Cong could most easily draw recruits. The only information even remotely relevant were the statistics on Viet Cong strength, and even if you did not believe the statistics were reliable, they indicated the government was in trouble. Early in 1966, intelligence was estimating regular Viet Cong strength at 16,000. Now they were estimating 23,000. Yet since early 1962 there had been 36,368 Viet Cong killed and 9228 captured—or so the statistics said. Where were all the Viet Cong coming from? The best estimate for the infiltration routes was 3500 since early 1962, and the evidence was that the rate had gone down in the last six months. The conclusion was inescapable that the rate of recruitment *inside* South Vietnam had actually been going up—even before the Buddhist crisis.

he would recommend deciding right now to introduce American combat forces to fight the Viet Cong themselves.

There was an awkward silence after that. Introducing American ground forces into Vietnam and becoming involved in the "land war in Asia" that MacArthur had warned against was one thing everyone knew Kennedy wished to avoid. The specter of it raised Robert Kennedy's question in everyone's minds—was this the time to withdraw entirely?

Rufus Phillips began his report by saying that he had known Diem, Nhu, and the others prominent in the Vietnamese Government for ten years, and since he had been in charge of the American support to the strategic hamlet program, he felt that he had also gotten to know the mood of the rural areas. He said that Nhu had lost the confidence and respect of the military officers and the civil service. They did not support the government with Nhu in it, and would not support the government at all if they had an alternative. There was now a crisis of confidence in Vietnam, not only between the Vietnamese people and their government, but between the Vietnamese people and the United States. The Vietnamese felt that Diem was in power only because of American support— that the United States was ultimately to blame. They might like to see Diem remain if it were possible, but they were unalterably opposed to the Nhus and the present government. The United States was under an obligation to adopt measures that would bring about a change. He had had this view from them all—and he named an impressive list of Vietnamese officials.

As for the military, with all due respect to General Krulak's report, he felt that American military advisers were not able to give credible evidence on political attitudes. They were under a directive not to talk politics with their Vietnamese counterparts and the Vietnamese knew this.

Krulak interrupted to say that the advisers might not be good on politics or have an entree to the palace, but they were good on telling whether the war was being won, and they said that the war was going well.

Phillips said that the war had, indeed, been going well in the I, II, and III Corps areas, but that it was emphatically not going well in the IV Corps, the crucial delta. The strategic hamlets there were being chewed to pieces by the Viet Cong. Fifty hamlets had been overrun in the last few weeks. And what made it all so significant was that the effects of the Buddhist crisis had not yet reached the delta—the deterioration of the war effort in the delta was not connected with political developments and repression of the Buddhists. Not yet.

Krulak interrupted again to say that Phillips was putting his judgment ahead of General Harkins and that he, Krulak, would take Harkins over Phillips. The war was *not* being lost in a military sense.

There was, said Phillips, a great deal of activity in the delta, all bad. The strategic hamlets were not being protected. They were being overrun wholesale. Furthermore, this was not a military war, but a political war. It was a war for men's minds more than a battle against the Viet Cong, and it was being lost. On this note, the meeting ended.[2]

BACKLASH FROM CAPITOL HILL

We began to have more trouble with the Congress, where the feeling of outrage and impatience was sharp. In the first week of September, I was called before the Senate Subcommittee on the Far East and given a rough time. Even the senators most friendly to Diem warned of further aid cuts if he did not move to ease the political position he had put us into. Senator Frank Church said that at some stage he intended to introduce a resolution calling for an end to aid for the government of South Vietnam unless it abandoned its policies of repression against its own people and made a determined and effective effort to regain their support. I begged him not to put it in without first checking with the Executive Branch on both wording and timing, and Church agreed—but only with the warning that any delay had to be very short.

AND AGAIN, TV

The "action-forcing" dynamics of mass communications took over again. On September 9, NBC launched its half-hour news program, and, inevitably, again the President was asked about Vietnam. "We are using our influence," he said, "to persuade the government there to take those steps which will win back support. That takes some time and we must be patient, we must persist." Would we cut our aid? "I don't think we think that would be helpful at this time," the President responded. "If you reduce your aid, it is possible you could have some effect upon the government structure there. On the other hand, you might have a situation which could bring about a collapse. Strongly in our mind is what happened in the case of China at the end of World War II, where China was lost, a weak government became increasingly unable to control events. We don't want that."

By the time of his news conference on September 12, 1963, his thinking had apparently gone a little further, and he spoke in sharper tones. "What helps to win the war, we support; what interferes with the war effort, we oppose. I have already made it clear that any action by either government which may handicap the winning of the war is inconsistent with our policy or our objectives. This is the test which I think every agency and official of the United States Government must apply to all of our actions, and we shall be applying that test in various ways in the coming months, although I do not think it desirable to state all of our views at this time.

"But we have a very simple policy in that area," he went on to say. "In some ways I think the Vietnamese people and ourselves agree: we want the war to be won, the Communists to be contained, and the Americans to go home. That is our policy. I am sure it is the policy of the people of Vietnam. But we are not there to see a war lost, and we will follow the policy which I have indicated today of advancing those causes and issues which help win the war."

This statement took us a bit farther down the road. "What helps to win the war, we support; what interferes with the war effort, we oppose" became a policy guideline, along with "changes in policy, and, perhaps, personnel." But there had been no concrete decisions at the September 10 meeting, and those of us who carried responsibility at the State Department prepared a paper presenting two alternative courses of action. One of these was to swallow everything that had happened, and adopt a policy of reconciliation—to go to Diem and extract from reconciliation whatever we could. The alternative was to adopt a policy of "pressures and persuasion"—a program of gradually increasing pressures in phases while at the same time inviting negotiations. The "pressures" were to include selective cuts in aid and other measures that would exert pressure as well as serve as concrete expressions of United States disapproval.

The "pressures and persuasion" track started off mildly, so mildly in fact that it hardly seemed distinguishable from "reconciliation." But, as I tried to make clear in a covering memorandum, Phase One of the "pressure and persuasion" track began with the requirement that the United States maintain a public posture of disapproval, while the reconciliation track required a public posture of acquiescence to the Diem regime's actions and even some effort by the United States to put those actions in as favorable a light as possible. They were true alternatives. If the reconciliation track did not work, it would not be possible to switch to "pressure and persuasion"—unless Diem and Nhu did something else outrageous that created a new situation. On the other hand, it *would* be possible to switch from "pressure and persuasion" to reconciliation at any time during the first two phases—but it would become increasingly difficult to do so in the absence of major concessions on the part of Diem, and impossible once we had entered the later phases. We did not believe that "reconciliation" would work, and our recommendation was to start on the first phases of "pressures and persuasion" and then take another look before going on.

And just at this time, the commanding officer of the Australian military mission to Vietnam, Colonel Serong, paid a visit to Washington and cast still more doubt on the Pentagon's contention that the "shooting war" was going well. The graphs of indicators that he considered key had either leveled off or showed a downward trend since June, even before the attack on the pagodas. The Viet Cong, for example, were capturing two weapons for every one they lost. It was true that the Viet Cong had not really exploited the situation created by Buddhist unrest, but he felt the reason was that things were really going so well for them that the smart thing for the Viet Cong to do was to let it continue to boil and avoid frightening people into thinking the Viet Cong might take advantage of it. The strategic hamlet program, furthermore, was pushing out too fast along the roads, the radial lines, and leaving pockets of Viet Cong control in between. If something was not done to pull back and develop a lateral, "oil blot" approach, the overextended hamlets would provide the Viet Cong with a great opportunity. It seemed clear that, whenever the Viet Cong considered that the time was ripe, they would strike at the overextended hamlets with even more effectiveness than they were already doing and capture a lot of weapons and ammunition in the process.

The next meeting of the NSC, later in September, was merely a repetition of the arguments—and the frustrations—of the previous meeting. Again, McNamara proposed a visit to Vietnam to "get the facts"—only this time it was to be McNamara himself who went, accompanied by General Taylor.

Again, one might ask what new questions could be put, what new officials consulted, and what a Washington delegation could accomplish that the Saigon mission couldn't. What "facts" could the Secretary of Defense get? He could talk to the same American military advisers that General Krulak had talked to, fly over the same terrain, and receive the same warm assurances from the same self-interested Vietnamese officials who owed their positions to Diem. An American Secretary of Defense could hardly drift quietly around interviewing the Vietnamese man in the street, much less the Vietnamese man in the paddy field. But, again, it was difficult to fight a proposal to "get the facts."

The State Department was uneasy about too many high-level visits to Vietnam, as already related, and especially by so high level an official as the Secretary of Defense. Visits attracted headlines showing how concerned we were about the situation, for one thing. But even worse, high-level visits tended to lock U.S. prestige tighter and tighter to the course of events. This was McNamara's third visit to Vietnam, and each one made the struggle there look more and more like an American war.

The President knew all this, as mentioned before, but he felt he had to pay the price. The Joint Chiefs of Staff and the military "brass" did not like the policy of keeping the struggle in Vietnam limited or the attempt to emphasize importance of the political aspects of the struggle. But they had not yet moved into open opposition, and there was still a chance that they could be persuaded to go along with the President's policy. If the JCS and the higher-ranking generals did move into open opposition, on the other hand, they could muster powerful support in the Congress and the split inside the American government might develop into the kind of nationwide political civil war that had paralyzed America during the McCarthy era. The President indicated that he felt he had to keep the JCS on board, that the only way to keep them on board was to keep McNamara on board—and that the only way to do that, apparently, was to let him go to Vietnam himself.

LEAKS AD HOMINEM

It was in this interregnum of tension, when the decisions seemed to be up in the air, that the politics of policy-making in both Washington and Saigon reached the most unpretty stage of all. In Saigon, for example, there were stories and rumors that questioned the loyalty and patriotism of American officials, as well as their judgment. Alsop had attacked his fellow reporters, as mentioned above, and Marguerite Higgins had suggested that some American reporters wanted to see the war lost to prove they were right. The attacks on Halberstam were particularly vicious— suggesting every possible failing from being pro-Communist to being pro-Fascist. But the one he resented most of all he attributed to either General Krulak or Marguerite Higgins, or both, since they were friends. The way the story came back to Halberstam was that Krulak told a *Time* reporter that when Miss Higgins was in Saigon "young" Halberstam had met her at a bar, had shown her a picture of some dead bodies, had asked if she had ever seen a dead man, and had then burst into tears.[3] Halberstam was young and he was far from being completely right about Vietnam, but he had seen a full quota of bodies, and he resented the implied slur on his manhood deeply.

CIA was accused of taking matters into its own hands. The military were accused of falsifying information—or being duped. John Richardson was accused of aiding Nhu against the orders from Washington.

John Mecklin also came under fire. After the assault on the pagodas, Halberstam and Sheehan asked Mecklin if they could stay at his house. They had reason to be fearful for their safety, and Mecklin welcomed them. But over the next few weeks, there were suggestions that Mecklin had made the arrangement to facilitate leaks against other agencies. Mecklin himself reports that he was told that even the head of CIA in Washington and the Secretary of State had complained to Ed Murrow, Chief of USIA.[4]

Generally speaking, these *ad hominem* attacks and viciously distorted leaks came not from the top levels of the different departments and agencies, but from people down the line who believed passionately but did not know the whole story. While McNamara and Taylor were on this particular trip, for example, someone in the Pentagon leaked a highly distorted version of the August 24 cable and the circumstances surrounding it—making me the principal culprit. But as far as the principals in the Pentagon were concerned, such an attack was shameful and an embarrassment.

This particular episode, in fact, casts some light on the dynamics of leak and counterleak as played out in the peculiar working methods of at least one of the weekly news magazines. The story was leaked to two of these, and, routinely, each sent their State Department correspondent around to inquire. After very serious consideration by all concerned, it was decided that the interests of the United States would best be served if the correspondents were shown some of the actual documents—things were tense enough without a news-magazine story adding to the bitterness. Both correspondents wrote it all out with complete accuracy. One magazine killed the story, but the other ignored its correspondent's "file" completely—in spite of the fact that he had seen the actual documents. David Halberstam remarks in his book that the correspondents of some of the news magazines spend an inordinate amount of their time apologizing to sources about the way stories turn out. I was amused that this particular correspondent came around a day before publication with an advance copy of the magazine, which he threw down on my desk. "My editors," he said, "are more interested in a good story than they are in the truth."

And here again, the dynamism of mass communications began to operate. Some unknown State Department official became incensed at what he thought was underhanded tactics and decided to come to the defense of those attacked—although they would have preferred to be their own defenders. Again, he was apparently someone who knew only part of the story—for he assumed that the attack had come from CIA, instead of the Pentagon, and he retaliated by leaking a damaging story to Max Freedman that CIA was "freewheeling" in Vietnam. Freedman had also been distressed at the way things were going and printed the story, which he had every reason to believe was accurate. The result was to increase the bitterness all around, and complicate our problem still more. And so it went, with bitterness added to bitterness.

MCNAMARA'S TRIP—AND REPORT

McNamara conducted a whirlwind tour of Vietnam, boring in with difficult questions to the squirming briefers. And to his everlasting credit, he came back doubting the statistics he loved so well—or at least recognizing that unquantifiable political factors might be more important than he had been willing to believe before. The report that McNamara and Taylor submitted stoutly maintained that the "shooting war" was making "great progress and continued to progress." But, it went on, there were serious political tensions in Saigon and "perhaps" elsewhere in Vietnam [meaning outside the cities], where the "Diem-Nhu government is becoming increasingly unpopular." It went on to say that an increasing number of officers were becoming hostile to the government—although they continued to be more hostile to the Viet Cong. Most importantly, the report acknowledged that further repressive actions by Diem and Nhu would change the "present favorable military trends." But the most vital point of all was the judgment offered on the question of a policy of pressure on the Diem-Nhu government. It was not clear that pressure would move Diem and Nhu toward moderation—it might, indeed, increase their obduracy. But the judgment in McNamara's report was that unless the United States did exert such pressures Diem and Nhu were almost certain to continue their past patterns of repressive behavior. Under questioning, in fact, McNamara said that he thought we couldn't even persuade Diem to take the most routine military advice of moving a division without accompanying it with a set of pressures.

But there was a price that Kennedy had to pay for all this. McNamara and Taylor had come a long way in recognizing that political factors were more important in Vietnam than they had been willing to admit, but they had not come far enough to recognize that political factors were fundamental and overriding. They still really believed that the war was being won. They still really believed that military measures would suffice. And they still really believed in statistics. They had come to agree that a continuation of Diem's and Nhu's repressive policies would be disastrous, but they were adamantly clinging to the idea that a military approach to guerrilla warfare was the right approach. Their proposal was implicit rather than explicit, but it was clear. McNamara and the Joint Chiefs would agree to a policy of "pressure and persuasion" on the Diem regime, which they now thought was necessary, but they would agree only if the White House and the State Department would in turn agree to a public announcement that the Pentagon was right about how the "shooting war" had been going. McNamara's tone, when he read the proposed language of the announcement to the NSC meeting on his return October 2, was almost brusque, as if he was delivering an ultimatum:

"The military program in South Vietnam has made progress and is sound in principle, though improvements are being energetically sought . . .

"Secretary McNamara and General Taylor reported their judgment that the major part of the United States military task can be completed by the end of 1965. . . . They reported that by the end of this year [1963] the U.S. program for training Vietnamese should have progressed to the point that one thousand U.S. military personnel assigned to South Vietnam can be withdrawn.

"The political situation in South Vietnam remains deeply serious. The United States has made clear its continuing opposition to any repressive actions in South Vietnam. While such actions have not yet significantly affected the military effort, they can do so in the future."

The statement was released from the White House immediately after the NSC meeting. It was a statement that came to haunt Secretary McNamara and the whole history of American involvement in Vietnam. And the real tragedy is that many of the ranking American officers in Saigon and the Pentagon believed it.

The recommendations on the military side were, first, for Harkins to review with the Vietnamese the military changes needed to complete the military campaign in the northern and central portions of South Vietnam by the end of 1964 and in the delta by 1965; and, second, to establish a training program to permit the Vietnamese to take over all functions being performed by Americans so that the "bulk of United States military personnel" could be withdrawn by 1965.

On the political side, the program of pressures would be, initially, to withhold funds for the commodity import program; to hold up approval for aid loans that had been requested for the Saigon water works and power plant; and to stop payments to Colonel Tung and the Special Forces until they were assigned to military control and used to fight the Viet Cong. Lodge would maintain his policy of cool correctness, and inquiries from Vietnamese officials about any of these matters would be met with the suggestion that President Diem might wish to take up the matter, whatever it was, with the Ambassador. When and if Diem did "take the matter up with the Ambassador," Lodge would take the opportunity to discuss the three basic issues causing the strain in our relations and impairing the war effort—the need for drastic improvement in the Vietnamese military effort; the crisis of confidence among the Vietnamese people caused by Diem's policy of repression and police-state methods; and the crisis of confidence among the American people and government.

No formal announcement would be made of the decision to apply pressures, although both Diem and the key military leaders would be informed of each cut as it was made. Since the public statement avoided any reference to pressures, Diem had a full opportunity to come around without any loss of face. When the specific measures we were taking did become known—as they eventually would—we would simply point to the President's TV statement that "What helps the war, we support; what interferes with the war effort, we oppose."

Forrestal asked me how I would bet on the outcome. My feeling was that there was about a 40 per cent chance that Diem would come around, a 40 per cent chance that he wouldn't and the generals would move to take over, and a 20 per cent chance that nothing would happen at all. If nothing at all happened, it seemed clear that within six months to a year the Viet Cong would control the country—or we would have to take over the war with American ground forces, which President Kennedy was convinced would be a tragic error. But the real hell of it was that, even if something did happen, the situation might still come to that choice. The Kennedy administration had developed a strategic concept for fighting guerrilla warfare, an idea for a political program into which military measures were meshed, but we had failed so far to convince the Diem regime or even the top levels of the Pentagon to give it a fair trial. If something did happen in Vietnam, all it meant was that we would have a second chance.

NOTES

[1] Mecklin details his report to this NSC meeting in *Mission in Torment*, p. 210.
[2] Only occasionally was there any relief from the tension. But the occasions did occur. One was a paper written by James Thomson, then Special Assistant in the Bureau of Far Eastern Affairs, which was clandestinely circulated to those of the participants who would enjoy it:

MINUTES OF THE *NEXT* HIGH-LEVEL MEETING ON VIET-NAM

"The Secretary of State opened the meeting, in the absence of the President, by urging that priority be given to the key question of the past thirteen hours: How did we get here, and Where do we go from here?

"On the one hand, he said, it was important to keep moving forward. But on the other hand, we must deal with things as they are.

"The Secretary of Defense concurred but felt that we must not permit the views of a handful of neurotic Saigon intellectuals to distract us from the major goal, which was to get on with the war. He asked General Krulak to report on his latest sampling of opinion among the trainers of Vietnamese secret police at Fort Belvoir.

"General Krulak reported that morale among the trainers at Fort Belvoir was at an all-time high. Many felt that we had turned a corner, and all were intent on moving on with our objectives.

"Mr. Hilsman asked if General Krulak had had an opportunity to talk to the Vietnamese at Fort Belvoir as well as the trainers.

"Ambassador Nolting interjected the comment that Mr. Hilsman had expressed doubts about the Vietnamese at Belvoir ten months ago. He wondered, in view of this fact, whether Mr. Hilsman's question was relevant.

"General Krulak responded that the American trainers had advised him to refrain from talking with the Vietnamese since their views were well known to the trainers, and conversation would distract them from the purpose at hand, i.e., to win the war.

"Governor Harriman stated that he had disagreed for twenty years with General Krulak and disagreed today, reluctantly, more than ever; he was sorry to say that he felt General Krulak was a fool and had always thought so.

"Secretary Dillon hoped that press leaks on the cost of opinion-sampling at Fort Belvoir would be kept to a minimum as the dollar reserve problem was acute. He, for one, was against moving forward until the risks had been calculated.

"General Taylor said that if risks were involved, 'You can count me out.'

"The Secretary of State re-phrased the basic question in terms of Saigon's 897. What were we to do about the 500 school-girls who were seeking asylum in the American embassy?

"(At this point, the President entered the room.)

"The President said that he hoped we were not allowing our policies to be influenced by immature twelve-year-old school-girls, all of whom were foreigners. He felt that we must not lose sight of our ultimate objective, and in no state was the Vietnamese vote worth very much.

"The Attorney General said that it was high time to show some guts, and here was a good place to begin. 'After all,' he said, 'I too am a President's brother.'

"The Secretary of Defense heartily concurred; as a former businessman, he said, he knew the importance of getting on with business as usual.

"Mr. Hilsman raised the question of disaffection among ninety percent of the soldiers, as reported in Embtel 898. Was not an action plan, phase by phase, now clearly necessary?

"The Vice President said that he had lived with both affection and disaffection in Texas and the Senate for thirty years, and he felt we could ride this one through. We must not lose our sense of humor, he said.

"The President asked that inter-agency committees be put to work on the nature of our dialogue with Diem, and he suggested that the EXCOM meet again in a week or so. Next time, he said, he hoped there would be a good map of Viet-Nam available."

It was just the kind of self-mockery President Kennedy appreciated, and when Forrestal showed it to him, he roared with laughter.

³ Halberstam, *op. cit.*, p. 268.

⁴ Mecklin, *op. cit.*, p. 185.

CHAPTER 33

Götterdämmerung: The Coup
Against Diem

ALTHOUGH in agony, a decision had finally been made. Now it was up to Henry Cabot Lodge.

Many New Frontiersmen had had their doubts about Lodge. It was not just that he was a Republican. Somehow, his performance as Ambassador to the United Nations in the Eisenhower administration had been too much like Dulles's as Secretary of State—too moralistic, too much of just anti-Communism without positive appeals. There had been criticism of Lodge from the Republicans, too—that he had not been energetic enough in the 1960 campaign, insisting on an afternoon nap no matter what. But for the task in Saigon at this particular juncture of history, he was superb. He knew how to be a public figure, to combine statesmanship with press relations and domestic politics. He had the supreme self-confidence and coolness of a Boston Brahmin, of both the Cabots and the Lodges. And he had an intuitive sense of prestige and "face" and the role they played in an Asian society.

He handled the press, with which there had been such roiled relations, with a masterly touch. As soon as the greetings were over the day he stepped off the plane and he saw the waiting newsmen, he stepped forward to talk to them. Thereafter, he saw them regularly, usually one by one at lunch. He did not try to argue with them, as Nolting had done. He listened to them, and he gave them stories that he wanted to see in print. "The leak," he said, "is the prerogative of the Ambassador. It is one of my weapons for doing this job." Even in Washington, it was clear that it was Lodge who was doing most of the leaking. The only trouble was that Lodge's interest did not always completely coincide with Washington's and there were times when the steady flow of all-too-revealing information leaking from Saigon drove Kennedy close to distraction. The press, of course, thrived on this steady diet of authoritative leaks. Thus Lodge was served not only by the stories that put pressure where he wanted it put —and the target was as often an American agency as it was Vietnamese —but by the gratitude of the reporters. But what completely won over the hard-core group of pressmen who were so pessimistic about the possibility of winning with the Diem regime and so disgusted with the blind optimism of Harkins' headquarters was that Lodge seemed to agree with them. The problem of the relations between the press and the embassy, at least, was solved, and Lodge was never once subjected to a hostile story from the permanently assigned reporters.

Lodge's strategy of remaining cool and aloof, of keeping a door open for Diem, but making him take the first step toward it, had a cunning shrewdness that all Asians appreciated, whether camel drivers, village headmen, or Confucian scholars. It showed that the Bostonian leader could be just as mandarin as the Vietnamese leader. "The techniques not only preserved but exploited American dignity," John Mecklin later wrote in admiration, "in effect turning an Asian characteristic against Asians, yet it never closed the door to reconciliation—on American terms." Writing to me about this "posture of silent disapproval" at the time, Lodge said that he had "never realized before in my life how much attention silence could attract." When Madame Nhu first heard of Lodge's appointment, she exclaimed in dismay, "They have sent us a proconsul!" She was right.

Forrestal and I had suggested to the President that he might consider appointing as Ambassador a "civilian public figure whose character and reputation would permit him to dominate the representatives of all other departments and agencies." Lodge was certainly such a man. It had been suggested, for example, that the recall of the CIA station chief, John Richardson, might be an effective pressure on Nhu. Richardson was close to Nhu personally. Nhu himself would interpret Richardson's recall as a signal that the United States really did mean business and that CIA views were no longer predominant in the councils of the United States. Everyone in Vietnam knew him as a defendant of the Diem-Nhu regime. Both Nhu's henchmen and his opponents would correctly read the meaning of Richardson's recall. It would help signal our determination not to co-operate with a government that continued to leave Nhu in a position of predominance.

Lodge decided it was a good idea. He sent a cable to McCone with a copy to the President requesting Richardson's recall. Having a national figure from the opposition party in a sensitive post like Saigon put a "bipartisan" cloak over policy there, but it also made it very difficult to refuse a specific request from that national figure. But in this case, the President had no problem, for he agreed with what Lodge was trying to accomplish by this move. What one Republican in a Democratic administration proposed another could hardly veto, and McCone acquiesced —although it caused him pain. John Richardson departed from Saigon on October 5, and all the predictions about how his departure would be interpreted turned out to be correct.

EVENTS IN VIETNAM

In Vietnam, in the meantime, events had also been moving. Tri Quang was in asylum in the American Embassy, and two other priests remained in the buildings of the aid mission, as described above. But a Buddhist underground had survived and was actively distributing leaflets—and, as it turned out, laying other plans. There continued to be demonstrations by Buddhists and students—and the secret police continued their arrests. Then, on October 5, at noon in the central market place of Saigon, another monk burned himself to death—the first self-immolation since the raid on the pagodas. American newsmen had been tipped off that "something big" was going to happen, and they were on hand. The secret police attempted to smash their cameras, and there was a knock-down, drag-out brawl before the Americans got away. Lodge immediately made the kind of strong protest that the newsmen had always wished for Nolting to make.

The regime stepped up its repression and brutality, and gave it a peculiarly anti-American twist. A Vietnamese co-ed at the University of Hué, to give just one example of many, was arrested and cruelly tortured in disgusting ways on the charge of being an American agent because she was a regular visitor to the United States Information Service library. Over and over again, Nhu planted rumors that this or that American installation was to be attacked by a "mob"—to annoy the Americans by forcing them to take defensive measures and to work on their nerves. In Washington, we decided that in his paranoiac state of mind Nhu was capable of almost anything, and the President ordered elements of the Seventh Fleet to stand off Saigon—over the horizon out of sight, but close enough to help our people if there was trouble. On October 27, still another monk burned himself to death—this time in front of the Saigon cathedral just as the communicants were coming out from mass.

MADAME NHU TAKES A TRIP

Madame Nhu had set about on a world trip, apparently in hopes of emulating Madame Chiang Kai-shek's feat in the 1940s of creating public support and sympathy in the United States that could influence policy in favor of her husband's regime. Certainly the elements for creating a "Diem-Nhu lobby" were present. There was always the chance of a Catholic faction, although it never materialized.* Beyond this, Gold-

* After it was all over, the Vatican expressed its appreciation to Lodge. Many Catholics feared that if Diem and Nhu had gone on with their policies of repression, Vietnam would have turned into a religious civil war in which Catholics would inevitably have suffered.

water, Dodd, and others in the Senate, Speaker McCormack in the House, various newspapers ranging from the Hearst chain to *Time* magazine, and the usual group of "hard-line" columnists like Alsop and Higgins—all had supported Syngman Rhee and Chiang Kai-shek, and they had all expressed sympathy, in larger or smaller degree, for Diem. When Madame Nhu asked for a visa, in other words, there were persuasive objections to granting it (these same objections, in fact, led the Johnson administration to deny a visa for a trip by Madame Nhu in later years). But Kennedy felt that denying her a visa would make the administration look as if it didn't trust the good sense of the American people. It was preposterous that the powerful United States was afraid of a beautiful woman, even though she was acid-tongued.

As it turned out, the President was profoundly right. Madame Nhu's intervention not only failed to mobilize a "Diem-Nhu lobby"; it turned the general public even more sharply against her and her family. Even before she got to the United States, while still in Rome, she commented that "the junior officers of the United States military mission are acting like little soldiers of fortune." It was just the kind of opportunity Lodge was waiting for, and he promptly broke his silence. "It is incomprehensible to me," he said in a public statement, "how anyone can speak so cruelly. These men should be thanked and not insulted. These junior officers are risking their lives every day. Some of them have been killed side by side with their Vietnamese comrades." Too late, Madame Nhu saw her error—and retreated into confused "clarifications." But she had not learned the lesson. When she arrived in New York, she accused USIA, the Voice of America, the New York *Times,* AP, and UPI of "working feverishly" to overthrow the Diem regime. On TV she said that the American government was following "the new fashion of liberalism, which is much closer to Communism than we are." She toured the whole country, making these charges and others, including the charge that the Buddhist burnings were a "communist-inspired plot." In most of the cities, her father, the former ambassador who had resigned in protest after the pagodas had been defiled, followed her by a day or two as a sort of one-man "truth squad" arguing that "there is no possibility at all of victory over the Communists under the present regime." It was a fantastic spectacle, and in the end public opinion polls showed that the American people disapproved of Madame Nhu by as much as thirteen to one.

THE TENSION MOUNTS

By the last week in October 1963 the tension in Saigon was at a peak, and little straws began to point to a break one way or another. There were two hints that Diem might be thinking about a change. Quite suddenly, Diem asked Lodge to accompany him to Dalat, the mountain resort, for the inauguration on October 27 of an atomic energy laboratory which had been financed by American aid. The last time they had seen each other had been almost a month before, on the occasion of McNamara's visit, and there was hope that this invitation might signal a change. On the plane, Diem talked not of policy matters but of the land and people of Vietnam, and Lodge found it fascinating. The only real hint of a possible change in outlook, however, was the fact of the invitation. Given his policy of making Diem come to him, Lodge was able to make only oblique reference to our hopes for some concession.

A possibly more substantial hint came on the morning of November 1. Admiral Felt was in Vietnam for a short inspection, and he paid a very brief courtesy call on President Diem as he departed, accompanied by the Ambassador. Just as they were leaving, Diem signaled Lodge to remain—and he said something to the effect that he wanted to have a chance sometime to discuss what it was that the United States wanted. Ironically, the report of this conversation, which was sent by routine priority cable, did not arrive in Washington until it was all over—for it was sidetracked for the very high priority "flash" messages that pre-empted the wires.

The other straws in the wind indicated that the key military leaders had reached a "national" decision and were planning some action against either Nhu or the regime itself very shortly. One of the generals, whom the others had apparently appointed for the purpose, contacted an American official and told him that a decision had been made and plans laid—but he would not say what or when or give any details whatsoever. He said that the generals wanted the United States Government to know that they were counting on what the United States had said in the past about such matters being a Vietnamese decision and counting on the United States neither to betray them nor to try to thwart their move when it was made. There was no date set, but they said they would give us ample warning.

Further efforts to find out more about all this yielded conflicting information. One story was that the generals were planning to seize or kill Nhu and keep Diem in office; another was that they would attempt a lightning stroke seizing both Diem and Nhu at the end of a meeting; a third story was that they were going to encircle Saigon with military units and fight it out with the presidential guard.

In Washington, the NSC met on October 29 to consider the conflicting reports. Lodge was due to leave Vietnam for consultations in Washington, and there was an immediate question as to whether he should postpone his visit.

There was certainly not much reason to believe that Diem had decided to come around. And the straws pointing toward a coup might well be just one more of Nhu's tricks. The Attorney General said that he felt that it was all very thin information indeed. It was a real quandary. It was hard to see that it was in the United States' interest if something started the end of which no one could see. If there was a coup attempt, the Attorney General went on, no one knew whether or not it would end up in a civil war from which only the Communists would benefit. If it succeeded, no one knew what kind of man would come to head the government, or whether he would be better or worse than Diem. On the other hand, if we went to Diem and told him of these hints, he might very well launch a blood bath among the generals that would ruin the war effort overnight. It was difficult to see where the United States' interest lay. It was important that the decisions in such matters be Vietnamese, the Attorney General concluded, but the United States would get the blame no matter what happened. It might be wise to try to find more about what was going on.

The Pentagon representatives still held the view that the war was going well and that any rocking of the political boat would inevitably affect the war effort adversely. The CIA representatives agreed.

The decision was to attempt to find out more about what the generals had in mind—or whether this was all some more of Nhu's shenanigans. As to the question of Lodge's trip, the wisest thing to do was to leave it up to him. A military airplane was dispatched to stand by for Lodge's use.

It was November 1 in Saigon. At noon, Admiral Felt was preparing to board his aircraft, following his call on President Diem. General Tran Van Don, acting chief of the Vietnamese armed forces, there to see Felt off, was nervously looking at his watch. As they took off Felt remarked that he had never seen Don chew gum before.

A large number of troops were observed moving through Saigon's streets beginning at 1:30 P.M. Then, at exactly 1:45, General Don telephoned General Joseph Stilwell, Jr., Harkins' deputy, to say that all the Vietnamese generals were together at the Joint General Staff Headquarters in Saigon and that a coup was underway—this was the promised warning.

Within half an hour, shortly after 2 A.M. Washington time, which is exactly twelve hours behind Saigon, I was awakened by the State Department duty officer and told of the "flash" message that had arrived. I spent the rest of the night in the "operations center" of the State Department.

An American CIA official who had spent many years in Vietnam made his way to the Vietnamese headquarters, and since he was so well known and trusted they let him stay and permitted him to keep the embassy informed of events by telephone. And the embassy in turn sent

the messages "flash" to Washington. The American official learned that
the generals had been working for some time toward making this
decision unanimous, and that, as mentioned earlier, the key had been
General Dinh, the excitable commander of the forces in Saigon. When
he came over to the view of the rest of the generals, they all took the
"blood oath" and serious planning had begun. The only senior officer
not involved was the commander of the Navy, who had been taken into
custody and—apparently by accident—shot.

The troop movements were carried out with precision. Some units
took up blocking positions in case Diem and Nhu succeeded in persuading provincial troops to come to their rescue. Others occupied the two
radio stations, the police stations, the post office, which was the terminus
for telephone and telegraph communications, the airport—and still others
took up positions for an assault on the palace and the barracks of the
palace guard.

The generals telephoned Diem and Nhu and requested that they
surrender, each of the generals talking in turn to convince them that all
the higher-ranking officers were against them. But Diem and Nhu refused.

At 4:30 in the afternoon, Diem telephoned Ambassador Lodge—who
expressed concern for Diem's physical safety and asked about the
General's offer of safe conduct out of the country and whether there
was anything Lodge could do about this. Diem's only response was to
say that he was Chief of State and that he was attempting to re-establish
law and order.

The generals reached Diem and Nhu on the telephone again at
4:45, putting Colonel Tung on the phone to say that he and the Special
Forces had surrendered and to convince them that the situation was
hopeless. Tung was then taken outside and shot.

At 5:15, General Minh, the senior general, called again, offering another
chance for surrender before the palace was bombed. Diem hung up.

Diem and Nhu spent several hours calling every command post they
could reach trying to find someone who would come to their support—
without success.

At 3:30 A.M., a full-scale attack was launched on the palace, and its
defenders surrendered soon thereafter.

Diem and Nhu had escaped through a tunnel the night before and
were hiding in the home of a rich Chinese friend in the twin city of
Cholon, where they had long since set up a communications center.
When their hideout was discovered, they escaped again to a small
Catholic church nearby, and it was there that they were finally captured.
They were taken to headquarters in an armored personnel carrier—but
were shot and killed sometime during the journey.

THE UNDERSIDE OF THE ROCK

The adage that it is unwise merely to wound a king is Asian as well as
Western, and the murder of Diem and Nhu may have been part of the
generals' "blood oath." But it shocked President Kennedy and the rest
of us in Washington. However, it was only after their deaths that the full
extent of their reliance on police-state methods, torture, and murder
came to light. The prisons were opened and with the release of the
prisoners came a flood of ugly stories of fiendish torture. Days later,
some prisons that had been entirely secret were discovered and their
occupants released, with the most pitiful of the stories of torture coming
from the young women. On the estate of Ngo Dinh Can, the brother
who was overlord of Hué, were found the graves of dozens and dozens
of torture victims who had succumbed.

There were riotous celebrations throughout Vietnam. Singing bands of
young people went marching about, cheering Americans as they had never
been cheered before. "If an election for President of Vietnam were held
right now," more than one Vietnamese told an American friend, "Henry
Cabot Lodge would win by a landslide." Cheering mobs burned down
the offices of the *Times of Vietnam*. Madame Nhu had served as the
model for some statues she had erected of the Trung sisters, ancient
Vietnamese heroines like Joan of Arc who had led armies against the
Chinese, and the mob broke them up—dragging the head that most
resembled the madame through the streets. It was lucky that she was out
of the country. All over Vietnam the pictures of Diem were torn down—
in a few days all reminders of him and his regime were gone.

The Viet Cong took advantage of the preoccupation of the new
regime with matters in Saigon to consolidate their holdings in the countryside and move into new ones. The new regime also set about to replace
the incompetent and politically dangerous among the Diem-Nhu political
appointees at the district and province levels and to reward its own
men—and the Viet Cong also made the most of the resulting confusion.

The past mistakes that cost most dearly were Diem's practice of
insisting on maintaining outposts in impossible places to show the flag,
and Nhu's insistence on proliferating strategic hamlets in disregard of the
"oil blot" principle. Diem, for example, insisted on maintaining one
outpost of sixty men with their dependents in an impossible position
twelve kilometers from Cambodia, where the Viet Cong had a base,
and fifty kilometers from the nearest reinforcements. The inhabitants
were so desperate that helicopters bringing them supplies had to hover
out of reach to keep from being dragged down by would-be escapees.
After the coup, the secret of why they had survived so long came out—
each evening they had put a box of U.S. M-1 ammunition outside the

gates. For months in that part of Vietnam, the United States had supplied both sides.

Now that Diem and Nhu were gone, the Viet Cong assumed, correctly, that the new military regime would pull back these indefensible outposts and hamlets that served only as storage places for arms and ammunition the Viet Cong could seize whenever they wished. There was a race to see who would get to them first, the government or the Viet Cong. The result was probably a tie, but even a tie gave the Viet Cong a new and greater supply of American weapons.

But the greatest shocks were not how effectively the Viet Cong moved to take advantage of the Diem-Nhu regime's past mistakes but the discovery of just how wild the statistics really were on which the United States had based so much optimism. On October 22, 1963, before the coup, the Bureau of Intelligence and Research had analyzed the statistics and concluded, not only that the trend was downhill, but that the statistics had started downhill in July, before the attack on the pagodas. The number of attacks initiated by the Viet Cong had increased steadily since July, and, significantly, so had the number of attacks by large Viet Cong units of company or battalion size. Viet Cong casualty rates had been going steadily down, so had the rate of Viet Cong defections. The conclusion was that the government's military position may have been set back to what it had been six months to a year earlier. General Krulak had been furious at this conclusion and persuaded the Pentagon to present a stiffly formal complaint. The argument was that the unfavorable statistics were the result of the Viet Cong being "compressed" into a progressively smaller area, and that the really significant statistics were the number of strategic hamlets and the increased pace of attacks initiated by the government.

But when the coup drew back the curtain, both sides of the argument were amazed at what the true picture really was. First, the Viet Cong had not really been "compressed" into the delta, but were merely lying low in the other regions while they concentrated on infiltrating strategic hamlets and gaining control from within. As R. K. G. Thompson had warned, the places to worry most about were where the Viet Cong could be expected to be active but weren't.

Second, a high percentage of attacks initiated by the government—the statistic on which so much American optimism had been based—had been mounted against "targets" where the Viet Cong were known *not* to be, as a means of inflating the statistics without risk of the casualties that would rouse Diem's ire. One division adviser, for example, estimated that as many as a third of his division's actions had been such sham affairs.

Third, the statistics on the number of strategic hamlets and on the number of villages under effective government control were completely false. Vice-President Nguyen Ngoc Tho, for example, informed us that of the 8600 strategic hamlets claimed under the Diem regime, only about 20 per cent actually met the standards. In Long An, a heavily populated province occupying a strategic position in the delta, the Diem regime reported 219 strategic hamlets—but only 45 could be so identified after the coup. And the statistics on the number of villages effectively controlled by the government were even worse. In one district in the Seventh Division area of the delta, which is a typical example, the district chief had reported that he controlled all twenty-four hamlets—but he now admitted that he controlled only three.

"Ah, les statistiques!" one of the Vietnamese generals exclaimed to an American friend. "Your Secretary of Defense loves statistics. We Vietnamese can give him all he wants. If you want them to go up, they will go up. If you want them to go down, they will go down."

CHAPTER 34

If Kennedy Had Lived?

IN THE STATE DEPARTMENT, we were convinced that the only way the Viet Cong could be defeated in a permanent, political sense was through a political and social program to which military measures were subordinated. The only sure success in guerrilla warfare was to win over the peasants, so they could be armed to defend themselves. This meant that the heart of an effective counterinsurgency program would have to be something like R. K. G. Thompson's notion of strategic hamlets, so it was particularly distressing to find Thompson himself highly alarmed at what now came to light. Thompson had visited several of the delta provinces and found the situation desperate. In Long An, for example, the district capitals and the main road south to My Tho were being threatened. Only a handful of strategic hamlets with an armed militia remained, and morale was very low. The deterioration, he concluded, had started by July at the latest, and it had accelerated in the few weeks preceding the coup. All along, the situation had been much worse than even the pessimists had thought and was now worsening even faster as the Viet Cong took advantage of the confusion following the coup.

The major weakness of the program under the previous regime, Thompson reported, had been the lack of over-all, strategic direction and Nhu's policy of creating hamlets haphazardly all over the country. In only two provinces of all Vietnam was there a solid bloc of them. Instead of the hamlets on the perimeter of the advance forming a front line against the Viet Cong that could be bolstered by regular troops, almost every hamlet was in the front line and vulnerable to Viet Cong attack.

A second weakness, he said, was that there had been no real effort to isolate the population from the Viet Cong by eliminating Viet Cong agents and supporters inside the strategic hamlets and by imposing controls on the movement of people and supplies. Even if some Viet Cong supporters and agents had moved out at the time when the strategic hamlet was created, they subsequently had no difficulty repenetrating the hamlet and continuing subversion.*

* The fundamental answer to the question of "How do you know if you're winning" is whether or not the government can effectively protect the people and minor government officials from acts of terrorism. All statistics from Vietnam are slippery,

The third weakness, according to Thompson, was that the military operations, particularly in the delta, were not designed to support the hamlet program. (Too much of the military effort went into "seek-and-destroy" operations, and too little into "clear-and-hold.")

Thompson urged that firm and rapid action was required by the new government to save the strategic hamlet program and to prevent the Viet Cong from gaining control of the rural population. The new government had to face up to the dilemma of reconciling the need to prosecute the war with vigor and resolution with the measures required to win the hearts and minds of the peasants. The whole problem, he felt, hinged on the new government's approach to the rural population.

In the State Department, we were acutely conscious that all these stormy events meant only that there was one more chance to carry out an effective counterguerrilla program. And we fully agreed with Thompson that Vietnam was a political problem of winning the allegiance of the people rather than a military problem of killing Viet Cong. But the rest of Washington also had to be convinced if the United States was to be effective in persuading Saigon. "The problem of Vietnam," we wrote in a memorandum which we circulated widely within the government, "is no different from what it was two years ago. The Viet Cong capability for action is based largely on their access to recruits, supplies, and intelligence from the villages of South Vietnam. Cadres, technical personnel, and specialized equipment are infiltrated from North Vietnam, but we have thus far no reason to believe that the Viet Cong have more than a limited need for outside resources. Our main effort must therefore be directed at cutting the links between the Viet Cong and the South Vietnamese villagers. The strategic concept for an effective counter-guerrilla program must be based on certain fundamental principles . . .

"The problem presented by the Viet Cong is by no means just a military problem. It is more accurately described as a problem in effectively coordinating military action with political and economic and

---

but figures on assassinations and kidnapings are more likely to reflect fewer than the actual total, which makes the official figures, given below, even more alarming. The rise in kidnapings in particular indicate that the Viet Cong had grown strong enough to "brainwash" rather than just kill.

VIET CONG TERRORISM AGAINST CIVILIANS

	Assassinated	*Kidnaped*	*Total*
1957–59	432	580	1,012
1960	1,400	700	2,100
1961	1,000	2,000	3,000
1962	1,719	9,688	11,407
1963	2,073	7,262	9,335
1964	1,795	9,554	11,349
1965	1,895	12,778	14,673

social measures. The first essential is to provide the villager with physical security, so that he has a choice of refusing to cooperate with the Viet Cong. . . . The second essential is to set up a system of government services and assistance that will break up the villager's isolation, tie him into the governmental structure, and earn his political support. To achieve these purposes a well-coordinated program must be conducted that combines military 'clear-and-hold' operations with a strategic hamlet program, no matter what its name is. To be effective, it must be based on a national plan that establishes priorities for operations beginning in the more secure areas and extending outward to the less secure.

"Operating within this national plan, regular forces should concentrate not on pursuing guerrillas and killing them, but on clearing them from the priority areas and holding those areas until strategic hamlets can be established. Provisions for the physical defense of the hamlet, the training of village defenders, and so on, should be combined with an adequate police program, identity cards and curfew hours to control the movement of goods and people . . . All this should enable the villagers themselves to deal with individual Viet Cong and with small Viet Cong units. Roving civil guard patrols, especially trained in counter-guerrilla warfare and night action should reduce or prevent the concentration of sizeable Viet Cong bands in the neighborhood of established villages. If a large group does slip through, each hamlet must have rapid means of communication, and the regular forces and civil guards must be able to respond immediately both day and night.

"With the establishment of a reasonable degree of security, economic and social projects at the village level must be pushed vigorously and rapidly . . . to win the allegiance and support of the people. . . .

"The infiltration problem is special. . . . While infiltration has played a relatively minor role in supporting Viet Cong activity, action to control and disrupt it has long been recognized as necessary. In such terrain, bombing would not be effective . . . [Because of this, we] recommended to the Diem government in 1961 the assignment of ranger units to patrol duties in the jungles and mountains along the borders of Laos and Cambodia, themselves using the tactics of the guerrilla to fight the guerrilla. This recommendation was never put into effect . . . we should press the new government to proceed rapidly . . ."

But getting a consensus among the agencies in Washington on the recommendations we should make to the new government in Saigon was proving to be a formidable task. The Joint Chiefs of Staff, smarting under the revelations coming out of Saigon, which destroyed the basis for past American optimism, began to talk again of the infiltration routes and of "striking at the source of the aggression."

After President Kennedy's death, the pressure was renewed. General Curtis L. LeMay, Chief of Staff of the Air Force, was particularly vigorous in advocating the bombardment of North Vietnam. "We are swatting flies," LeMay said, "when we should be going after the manure pile." General Thomas S. Power said that with conventional bombs alone the Strategic Air Command, which he headed, and its B-52s could "pulverize North Vietnam," and he made a special trip to Washington to plead the case for bombing not only North Vietnam but the Viet Cong and their bases *in South Vietnam.*

In the State Department, Walt Rostow presented to the new President, a well-reasoned case for a gradual escalation, and soon thereafter a proposal was put forward by the Pentagon and the CIA for a program of low-level reconnaissance over Laos and for a program of increased military pressures of various sorts on the north.

The proposal for low-level reconnaissance over Laos—with the implication that bombing would follow if targets were spotted—had been made before. But Harriman, Forrestal, and I had fought it steadily. In the first place, we were worried about the effects on Laos itself. The Geneva agreements of 1962 had achieved a precarious neutrality for Laos that so far both sides had respected in its broad outlines. There was a *de facto* partition rather than an effective government of national union, but by and large the Communists had stayed on their side of the line of partition. If the United States openly violated the Geneva agreements of 1962 and gave the Communists an excuse, they might well begin again to nibble away at the non-Communist position.

But we were also worried about the effects of an escalation on the struggle in Vietnam as well. Bombing the infiltration routes seemed promising at first sight, but the more we thought about it the more our doubts increased. The North Vietnamese, of course, had used the routes through Laos in violation of the Geneva agreements, and both reconnaissance and bombing could be justified on these grounds. But the Communists had kept their use of the trails at a very low level. At least 5000 men a month could be infiltrated over the Ho Chi Minh trails— over 60,000 a year. Yet from 1960 on, the monthly average had been only 650 and the yearly average only 7850. More important, the personnel coming over the routes were not North Vietnamese, but still only the pro-Communist southerners who had gone north in 1954 and were returning to serve in the Viet Cong as cadre. And as for supplies, so far the only equipment that had come over the infiltration routes was radios, codes, medicines, and a very limited amount of specialized equipment such as recoilless rifles. Even though this infiltration of men and supplies was small, it still constituted aggression and some sort of case could be made to justify bombing the north.* But it was in the

---

* Even though Hanoi triggered the Viet Cong insurrection by infiltrating cadres and key items of supply and even though they commanded and directed the effort, it should be noted that they would not have been successful in starting the insurrection if there had not been a substantial core of resistance already in existence among the

United States' interest, it seemed to us, to continue what amounted to a tacit agreement that we would refrain from bombing and the North Vietnamese would observe their self-imposed limitation not to infiltrate large numbers of northerners or North Vietnamese regular troops. Bombing could not "cut off" infiltration routes that consisted only of jungle trails, and the amount of men and equipment coming over them could be vastly increased in the teeth of the heaviest kind of pounding by bombers. If we openly violated the Geneva agreements, it would be politically easier for the Communists to violate them even more openly, actually increasing their infiltration through Laos.

To Harriman, Forrestal, and me the conclusion seemed obvious. If we raised the ante by bombing, the North Vietnamese would respond by increasing the use of the infiltration routes to include northerners. We would be no better off than before and perhaps worse, and we would be paying the international political cost for nothing.

The way to deal with the infiltration routes, in our judgment, was on the ground, by using ranger companies as counterguerrilla guerrillas, ambushing along the trails. Since over half of the distance of the Ho Chi Minh trails from North Vietnam to the delta was inside South Vietnam, these could be chewed up with no violation of the Geneva agreements at all. To help protect the more northern portions of South Vietnam, it might be necessary to do the ambushing in Laos. But there was a world of international political difference between a black-clad company of South Vietnamese rangers ambushing a black-clad unit of Viet Cong infiltrators on a jungle trail in Laos and *American* jets dropping bombs in Laos. Militarily, ambushing was more effective than bombing and politically it was less costly.

These were our objections to the proposals for bombing the infiltration routes in Laos. Our objections to the proposals for a large-scale bombing program inside South Vietnam were even more basic. A bombing program conducted solely by Americans against targets in South Vietnam violated the most fundamental principle of a strategic concept that was based on the idea of winning the allegiance of the people. In the first place, if Americans did the bombing it would give powerful support to the Viet Cong charge that the United States' purpose in Vietnam was a new form of colonialist-imperialism, and help them enlist the forces of nationalism on their side. In the second place, bombing would greatly increase the difficulty of a program to win the people. Air power and artillery are essential for close-in support for a unit locked in combat with a Viet Cong unit. In very special circumstances, when the intelligence was beyond question, artillery and bombers might also be used to good

people of South Vietnam and a framework of native Communist leadership there. As it happened, Hanoi did fire the starting gun; Hanoi did supply key items of supply; and Hanoi did exercise command and over-all direction.

effect against Viet Cong jungle hideouts and base areas. But what was bound to be bad was preparatory bombing prior to helicopter landings or "interdiction" bombing of "suspected" Viet Cong areas. To repeat, more Viet Cong would be recruited than would be killed.*

* Here again, even the slippery statistics fom Vietnam provide an argument for a strategic hamlet, "pacification" approach to the problem of guerrilla warfare, as demonstrated in the following table. The first four vertical columns of figures in the table are official Pentagon figures; the last column, giving the number of Viet Cong recruited in *South Vietnam,* is derived by subtracting the number of infiltrators for the year from the total increase for that year—including killed and captured. The reader should note also that these figures are the official estimates as revised in the year 1966, after some of the totals of Viet Cong strength for past years had been raised. The figures on Viet Cong strength given in the chapters above were always the estimates of the time.

	Viet Cong Strength at year start	Viet Cong Killed each year	Viet Cong Captured each year	Viet Cong Infiltrated from North Vietnam each year	Viet Cong Recruited in South Vietnam each year
		(1960: 6,000)	(unknown)	(1959–1960: 4,500)	
1961	5,000 reg.				
	30,000 irreg.				
	35,000 total				
		12,000	(unknown)	5,400	34,600
1962	23,000 reg.				
	40,000 irreg.				
	63,000 total				
		21,000	5,500	12,400	31,100
1963	30,000 reg.				
	50,000 irreg.				
	80,000 total				
		21,000	4,000	7,400	29,600
1964	32,000 reg.				
	60,000 irreg.				
	92,000 total				
		17,000	4,200	7,400	45,800
1965	34,000 reg.				
	90,000 irreg.				
	124,000 total				

U.S. bombing of North Vietnam begun, February 17, 1965.
U.S. bombing of South Vietnam begun, February 19, 1965.

		35,000	5,900	19,000†	112,900–142,900
1966	75,000– 85,000 regular				
	100,000–120,000 irregular				
	40,000 political cadre				
	215,000–245,000 total				

† This figure includes ten North Vietnamese regiments, which began to infiltrate into South Vietnam after the bombing of the north.

If bombing the south were accepted as just another routine weapon in the arsenal—no matter how stringent the "rules of engagement"— civilian casualties would be bound to occur in numbers that would be politically excessive. Two years later, in fact, after President Johnson decided to bomb South Vietnam, Clement J. Zablocki, Chairman of the House Foreign Affairs Subcommittee on the Far East, returned from a trip to Vietnam to announce that, although complete statistics were not available, he estimated that a "ratio of two civilians [killed] to one Viet Cong is likely" and that on some "search-and-destroy" operations the ratio was six civilians to one Viet Cong.

The argument over whether or not to launch a large-scale bombing program in South Vietnam was really a symbol of the basic disagreement over the nature of guerrilla warfare. Was revolutionary warfare on the guerrilla model no different from orthodox, regular war in its fundamentals or was it something new, a political struggle with terroristic and military aspects? "Interdiction" bombing—hitting communications routes and "suspected" enemy installations—is an ordinary tool of regular warfare, for example. Yet interdiction bombing is inevitably indiscriminate, bringing death and destruction to the population living in the theater of war. So is artillery fire, except for close support in areas removed from the population. So are large-scale military operations, when battalions and regiments of ground forces sweep a countryside. And so are all the other means of large-scale, regular warfare. These costs will be cheerfully borne by a population if the enemy army is a hated invader. It is a cost that can be tolerated by one side if the opposing army and the population in the theater of war are one and the same united enemy. But it is a cost that may not be tolerable if the allegiance of the population is the true objective. For the means of regular warfare tend to create a hostile population if one did not exist in the beginning.

Bombing North Vietnam itself also raised thorny problems. North Vietnam had only thirty-five or so industrial plants and power installations, which they had acquired through much sacrifice, and it was probably the risk of losing these that had deterred Hanoi from infiltrating their 250,000 regular North Vietnamese troops into South Vietnam. Once these factories and power plants were destroyed, they would have nothing left to lose. And the closer American power got to the border of China, the greater was the possibility of a massive intervention by "Chinese People's Army Volunteers," as had happened in Korea.

A more limited bombing program, attacking only military installations and communications routes in North Vietnam, ran much less risk of causing Chinese Communist intervention. Both the Soviets and the Chinese could be expected to step up their aid and might even bring in volunteers to man antiaircraft units and to pilot fighter planes, but probably not much more. The full strength of the North Vietnamese armies would probably not be infiltrated to the south in response to limited bombing. But as a way of matching the escalation initiated by the United States and in retaliation for it, they might begin to introduce battalions of North Vietnamese regulars into the south.*

* When President Johnson decided to bomb North Vietnam in February 1965, those officials who favored the decision did so for different reasons. Some thought it would so punish North Vietnam as to cause Hanoi to end the struggle. Others doubted this, but favored the bombing on the grounds that it would cut off the flow of supplies and infiltrators or severely reduce it. Still others favored bombing the north on the grounds that it would make the whole North Vietnamese effort more costly and painful, even if it did not stop the flow of supplies and men, and that this would improve morale in South Vietnam. The public position, however, tended to justify the bombing as a retaliation for attacks on American installations in South Vietnam, such as the attack on the American barracks at Pleiku, or as a retaliation for increased use of the infiltration routes, to include North Vietnamese as well as ex-southerners. Many outside observers felt that all this was merely a rationalization and excuse—that the decision was made on the grounds described above and then delayed until a suitable incident provided the justification. In any event, the public case was weak. First, there had been attacks on Americans and American installations all along—a grenade was thrown at Ambassador Nolting in 1961, for example; there was an attack on the American Special Forces camp at Plei Mrong in 1962, and so on. Second, as the table in the footnote on page 529 shows, the number of people coming over the infiltration routes remained fairly steady, ranging from 5,400 to 12,400 from 1961 until after the bombing of North Vietnam in 1965, after which it jumped to 19,000 for 1965 and something over 60,000 for 1966. Third, the evidence that there had been such a significant introduction of North Vietnamese in 1964 as to justify retaliation is unconvincing. What evidence there is has been assembled in the Department of State's white paper, *Aggression From the North, The Record of North Vietnam's Campaign to Conquer South Vietnam*, which was issued in February 1965, to present the case for the bombing. No captured documents, equipment, or materials are presented that indicate either the presence of North Vietnamese regular units or of individual North Vietnamese in significant numbers. The white paper was able to present the case studies of only four captured infiltrators who were ethnic North Vietnamese. No evidence was presented of the presence of regular North Vietnamese units except the allegations of two of these and two other captured Viet Cong of southern origin.

Privately, some government officials have argued that the bombing should have been justified not so much by the presence in South Vietnam of regular North Vietnamese units *prior to* the bombings, but by the assembling of these units in North Vietnam and Laos in *preparation* for infiltrating into South Vietnam. It could be equally well argued, however, that the assembling of the North Vietnamese regular units on the borders of South Vietnam was an attempt to deter the United States from escalating the struggle by threatening to retaliate for any bombing by introducing regular forces into the south.

Although it was not offered publicly at the time, another reason for the decision to bomb North Vietnam was probably the conviction that the struggle in the south was at a crisis point and the whole of South Vietnam would be lost unless desperate measures were taken promptly. Here again, however, the starting assumption that a guerrilla struggle is a war like any other, that it is basically military in character, may have led to a wrong conclusion and unjustifiably created the feeling of near-panic of the time. The struggle had indeed gone badly in 1964. But the assumption that it was a war made people assume that the Viet Cong success in the highlands meant

There were also political drawbacks to bombing North Vietnam. Any bombing of the north would be an escalation at American initiative and a violation of the Geneva accords at a time when prudence demanded that the United States should hold to a posture of restraint. Any other course would be bad international politics, raising questions about America's sense of responsibility among both neutrals and our allies. A posture of restraint was also essential in order to preserve as much of the 1954 Geneva accords as possible. For the 1954 Geneva accords would become, as they had in Laos, the basis for any negotiated settlement—and a negotiated settlement was probably the most likely outcome even if the effort in Vietnam were successful.

Another predictable result, it seemed to us, was that there would be formidable pressure from our allies and from a significant segment of domestic opinion pushing us toward offering to negotiate *prematurely*. If negotiations took place before there had been progress in winning the allegiance of the peasants, especially in the delta, the result would be the neutralization of Vietnam, which in those circumstances would be tantamount to the Viet Cong taking over completely.*

Bombing the north would also put an obstacle in the way of furthering the *détente* with the Soviet Union, and make it difficult for the Soviets to follow their own national interest regarding Southeast Asia, which was to press Hanoi to keep the struggle damped down. And bombing the north would add force to the Chinese argument for more belligerent Communist policies, and strengthen their hand in the Sino-Soviet dispute.

But above and beyond all these unwelcome consequences, bombing the north would be a mistake for the fundamental reason that it probably would not work. The advocates of bombing believed that it would force North Vietnam to quit or that it would cut the flow of supplies to the south and make it impossible for the Viet Cong to continue. All-out bombing of the cities of North Vietnam might force Hanoi to quit, but that kind of massive bombing would also run too great a risk of massive Chinese intervention. Limited, measured bombing, on the other hand, could not hurt the North Vietnamese economy enough to matter. Nor

---

that they were about to "cut the country in half." If the starting assumption had been that a guerrilla struggle is basically political and that the true objective is to gain the allegiance and control of the population, then who controlled the under-populated highland territories would have been considered much less significant than who controlled the people in the delta. And although things had not been going well in the delta in 1964, they were not yet so serious as to require such measures of desperation.

* As it happened, the decision to bomb North Vietnam was made in February, and by April the pressures had become so strong that President Johnson felt obliged to put forward the offer to negotiate in his speech at Baltimore. Unaccountably, however, Hanoi did not accept, and the large-scale introduction of American ground forces beginning in July radically altered the entire situation.

could any bombing, no matter how heavy, "cut" the flow of supplies. Most of the supplies for the Viet Cong, like the recruits, came from the villages of the *South*—the Viet Cong required only five or six tons of supplies a day from the outside world.[1] This was an amount that could be carried by three or four trucks or one large sampan or 150 coolies. Of course bombing the supply routes would hurt the Communists. They would have to travel at night. They would have to spend time and energy filling in craters in the roads, putting their supply dumps in camouflaged underground warehouses, and repairing bridges. But bombing does not "destroy" an underdeveloped economy, in which trade is often conducted by barter. Nor does bombing "destroy" communications lines that are really dirt roads and jungle trails with timber bridges that are usually sited where there was an old ford anyway. In a country like North Vietnam, bombing communications routes would do little more than make the enemy put more effort into maintaining the flow of supplies, an effort mainly requiring manpower. And manpower was the one thing that the North Vietnamese and their Chinese allies had plenty of.

There was a real question, in sum, whether the results of bombing would be substantial enough to justify the loss of the expensive American airplanes that would inevitably be shot down and the lives of the pilots that would be lost along with them. It seemed more likely that it would not be American air power alone that would deter the Communists from escalating the struggle by infiltrating regular North Vietnamese units and more supplies, but the totality of American power, including especially American ground power.

The fact of the matter was that Asians tended to interpret the use of air power *alone* as a weak response, even though they feared air power. The United States had so often flirted with the idea of "immaculate" war in Asia, war fought in the air above the muck and blood of jungle fighting, that Asians thought of air power alone as a bluff. In the circumstances, the only thing we could really be sure would impress either Communist or non-Communist Asians was ground forces.

But again, the purpose would be not to use American ground forces to take over the war effort, for that would be politically self-defeating. The purpose in using American ground forces would not be for the United States to escalate the level of fighting but to deter the Communists from escalating it. We suspected that the claims of vastly increased use of the infiltration routes was nothing more than a repetition of the "built-in excuse for failure" that President Kennedy had predicted. (It turned out, in fact, that fewer infiltrators had come over the trails in 1963 than in 1962.) But if the information when it came in did indeed show that the North Vietnamese had stepped up their use of the infiltration routes, our proposal was to put a division of American ground forces into

Thailand as a warning and couple it with communications to North Vietnamese representatives in the various Communist and neutral capitals. If the warning was not heeded, that division could be moved right up to the Laos border, and a second division introduced into Thailand. If that set of warnings was also ignored, a division could be introduced into Vietnam, and so on—not to fight the Viet Cong, which should remain the task of the South Vietnamese, but to deter the north from escalating.

But these recommendations ran head on into the objections of the "never again" school of thought in the Pentagon that opposed any limitations on the use of force if force were to be used, and the result was another impasse. And once again, as he had in such circumstances before, McNamara proposed that he himself visit Vietnam.

President Johnson did not share our misgivings that McNamara's frequent trips to Vietnam tended to turn the struggle into an American war nor our doubts about what such a high-level visitor might find out, and he quickly approved McNamara's proposal. Accompanied by John McCone, McNamara spent December 19 and 20, 1963, in Vietnam and returned to say that he had found no evidence of an increased use of the infiltration routes. He did not at that time join those who advocated bombing of the north. But he did recommend that a committee of specialists be designated to develop a list of targets and lay the groundwork for a future decision to bomb the north.

President Johnson had been pressing hard for quick results in Vietnam. One of his first instructions had been for everyone in the administration to ask himself each day what he had done toward victory there and to remind everyone that Vietnam was "the only war we've got." He was accordingly in complete sympathy with the general approach McNamara recommended, and he appointed an interdepartmental committee to develop the list of bombing targets, a committee which in February became the new Vietnam task force. Although I had submitted a memorandum opposing Rostow's proposal to bomb North Vietnam, there was no further opportunity provided to present the arguments against moving in this direction. A concession was made, however, in the appointment of William H. Sullivan, in whom both Harriman and I had great confidence, as chairman of the new committee.

A PERSONAL DECISION

President Kennedy was killed on November 22. In the weeks that followed, everyone in the government was frantically busy, and time to think about anything except the immediate task was an unknown luxury. Finally, on January 18, 1964, my wife and I boarded an airplane to meet a long-standing engagement to give a speech in Canberra and to visit Australia and New Zealand. It took five hours to fly to San Francisco, and another four and a half to Honolulu. There, thankfully, we had two days on the beach at Waikiki. It was another eight hours' flying time to Fiji, and four hours more to Sydney. And by the time the plane had begun to circle the Sydney airport, I had decided that I must resign.

My reasoning was basic. The style of Roosevelt and Kennedy was to build into the situation around them conflicting advice, to have men around who had opinions of their own, and to encourage them to articulate their positions vigorously. In this freewheeling environment, they hoped to have all aspects of a question fully explored and to preserve for themselves the whole range of choices. The tasks of the presidency, however, are burdensome, and each new president must find his own way of coping with them. President Johnson seemed to prefer a more hierarchical way of handling the job, and from both the people he turned to for advice on Vietnam and his own approach to the problem it seemed clear that his natural instinct was toward attempting a military solution to the question of Vietnam, although hedging it with political qualifications. I was sure that the United States under his direction would not leap irresponsibly into a policy of military escalation, but it was obviously going to take the military path—even though it climbed the ladder of escalation slowly and deliberately.

On the other hand, I was deeply convinced that the political approach was the wiser course. The human costs of a military approach to Vietnam, both for Americans and Vietnamese, would be much greater, in my judgment, and success less likely—especially in the permanent sense of achieving a politically viable outcome. A military course of action in Vietnam would impede also the slow but significant movement toward a *détente* with the Soviet Union that President Kennedy had set in motion with the test ban treaty following the Cuban missile crisis. And a military approach would put enormous obstacles in the way of working toward a more realistic, "open door" policy toward Communist China, as we had planned.

It seemed to me that I had only three choices. I could acquiesce and stay on with the administration, if not as Assistant Secretary, then in some other capacity—although my influence would then be no more than that of a clerk. Second, I could stay on and fight. But I would not only lose, but would be so cut up in the process that anything I said thereafter would be regarded as sour grapes. Or I could leave before the issue was fully joined and at least preserve a voice as a private citizen.

On my departure, I sent the Secretary of State a memorandum with copies to the President, McGeorge Bundy, the Secretary of Defense, and the others recapitulating the case described in the pages above for a political approach to guerrilla warfare and for the use of American power not to escalate but to deter the Communist side from escalating. A few sentences of that memorandum may be worth repeating:

"My own preference would be . . . [for] covert, or at least deniable,* operations . . . with the objective, since these are only pinpricks, not of forcing North Vietnam to its knees but of keeping the threat of eventual destruction alive in Hanoi's mind. Then, after we had made sufficient progress in the Delta so that all concerned began to realize that the Viet Cong were losing the support of the population, and that their ability to continue the war depended solely on North Vietnamese support, I think we should indicate as much privately to the North Vietnamese and follow this by selected attacks on their infiltration bases and training camps.

"In my judgment, significant action against North Vietnam that is taken before we have demonstrated success in our counter-insurgency program will be interpreted by the Communists as an act of desperation, and will, therefore, not be effective in persuading the North Vietnamese to cease and desist. What is worse, I think that premature action will so alarm our friends and allies and a significant segment of domestic opinion that the pressure for neutralization will become formidable."

No one, of course, can know for sure what President Kennedy would have done in the future—had he lived. But his policy had been to keep the fighting as limited as possible, to urge the new government to pursue an effective counterguerrilla program designed to protect the people and win their allegiance. He preferred to treat the problem of Vietnam as something other than war and to avoid getting American prestige so involved that the United States could not accept a negotiated settlement along the lines of the Geneva accords on Laos—when and if the Vietnamese desired it. When President Kennedy died, there were just over sixteen thousand American advisers in Vietnam. When the Geneva accords on Laos were signed, there were 666 American advisers there—about the same proportion relative to the size of the country. In any event, President Kennedy made it abundantly clear to me on more than one occasion that what he most wanted to avoid was turning Vietnam into an American war. He was skeptical of a policy of escalation and of the effectiveness of an air attack on North Vietnam. If the North Vietnamese had vastly increased their use of the infiltration routes, so as to include large numbers of North Vietnamese soldiers and regular North Vietnamese units, he might well have introduced United States ground forces into South Vietnam—although I believe he would not have ordered them to take over the war effort from the Vietnamese but would have

* E.g., the use of black-clad South Vietnamese ranger companies to impede the infiltrators in Laos, rather than American jet bombers.

limited their mission to that of occupying ports, airfields, and military bases to demonstrate to the North Vietnamese that *they* could not win the struggle by a policy of escalation either. President Kennedy's policy, in sum, was to meet the guerrilla aggression within a counterguerrilla framework, with the implied corollary that if the Viet Cong could not be defeated within a counterguerrilla framework and the allegiance of the people of Vietnam could not be won, then the United States would accept the resulting situation and would be free to enter negotiations without fatal consequences to our position in the rest of Asia. But President Kennedy did not live, and no one can say with absolute certainty what he would or would not have done.

NOTES

[1] In early 1966, when the size of the Viet Cong forces had almost trebled, the Pentagon estimate of Viet Cong *needs* from outside South Vietnam was twelve tons per day.

X

THE MAKING AND MANAGING
OF FOREIGN POLICY

"Underneath our images of Presidents-in-boots, astride decisions, are the half-observed realities of Presidents-in-sneakers, stirrups in hand, trying to induce particular department heads, or congressmen, or senators to climb aboard."

—RICHARD E. NEUSTADT

"Politics is a strong and slow boring of hard boards. It takes both passion and perspective. Certainly all historical experience confirms the truth—that man would not have attained the possible unless time and again he had reached out for the impossible. But to do that a man must be a leader, and not only a leader but a hero as well . . ."

—MAX WEBER

CHAPTER 35

Power, Politics, and Policy-Making

THE MAKING of foreign policy is a political process. When decisions are made on the big questions, questions requiring sacrifices by the nation or the concentration on one set of objectives at the cost of neglecting others, there is struggle and conflict. At the same time, there is a "strain toward agreement,"[1] an effort to build a consensus, a push for accommodation, for compromise, for some sort of agreement on the policy decision. There are independent participants in the process who may be able to block a policy, or sabotage it, or at least to snipe away at it from the sidelines. There may be other men whose active, imaginative support and dedicated efforts are required if the policy is to succeed, and it may take concessions aimed directly at them and their interests to enlist this kind of willing co-operation. And, finally, there is in all participants an intuitive realization that prolonged intransigence, stalemate, and indecision on urgent and fundamental issues might become so intolerable as to threaten the very form and system of governance.

THE CONCENTRIC RINGS OF DECISION-MAKING

Political scientists in America clung for generations to an ideal of decision-making in democracy in which the electorate was to decide among rival policies as well as choosing among rival leaders. The view was most eloquently voiced by Woodrow Wilson, when he was still a professor, in his book, *Congressional Government*. Wilson pined for the logic and clearly fixed responsibilities of parliamentary government modeled on what he conceived to be the British system of his day. He admired the party discipline the British displayed and the clear-cut choices their system at least *appeared* to offer the electorate. Congress, on the other hand, appalled him. He was convinced that its noisy and often undignified procedures were an unsurmountable obstacle to good government. Its untidiness outraged his Calvinist soul.

The truth of the matter is that the British system never did work the way Wilson and his intellectual followers thought it did. If it had, the results would undoubtedly have been disastrous. The few examples where the two parties momentarily approximated the ideal and offered grand alternatives which they insisted on following have not been happy ones.

The postwar nationalization and denationalization of steel as the Labour and Conservative parties came in and out of office are only suggestive of the wrenches the British economy and society would have been subjected to. Instead of offering grand alternatives, the parliamentary system, like the congressional system, works to find compromises that blur the alternatives rather than sharpen them.

The great fallacy in the Wilsonian ideal was to suppose that all the electorate would be equally interested in all subjects and acquire the specialized information and knowledge to choose intelligently between the alternatives. But when the interests of political scientists turned to empirical work, it quickly became clear that different segments of the public were interested in different things. As Gabriel Almond wrote in the *American People and Foreign Policy,* there is not one public but many. Within the general public, there is a division of labor—one "attentive public" for agricultural policy, another for Latin American affairs, and perhaps still another for policy toward Asia. Informed and interested groups follow each policy area, but the "general" public becomes involved in a particular policy only rarely. Ending the Korean War became a major issue in the election of 1952, but war touches all our lives, and examples of foreign policy issues that directly influenced the outcome of elections are rare.[2]

Approached from the other direction—from the Washington end, as this book does—the policy-making process presents itself as a series of concentric circles.[3] The innermost circle, of course, is the President and the men in the different departments and agencies who must carry out the decision—staff men in the White House, the Secretaries of State and Defense, the Director of CIA, and the Assistant Secretaries of State and Defense who bear responsibility for whatever the particular problem may be. Some matters never go beyond this circle, but even here the process is political—the "closed politics" of highly secret decision-making.[4] The decision in September of 1962 about how many U-2 flights would be made over Cuba and how many around its periphery is an example. There were conflicting interests among the State Department, the Defense Department, and the CIA. The power of those representing different views influenced the decision and so did the possibility that the result might affect the future power position of the different participants. As it was, there was at least a tentative effort to shift the blame to the Secretary of State by asserting that the Soviet missiles would have been discovered sooner if that decision had gone the other way. If the crisis had turned out badly for the United States, the effort to shift the blame would have been massive.

Beyond this innermost circle lie other departments of the Executive Branch, and other layers within the agencies and departments already involved, including presidential commissions, scientific advisory panels, and so on. Even though the debate might still remain secret from the press, the Congress, and the public, these second layers soon become involved. In the Laos crisis of 1962, for example, the debate over whether or not to send American troops directly into Laos from Thailand continued for weeks. It was all still top secret, but more and more people became involved in the "closed politics" of the decision. Specialists in the State Department's Bureau of Intelligence and Research and in the Policy Planning Staff, similar specialists in CIA and the Defense Department became aware of the debate and pushed forward additional information in their province of responsibility that bore on the subject or wrote interpretive memoranda that might have an influence one way or another. People in the RAND Corporation, as we saw, learned of the struggle, and rushed copies of their study of the logistical capacity of the transportation routes in Laos to people they knew would use it to good advantage. The longer a policy debate goes on, no matter how delicate the issue is, the more people will become involved until eventually the debate spills over into the public domain. It is for this reason that there is sometimes an incentive to avoid "forward thinking" or any other form of contingency planning. For example, Secretary Rusk, in that same Laos crisis of 1962, wished to avoid even asking the President for a decision about whether or not we would order American forces into Laos if the Communists continued their nibbling tactics.

THE PUBLIC ARENA

The next arena is the public one, involving Congress, the press, interest groups, and—inevitably—the "attentive publics." In this arena, a decision on policy may be made in any one of several ways. The Cuban missile crisis became public, but it never did enter the public arena for decision. The decision was made in the arena of "closed politics," and although the President had always to consider the effects and reactions and repercussions in the wider public arena, the crisis moved too fast for a public debate to catch up. Policy toward Indonesia during the confrontation with Malaysia became public in a variety of ways—focused especially through Congress's authority over appropriations—but it remained the province only of those very few in the Congress, the press, and so on who had already had a developed interest. Important though reaching an understanding of the emerging nations might be in the long run, for most Americans the problem of Indonesia remained esoteric. Like blue cheese, it was an acquired taste.

In the Congo crisis, in Laos, in China policy, in Vietnam—in all of these a wide variety of people became involved in one way or another.

The debate over Vietnam, to cite the most vivid example, took place in the National Security Council, in the halls of Congress, in the press, in academic journals, inside the United States Mission in Vietnam, within each of the departments and agencies of the Executive Branch in Washington, and so on and on. The battle lines were drawn between the State Department and the Defense Department, but alliances also cut straight across the institutional boundaries. Individual members of the embassy and of CIA shared the views of a segment of the press, represented by Halberstam and Sheehan, while other members of the embassy and CIA were allied with the opposing segment of the press, represented by Alsop and Higgins. Some members of Congress, such as Senator Church, shared the view of a group in the State Department opposed by other members of Congress allied with others in the Executive. And inevitably the activities of a group in one institution supported the activities of its allies in the other—with or without any attempt at connivance. In Saigon, one group leaked to Halberstam and the other to Higgins. In Washington, Senator Church put in his resolution in the hopes of strengthening the hands of those he agreed with in the State Department—although they did not ask for it and even felt obliged to urge him to hold back.

And there was also the "strain toward agreement"—the effort to reach a consensus, to work out a compromise, to enlist the support of others standing at the edge of the debate. Considering the depth of the disagreement in some of the problems we have examined—Laos, Vietnam, China policy, and the Congo, for example—the remarkable thing is not that there was conflict, but that there was sufficient accommodation to make a decision possible. And the extent of accommodation and consensus would probably look even more remarkable if the scope of the inquiry were broadened to include the other great issues of foreign policy since World War II—the Marshall Plan, NATO and the containment of the Soviet Union, and the bitter interservice quarrels over weapons and military strategy.

CHARACTERISTICS AND CONSEQUENCES OF THE SYSTEM

The fact that policy is made through a political process of conflict and consensus-building accounts for much of the untidiness and turmoil on the Washington scene. The issues are important; there are rival policies for dealing with them; and the rival policies are sponsored by different groups of advocates competing for the approval or support of a variety of different constituencies. Attracting the attention of such varied audiences requires something dramatic. It takes effort, and many comings and goings, to enlist allies and forestall opponents. A high noise level is a natural consequence of the system itself.

THE "LEAK"

Consider, for example, the seemingly endless leaks of secret information. Many are not leaks at all. Sometimes a leak is really a trial balloon, launched anonymously in a "background" press conference to test the possibility of building a consensus without the penalty of making a full-scale attempt and failing.

Sometimes information leaks, not because the policy-makers want it to, but because the press drills a hole. There is a deeply idealistic conviction in the Washington press corps that they have a duty to inform the wider public of what the government is doing.[5] A selfish interest is added by the fact that conflict and disagreement within the government puts their stories on the front page. And there are always, as we saw in the case of Vietnam, Laos, and the others, some in the press who are just as passionately committed to a particular policy view as any of the officials inside the government and just as anxious to influence the policy decisions.

All these are high incentives, and many a "leak" is just hard digging by diligent and dedicated reporters. My favorite example occurred in the wake of the Cuban missile crisis, when there were so many charges of "managing the news" that both the press and the policy-makers were a little touchy. There had been an exchange of cables in which Khrushchev had finally made a concession on withdrawing troops. Just about this time, a reporter from the New York *Times* and one from the Washington *Post* cornered McGeorge Bundy at a reception and pushed him hard about "news management." Irritated, Bundy said that he knew something that would sooner or later be released and that it would make a big headline—but that the press would *not* be told until the government was good and ready. The two reporters were equally irritated, and each went back to his office and called in as many of his colleagues as he could reach. After talking it over, each group developed two or three ideas about what it might be that Bundy was holding back—and the possibility that it might be a cable from Khrushchev about something to do with Cuba was naturally on both lists. Each set of reporters began to make telephone calls—asking officials if it was true that the cable from Khrushchev had said thus and so—trying a different idea each time. "Oh, no, no, no," one or another official would say, falling into the trap, "It wasn't like that at all." By the time several different officials had "corrected" what would have been a damaging story, both sets of reporters had full and accurate accounts of what was in the cable.

Many "leaks" are of this order. Some others are sheer accident. But then there are true leaks, deliberate and knowing. But even these are not really blabber-mouthed irresponsibility, but more often attempts by men who are deeply convinced, rightly or wrongly, that their cause is over-whelmingly just. They believe that they have both the right and the duty, if their inside effort has failed, to use the public channel—to force an issue or policy alternative up to the level of decision, to outflank the proponents of a rival view, or to appeal a decision to a higher tribunal and a wider public. And they will have sympathetic encouragement from allies in both the press and the Congress.

THE OVERSIMPLIFICATION OF THE POLICY DEBATE

The fact that policy is made in a political process of conflict and consensus-building also accounts for some of the other apparent absurdities of the Washington scene. Often the public debate on foreign policy is childishly oversimplified, for example. The problem of Sukarno and Indonesia was far more complicated than Congressman Broomfield pictured it when he called Sukarno a "Hitler," and the problem of Tshombe and the secession of Katanga was not just a question of the "good guys" versus the "bad guys" as Senator Dodd's speeches implied. Both Broomfield and Dodd probably understood this as well as anyone else. But if the debate is taking place in front of a variety of audiences whose attention is easily diverted, then the alternatives must be very clear-cut, simple, and dramatic and the arguments painted in colors that are both bold and bright.

Another consequence of the multiplicity of constituencies involved in policy-making is that more and more problems are thrown into the White House. It is only the presidency—the President himself, his immediate aides in the White House, or *his* men in the departments and agencies—that can consider the whole broad range of interconnections between conflicting interests and demands. Judging these interconnections from the point of view of the President requires someone who partakes of the pressures *on* the President—facing Congress, the press, and the demanding interest groups—and who has his own future tied to the President and his administration. It was only the President himself or someone who identified with him rather than the particular department or agency in which he served, for example, who could ask, as President Kennedy so often asked, "How can we justify fighting a war with American troops in Southeast Asia, which is nine thousand miles away, when we can't justify it in Cuba, which is only ninety miles away?"

All this means that competition for attention at the decision-making level of government becomes more intense. Before a new problem or proposal can be raised to the level of decision, it must jostle out hundreds of others. And what might be called the "jurisdictional" effect of bureaucracy tends to increase still more the number of problems that must elbow their way right to the very top. The essence of bureaucracy is specialization of function and a division of labor and responsibility accordingly. This device is indispensable in managing large-scale enterprises. But it presents peculiar difficulties when it comes time to fix responsibility for problems that cut across jurisdictional lines—which foreign policy problems tend to do in any age and especially so in time of external threat when both military and economic instrumentalities are prominent. More often than not, complex problems arising out of interaction, as between military and political considerations, can be "recognized" as problems in an official sense only at the top. The heart of the problem of guerrilla warfare, for example, lies at the intersection of political and military factors. No one department or agency can begin to cope, and the whole problem can be faced only at the level of the presidency. Since the solution is the same mixture, carrying out the policy in the field requires the same type of over-all authority—presenting a problem in implementation for which the American form of government is ill-equipped.

A policy-making system that revolves around developing a consensus among a wide range of participants also puts a high premium on effective communication and an even higher penalty on a failure of communication. In the first round of the Congo crisis, for example, Mennen Williams and the "New Africa" group were defeated mainly because they had neglected to communicate effectively what it was they were trying to do and why to the Washington constituencies that might have been their allies. Achieving sophisticated policies is not just a problem of policy planning by an elite staff, but also one of persuading and educating. What is more, there seems to be no one place where these tasks can be accomplished fully, since there are too many participants too widely scattered to be reached by the communications resources available to any one group of participants, except, perhaps, those available to the White House itself.

The need for wide support sometimes leads to overselling a policy proposal in the sense of claiming too much for it. This happened to some extent in the case of Kennedy's policy of neutralizing Laos and even more in the case of Vietnam. But the classic example would be the foreign aid program as a whole. Foreign aid was supposed to create military allies and at the same time ensure democratic regimes as economic development was achieved. But both of these claims created false expectations at home that eventually eroded support for foreign aid not only among conservatives but among the very liberals who were the most ardent backers of the aid program.

Paradoxically, the need for wide support for a foreign policy sometimes creates an incentive *not* to communicate effectively, to be a little fuzzy in articulating policy and its possible outcomes. Different groups climb aboard a particular policy for different reasons, sometimes because of a differing estimate of just what the true outcome of a policy will be. The politician in a President has a need at times to postpone a decision until there is time to build a consensus, or to proceed in painfully slow increments for the same reason. Every President has occasionally been accused of obfuscation and indecisiveness. Some of Lincoln's cabinet members despaired of getting a decision from him, and similar incidents are told of both Roosevelts, Wilson, and the other presidents with a reputation for strength and decisiveness. As an executive and the leader of a large and complicated organization, the President needs to be articulate and precise; as a politician, he may need to be vague. And inevitably there is tension between the two.

The effort that must go into "selling" a policy that requires wide support, the tension between the need for articulation and the need for fuzziness, the difficulty in getting some kinds of problems "recognized" except at the top, and the competition for the attention of the many constituencies and levels of government all combine to put obstacles in the way of any attempt at systematic policy-making. Some issues or proposals are the subject of massive concentration, while others are neglected almost entirely. There is a tendency to bounce from the crest of one crisis to the crest of another, and a bias toward postponing final choice among the possible alternatives until the new crisis forces decisions that are mainly reactions, the children of events rather than their master. Because so many different people and so many different constituencies are involved, it takes the urgency of crisis to force attention and point up the necessity for the mutual concessions and accommodation out of which consensus on a policy is reached.

INCREMENTALISM

There is also a tendency to decide as little as possible.[6] Partly this is because of the impossibility, as Charles E. Lindblom has pointed out, of the task of giving rational consideration to the whole wide range of goals and the multiplicity of alternative means for achieving them and calculating the myriad of consequences and interactions.[7] Policy, as Lindblom says, tends to proceed in a series of incremental steps, tentative and easily reversible. But it seems clear that this is true, not only because of the impossibility of analyzing the grand alternatives rationally, but also because of the political process of consensus-building by which policy is made. The acquiescence of a key constituency might be given for what could be regarded as a tentative, reversible experiment when it would be withheld for a grand leap.

All of this—the bouncing from crisis to crisis, the overselling, the incrementalism—leads to what might be called a discontinuity of policy development. There are gaps in both analysis and policy as a result of the working of the system itself. The Sino-Soviet dispute showed that the Communist world was not the monolith it was supposed to be, but policy based on the assumption that it was a monolith continued through the sheer inertia of the process itself. Guerrilla warfare showed the inadequacy of strategic thinking, but a massive conventional military effort continued to dominate strategy in Vietnam long after a more sophisticated concept had been worked out. Americans feel that they have been too often surprised by the turn of international events, and they tend to blame intelligence, on whom, they feel, so much effort has been lavished to what seems so little avail. But the real reason for their being surprised seems more likely to be here, in the discontinuities growing out of the very nature of the policy-making process.

ADVANTAGES OF THE PROCESS

But in spite of the untidiness and turmoil of the politics of policy-making in Washington, such an open process of conflict and consensus-building, debate, assessment, and mutual adjustment and accommodation can be solidly effective in the assessment of broad policy alternatives if the conditions are right. The conditions are, first, that the subject is one on which the competing groups of advocates are knowledgeable. Second, both the participating constituencies within the government and the "attentive publics" outside must be well informed. Third, all levels of government, those who will carry out the policy as well as those who decide it, must be responsive to the decision and persuaded by it. Under these conditions, the chances are good that the policy will be wise, that the effort and sacrifice required will be forthcoming, and that the work of carrying out the policy will go forward intelligently and energetically. An example is the development of United States policy toward Europe in the years following World War II—the broad policy highlighted by the Truman doctrine, the Marshall Plan, and the establishment of NATO—which successfully halted the slide of Western Europe into Soviet domination and eventually helped to bring it to security and prosperity. The advocates of rival policies, the constituencies inside the government, and the attentive publics outside were equipped with a frame of knowledge about Europe and its problems against which to test proposed policies, and the results were good.

An example of the opposite is the story of China policy—which for so long reflected a lack of the necessary frame of knowledge for intelligent debate at every level, within the government and outside it. Even the Assistant Secretary of State for Far Eastern Affairs at the time, Dean Rusk, could argue, as we saw, that the Chinese Communist regime might be a "colonial Russian government" but that it was "not Chinese." China policy also illustrates how a doctrinaire rigidity can take over and substitute for a frame of knowledge. The Committee of One Million and its allies in Congress and the press, for example, were still insisting that Communism was a "passing phase" on the mainland long after an ordinary citizen would have taken the common sense view that the Communists had been in control too long to be considered merely a "passing phase" even if they were successfully ousted.

Interestingly enough, the point seems to hold even when the needs of secrecy and speed keep the process circumscribed—when the decision is made in a process of "closed politics" rather than open. In the Cuban missile crisis the number of participants was small. But the frame of knowledge was there, the alternative views were expressed, the debate was wide-ranging, and the presence of competing interests and the wider implications were felt even though the representation was limited. One has the impression, for example, that the President decided against an air strike in his own mind almost immediately, and that the long discussion of it over the next few days was to try to bring the "hawks" around and, failing that, at least to have the record show that their alternative was given a full and complete hearing. The result was a policy decision that not only was successful but seems as wise under the scrutiny of hindsight as it did at the time.

The obvious example from the Kennedy administration of a decision made in "closed" politics that suffered from an inadequate frame of knowledge was, of course, the Bay of Pigs. But what is worth pondering is that, unlike the case of China policy, the necessary knowledge was in fact available in Washington. The trouble was different. In the Cuban missile crisis the demands for secrecy kept the number of participants small, but all the different viewpoints, constituencies, and centers of expertise were still represented. In the Bay of Pigs decision, however, secrecy resulted in the exclusion not only of rival advocates but also of centers of expertise and prevented debate before the full range of governmental constituencies.

SOME THEORETICAL IMPLICATIONS

This is not intended to be a book of political science theory, but some further comment on theoretical implications may be in order.

One is the similarity between decision-making about foreign policy in Washington and decision-making on the international scene.[8] We have spoken of policy-making in Washington as a political process, one of conflict and consensus-building. People tend to think of war as the principal mode of conflict between nations and thus to assume that conflict between nations is fundamentally different from the conflict within a single country or in private lives. Yet even in the "total" wars of recent times, the use of force is limited. Mankind uses force against some natural enemies with the full intention of exterminating them—as the wolves in England were exterminated or the snakes in Ireland. But except for Hitler's maniacal policy toward the Jews, no modern nation has deliberately set about to destroy another people. Physical violence, in fact, is not really a very common state of affairs between nations. In the history of most nations the years of peace far outnumber the years of war. Even when conflict is the dominating theme in a set of relationships, statecraft is not really concerned as much with physical violence, the military art, as it is with threats of physical violence, or still more accurately with manipulating all the varied forms of power—since physical violence is only one of several means that nations use to coerce or influence one another.

It is on the conflict in international affairs that a pure power theory of world politics focuses. Yet for all its utility in explaining the maneuverings of states, a pure power theory has limitations. Without a sizable list of inelegant qualifications, it cannot account for the long periods of peace in international relations, for the stability of certain friendships, and for the not uncommon occasions when nations knowingly relinquish positions of power. For the practical purposes of estimating the consequences of different policies and so of choosing between them, a pure power theory of politics is a cumbersome and uneconomic tool.

The difficulty comes from the multiplicity of values shared by people on both sides of national boundaries—peace, security, prosperity, self-determination, and the sanctity and freedom of the individual. Thus one nation's gain is not always another's loss, and accommodation and concerted action occur almost as frequently in international affairs as conflict.[9]

The obvious example of nations acting in concert are alliances for security against a common enemy. But nations also act in concert for a variety of lesser purposes—to regulate trade, to counter economic depressions, to conserve such natural resources as fisheries, to combat crime, and to provide international postal and other services.

There is accommodation between adversaries, too. Rival nations often agree, formally or tacitly, to respect spheres of exclusive influence, to act together in neutralizing a third country, or to refrain from bringing certain matters into the arena of competition. The bitterest rivals have a stake in restricting their competition to means that are appropriate to the goals at issue and in avoiding measures that will bring about the sacrifice of things more cherished than those to be won. Even nations at war have reached agreements. Gas was outlawed in World War II, although not all the participants had signed the convention on the rules of war. In the Korean War there was a tacit agreement to respect sanctuaries. The United Nations forces refrained from bombing north of the Yalu and the Communist forces conformed by avoiding Pusan and our bases in Japan. In Vietnam, there was until 1965 a tacit agreement that the United States would refrain from bombing North Vietnam and the North Vietnamese would refrain from infiltrating their regular battalions into the south.

Thus international politics has a mixture of conflict and accommodation similar to that in domestic politics. As a consequence, the business between nations, like the business of reaching decisions within a single nation, requires techniques for persuasion, negotiation, and bargaining as well as for manipulating power.

The practitioners of statecraft, the operators in foreign offices and embassies do not make a practice of generalizing about the "decision-making procedures of world politics" or the "international decision-making system." Neither do they comment on the resemblance between international politics and a process of consensus-building. Yet, faced with the problem of *doing* something in international affairs—whether it is trying to bring about a Geneva conference on Laos or implementing a decision to blockade Cuba—any practitioner, from desk officer to assistant secretary, would unerringly tick off the steps to be taken. Nation A would have to be consulted in advance; Nations B and C would have only to be informed. *This* line of argument should be taken in the UN; *that* line of argument with the press. Moscow should be told *this* at *that* stage; Paris should be handled in a different way. Practitioners may not generalize about the "international decision-making system," but they know how to operate it.

THE NATURE OF POLITICS

A second theoretical comment that might be made is on the nature of politics. How one defines politics depends very much on what analytical purposes one has in mind. Politics has been defined as the struggle to determine "who gets what, when, and how" for one analytical purpose.[10] It has been defined as a struggle for power, pure and simple, for other purposes.[11] And there are still other definitions.[12] Most of them are reasonably valid and useful for particular purposes, and most of them are not completely satisfactory for all purposes. And it is probably not necessary to strain for the perfect definition. Most people have a common sense definition that is good enough. People speak of "office politics," for example, and everyone knows what they mean. As a general rule, people assume that politics is concerned with power, that it is more likely than not concerned with matters of government, and that political decisions of the largest moment are concerned with the ordering and regulating of society itself. In its broadest meaning, politics concerns the activities and relationships of groups of people as groups.

POLITICS AS GROUP DECISION-MAKING

For the purpose of analyzing the making of foreign policy, it seems most useful to look at a political process as a device for making group decisions, a procedure by which a group of people can decide what they should do as a group, the goals they should seek and the means for achieving them, or how they should divide among themselves those benefits already available. Politics would be concerned both with the making of such decisions and the maneuvering to acquire the power and influence to affect them.

There are, of course, other devices for the making of group decisions —judicial and administrative procedures, for example, in which decisions are made by the interpretation, guided by precedent, of sets of laws, policies, rules, and regulations, or, perhaps, by tribal customs.

One can conceive of group decisions made in a purely hierarchical way, in which only the head man had a vote. At the other extreme, one could also conceive of a pure type of democratic decision-making in which there was no leader at all, and decisions were made unanimously or by the majority, with each man really having only one vote and no influence other than his vote. But the real world is more complex. It differs from the pure hierarchical model of decision-making in that more than one person has power or influence on decisions and from the pure democratic model in that the participants have differing amounts of power and influence. The active co-operation of some people may be required for a decision, as we have seen, while only the acquiescence of others may be necessary. Some participants might have to give formal approval before some decisions could be made; and on other decisions these same people might be safely ignored.

Also, several different forms of group decision-making might be operative at the same time. Within a single department of the government, some decisions are made by hierarchical procedures, some by judicial, and some by political—and perhaps some by a combination of all three. Not infrequently officials are called upon to play roles appropriate to every possible form of decision-making in swift and bewildering succession with few cues as to when the scene is changing.[13]

CHARACTERISTICS OF A POLITICAL PROCESS

Three characteristics distinguish a political process of decison-making from other ways of making group decisions. In the first place, politics implies a diversity of goals and values that must be reconciled before a decision can be reached. It is not just a question of whether this or that value should be pursued, but what mixture of values should be pursued.

It also implies alternative means for achieving values whose precise effects may be in dispute. There is never a political debate over the tensile strength required for the truss members of a bridge, which can be determined with great exactitude. But there frequently is a political debate over the economic and social effects of locating the bridge at one place on a river rather than another, which cannot be determined with such exactitude.

Frequently, a debate over the probable effects of alternative means is really a mask for a disagreement about goals that remains unspoken. But in the making of foreign policy, at least, it is noteworthy how often the debate is truly over means and predictions about what a particular means will or will not accomplish. In the Cuban missile crisis, in the Congo crisis, in China policy, in the Laos crisis, in South Vietnam—in all of these there was by and large agreement about the general objective and the debate was over which means would best accomplish the objective at what risk and at what cost.

Politics, in other words, begins to come to the fore when there is disagreement (1) about the goals the group should seek as a group, or (2) about the effects of alternative means for achieving the goal, or (3) about the rules governing competition between individuals and subgroups, or (4) about the allocation of benefits held or distributed by the group as a whole, or (5) about the sacrifices required by different segments of the group as a whole. It is not competition alone that produces politics. If there is substantial agreement, for example, that unrestrained economic enterprise shall govern the distribution of material benefits, then the competition will take place in other than political terms. It is when there is disagreement about the rules for economic competition that politics begins.

A second characteristic of a political process is the presence of competing clusters of people within the main group who are identified with each of these alternative goals and policies. In the policy-making arena, for example, we have found not just the traditional political parties, but subgroups of many kinds, including some that lie within the government as well as outside it—frequently entirely informal alliances that cut across departmental or institutional lines, including the line between the Executive and Congress. In the Congo crisis, as we saw, this pattern was particularly sharp. The "New Africa" group had friends and allies in the Congress, in the press, and in the "attentive publics," while the "Old Europe" group found an entirely different set of allies in the Congress and the press, bolstered by those in the Pentagon. But the same pattern of subgroups and informal alliances ran through each of the other major policy disputes, sometimes more and sometimes less prominently.

In a political process, finally, the relative power of the different groups of people involved is as relevant to the final decision as the appeal of the goals they seek or the cogency and wisdom of their arguments. It was the political power that the China Lobby could muster at the height of its influence, to cite the most obvious example, that bound policy so tightly for so long and not the persuasiveness of the argument. Who advocates a particular policy is as important as what he advocates.

Viewing policy-making as a political process in the sense described by these characteristics illuminates the diversity and inconsistency of the goals that national policy must serve, as pointed out in the first chapter of this book, and calls attention to the powerful but sometimes hidden forces through which these competing goals are reconciled. It helps explain, as we said, why the push and pull of these crosscurrents are sometimes dampened or obscured, and why they are sometimes so fiercely public. And the roles of such *"unrational"* procedures as bargaining also become more clear.

POLITICAL POWER

A third, and final, theoretical comment that might be made here is on the nature of political power as illuminated in the making of United States foreign policy. It seems beyond dispute that power is a factor in any political process. Everyone recognizes the obvious fact that some people have more power than others, and all the great social thinkers have devoted their attention to the nature of power. As Robert A. Dahl has pointed out, the existence of so much comment arouses two suspicions.[14] The first is that where there is so much smoke there must be fire and some "Thing" that can be called power must exist. The second suspicion is that "a Thing to which people attach many labels with subtly or grossly different meanings in many different cultures and times is probably not a Thing at all but many Things . . ." It is in the spirit of this notion that political power is probably many different things—and without attempting any general or systematic essay on power in the United States—that attention might be drawn to a few of the implications of the case studies of foreign policy issues related in this book.

THE POWER OF CONGRESS

Consider the power that congressmen exercise in the making of foreign policy. In their exploration of the policy-making machinery of government, Senator Jackson and his subcommittee forestalled a number of moves toward reorganizing the "machinery" of the government and killed such ideas as creating a "Vice-President for Foreign Affairs." Second, they made an effective case for giving the State Department and the Secretary of State the central role. Even though neither the department nor the Secretary took up the opportunity presented, and the President, aided by McGeorge Bundy and the White House staff, had to fill it himself, it was the Jackson Subcommittee that was mainly responsible for giving them the opportunity. Yet Senator Jackson accomplished this, not by legislation, but by commissioning staff studies and by holding hearings to serve as a platform for people with ideas. It was, in effect, an exercise in semiformal and public consensus-building.

Senator Keating in the Cuban missile crisis and Senator Dodd in the Congo crisis played similar roles. The benefit to these particular senators of picking up a foreign policy issue in just the way they did is obvious. Senator Keating had been a member of the House for many years representing an upstate district. As senator, he needed to become known in New York City and to build a "statesman" image to overcome his rather parochial, conservative record as an upstate congressman. Senator Dodd had the problem of representing a state that borders New York City and houses commuters who listen to its radio and TV and read its newspapers. How does a senator from either Connecticut or upstate New York get on New York City's radio and TV and on the front page of the New York *Times?* Picking up a continuing foreign policy issue and being the focal point for opposition to State Department policy is not only an effective way, but it is politically cheap. Both Cuba and the Congo offered an opportunity for the senators to take a strong anti-Communist stand, which is always popular, without risk of alienating anyone except the State Department—and, as far as the voters of New York and Connecticut were concerned, this was itself undoubtedly a plus.

But what effect did Keating and Dodd have on the substance of foreign policy? Keating attracted attention to the possibility of the Soviets putting missiles in Cuba, but the government was already so sensitive to that possibility it was quivering. Actually, Keating and Goldwater between them almost caused the agreement with the Soviets about withdrawing their troops to break down, which was certainly not in either their interest or the nation's. And Dodd was never able to force the government to adopt his policy for the Congo, that of supporting Tshombe and the secession of Katanga. Yet their activities were always a factor to be taken account of in the policy discussions—and policy was at times either adjusted to accommodate some element of their view so as to disarm them or presented in such a way as to forestall them. For even though Keating and Dodd did not become the rallying points for an alternative policy, they had the potential for doing so, especially if the policy the government was actually pursuing failed dramatically.

In Vietnam, during President Kennedy's administration, Congress did not play a large role. There was pressure from the liberals to dissociate the United States from President Diem, but after the Buddhist crisis dissociation also became the general direction of official policy. The conservatives of both parties agreed with the "war hawk" view that advocated bombing North Vietnam and the United States taking over direction of the struggle from the Vietnamese, but they did not make a great effort to get the policy adopted. The irony is that one of the main reasons this group did not push harder for stepping up the war was that the Pentagon, their main ally in the Executive Branch, kept stubbornly insisting that the war was already being won. If the war was already being won, there was no need to bomb the north and take over responsibility from the Vietnamese.

Congressman Broomfield attempted to cut off all aid to Sukarno's Indonesia, even though the aid was mainly designed to strengthen the army's capacity to deal with the Communists when the showdown came. But he could not, in fact, change policy. President Kennedy would have signed the determination that the aid was in the national interest and gone ahead. Although President Johnson refused to sign and, in effect, adopted Broomfield's policy, he did it, not in response to pressure from Broomfield and Congress, but because the policy conformed to his own view. But here again, Broomfield's position had at least to be considered by President Kennedy—if only as a potential rallying point for opposition should effective opposition really be aroused.

In all these examples, the influence and power of Congress were indirect or limit-setting rather than direct or initiative-taking. In domestic policy, Congress occasionally can take the initiative and force a new policy according to its tastes, but rarely so in foreign policy. In foreign policy, the Executive calls the tune—and there are reasons. In the first place, it is the Executive who controls the detailed flow of information from overseas. There need be no conscious intention to suppress one kind of information and emphasize another to accomplish the same result as deliberate suppression and emphasis. No one deliberately distorted the information on the way the war was going in Vietnam, for example, but it was distorted. The policy position of the Executive will have its effect on the way information is presented, even when passions run less deep than they did over Vietnam. In such a massive flow of information, merely winnowing the raw data down to what one man could conceivably absorb would of itself present a partisan picture of the situation.

The increasing technicality of foreign affairs also robs the Congress of its power. Understanding the Buddhists in Vietnam, the nature of the new nationalism, the complexities of the Sino-Soviet dispute, and so on requires expert knowledge; and it is the Executive who has the greater command of experts. As a consequence, it is the Executive who sets the framework in which policies are discussed, who defines the problems we will essay as a government and the alternatives from which we choose the courses of action to meet them.

This command of both information and expertise gives to the Executive the intellectual initiative in making foreign policy. The Congress as a whole can criticize; it can add to, amend, or block an action by the Executive. But Congress can succeed only occasionally in forcing Executive attention to the need for a change in policy, and rarely can it successfully develop and secure approval from the public for a policy of its own.

The Executive also has an "instrumental" initiative in foreign affairs. It is the Executive who carries out a policy, who deals with problems face to face. In doing so, the Executive must inevitably make a host of secondary decisions that can and do set new lines of policy. Here again, this is especially true in foreign policy. It is the Executive who conducts negotiations with other powers, and in these negotiations it can make promises and commitments that Congress cannot fail to honor. Frequently, indeed, the Executive may proceed without any formal reference to Congress at all. Kennedy concluded the Laos agreements of 1962 without formal reference to Congress. Eisenhower's commitment to South Vietnam in 1954 was not formally referred to Congress; and neither was Kennedy's in 1961. And there is a host of other examples: Roosevelt's destroyers-for-bases deal with Great Britain; the Yalta agreement, which so many Congressmen resented for so long; Truman's decision to meet the blockade of Berlin with an airlift; and his even bolder decision to resist Communist aggression in Korea with troops as well as with material aid.

But this power of the Executive to proceed in some matters without reference to Congress, or even to evade the expressed desires of Congress, is only part of the story. Congress has little direct control over foreign policy, and it can take few initiatives. It participates only fitfully in the actual formulation of foreign policy and takes formal action only in approving or rejecting appropriations, treaties, resolutions, and in confirming the appointments of ambassadors and high officials. Yet it is equally clear that Congress—subtly and indirectly, but nevertheless effectively—plays a decisive role in setting the tone of many policies and the limits on many others.

The most dramatic example of the power of Congress to set the policy tone is the case of China policy. Congress and Congressmen took the lead in solidifying a national consensus on a rigid policy toward Communist China, and the viciousness of the McCarthy era set it in concrete. Once this kind of wide consensus is set, inertia rules. It then takes almost heroic action to overcome even the mildest congressional resistance. President Kennedy wished to bring about a change in China policy, but progress was painfully slow. In the beginning of his administration, he sought to start by recognizing Mongolia, but the Nationalists objected and their friends in Congress quickly shot the proposal down.

Nothing dramatic or specific would have been accomplished by recognizing Mongolia—the effects would have been symbolic and psychological, indicative of a *coming* change in China policy. And this was the trouble, for when the purpose is a change in policy against a massive inertia of the kind surrounding policy toward China, it is essential to have quick results to point to and beat off the counterattacks.

Legally and constitutionally, President Kennedy could have gone ahead and recognized Mongolia. But he would have had to be willing to take the consequences, not just angry speeches and threats of impeachment, but retaliatory action on a whole range of other matters over which Congress has more direct legal and constitutional power. In a very real sense, the peculiarly negative, limit-setting power of Congress over foreign policy is the power of deterrence and the threat of "massive retaliation."

THE SOURCES OF POWER

We have argued that policy-making is a political process, and on the face of it power and politics are intertwined. Yet power is a crude concept, as we have said, and it fails to satisfy as an explanation of the mixture of both conflict and accommodation that is present, of the motives that presumably lie behind the decisions on foreign policy, or of the techniques that are used to achieve agreement or acquiescence on a policy.

If it is correct to say that the peculiar province of politics is matters in which there is disagreement about either group goals and values or the rules of competition and allocation of those individual values and interests that are regulated by the group, then power need not be quite so central in either domestic politics or international. Power need not be the motive force for most participants, nor the cause of politics, nor even a necessary condition, but only one of the more pervasive and perhaps decisive of the several instruments of politics.

At certain times and in certain places, military power, for example, may be starkly central in domestic affairs—civil war is the obvious example. But to the extent that military strength is a *source* of power on the domestic scene, the mechanism is not so crude. In the making of foreign policy in the cases studied here, there was a policy view and position from what President Eisenhower called the "military-industrial complex" on some issues, such as Laos and Vietnam, in both of which there was a large military stake. And in these cases power was clearly exerted in support of that view and position. But as a force the "military-industrial complex" was loosely organized, amorphous—more potential than structured. Nothing in any of the foreign policy issues examined here, certainly, resembles in the slightest the "power elites" described in Marxist and neo-Marxist literature. The oil companies had a huge investment in Indonesia, for example, but their inclination was not to push the United States into greater involvement but to get themselves out. More than once it was only because of the urgings of the United States Government that American businesses were persuaded to stay in Indonesia as long as they did.

In the domestic scene, clearly, power has more varied and subtle sources than in either force and violence or wealth and class. Power grows not only "out of the barrel of a gun," as Mao Tse-tung would have it, but also in legitimacy, in legal authority, in expertise, and in special interest that is recognized as legitimate, such as the interest of the farmer in agricultural policy or the banker in monetary policy. It is so varied and subtle in its sources, indeed, that one wonders whether "power" is the most useful word.

Power can be the negative power that Congress has of making life difficult for the President if one of its treasured views is ignored. It can be the legal and constitutional right to decide in a formal sense, which is usually the President's in foreign affairs but sometimes belongs to Congress. It can be influence, in the sense of having the ear of the President or the respect of the leaders of Congress without holding any office at all. It can be the ability to have one's views at least taken into account because one represents a special interest group like the farmers, as we said, whose legitimacy is recognized. It can also be the ability to have one's views taken into account simply because one has convinced the world that one speaks for a wider public and that there will be political consequences if one is ignored. An example is Marvin Liebman, who as Executive Secretary of the Committee of One Million could get a hearing because he was accepted as the spokesman for the China Lobby and presumably for a wider public that supported the views of Chiang Kai-shek. It can also be the ability to have one's views taken into account because of one's personal expertise. When George Kennan speaks about policy toward the Soviet Union, for example, the government listens even when it abhors the advice offered and refuses to take it. Power can also come simply because one has a "platform" which gives one the opportunity of enlisting a particular constituency. An Adlai Stevenson or a Chester Bowles out of office can influence policy by their ability to command a hearing before "liberals" and the possibility that they might swing the whole constituency with their persuasiveness. A scientist who is completely unknown outside the scientific community might develop such leverage—and if the subject matter concerned a scientific question, the leverage might be overwhelming. No president would lightly go against the consensus of scientists on a matter in the area of their specialty.

Within the Executive Branch itself power comes to some people because they enjoy the confidence of the President. Power also comes from using a "job platform" so that it fills a larger need, which can bring still wider responsibility and more power. The position and title—the "platform"—that McGeorge Bundy occupied in the Kennedy administration existed in Eisenhower's day, but it was Bundy who made it powerful. Power comes from expertise, from representing a particular constituency, whether within or outside the government, from institutional backing, and from statutory or designated authority and responsibility. The mere title of the Secretary of State gives him authority, in addition to what he acquires through statute and custom.

The richness of the sources of power over the making of foreign policy goes back to the nature of the political process of conflict and consensus-building by which policy is made. Within the government and outside it, to repeat, there are different constituencies with a stake in the outcome. The State Department may have jurisdiction over the general problem, for example, while the Pentagon must implement one aspect of it and the Agency for International Development another. Even if the President's prestige and position are not involved, his approval may be a legal or a political necessity. This may be true of Congress, also. If so, the outside constituencies are likely to be drawn in—interest groups, newspapermen, academic commentators, and the still wider constituency of the particular "attentive public."

In a major problem of foreign affairs, as we have said, the advocate of a particular policy—even if there is neither a rival advocate nor a rival policy—must build a consensus to support his policy in the different constituencies within the government and frequently outside as well. He needs the active co-operation and support of some, the formal or informal approval of others, and at least the acquiescence of still others. He may prevail over the active opposition of one or another constituency, but rarely if it is from within the government and the enterprise is large. For even passive opposition can bring a large and complicated enterprise to failure, not by sabotage, but simply lack of enthusiasm. When there are rival advocates or rival policies, on the other hand, there is not only debate before the different constituencies, but competition for their support. Alliances are formed, and all the techniques of consensus-building appear—persuasions, accommodation, and bargaining.

Over some of this at certain times, the President may merely preside—if it is a matter of slight interest to him and has little impact on his position. But if *he* is an advocate or if the outcome affects *his* position and power, then the President, too, must engage in the politics of policy-making. In the field of foreign affairs, the President's power is immense. His is the constitutional authority as Commander-in-Chief. His is the monopoly in dealing with other states. But he, too, must build a consensus for his policy if it is to succeed. He must bring along enough of the different factions in Congress to forestall revolt, and he must contend for the support of wider constituencies, the press, interest groups, and "attentive publics." Even within the Executive Branch itself, his policy will not succeed merely at his command, and he must build co-operation and support, obtain approval from some, acquiescence from others, and enthusiasm from enough to carry it to completion. This is the truth that so amused President Truman when he said that Eisenhower would find that the presidency was not "a bit like the Army." It is the truth that President Kennedy had in mind when he joked about the "inner club." It is the "half-observed realities," as Neustadt says, underneath our images of "Presidents-in-boots, astride decisions"—the realities of "Presidents-in-sneakers, stirrups in hand, trying to induce particular department heads, or congressmen, or senators to climb aboard."[15]

NOTES

[1] The phrase is Warner R. Schilling's. See his "The Politics of National Defense: Fiscal 1950" in Schilling, Hammond, and Snyder, *Strategy, Politics, and Defense Budgets*, 1962, p. 23.

[2] Even if foreign policy *issues* do not seem to play a very important role in elections, the electorate apparently wants its candidates for national office to have qualifications or experience that show *competency* in foreign affairs. See Angus Campbell, and others, *The American Voter*, 1960, 1964.

[3] The theoretical model of the policy-making process that follows owes much to the work of Gabriel A. Almond, especially his *American People and Foreign Policy*. An earlier attempt at this model—influenced not only by Almond, but also by Charles E. Lindblom's article, "The Science of 'Muddling Through,'" and the works of Robert A. Dahl—is contained in my 1958 and 1959 articles, "Congressional-Executive Relations and the Foreign Policy Consensus," and "The Foreign Policy Consensus: An Interim Research Report," which are cited in the preface. The model as presented here draws on the subsequent work of Warner R. Schilling, "The Politics of National Defense: Fiscal 1950," *loc. cit.;* Samuel P. Huntington, *The Common Defense*, 1960; and Thomas Schelling, *The Strategy of Conflict*, 1960; as well as the later work of Almond, Dahl, and Lindblom.

[4] The phrase is C. P. Snow's. See his *Science and Government*, 1960, 1961.

[5] Bernard C. Cohen, *The Press and Foreign Policy*, 1963.

[6] On this point, see Warner R. Schilling, "The H-Bomb Decision: How to Decide Without Actually Choosing," *Political Science Quarterly*, March 1961.

[7] Charles E. Lindblom, *The Intelligence of Democracy*, Chapter 9.

[8] Others who have commented on the parallel between domestic and international politics are: Nicholas John Spykman, *America's Strategy in World Politics*, 1942; W. T. R. Fox in his lectures at Yale and Columbia; and Warner R. Schilling, *op. cit.*

[9] For descriptions of international politics in which both conflict and accommodation appear, see the following, among others: Nicholas John Spykman, *op. cit.;* W. T. R. Fox, *The Superpowers*, 1944; Hans J. Morgenthau, *Politics Among Nations*, 1962;

Arnold Wolfers, "The Pole of Power and the Pole of Indifference," *World Politics*, October 1951; and Thomas C. Schelling, *op. cit.*

[10] Harold Lasswell, *Politics: Who Gets What, When, How*, 1958.

[11] Charles E. Merriam, *Political Power: Its Composition and Incidence*, 1934; Hans J. Morgenthau, *op. cit.*, 3rd edition, 1960.

[12] Although they by no means exhaust the list, three others might be noted here: first, V. O. Key's definition of politics as the "human relationship of superordination and subordination, of dominance and submission, of the governors and the governed" (*Politics, Parties, and Pressure Groups*, 4th edition, 1958); David Easton's as the making and executing of the "authoritative," that is, legally binding, decisions in a society (*The Political System: An Inquiry into the State of Political Science*, 1953, and "An Approach to the Analysis of Political Systems," *World Politics*, April 1957); and Gabriel A. Almond's as "that system of interactions to be found in all independent societies which performs the functions of integration and adaption (both internally and vis-à-vis other societies) by means of the employment, or threat of employment, of more or less legitimate physical violence" (*The Politics of the Developing Areas*, 1960).

[13] On the overlapping of different forms of decision-making and the psychological problems posed for the individual, see Robert A. Dahl, "Hierarchy, Democracy, and Bargaining in Politics and Economics," in *Research Frontiers in Politics and Government*, the Brookings Institution, Washington, D.C., 1955.

[14] Robert A. Dahl, "The Concept of Power," *Behavioral Science*, July 1957.

[15] Richard E. Neustadt, "White House and Whitehall," *The Public Interest*, No. 2, Winter, 1966.

CHAPTER 36

Improving the Policy "Machinery"

FOREIGN POLICY is politics, and politics is a "slow boring of hard boards." There is probably no quick or easy way of making improvements. Certainly tinkering with the organizational "machinery" is not going to help very much. The debate about how to "organize for national security" that preceded the Kennedy administration reached the conclusion, as described in Chapter 2, that the problems of national security policy were not going to be solved by reorganizing the government. "Super-staffs and super-secretaries" were no way out, it was clear, and neither was strengthening the National Security Council or creating a "vice-president for foreign affairs." And certainly nothing happened in the Kennedy administration that would alter that conclusion. In fact, the major recommendation that came out of the debate about organizing for national security—that the prime voice and co-ordinating power should center in the Department of State—in practice only proved the validity of the conclusion that reorganizing was no solution. Merely assigning power to the State Department did not guarantee that the Secretary and the Department would use it.

All this, of course, does not mean that changes in organization do not affect policy. Organizational changes usually follow a shift in power, as for example, the changes in the way intelligence problems were handled in the State Department followed CIA's loss of power in the aftermath of the Bay of Pigs. But changes in organization can in themselves bring about an increase or decrease of power and alter the weight that one set of considerations will have over another in policy deliberations. But whether the result is better or worse policy depends on your point of view, on whose interests are being given additional weight. What is an "improvement" in this sense to one person may not be to another.

Some improvements are undoubtedly possible in organizational structure that everyone would agree were improvements. Ways might be found, for example, to make the communications process among participants in the making of policy quicker and easier. There might also be organizational changes that could bring more precision in assigning the flow of work, or in the effectiveness of applying the proper expertise at the proper stage. But these are not of fundamental importance and would result in only marginal improvement in the foreign policies that came out the other end.

PREDICTION AND KNOWLEDGE

Effective foreign policy depends on the capacity to predict events in the social affairs of men, and a better capacity to predict would mean better and more effective foreign policy. But more is required than simple factual information. Predicting the outcome of alternative policies requires knowledge in the sense of an ability to identify and weight the different factors bearing on the particular situation and an understanding of the dynamism by which those different factors interact.[1] In the Middle Ages, for example, no one foresaw the Black Death, the great plague that swept Europe, or knew what to do about it after it came. Yet when men learned that germs cause disease and the means by which germs are transmitted, they could not only treat individual cases of the plague, but could foresee that an increase in filth in the cities and the rats that live on it would create the conditions for an outbreak of the plague and indicate the measures needed to head it off.

There is no doubt that knowledge in this sense of the ability to make sound predictions is the crux of the matter. The debate in the Kennedy administration over Vietnam policy, for example, revolved around rival analyses about the nature of guerrilla warfare and predictions about the effects of alternative ways of dealing with it. In China policy, the debate centered on the analysis of the nature of Chinese Communism, its capacity to change Chinese society, and whether or not it was a "passing phase" as well as on predictions about the effects of the rival policies of "isolating" Communist China or maintaining an "open door" for a lessening of hostility and eventual accommodation. And so it was through all the other cases—the Cuban missile crisis, the Congo, Laos, and Indonesia. The crux of the debate in each instance turned on an analysis of the factors bearing on the problem and on predictions about the consequences of alternative ways of dealing with it.

More and better knowledge of the kind that permits accurate prediction is undoubtedly the most important single thing that is needed for the improvement of foreign policy. But here again, there is no quick or easy solution. If there was a wide and obvious gap between the pool of basic knowledge available in the universities, say, and what was actually used in informing governmental decisions, something dramatic might be done. But this particular gap, the gap between the knowledge of experts in government and experts outside, is infinitesimal. Take, for example, the field of "Sovietology." The great body of what is known about the Soviet Union and the workings of Soviet society is shared—and subscribed to—by Soviet specialists within and outside the government. By and large, in fact, the personnel themselves are interchangeable and frequently do shift back and forth. What disagreements there are in the field of "Sovietology" are not between government experts and academic experts but between one group of specialists cutting across both government and academia and another, also cutting across both government and academia. And what is really remarkable is how small the area of disagreement is, how accurate are their judgments about Soviet reactions and behavior, and how few are their failures at prediction—no matter how harshly their role in the Cuban missile crisis is judged.

New and better knowledge is needed, but how can it be developed? Certainly the attempts to institutionalize the effort within government have not been very fruitful. It was this need for knowledge and foresight, according to Dean Acheson, that led General Marshall when he was Secretary of State to establish in 1947 the Policy Planning Staff, a group of about a dozen top-level specialists under an assistant secretary.[2] But in practice, the Policy Planning Staff did not work out to be the panacea some had hoped for. It proved to be a useful pool of talent that could be tapped in time of crisis—as its second chief, Paul Nitze, for example, was pulled out for the negotiations after Mossadegh and his government nationalized oil in Iran. Its members have also contributed "think-piece" memoranda, which have been neither better nor worse, on the average, than similar thoughtful memoranda written in the action bureaus, in the intelligence agencies, or by outside scholars and writers. But none of this, no matter how well done, fulfills the concept of a "planning" staff, and yet beyond this the Policy Planning Staff has done very little.

What is "planning"? Men building a dam or a bridge can plan in a long-range and very precise sense. They can predict the forces that the dam or bridge must withstand and determine with great accuracy the materials and strength needed for each part of the structure. In building a dam or a bridge, men can also draw blueprints and develop a schedule for the work to be done that will permit them to specify months in advance the exact dates on which cement, for example, should be ordered and delivered. Some military planning is also of this nature, such as providing port facilities and hospitals and stockpiles of ammunition and so on. But beyond the field of logistics, military planning is limited—for the fundamental reason that there is an enemy who has some choice in the matter too. In war, the only long-range "planning" that can be done apart from logistics is the making of very broad strategic choices.

Long-range planning in foreign affairs is more similar to this kind of military planning than it is to either logistics planning or the kind of planning used to build a dam or a bridge. It is, essentially, analyzing the nature of the problem and making broad strategic choices for dealing with it. Secretary Dulles in his 1957 speech about Communist China, for example, which argued for a strategy of isolating the Chinese Communists was one strategic choice. The "open door" speech of 1963, which argued for an alternative strategy of "firmness and flexibility" leading toward an eventual accommodation, was another strategic choice. The choice in dealing with Indonesia and Sukarno was the United States posture toward the "new nationalism," whether it could be brought into constructive channels or would respond only to firmness. In Vietnam, the problem was how to treat guerrilla warfare, as we have said—as fundamentally a political problem or as fundamentally a war.

Short-range planning in foreign affairs is working out the moves and countermoves in the midst of an ongoing situation, of developing instructions for an ambassador or orders for the fleet. Should the United States move troops into Thailand in response to the Communists' violation of the cease-fire in Laos, and if so what will the Communists then do? Should the United States use an air strike to take out the Soviet missiles in Cuba, confine its action to diplomatic moves, or begin with a blockade? In China policy, should the United States lift travel restrictions on Americans, push for Chinese participation in disarmament talks, and recognize Mongolia, and if so, what will be the Chinese response?

But both the making of broad strategic choices in foreign affairs and this shorter-range form of making contingency calculations of move and countermove are at the political heart of policy-making. Consequently, the truth of the matter is that both of these kinds of "planning" are done at several places at once—by the advocates of the rival policies and their allies. In the Laos crisis of 1962, for example, one set of "plans" of what the United States should do if the Communist side continued to violate the cease-fire in spite of our having put troops in Thailand was prepared in the Pentagon and another was prepared by the Bureau of Far Eastern Affairs and their allies in the State Department's Intelligence Bureau. In the struggle over Vietnam policy, one strategic concept for fighting the guerrillas was developed out of the work of Thompson in Saigon, people in the Intelligence Bureau at the State Department and in the White House, and military people at the Special Forces center at Fort Bragg—but all this "planning" was overridden by the "planning" for traditional warfare that took place in the military headquarters at Saigon. In the Congo crisis, "planning" took place most of the time in the Bureau of African Affairs, but every now and again it was done elsewhere—in the bureau responsible for UN affairs, in the Intelligence Bureau, and occasionally, to be completely accurate, in the office of Senator Dodd.

At one time or another, the Policy Planning Staff "planned" in this sense as the ally of one or another set of advocates, but it succeeded in being the *principal* advocate and planner in very few cases. The Multilateral Force for NATO and the earlier Developmental Loan Fund are two outstanding examples, and it is instructive of the politics of statecraft that both of these problems were bureaucratic orphans, matters that cut across the regular responsibilities of both the regional and the functional offices of the State Department.

Policy is made in a political process for good and sufficient reasons, and so long as these basic reasons persist, attempts at institutionalizing "planning" or "foresight" or "wisdom" are likely to fail. Some improvements, of course, can be made. A climate of receptivity to new ideas and knowledge can be created rather easily, for example, and creating such a climate of receptivity can have important consequences as people are encouraged to experiment with new ideas and to put them forward. Although it was partly nullified in the State Department by the attitude at the top, President Kennedy established this climate of receptivity at the beginning of his administration very quickly. His actions showed that he was reading people's memos, and he called up "little" men on the phone, all of which created an excitement that the bureaucracy had not known for many years. Government can also do more to encourage research and the development of new knowledge in political and social affairs. The Defense Department, for example, spends billions of dollars supporting research in the physical sciences, but it was not until the Kennedy administration that the State Department obtained money for supporting research in foreign affairs, and as it was, Congress appropriated less than one hundred thousand dollars for the purpose. Something might also be done to direct research and the work of increasing basic knowledge to questions that are more immediately relevant to the issues of foreign policy. Much of the work in the universities on social, political, and economic matters, for example, would benefit from a better understanding of the issues as the policymaker must view them. Not only would the results be of more utility to governmental decisions, but the research itself would benefit in a purely scholarly sense by a sharpening of its perspectives.

But important though the results of these kinds of effort might be in the long run, the immediate results would not be any very dramatic improvement in United States foreign policy. The making of foreign policy is a groping effort at understanding the nature of the evolving world around us. It is a painful sorting out of our own goals and purposes. It is a tentative, incremental experimentation with various means for achieving these purposes. It is an unremitting argument and debate among various constituencies about all of these questions and an attempt to build a consensus on how the United States as the United States should decide on these questions and what action it should take. And none of these several activities is the kind that will yield to organizational or institutional gimmicks.

PERSONNEL

One other possible area for improvement in United States foreign policy is people. Other things being equal, good people make good foreign policy and better people make better foreign policy.

There is a wide variety of people who make foreign policy, as we have seen—the press, interest groups, attentive publics, congressmen—but within the Executive Branch itself, where something concrete could be done, the "people who make foreign policy" fall into two general groups. One group is made up of career officials in the foreign service, the civil service, and the military services. The other group are presidential appointees and the people they bring with them—the group of officials who make up an "administration."

There was a time when the quality and training of people in the career group were undoubtedly not as good as they should have been. But much has been done in the years since World War II, not only to broaden the foreign service and the career civil service, but to improve the knowledge and training of everyone concerned with foreign affairs and national security, civilian and military. Pay, retirement, and other benefits have made a government career more attractive. Qualifications have been raised. Mid-career training is provided, not only at the Foreign Service Institute and the service war colleges, but also by new legislation that permits agencies to send officials to private universities for special training. The task of maintaining high standards in the career services and of seeking new ways to improve training is never completely ended, but by and large the United States can be proud of its career services, both civilian and military. The people in them are able, well trained, and dedicated professionals, and although there are things that can be done to help them and to maintain the present high standards, none will bring any marked improvement in the quality of foreign policy.

THE FRONT MEN

As far as the second group of people are concerned—the group of people who make up an "administration"—the thing to mark down first is the function they perform. One aspect of their function is to be the President's man, the representative of the administration. If he is in a staff job in the White House, this is the total of the presidential appointee's function. He is expected to jab and prod and push all the different bureaucracies. He must make sure they produce the data, the recommendations, and so on that the President should have to make decisions. And he must follow up decisions to make sure the bureaucracies take timely and effective action to carry them out once they are made.

The presidential appointee who heads a department, agency, or bureau or serves in a line job in one of them—a secretary or director or assistant secretary—is expected to shape and mold the bureaucracy to the President's needs. He must represent political management, represent the top level of the administration in the form either of the President or the cabinet member in whose department he serves. But if the presidential appointee in the line job is the President's man with the careerists, he should also be the careerists' man with the President and the top levels of the administration. He should represent the specialists' view to the President and his cabinet officers and be the vehicle for their expertise. He must be the judge of whether what they have to say should be laid before the highest councils, but when he does decide that their views should be heard, he ought to be their unrelenting champion. The head of a department or bureau or agency and the presidential appointees who serve in them *should* run interference for their organization and its careerists. Otherwise, in a political process of decision-making, their expertise will go unheard.

All this applies to the cabinet member—the secretary heading a department or the director of an independent agency. It also applies in general to lower-ranking presidential appointees. Some of these, in fact, may have a relationship to the President almost exactly similar to that of a cabinet member. In the Kennedy administration, for example, Mennen Williams enjoyed this status as Assistant Secretary for African Affairs. The President was deeply interested in the problems of Africa, and Mennen Williams was a public figure in his own right. The result was that Williams had a special status and a special relationship to both the President and the Secretary of State. The position of the Assistant Secretary for Middle Eastern Affairs, held by Phillips Talbot, on the other hand, was less independent, more closely tied to the position of the Secretary of State than to the President.

Inevitably, most presidential appointees come to identify with the organizations they head and to represent the men and women who make up these organizations, whether they represent them well or badly. This is one source of the tension between presidents and cabinet ministers, which has been so often remarked upon. It is also a reason that presidents must go consensus-building in the Executive Branch as well as in the wider rings of policy-making.

Another source of the tensions between presidents and their appointees is the fact that presidents so often seek their men precisely because they represent an outside, public constituency. President Kennedy chose Mennen Williams for the Africa post because he represented liberal opinion in the United States—which was also the reason he preferred

Adlai Stevenson at the UN. He chose John McCone—an Irish Catholic, a Republican, and a millionaire shipbuilding tycoon—to head the CIA precisely to make the conservatives in business, in industry, the military, and Congress feel that they and their foreign and defense policy interests would be represented. Having chosen men because of their affiliations with particular constituencies, a president can hardly be surprised if they speak for that constituency in the internal policy debate.

The function of these men, in sum, is to be the advocates of policy and to represent the different bureaucratic constituencies inside the government and the public constituencies of special interests and attentive publics outside of government. It is their function to force an issue up to decision, to try to make the government face up to an emerging problem. It is their function to put forward an alternative policy and to become identified with it. They are the "front men." They are the men who will become public figures if they are not already.

A "front man" need not be a specialist in a particular subject, but if he lasts he is or will become a specialist in using specialists, in knowing when the specialists are right and should be backed, and when they are caught up in their own parochialism. It is the front man who pushes for a particular policy at different places inside the government and outside, with higher officials and lower, with other agencies, in congressional hearings, in backgrounders with the press, in public speeches, and in endless struggles over countless pieces of paper. It is the front man who is the leader of a constituency, the sponsor of a policy, and the builder of a consensus for it. Career men down the line may push a particular policy with unrelenting passion; they may be advocates to the core fiber of their being, but it is this front man who is *the* advocate. The *function* of advocacy is his. He is the man who runs interference by the nature of his job. Out in front, as he is, he is the one who first feels the blast of political heat. And above all, in consequence, the front man is expendable.

THE FRONT MAN AS AN "IN-AND-OUTER"

It is the high expendability of the front men—as well as the fact of their identification with a particular president and his administration, which are, after all impermanent—that accounts for their being dubbed the "in-and-outers."[3] Unlike J. Edgar Hoover, who has headed the FBI for over forty years, there is no example of someone who was always "in" the foreign affairs field in the sense of holding high office. But the term "in-and-outers" does have some misleading connotations, especially the implication that there is a ladder and that men come in and out to gradually increasing responsibilities and experience. Many do. Dean Acheson started as Assistant Secretary of the Treasury under Roosevelt.

He went out in a disagreement over fiscal policy, then came back as Assistant Secretary for Economic Affairs in the State Department. He was then Assistant Secretary for Congressional Relations, then Under Secretary, and out again. Finally, he came back as Secretary of State under President Truman. W. Averell Harriman started very near the top, but he gained in experience by serving in every Democratic administration since Roosevelt's, being out of the foreign affairs area of government only during the Eisenhower years. Dean Rusk was Assistant Secretary for UN Affairs in the Truman administration, Deputy Under Secretary, and Assistant Secretary for Far Eastern Affairs. He went out to head the Rockefeller Foundation, and then came back again to be Secretary of State. Other, completely random examples are the following: Henry L. Stimson, Chester Bowles, Allen Dulles, Paul Nitze, Adolf Berle, George W. Ball, McGeorge Bundy, Arthur H. Dean, Robert A. Lovett, Douglas Dillon, J. Kenneth Galbraith, John J. McCloy, and John McCone.

Some front men come in only once. Henry A. Wallace, for example, held three positions the first time in—Secretary of Agriculture, Vice-President, and Secretary of Commerce—but he never came back once he went out. Eisenhower's Secretary of Agriculture, Ezra Taft Benson, and his Secretary of Defense, Charles E. Wilson, had never held government posts before their appointments as cabinet members. Neither had Kennedy's Secretary of Defense, Robert S. McNamara.

Where do the front men come from? Many have come from Wall Street—Henry L. Stimson, James V. Forrestal, Paul Nitze, Douglas Dillon. Some from politics—G. Mennen Williams and James F. Byrnes. Some came from the law—Dean Acheson, George W. Ball, and Arthur H. Dean. Some came from a combination of law and politics—Adlai E. Stevenson. Some have come from business and industry—Charles E. Wilson, and Averell Harriman and Chester Bowles, the last two having an interim period in politics. Some have come from academia and the foundation world—Dean Rusk, McGeorge Bundy, Adolf Berle, Philip C. Jessup, and J. Kenneth Galbraith. Some have come from the career service—Robert Murphy, who went pretty steadily up and went out only on retirement. Coming from the career service, Murphy was an "up-and-outer" rather than an "in-and-outer." And George F. Kennan was both. He rose to prominence as Ambassador to the Soviet Union and head of the Policy Planning Staff, left for an academic post, and returned as Ambassador to Yugoslavia. Some of the front men are really "up-and-backers" or "up-and-to-one-siders"—Charles E. Bohlen, for example, who was at the heart of policy-making in the Truman years, sat out the Eisenhower administration as Ambassador to Manila, and returned to the heart of policy-making in the Kennedy administration. There are also the "in-and-outers" and "up-and-backers" from the military—Maxwell Taylor, James Gavin, Walter Bedell Smith, George C. Marshall, Lucius Clay—

all of whom held high civilian office after reaching prominent military positions.

These "front men" as we have said, are key in making foreign policy *effective*. They are the ones who kick and push and shove to get the government to recognize a problem and face up to the policy choices rather than drift in indecision. They are the ones who sponsor policy alternatives, who do the work of enlisting support, arguing, selling, persuading, and building a consensus around a particular course of action. It is their leadership or lack of it that determines whether a decision will be vigorously or indifferently carried out.

The effectiveness of foreign policy depends peculiarly on the front men. If their quality, training, and progressive experience can be improved, so will foreign policy. The nation should clearly pay careful attention to their upbringing, care, and feeding.

But here again there is no simple solution. To an American, for example, the British parliamentary system seems to provide a neat solution to the problem of providing an obvious ladder, early selection, and progressive experience for policy leaders. There is an opportunity to start early. Men may run for parliament from any district without residence requirements, and an able man may get a seat while still very young. There is opportunity to work up. The member sits on the back benches and learns, eventually earning a position as parliamentary undersecretary where he can work from inside the great departments. If he is an apt pupil with sufficient luck, sooner or later he will get a cabinet post.[4] And there is provision for the "out" period that permits him to develop and work in the field of his major interest. When his party is out of power he still has a seat in parliament from which he can participate, study, and follow developments in his special field. Most importantly of all, there is the clear expectation on his part, by his constituency, his colleagues, and his adversaries that he will in fact be back.

To an American all this seems a marvelous system for the upbringing of "front men." But to an Englishman, on the other hand, it does not always look quite so wonderful. To him, the system sometimes seems to ensure that there will never be any new blood. Responsibility for policy-making alternates between two small groups of familiar people in a tight procedure that works against any possibility of new faces and fresh ideas. More than one Englishman has commented on how difficult it would be for a new British government to bring into high and influential posts such a glittering array of new, young, and vigorous people full of verve and fresh ideas that the Kennedy administration assembled. The old, familiar "shadow cabinet," they complain, merely replaces the old, familiar cabinet—and back and forth in a dull minuet. Once in a while a single new face can be brought in, but only by the ponderous device of forcing a resignation in a safe seat and holding a by-election or by having the man elevated to the peerage and given a seat in the House of Lords.

In the United States there are a few things that might be done to improve matters. The attractions of going "in" or "up" can be increased, and the risks of having no place to go "out" or "back" can be reduced. Perhaps other measures can be taken to ease the lot and improve the incentive of the "front men." But it is difficult to conceive of any very radical changes in their recruitment, training, or conditions of servitude. And so here again, the somewhat pessimistic conclusion seems inescapable —that there is no easy route to dramatic improvement.

And so it goes. Knowledge can and should be increased and made available at all levels of participation, inside and outside the government and among the attentive publics—but the improvement in foreign policy will be slow. Communications and the flow of information among all participants at all levels can and should be improved—and the results will be good but not dramatic. Policy is made in a political process involving debate among rival advocates before a variety of constituencies, and the wisest course is probably to concentrate on trying to maximize the strengths of the system rather than changing it. Secrecy should in general be mistrusted, although it is sometimes necessary. Expertise should be given a full hearing, but experts themselves should be watched, at least for the narrowness of their interest. Deliberate heed should be paid to the role of the process itself, the need for debate and the involvement of all those who have a legitimate interest or contribution. The best way to improve policy, in a word, is probably to conduct it with an eye—but a highly discriminating eye—to the political realities of the process by which it is made.

"DEMOCRACY" IN THE MAKING OF FOREIGN POLICY

One final word should be added. All these considerations have been about the "effectiveness" of foreign policy, not whether it was "good" or "bad." Whether foreign policy is "effective" turns on whether or not the government recognizes an emerging problem and faces up to it; whether or not the policy adopted is in fact the alternative most likely to achieve the desired goal; and whether or not the decision is vigorously and efficiently carried out. The results, however, can be either "good" or "bad" depending on one's particular goals and interests—which is why the making of foreign policy is a political matter. And this involvement of the values and interests of the different segments of society in turn raises the question of "democracy" in the making of foreign policy.

The relative openness of the process of policy-making as we have seen it in the particular cases related in this book, the variety of constituencies, and the strain toward consensus provide at least for the possibility that different views of what is "good" and what is "bad" will be heard. By and large the very existence of these different constituencies —including the constituency of the press with its peculiar interest in conflict and disagreement—ensures that most of the major foreign policies will continue to be decided in the relatively open process of "conflict and consensus-building" and that the full range of different views will be represented even when the number of participants is restricted for reasons of security. But this still permits an occasional decision to be made in an inner circle that excludes major constituencies and major bodies of knowledge and expertise—as the Bay of Pigs so vividly illustrates. President Kennedy used to say, as mentioned earlier, that a domestic failure would hurt the country, but that a failure in foreign affairs could kill it. Yet it is in foreign affairs that "closed" decisions like the Bay of Pigs are most possible, for the President's power to take independent action is far greater in the field of foreign affairs than it is in domestic matters.

Once burned by the Bay of Pigs, President Kennedy made sure that his decisions in the Cuban missile crisis, in sending troops to Thailand in the Laos crisis, and so on, were taken only with the full range of both the interested constituencies and the relevant expertise, even though secrecy demanded that the decision be "closed" in a public sense. But an egocentric president, a man who saw himself as infallible and whose thirst for power had excluded independent-minded men from his administration or muted their voices, could make a particular decision without considering the range of constituencies at any time and could succeed in making the process itself much less open than it normally is—at least for a time.

And once more there is no simple or easy solution. No constitutional amendment will give this guarantee, and neither will reorganizing and strengthening the National Security Council. And any other alternative— such as giving Congress a more direct role—would probably make it impossible to move quickly and effectively in time of crisis. The Cuban missile crisis, for example, could not have been effectively handled by a congressional committee. As a practical matter, the nearest thing we have to a guarantee that foreign policy will continue to be made in this relatively open, "democratic" process of "conflict and consensus-building" is the way that men get to be President of the United States. And that, in fact, may be guarantee enough, at least for normal circumstances. A man who can last through the long, hard climb up the ladder of American politics to the pinnacle of the presidency must have an urge to power. But it is also unlikely that a man could come within reach of the presidency who did not have at the center of his character a sympathy for the range of values among Americans and a natural instinct for the political process of "consensus-building." For there is nothing quite like the buffeting and merciless public scrutiny of political life in America to expose the weaknesses of human character.

NOTES

[1] For discussions of the role of facts and the role of theory, see Morris R. Cohen, *Reason and Nature*, 1959, and my own *Strategic Intelligence and National Decisions*, 1956.

[2] Dean Acheson, "The President and the Secretary of State," in *The Secretary of State*, edited by Don K. Price for the *American Assembly*, 1960, p. 48.

[3] Credit for the term seems to belong jointly to Richard E. Neustadt and Adam Yarmolinsky—both of them "in-and-outers" themselves. See Richard E. Neustadt's "White House and Whitehall," already cited, and Adam Yarmolinsky, "Ideas into Programs," both of which appear in *The Public Interest*, No. 2, Winter, 1966.

[4] Neustadt, in his "White House and Whitehall," argues that the *function* of the President's men as described above is shared in Britain between these members of Parliament and the senior civil servants, who are different in this respect from American senior civil servants. My demurrer would be that to the extent that this function is managerial, we have senior civil servants like this too—for example, Loy Henderson. And to the extent that it is policy-making, they have their "Chip" Bohlens—men who go up and, if not back, at least sideways. See, for example, C. P. Snow's tale of the alternation of Tizard and Lindemann in the post of Science Adviser, *op. cit.*

The Statecraft of John F. Kennedy

A DEFINITIVE JUDGMENT of the statecraft of John F. Kennedy could probably not be written by a person who lived close to the events of his administration, and it is even less likely that a person personally committed to Kennedy, the man, could do so. This book, furthermore, has been concerned only with foreign policy, and even then it makes no attempt to deal with all the problems of foreign policy in the Kennedy administration, but concentrates on those issues and problems of which I had some personal knowledge. For all these reasons, to attempt anything very ambitious here at the end would be inappropriate, and the most that can be done is to offer reflections arising out of these particular events and experiences.

In my admittedly committed view, President Kennedy did not make many serious errors in foreign policy. But he did make some. The Bay of Pigs was a disaster—explainable, perhaps, but not excusable. The only thing that can be said as some small compensation is that Kennedy learned from it.

Vietnam requires a more complicated judgment. Senator Fulbright and others have suggested that President Eisenhower's original commitment to South Vietnam was a mistake and that President Kennedy's renewal of that commitment in 1961 was too. It may be—although I would not share Fulbright's view. But the commitment Eisenhower and Kennedy made was to support the South Vietnamese with economic and military aid, training personnel, support units such as helicopter squadrons, and military and civilian advisers. This was a large and serious commitment, but it was still vastly different from a commitment to engage in war using American troops. And one step need not necessarily make the next inevitable. So long as the military struggle in Vietnam remained essentially Vietnamese, United States prestige in Asia would not have been seriously affected by a negotiated settlement along the lines of the Geneva agreements on Laos, which actually increased our prestige in Asia, or even by the eventual success of the Viet Cong if the South Vietnamese Government failed to win the allegiance of the villagers. It is a reasonable argument that not only would United States prestige remain unaffected but so would the United States strategic position in Asia.

In contrast to this view, Secretary Rusk later suggested that President Kennedy erred in not putting up more "blue chips" at the very beginning.[1] His argument implies that from the beginning the goal of the United States in Vietnam should have been victory and that Hanoi should have been made to realize that rather than suffer defeat the United States would in fact turn the struggle into an American war, as it became in 1965, some fifteen months after Kennedy's death. But President Kennedy saw the American purpose in Vietnam as more limited than this. The only politically viable future he could see for any of the countries of Southeast Asia was true independence, achieved principally through their own efforts. "In the final analysis," he said at a news conference on September 2, 1963, "it is their war. They are the ones who have to win it or lose it. We can help them; we can give them equipment; we can send our men out there as advisers; but they have to win it, the people of Vietnam, against the Communists." No amount of force could prevent the north from infiltrating a few thousand ex-southerners a year into South Vietnam. But if the people turned against the Communists and toward the government in Saigon, these few thousands would be unimportant. What President Kennedy wanted to do was to use American power to give the South Vietnamese the chance to win the allegiance of the people, to use American power to deter the Communist north from doing any more than infiltrating a few thousand ex-southerners, to deter them from escalating the struggle into a larger war. And the evidence indicates, as described above, that Hanoi did not send any North Vietnamese regular units south until 1965, after the United States decision itself to escalate the war by bombing the north. The sequence of events, in other words, argues that President Kennedy used enough "blue chips" to accomplish the purpose that he intended, yet avoided using so many as to change the nature of the struggle.

If Vietnam does represent a failure in the Kennedy administration, it was a failure in implementation. A strategic concept of great promise for meeting guerrilla warfare was developed under President Kennedy— a concept that has looked more and more appropriate in the light of subsequent events. But although many people in the Pentagon, in the Special Forces, and elsewhere in the armed services—especially among company and field-grade officers—became enthusiastic believers in the concept as a result of their personal experiences in the field, Secretary McNamara, the Joint Chiefs of Staff, and many general officers were never more than lukewarm. General Harkins, for example, the commander in Vietnam, always acknowledged the importance of winning the allegiance of the people. But he never saw that the central principle of the concept was the need to subordinate military measures to a political and social program. What he apparently believed was not only that a regular war should be fought in Vietnam, but that it could be fought parallel to the necessary political and social program without destroying that program—which was probably a mistake. In any case, General Harkins was content to leave to someone else both the problem of pursuing the political and social struggle and the problem of seeing that military measures did not destroy it. As a result, the strategic concept was never fully implemented and military factors were emphasized over political.

If the Secretary of Defense had had the gift of wisdom in addition to his other extraordinary talents, if he had been less self-confident and dominating, the political side might have received more emphasis. But no cabinet minister can be faulted for presenting his own and his department's case with all the eloquence and vigor at his command, no matter how parochial it may be, and the real blame rests with the Secretary of State and his department. Here again, as in the Bay of Pigs, the Secretary and the Department of State failed to stand up and make the case for the political side of the equation with the strength, vigor, and determination with which Secretary McNamara and the military chiefs made the case for the military side.

While President Kennedy lived, the result was not as bad as it might have been. His freedom of maneuver and choice was reduced, but he succeeded in keeping both the "militarization" and the "Americanization" of the struggle in Vietnam within tolerable limits. And he did it pretty much on his own. The top-ranking military people pressed continually for measures that would escalate the war, and although Secretary McNamara vigorously and effectively opposed the more extreme proposals, he was basically sympathetic to the general strategy of escalation. So was Secretary Rusk.

President Kennedy was aware of the extraordinary difficulties in implementing a new and radically different concept for meeting guerrilla warfare, as he was of the need for the concept itself. He was also fully sensitive to the fact that the concept was not enough and that it also depended on the men he chose to carry it out. President Kennedy felt that he could not overrule the Joint Chiefs of Staff's nomination of General Harkins and reach down into the list of younger generals for a "Special Forces type" or a man who had had experience with the more political and less orthodox situations in which military force plays a role. His answer to the problem was to look for a civilian public figure of great stature to be ambassador and head of the entire United States effort in Vietnam. The result was Henry Cabot Lodge.

It could be argued that, even though President Kennedy cannot be fairly criticized for renewing President Eisenhower's limited commitment for aid and advisers or for refusing to put up more "blue chips" at the beginning, he could be criticized for these two appointments. It does seem probable that a younger general with a special background in guerrilla warfare would have been more effective in implementing the strategic concept than General Harkins. And although Ambassador Lodge was superb in dealing with Diem and Nhu, he was criticized in later years for what seemed to be an abdication of leadership to the military commanders. But if President Kennedy had overruled the Joint Chiefs and reached down the list for a younger man at the time of the Harkins appointment, there would have been much bitterness, which might have hampered the effort in Vietnam even more. President Kennedy was betting on a long, slowly paced effort in Vietnam, and no one will ever know if he was right in his judgment on this and on the people he chose to carry out the program. Nhu had taken over the name of the strategic hamlet program for his own neo-Fascist purposes, and so long as he and Diem dominated Vietnam the strategic concept was never given a fair trial. The downfall of the Diem regime gave Vietnam and the United States a second chance to carry out an effective program to defeat the Communist guerrillas and win the people. Ambassador Lodge and whomever Kennedy might have chosen to replace General Harkins, whose tour of duty was coming to an end, might well have done the trick—if Kennedy had lived.

With the certain exception of the Bay of Pigs and the possible exception of this one aspect of Vietnam, it seems to me that President Kennedy made no strategic mistakes in dealing with the problems we have examined here. A detailed study of the Alliance for Progress and Latin America, the problems he faced in the Middle East, and Berlin and Atlantic policy might reveal other errors. But the rest of the major policy decisions reviewed here seem good. The neutralization of Laos and the Geneva agreements of 1962 were, in my view, a triumph of statecraft— precisely because Laos was such an unholy mess, such an impossible combination of rival factions, difficult terrain, and inadequate power. No matter what happens in the future, to have steered past either abandoning Laos or letting it be the cause of a major military confrontation, to have succeeded in putting it to one side for the whole of his administration and beyond—this required not only wisdom on the part of a president, but nerve.

The Congo, too, was a success, and although not so fateful as some of the other problems, it was in many ways thornier and more tangled.

On China policy, no one can tell whether or not the direction in which the Kennedy administration was moving was correct in its assumptions about Communist China and whether or not the policy would have succeeded. This is especially true since any policy moving toward an accommodation between Communist China and the United Stated depended fundamentally on keeping the struggle in Vietnam severely limited. All that can be said is that Kennedy intended to keep Vietnam limited and that there was both purpose in his new China policy and an urge to magnanimity and therefore, one hopes, an element of wisdom.

President Kennedy's reading of Indonesia and the forces of the new nationalism there was borne out by subsequent events. It is not Communism but nationalism—tempestuous and troublesome though it is— that is the wave of the future in Indonesia.

The Cuban missile crisis, finally, was a dazzling success. And so, most importantly, was the follow-up—the nuclear test ban treaty and the measured steps toward a *détente* with the Soviet Union. If Kennedy had not been killed and the Vietnam struggle had been kept below the level of war, the Cuban missile crisis and the growing *détente* that followed it might have marked a turning point in history—and it is not impossible that the trend started at Cuba may yet be renewed.

All this has been concerned with Kennedy's management of affairs, his capacity for analysis, his sense of strategy, and his willingness to search out and follow the currents of history. It illustrates that Kennedy understood that the true art of statecraft is not always to adjust to events or always to attempt to dictate them, but to distinguish between those to which we must adjust and those which we may influence.

Beyond this, Kennedy also had the prime ingredients of wisdom—a doubt that anyone, including himself, could be infallible, and a respect for human weakness. He had a large perspective, a sense of the ebb and flow of events, that permitted him to look beyond the immediate crisis— as he looked beyond the Soviet affront in putting missiles into Cuba to the opportunity the resolution of the crisis gave mankind for alleviating the dangers of nuclear war. Both of these qualities helped him in dealing with the untidiness, the inconsistencies and internal contradictions of foreign affairs. He had an inner calmness, a slightly detached, cool, and objective view of himself and those around him that freed him from compulsiveness. There was in his make-up a high idealism, but this was coupled with a wry capacity for laughing at himself that made him impervious to flattery and contemptuous of any form of sycophancy, which are great assets in judging between competing views.

In spite of his coolness and clean intelligence—and partly because of them—President Kennedy had a capacity to attract able men to work with him and to excite their loyalties, to win their personal commitment to strive in a great cause. Men who were part of those gallant Kennedy years will call it their great adventure, to be recounted in their age.

Kennedy's capacity to elicit personal commitment naturally had its obverse, and he had his enemies. No one moves a nation without opposition—a public figure without enemies is a political eunuch. But if Kennedy had his enemies, they were good and passionate enemies and by and large the right ones, in that they stood for an outmoded *status quo*.

All these qualities ensured the loyalties of his own men. But statesmanship is a higher art than partisan leadership, and Kennedy could also reach across and establish a relationship with adversaries. It was based not only on an instinct that one ought to avoid cornering an enemy but a reasonableness, an openness, a largeness of spirit that permitted him to understand how the other fellow might see things differently. "I suppose," he said once in the days immediately following the Cuban missile crisis, "that we ought never to forget the possibility that the Soviets really believe what their propagandists write." Kennedy was tough and determined, but he also had magnanimity.

But above all else, President Kennedy had a vision of the future and a capacity for communicating it to the world's peoples. Kennedy was an idealist, but not an ideologue; the old ikons were being broken on all sides, and Kennedy's gift was to approach the world in new words and new sincerity. As he said over and over again in the election campaign of 1960, he wanted to get America moving not only for its own sake but so that it could provide the "inspiration and leadership" to get the world moving, too. He saw not only a world of peace and mutual respect, with a "world economy in which no nation lacks the ability to provide a decent standard of living for all its people," but also a world meeting new demands, overcoming new crises, realizing a new fulfillment for men. In words that rang loud in the ears of the emerging peoples, he spoke— as in his great American University speech—of a "world of diversity" in which each nation could develop its full potential in its own way and in peace.

The agony of grief that swept the emerging countries—Asia, Africa, Latin America—testifies that he had touched the peoples there as no other American since Franklin D. Roosevelt. But their grief was more than sorrow at the loss of a man who understood them and their aspirations. It was the promise they sensed in the combination of his understanding, his abilities, and his vision for the world. More was killed in Dallas than just the man.

Foreign policy is politics. But in politics, as Max Weber said, "man would not have attained the possible unless time and again he had reached out for the impossible. But to do that a man must be a leader, and not only a leader but a hero as well." John F. Kennedy was a leader. And he was a hero as well.

NOTES

1 Henry F. Graff, "Teach-In on Vietnam, the President, the Secretary of State, the Secretary of Defense and Under Secretary of State," the New York *Times Magazine*. March 20, 1966, p. 131.

Index